THE ROUTLEDGE COMPANION TO REMIX STUDIES

The Routledge Companion to Remix Studies comprises contemporary texts by key authors and artists who are active in the emerging field of remix studies. As an organic international movement, remix culture originated in the popular music culture of the 1970s, and has since grown into a rich cultural activity encompassing numerous forms of media.

The act of recombining preexisting material brings up pressing questions of authenticity, reception, authorship, copyright, and the techno-politics of media activism. This book approaches remix studies from various angles, including sections on history, aesthetics, ethics, politics, and practice, and presents theoretical chapters alongside case studies of remix projects. *The Routledge Companion to Remix Studies* is a valuable resource for both researchers and remix practitioners, as well as a teaching tool for instructors using remix practices in the classroom.

Eduardo Navas is the author of *Remix Theory: The Aesthetics of Sampling* (Springer, 2012). He researches and teaches principles of cultural analytics and digital humanities in the School of Visual Arts at The Pennsylvania State University, PA. Navas is a 2010–12 Post-Doctoral Fellow in the Department of Information Science and Media Studies at the University of Bergen, Norway, and received his PhD from the Program of Art and Media History, Theory, and Criticism at the University of California in San Diego.

Owen Gallagher received his PhD in Visual Culture from the National College of Art and Design (NCAD) in Dublin. He is the founder of TotalRecut.com, an online community archive of remix videos, and a cofounder of the Remix Theory & Praxis seminar group. He is the author of a number of research papers and book chapters on remix culture, intellectual property, and visual semiotics. Owen is a lecturer of Web Media at Bahrain Polytechnic.

xtine burrough makes participatory projects for networked publics. Her creative practice includes interventions with crowd workers, and recoveries of feminist texts through mediation. She uses appropriation and remix as strategies for poetic communication. She has presented works and ideas at Abandon Normal Devices, Electrofringe, Eyebeam, FutureSonic, IgniteLA, ISEA, and Machine Projects. xtine is an associate professor at The University of Texas at Dallas, and editor of the *Visual Communication Quarterly*.

THE ROUTLEDGE COMPANION TO REMIX STUDIES

Edited by
Eduardo Navas, Owen Gallagher,
and xtine burrough

Routledge
Taylor & Francis Group

NEW YORK AND LONDON

First published in paperback 2017
First published 2015
by Routledge
711 Third Avenue, New York, NY 10017

and by Routledge
2 Park Square, Milton Park, Abingdon, Oxon OX14 4RN

Routledge is an imprint of the Taylor & Francis Group, an informa business

© 2015, 2017 Taylor & Francis

Library of Congress Cataloging in Publication Data
The Routledge companion to remix studies / edited by Eduardo Navas, Owen
Gallagher, and xtine burrough.
pages cm
Includes bibliographical references and index.
1. Appropriation (Arts) 2. Remixes--History and criticism. I. Navas, Eduardo. II.
Gallagher, Owen. III. Burrough, Xtine.
NX197.R38 2015
700.9'04—dc23
2014022804

ISBN: 978-0-415-71625-3 (hbk)
ISBN: 978-1-138-21671-6 (pbk)
ISBN: 978-1-315-87999-4 (ebk)

Typeset in Goudy
by Swales & Willis Ltd, Exeter, Devon, UK

CONTENTS

CONTENTS

CONTENTS

CONTENTS

ACKNOWLEDGMENTS

A major project such as an anthology for a field of studies is made possible thanks to the collaboration of many individuals who unselfishly support a book's eventual publication. For this reason, we would like to thank all of the contributors who accepted our invitation to participate and write a text that went through a long editing process. We would like to thank our editor at Routledge, Erica Wetter, for considering the proposal of a reader, and the editorial board at Routledge, who offered us this major project by inducting what was once a smaller proposal into part of the Routledge Companion series. We also thank Simon Jacobs, Editorial Assistant at Routledge, who oversaw the book's process during its early stages, reviewed it, and prepared it for its final production. We thank the remix community, who participated in a survey we distributed during the proposal stage of this project. Their feedback was vital in determining the feasibility of a publication of this magnitude.

—Eduardo Navas, Owen Gallagher, and xtine burrough

I would like to thank Graeme Sullivan, Director of The School of Visual Arts at The Pennsylvania State University, for his support in the last two years that led to the eventual publication of *The Routledge Companion to Remix Studies*. I also thank Lev Manovich for his ongoing support in my research and activities. His unselfish critical feedback has always proven fruitful for all aspects of my practice. I also thank my family, especially my wife and partner, Annie Mendoza, who gave me moral support and the time needed to finish such a long-term project. And I thank my two sons Oscar Eduardo and Oliver Antonio for constantly reminding me what is ultimately important in life.

—Eduardo Navas

I wish to extend my gratitude to Dr. Paul O'Brien and Professor Jessica Hemmings of the Faculty of Visual Culture, and Professor Des Bell, Head of Academic Affairs and Research at the National College of Art and Design (NCAD), Dublin, for their guidance and support of my research over the past few years, leading to the publication of this volume. I also thank Brendan Muller, Web Media Programme Manager, for his support of my involvement in this project while simultaneously lecturing at Bahrain Polytechnic. I would like to thank my parents, Brendan and Frances Gallagher, for their unwavering encouragement and most importantly, I thank my wife, Aoife, and my daughters, Jennifer and Rebecca, for their love and support throughout this process.

—Owen Gallagher

ACKNOWLEDGMENTS

To my husband and partner, Paul Martin Lester, our two sons Parker and Martin, and to my parents Viola and Bill: the phrase "thank you" barely captures the essence of my gratitude. Your support, encouragement, wisdom, and silliness sustained me in this project, as it always does. I would also like to fondly acknowledge my peers, as well as my life-long mentors, Christopher James, Steven Kurtz, and Humberto Ramirez for their ongoing support . . . and silliness.

—xtine burrough

FIGURES

TABLES

CONTRIBUTORS

Janneke Adema is a Research Fellow in Digital Media at Coventry University where she is writing a PhD thesis on the future of the scholarly monograph. She is the author of the OAPEN report *Overview of Open Access Models for eBooks in the Humanities and Social Sciences* (2010) and has published in *New Formations*, *The International Journal of Cultural Studies*, *New Media & Society*, *New Review of Academic Librarianship*, *Krisis: Journal for Contemporary Philosophy*, *Scholarly and Research Communication*, and *LOGOS*, among other publications. Together with Pete Woodbridge she has coedited a living book on *Symbiosis* (Open Humanities Press, 2011). Her research can be followed on www.openreflections.wordpress.com.

Mark Amerika is an artist whose work has been exhibited internationally at venues such as the Whitney Biennial of American Art, the Denver Art Museum, the Institute of Contemporary Arts in London, and the Walker Art Center. In 2009–10, The National Museum of Contemporary Art in Athens, Greece, hosted Amerika's comprehensive retrospective exhibition entitled UNREALTIME. In 2009, Amerika released *Immobilité*, generally considered the first feature-length art film ever shot on a mobile phone. He is the author of many books including *remixthebook* (University of Minnesota Press, 2011; remixthebook.com) and his collection of artist writings entitled *META/DATA: A Digital Poetics* (MIT Press, 2007). His latest art work, Museum of Glitch Aesthetics (glitchmuseum.com), was commissioned by the Abandon Normal Devices Festival in conjunction with the London 2012 Olympics. The project was recently remixed for his survey exhibition, Glitch.Click. Thunk, at the University Art Galleries at the University of Hawaii. Amerika is a Professor of Art and Art History at the University of Colorado at Boulder. In Fall 2013, he was the Labex-H2H International Research Chair at the University of Paris 8. More information can found at his website, markamerika.com and at his Twitter feed @markamerika.

Kevin Atherton is an artist, fine art educator, and writer. A pioneering video and performance artist in Britain in the 1970s, in the 1980s Atherton went on to contribute to the redefinition of public art in the UK through his emphasis on the importance of site-specificity and produced a number of permanent public sculptures in a variety of media for a range of locations in the UK. In the 1990s he was Head of Fine Art Media at Chelsea College of Art, London where he established and ran the research project "Virtual Reality as a Fine Art Media" and in 2014, after 15 years of teaching in the Fine Art Faculty, he retired as the Head of Post Graduate Pathways at the National College of Art and Design, Dublin. In 2014–15 he exhibited a new version of *In Two Minds* in the exhibition "Primal Architecture" at the Irish Museum of Modern Art, Dublin.

Patricia Aufderheide is University Professor in the School of Communication at American University in Washington, DC. She is the coauthor with Peter Jaszi of *Reclaiming Fair Use: How to Put Balance Back in Copyright* (University of Chicago Press, July 2011), and author of, among others, *Documentary: A Very Short Introduction* (Oxford, 2007), *The Daily Planet* (University of Minnesota Press, 2000), and of *Communications Policy in the Public Interest* (Guilford Press, 1999). She has been a Fulbright and John Simon Guggenheim fellow and has served as a juror at the Sundance Film Festival among others. Her awards include the Preservation and Scholarship award in 2006 from the International Documentary Association, a career achievement award in 2008 from the International Digital Media and Arts Association, and the Woman of Vision Award from Women in Film and Video (DC) in 2010.

Mette Birk is a graduate from the Department of Media, Cognition, and Communication at University of Copenhagen. She has been active within the Remix Theory & Praxis online seminar group and on behalf of this group presented a paper on artist motivations at the Remix Cinema Workshop hosted by the Oxford Internet Institute. In 2012 she wrote her dissertation on ethics in video remixing communities as a follow up on her bachelor's thesis on motivations among trailer remixers. Currently she is working as a media researcher at the Danish Broadcasting Corporation with a primary focus on younger demographics.

Margie Borschke is a Senior Lecturer in Journalism and Media at Macquarie University in Sydney, Australia. Her research focuses on media use and circulation with an emphasis on questions related to copies, copying practices, and material culture.

Jonah Brucker-Cohen is an award-winning researcher, artist, and writer. He received his PhD in the Disruptive Design Team of the Electronic and Electrical Engineering Department of Trinity College Dublin. He has taught at Lehman College, New York University, Trinity College Dublin, Parsons The New School for Design and more. His work and thesis is titled *Deconstructing Networks* and includes creative projects that critically challenge and subvert accepted perceptions of network interaction and experience. His work has been exhibited and showcased at venues such as San Francisco Museum of Modern Art, MOMA, ICA London, Whitney Museum of American Art (Artport), Palais du Tokyo, Tate Modern, Ars Electronica, Transmediale, and more. His writing has appeared in publications such as *WIRED, Make, Gizmodo, Neural*, and more. His Scrapyard Challenge workshops have been held in over 14 countries in Europe, South America, North America, Asia, and Australia since 2003.

xtine burrough is a media artist and educator. She has authored, coauthored, edited, and coedited several books including *Foundations of Digital Art and Design* (New Riders, 2014) and *Net Works: Case Studies in Web Art and Design* (Routledge, 2012). She uses social networking, databases, search engines, blogs, and applications in combination with popular sites like Facebook, YouTube, or Mechanical Turk, to create Web communities promoting interpretation and autonomy. xtine is passionate about creating works that transform social experiences. She is a Webby Honoree, has received a Terminal commission and an award from the UK Big Lottery fund. She is an associate professor at California State University Fullerton, where she bridges the gap between histories, theories, and production in new media education. Her website is missconceptions.net.

Vito Campanelli (www.vitocampanelli.eu) is a writer and a new media theorist. His main research interest is technological imaginary. He is also a freelance curator of digital culture events and cofounder of MAO—Media & Arts Office. His essays are regularly published in international journals.

Roy Christopher was assistant editor of Paul D. Miller aka DJ Spooky's edited collection *Sound Unbound: Sampling Digital Culture and Music* (MIT Press, 2008). His first book is an anthology of interviews entitled *Follow for Now: Interviews with Friends and Heroes* (Well-Red Bear, 2007), which *Disinformation* named one of the most important books published in 2007, and which Erik Davis called, "a crisp and substantial remix of the major memes of the last decade or so." Christopher is currently a Visiting Lecturer in the Department of Communication at The University of Illinois, Chicago and a PhD candidate in Communication Studies at The University of Texas, Austin. He is also working on a book about technological mediation and culture, titled *The Medium Picture* and will be out in the near future on Zer0 Books. He lives in Chicago and writes regularly at roychristopher.com.

Scott H. Church frequently teaches courses in popular culture, music, and media studies. His research primarily uses cultural criticism, aesthetics, and rhetorical theory as analytic lenses for digital media and mediated popular texts, as evidenced by his 2013 dissertation "All Living Things are DJs: Rhetoric, Aesthetics, and Remix Culture." During his graduate studies in the Department of Communication Studies at the University of Nebraska, Lincoln, his research earned him the departmental Phyllis Japp Scholar Award, a top paper honor from the Western States Communication Association, and a competitive invitation to present his research on remix at the National Communication Association's Doctoral Honors Seminar. His research has also been published in *The Information Society* and *The Journal of Information Technology & Politics*. He currently teaches at the University of Utah and resides in the Salt Lake Valley with his wife and four children.

Olivia Conti is a PhD student in Rhetoric, Politics, and Culture in the Department of Communication Arts at the University of Wisconsin—Madison. Her research focus is digital rhetoric, specifically the ways in which users encounter and attempt to shape policy through their everyday online behavior and content production.

Desiree D'Alessandro is a professor at the University of Tampa where she teaches classes in art and technology, digital video production, and digital citizenship. She has exhibited works at the Santa Barbara Museum of Art and Contemporary Arts Forum in California and the Brevard Art Museum, Atlantic Center for the Arts, and Tampa Museum of Art in Florida. Additionally her video works have screened at the European New Media Art Festival in Germany, the Experiments in Cinema Festival in New Mexico, the RE/Mixed Media Festival in New York, the Rogue Political Remix Festival in California, and the Festival of the Moving Image in Florida. Her writing has been published in *ArtUS* and *Transformative Works and Cultures* and she has presented at diverse conferences including the Open Video Conference in New York, International Conference on Arts and Humanities in Hawaii, Media Fields: Contested Territories in California, and Digital (De-)(Re-) Territorializations in Ohio.

Cicero Inacio da Silva has been a leading researcher in the Brazilian digital media art field for more than 20 years. He coordinates the Software Studies Initiative group in Brazil in partnership with the University of California, San Diego (UCSD) and City University of New York (CUNY). He was digital art curator for the Brazilian Digital Culture Forum, digital communities honorary mention at the Prix Ars Electronica in 2010. He was a visiting researcher at the Center for Research in Computing and the Arts (CRCA/UCSD) from 2006 to 2010 and a visiting scholar at Brown University (2005). He was a digital media art curator for several media art festivals including the Electronic Language International Festival (FILE) and the Digital Culture Festival in Brazil. His vitae includes associations with key digital media thinkers such as Ted Nelson, Lev Manovich, and George Landow. He currently holds an appointment as a digital media tenured adjunct professor at the Federal University of São Paulo (UNIFESP).

Jesse Drew's research and practice centers on alternative and community media and their impact on democratic societies, with a particular emphasis on the global working class. His audiovisual work, represented by Video Data Bank, has been exhibited at festivals and in galleries internationally. *Open Country* is his current film project, a feature documentary on the politics of American Country music. His writings have appeared in numerous publications, journals, and anthologies, including *Resisting the Virtual Life* (City Lights Press, 1995), *At a Distance* (MIT Press, 2005), *Collectivism After Modernism* (University of Minnesota, 2007), *West of Eden* (PM Press, 2012). His new book is *A Social History of Contemporary Democratic Media* (Routledge, 2013). He is currently professor of Cinema and Technoculture at UC Davis, where he teaches media archaeology, radio production, documentary studies, electronics for artists, and community media. Before coming to UC Davis he headed the Center for Digital Media and was Associate Dean at the San Francisco Art Institute.

Nicola Maria Dusi, PhD in Semiotics, is Senior Lecturer of Media Semiotics at the University of Modena and Reggio Emilia (Italy), Department of Communication and Economics. He is the author of the semiotic essay *Il cinema come traduzione* (Turin: Utet, 2003). He coedited the essay *Remix–Remake. Pratiche di replicabilità* (Rome: Meltemi, 2006) and the essay *Matthew Barney: Polimorfismo, multimodalità, neobarocco* (Milan: Silvana Editoriale, 2012). He also coedited some monographic issues of international journals: *Versus* (85–87, 2000) dedicated to "Intersemiotic Translation"; *Iris* (30, 2004) dedicated to "Film Adaptation: Methodological Questions, Aesthetic Questions"; and *Degrés* (141, 2010) about "Dance Research and Transmedia Practices."

Emily Erickson is an award-winning teacher who specializes in media law and has taught and developed several original communications courses as well. Her research focuses on First Amendment jurisprudence and the role of journalists in public records policy, an interest propelled by her work in helping create Alabama's first freedom of information group. She is the coeditor of *Contemporary Media Issues* and has published legal and communications research in a number of academic journals. In 2014 she authored "The Watchdog Joins the Fray: The Press, Records Audits, and State Access Reform" for *Journalism & Communication Monographs*.

Eric S. Faden is an Associate Professor of English and Film/Media Studies at Bucknell University (Lewisburg, PA). He studies early cinema and digital image technologies. He also creates film, video, and multimedia projects that imagine how scholarly research might appear as visual media. These works appear in a variety of modes including traditional documentary, scholarly video essays, and avant-garde remixes. In addition, he also works as a commercial filmmaker with a broad range of clients from a biotech start-up to a US Federal Judge as well as advocacy groups like the Electronic Frontier Foundation and the Independent Film & Television Alliance.

Rachel Falconer is a curator, writer, and producer operating at the intersections of technology, networked behavior, and contemporary art. She is Head of Art and Technology at The White Building (London's center for art, technology, and sustainability) and structures an internationally acclaimed residency program in association with Eyebeam, LUX, The Goethe-Institut, IASPIS, and Bloomberg. As coeditor at Furtherfield she regularly contributes articles to the Furtherfield network and is a founding member of the collective Hardcore Software. She is regularly invited to participate in exhibitions, panel discussions, and events in her field—including at the Tate, the Barbican, the Royal College of Art, Rhizome, Furtherfield, and Goldsmiths University. Her practice is hybrid and interdisciplinary in approach, and she draws on her international experience in the viral advertising and gaming industries to inform her systems-based practice. Her ongoing research focuses on the pathologies surrounding distributed knowledge production and consumption and networked behavior patterns.

Katharina Freund completed her PhD in digital communication at the University of Wollongong in Australia. Her dissertation analyzed the online community of fan vidders, discussing how fanvids reimagine televisual texts. She is now pursuing an alt-ac career as a digital learning developer at the Australian National University and writes about fanvids and online communities in her spare time.

Owen Gallagher received his PhD in Visual Culture from the National College of Art and Design (NCAD) in Dublin. He is the founder of TotalRecut.com, an online community of video remixers and archive of remix videos. He is a co-founder of the Remix Theory & Praxis seminar group and author of a number of research papers, articles and book chapters on remix culture, intellectual property, and visual semiotics. He is a lecturer of Web Media at Bahrain Polytechnic, where he teaches audio and video postproduction, 3D animation, and advanced interactive applications, as well as producing and publishing his own remix videos.

Nate Harrison is an artist and writer working at the intersection of intellectual property, cultural production, and the formation of creative processes in modern media. He has both exhibited and lectured internationally. He serves on the faculty at the School of the Museum of Fine Arts, Boston. He is the recipient of the 2011 Videonale Prize as well as the 2013 Hannah Arendt Prize in Critical Theory and Creative Research. He is completing his doctoral dissertation "Appropriation Art and Intellectual Property: Rethinking Authorial Agency in Postmodernity and Beyond" at the University of California, San Diego.

Martin Irvine is the Founding Director of the graduate program in Communication, Culture, and Technology at Georgetown University where he has been a professor for over 20 years. His research, publications, and teaching span a wide range of fields, including classical and modern languages and literature, philosophy, semiotics, art history, media theory, and the Internet and digital media. He has a PhD from Harvard University, where he also learned computing and became the first liberal arts student to write a dissertation on a computer. He has been a pioneer and advocate of Internet and Web computing in the university since the early 1990s. He has recently published on street art and the city, and is currently working on a book that presents a new interdisciplinary view of semiotics and media theory. He has also been active in the art and music communities as a gallery curator and promoter of contemporary music.

Elisa Kreisinger is a Brooklyn-based pop culture hacker mashing up *Mad Men* into feminists and *The Real Housewives* into lesbians. Her 2012 US Copyright Office testimony helped win crucial exemptions to the Digital Millennium Copyright Act, decriminalizing DVD ripping for artistic statements. She is a contributor to *The Book of Jezebel* and *The Future of Now: Making Sense of Our Always On, Always Connected World*. A former fellow at the Center for Social Media at American University and artist-in-residence at Public Knowledge and Eyebeam Art and Technology Center, Elisa currently speaks around the world on the power of remix and remaking pop culture.

J. Meryl Krieger's research into remix and mashup video is a logical extension of earlier research. She began exploring the ways that media creators and culture producers interact with recording and production technologies, first in face-to-face audio recording sessions and later in online production spaces. Her current research explores how creative and improvisatory modes of performance are translated through online media technologies including remixing, pre-, and postproduction issues of crowdfunding and crowdsourcing, and the impact of these technologies on local performing communities in the United States. She teaches part-time on issues of gender, technology, and popular culture as sociological issues at Indiana University-Purdue University, Indianapolis.

John Logie is an Associate Professor of Rhetoric in the Department of Writing Studies at the University of Minnesota in Minneapolis. His work has centered on authorship, copyright, and rhetorical invention, with a particular emphasis on these topics as informed by the advent of networked digital media. His 2006 book *Peers, Pirates, and Persuasion: Rhetoric in the Peer-to-Peer Debates* (Parlor Press) focused on the mischaracterizations of peer-to-peer technologies as facilitators of "piracy" and "sharing." This book was made freely available (and remains freely available) via a Creative Commons license. His work is directed at maximizing access to creative work—for creators and consumers—by streamlining and recalibrating copyright laws to reflect the realities of twenty-first century technologies.

Diran Lyons produces political remix videos which have been featured by *Billboard*, *Boing Boing*, *Entertainment Weekly*, *Huffington Post*, *Mashable*, *MSN*, *NY Magazine*, *OC Weekly*, *SF Weekly*, *Slate*, *Time*, *VIBE*, *WIRED*, and the IMDb most popular short film ratings, where he was the first remix artist ever to reach Number One. Examples of his remix work have been presented at Ars Electronica in Linz, Austria, Cut Up at Museum of the Moving Image in New York, and ROFLcon at Massachusetts Institute of Technology. Lyons's participation in notable film festivals and video exhibitions includes LA Shorts Fest in Hollywood, CA; Athens Video Art Festival in Athens,

Greece; RE/Mixed Media Festival in Brooklyn, NY; Antimatter Film Festival in Victoria, British Columbia, Canada; Reuse Aloud at The NewBridge Project in Newcastle Upon Tyne, UK; SAME OCEAN at The Armory Center for the Arts in Pasadena, CA; among others. His viral video *99 Problems (Explicit Political Remix)* won the Pirate Flix Video Remix contest, juried by Cory Doctorow.

Lev Manovich is the author of Software Takes Command (Bloomsbury Academic, 2013), *Soft Cinema: Navigating the Database* (MIT Press, 2005), and *The Language of New Media* (MIT Press, 2001) which was described as "the most suggestive and broad ranging media history since Marshall McLuhan." Manovich is a Professor at The Graduate Center, City University of New York (CUNY), and a Director of the Software Studies Initiative which works on the analysis and visualization of big cultural data. In 2013 he appeared on the List of "25 People Shaping the Future of Design" (between Casey Reas at no. 1 and Jonathan Ive at no. 3).

Conor McGarrigle is an Irish new media artist, researcher, and educator working at the intersection of digital networks and real space. His work is concerned with the integration of digital technologies into the everyday, the spatial implications of location-aware mobile devices, and the social, political, and cultural implications of big data. His practice is characterized by urban interventions mediated through digital technologies that explore the avant-garde legacy of walking as art reimagined for the smartphone age. Projects have included a drive along the longest street in the US documented by satellite, data mining Vine to create a 24-hour portrait of social media as performance, iPhone apps that create spatial remixes of literary texts and augmented reality mappings of the geography of the Irish financial collapse. His work has been exhibited in over 70 exhibitions worldwide including the 2011 Venice Biennale, Fundació Miro in Mallorca, the St. Etienne Biennale, EVA International, SIGGRAPH, Site Santa Fe and FILE São Paulo. He is an Assistant Professor in the Emergent Digital Practices program at the University of Denver.

Kembrew McLeod is a writer, filmmaker, and Professor of Communication Studies at the University of Iowa. He has published and produced several books and documentaries about music, popular culture and copyright law—including *Pranksters* (New York University Press, 2014) and *Freedom of Expression®* (University of Minnesota Press, 2007), which received the American Library Association's Oboler book award. *Copyright Criminals* aired on PBS's Emmy Award-winning documentary series *Independent Lens*, and his writing has appeared in *The New York Times, Los Angeles Times, Village Voice, Slate, Salon, SPIN,* and *Rolling Stone.*

Eduardo Navas is the author of *Remix Theory: The Aesthetics of Sampling* (Springer, 2012). He implements methodologies of cultural analytics and digital humanities to research the crossover of art and media in culture. He has been a juror for Turbulence. org (Boston) in 2004, Rhizome.org (New York City) in 2006–07, and Terminal Awards in 2011. He was a nominee for the 2005 Rockefeller Foundation New Media Fellowship. Navas was also consultant for Creative Capital (NYC) in 2008–09. He was Gallery Coordinator, Researcher and Senior Writer for gallery@calit2, UC San Diego in 2008. He has lectured on art and media theory, and art history, as well as studio practice at various colleges and universities in the United States. Navas currently researches and teaches in The School of Visual Arts at The Pennsylvania State University, PA. Navas is a 2010–12 Post-Doctoral Fellow in the Department of Information Science and Media Studies at the University of Bergen, Norway. He received his PhD from the Program of Art History, Theory, and Criticism at the University of California in San Diego.

Rachel O'Dwyer is a lecturer in the school of computer science in Trinity College Dublin where she teaches masters courses in media theory, technology studies, and physical computing. She is the founding editor-in-chief of the journal *Interference* (www.interferencejournal.com), the leader of the Dublin Art and Technology Association and the curator of the openhere festival (www.openhere.data.ie). She is a regular contributor to *Neural* magazine (www.neural.it) and has published broadly on issues including open source, the digital commons and sound studies, most recently in *Fibreculture* and *Ephemera*.

Paolo Peverini is assistant professor in Media Semiotics at Luiss Guido Carli University of Rome, Department of Political Science and member of CMCS (Centre of Media and Communication Studies "Massimo Baldini"). In 2013, as a visiting professor, he participated in the XIX Colóquio do Centro de Pesquisas Sociossemióticas. He gave lectures at the University Tuiuti do Paraná of Curitiba and at the ESPM of São Paulo. His publications include *Social guerrilla. Semiotica della comunicazione non convenzionale* (in press), "Environmental issues in unconventional social advertising. A semiotic perspective" (*Semiotica* vol. 2014, issue 199), "A efetividade das imagens na comunicação de interesse público: estratégias de veridicção" (*19° Caderno de Discussao do Centro de Pesquisas Sociossemioticas PUC-SP*), "Manipulaciones en la red. El mashup como consumo creativo" (*Revista de Occidente*, n° 370, 2012), *I media: strumenti di analisi semiotica* (2012), *Unconventional. Valori, testi, pratiche della pubblicità sociale* (2009), *Il videoclip. Strategie e figure di una forma breve* (2004).

Gustavo Romano is an artist and curator who was born in 1958 in Buenos Aires, and lives and works in Madrid. In 1995 he founded Fin del Mundo, one of the first platforms for net art in Latin America. He was curator of the Virtual Space of the Centro Cultural Center of Buenos Aires, where he created and directed its Medialab. In 2006 he published the book *Netart.ib*, an overview of digital production in Ibero-America. He coordinates the NETescopio project, an archive of digital works of the MEIAC, a contemporary art museum in Spain. As an artist he has taken part in numerous international events, among them the 7th Havana Biennale; the 1st Singapore Biennale; the 2nd Mercosur Biennale; the 1st Fin del Mundo Biennale, Ushuaia [Argentina]; la Videonale 11, Bonn; Transmediale 03 Berlin; Ars Electronica 97, Vienna; Madrid Abierto; Transitio MX. He has received numerous prizes, among them, a Guggenheim Fellowship and a VIDA Prize of Telefonica Foundation.

Byron Russell is an artist, writer, and educator deeply interested in the creative potential and human implications of technology. In addition to remix theory, practice, and curating, his artistic practice includes site-specific interactive installations, the most recent of which, "The Master Control Station and Heptagon Server Monolith," was exhibited at the 2014 Bay Area Maker Faire and received an Editor's Choice award. An adjunct faculty member at Fresno City College, he teaches digital video production, 2D and 3D animation and storyboarding. He received his BA in Art from Pomona College and his MFA in Motion Picture Producing from the Peter Stark Program of the USC School of Cinema/Television.

Aram Sinnreich is an assistant professor at Rutgers University's School of Communication and Information, and the author of the 2010 book *Mashed Up: Music, Technology and the Rise of Configurable Culture* (University of Massachusetts Press), as well as the 2013 book *The Piracy Crusade: How the Music Industry's War on Sharing Destroys Markets and Erodes Civil Liberties* (University of Massachusetts Press). He has written about music, media, and technology for *The New York Times*, *Billboard*, and *WIRED*, has testified as an expert witness in several cases including the Supreme Court file sharing suit *MGM vs. Grokster*, and has offered his expertise as an analyst and consultant to hundreds of companies, from the Fortune 500 to fledgling startups, since 1997. Sinnreich holds an MS from the Columbia University School of Journalism, as well as an MA and a PhD in Communication from the USC Annenberg School for Communication & Journalism.

Stefan Sonvilla-Weiss is professor and head of the international Master of Arts program ePedagogy Design—Visual Knowledge Building at Aalto University/School of Art and Design, Helsinki. For the last 20 years he has worked as art and design teacher, media artist, graphic designer, author, multimedia-developer, and university professor. His international activities as researcher, artist, and speaker brought him to many institutions around the world, including Oxford University—Internet Institute, Seoul National University—Design Talks, National Institute of Multimedia Education Tokyo, University of the Arts London, Zurich University of the Arts, University of Arts and Industrial Design Linz, ZKM Karlsruhe. He is the author of *Synthesis & Nullification. Works 1991–2011* (Springer, 2012), *(In)visible. Learning to Act in the Metaverse* (Springer, 2008), *Virtual School—kunstnetzwerk.at* (Peter Lang, 2003), and he has edited Mashup Cultures (Springer, 2010) and (e)*Pedagogy Design—Visual Knowledge Building* (Peter Lang, 2005).

Monica Tavares is Associate Professor at the Department of Visual Arts at School of Communications and Arts at University of São Paulo, Brazil. She is a Visiting Scholar at Cornell University (2013–14) and at Pennsylvania State University (2008–09). She received a PhD in Arts from the University of São Paulo (2001) and a Master's degree in Multimedia from the State University of Campinas (1995). She is a licensed architect from the School of Architecture and Urbanism at Federal University of Bahia (1982) and has experience in communication, focusing on visual communication, acting on the following subjects: design, media art, and aesthetics.

Tom Tenney is a New York-based producer, arts journalist, educator, and the founder and director of the RE/Mixed Media Festival. His work as a producer, director, and performer has been seen in New York, Chicago, Los Angeles, Boston, and several cities throughout Europe. Tom received his MA in Media Studies from the New School in NYC and his BFA (Bachelor of Fun Arts) from Ringling Brothers & Barnum & Bailey Clown College. He has been a guest lecturer at the School of Visual Arts (SVA), and currently teaches a variety of media studies courses at Hofstra University.

Tashima Thomas is a PhD candidate in the Art History department at Rutgers, the State University of New Jersey. She specializes in the art of the African Diaspora in the Americas and her work focuses on food pathways, commodity fetishism, and the consumption of culture. She holds a BA in Art History from the University of Houston and an MA in Art History from San Diego State University. She is a Ford Foundation Pre-Doctoral Fellow and the recipient of the Goldman Sachs Multicultural Afrolatino Junior Fellowship at the Smithsonian. Her interests include: visual culture, fashion, film, music, food studies, popular culture, remix theory, and critical race theory.

Erandy Vergara is an independent curator and a PhD candidate in Art History at McGill University. She is a recipient of the Doctoral Fellowship from the SSHRC and the FQRSC. Her research interests include media art, global art histories, curatorial studies, Latin American studies, postcolonialism, and critical race studies. Her writing has been published in books and journals including: "[Ready] Media: Towards an archeology of Media and Invention in Mexico" (2013), and "Points, Pixels and Inches: Fragments of a Discourse of Digital Images." Some of her curatorial projects include "Parallel Visions" held at the Manchester Digital Laboratory, UK, and "Curating Mexican Video Art: A Historical Survey," held at the Laboratorio Arte Alameda, Mexico. She blogs at http://heartelectronico.org.

Nadine Wanono has a research tenure position at the CNRS: Institut des Mondes africains. She took part in the workshop organized by Jean Rouch in Mozambique (1977–79). She conducted her field work among the Dogon people in Mali, where she produced several films which were selected by numerous ethnographic film festivals and broadcast on Arte. As Visiting Associate Professor at UCSB, she started research on the role and impact of digital technologies in visual anthropology. In 2005–07, she conducted a seminar on the subject *Singularités et Technologie*. From 2011 she initiated a collaboration with Le Cube, digital art center (www.lecube.com), to present an encounter entitled Digital Anthropologies. In 2012, she coedited a special issue of the *Journal des anthropologues* entitled Creation and Transmission in Visual Anthropology, No. 130/131.

INTRODUCTION

Eduardo Navas, Owen Gallagher, and xtine burrough

The Routledge Companion to Remix Studies includes a set of selected texts from different fields of research that reflect on the history and ongoing development of remix culture. The chapters offer varied critical and historical approaches to the act of remixing, thus making evident the direct connection of remix studies to previous schools of thought. Remix studies is the result of a long process of rich cultural production directly informed by computing technology. However, while remix, as an activity and a scholarly pursuit, enjoys much international attention, it has no concrete paradigm of reference. Its interdisciplinary nature demands a fragmented approach that is self-aware of its main role as a point of entry to enrich ongoing discourse in the respective fields that use it to expand their specific research interests. Consequently, *The Routledge Companion to Remix Studies* aims to function as a framework that extends beyond book form to support a growing community by offering a concrete point of reference based around ongoing discussions and online resources.

The motivation to develop a remix studies reader came out of our many exchanges with other like-minded researchers. We have been active at international conferences such as the Remix Cinema Workshop (Oxford, 2011) and the Open Video Conference (New York, 2010), Bastard Pop Conference at Museo Universitario del Chopo (Mexico City, 2013), as well as the Remixed Media Festival (New York City, 2012, 2014) among others. During 2009–2011, a series of seminars organized by Owen Gallagher developed international interest to the point that researchers, professors, and graduate students from different parts of the world joined the discussions. It became evident that certain themes recurred, and this led us to consider editing this book as a demonstration of remix as a rich, scholarly field of research.

Remix studies branches out of remix culture, an organic international movement that began around the late Nineties, which is closely linked to open source and do-it-yourself (DIY) activities that became relevant on the Internet around that time. Copyright lawyer and activist Lawrence Lessig contributed to making the term "remix culture" popular when he founded Creative Commons in 2001. The fundamental concept of remix culture is based on the act of using preexisting materials to create something new as desired by any creator—from amateurs to professionals. As a practice, remix was first made popular in music communities, such as disco and hip hop, beginning in the 1970s, initially in New York City. The creative activity of remixing music became a trend that eventually spread to major cities all over the world. Though this is often a popular understanding of the roots of remix, some contributors in this publication question this usual contextualization. Various remix theorists argue that positive attitudes relating to musical remixes changed how people understood their creative output and its relationship to intellectual property. Needless to say, the premise of remixing has led to major legal conflicts between the private sector and growing social media communities on the Internet.

For such reasons the focus of many conferences and much of the literature on remix deals with issues that bring together copyright and cultural production based on interdisciplinary approaches by activists, who may be lawyers or economists, as well as cultural critics, computer engineers, and artists. Due to the interdisciplinarity of remix culture, remix studies is becoming a complex field. Its position in relation to other contemporary fields of research, especially the digital humanities, is ripe for analysis. Many researchers who attend conferences and write about remix culture align themselves with this paradigm, including the editors of this publication.

The Routledge Companion to Remix Studies is primarily written for scholars (including researchers, lecturers, and students) interested in some or all aspects of remix studies, across a range of academic disciplines. Such fields include art education, art history and theory, communication studies, composition and rhetoric studies, critical theory, design, digital humanities, media and cultural studies, musicology, new media studies, studio art practice, visual culture, and among many others in diverse fields in the humanities and social sciences. We also aim for this collection to be accessible and of interest to media professionals, amateur remix practitioners and members of the general public with an interest in remix. In short, the only prerequisite for anyone who wants to engage with this book is a basic interest in remix—as an activity, as a discourse, or both.

The essays comprising this volume demonstrate that creative production is a political activity. For remixers, there is often friction between creative freedom, intellectual property, and copyright law. For this reason many, if not most, of the texts included reflect directly or indirectly on the implications of intellectual property and creativity. A few texts expose polemical instances of fair use injustice, while others shed light on possibilities to compromise while pushing for more open spaces that support collective-critical reflection. Others are more radical, and demand or, at least, make a strong case for radical changes to intellectual property laws, while developing a more historically informed attitude toward collective creativity.

This very publication is not exempt from the politics of authorship and copyright. In effect, the 41 chapters that comprise this volume are published with one of the most traditional copyright contracts between author and publisher. This certainly is a paradoxical position. As editors, we tried to negotiate for a more flexible contract to the best of our abilities, but we were not successful (again, compromise is at play and readers should understand that this volume is among others in the "Companion" series that Routledge has developed with the same copyright policy). As a result some contributors left the project, while others stayed because, like us, they believe in the debate this publication can lead to, even under a traditional copyright agreement. One of the reasons we were unable to include the work of some contributors we initially approached is that they wished for the book, or at least their contribution, to be released under a less restrictive copyright agreement, from nonexclusive terms to a "copyleft" Creative Commons license. Such uncompromising ideals are admirable, and we understand the position our peers have taken in this regard. However, our hope is that because this book is published with a traditional copyright, it will help to draw attention to and encourage discussions among the remix community, publishers, and media corporations, about the complex intellectual property issues facing creators in the contemporary media environment.

Another reason we believe that publishing these essays with Routledge as a scholarly book with a traditional copyright is a positive step toward a more open future for creativity is that, in our view, such a publication will function well within spaces that resist radical change—as opposed to trying to create change from the outside. For this reason the *Companion* is designed to be read by practitioners, scholars, and researchers, who are already involved in remix studies as well as others who generally may not be interested in the field itself, but who share a concern with the issues it faces. Our aim is to bring these individuals together, or at least make them aware of issues that are not fully being discussed in their respective fields using the same language. We hope that *The Routledge Companion to Remix Studies* becomes a concrete stepping stone that functions from within the very system that all of its contributors are trying to change for the future of creativity in an increasingly networked culture.

This volume is not just a book. We expect to produce ongoing discussions and resources online to encourage users to engage with the content in an interactive way. The book's companion website, www.remixstudies.com, will act as the central hub through which readers may find additional chapter content, classroom resources, discussion forums, seminars and expanding archives of remixed media. We hope to use the website to facilitate a growing network of scholars interested in remix studies, to share ideas and content and engage in meaningful discourse with like-minded individuals.

Given the many facets of remix and its interdisciplinarity in research and practice, *The Routledge Companion to Remix Studies* is organized into five major parts: History, Aesthetics, Ethics, Politics, and Practice. The chapters under each heading, while certainly relevant to the focus of their respective parts, more often than not crossover to other areas. It is also worth noting that quite a few of the texts adopt differing positions and also contextualize the history of remix with multidisciplinary emphases on important cultural moments. The anthology in effect begins to function more like a contextual collage that sheds light on the complexity of remix as a cultural and political activity.

> Practice part contributions that relate to the History part include Chapter 33 by Nate Harrison, Chapter 40 by Jesse Drew, and Chapter 41 by Kevin Atherton.

Part I: History

The History part includes essays that reflect upon and reconsider the history of remix. While the concept of remixing was originally made popular in music culture during the late 1970s, throughout the 1980s and 1990s the act of recombining preexisting material was, as it still is, often used to reference and contextualize prior acts of recombination in all forms of media. One of the aims of this part is to provide a critical analysis of the complex history of remix in relation to other theories of recombination. The chapters assess how principles of remix have been at play from the early days of rhetoric to our contemporary times of media saturation.

The part opens with Martin Irvine's contribution "Remix and the Dialogic Engine of Culture: A Model for Generative Combinatoriality" which makes a clear case for remix as part of a rich history of communication relying on hybridity and recombinational strategies that has been in place well before the concept of remix was being used to discuss hybrid works. Irvine relies on concepts of dialogism as well as cognitive research. Particularly, he cites the research of Mikhail Bakhtin and Charles Sanders Peirce to trace how meaning is created, recontextualized, and extended in all forms of communication. Irvine's argument is that the elements at play in remix include a broad set of variables closely linked to semiosis and linguistics. Scott H. Church, in his text "A Rhetoric of Remix," repositions remix as a form of mimesis—or, at the very least, an extension of the long tradition of rhetorical practice. He specifically focuses on the work of Isocrates to develop a comparative analysis of remix and rhetoric. Church argues that remix is part of a long tradition that should be understood as part of a complex web of activities at the very foundations of Western tradition.

Stefan Sonvilla-Weiss's contribution "Good Artists Copy; Great Artists Steal: Reflections on Cut-Copy-Paste Culture," focuses on major shifts of the early modern period and industrialization that clearly expose our necessity to collaborate and produce cultural artifacts and meaning. He argues that the printing press already exposed the contradiction of creativity currently at play in contemporary times for collective production. Consequently, he offers an elaborate conceptual map, beginning in the nineteenth century, of major developments that inform the act of remixing as it is currently understood across the history of various disciplines in the humanities. Vito Campanelli's "Toward a Remix Culture: An Existential Perspective" relates the research of Vilém Flusser to remix as a rhetorical practice, and proposes the argument that a creative work is never completed but rather is constantly passed on to others for further elaboration. His text evaluates how basic elements of remix were already at play in the theories of Flusser and are more than evident in the way creative production is at play in the time of telematics. Kembrew McLeod's "An Oral History of Sampling: From Turntables to Mashups" is a textual collage consisting of quotes by DJs, musicians, and artists taken from his published research. His essay explores the complex process of creativity and intellectual property; it puts into practice the multilayered issues at play in the act of sampling music. The quotes are by some of the most important figures in the history of R&B and hip hop. The excerpts range from basic creativity to whether or not sampling is a justified act that should be paid for. Cicero Inacio da Silva's "Can I Borrow Your Proper Name? Remixing Signatures and the Contemporary Author" revisits the concept of the author as theorized by Jacques Derrida, Roland Barthes, and Michel Foucault among others in order to reflect on how remix is dependent on assumptions of authorship being integral to the process of recombination. Remix is a ripe space where the role of the author has been questioned, as da Silva explains, and for this reason he offers a detailed analysis of how authorship and remix are intertwined and develop meaning that constantly appears to deconstruct itself. He repositions and revitalizes remixing as a paradoxical complement to authorship.

Margie Borschke evaluates the limitations of remix. Her text "The Extended Remix: Rhetoric and History" argues that remix has been contextualized within a specific and limited framework that makes it specific to digital culture. Borschke reviews the relationship of analog to digital recordings and how their material differences are part of a complex practice that goes well beyond a narrow understanding of remix as something that is relatively new. She particularly takes on the arguments of Lawrence Lessig to question assumptions of a specific type of progress that appears to be concerned with the "new" which is proposed as a means to recover basic acts of creativity that, in the past, were considered "natural." Eduardo Navas closes the part with "Culture and Remix: A Theory on Cultural Sublation." Navas looks at different definitions of the term *culture* to evaluate its relation to the act of remixing in historical terms. He explains that the reason our awareness of remix has emerged in recent times is due to the overlapping of two layers of cultural production that introduce and recycle material we produce. His text aims to shed light on how and why the assimilation of new material appears to be an inevitable process.

Many of the texts above certainly cross over in interests and share questions that make a case for a historical understanding of remix. Many, if not most, chapters also contradict each other or take on divergent views on the history of remix: where it comes from and where it may be going. This first part serves as a precedent to the multilayered contextual collage that is evident in the parts that follow.

Part II: Aesthetics

This part is concerned with the production and reception of remix in visual culture. How the aesthetics of diverse communities influence remix is a key area of exploration, as is the question of whether or not remix can be considered an art form in its own right, or if it is merely derivative of other fields of artistic practice. Consequently, issues of specialization, and the crossover from one creative field to another are central to gain-

> Practice part contributions that relate to the Aesthetics part include Chapter 31 by Gustavo Romano and Chapter 32 by Jonah Brucker-Cohen.

ing a sense of the type of aesthetics that have developed in relation to the act of remixing. How remix may play a role in redefining our basic experiences is a key issue among chapter contributions.

Lev Manovich, in his essay "Remix Strategies in Social Media," takes a systematic, yet sprawling survey of remix and software and the growth of social media. Manovich focuses on how software is linked to creative and social production. In effect, he evaluates the shifts in an ever-evolving global landscape during which he develops the key question: "What is media after software?"—especially when considering social networking and media sharing. Nicola Maria Dusi's "Mixing Movies and Trailers Before and after the Digital Age," surveys several video mashups known as "sweded videos." These are videos shot mainly by fans who recreate key scenes from selected films. Dusi implements a semiotic reading in order to take assessment of the evolution of sweded trailers and films particularly during the rise of YouTube, which has enabled the sharing of fan produced material. Erandy Vergara, in her chapter, "Remixing the Plague of Images: Video Art From Latin America in a Transnational Context" makes a direct connection between creative strategies explored by remixing as understood in music and video reediting. Vergara examines the artworks of four Latin American artists to illustrate the internationalization of remix as a form of creative discourse that can be used for divergent creative purposes. She sees the videos as metacommentaries on remix itself that also expose the bombardment of images on a global level. In effect, Vergara's analysis provides insight to the complex politics of creative production in Latin American culture and beyond.

Tashima Thomas's essay "Race and Remix: The Aesthetics of Race in the Visual and Performing Arts" provides an in-depth postcolonial reading on casta paintings, Carmen Miranda, and the film *Pirates of the Caribbean*. Thomas implements a critical reading of race using remix as a theoretical framework for her three case studies, which she dubs as the Casta Grandmaster Remix, The Banana Remix, and the Monster Mash Remix, respectively. The result is the exposition of postcolonial conflicts that at first glance may appear to be part of the past, but as Thomas makes clear, are still quite prevalent in contemporary media representation of race and specifically blackness. Monica Tavares's "Digital Poetics and Remix Culture: From the Artisanal Image to the Immaterial Image" explains the process of remixing according to three cultural stages: the preindustrial, the industrial, and the post-industrial. These three stages are respectively linked to three forms of production: the artisanal, the technical, and the technological. Tavares argues that contemporary culture functions under a type of metaproduction that is character-istic of remix culture, and which is closely informed by material potentialities of digital media. Roy Christopher's chapter "The End of an Aura: Nostalgia, Memory, and the Haunting of Hip Hop" deals with the question of memory in a time of digital mass reproducibility. His inquiry is realized as an actual literary critical performance. Christopher's text by and large comprises a series of quotes by divergent authors, ranging from cyberpunk to hip hop, which take the shape of an intertextual collage that turns into a case study of authenticity in the time of constant digital reproduction. Byron Russell's "Appropriation Is Activism" is an exploration of the possibilities of the critical remix. Russell establishes a remix as distinct from its sources, new, and therefore origi-nal. He then argues that the critical remix emerges as a metagenre within remix itself. Critical remix for Russell can serve as a pivotal space to explore the connection between creativity and its politics in direct relation to the politics of culture at large. This poten-tial of the political remix is what Russell finds promising for the future of creative production.

The texts in this part range from the evaluation of the cultural importance of software to issues of race and ethnicity, as well as the politics of aesthetics as part of remix and beyond. Some of the chapters delve deep into history and politics, which makes it more than evident that a few of them would also fit or complement texts in other parts of this volume. In effect, this clarifies how evaluating remix—even with a focused lens such as aesthetics—cannot be approached with a particular and narrow research methodology. Remix demands an interdisciplinary approach to its articulation.

Part III: Ethics

Practice part contributions that relate to the Ethics part include Chapter 34 by xtine burrough and Emily Erickson, Chapter 35 by Desiree D'Aless-andro, and Chapter 38 by Eric S. Faden.

This part is concerned with ethical issues in remix culture. Issues such as those surrounding the unauthorized appropriation and reuse of copy-righted content by remixers, whether or not con-tent producers should make their work available for universal reuse, and the changing concepts of privacy and freedom of expression in the face of increasing cultural protectionism are explored in an attempt to present a balanced perspective on remix culture. In framing these issues, questions related to authorship, copyright, origi-nality, and the changing nature of audiences in the production/consumption dichotomy are considered, establishing the role of ethics in remix.

Aram Sinnreich's "The Emerging Ethics of Networked Culture" reflects upon the relationship between ethics and configurability. Sinnreich sees the definition of ethics as a challenge to take head-on in a time when extremists may propose that *nothing has changed*, or that *everything is different*. As opposed to imposing an a priori view of ethics, he decides to observe how ethics are practiced in configurable culture by its participants. He accomplishes this with an evaluation of a set of surveys that expose how complex attitudes appear to be emerging in configurable culture, and how gender, ethnicity, and class inform ethical decisions. Mette Birk, in her chapter "The Panopticon of Ethical Video Remix Practice," similarly to Sinnreich, also looks at the attitude toward redistribution of remixed production. Birk distributed a survey that, she argues, makes evident how people appear to self-impose particular attitudes and views on creativity in relation to the reuse or repurposing of someone else's creative material. Birk references the work of Michel Foucault to make sense of this apparent attitude. She deliberately refrains from recommending a possible "best practice" for creative production, and leaves the reader to ponder the many questions her findings reveal. Janneke Adema's "Cutting Scholarship Together/Apart: Rethinking the Political-Economy of Scholarly Book Publishing" is a direct reflection on the act of cutting and remix in relation to the complexity of authorship and the future of the book. Adema redefines cutting in order to propose an alternative approach to the economy of the scholarly book; one that would be more open to real ethical change while also acknowledging its shortcomings. She considers her contribution a performative text: the actual result of the very frictions she sets out to examine. Patricia Aufderheide's "Copyright and Fair Use in Remix: From Alarmism to Action" demystifies some of the assumptions about YouTube's practice of video take-downs. She explains that in reality there actually is minimal prosecution of people who upload material that corporations consider infringement of their copyright. What actually takes place quite often, Aufderheide argues, is self-censorship due to lack of knowledge of fair use by YouTube users. To shed light on these issues Aufderheide offers two case studies that demonstrate how users can strengthen their understanding of copyright laws to exercise their rights, while also functioning under copyright law as defined.

Katharina Freund looks at the history and ever-evolving idiosyncrasies of vidding in her essay "I Thought I Made A Vid, But Then You Told Me That I Didn't: Aesthetics and Boundary Work in the Fan Vidding Community." Freund's pivotal event and point of reference is the 2009 VividCon Convention (Chicago), which she uses as a starting point to reflect on how the vidding community shares aesthetics and ethics that in the past were practiced by a few who would convene periodically. She notes that such a tradition has moved on to become networked via the Internet, and evaluates the implications that this reality brings to a group who, in the past, has demonstrated insular tendencies. To make sense of the complexity of such a shared culture, Freund reviews the early history of vidding, and how it changed drastically due to the uploads of vids to YouTube, leading to contentions that remain unresolved. John Logie revisits assumptions of authorship in his chapter "Peeling the Layers of the Onion: Authorship in Mashup and Remix Cultures." He provides a detailed analysis of "No Fun/Push It" credited to the duo 2 Many DJ's; a mashup of two compositions under the same names by The Stooges and Salt-n-Pepa respectively. Logie traces in detail the many "authors" that contributed to the songs and the eventual mashup, which initially may appear to consist of three authorial figures, but when examined more closely a Pandora's box opens, and a compelling case for a better understanding of how creativity is much more complex becomes more than evident, because the production of such songs is the result of a multilayered network of citations. Mark Amerika takes on himself in "remixthecontext (A Theoretical Fiction)." In this metafictional text Amerika questions the ethical relationship of the author and the publisher. He literally remixes selections of his previous reflections to deconstruct the limitations and ongoing negotiations of copyright granted by publishers to authors who agree to release their creative material with them. The result is a self-reflexive text that puts into practice the very issues that are in effect currently across the arts, and particularly, in his case, literary practice.

As it is evident in other parts, the Ethics part is diverse in the approaches that contributors implement to reflect on the ethics of remix. Some contributors take a distanced approach by making use of surveys with a clear position as detached researchers, who may share some insiderism with the culture they analyze, while others immerse themselves fully into the subject of analysis—their writing becomes part of, if not the very subject of, analysis. It is this fluttering between being inside or outside of culture that makes the chapters in this part rich subjects worthy of careful contemplation in direct relation to the foundations of an ethical practice.

Part IV: Politics

Practice part contributions that relate to the Politics part include Chapter 30 by Tom Tenney, Chapter 36 by Owen Gallagher, Chapter 37 by Elisa Kreisinger, and Chapter 39 by Diran Lyons.

This part is concerned with the role of remix as a techno-political tool of media activism. It explores the extent to which remix may be considered effective in the service of various social and political causes. Remix is a contemporary practice enabled by the convergence of digital networking technologies, the affordability of digital media production and distribution tools, and the proliferation of access to ever-expanding online archives of spreadable digital media content. The convergence of such factors has resulted in an unprecedented democratization of the tools and techniques previously available to an exclusive minority of well-funded producers. Contributions explore the shifting balance of power in the contemporary media landscape and consider the implications of the remixer's increasing potential to reach audiences of millions with political messages. They also evaluate how such potential is in the process of being co-opted by the very system that remixers, invested in critical practice, aim to reshape.

Rachel O'Dwyer, in her contribution "A Capital Remix," evaluates how strategies of remix as an act of resistance are in fact being used by corporations for profit. O'Dwyer outlines such processes by reviewing the history and theory that shapes how the term is currently understood. She argues that material used to create remixes is artificially made scarce by way of copyright laws, which then place actual remixes in a similar position to goods for which people would compete. O'Dwyer then takes apart the cultural frictions that this artificial scarcity creates for the practice of remix. Paolo Peverini's "Remix Practices and Activism: A Semiotic Analysis of Creative Dissent" applies a semiotic reading to video mashups. Peverini approaches audiovisual works as texts which can be understood in depth as a complex system of communication. He first defines remix in terms of semiotics then applies his theory to two case studies, which are the campaigns of Greenpeace and Wikileaks. With these examples Peverini aims to demonstrate how the hybrid production found in remix practice is increasingly aimed at not only addressing but also engaging the receiver as a proactive thinker. Olivia Conti's "Political Remix Video as a Vernacular Discourse" explores the relation between video mashups that take on political issues. Conti evaluates how the vernacular is at play in remixes. Semiotics is the methodology of choice to examine how meaning in video mashups is comprised of multiple layers that may contradict while also deepening the understanding of the mashups themselves. In "Locative Media as Remix" Conor McGarrigle discusses how privacy is changing in the era of GPS technology. McGarrigle views the rise of locative data with the potential to be used for "data-powered critique." To make sense of this potential his reflection on data and privacy is developed with an awareness of issues of surveillance raised by the case of Edward Snowden. McGarrigle looks at the early production of locative media that utilized the technology to propose a critical practice that may at this point be more relevant than ever to be able to work proactively within the current system of constant tracking.

J. Meryl Krieger, in her chapter "The Politics of John Lennon's "Imagine": Contextualizing the Roles of Mashups and New Media in Political Protest" analyses a mashup of John Lennon and Occupy with the Arab Spring. Krieger argues that there is a lack of rigorous analysis of the relation between remixes and mashups as they intersect in political activism—specifically protest movements. To reify her case she provides an in-depth analysis of John Lennon's "Imagine" in protest movements prior to the age of YouTube, and then explains how the history of protest and the song by Lennon culminate in the mashup "Imagine This." Krieger's interest is to shift the tendency to consider mashups and remixes as static objects to viewing them as ongoing subjects of discourse that contribute to day-to-day political activism. Nadine Wanono's "*Détournement* as a Premise of the Remix from Political, Aesthetic, and Technical Perspectives" reflects upon the history and legacy of the Situationist International in direct juxtaposition to remix practices. This essay is in part personal reflection as Wanono worked closely with Jean Rouch, a French intellectual and educator who was largely connected to and inspired by the works of the Situationists. Wanono provides a brief and concise history of the concept *détournement* to explain how its principles are quite relevant to the way new media and remix emerged and currently function. Her contribution makes eloquent connections between code, activism, scholarly research, and remix in all its forms. Rachel Falconer recontextualizes the polymath as a remixer in her chapter, "The New Polymath (Remixing Knowledge)." A polymath is a person who is adroit at several tasks and/or fields of production. Falconer traces the history of the polymath and makes a compelling case for it to be seen as a "DJ of thought" who is critically conscious of the many challenges that networked culture presents. Falconer develops a critical model for the cultural producer of the future who will be constantly tested in various operational spaces.

The chapters in this part are quite diverse in their focus, yet they share a clear urgency in understanding how a critical practice is needed in order for remixers to be effective contributors to the global culture emerging during the first half of the twenty-first century. The texts fit multiple themes, continuing to demonstrate how remix demands a constant questioning of itself—so that its subversion by the very system it aims to critique is not successful.

Part V: Practice

This part offers chapters written by remix practitioners. The authors—often artists or remix practitioners themselves—include their first-person stories about festivals, exhibits, music productions, and video mashups, as well as performances and installations.

Contributors range from event organizers and video artists to interdisciplinary activists who thrive on the threshold of various disciplines. Many of the contributions, particularly the last few, tend to focus on video mashups. This emphasis should be considered representational of the overall prevalence of mashups in remix culture. Remix may have started in music—and much of the most polemical and popularized contestation of copyright may be found there due to the stakes major corporations have on intellectual property, but it is in video remixes where one can find the seeds of pervasive resistance—that is specifically and deliberately self-reflexive of the limitations of the very product that such mashups share. This defines the overall contextualization of remix throughout this volume. It is this context that informs the works discussed by the practitioners contributing to this part.

Tom Tenney, director of The RE/Mixed Media Festival, in his chapter "Crises of Meaning in Communities of Creative Appropriation: A Case Study of the 2010 RE/Mixed Media Festival" shares his experience in organizing the multidisciplinary event which has taken place successfully for more than four years. Tenney discusses his early influences and how they came to shape his attitude toward the practice of remixing. He also elaborates on the challenges and achievements of The RE/Mixed Media Festival in relation to bigger questions of the future of creativity and the politics of copyright. Tenney's contribution is a testament to the complex process that collaborative projects demand of organizers who often have to develop many skills to make several elements function together to succeed in producing a large festival. Gustavo Romano, in his chapter "Of Re/appropriations," provides a theoretical and personal account of the process of curating the exhibit titled Re/appropriations, for the MEIAC museum in Badajoz, Spain. The artworks included in the exhibit are also archived as part of the museum's online database known as NETescopio. Romano shares his definition of remix to explain how he used it to curate the exhibition. His essay is an entry point into an interdisciplinary practice, which brings together the roles of artist and curator: a necessary combination in the field of new media, given that, to this day, the field does not have enough curators to do justice to the ever-increasing production by emerging new media artists—particularly those who rely heavily on remix practices. Jonah Brucker-Cohen discusses the limitations of current interface design, and its potential in "Aesthetics of Remix: Networked Interactive Objects and Interface Design." He discusses selected projects of his own and others to demonstrate the potential of remix as an attitude in the production of software in order to enhance the possibilities of user interfaces. His research in effect opens a space to reflect on the aesthetics of software in an evidently emerging hybrid culture.

In Nate Harrison's chapter, "Reflections on the Amen Break: A Continued History, an Unsettled Ethics," the author shares his own experience of having his metacommentary, a brief documentary on the history of the Amen Break, become remixed into actual music tracks, as well as being potentially plagiarized in an article by a major online publication. Harrison's account makes a strong case for the creative process to be deemed as an ongoing fragmentation that can only attain meaning when it is shared, shaped, and reshaped by participants in a cultural space. xtine burrough and Emily Erickson share their collaboration—"Let's Go Crazy" video activism on YouTube—between burrough's new media production and Erickson's media law classrooms, in their chapter "Going Crazy with Remix: A Classroom Study by Practice via Lenz v. Universal." The student-created remixes of Lenz's dancing baby video created a platform for students to interact directly with Stephanie Lenz (of Lenz v. Universal) while learning about remix, appropriation, copyright, and fair use. Desiree D'Alessandro, in her chapter "A Remix

Artist and Advocate" describes selected video mashups she produced during the last few years to share how she confronted copyright infringement allegations at the university where she was pursuing a master's degree. D'Alessandro uses her own experience as an entry point to reflect on the politics of remix in terms of remix culture, as defined by Lawrence Lessig and the premise of free culture as defined by Creative Commons. Owen Gallagher's chapter "Occupy/Band Aid Mashup: 'Do They Know It's Christmas?'" reflects on his own practice as a producer of critical remix videos (CRV), focusing on his CRV "Occupy/Band Aid Mashup" as a case study. In his analysis, Gallagher considers the contrast between Western and Middle Eastern media representations of the Occupy movement and the Arab Spring uprisings, against a backdrop of cultural obsession in relation to which song will be the Christmas number one in the music charts. Gallagher argues that CRVs represent an authentic opportunity for activist remixers to have their voices heard on a global stage, utilizing the full potential of digital networking and mobile technologies, as well as spreadable media content and online distribution platforms.

Elisa Kreisinger's essay "Remixing the Remix" is a self-reflexive account of her production of "Queer Carrie," and other *Sex and The City* video mashups, along with "Don Loves Roger," a video remix of *Mad Men*. Kreisinger makes use of queer theory and feminist practice as a means to open a space for debate in which the representation of diverse cultures that may appear on the fringes is noted as elemental, and necessary for a promising development of diversity in culture as a whole. Eric S. Faden's "A Fair(y) Use Tale" explains how he and undergraduate students at Bucknell University remixed footage from Walt Disney cartoons, to create a critical commentary on copyright and fair use. Faden shares in great detail how and why he was never sued by the Walt Disney Company, and why up to the time of this publication he and his students still experience freedom of expression. In his case study "An Aesthetics of Deception in Political Remix Video" Diran Lyons discusses the principles of political remix and how he contributes to this tradition. Lyons discusses his creative production for selected video mashups that comment on the politics of George Bush, John McCain, Mitt Romney, and Barack Obama. The remixer holds a stern position against all politicians who profess empty slogans of major paradigm shifts, whether they are Republicans or Democrats alike.

"Radical Remix: *Manifestoon*" by Jesse Drew is a remix of US-produced cartoons remixed to support a voice-over narrative of Marx and Engels's *The Communist Manifesto*. Drew produced the video mashup under the tradition of political remix as a critical commentary and reflection on the politics after the fall of the Soviet Union. As Drew explains, he was quite surprised how relevant words written in the nineteenth century sounded in the 1990s. In his essay Drew also shares the unexpected viewership and worldwide recognition *Manifestoon* received once it was uploaded to YouTube by an anonymous person without his permission. Kevin Atherton's "*In Two Minds*" is a critical reflection on the remixing of a 1978 performance more than 30 years later, in 2014. Atherton performed himself having a discussion with footage of himself from 1978. The first time he performed this piece in 2013, he realized that the concept of conversing with footage from decades back in front of an audience was a rich ephemeral experience full of potential for the reflection on issues of original experiences and their recontextualization into the future. This was possible, as Atherton explains, because unlike most performances in the Seventies, his was documented. In a sense, Atherton touches on the richness of the recorded object in similar fashion to DJs who realized that there is great potential in the creative mix of a record, and even more in its remix.

Not surprisingly, the chapters included in the Practice part demonstrate a wide range of diversity. Many of them would complement the other themes included in this book (in fact some are mentioned in chapters blanketed beneath other themes), thus illustrating that remix remains an interdisciplinary practice among divergent cultural producers from a variety of scholarly and/or production backgrounds. We hope readers will notice how the artists and producers included in this part put into action the many ideas discussed and theorized in the other four areas (History, Aesthetics, Ethics, and Politics) of the book. Toward this goal, we have included notes in the sidebar throughout the text to indicate where themes that arise in the first four parts are further articulated, from a practitioner's point of view, in the Practice area of the text.

While this manuscript is in no way conclusive on the nature of remix studies—we considered other themes and certainly there are new themes that emerge each year—our goal is to create a baseline anthology for students, practitioners, and digitally empowered citizens interested in remix to understand it as a discourse and practice. We hope you will join us online at remixstudies.com and continue to develop this important area of research, practice, and online communication.

Part I

HISTORY

1

REMIX AND THE DIALOGIC ENGINE OF CULTURE

A Model for Generative Combinatoriality

Martin Irvine

Is the cliché "everything is a Remix" more than trivially true? The terms Remix, appropriation, sampling, and mashup are used so generally, in so many contexts, and at different levels of description that they don't provide a useful vocabulary for explanation.[1] "Remix" has become a convenient metaphor for a mode of production assumed (incorrectly) to be specific to our post-postmodern era and media technologies (though with some earlier "precursors"), and usually limited to describing features of cultural artifacts as "outputs" of software processes (especially in music, video, and photography). "Remix" and related terms are used for *genres and techniques of composition* (collage, assemblage, music Remix, appropriation), artistic *practices* (with a variety of self-reflexive, performative, and critical strategies), media and technology *hybridization* (new combinations of software functions, interfaces, and hardware implementations), and *cultural processes* (ongoing reinterpretation, repurposing, and global cross-cultural hybridization).[2] What connects all these manifestations of Remix, hybridity, and creative combinatoriality? What else is "Remix" telling us if we open up the cultural black box?

See Chapter 33 for Nate Harrison's "de-black-boxed" discussion of the Amen Break as it relates to Remix practice and culture.

Riffing on the great, often-referenced, soul album by Marvin Gaye, *What's Going On* (1971), we can say that there's always been a "deep Remix" going on at multiple levels simultaneously, and we need to find ways of bringing these ordinarily unconscious and ubiquitous processes up for awareness and description.[3] "Remix" in all of its manifestations needs to be turned inside out, reverse engineered, and de-black-boxed, so that it can reveal the dynamic, generative processes that make new (re)combinatorial expressions in any medium *possible*, *understandable*, and *necessary*.

Working toward this end, I will introduce a new synoptic view of concepts and research approaches for a more complete description of the *generative dialogic principles* behind Remix and all forms of hybrid combinatoriality. I will demonstrate how Remix, appropriation, and hybrid works implement the same *normative* processes that enable combinatoriality in all expression and are not special cases requiring genre- or medium-specific justification. Making these foundational processes understandable allows us to reposition Remix and hybrid works in the living continuum of culture, thus enabling this creative principle to do much more important critical work for us in an era of intense debates about the status of authors, artists, individual works, the cultural archive, intellectual property, and common culture.

My de-black-boxing of "Remix" draws from an interdisciplinary knowledge base with extensible methods for revealing how all works in a culture are necessarily constituted in ongoing dialogic chains and networks. The approach that I develop here expands on the concept of dialogism from Bakhtin, socio- and cognitive linguistics, generative models of meaning-making (*semiosis*) from Peircean foundations in semiotics and recent interdisciplinary work, and the generative-combinatorial-recursive models of language and symbolic cognition from linguistics and the cognitive sciences.[4]

Of course, all these fields have extensive bibliographies and complex histories of research and debate, and any summary of common areas of interest will risk eliding over intra- and interdisciplinary disputes and disagreements. I will only be able to outline a conceptual map of this interdisciplinary terrain here, and suggest some ways to mobilize these combined resources for new research. My approach is motivated by two central questions: (1) what makes dialogic, combinatorial expressions in any symbolic form *possible*, *meaningful*, and *necessary* in living cultures, and (2) how can we develop a fuller description of the generative-creative principles underlying Remix and hybrid works for more compelling arguments in the context of current debates?

An Overview of the Conceptual Repertoire: Meaning Generation, Dialogism, Combinatoriality, and Recursion

The idea of culture as a process of reinterpreting and reusing inherited resources has often been noted and emphasized by many recent scholars:[5] "[C]ulture is a complex process of sharing and signification. Meanings are exchanged, adopted, and adapted through acts of communication—acts that come into conflict with intellectual property law."[6]

Although the general concept of new cultural expressions created in a continuum of interpretive responses is well recognized, the underlying normative and necessary generative principles for cultural expression remain vaguely understood and poorly defined.

The question of *generativity* in culture was usefully defined by Yuri Lotman, the founder of an important school of thought in cultural semiotics:

> The main question of semiotics of culture is the problem of meaning generation. What we shall call meaning generation is the ability both of culture as a whole and of its parts to put out, in the "output," nontrivial new texts. New texts are the texts that emerge as results of irreversible processes . . . , i.e. texts that are unpredictable.[7]

"Texts," of course, designate any form of organized symbolic expression, and "nontrivial new texts" are those emerging from the generative dialogic process (nonrepetitive expression), expressions in any medium that expand into other networks of meaning in unanticipated ways.[8]

Finding adequate ways to describe the generative processes behind all the *observable* features of expression in a culture is difficult because we can't catch ourselves in the routine and spontaneous process of making meaningful expressions because we produce them unconsciously and non-self-reflexively. Just as we are ordinarily unaware of the grammatical, semantic, and pragmatic rules and codes that allow us to generate new expressions in unforeseen new contexts of meaning in our own native language, "Remix" in all of its forms sits on top of ongoing, generative, dialogic, and combinatorial processes that make all our symbolic systems from language to multimedia possible but *unobservable* during the process of expression and understanding itself. We have to reverse-engineer the observable outputs and de-black-box the meaning processes that made the expressions possible.

The underlying dialogic and intersubjective processes are not visible as *features* of expressions because they form the grounds of their possibility per se. Consequently, we cannot account for how and why Remix and explicit combinatorial forms of expression are as recurrent, meaningful, and prominent as they are by merely describing observable, surface features (e.g., instances of expressions with "sources"). Thinking of relations among cultural expressions and artifacts in terms of itemizable sources usually devolves into making inventories of "originals," "copies," and "derivations." Works become reified, productized totalities, outputs from cultural-technical black boxes with preprogrammed ownership labels.

Participating in this "sources and derivations" discourse, with the level of description it imposes as natural and obvious, is a form of what Pierre Bourdieu has termed "collective misrecognition."[9] We are continually socialized into maintaining—under heavy ideological pressure—ways of preserving the *misrecognition* of sources, authors, origins, works, and derivations in order to sustain these *social* categories as *functions* in the political economy and the intellectual property legal regime for cultural goods.[10] We need to pry all this loose, breaking the cycle of misrecognition, with a different concept base for more useful levels of description and analysis.

A Generative Model of Meaning-Making

For all the meanings we use in seemingly transparent ways every day, our symbolic faculties use parallel architectures of rules and procedures for combining components into meaningful wholes. To understand the necessary processes in these combinatorial structures we need to start from an *extensible* model of meaning that usefully holds for descriptions across symbolic systems (like language, images, and musical sounds in their multiple genre-specific combinations). Students in the humanities and social sciences are familiar with the French poststructuralist schools of thought that work from Ferdinand de Saussure's model of signification,[11] but a far more productive model is provided by C. S. Peirce. Peirce's model for the generative meaning-making process, which he termed *semiosis* (symbolic productivity), continues to provide new insights in many fields of research.[12]

Peirce's specialized terms are often a barrier to appreciating what he was figuring out, and I'll only point out some top-level terms and concepts important for this chapter. Throughout his career, Peirce sought out ways to describe his key insights about symbolic productivity as a dynamic activity depending on simultaneously perceptible, cognitive, dialogic, pragmatic, and intersubjective functions.[13] He zeroed in on the central problem of symbolic thought, meaning-making, and conceptual knowledge with a model that unifies production, creation, encoding, or expression (from the side of meaning generation) with interpretation, reception, or decoding (from the side of meaning understanding).

Early in his career, Peirce discovered that a sign is "something by knowing which we know something more,"[14] and that meaning cannot be "in" anything but can only be explained as an ongoing cognitive *activity* or *process* (*semiosis*) activated by human subjects connected by collective uses of symbols. Human symbol systems—from language and mathematics to pictorial images or musical sounds—incorporate a structure and a process enabling anyone to think with others and form nodes of cognitive relations in concepts that always seek completion in further relations. Meaning and learning are thus closely related in our dependence on intersubjective symbolic-conceptual steps that develop through and in time:[15]

> Thought . . . is in itself essentially of the nature of a sign. But a sign is not a sign unless it translates itself into another sign in which it is more fully developed . . . . Thought must live and grow in incessant new and higher translations, or it proves itself not to be genuine thought.[16]
>
> Symbols grow. They come into being by development out of other signs . . . We think only in signs . . . A symbol, once in being, spreads among the peoples. In use and in experience, its meaning grows.[17]

What are the consequences, then, if thought and meaning are symbolic processes continually emerging through time and always embodied in material-symbolic form? In Peirce's primary elucidation of meaning-making, "the meaning of a sign is the sign it has to be translated into."[18] Meanings "grow" in a recursive process in the sense that from one state of symbolic representations we develop higher or more inclusive concepts that can only be expressed or represented in further signs.[19]

By redefining human symbolic activity (*semiosis*, meaning productivity) in a continuum of collective uses and interpretations over time, we find that meanings are what someone *does* or *activates* by participating as a semiotic agent in a social-cognitive position with others (through conversation, writing, music, artworks, any shared cultural genre). Expressions and cultural artifacts can only function as meaningful, and recognizable as such, in *intersubjective* activity that connects expressions understood (past or prior cognition symbolically realized) to meanings developed in further symbolic combinations (connecting and projecting meanings toward future cognition and ongoing meaning-making).

Peirce's key insight was combining the *standing-for* relation in the symbolic structure with generative sequences of intersubjective *symbolic cognition* as the ground of meaning: A sign, or *representamen*, is something that stands to somebody for something in some respect or capacity. It addresses somebody, that is, creates in the mind of that person an equivalent sign, or perhaps a more developed sign. That sign which it creates I call the *interpretant* of the first sign.[20] Meaning-vehicles like words, statements, images, and musical forms are used to convey meaning because they *stand for* something interindividually cognitive, and only for (in relation to) a cognitive agent, a meaning subject, an interpreter in an interpretive community, who recognizes the kind of sign and its conceptual symbolic possibilities (for example, the multiple ways that words, images, and musical sound patterns invoke meanings for those in an interpretive community). Meaning-making can only happen through communally cognitive, intersubjective, rule-governed processes unfolding in and through human lived time.

How we build or associate meanings from the *standing-for* relation forms the third part of Peirce's meaning triad, which he termed the *interpretant* (that by means of which meaning or interpretability is disclosed), a cognitive step forming one node of relations in the unfolding development of meaning. In one of his well-known formulations of the model he states:

> A sign stands for something to the idea which it produces, or modifies . . . The meaning of a representation can be nothing but a representation . . . . Finally, the interpretant is nothing but another representation to which the torch of truth is handed along; and as representation, it has its interpretant again. Lo, another infinite series.[21]

The conceptual networks (*interpretants*) activated through making meanings in symbolic relations are thus not privately in anyone's mind or in the perceptible *properties* of sign vehicles like the sounds of a language, written characters, or the visual information we perceive from images. Peirce observed that whenever we "get" a meaning, it is always representable or expressible in additional signs in ongoing sequences (even in individual thought). Peirce's model of the ongoing development of meaning is known as *infinite semiosis*; that is, meanings unfolding in open-ended, unlimited sequences and conceptual networks with interpretive paths that are unpredictable from any one state in time.[22] The necessary structure of the symbolic process in human thought is thus always already dialogic, entailing interpretations of prior signs (an "input," as it were, from prior structures of meaning), the "meaning" of which (a new subsequent "output" meaning structure, the "interpretant") can only be expressed, represented, instantiated, or developed in further signs.

Translating Peirce's concepts into our current vocabulary, we can say that symbolic forms of expression—like understood images or a movie narrative—are a medium or interface for combining something individually *perceptible* with something intersubjectively *cognitive*. Since we live collectively in and through time, symbolic expressions in all media sustain continuities in social, communicable states of thought. This necessary structure of meaning-making developing symbolically and socially in lived temporal contexts is the ground of possibility for all our meaning and communication systems: the symbolic function cascades out through the multiple orders of conceptualization we use every day from language and writing to visual media and software-produced artifacts (Figure 1.1).

Emerging in recursive symbolic processes, meaning isn't something reified or fixed in any one set of material-perceptible tokens (as expressions "in tangible form," in the copyright definition). Expressible meaning develops in new interpretations *unpredictable* from the state of meanings realized at any one point in time. For Peirce, this recursive, future-directed continuum of meaning-making is *dialogic*:[23] "All thinking is necessarily a sort of dialog, an appeal from the momentary self to the better considered self of the immediate and of the general future."[24]

> Thought is what it is only by virtue of its addressing a future thought which is . . . more developed. In this way, the existence of thought now depends on what is to be hereafter; so that it has only a potential existence, dependent on the future thought of the community.[25]

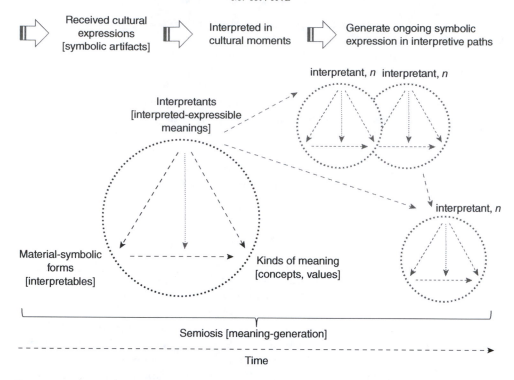

Figure 1.1 Extending C. S. Peirce's model of semiosis as a generative process (diagram courtesy of Martin Irvine)

Any cultural artifact thus forms a dense node in a network of symbolic relations and future-directed meanings in the semiosic continuum. Any work represents stored-and-forwarded semiosis, a momentarily resumed dialogic development of possible meanings interpretable in a community, meanings *made* by instantiating continually additive interpretability. A cultural work is thus an interface to the cumulative deep Remix that makes it possible.

In the complex bundles of symbolic functions in contemporary genres and media forms, we see the emergent process of meaning generation unfolding countless times every day. A news show typically begins by interpreting sources of mediated information, and then the interpretive output—the news show—will be in the form of *another mediated representation* in an open sequence. Further, using the codes of irony and parody, the whole genre of a news show and its framing of content can be reinterpreted like *The Daily Show*. New songs get released into the popular music stream every day, and musicians in every genre are always tacitly saying, "yeah, yeah, we know all *that* (prior instances of the genre, prior ways they are taken to mean), it's all in there, been there, done that; but what about *this?*" (the new piece, a new combinatorial expression that presupposes the already-expressed). We can catch ourselves in the daily, ordinary semiosic process every time we or others say, "in other words . . . ", "what he meant was . . . ," "that scene in the movie is so Hitchcockian," "that song is riffing on The Beatles . . . "

So, the first steps toward uncovering the generative structure of meaning-making gives us an important, generalizable, productive law of semiosis: *the interpretation (meaning) of a set of signs will always take the form of another set of signs.* The "outputs" of *meanings understood* become new "inputs" for further *meaningful expressions* that, when received by others, align productively with other meaning nodes activated by other meaning agents in a culture. Meaning, writ large, is always *Remix+*: meaning emerges through a "Remix" of symbolically structured "inputs" restructured into further "outputs" with a "value-add," a development of additional conceptual relations and contexts for other routes in a meaning network.

Generative Dialogism

Most artists, writers, and musicians know intuitively that they work from generative dialogic principles that enable new combinations and hybrid expressions in the genres that they work with. Herbie Hancock recently described the well-known dialogic hybridization in jazz in his own way:

> The thing that keeps jazz alive, even if it's under the radar, is that it is so free and so open to not only lend its influence to other genres, but to borrow and be influenced by other genres. That's the way it breathes.[26]

Jazz has long been the paradigm of a generative art form based on responses to, and reinterpretations of, expressions by other musicians and ongoing fusion with other genres, sounds, and traditions both in live performance and studio compositions.[27] With its ever-accruing encyclopedia of music resources and intertextual relations, jazz exemplifies a form of *practiced dialogism* that opens up the deeper underlying generative processes in other cultural forms. The concept of dialogism is essential for building an extensible model of interindividual meaning-making that also explains the necessity of linking new expressions to those of others and to prior expressions in the memory system formed by a culture's accrued artifacts.[28]

Peirce redescribed meaning-making as a conceptual-dialogic process that necessarily projects prior interpretable meaning units into future-oriented interpretable meaning units. Bakhtin's discovery is parallel to Peirce's but emerged from analyzing expressions in social use, in living conversations and in dialog representing different voices and points of view in written genres. Bakhtin discovered that we are always referencing, assuming, quoting, embedding, and responding to the expressions of others, whether in direct references or as a background of unexpressed presuppositions.[29] Everything expressed in social situations and in larger cultural contexts is fundamentally grounded in otherness—others' words and others as receivers of, and responders to, anything expressed. Anyone's expression in speech and written genres is always inhabited by the words of others, other voices and other contexts in time or place, and others different in identity from one's own:

> When we select words in the process of constructing an utterance, we by no means always take them from the system of language in their neutral, *dictionary* form. We usually take them from *other utterances* [author's emphasis] . . . Each utterance is filled with echoes and reverberations of other utterances to which it is related by the communality of the sphere of speech communication. . . . Each utterance refutes, affirms, supplements, and relies on the others, presupposes them to be known, and somehow takes them into account.[30]

In Bakhtin's terms, anything one says is always already hybrid and *heteroglot* (formed with "other[s'] speech"): both spoken and formal written genres always have otherness and others built in.

In Bakhtin's key insight, the minimal unit of expression and meaning is the "dialogized utterance," an expression in a living context that necessarily emerges from a background of prior statements and anticipates other responses in a Janus-like structure of past and future, self and others. All forms of cultural expression have *addressability* and *answerability* built in: expressions are simultaneously a response to, and an anticipation of, ongoing dialogic meaning. Living dialog is always "oriented toward a future answerword," and the "already-spoken" anticipates a future response linked in reciprocal dialogic presupposition.[31]

The dialogic principle thus extends beyond local situations of expression to the continuum of reinterpretations in cultural forms through historical time (as also recognized by Peirce). Scaled up to the level of cultural genres, texts, and media artifacts, dialogism becomes *intertextuality* and *intermediality*, that is, networks of expressions, prototypical works, encyclopedic cross-references, and genre types that presuppose and entail each other and provide the links for meanings in new combinatorial nodes.[32] "Intertextuality" is often invoked less usefully for describing "borrowing," "sources," and "influences" in recognizable recurrences (features which are, again, surface indicators of deeper, presupposed relations), but *intertextuality* and *intermediality* have greater heuristic value for uncovering generative, dialogic processes.

The dialogic principle has also been productively developed for focused empirical research in sociolinguistics, discourse studies, and pragmatics, yielding a wealth of evidence confirming Bakhtin's central hypothesis.[33] Deborah Tannen has done extensive research on "dialogicality" in everyday conversations: we always find repetition of phrases, reporting and embedding others' speech, and ongoing intertextuality (speakers in conversations presupposing and referencing prior expressions outside the current frame of conversation).[34] This kind of dialogism is a "spontaneous feature" in live discourse, and not (only) a feature of self-conscious literary forms. For conversations to be what we experience them to be, we necessarily "Remix" others' words and phrases with our own to establish conversational continuities, mark social relations among speakers, negotiate meanings, and make responses that are open to further responses.

The conclusions from research in multiple fields show that the dialogic principle is a built-in constitutive feature already in place *before* any specific language use or expression in other symbolic forms is possible. An individual person's meanings, cognition, and expression require and presuppose a community of *others*: others' expressions are necessary as structured "inputs" that initiate and perpetuate participation as an intersubject with other members of a cultural community. In Lotman's description, "the *dialogic situation* [author's emphasis], precedes both real dialog and even the existence of a language in which to conduct it: the semiotic situation precedes the instruments of semiosis."[35] The dialogic principle is thus not an *effect* or perceptible *property* of discourse and symbolic expression, but is a *precondition* for its possibility per se.

Since all symbolic systems of expression are intersubjective, interindividual, collective, and other-implicated, we find that the dialogic principle and semiosis, as enacted and activated by people in cultural communities, are the "sources" of remixes, hybrid recombinations, and appropriations. Generative dialogism provides the environment, milieu, or medium of *situated meaning transformations*. The dialogic principle is the generative engine of culture, and all living cultures are always already dialogic. Dialogic hybridization is thus the default (always on) state of culture. There is no "there" there outside the dialogic network.

Generativity and Recursion

Generative and cognitive linguistics provide important models for explaining productivity and combinatoriality in language extensible to other symbolic systems. Any speaker in any language community can generate an unlimited (infinite) set of new expressions from the limited (finite) resources of the language.[36] This principle is known as "discrete infinity," the capacity for infinite (unlimited, open-ended) expression from finite means. Language is composed of formally discrete constituents (words and grammatical structures), but the possibilities for new combinations of words in new statements expressing new concepts in new contexts are unlimited. This productivity/creativity is possible because language is a system of *symbolic functions* (words and phrases as tokens for abstract and generalizable concepts, not signals corresponding to unique entities) and *rules for syntactic combinatoriality*. Seeking ever simpler unifying principles for language, Noam Chomsky most recently uses the term "unbounded *Merge*" as the unifying operation for rule-governed combinatoriality:[37] "In its most elementary form, a generative system is based on an operation that takes structures already formed and combines them into a new structure. Call it *Merge*. Operating without bounds, Merge yields a discrete infinity of structured expressions."[38]

Parallel principles for combining structures within structures are found in all symbolic systems, though not with a formal one-to-one mapping of features from language architectures to those in other systems.[39]

The ability to generate unlimited sequences of rule-governed combinatorial structures depends on recursion, which is now widely recognized as an essential cognitive capacity that unites language, memory, and all other forms of symbolic cognition and expression.[40] The terms "recursion," "recursive function," and "recursive process/procedure" are used in several ways across the disciplines. In mathematics and algorithm theory, recursion is a logical design for looping a *function* (a software routine or process) by calling (*invoking*) itself to use its outputs as new inputs in computable processes. Recursive routines are built into every software program we use (and all those running behind the scenes). In our context, we will use the concept of recursion in the specific senses developed in cognitive linguistics. Language, other sign systems, and memory in human cognition depend on multiple kinds of recursion, both recursive processes and recursively applied rules.

Recent research in linguistics and cognitive science focuses extensively on recursion as a (if not *the*) defining feature of language in its architecture for enabling us to produce unlimited new combinations of statements of any length and for creating unlimited larger patterns of connected discourse.[41] This productive field of research provides valuable analytical and empirical methods that can be extended to the study of other symbolic systems in culture. As forms of rule-governed compositions, all genres of Remix and hybrid combinatorial works implement recursive processes and recursively applied rules from the larger symbolic systems of which they are part.

Pinker and Jackendoff sum up an accepted view in linguistics: "Recursion consists of embedding a constituent in a constituent of the same type, for example a relative clause inside a relative clause."[42] For example, any English speaker can nest phrases like "the boy who loved the girl who lived in a house that had a garden that had rabbits that ate the carrots that the girl planted that . . . " in open-ended grammatical structures limited only by the speech situation. (This means there can be no "longest sentence," "longest narrative," or "longest song" since we can always loop in another constituent of like form.) Likewise, any musician competent in a musical genre can expand a composition or performance by embedding new phrases of like form within the structures of a composition in unlimited ways. (As fans may either love or loathe, a jam band can play for hours.) From this underlying feature of recursively open combinatoriality in language, we can extrapolate a generalizable rule for expression in other symbolic forms: *in the compositional structure of a form, embed a constituent (structure) within a constituent (structure) of the same type, repeat n number of times as expressive needs require.* As we shall see, this generative rule describes recursive constituent embedding, nesting, or looping implemented in the structures of many cultural forms.

The recursive processes that enable symbolic cognition and rule-governed combinatoriality are also the key processes behind dialogism. A syntactic recursive procedure explains how and why embedded combinations must always follow a rule for the "fit" of units within an expression (a structure fits a "slot," a placeholder, within a like structure). However, a recursive procedure does not specify the *source* of the "constituent of the same type" in open combinatorial structures. The generative processes enable speakers/writers to combine units expressed as their "own" phrases within spontaneous discourse and/or as units representing embedded allusions, references, or quotations from other expression, recent or past, combined in the appropriate structural slots. Dialogism thus happens at an interface between the underlying formal generative-recursive processes and the specific symbolic forms of cultural genres and their situated contexts of social use.

Since the structures for assuming, referencing, and quoting others' and prior expression are built in, constitutive features of language as our primary intersubjective-symbolic system, then it should be intuitively clear how these recursive quotational embedding functions are distributed in multiple levels through other equally dialogic symbolic systems like music, written genres, film, and the visual arts. We use the recursive embedding function in forms we see every day: embedding "others' expression" as quotations, citations, or references in conversation and written genres (first-order dialogism), inserting appropriated "sources" in a genre of assemblage or collage within the genre's compositional structures, using quoted or sampled musical "constituent" units combined in the structures of a musical piece (e.g., as foregrounded in compositions developed with software enabled rerecording methods). We can generate unlimited combinations of meaning structures through the formal processes of syntactic recursion, and the dialogic principle explains what drives or motivates necessarily combinatorial expressions as the *situated, ongoing meanings* produced by members of a culture.[43]

Recursion is thus a unifying principle for the analysis of symbolic processes and expression in multiple disciplines. Recursion explains *how* we embed and combine units of meaning in language and other symbolic forms (the underlying syntactic, semantic, and semiosic dimensions). Dialogism explains *why* embedding "other(s') expression" is necessary in all forms of discourse and in the continuum of cultural genres over time (the pragmatic, social, and situated contextual dimensions). Dialogism, semiosis, and recursion form a powerful set of concepts and testable hypotheses that account for collective, intersubjective, and generative processes of meaning-making in cultural expressions, processes that extend into longer continuums of cultural time, history, and ongoing reinterpretation of cultural artifacts. The deep Remix begins in these intersubjective and collective symbolic processes and cascades out in all the specific expressive forms that we experience in a culture.

Collective Meaning Resources and the Cultural Encyclopedia

Our symbolic systems and media implement different component structures (e.g., language and discourse units, structures for image genres, and multimodal units in time-based media like music and film) in *parallel architectures* for combinations at different levels or layers of meaning.[44] There are two primary levels of meaning formation: the *lexicon* (dictionary-level vocabulary units, any system of minimal constituents and meanings) and the *encyclopedia* (multiple levels of conceptual organization, background knowledge, and symbolic associations, including the codes for individual genres).[45] We can analyze words and phrases combined in the syntax and discourse structures of spoken and written genres, and, by analogy, describe an artist's or musician's "vocabulary" (minimal constituent units) used in combinatorial structures. But what any specific composition *means* in a culture (for example, a text, the combined lyrical and musical form of a song, or the components of a visual artwork) isn't derived by adding up dictionary-like look-ups for the components. Rather, we create artifactual meanings in patterns generated from organized symbolic relations and shared knowledge at another level—networks of meaning that function like a cultural encyclopedia distributed through, and implementable across, all symbolic forms, genres, and media. This parallel architecture in meaning-making is summarized in Table 1.1.

For example, the *Mona Lisa* is, on one level, an instance of an Italian Renaissance commissioned portrait with its genre-specific vocabulary of minimal compositional units, but what the painting *means* (in all the senses of meaning in a culture) comes only through the way interpreters in cultural communities access encyclopedic relations of symbolic value and accrued significance "outside" the vocabulary of the painting. What the *Mona Lisa* means for us is what we can express in networks of interpretants (dialogic expressions) accessible in a shared cultural encyclopedia (some major interpretants of which are other *paintings* that reference, presuppose, parody, or riff on the historical exemplar).

Research in cognitive semantics and semiotics shows that we make meaning by multiplexing levels of *conceptual* combinatorial processes in active "online" real-time interpretation (Peirce's concept of *semiosis* as opening onto networks of *interpretants* in

Table 1.1 Levels in the parallel architecture of generative combinatoriality

Lexicon: Minimal constituents, vocabulary units of meaning composed in the grammar/ syntax of a symbolic system	Combination of constituent units in rule-governed, unlimited recursive structures for dialogic embedding and future answerability.
Encyclopedia System of culturally organized meanings and values, codes, genres, symbolic associations	Combination and hybridization of genres, types, categories, and concepts in network-like reconfigurable nodes of symbolic relations. How the contents of a cultural archive are organized into categories of meaning.

symbolic cognition): (1) we move up and down nested levels of conceptual generalization or abstraction (termed semantic frames or schemes), (2) we combine, merge, or blend concepts to form new ones (as in metaphors and hybrid genres), and (3) we interpret specific instances (tokens) of cultural genres (types) through shared codes and encyclopedic knowledge (genres as types with collectively understood rules and codes and a shared cultural knowledge base of prototypes—famous versions, exemplars—of a type).[46] Distinguishing the functions of this parallel architecture allows us to present a more complete description of what happens in active uses of meaning resources. Symbolic structures enable us to generate meanings by combining concepts that are not present in any specific instance, but supplied by engaging multiple cognitive levels in the parallel architectures of symbolic functions.

For an everyday example, most people following popular music will easily be able to express interpretive statements at multiple levels of meaning by invoking concepts in nested type categories—often mapped out in a hierarchical tree structure—that frame a pop song *as* a pop song in contexts of meaning (read "=>" as "is an instance of"):

Jay-Z song (+/− other associates) →

celebrity rap star song in relation to others in the genre →

rap/hip hop genre types and subtypes and symbolic values →

commercial pop song and music industry market categories →

hip hop positioned in celebrity culture and other popular culture artifacts (video, TV, etc.) →

global popular culture . . .

The conceptual frames depend on a cultural (and subcultural) encyclopedia of collective knowledge, values, and codes that provide the collective ground for interpretable meanings. Someone unfamiliar with hip hop music genres and recent pop culture will not get what is going on in a Jay-Z song, but the musical codes and background knowledge are publically available to learn. Similarly, a painting by Andy Warhol is not interpretable without some familiarity with the genre categories of modern art, some background in the vocabularies of representation and the presupposed cultural encyclopedia, and knowledge of the dialogic situation in the artworld that Warhol participated in. And, of course, since the dialogic continuum is ongoing, what a Warhol painting can mean today is part of an accruing socially accessible encyclopedia of symbolic associations and values (the reception history of an artist or work), forming networks of meaning that were unanticipated in the 1960s but are now part the dialogic situation that frames our interpretations. While all societies have regulating ideologies and social structures that create unequal access to knowledge and symbolic resources, the cognitive abilities for meaning generation and expression are, at all levels of this parallel architecture, intersubjective, interindividual, collective, and necessary, and vary only in individual competencies.

Remix+

Mobilizing these conceptual resources, we can redescribe Remix, appropriation, and hybrid works as genre implementations of the underlying generative, dialogic, recursive principles in the symbolic systems of a culture independent of any specific instantiation in a tangible medium. Remix as a form of ongoing dialogism is *Remix+*, not bundles of repetitions, plagiarisms, copies, or technically generated clones, but value-add interpretive nodes (instantiating a time + meaning shift or increment, the "+") formed by necessary generative, combinatorial processes in the dialogic situations of a community. Remix and hybrid works are articulations in forms that emerge from *necessary, normative* principles: (1) implementing generative principles for open, recursive combinatoriality of constituent units within rule-governed meaning systems, (2) the intersubjective, interindividual, and other-implicated grounds of meaning and expression (semiosis and dialogism as parallel generative processes), (3) the dialogic ground for appropriating and quoting other(s') expression in ongoing interpretations of a culture's artifacts through an intertextual/intermedial collective encyclopedia, and (4) generative processes that encode and externalize *future-projecting collective memory* in structures of meaning destined for reuse in the continuum of cultural expression.

These deep Remix principles also explain why all cultures are experienced as incomplete, never finalized, and in need of continual additions, supplements, and renewal of meaning (else why the proliferation of new expressions and works?).[47] Generative dialogism manifests itself in all the ways that cultural members develop sequences of recombined, additive, and accruing meanings that map out new, additional routes through a culture's symbolic networks. *Remix+* means that cultural expression is unfinalizable and always future-oriented, as Bakhtin recognized:

> Nothing conclusive has yet taken place in the world, the ultimate word of the world and about the world has not yet been spoken, the world is open and free, everything is still in the future and will always be in the future.[48]

Remix and Dialogism in Cultural Genres: Meaning Generation in Music

There are many ways that we can use these concepts and methods heuristically for analyzing exemplary works as interfaces to the architecture of generative dialogism in the symbolic systems within which a work is created and received. The contentious issues in high-profile cases of music sampling and appropriation art have been well-treated by many scholars,[49] and many examples are now over-determined in the discourse and not as useful as paradigms of normative meaning-making processes. I would like to show how we can mobilize these ideas for analyzing mainstream examples in music and visual art to uncover the normative, generative, combinatorial, dialogic principles underlying all cultural genres. The value of any theory is its ability to generate testable hypotheses that explain what we can't explain in other ways.

Miles Davis's *Kind of Blue* (1959) is the most commented on jazz album in history, forming a dense node of cultural meanings and values expressed both in interpretive discourse and in hundreds of appropriations and elaborations by many other musicians in the dialogic continuum of contemporary music.[50] The album is an interface to a dialogic moment of major reinterpretations of the cumulative, inherited musical encyclopedia (African American blues roots, jazz and bebop reinterpretations, and music theory in the European–American classical tradition). Combining the vocabularies and symbolic values of African and European traditions, Davis positioned the hybrid improvisational form of the music in the dialogic situation of the 1950s where the musi-cal forms were understood to symbolically encode ethnic-cultural identity and values. Creating this specific interpretive node as a hybrid form that combined conflicting registers in the encyclopedic meaning system meant adding value to both identity terms, African and American, as many other jazz musicians also affirmed.

Jazz improvisation is highly structured, difficult to master, and involves combinations of learned and continually practiced model forms and phrases that become structures in a generative grammar for "composing in the moment." Musical improvisation is a direct analog of the "discrete infinity" through generative combinatoriality studied in lan-guage.[51] The *Kind of Blue* sessions are unrehearsed ensemble improvisations done in one take, developed in real-time only from musical "sketches" of the formal structures. The songs are thus simultaneously compositions and performances, snapshots of expressive, open, rule-governed combinatoriality in the grammar of the musical forms.[52] In each bar of the recorded performances, we can hear the results of the generative-recursive processes used to combine rhythms, tones, phrases, harmonization, and styles from a common vocabulary selected for contextually specific functions. In improvisation, the Janus-like generative combinatorial structure provides the spaces for *quotations from the future*, the about-to-be, but not-yet-said, in dialog with the live conversation of perfor-mance and with the larger traditions internalized by the musicians. The symbolic form, activated in real-time, enables structured anticipations: projected *future* expressions as possibilities in the form are already in *memory* in the present moment.

Building on postbebop developments in jazz, Davis experimented with an additional interpretive concept: the generative potential of improvising through types of scales fundamental to classical music theory (scale *modes*). The "grammar" for each tune on *Kind of Blue* was based on a blues-rooted structure, but with a novel way to play impro-vised solos by following a classical scale rather than the blues-to-bebop tradition of developing freer-form extempore melodies following complex chord changes.[53] Davis commented that this approach opened "infinite possibilities" for new expression within the formal constraints, and the musicians refocused on the values of tone, timbre, and "space" within the form.[54]

"All Blues," the fourth track on the album, channels the values of the deep blues tradition and reinterprets the canonical blues chord progression through a modal scale and in 6/8 time.[55] A musicological description reveals how the *formal* (grammatical) combinations were motivated by the symbolic value of combining *encyclopedic* mean-ings. The lexicon and grammar of the blues are inextricably connected to the larger cultural encyclopedia of meanings and values associated with the form. Iconic songs by Robert Johnson and others in the Delta blues diaspora encode a form stabilized in a template of chord progressions, a form that provided the generative structure for multi-ple combinatorial variations in jazz and further extensions in R&B and rock genres.[56]

In "All Blues," Davis appropriates and reinterprets a distinctive feature in the blues tradition: the "blues shuffle" pattern defined by playing notes from the fifth to the sixth and flat seventh scale degrees of a chord in a rhythmic ascending and descending riff on the bass notes (a pattern with variations used in countless blues, jazz, boogie, soul, and rock styles). Davis takes this Delta roots pattern known by all jazz musicians for a 12/32 bar blues form, slows the tempo, reharmonizes the scale riff, and prescribes the Mixolydian scale mode for the improvised solos (a scale with notes we "feel" as minor). The musicians performed new, unrehearsed, improvised solos using the modal scale over the reinterpreted blues chord progression performances that have been widely studied, analyzed, and debated for understanding the astonishing skill demanded in these rein-terpretations of a musical form. All the levels of generativity, recursive combinatoriality, dialogism, and encyclopedic encoding are openly engaged. The compositions on *Kind of Blue* represent interpretive remixes on multiple levels. They are hybrid forms that affirm the generativity of the musical structures (jazz = unlimited creativity) in the dialogic situation of the culture and also renew the music's meanings in the larger cultural encyclopedia for both African American and European traditions.

Turning to interpretive Remix genres based on sampling, quotation, and encyclopedic cross-referencing in contemporary musical forms, we find that the *technical* means for combinatoriality can be used to disclose the underlying recursive, generative, dialogic processes of the expressive forms. The cultural, historical, and technical roots of con-temporary Remix in Jamaican dub, techno, and DJ and hip hop cultures have been widely studied, and the creative functions of sampling, quoting, and referencing in popu-lar music are now commonplace knowledge.[57] Sample and source hunting have now been converted into a fan-driven marketing device on websites like whosampled.com (and accompanying mobile app), which claims to "explore the DNA of music" through users' identifications of "direct connections" among a song's samples, remixes, and covers.[58]

Rather than analyzing an example here, I invite readers to make any selection of sam-ple-based songs to use as an *interface* to the shared combinatorial and dialogic processes in the parallel architectures that made the songs possible. As an interface to, and implemen-tation of, collective and intersubjective meaning processes, a Remix work can be used to reveal how the recombinations and embedded constituent musical vocabulary units (facil-itated in automated software procedures for digital media) are motivated not by the tech-nology but by the *dialogic contexts* of the musical form and the situations of production and reception in the genre's reception communities where the meaning is made.

Remix in explicit quotational and appropriation genres use the recursive combinato-rial function for embedding constituent phrases as recognizable *dialogically positioned* units of "other's" expression (quotations of prior and contemporaneous expressions with built-in addressivity and answerability). The combinatorial and dialogic process requires: (1) selecting syntactically possible units in contexts of prior symbolic relations and encyclopedic values (identifying and selecting "answerable" combinable constituent units represent initial interpretive process for linking token to typed meaning), and (2) recontextualizing the selected unit by embedding it in the compositional structure of the new expression, a meaning environment that opens up additional encyclopedic meaning relations that were not active in the situation of the prior expression. Context is all—in every sense of the term.

For both the composer and audiences in the cultural community, the selections of combinatorial units are motivated by how they can function dialogically in new or dif-ferent contexts of meanings associated at the encyclopedic level, not as self-same *copies* or *repetitions* of the already-expressed in their *disquotational* lexical form (that is, in their prior "authored" form). The recontextualized units work as synecdoches (parts for the whole), not only for other songs and artists but as tokens for whole genres, styles, tradi-tions, concepts, and cultural values. The Remix work reveals how the dialogic process engages our encyclopedic competencies by foregrounding subsets of the musical-cultural lexicon in the combinatorial structures, sets of embedded meaning units symbolically linked to a shared cultural encyclopedia of musical meanings, values, and signature, prototypical sounds.

Daft Punk's *Random Access Memories* (*RAM*) (2013) is a compendium of orchestrated combinatoriality and recontextualization, a paradigm of creative *Remix+* through the generative structures of the musical genres and the affordances of the recording studio. For *RAM*, the musicians, Guy-Manuel de Homem-Christo and Thomas Bangalter, known as "the Robots" in the music world for their techno and voice-processed sounds, used all the resources of state-of-the-art audio technology to recover and mix the symbolic *sounds* of music genre elements in prototypical analog studio recordings from the 1970s to the 1980s.[59] Working collaboratively with many other musicians and audio engineers at multiple recording locations, they mixed recorded instrument tracks (notably funky rhythm guitar and bass), live recordings of drum tracks, analog modular synthesizers, Vocoder programming, and live orchestra recordings.[60] The integration of analog sound and digital production is seamless, even to the point of knowledgeable listeners being unable to distinguish software-simulated analog sounds from those recorded from instruments.[61]

In concept and production, the album represents a deep Remix of the symbolic features of sounds now standardized in digital samples (beats, bass grooves, riffs, percussion) but detached from how they were made. The musicians *desampled* sampling, reverse engineering the library of prototypical sampled sounds (now available as digital clones and clichés on any laptop) by re-producing and re-capturing the symbolic audio properties of the sounds that made them so *sampleable* as genre synecdoches in the first place. As Bangalter explains:

> The idea was really having this desire for live drums, as well as questioning, really, why and what is the magic in samples? Why for the last 20 years have producers and musicians been extracting these little snippets of audio from vinyl records? What kind of magic did it contain?[62]

The "magic" was in the symbolic properties of the musical sound elements now standardized as recomposable, replicable, sampled sound units. The musicians use the technical means in recording and audio production to expose the symbolic properties of combinable sounds now taken for granted as "in the mix," sounds that were sampled because they encoded specific sound values from specific instruments and audio technologies in their time and place.[63] In effect, Daft Punk de-black-boxed Remix to reveal how embeddable constituent units are used symbolically in the combinatorial processes of the forms.

In *RAM*, we can observe how a recombinatorial mix—as an interpretive, dialogic process, not simply a technical product—is a reactivation of symbolic forms in a continuum of value-add interpretation, new expression as *Remix+*. Without using explicit, quotational sampling, Daft Punk produced an interpretive Remix of styles and genres by sonic tokenization, re-producing the symbolic values of constituent elements, in a large network of encyclopedic referencing and allusion. The dialogic network of *RAM* extends to major concept album collaborative productions like The Beatles' *White Album*, Michael Jackson's Quincy Jones-produced *Thriller*, Pink Floyd's *The Dark Side of the Moon*, and Fleetwood Mac's *Rumours*. You don't need to directly sample segments from The Beatles' "A Day in the Life" or a specific James Brown funk groove to invoke these works and their values in the collective cultural encyclopedia. *RAM* reveals the generative dialogic, combinatorial engine at work in a large collective, distributed network of cultural agents, recent and past. Fully aware of the dialogic foundations of music culture and their role as encyclopedic interpreters projecting musical expressions into the future, Daft Punk set out "to make music that others might one day sample."[64]

Combinatoriality Visual Art

Remix in all its forms is an accepted *fact*, not a *problem*, in the contemporary art world. Art history is now widely accepted as a history of reinterpretations, appropriations, cross references, dialogic presuppositions, and recontextualizations. Although a canonical topic of postmodern theory, appropriation and hybrid genres are not *products* or *effects* of postmodernism, the exposure of these forms in critical debates has opened up the dialogic and combinatorial processes behind all art genres.[65] Although widely studied from multiple approaches, artworks based on appropriation and mixed sources are still too-often discussed as patchworks of isolated atomic units "taken" from other artifacts of expression, not as rule-governed genre implementations of dialogism developed in the combinatorial processes of the symbolic forms. Parallel with the generative processes in other media of expression, new combinatorial structures in visual art are motivated by the dialogic situations of a culture community within which the artifacts become new nodal positions for interpretive routes in the encyclopedic network.

As in the discussion of Remix in music genres above, I invite readers to use the conceptual resources developed here to investigate works by artists that can be used as interfaces to the generative and collective meaning processes of their symbolic forms. For example, we can map out a dialogic continuum in genre hybridization, recontextualization, and interpretive appropriation in the works of Robert Rauschenberg and Andy Warhol (from the 1950s to the 1980s) and Shepard Fairey and contemporary street artists (from the 1990s to the present), a dialogic continuum that continues in most contemporary art.[66] A Google image search on these artists will provide many examples that can be studied and compared for further analysis. Working with well-established concepts in their artistic communities of practice, these artists developed exemplary ways to follow deep Remix principles, working intuitively and heuristically through the generative, recursive combinatorial rules for the symbolic systems in art genres to create hybrid forms as nodes in new networks of meaning.

Rauschenberg's lifelong practice illustrates how the generative principles described in Chomsky's "unbounded Merge," unlimited semiosis, and dialogism can be expanded to explain the generative, recursive combinatorial principles underlying the symbolic structures of visual art. In the late 1950s and early 1960s, Rauschenberg discovered and exploited a generative principle implicit in the grammar of modern art: with the redefinition of painting in modernism taken for granted, the constituent combinable vocabulary units in the form of a composition could come from any source or medium because combinatorial rules provide the "slots" or placeholders for embedding visual units, but do not determine the source, type, or medium for what can become meaningfully combined. Parallel with Warhol's appropriation of photographic reproduction for painting, Rauschenberg saw that image constituents in a composition—embeddable units within other units—can come from any source—reproduced photographs from the mass media, magazine pages, and photo reproductions of other art works.[67] Photomechanical screenprinting techniques allow multiple reuses of constituent image units in combinations within and across compositions in serial form, effectively erasing the boundaries between painting and printmaking and uniting them as image making technologies for appropriating image units from both the museum archive of art history and from every form of mass media imagery in popular culture.[68] Graphic and painterly marks or gestures can be quotational (from other sources) or directly imposed on a canvas or other material substrates. A combinatorial unit in a structure can also be a material object or thing—not representations of things but found objects from the city that function as synecdoches of the dense, accumulated meanings of urban experience.

Rauschenberg called his new hybrid combinations "combines," that is, combinatorial meaning platforms that simultaneously engage the grammar and vocabulary for two-dimensional genres and media (painting, printmaking, drawing, photography, collage) and three-dimensional meaning structures (sculpture, assemblage, found objects). The combined grammars and vocabularies of the forms expanded contextual possibilities and opened up further networks of meaning for what artworks could be. In many ways, all contemporary art is post-Rauschenberg in the sense of being motivated by exploring all possibilities of hybrid combinatoriality in the generative logic of a form and ways of using the combinable units as material synecdoches in contexts for configuring other, new, or additional encyclopedic meanings in an artist's dialogic situation.

For a moving global index of Remix, hybridity, and dialogism in contemporary visual culture, street art exemplifies the generative combinatorial "unlimited creativity" principle of ever-renewable expression.[69] Shepard Fairey and other contemporary street artists around the world take the always already hybrid context of art-making and visual culture for granted and work in the expanded dialogic environment of city streets with the symbolic structures of urban visual space.[70] Since source material is everywhere, the dialogic situations of street art in urban locations motivate the interpretive remixes. Street artists use the city as a visual dub studio, extending the combinatorial principles from multiple image and graphic genres to expand appropriation, Remix, and hybridity in every direction: image sources, contemporary and historical styles, local and global cultural references, remixed for contexts and forms never anticipated in earlier postmodern arguments. Street art also assumes a foundational dialogism in which each new act of making a work and inserting it into a street context is a response, a reply, an engagement with prior works and the ongoing debate about the public visual spaces of a city. As dialog-in-progress, it anticipates a response, public discourse, commentary, and new, additional works of *Remix+*. The city is seen as a living historical palimpsest open for new inscription, rewrite culture in practice. Like jazz, street art opens onto a collaborative, participatory generative process, a dialogic engine for intuitive improvisations always open to hybridization in ever-renewable future-directed expression.

Conclusion

From the knowledge base outlined here, we have seen how the principles of generative dialogism and recursive, rule-governed unlimited combinatoriality are necessary and normative in all symbolic systems and generate the material forms of expression used in a culture. Whether we consider combinatorial elements at the level of embedded quotational constituents or in the deep Remix of symbolic resources whose meaning is contingent on networks of presupposed works, genres, and styles with complex encyclopedic relations, all levels of combinatoriality are equally generated from necessary combinatorial functions motivated by the dialogic situations of communities in time and place. All meaning systems from language to multimedia are based on generative, intersubjective and other-implicated processes that precede any specific material implementation.

So, yes, we can't *help* but Remix in forms of *Remix+*, regardless of the historical state of technical mediation. Our current technologies enable us to implement and automate *preexisting symbolic functions* that are in place before using technical tools for recombining tokens of expression. Since we're born into a generative symbolic continuum already in progress, we always dialogically, collectively "quote ourselves" to capture prior states of meaning as inputs for new interpretations in new contexts in materially reimplementable, remixable ways. In Lotman's apt definition, "culture [is] the nonhereditary memory of the community"[71] materialized in the continuum of encoded artifacts of expression. Cultural artifacts in all media bundle the functions of meaning-making into durable externalizations of intersubjective and collective cognitive processes that enable the renewable continuum of human cultures in the sequences of their historically, dialogically situated "rewritable" forms.[72] Instead of starting from the assumption that genres of Remix with explicit quotations are a special case (troubling the ideologies of the autonomy of the work and the artist/author) requiring justification, explanation, or special pleading, Remix can do much more important cultural work when redescribed as *Remix+*, an implementation of the normative generative, intersubjective, and collective meaning-making processes underlying all forms of expression in any medium.

The evidence from the knowledge base outlined here allows us to change the starting point in descriptions of Remix and hybrid expressions "in tangible form." In a Copernican reorientation of the point of observation, if we recenter the conversation by starting with the necessary intersubjective principles as defined in generative, recursive combinatoriality, unlimited meaning generation (semiosis), and dialogism, then the material form of an expression appears as a moment of orchestrated combinatoriality in the ongoing interpretive, collective, meaning-making processes that necessarily precede and follow it. This new orientation can counter misrecognitions about originary authorship and proprietary artifacts that sustain copyright law and confuse the popular understanding of Remix as something outside the normative and necessary structures of meaning-making in ordinary, daily expression.

This new point of view reveals that any work produced and received in a culture, when decrypted from the copyright ontology force field of assignable property, is, necessarily, a materialized symbolic structure encoding an interpretive dialogic pattern of combinatorial units, meanings, values, and ideas that came from somewhere and are on their way to somewhere else. In the context of debates over copyright reform in the interests of common culture, this knowledge base provides important scientific support for stronger fair use practices that counter the ideologies for "long and strong copyright,"[73] and can enable better-informed debate about novelty (how/when/why is an expression "new"?) and the criteria for proprietary ownership of forms of expression. Legal and economic definitions of cultural property must be re-synced with these fundamental facts of collective, dialogic meaning-making and mediated forms of cultural expression.

I propose this outline for a new interdisciplinary model and reorientation of starting points as an open-ended research program that can be tested and developed in our research communities for Remix studies and for the generative principles of creativity more broadly. When de-black-boxed and reverse engineered with the conceptual models outlined here, Remix and hybrid works have much more to tell us—not as reified products, but as *interfaces* to the generative, collective, and unfinalizable meaning-making processes that enable cultures to *be* cultures.

Notes

1 "Remix" as a technical artifact and as a more general metaphor is widely used, notably: Kirby Ferguson, *Everything Is a Remix*, 2010–14, http://everythingisaremix.info; Brett Gaylor, *Rip: A Remix Manifesto*, DVD (The Disinformation Company, 2009); Jonathan Letham, "The Ecstasy of Influence: A Plagiarism," *Harper's Magazine*, February 2007; Lawrence Lessig, *Remix: Making Art and Commerce Thrive in the Hybrid Economy* (New York: Penguin Press, 2008). Full documentation of the bibliography and access to source materials for this essay are available on this resource page: http://www9.georgetown.edu/faculty/irvinem/Remix/.

2 These topics are discussed from different disciplinary perspectives in Kembrew McLeod and Peter DiCola, *Creative License: The Law and Culture of Digital Sampling* (Durham, NC: Duke University Press, 2011); Kembrew McLeod and Rudolf Kuenzli, eds., *Cutting Across Media: Appropriation Art, Interventionist Collage, and Copyright Law* (Durham, NC: Duke University Press, 2011); Eduardo Navas, *Remix Theory: The Aesthetics of Sampling* (Vienna: Springer, 2012); Paul D. Miller (DJ Spooky), *Rhythm Science* (Cambridge, MA: MIT Press, 2004); Mark Amerika, *remixthebook* (Minneapolis, MN: University of Minnesota Press, 2011); Martha Woodmansee and Peter Jaszi, eds., *The Construction of Authorship: Textual Appropriation in Law and Literature* (Durham, NC: Duke University Press, 1994); Nicolas Bourriaud, *Postproduction: Culture as Screenplay: How Art Reprograms the World*, 2nd ed. (New York: Lukas & Sternberg, 2005); Lev Manovich, *Software Takes Command: Extending the Language of New Media* (London: Bloomsbury Academic, 2013).

3 Lev Manovich has developed the concept of "deep remixability" in software and media in Software Takes Command.

4 My approach presupposes the background of the canonical arguments in structuralism, poststructuralism, postmodern cultural theory, and communication theory, but I will focus here on exploring the potential of a broader interdisciplinary model. The concepts and methods of the French poststructuralist tradition (Barthes, Foucault, and Derrida) and the core theories in semiotics (Peirce, Jacobson, Greimas, and Eco) are treated extensively in our scholarly literature and require no further elaboration here.

5 See Lessig, *Remix*; Letham, "The Ecstasy of Influence: A Plagiarism." Lawrence Lessig, *Free Culture: The Nature and Future of Creativity* (New York: Penguin Press, 2005); Siva Vaidhyanathan, *Copyrights and Copywrongs: The Rise of Intellectual Property and How It Threatens Creativity* (New York, NY: New York University Press, 2001); Woodmansee and Jaszi, *The Construction of Authorship*; McLeod and DiCola, *Creative License*; McLeod and Kuenzli, *Cutting Across Media*.

6 McLeod and Kuenzli, *Cutting Across Media*, 2.

7 Quoted in Peeter Torop, "Semiosphere And/as the Research Object of Semiotics of Culture," *Sign Systems Studies* 33, no. 1 (March 2005): 169.

8 See Yuri M. Lotman, *Universe of the Mind: A Semiotic Theory of Culture*, trans. Ann Shukman (Bloomington, IN: Indiana University Press, 1990); Yuri M. Lotman and B. A. Uspensky, "On the Semiotic Mechanism of Culture," *New Literary History* 9, no. 2 (Winter 1978): 211–232.

9 See Pierre Bourdieu, *Language and Symbolic Power*, trans. John B. Thompson (Cambridge, MA: Harvard University Press, 1991), 153–154, 214–216; Pierre Bourdieu, *Practical Reason: On the Theory of Action* (Stanford, CA: Stanford University Press, 1998), 96–102, 120–122.

10 On author function in copyright and political economy contexts see: Woodmansee and Jaszi, *The Construction of Authorship*; Patricia Aufderheide and Peter Jaszi, *Reclaiming Fair Use: How to Put Balance Back in Copyright* (Chicago, IL: University Of Chicago Press, 2011), 16–33.

11 Most work in French and Anglophone semiotics and cultural theory develops or critiques the theory of Ferdinand de Saussure, *Course in General Linguistics*, trans. Roy Harris (Peru, Il: Open Court, 1986) (published in French in 1916). For context and background, see Winfried Nöth, *Handbook of Semiotics* (Bloomington, IN: Indiana University Press, 1990); Umberto Eco, *A Theory of Semiotics* (Bloomington, IN: Indiana University Press, 1976); Paul Cobley, ed., *The Routledge Companion to Semiotics* (Abingdon, UK: Routledge, 2009).

12 Peirce's approaches have been elaborated in many fields including learning theory and computation and information theory, and provide a valuable heuristic model for the central questions of this essay. For other applications and extensions, see Robert Hodge and Gunther Kress, *Social Semiotics* (Ithaca, NY: Cornell University Press, 1988); Andrew Lock and Charles R. Peters, eds., *Handbook of Human Symbolic Evolution* (Oxford: Oxford University Press, 1996); Eco, *A Theory of Semiotics*.

13 Eco, *A Theory of Semiotics*; Umberto Eco, "Peirce and the Semiotic Foundations of Openness: Signs as Texts and Texts as Signs," in *The Role of the Reader: Explorations in the Semiotics of Texts* (Bloomington, IN: Indiana University Press, 1979), 175–199; Susan Petrilli and Augusto Ponzio, *Semiotics Unbounded:*

Interpretive Routes Through the Open Network of Signs (Toronto: University of Toronto Press, 2005); T. L. Short, *Peirce's Theory of Signs* (Cambridge: Cambridge University Press, 2009); Roland Posner, Klaus Robering, and Thomas A. Sebeok, eds., *Semiotik/Semiotics: A Handbook on the Sign-Theoretic Foundations of Nature and Culture*, 13.1 (Berlin: Mouton de Gruyter, 1997). I am especially indebted to the work of Eco's expositions of Peirce and to Petrilli and Ponzio in their productive synthesis of Peirce and Bakhtin in *Semiotics Unbounded*.

14 Charles Sanders Peirce, *Collected Papers of Charles Sanders Peirce*, 8 Volumes, ed. Charles Hartshorne, Paul Weiss, and A. W. Burks (Cambridge, MA: Harvard University Press, 1931), Vol. 8, p. 332.

15 All references to the works of Peirce are from the standard editions: Charles Sanders Peirce, *Collected Papers of Charles Sanders Peirce*, 8 Volumes, ed. Charles Hartshorne, Paul Weiss, and A. W. Burks (Cambridge, MA: Harvard University Press, 1931), henceforth *CP*; and Charles S. Peirce, *The Essential Peirce: Selected Philosophical Writings (1867–1893)*, ed. Nathan Houser and Christian J. W. Kloesel, Vol. 1 (Bloomington, IN: Indiana University Press, 1992); Charles S. Peirce, *The Essential Peirce: Selected Philosophical Writings (1893–1913)*, ed. Nathan Houser and Christian J. W. Kloesel, Vol. 2 (Bloomington, IN: Indiana University Press, 1998).

16 Peirce, *CP*, Vol. 5, p. 594.

17 Peirce, *CP*, Vol. 2, p. 302.

18 Peirce, *CP*, Vol. 4, p. 132.

19 This "classic" reading of Peirce's ideas is well-described by Eco; see Eco, "Peirce and the Semiotic Foundations of Openness: Signs as Texts and Texts as Signs."

20 Peirce, *CP*, Vol. 2, p. 228.

21 Peirce, *CP*, Vol. 1, p. 339.

22 Peirce saw semiosis as being formally open and unlimited though constrained by the rules, codes, and conventions of a symbolic system, the pragmatic situations of expression, and the motivation to find conceptual conclusions. See Eco, A Theory of Semiotics, 66–73; Umberto Eco, "Unlimited Semeiosis and Drift: Pragmaticism vs. 'Pragmatism,'" in *The Limits of Interpretation* (Bloomington, IN: Indiana University Press, 1990), 23–43; Jorgen Dines Johansen, *Dialogic Semiosis: An Essay on Signs and Meanings* (Bloomington, IN: Indiana University Press, 1993); Susan Petrilli, "Dialogism and Interpretation in the Study of Signs," *Semiotica* 97, no. 1/2 (January 1993): 103–118.

23 This important aspect of Peirce's thought is more fully explored in studies by Petrilli and Ponzio: Augusto Ponzio, "Sign, Dialogue, and Alterity," *Semiotica* 173, no. 1/4 (January 2009): 129–154; Petrilli, "Dialogism and Interpretation in the Study of Signs"; and Petrilli and Ponzio, Semiotics Unbounded.

24 Charles S. Peirce and Victoria Welby, *Semiotic and Significs: The Correspondence Between Charles S. Peirce and Lady Victoria Welby*, ed. Charles S. Hardwick (Bloomington, IN: Indiana University Press, 1977), 195.

25 Peirce, *Essential Peirce*: Vol. 2, p. 241.

26 Cited in Nate Chinen, "So Many Sounds, but Jazz Is the Core: Herbie Hancock Is the Emissary of an Art Form," *The New York Times*, November 27, 2013, sec. Arts/Music, http://www.nytimes.com/2013/12/01/arts/music/herbie-hancock-is-the-emissary-of-an-art-form.html.

27 On the dialogic improvisational structuredness of jazz, see Paul Berliner, *Thinking in Jazz: The Infinite Art of Improvisation* (Chicago, IL: University of Chicago Press, 1994).

28 For semiotics, the implications are usefully described by Petrilli and Ponzio, *Semiotics Unbounded*, and the wider applications in cognitive science and discourse studies are developed in Paul Thibault, *Agency and Consciousness in Discourse: Self-Other Dynamics as a Complex System* (London: Continuum, 2004).

29 For Bakhtin's major statements, see M. M. Bakhtin, *The Dialogic Imagination: Four Essays* (Austin, TX: University of Texas Press, 1992); M. M. Bakhtin, *Speech Genres and Other Late Essays*, ed. Caryl Emerson and Michael Holquist, trans. Vern W. McGee (Austin, TX: University of Texas Press, 1986); Mikhail Bakhtin, *Problems of Dostoevsky's Poetics*, ed. Caryl Emerson (Minneapolis, MN: University of Minnesota Press, 1984).

30 Bakhtin, *Speech Genres and Other Late Essays*, 87, 91.

31 See Bakhtin, *The Dialogic Imagination*, 280.

32 There is a vast literature on intertextuality and intermediality; for orientations to the use of the concept here see: Petrilli, "Dialogism and Interpretation in the Study of Signs"; Umberto Eco, "Metaphor, Dictionary, and Encyclopedia," New Literary History 15, no. 2 (Winter 1984): 255–271; Lotman and Uspensky, "On the Semiotic Mechanism of Culture"; Norman Fairclough, "Discourse and Text: Linguistic and Intertextual Analysis Within Discourse Analysis," Discourse & Society 3, no. 2 (April 1, 1992): 193–217.

33 Accessible introductions to major topics include: Yan Huang, *Pragmatics* (Oxford: Oxford University Press, 2007); Teun A. van Dijk, *Text and Context: Explorations in the Semantics and Pragmatics of Discourse*

(London: Longman, 1977); Talmy Givón, *Context as Other Minds: The Pragmatics of Sociality, Cognition, and Communication* (Amsterdam: John Benjamins, 2005).

34 See Deborah Tannen, *Talking Voices: Repetition, Dialogue, and Imagery in Conversational Discourse*, 2nd ed. (Cambridge, UK: Cambridge University Press, 2007); Deborah Tannen, "Intertextuality in Interaction: Reframing Family Arguments in Public and Private," *Text & Talk* 26, no. 4/5 (July 2006): 597–617; Deborah Tannen, "Abduction, Dialogicality and Prior Text: The Taking on of Voices in Conversational Discourse" (presented at the Annual Meeting of the Linguistic Society of America, Baltimore, MD, 2009), http://faculty.georgetown.edu/tannend/lsa%20plenary%20written%20version.pdf.

35 Lotman, *Universe of the Mind*, 143–144.

36 Ray Jackendoff provides excellent guides to the current state of research and recent debates; see Jackendoff, *Foundations of Language: Brain, Meaning, Grammar, Evolution* (New York, NY: Oxford University Press, USA, 2003); Ray Jackendoff, "Linguistics in Cognitive Science: The State of the Art," *Linguistic Review* 24, no. 4 (December 2007): 347–401; Ray Jackendoff, "What Is the Human Language Faculty? Two Views," *Language* 87, no. 3 (2011): 586–624. Much of the recent debate on language and recursion expands or critiques Chomsky's theory since the Minimalist Program; see: Noam Chomsky, *The Minimalist Program* (Cambridge, MA: MIT Press, 1995) and Noam Chomsky, "Approaching UG From Below," in *Interfaces + Recursion = Language? Chomsky's Minimalism and the View From Syntax-Semantics*, ed. Uli Sauerland and Hans-Martin Gärtner (Berlin: Mouton de Gruyter, 2007), 1–29.

37 The "unbounded Merge" operation is a key feature of Chomsky's recent theory; see Chomsky, *The Minimalist Program*.

38 Chomsky, "Approaching UG From Below," 5.

39 Chomsky states:

> The conclusion that Merge falls within UG [Universal Grammar] holds whether such recursive generation is unique to FL [the Faculty of Language] or is appropriated from other systems . . . [I]t is interesting to ask whether this operation is language-specific. We know that it is not.
>
> (Chomsky, "Approaching UG From Below," 7)

For applications and examples, see Ray Jackendoff and Fred Lerdahl, "The Capacity for Music: What Is It, and What's Special About It?," *Cognition* 100, no. 1 (May 2006): 33–72; Fred Lerdahl and Ray S. Jackendoff, *A Generative Theory of Tonal Music* (Cambridge, MA: MIT Press, 1996); Jean Nattiez, *Music and Discourse: Toward a Semiology of Music* (Princeton, NJ: Princeton University Press, 1990); Raymond Monelle, *Linguistics and Semiotics in Music* (Chur, Switzerland: Harwood Academic, 1992).

40 See Pauli Brattico, "Recursion Hypothesis Considered as a Research Program for Cognitive Science," *Minds and Machines* 20, no. 2 (July 1, 2010): 213–241; Michael C. Corballis, *The Recursive Mind: The Origins of Human Language, Thought, and Civilization* (Princeton, NJ: Princeton University Press, 2011); Steven Pinker, *The Language Instinct: How the Mind Creates Language* (New York, NY: William Morrow & Company, 1994), 122–126, 201–206, 377–380.

41 See Marc D. Hauser, Noam Chomsky, and W. Tecumseh Fitch, "The Faculty of Language: What Is It, Who Has It, and How Did It Evolve?," *Science* 298, no. 5598, New Series (November 22, 2002): 1569–1579; Steven Pinker and Ray Jackendoff, "The Faculty of Language: What's Special About It?," *Cognition* 95, no. 2 (March 2005): 201–236; Harry van der Hulst, ed., *Recursion and Human Language* (Berlin: De Gruyter Mouton, 2010); Uli Sauerland and Hans-Martin Gärtner, eds., *Interfaces + Recursion = Language? Chomsky's Minimalism and the View From Syntax-Semantics* (Berlin: Mouton de Gruyter, 2007); and Corballis, *The Recursive Mind*.

42 Pinker and Jackendoff, "The Faculty of Language," 211.

43 Pinker and Jackendoff emphasize that recursion and syntactic structures support meaning in expression: "The only reason language needs to be recursive is because its function is to express recursive thoughts. If there were not any recursive thoughts, the means of expression would not need recursion either." Pinker and Jackendoff, "The Faculty of Language," 230.

44 See Jackendoff's parallel architecture model: Jackendoff, *Foundations of Language*, 107–264; and Jackendoff, "The Parallel Architecture and Its Place in Cognitive Science," in *The Oxford Handbook of Linguistic Analysis*, edited by Bernd Heine and Heiko Narrog, 643–668.

45 For introductions to the descriptive levels of lexicon and encyclopedia see: Vyvyan Evans and Melanie Green, *Cognitive Linguistics: An Introduction* (Edinburgh: Edinburgh University Press, 2006); and Dirk Geeraerts, ed., *Cognitive Linguistics: Basic Readings* (Berlin: Mouton de Gruyter, 2006); Jackendoff, *Foundations of Language*, 271–293; Ray S. Jackendoff, *Language, Consciousness, Culture: Essays on Mental Structure* (Cambridge, MA: MIT Press, 2007), 43–75; Eco, *A Theory of Semiotics*, 84–120; Umberto Eco,

Semiotics and the Philosophy of Language (Bloomington, IN: Indiana University Press, 1984), 68–86, 97–108, 124–129; and Eco, "Metaphor, Dictionary, and Encyclopedia."

46 See Gilles Fauconnier and Mark Turner, *The Way We Think: Conceptual Blending and the Mind's Hidden Complexities* (New York, NY: Basic Books, 2002); George Lakoff and Mark Johnson, *Metaphors We Live By*, 2nd ed. (Chicago, IL: University of Chicago Press, 2003); Ray S. Jackendoff, *Semantics and Cognition* (Cambridge, MA: MIT Press, 1985); Ray Jackendoff, *Meaning and the Lexicon: The Parallel Architecture (1975–2010)* (New York, NY: Oxford University Press, 2010), 1–39; Givón, *Context as Other Minds*.

47 This is a central thesis of Lotman and Uspensky, "On the Semiotic Mechanism of Culture."

48 Bakhtin, *Problems of Dostoevsky's Poetics*, 166.

49 See Joanna Demers, *Steal This Music: How Intellectual Property Law Affects Musical Creativity* (Athens, GA: University of Georgia Press, 2006); Lawrence Lessig, *The Future of Ideas: The Fate of the Commons in a Connected World* (New York, NY: Vintage, 2002); Rosemary J. Coombe, *The Cultural Life of Intellectual Properties: Authorship, Appropriation, and the Law* (Durham, NC: Duke University Press, 1998); Kembrew McLeod, *Freedom of Expression®: Resistance and Repression in the Age of Intellectual Property* (Minneapolis, MN: University of Minnesota Press, 2007); Vaidhyanathan, Copyrights and Copywrongs; Woodmansee and Jaszi, The Construction of Authorship; William Patry, Moral Panics and the Copyright Wars (New York: Oxford University Press, 2009); Aufderheide and Jaszi, *Reclaiming Fair Use*, 34–93.

50 See Ashley Kahn, *Kind of Blue: The Making of the Miles Davis Masterpiece* (Cambridge, MA: Da Capo Press, 2007); Richard Williams, *The Blue Moment: Miles Davis's Kind of Blue and the Remaking of Modern Music* (New York: W. W. Norton, 2010).

51 See Berliner, *Thinking in Jazz*; Peter W. Culicover, "Linguistics, Cognitive Science, and All That Jazz," *Linguistic Review* 22, no. 2/4 (June 2005): 227–248; P. N. Johnson-Laird, "How Jazz Musicians Improvise," *Music Perception* 19, no. 3 (March 2002): 415–442.

52 On the generative principles in improvisation, see Berliner, *Thinking in Jazz*; and Aaron Berkowitz, *The Improvising Mind: Cognition and Creativity in the Musical Moment* (New York: Oxford University Press, 2010).

53 For general background, see Ted Gioia, *The History of Jazz*, 2nd ed. (New York: Oxford University Press, 2011), 271–274; and Kahn, *Kind of Blue*; and on the use of the modal scales, see Samuel Barrett, "Kind of Blue and the Economy of Modal Jazz," *Popular Music* 25, no. 02 (2006): 185–200.

54 Miles Davis interview, in Paul Maher and Michael K Dorr, eds., *Miles on Miles: Interviews and Encounters with Miles Davis* (Chicago, IL: Lawrence Hill Books, 2009), 18.

55 For background, see Kahn, *Kind of Blue*, 142–152.

56 On the history and forms of blues, see Ted Gioia, *Delta Blues: The Life and Times of the Mississippi Masters Who Revolutionized American Music* (New York: W. W. Norton, 2008); Alan Lomax, *The Land Where the Blues Began* (New York: Delta/Dell, 1994).

57 Useful studies and background include: Miller (DJ Spooky), *Rhythm Science*; Christoph Cox and Daniel Warner, eds., *Audio Culture: Readings in Modern Music* (New York: Continuum, 2004); Michael Veal, *Dub: Soundscapes and Shattered Songs in Jamaican Reggae* (Middletown, CT: Wesleyan University Press, 2007); Jeff Chang, *Can't Stop Won't Stop: A History of the Hip Hop Generation* (New York: St. Martin's Press, 2005); Mark Katz, *Groove Music: The Art and Culture of the Hip-Hop DJ* (Oxford: Oxford University Press, 2012); Navas, *Remix Theory*; David Dworsky and Victor Köhler, *PressPausePlay*, Documentary Film (House of Radon, 2011).

58 See http://www.whosampled.com.

59 See Simon Reynolds, "Daft Punk Gets Human With a New Album," *The New York Times*, May 15, 2013, sec. Arts/Music, http://www.nytimes.com/2013/05/19/arts/music/daft-punk-gets-human-with-a-new-album.html; Geeta Dayal, "Daft Punk's Random Access Memories," *Slate*, May 21, 2013, http://www.slate.com/articles/arts/music_box/2013/05/daft_punk_s_random_access_memories_reviewed.single.html; Andre Torres, "Quantum Leap: Daft Punk Go From Sampling Disco Records to Creating Disco Records," Wax Poetics (55), 2013, http://www.waxpoetics.com/features/articles/quantum-leap.

60 The major collaborations are well-documented in a series of videos about the production of the album. See *Daft Punk | Random Access Memories | The Collaborators: Nile Rodgers*, 2013, http://www.youtube.com/watch?v=da_Yp9BOCaI&feature=youtube_gdata_player; *Daft Punk | Random Access Memories | The Collaborators: Giorgio Moroder*, 2013, http://www.youtube.com/watch?v=eYDvxo-M0OQ&feature=youtube_gdata_player; *Daft Punk | Random Access Memories | The Collaborators: Pharrell Williams*, 2013, http://www.youtube.com/watch?v=6QVtHogFrI0&feature=youtube_gdata_player.

61 If you listen to RAM with good audio equipment you will hear a different quality of sound from Daft Punk's earlier recordings and from most popular music releases. Rhythm, groove, and beat elements

(which are now emulated or simulated in digital loops and samples in techno and dance music) are mixed almost entirely from live recordings by musicians.

62 Kerry Mason and Thomas Bangalter, "Daft Punk on EDM Producers: 'They're Missing the Tools' (Interview)," Text, *Billboard*, May 6, 2013, http://www.billboard.com/articles/columns/code/1560708/daft-punk-on-edm-producers-theyre-missing-the-tools.

63 On the technical details of the album production, see Paul Tingen, "Daft Punk: Peter Franco & Mick Guzauski: Recording Random Access Memories," *Sound on Sound*, July 2013, http://www.soundonsound.com/sos/jul13/articles/daft-punk.htm.

64 Reynolds, "Daft Punk Gets Human With a New Album."

65 For useful compendiums of sources on appropriation and interpreting a cultural archive, see David Evans, ed., *Appropriation* (London & Cambridge, MA: Whitechapel & MIT Press, 2009); Charles Merewether, ed., *The Archive* (Cambridge, MA: MIT Press, 2006); other important studies include Douglas Crimp, *On the Museum's Ruins* Cambridge, MA: MIT Press, 1993; Martha Buskirk, *The Contingent Object of Contemporary Art* (Cambridge, MA: MIT Press, 2003); Bourriaud, *Postproduction*; Nicolas Bourriaud, *Altermodern: Tate Triennial* (London & New York: Tate Publications & Harry Abrams, 2009); McLeod and Kuenzli, *Cutting Across Media*.

66 I treat the continuum of appropriation from postmodern art to street art in Martin Irvine, "The Work on the Street: Street Art and Visual Culture," in *The Handbook of Visual Culture*, ed. Ian Heywood and Barry Sandywell (London: Berg, 2012), 235–278.

67 On Rauschenberg's combinatorial methods, see Branden W. Joseph, *Random Order: Robert Rauschenberg and the Neo-Avant-Garde* (Cambridge, MA: MIT Press, 2003); Branden W. Joseph, ed., *Robert Rauschenberg* (Cambridge, MA: MIT Press, 2002); Robert Rauschenberg, *Robert Rauschenberg: Works, Writings and Interviews*, ed. Sam Hunter (Barcelona, Spain & New York: Ediciones Polígrafa & D.A.P./Distributed Art Publications, 2006); Crimp, *On the Museum's Ruins*.

68 See Crimp, *On the Museum's Ruins*; Rosalind Krauss, "Perpetual Inventory," *October* 88 (Spring 1999): 87–116; Robert S. Mattison, *Robert Rauschenberg: Breaking Boundaries* (New Haven, CT: Yale University Press, 2003).

69 Books and catalogues can't keep up, so the best real-time index to global street art are the many websites devoted to the form and movement. See especially: http://www.woostercollective.com (and their projects and books); http://blog.vandalog.com; http://www.brooklynstreetart.com (more than Brooklyn).

70 See Irvine, "The Work on the Street: Street Art and Visual Culture" for a study of the dialogic contexts of street art.

71 Lotman and Uspensky, "On the Semiotic Mechanism of Culture," 213.

72 Lawrence Lessig has developed arguments about "Read Only"/"Rewrite" cultures, but his view is based on the properties of technologies rather than on the underlying and necessary principles of symbolic systems that precede a specific technical implementation; see Lessig, *Remix*.

73 See the excellent proposals for stronger fair use in Aufderheide and Jaszi, *Reclaiming Fair Use*.

Bibliography

Amerika, Mark. *remixthebook*. Minneapolis, MN: University of Minnesota Press, 2011.

Aufderheide, Patricia, and Peter Jaszi. *Reclaiming Fair Use: How to Put Balance Back in Copyright*. Chicago, IL: University of Chicago Press, 2011.

Bakhtin, Mikhail. *Problems of Dostoevsky's Poetics*. Minneapolis, MN: University of Minnesota Press, 1984.

——. *Speech Genres and Other Late Essays*. Austin, TX: University of Texas Press, 1986.

——. *The Dialogic Imagination: Four Essays*. Austin, TX: University of Texas Press, 1992.

Baraka, Amiri. *Blues People: Negro Music in White America*. New York: William Morrow and Company, 1963.

Barrett, Samuel. "Kind of Blue and the Economy of Modal Jazz." *Popular Music* 25, no. 02 (2006): 185–200.

Barthes, Roland. *Elements of Semiology*. New York: Hill and Wang, 1973.

——. "From Work to Text." In *Image, Music, Text*, translated by Stephen Heath, 155–164. New York: Hill and Wang, 1988.

Berkowitz, Aaron. *The Improvising Mind: Cognition and Creativity in the Musical Moment*. New York: Oxford University Press, 2010.

Berliner, Paul. *Thinking in Jazz: The Infinite Art of Improvisation*. Chicago, IL: University of Chicago Press, 1994.

Bourdieu, Pierre. *Language and Symbolic Power*. John B. Thompson, trans. Cambridge, MA: Harvard University Press, 1991.

———. *Practical Reason: On the Theory of Action*. Stanford, CA: Stanford University Press, 1998.

Bourriaud, Nicolas. *Postproduction: Culture as Screenplay: How Art Reprograms the World*. 2nd ed. New York: Lukas & Sternberg, 2005.

———. *Altermodern: Tate Triennial*. London & New York: Tate Publications & Harry Abrams, 2009.

Boyle, James. *Shamans, Software, and Spleens: Law and the Construction of the Information Society*. Cambridge, MA: Harvard University Press, 1996.

Brattico, Pauli. "Recursion Hypothesis Considered as a Research Program for Cognitive Science." *Minds and Machines* 20, no. 2 (July 1, 2010): 213–241.

Buskirk, Martha. *The Contingent Object of Contemporary Art*. Cambridge, MA: MIT Press, 2003.

Chang, Jeff. *Can't Stop Won't Stop: A History of the Hip Hop Generation*. New York: St. Martin's Press, 2005.

Chinen, Nate. "So Many Sounds, but Jazz Is the Core: Herbie Hancock Is the Emissary of an Art Form." *The New York Times*, November 27, 2013, sec. Arts/Music. http://www.nytimes.com/2013/12/01/arts/music/herbie-hancock-is-the-emissary-of-an-art-form.html.

Chomsky, Noam. *The Minimalist Program*. Cambridge, MA: MIT Press, 1995.

———. "Approaching UG From Below." In *Interfaces + Recursion = Language? Chomsky's Minimalism and the View From Syntax-Semantics*, ed. Uli Sauerland and Hans-Martin Gärtner, 1–29. Berlin: Mouton de Gruyter, 2007.

Cobley, Paul, ed. *The Routledge Companion to Semiotics*. Abingdon, UK: Routledge, 2009.

Coombe, Rosemary J. *The Cultural Life of Intellectual Properties: Authorship, Appropriation, and the Law*. Durham, NC: Duke University Press, 1998.

Corballis, Michael C. "The Uniqueness of Human Recursive Thinking." *American Scientist* 95, no. 3 (June 2007): 240–248.

———. *The Recursive Mind: The Origins of Human Language, Thought, and Civilization*. Princeton, NJ: Princeton University Press, 2011.

Cox, Christoph, and Daniel Warner, eds. *Audio Culture: Readings in Modern Music*. New York: Continuum, 2004.

Crimp, Douglas. *On the Museum's Ruins*. Cambridge, MA: MIT Press, 1993.

Culicover, Peter W. "Linguistics, Cognitive Science, and All That Jazz." *Linguistic Review* 22, no. 2/4 (June 2005): 227–248.

Daft Punk | Random Access Memories | The Collaborators: Giorgio Moroder, 2013. http://www.youtube.com/watch?v=eYDvxo-M0OQ&feature=youtube_gdata_player.

Daft Punk | Random Access Memories | The Collaborators: Nile Rodgers, 2013. http://www.youtube.com/watch?v=da_Yp9BOCaI&feature=youtube_gdata_player.

Daft Punk | Random Access Memories | The Collaborators: Pharrell Williams, 2013. http://www.youtube.com/watch?v=6QVtHogFrI0&feature=youtube_gdata_player.

Dayal, Geeta. "Daft Punk's Random Access Memories." *Slate*, May 21, 2013. http://www.slate.com/articles/arts/music_box/2013/05/daft_punk_s_random_access_memories_reviewed.single.html.

De Saussure, Ferdinand. *Course in General Linguistics*. Roy Harris, trans. Peru, IL: Open Court, 1986.

Demers, Joanna. *Steal This Music: How Intellectual Property Law Affects Musical Creativity*. Athens, GA: University of Georgia Press, 2006.

Derrida, Jacques. *Of Grammatology*. Baltimore, MD: Johns Hopkins University Press, 1997.

Dworsky, David, and Victor Köhler. *PressPausePlay*. Documentary Film. House of Radon, 2011.

Eco, Umberto. *A Theory of Semiotics*. Bloomington, IN: Indiana University Press, 1976.

———. "Peirce and the Semiotic Foundations of Openness: Signs as Texts and Texts as Signs." In *The Role of the Reader: Explorations in the Semiotics of Texts*, 175–199. Bloomington, IN: Indiana University Press, 1979.

———. "Metaphor, Dictionary, and Encyclopedia." *New Literary History* 15, no. 2 (Winter 1984): 255–271.

———. *Semiotics and the Philosophy of Language*. Bloomington, IN: Indiana University Press, 1984.

———. "Unlimited Semeiosis and Drift: Pragmaticism vs. 'Pragmatism.'" In *The Limits of Interpretation*, 23–43. Bloomington, IN: Indiana University Press, 1990.

Evans, David, ed. *Appropriation*. London & Cambridge, MA: Whitechapel & MIT Press, 2009.

Evans, Vyvyan, and Melanie Green. *Cognitive Linguistics: An Introduction*. Edinburgh: Edinburgh University Press, 2006.

Fairclough, Norman. "Discourse and Text: Linguistic and Intertextual Analysis Within Discourse Analysis." *Discourse & Society* 3, no. 2 (April 1, 1992): 193–217.

Fauconnier, Gilles, and Mark Turner. *The Way We Think: Conceptual Blending And The Mind's Hidden Complexities*. New York: Basic Books, 2002.

Ferguson, Kirby. *Everything Is a Remix* (Parts 1–4). Documentary videos, 2010–14. http://everythingisaremix.info.

Gaylor, Brett. *Rip: A Remix Manifesto*. DVD. The Disinformation Company, 2009.

Geeraerts, Dirk, ed. *Cognitive Linguistics: Basic Readings*. Berlin: Mouton de Gruyter, 2006.

Gioia, Ted. *Delta Blues: The Life and Times of the Mississippi Masters Who Revolutionized American Music*. New York: W. W. Norton, 2008.

———. *The History of Jazz*. 2nd ed. New York: Oxford University Press, 2011.

Givón, Talmy. *Context as Other Minds: The Pragmatics of Sociality, Cognition, and Communication*. Amsterdam: John Benjamins, 2005.

Hauser, Marc D., Noam Chomsky, and W. Tecumseh Fitch. "The Faculty of Language: What Is It, Who Has It, and How Did It Evolve?" *Science* 298, no. 5598. New Series (November 22, 2002): 1569–1579.

Hodge, Robert, and Gunther Kress. *Social Semiotics*. Ithaca, NY: Cornell University Press, 1988.

Huang, Yan. *Pragmatics*. Oxford: Oxford University Press, 2007.

Hulst, Harry van der, ed. *Recursion and Human Language*. Berlin: Mouton de Gruyter, 2010.

Irvine, Martin. "The Work on the Street: Street Art and Visual Culture." In *The Handbook of Visual Culture*, edited by Ian Heywood and Barry Sandywell, 235–278. London: Berg, 2012.

Jackendoff, Ray. *Foundations of Language: Brain, Meaning, Grammar, Evolution*. New York: Oxford University Press, 2003.

———. "Linguistics in Cognitive Science: The State of the Art." *Linguistic Review* 24, no. 4 (December 2007): 347–401.

———. "The Parallel Architecture and Its Place in Cognitive Science." In *The Oxford Handbook of Linguistic Analysis*, edited by Bernd Heine and Heiko Narrog, 643–668. New York: Oxford University Press, 2009.

———. *Meaning and the Lexicon: The Parallel Architecture (1975–2010)*. New York: Oxford University Press, 2010

———. "What Is the Human Language Faculty?: Two Views." *Language* 87, no. 3 (2011): 586–624.

Jackendoff, Ray, and Fred Lerdahl. "The Capacity for Music: What Is It, and What's Special About It?" *Cognition* 100, no. 1 (May 2006): 33–72.

Jackendoff, Ray S. *Semantics and Cognition*. Cambridge, MA: MIT Press, 1985.

———. *Language, Consciousness, Culture: Essays on Mental Structure*. Cambridge, MA: MIT Press, 2007.

Johansen, Jorgen Dines. *Dialogic Semiosis: An Essay on Signs and Meanings*. Bloomington, IN: Indiana University Press, 1993.

Johnson-Laird, P. N. "How Jazz Musicians Improvise." *Music Perception* 19, no. 3 (March 2002): 415–442.

Joseph, Branden W. *Random Order: Robert Rauschenberg and the Neo-Avant-Garde*. Cambridge, MA: MIT Press, 2003.

———, ed. *Robert Rauschenberg*. Cambridge, MA: MIT Press, 2002.

Kahn, Ashley. *Kind of Blue: The Making of the Miles Davis Masterpiece*. Cambridge, MA: Da Capo Press, 2007.

Katz, Mark. *Groove Music: The Art and Culture of the Hip-Hop DJ*. Oxford: Oxford University Press, 2012.

Krauss, Rosalind. "Perpetual Inventory." *October* 88 (Spring 1999): 87–116.

Lakoff, George, and Mark Johnson. *Metaphors We Live By*. 2nd ed. Chicago, IL: University Of Chicago Press, 2003.

Lerdahl, Fred, and Ray S. Jackendoff. *A Generative Theory of Tonal Music*. Cambridge, MA: MIT Press, 1996.

Lessig, Lawrence. *The Future of Ideas: The Fate of the Commons in a Connected World*. New York: Vintage, 2002.

———. *Free Culture: The Nature and Future of Creativity*. New York: Penguin Press, 2005.

———. *Remix: Making Art and Commerce Thrive in the Hybrid Economy*. New York: Penguin Press, 2008.

Letham, Jonathan. "The Ecstasy of Influence: A Plagiarism." *Harper's Magazine*, February 2007.

Lock, Andrew, and Charles R. Peters, eds. *Handbook of Human Symbolic Evolution*. Oxford: Oxford University Press, 1996.

Lomax, Alan. *The Land Where the Blues Began*. New York: Delta/Dell, 1994.

Lotman, Yuri M. *Universe of the Mind: A Semiotic Theory of Culture*. Ann Shukman, trans. Bloomington, IN: Indiana University Press, 1990.

Lotman, Yuri M., and B. A. Uspensky. "On the Semiotic Mechanism of Culture." *New Literary History* 9, no. 2 (Winter 1978): 211–232.

Maher, Paul, and Michael K. Dorr, eds. *Miles on Miles: Interviews and Encounters with Miles Davis*. Chicago, IL: Lawrence Hill Books, 2009.

Manovich, Lev. *Software Takes Command: Extending the Language of New Media*. London: Bloomsbury Academic, 2013.

Mason, Kerry, and Thomas Bangalter. "Daft Punk on EDM Producers: 'They're Missing the Tools' (Interview)." *Billboard*, May 6, 2013. http://www.billboard.com/articles/columns/code/1560708/daft-punk-on-edm-producers-theyre-missing-the-tools.

Mattison, Robert S. *Robert Rauschenberg: Breaking Boundaries*. New Haven, CT: Yale University Press, 2003.

McLeod, Kembrew. *Freedom of Expression®: Resistance and Repression in the Age of Intellectual Property*. Minneapolis, MN: University of Minnesota Press, 2007.

McLeod, Kembrew, and Peter DiCola. *Creative License: The Law and Culture of Digital Sampling*. Durham, NC: Duke University Press, 2011.

McLeod, Kembrew, and Rudolf Kuenzli, eds. *Cutting Across Media: Appropriation Art, Interventionist Collage, and Copyright Law*. Durham, NC: Duke University Press, 2011.

Merewether, Charles, ed. *The Archive*. Cambridge, MA: MIT Press, 2006.

Miller (DJ Spooky), Paul D. *Rhythm Science*. Cambridge, MA: MIT Press, 2004.

———, ed. *Sound Unbound: Sampling Digital Music and Culture*. Cambridge, MA: MIT Press, 2008.

Monelle, Raymond. *Linguistics and Semiotics in Music*. Chur, Switzerland: Harwood Academic, 1992.

Nattiez, Jean. *Music and Discourse: Toward a Semiology of Music*. Princeton, NJ: Princeton University Press, 1990.

Navas, Eduardo. *Remix Theory: The Aesthetics of Sampling*. Vienna: Springer, 2012.

Nöth, Winfried. *Handbook of Semiotics*. Bloomington, IN: Indiana University Press, 1990.

Patry, William. *Moral Panics and the Copyright Wars*. New York: Oxford University Press, 2009.

Peirce, Charles S. *The Essential Peirce: Selected Philosophical Writings (1867–1893)*. Edited by Nathan Houser and Christian J. W. Kloesel. Vol. 1. Bloomington, IN: Indiana University Press, 1992.

———. *The Essential Peirce: Selected Philosophical Writings (1893–1913)*. Edited by Nathan Houser and Christian J. W. Kloesel. Vol. 2. Bloomington, IN: Indiana University Press, 1998.

Peirce, Charles S., and Victoria Welby. *Semiotic and Significs: The Correspondence Between Charles S. Peirce and Lady Victoria Welby*. Edited by Charles S. Hardwick. Bloomington, IN: Indiana University Press, 1977.

Peirce, Charles Sanders. *Collected Papers of Charles Sanders Peirce, 8 Volumes*. Edited by Charles Hartshorne, Paul Weiss, and A. W. Burks. Cambridge, MA: Harvard University Press, 1931.

Petrilli, Susan. "Dialogism and Interpretation in the Study of Signs." *Semiotica* 97, no. 1/2 (January 1993): 103–118.

Petrilli, Susan, and Augusto Ponzio. *Semiotics Unbounded: Interpretive Routes Through the Open Network of Signs*. Toronto: University of Toronto Press, 2005.

Pinker, Steven. *The Language Instinct: How the Mind Creates Language*. New York: William Morrow & Company, 1994.

Pinker, Steven, and Ray Jackendoff. "The Faculty of Language: What's Special About It?" *Cognition* 95, no. 2 (March 2005): 201–236.

Ponzio, Augusto. "Dialogic Gradation in the Logic of Interpretation: Deduction, Induction, Abduction." *Semiotica* 153, no. 1/4 (February 2005): 155–173.

——. "Sign, Dialogue, and Alterity." *Semiotica* 173, no. 1/4 (January 2009): 129–154.

Posner, Roland, Klaus Robering, and Thomas A. Sebeok, eds. *Semiotik/Semiotics: A Handbook on the Sign-Theoretic Foundations of Nature and Culture.* 13.1. Berlin: Mouton De Gruyter, 1997.

Rauschenberg, Robert. *Robert Rauschenberg: Works, Writings and Interviews.* Edited by Sam Hunter. Barcelona & New York: Ediciones Polígrafa; D.A.P. & Distributed Art Publications, 2006.

Reynolds, Simon. "Daft Punk Gets Human With a New Album." *The New York Times*, May 15, 2013, sec. Arts/Music. http://www.nytimes.com/2013/05/19/arts/music/daft-punk-gets-human-with-a-new-album.html.

Sauerland, Uli, and Hans-Martin Gärtner, eds. *Interfaces + Recursion = Language? Chomsky's Minimalism and the View From Syntax-Semantics.* Berlin: Mouton de Gruyter, 2007.

Sebeok, Thomas A., and Marcel Danesi. *The Forms of Meaning: Modeling Systems Theory and Semiotic Analysis.* Berlin: Mouton de Gruyter, 1999.

Short, T. L. *Peirce's Theory of Signs.* Cambridge: Cambridge University Press, 2009.

Silverman, Hugh J. *Cultural Semiosis: Tracing the Signifier.* London: Routledge, 1998.

Tagg, Philip. *Music's Meanings: A Modern Musicology for Non-Musos.* New York: Mass Media Music Scholars' Press, 2012.

Tannen, Deborah. "Intertextuality in Interaction: Reframing Family Arguments in Public and Private." *Text & Talk* 26, no. 4/5 (July 2006): 597–617.

——. *Talking Voices: Repetition, Dialogue, and Imagery in Conversational Discourse.* 2nd ed. Cambridge, UK: Cambridge University Press, 2007.

——. "Abduction, Dialogicality and Prior Text: The Taking on of Voices in Conversational Discourse." Baltimore, MD, 2009. http://faculty.georgetown.edu/tannend/lsa%20plenary%20written%20version.pdf.

Thibault, Paul. *Agency and Consciousness in Discourse: Self-Other Dynamics as a Complex System.* London: Continuum, 2004.

Tingen, Paul. "Daft Punk: Peter Franco & Mick Guzauski: Recording Random Access Memories." *Sound on Sound*, July 2013. http://www.soundonsound.com/sos/jul13/articles/daft-punk.htm.

Tomalin, Marcus. *Linguistics and the Formal Sciences: The Origins of Generative Grammar.* Cambridge, UK: Cambridge University Press, 2006.

——. "Syntactic Structures and Recursive Devices: A Legacy of Imprecision." *Journal of Logic, Language and Information* 20, no. 3 (July 1, 2011): 297–315.

Torop, Peeter. "Semiosphere And/as the Research Object of Semiotics of Culture." *Sign Systems Studies* 33, no. 1 (March 2005): 159–173.

Torres, Andre. "Quantum Leap: Daft Punk Go From Sampling Disco Records to Creating Disco Records." *Wax Poetics*, 2013. http://www.waxpoetics.com/features/articles/quantum-leap.

Vaidhyanathan, Siva. *Copyrights and Copywrongs: The Rise of Intellectual Property and How It Threatens Creativity.* New York: New York University Press, 2001.

Van Dijk, Teun A. *Text and Context: Explorations in the Semantics and Pragmatics of Discourse.* London: Longman, 1977.

Veal, Michael. *Dub: Soundscapes and Shattered Songs in Jamaican Reggae.* Middletown, CT: Wesleyan University Press, 2007.

Williams, Richard. *The Blue Moment: Miles Davis's Kind of Blue and the Remaking of Modern Music.* New York: W. W. Norton, 2010.

Woodmansee, Martha, and Peter Jaszi, eds. *The Construction of Authorship: Textual Appropriation in Law and Literature.* Durham, NC: Duke University Press, 1994.

2

A RHETORIC OF REMIX

Scott H. Church

I urge all who intend to acquaint themselves with my speech, first, that it is a *mixed discourse*, composed with an eye to all these subjects.[1]

I'm always sampling loops and hooks, and cataloguing them and quantizing them, and then I try out different combinations all day long of those +samples.[2]

Remix is usually considered a technological, musical, and/or legal phenomenon. Literature regarding remix, for example, often gravitates to a description of digital sampling and its related legal or ethical ramifications. This chapter diverges from these approaches in several ways. I make the case for examining remix as a communicative practice, a frame that illuminates the rhetorical dimensions, persuasive possibilities, and cultural implications of remixed artifacts. Second, remix is usually thought of as a genuinely new phenomenon.[3] However, seeing remix as simply a function of the recombinatory capacities of digital media eludes the historical antecedents to remix found in the rhetorical tradition. When viewed in this light, remix practices hark back to the classical culture of collectivism, re-creation, and performance in cultural production.[4] Situating remix in a broader historical trajectory provides a richer sense of its location in contemporary culture.

Admittedly, remix and rhetoric appear to be an odd couple. After all, rhetoric is called "the art of speaking well," historically concerned with oral speech.[5] Classical rhetoric and digital culture, however, share some surprising similarities. Foremost, rhetoric and many forms of digital media are concerned with attracting and sustaining the attention of audiences, primarily by using style and aesthetics as vehicles for persuasion. When one considers the attention demands of information-abundant environments, rhetoric becomes an especially useful hermeneutic. For Richard Lanham, living in the information age is akin to drinking from a fire hose: the production of information has overwhelmed our ability to pay attention to it all.[6] Though rhetoric has traditionally been conceived of as the art of persuasion in speech, it might, following Lanham, be best considered as an "economics of attention."[7] Rhetoricians, in fact, have assumed that attention was a scarce resource all along, so rhetorical theory usually postulates how to "skillfully allocate"[8] that resource. Rhetoric has been defined as the "art of using language to help people narrow their choices"[9] and "attend to what we would like them to attend to."[10] In order to be persuaded, the audience must be given options and then be directed to focus its attention toward certain choices.

Both oratory and remix focus attention through *invention*, the process of discovering and generating novel arguments. Invention is both cognitive and collaborative. It is cognitive in the sense that the orator needs to mentally synthesize previously discovered arguments, and collaborative in the sense that the interaction of the orator and the audience may be crucial in formulating one's arguments. Invention is what makes the persuasive potential of remix possible because it entails the use of *creative imitation* and *sampling*; the remixer participates in a practice similar to the ancient orators, creating links between samples by exploiting and leveraging the audience's understanding of the samples in their original contexts. When DJs choose a sample of music, for example, their selection is rhetorical because they deem one sample to be more appropriate than another.

To further explore the link between rhetoric and remix, I will recast the classical rhetorician Isocrates as a protoremix artist. His liminal teachings suggest some rhetorical norms that antecede remix culture. I will then show how the mashups by Gregg Gillis, also known as the remix artist Girl Talk, can be understood as a digitally networked incarnation of Isocratic rhetoric.

Isocrates, Protoremix Artist

Isocrates is one of the most important classical philosophers of rhetoric—though he is less appreciated in our times than his contemporaries Plato and Aristotle. He lived in Greece from 435 to 338BCE and established a school for training the citizens in the practical art of speaking persuasively.[11] Isocrates was also one of the first to use writing—a new technology—to distribute pamphlets that publicized his ideas. Relating to his embrace of early technologies of communication, Kathleen Welch argues that Isocrates used innovative techniques we now associate with the digital age: "His writing fluctuates between eye dominance and ear dominance. He relies, in fact, on what we now regard as sampling, a musical construction defined by recording one musical text onto another."[12] Isocrates's pedagogy was similarly oriented toward inspiring others to use *imitatio* and sample the discourses of other admirable orators and leaders—two key Isocratic themes that can inform contemporary remix culture.

Prior to exploring these themes, it is worth noting that making the transition between Isocratic thought and contemporary remix is not always a seamless endeavor; the concepts may be understood differently for their respective times. Isocratic sampling, for example, had a certain function in classical rhetoric that does not translate exactly into the contemporary connotations of sampling in remix. However, there are striking parallels between both epochs that are well worth examining.

Imitatio

Classical imitation, also called *imitatio*, was key to Isocrates's teaching because it required the student to emulate a skilled orator and thus improve his or her own speech.[13] Contrary to the Romantic interpretation that imitation was the act of merely repeating or copying existing texts, John Muckelbauer argues that "imitation was the single most common instructional method in the West for well over two millennia."[14] Creative imitation was a productive and inventive process that spurred rhetorical invention primarily through interpretation, variation, creativity, and novelty.

Interpretation is not only critical to *imitatio*, it is useful to distinguish classical imitation from the Romantic framing that still permeates contemporary understandings of the term. In classical times, creative imitation of other orators allowed neophytes to gain experience by isolating what was appropriate for each situation, and then use it accordingly. Further, the student needed to exercise prudence in selecting the right model to imitate. One of the objectives of imitation was to create an exact replica of the model. However, if the model was flawed in some way, the student needed to be sufficiently conscientious to avoid imitating the weaknesses, interpreting instead the strengths upon which he or she could build. Similarly, contemporary remix is predicated upon *imitatio*; in order to create a mashup, the remixer will creatively appropriate and then transform the song by sampling it. In other words, remix enacts *imitatio*, not the reductive model of imitation qua imitation we often think of with contemporary art. Whereas the artistic process of imitation is labor-intensive, sampling performs *imitatio* when it removes the element of labor (traditionally understood) from the imitation and focuses rather on the express interpretation of the artifact. The remixer does imitate the source material insofar as it creates a contrast and thus evinces the novelty of the remix. Therefore, as in the time of Isocrates, the remixer is not engaging in mere repetition of the original song, but rather manipulating it in order to use it in a new context.

Imitatio was also an inventive practice because it yielded variation rather than exact reproduction.[15] This variation was closely related to the students' mandate to conduct research before imitation. Roman rhetorician Quintilian, channeling Isocrates's strategies of imitation, invited students of rhetoric to perform "an investigation of [an orator's] good qualities" before imitating them.[16] In effect, the student would create a mashup of the numerous good qualities of multiple model orators, thus paying tribute to them. Likewise, when remixers imitate artists by sampling their songs, they often do so to pay homage to that artist.[17] They acknowledge that the artist being sampled has created a memorable original piece worthy of being used as a sample. This imitation-as-homage model is a contemporary manifestation of Isocratic practices. Remixers also use variation by carefully and critically examining different songs to fit in the remix, often remixing songs until they are altered into unrecognizable samples. For example, the DJ El-P confesses, "If you can catch me [using familiar samples] then I haven't done my job."[18] To perform variation, DJs must exploit an interpretive repertoire spanning tempos, beats, samples, a cappella vocals and more.

Creativity was also essential to classical imitative practices. In fact, Isocrates viewed imitation as a "creative and productive process,"[19] determined by the inventiveness of the speaker in responding to those models in flexible and creative ways.[20] When taking the variation of differing models into account, the students were able to creatively manipulate the speech to tailor it to their own ends. Ultimately, the success of the imitation would be gauged by the speaker's innovative interpretation, coupled with the audience's sophisticated reception.[21] Knowing which portions of what speeches to imitate required a great amount of knowledge, but knowing how to reassemble those samples together into one unified discourse required a high level of creativity.

Therefore, novelty and holistic coherence were other desired by-products of a successfully elevated imitation. When students of rhetoric would imitate multiple orators and converge those examples into their own tailored oratory, "the whole [was] necessarily different from its parts."[22] Similarly, the remixer carefully crafts novel mashups intended to be greater than their constituent samples. As it was with creative imitation, novelty is also crucial to remix; a mashup could not be classified as such unless it were sufficiently novel. It contains the remixer's unifying voice, despite the fact that the mashup is composed of other songs entirely. Due to its levels of novelty and holism, elevated *imitatio* does not resemble the pejorative Romantic concept of imitation.

Sampling

Sampling as a musical practice rejects linear order and focuses instead on aesthetic appropriateness, which is governed by opportune timing, or *kairos*. Isocrates favored *kairos* in his rhetoric, proclaiming "oratory is good only if it has the qualities of fitness for the occasion, propriety of style, and originality of treatment."[23] This belief in "fitness for the occasion" also permeates contemporary remixes, especially when a remixer searches for an appropriate sample to use in a song. This ability to find two songs that blend well together is important for remix artists, especially in live situations where they more immediately adapt to their audiences.[24] Essentially, contemporary sampling works in tandem with classical *imitatio*. Instead of exerting the requisite mimetic labor as in the traditional imitation model, remixers productively interpret the samples they use in their mashups, thereby creatively modifying the samples for their use in a new context. Remixers engender *kairos* in their mashups to an even greater degree than Isocrates, as a sample will likely be placed in a certain portion of a mashup exclusively because it "sounds good" or that it "fits" in that place. By making ostensibly incongruous samples fit together, remixers also use the rhetorical strategies *novelty* and *surprise*—both of which can be observed in the mashups of Girl Talk. This primacy of appropriateness defines much of the aesthetic structure of mashups.

The remix artist's focus on appropriateness also parallels the classical belief that probability is more important than chronology. Classical rhetorician Takis Poulakos explains,

> To be artistic, a sequence of events must be governed by probability: one episode must follow *because* of another, not merely *after* another. Without probability, art loses its essential quality, since it is clear that "a poet's object is not to tell what actually happened but what could and would happen either probably or inevitably."[25]

In line with the Isocratic belief that *kairos* should dictate how discourse is crafted, probability is essential to musical sampling. Remixers choose samples that will fit together naturally in a way that, hopefully, encourages the listener to recognize their congruity. In other words, the listener will appreciate a good mashup, in part, because the smooth layering and musical similarities of the source samples emphasize their fit for the mashup. As Joanna Demers writes, "Materials that might have different tempi, rhythms, or keys are mixed in such a way as to make their combination seem necessary, almost inevitable."[26] Sampling manipulates the elements of the songs to align with each other, thus revealing their occluded congruity.

Isocrates participated in a discursive type of sampling that shared similarities with remix, particularly in its *kairotic* production, repetition, and transitions. Regarding *kairos*, he considered sampling to be a productive concept, proclaiming, "we should regard that man as the most accomplished in this field who can collect the greatest number of ideas scattered among the thoughts of all the rest and present them in the best form."[27] Likewise, musical sampling is usually decided by the use-value of the samples, without regard to copyright or other factors. Isocrates appears to have brought in samples of other speeches in his own, using what helped him make his particular points. He considered his work to be a "mixed discourse,"[28] composed of samplings of his own words from previous works as well as the words from others. In *Antidosis*, for example, Isocrates sampled not only his own writings but also those of Homer, Thucydides, and Socrates; in fact, it is essentially considered a remix of Plato's *Apology*.[29] This most important of Isocrates's works was a fictional trial in which he was charged to defend himself. In doing so, he argued that sampling allows him the easiest route for building his case for himself:

> I am charged with offending by my words, I think that I shall be in a better position to make you see the truth; for I shall present in evidence the actual words which I have spoken and written, so that you will vote upon my discourses, not from conjecture, but with clear knowledge of their nature. I cannot, however, present them all in complete form; for the time which has been allowed me is too short. But just as is done with fruits, I shall try to produce a sample of each kind. For when you have heard a small portion of them you will easily recognize my true character and appreciate the force of all my speeches.[30]

Isocrates, then, used discursive samples so that the audience could be aware of only his best and most representative work. Though not explicitly, this objective informs contemporary mashup culture as well; in particular, a song may be sampled because it is representative of an entire genre of music or a musical movement[31] or a name may be chosen because of its cultural connotations. Experimental artists the Tape-beatles, for example, named themselves as homage to the studio recording techniques of their appropriated-and-transformed namesake.[32] Music also has a powerful ability to represent emotions and it is perhaps even more effective than language for this purpose. Thus, for a remixer to sample a particular song allows him or her the unique ability to economically cull certain emotions from its audience. Or, the associations may resonate simply because they are gleaned from the "shared cultural resonance" of certain recordings.[33] In either case, remixers follow Isocrates by selecting only the best and most representative samples.

Isocrates's use of repetition and smooth transitions demonstrates a range of his rhetorical strategies that also mirror current sampling practices. In several of his discourses, Isocrates used both verbal and thematic repetition, unapologetically repeating past statements he had used previously—sometimes verbatim.[34] Repetition in oratory, after all, breeds a sense of familiarity to the audience with the ideas being expressed, thus "disarm[ing] readers and render[ing] them receptive."[35] Repetition also functions pedagogically. The orator can employ it with the objective of helping the audience remember and ultimately learn through its recall.[36] In a musical context, repetition is key for structural reinforcement; through recurring motifs, themes, and lyrics, the music is communicated to the listener as a bona fide song. Because repetition is foundational to pop music, remixers strategically employ it in remixing as well. Naturally, repetition entails important aesthetic choices for the sample to work. If the remixer wants to make the mashup sound palatable, he or she will use repetition to mimic the structure of pop music. In the case of samples, remixers often choose to flip the "figure/ground" distinction of a song.[37] This variation might entail that a drumbeat or looping bass line used in the background be grafted on top of another song's melodies. If a figure is to be "demoted" to the ground of another song, it must be looped continually throughout the song in order for it to achieve a semblance of the traditionally steady and constant ground. Thus, the listener can be reminded that the remix is a holistic musical statement like a pop song.

Isocrates also used smoothing transitions between discursive samples. At times, his source materials were quite fragmented and thus required a fluency with transitioning in order to make his discourses sound unified. George Norlin, a translator and editor of many of Isocrates's works, argued that Isocrates's ease with language betrayed an aptitude for creating beautiful prose that subordinated words to a larger unifying force.[38] In employing this holistic perspective, Isocrates paid particular notice to crafting syntactic connections, taking "infinite pains with composition—the smooth joining of part to part," thus creating a pleasurable final discursive product.[39] One of his major contributions was the periodic sentence, a linking of multiple words and phrases that, in lesser hands, would appear to be an ugly conglomeration to disrupt the flow of the argument. However, these long periodic sentences—often comprising half of a written page—were crafted to a degree that suppressed their fragmentation and amplified their unity.[40] Isocrates had the vision to inject artistry into his speech, which was executed through his ability to transition effectively. A remixer similarly needs to make aesthetic choices in order to aggregate many disparate samples and craft a unified final product larger than the samples contained therein. This holism and other Isocratic techniques are exemplified in the mashups of the remix artist Gregg Gillis, also known as Girl Talk.

Isocratic Rhetoric and Girl Talk's Mashups

The same tools rhetoricians use to produce and understand public address can also be employed to think through the implications of remix. One of the principal components of rhetoric, invention, is essential to both the traditional orator and the contemporary remix artist. For the classical orator, imitation yielded invention.[41] For the contemporary remixer, invention fosters creativity. By harnessing *kairos* as inventive inspiration for their mashups, remixers also unleash other important elements of invention, *novelty* and *surprise*.

Track five from Girl Talk's *All Day*, "This Is The Remix,"[42] clearly demonstrates rhetorical invention at work in remix. Early in the mashup, Bananarama's 1980s hit "Cruel Summer" is featured prominently along with Justin Timberlake, Lady Gaga, and Diddy—Dirty Money on top. Certainly the incongruities of the songs stem from the decades in which they were released, but the shared embrace of the genre of pop ties each together. An interlude from Genesis's 1980s smash "Tonight, Tonight, Tonight" follows, then Lil' Kim and Snoop Dogg's drum beats (featured in different songs) are sampled over the top of The Jackson 5's bass-driven "I Want You Back." And yet, surprisingly (is there any other way?), the 1970s R&B standard (with the help of Beastie Boys and a few others) transitions into Toadies's 1990s grunge rocker "Possum Kingdom." After a full minute and a half of Toadies (a veritable lifetime in the frenetic sampling world of Girl Talk), the closing strains of distorted guitar seamlessly segue into the pseudo-tribal rhythms of Simon and Garfunkel's "Cecilia." But where the a cappella sing-along break of "Cecilia" takes place, the drums are replaced by the rhythms from the introduction of U2's "Sunday Bloody Sunday." The match between both songs is so similar that once the original beat returns, both songs still overlap seamlessly. "Get Low" by Lil Jon and the East Side Boyz (feat. Ying Yang Twins), functions as binding glue here, offering vocal exclamations across the multiple samples and ensuring that the listener is still able to make the transition comfortably along with the mashup. In the next ten seconds, the mashup transports Grateful Dead's psychedelic rock of "Casey Jones" directly into

INXS's new wave sensation "Need You Tonight." Again, the transition is made possible by Gillis's immaculate layering; when one song transitions into another, the ongoing layers of complementary samples bridge the musical gap. In the closing seconds of the mashup, INXS's groove is supplemented by the sneeze-like yell that signifies The Clash's "Should I Stay or Should I Go," along with some LL Cool J thrown in for good measure. "This is The Remix," indeed.

This representative mashup indicates that few of these samples exist in any definable or predictable system. They are as disparate as Gillis's taste for music is eclectic. Indeed, many of the samples that play concurrently originated from clearly opposing genres. Still, when they are mashed up in such a manner, the connections seem natural. Because the DJ reframes the dissonance of clashing artists and genres as consonant by layering them together congruously, the clash is still apparent at an abstract level, but the listener can simultaneously oscillate from one sample to another.

"This is the Remix" also exhibits Gillis's use of novelty and surprise, each key components of rhetorical and aesthetic invention.[43] Enlightenment philosopher George Campbell wrote that a speech done properly will "excite in the mind an agreeable surprise, and that arising, not from anything marvelous in the subject, but solely from the imagery she employs, or the strange assemblage of related ideas presented to the mind."[44] Notable here is Campbell's statement that the audience will be delighted by the "strange assemblage of related ideas" presented by the orator; the literal application of these words to remix showcases how the practice sees novelty as essential to its persuasive ends. What is a mashup other than a "strange assemblage of related ideas"? In his related assemblage of strange ideas, bolstered by a relentless beat throughout, Girl Talk's mashups follow Isocratic practices of *imitatio* and sampling. Gillis's creative interpretation and variation of the source materials lead to the novelty and surprise of those mashups and thus their rhetorical potency.

Aesthetically speaking, Gillis's deliberate musical heresies have their purposes. In part, they are analogous to the functions of avant-garde art in that each of them questions the arbitrary classifications of art. Moreover—and more importantly to our digital age of information superabundance—these texts vie for our attention. A good remix artist will use invention to create a novel mashup, thereby grabbing our attention. Here's how it works: when Gillis mashes up incongruous samples, he not only persuades the audience that the clashing songs belong together, he does so through their congruity, thus erasing the dissonance embedded in the very idea of sampling. This strategy is reminiscent of a model of argumentation in which the orator is responsible for using language in a way to create a version of reality that will support whichever arguments he or she is constructing. Provocatively, Kenneth Burke describes the process in this way: "Even if any terminology is a *reflection* of reality, by its very nature as a terminology it must be a *selection* of reality; and to this extent it must also function as a *deflection* of reality."[45] Orators select from a wide array of arguments in their creative process to reflect reality as they select it (or desire the audience to see it), while choosing which aspects to deflect away from the audience's collective consciousness. Thus, the orator's task of using this *dissuasive* function of argumentative discourse is to move the audience to accept certain ideas while rejecting others as unacceptable.

Like rhetoric, remix also reflects, selects, and deflects reality. When the artist composes a remix, she or he is responsible for choosing the appropriate voices to be sampled and the parts of the composition to be added upon or subtracted from. This element of the remix process has spawned a subclassification called *selective remix*.[46] The process is tricky to maneuver because remixers must allow the original essence of the song to remain intact and yet transform it sufficiently to be considered something novel. Remix artists will consider the final product successful if they, like orators, can sustain the audience's attention as well as help persuade it that the aesthetic choices were appropriate.

The practice of selecting samples by their "due appropriateness to the [mashup] at hand"[47] is a contemporary application of the Isocratic notion of *kairos*. Gillis's selection of samples is based on their aesthetic appropriateness for the overall mashup, without explicit regard to potential ethical or legal issues.[48] However, this *kairotic* imperative presents a disjunction between *kairos* and the generic clash of the source materials: strictly based on their origins, these samples were never really considered that appropriate to be paired in the first place. Still, the belief that all materials are available for the benefit of art, culled from the open source ideology of the digital era, presents the challenge to make something beautiful and unified out of something so fragmented. Thus, despite the apparent disconnect between the belief in appropriateness and the clashing genres of the music, Girl Talk samples the sources anyway. Once the mashup is complete, it exhibits the elements of novelty and surprise to enhance the rhetorical function of its aesthetics. Girl Talk's mashups, facilitated by his process of imitative invention, function rhetorically by sublimating ethical issues into their transcendent aesthetic presentations via their strategic use of congruity.

In conclusion, this chapter has demonstrated a few ways that remix can be rhetorical. In using either remix or rhetoric to examine the other, both become mutually elucidated. Like the classical concept of invention, remix also uses classical rhetoric resources like *imitatio* and *kairos*. In this case study, I gestured to the rhetorical potential of remix by analyzing the aesthetic dimensions of one of Girl Talk's mashups. In his successful employment of *imitatio*, *kairos*, repetition, smoothing transitions, novelty, and surprise in his mashups, Gregg Gillis performs Isocratic rhetoric in a digital context and therefore demonstrates, perhaps ironically, that remix is not a new or strictly technological practice.

Notes

1 Isocrates, *Antidosis*, in *Isocrates Volume II*, trans. and ed. George Norlin (Cambridge, MA: Harvard University Press, 1929), 191 (emphasis added).

2 Gregg Gillis, quoted in Greg Kot, *Ripped: How the Wired Generation Revolutionized Music* (New York: Scribner, 2009), 166.

3 Margie Borschke argues that Lawrence Lessig's conception of remix reveals a bias of cyber-utopianism. Lessig sees the practice to be new and digital, both of which Borschke challenges. See Margie Borschke, "Rethinking the Rhetoric of Remix," *Media International Australia* 141 (November 2011): 17–25.

4 Thomas Pettitt, "Before the Gutenberg Parenthesis: Elizabethan-American Compatibilities," 2. Paper presented at MIT5: Creativity, Ownership, and Collaboration in the Digital Age, April 27–29, 2007, http://web.mit.edu/comm-forum/mit5/papers/pettitt_plenary_gutenberg.pdf.

5 This definition comes from the classical Roman rhetorician Quintilian. Peter Ramus, *Arguments in Rhetoric Against Quintilian: Translation and Text of Peter Ramus's Rhetoricae Distinctiones in Quintilianum*, ed. James J. Murphy, trans. Carole Newlands (Carbondale, IL: Southern Illinois University Press, 2010), 109.

6 Richard Lanham, *The Electronic Word: Democracy, Technology, and the Arts* (Chicago, IL: University of Chicago Press, 1993), 227.

7 Richard Lanham, *Economics of Attention: Style and Substance in the Age of Information* (Chicago, IL: University of Chicago Press, 2006), 21.

8 Lanham, *Economics of Attention*, 25.

9 Roderick P. Hart and Suzanne M. Daughton, *Modern Rhetorical Criticism*, 3rd ed. (Boston, MA: Allyn & Bacon, 2005), 2.

10 Lanham, *Economics of Attention*, xii–xiii.

11 Regarding the influence of Isocrates, George Norlin wrote: "[F]ew if any of the literary men of [Isocrates'] age, whether or not they were members of his school, were unaffected by his influence." George Norlin, "General Introduction," in *Isocrates Volume I*, ed. and trans. George Norlin (Cambridge, MA: Harvard University Press, 1928), xxix.

12 Kathleen E. Welch, *Electric Rhetoric: Classical Rhetoric, Oralism, and a New Literacy* (Cambridge, MA: MIT Press, 1999), 37.

13 John Muckelbauer, "Imitation and Invention in Antiquity: An Historical-Theoretical Revision," *Rhetorica: A Journal of the History of Rhetoric* 21, no. 2 (Spring 2003): 65.

14 Muckelbauer, "Imitation and Invention," 62.

15 Muckelbauer, "Imitation and Invention," 67.

16 Quintilian, quoted in Muckelbauer, "Imitation and Invention," 69.

17 DJs frequently use the music from artists and songs they admire and, in sampling it, want to pay tribute to the "greatness" of that particular song. Eduardo Navas, "Regressive and Reflexive Mashups in Sampling Culture," in *Mashup Cultures*, ed. Stefan Sonvilla-Weiss (New York: Springer, 2010), 166.

18 Quoted in Kembrew McLeod and Peter DiCola, *Creative License: The Law and Cultural of Digital Sampling* (Durham, NC: Duke University Press, 2011), 194.

19 Takis Poulakos, "Isocrates's Use of Narrative in the *Evagoras*: Epideictic Rhetoric and Moral Action," *Quarterly Journal of Speech* 73 (August 1987): 323.

20 Robert Hariman, "Civic Education, Classical Imitation, and Democratic Polity," in *Isocrates and Civic Education*, ed. Takis Poulakos and David Depew (Austin, TX: University of Texas Press, 2004), 229.

21 Hariman, "Civic Education," 230.

22 Muckelbauer, "Imitation and Invention," 75.

23 Isocrates, *Against the Sophists*, in *Isocrates Volume II*, trans. and ed. George Norlin (Cambridge, MA: Harvard University Press, 1929), 171. Though my discussion only focuses on Isocrates's use of *kairos*, he was greatly influenced by his teacher Gorgias, who is credited as the progenitor of the concept.

24 John Shiga, "Copy-and-Persist: The Logic of Mash-up Culture," *Critical Studies in Media Communication* 24, no. 2 (June 2007): 103.

25 Poulakos, "*Evagoras*," 324. Poulakos's quotation marks indicate a cited passage from Aristotle's *The Poetics*, trans. W. Hamilton Fyfe. Loeb Classical Library (London: Heinemann, 1927), ix.

26 Joanna Demers, *Listening Through the Noise: The Aesthetics of Experimental Electronic Music* (New York: Oxford University Press, 2010), 57.

27 Isocrates, *To Nicocles*, in *Isocrates Volume I*, ed. and trans. George Norlin (Cambridge, MA: Harvard University Press, 1928), 63.

28 Isocrates, *Antidosis*, 191. The fact that Isocrates's discursive use of (what we consider today to be) mashup logic appears as an anachronism again reveals the classical rhetoric roots of remix. It is the juxtaposition of the classical and the contemporary in Isocratic thought that, to Kathleen Welch, "puts him in a crucial place intellectually" (Welch, *Electric Rhetoric*, 38).

29 Isocrates quotes from Homer and Socrates in *Against the Sophists*, and echoes some of Thucydides's work in *Antidosis*. For further examples of Isocrates sampling Socrates, see *Antidosis*, pages 215, 237, and 365. For the argument that Isocrates remixed Plato, see Robert J. Bonner, "The Legal Setting of Isocrates' *Antidosis*," *Classical Philology* 15 (April 1920): 193. Bonner cites other scholars who have noticed a resemblance between both works, and that *Antidosis* contains a number of parallel passages to *Apology*. Yun Lee Too argues that Isocrates cites Plato in *Antidosis* "extensively and obviously." Yun Lee Too, *A Commentary on Isocrates' Antidosis* (Oxford: Oxford University Press, 2008), 24.

30 Isocrates, *Antidosis*, 215, 217.

31 A particular type of remix, which Eduardo Navas calls the "megamix," has the objective of sampling songs that are particularly representative of an entire time period. Navas, "Regressive Mashups," 166.

32 McLeod and DiCola, *Creative License*, 41.

33 Ibid., 101.

34 Welch, *Electric Rhetoric*, 38. Yun Lee Too, citing another study, gives citations from six of Isocrates's works that demonstrate his affinity for repetition. Yun Lee Too, *The Rhetoric of Identity in Isocrates: Text, Power, Pedagogy* (New York: Cambridge University Press, 1995), 53.

35 Too, *The Rhetoric of Identity*, 54.

36 Eric A. Havelock explains that in the classical era, "the task of the poetic education [was] to memorise and recall." Eric A. Havelock, *Preface to Plato* (Cambridge, MA: Harvard University Press, 1963), 207.

37 Aram Sinnreich, *Mashed Up: Music, Technology, and the Rise of the Configurable Culture* (Amherst, MA: University of Massachusetts Press, 2010), 87.

38 Norlin, "General Introduction," xv.

39 Norlin, "General Introduction," xv.

40 Norlin, "General Introduction," xvi.

41 Muckelbauer, "Imitation and Invention," 74.

42 The following description may be located at http://www.mashupbreakdown.com (accessed June 19, 2013), and clicking on track 5.

43 When discussing modern aesthetics, Umberto Eco speaks about "novelty" and "innovation" synonymously, arguing that aesthetic value is assessed in a work of art, in part, by the amount of novelty the artist exhibited. See Umberto Eco, "Innovation and Repetition: Between Modern and Postmodern Aesthetics," *Daedalus* 134 (2005): 191, 200.

44 George Campbell, *The Philosophy of Rhetoric*, originally published in 1776. Located in *The Rhetoric of Blair, Campbell, and Whately*, ed. James L. Golden and Edward P. J. Corbett (New York: Holt, Rinehart and Winston, 1968), 150.

45 Kenneth Burke, *Language as Symbolic Action* (Berkeley, CA: University of California Press, 1966), 45 (emphases are Burke's).

46 Navas, "Regressive and ReflexiveMashups," 159.

47 This quotation remixes Isocrates's justification of his *kairotic* philosophy in *Antidosis*, 191. The original word that has been bracketed out and replaced by "mashup" is "subject."

48 If I carry on the investigation of the parallels of Girl Talk's contemporary philosophy with the classical pedagogy of Isocrates, interesting points emerge. For example, Isocrates avoided teaching ethics, virtue, or justice because he believed that these lofty and abstract concepts were outside of his more pragmatic objectives in his teachings. Expanding this idea to remix culture, there is a possibility that the same logic informs Girl Talk. The expense of acquiring rights to hundreds of samples would run Gillis in the red to the tune of many millions of dollars. Thus, taking legal considerations into account is simply beyond the scope of Gillis and his relatively modest record label. He generally allows his releases to be downloaded for free and would not have the financial wherewithal to recoup his losses.

Bibliography

Bonner, Robert J. "The Legal Setting of Isocrates' *Antidosis*." *Classical Philology* 15 (April 1920): 193–197.

Borschke, Margie. "Rethinking the Rhetoric of Remix." *Media International Australia* 141 (November 2011): 17–25.

Burke, Kenneth. *Language as Symbolic Action.* Berkeley, CA: University of California Press, 1966.

Campbell, George. "The Philosophy of Rhetoric." In *The Rhetoric of Blair, Campbell, and Whately.* Edited by James L. Golden and Edward P. J. Corbett, 145–271. New York: Holt, Rinehart, and Winston, 1968.

Demers, Joanna. *Listening Through the Noise: The Aesthetics of Experimental Electronic Music.* New York: Oxford University Press, 2010.

Eco, Umberto. "Innovation and Repetition: Between Modern and Postmodern Aesthetics." *Daedalus* 134 (2005): 191–207.

Hariman, Robert. "Civic Education, Classical Imitation, and Democratic Polity." In *Isocrates and Civic Education.* Edited by Takis Poulakos and David Depew, 217–234. Austin, TX: University of Texas Press, 2004.

Hart, Roderick P., and Suzanne M. Daughton. *Modern Rhetorical Criticism.* 3rd ed. Boston, MA: Allyn & Bacon, 2005.

Havelock, Eric A. *Preface to Plato.* Cambridge, MA: Harvard University Press, 1963.

Isocrates. *To Nicocles.* In *Isocrates Volume I.* Edited and translated by George Norlin, 37–71. Cambridge, MA: Harvard University Press, 1928.

———. *Against the Sophists.* In *Isocrates Volume II.* Edited and translated by George Norlin, 159–77. Cambridge, MA: Harvard University Press, 1929.

———. *Antidosis.* In *Isocrates Volume II.* Edited and translated by George Norlin, 179–365. Cambridge, MA: Harvard University Press, 1929.

Kot, Greg. *Ripped: How the Wired Generation Revolutionized Music.* New York, NY: Scribner, 2009.

Lanham, Richard. *The Electronic Word: Democracy, Technology, and the Arts.* Chicago, IL: University of Chicago Press, 1993.

———. *Economics of Attention: Style and Substance in the Age of Information.* Chicago, IL: University of Chicago Press, 2006.

McLeod, Kembrew, and Peter DiCola, *Creative License: The Law and Cultural of Digital Sampling.* Durham, NC: Duke University Press, 2011.

Muckelbauer, John. "Imitation and Invention in Antiquity: An Historical-Theoretical Revision." *Rhetorica: A Journal of the History of Rhetoric* 21, no. 2 (Spring 2003): 61–88.

Navas, Eduardo. "Regressive and Reflexive Mashups in Sampling Culture." In *Mashup Cultures.* Edited by Stefan Sonvilla-Weiss, 157–177. New York: Springer, 2010.

Norlin, George. "General Introduction." In *Isocrates Volume I.* Edited and translated by George Norlin, ix–li. Cambridge, MA: Harvard University Press, 1928.

Pettitt, Thomas. "Before the Gutenberg Parenthesis: Elizabethan-American Compatibilities." Paper presented at MIT5: Creativity, Ownership, and Collaboration in the Digital Age, April 27–29, 2007, http://web.mit.edu/comm-forum/mit5/papers/pettitt_plenary_gutenberg.pdf.

Poulakos, Takis. "Isocrates's Use of Narrative in the *Evagoras*: Epideictic Rhetoric and Moral Action." *Quarterly Journal of Speech* 73 (August 1987): 317–328.

Ramus, Peter. *Arguments in Rhetoric Against Quintilian: Translation and Text of Peter Ramus's* Rhetoricae Distinctiones in Quintilianum. Edited by James J. Murphy. Translated by Carole Newlands. Carbondale, IL: Southern Illinois University Press, 2010.

Schaeffer, John D. *Sensus Communis: Vico, Rhetoric, and the Limits of Relativism.* Durham, NC: Duke University Press, 1990.

Shiga, John. "Copy-and-Persist: The Logic of Mash-up Culture." *Critical Studies in Media Communication* 24, vol. 2 (June 2007): 93–114.

Sinnreich, Aram. *Mashed Up: Music, Technology, and the Rise of Configurable Culture.* Amherst, MA: University of Massachusetts Press, 2010.

Timmerman, David M., and Edward Schiappa. *Classical Greek Rhetorical Theory and the Disciplining of Discourse.* Cambridge, NY: Cambridge University Press, 2010.

Too, Yun Lee. *The Rhetoric of Identity in Isocrates: Text, Power, Pedagogy.* New York: Cambridge University Press, 1995.

———. *A Commentary on Isocrates'* Antidosis. Oxford: Oxford University Press, 2008.

Welch, Kathleen E. *Electric Rhetoric: Classical Rhetoric, Oralism, and a New Literacy.* Cambridge, MA: MIT Press, 1999.

3

GOOD ARTISTS COPY; GREAT ARTISTS STEAL[1]

Reflections on Cut-Copy-Paste Culture

Stefan Sonvilla-Weiss

Remix culture is highly dependent on the abundance of cultural production and access to media objects by a large community. From an economic and organizational perspective, cultural artifacts in the broadest sense need to be inexpensive, widely distributed and easily accessible. This basically means that the individual gains the right to work on the source material without becoming endangered by infringements of laws or taboos.

From a historical point of view the accumulated body of recorded works of human art and knowledge was first achieved through the expansion of the printing press, which laid the foundation for the development of early modern science in the seventeenth century. A new self-conception in dealing with texts arose from discernible naming of authors, printers, page numbers and publishing years. Hence texts could be clearly referenced, which in turn served as the basis for creating new knowledge through critical review and supplementation of information.

These interweaving processes of combining existing and new material became a major principle and coercive element in scientific argumentation. Scientific publications always selectively refer to other scholarly works from which new schools and discourses evolve. New findings and knowledge bear on individual yet reproducible empirical knowledge—a supposition that is still controversial to this day. The development of the printing press made possible the standardization and comparison of text production in a freer and more critical way, and the possibility of simply transferring, for instance, a loss-free quotation from one sign vehicle to another, enabled a very early form of remix culture. Many of the punctuation conventions we know derive from this period, for example, how a quotation can be modified so that it remains a direct quote while seamlessly fitting into a new text.

In the late nineteenth century when the first reproduction of a photograph with a full tonal range in a newspaper was introduced, a new chapter in the mass diffusion of images

See Chapter 41 for Kevin Atherton's discussion on combining existing and new video footage of himself, spanning decades, in what becomes a recombinatory installation of self-driven questions and answers.

was opened. The newly developed reprographic technique allowed parallel printing of text and photographs that enhanced the qualitative and quantitative aspects of image reproduction in a flourishing printing culture.

Early experiments with direct-contact printing of objects placed on photographic plates, double exposures, and composite pictures made by darkroom masking were popular during the Victorian era. It was William Fox Talbot who, in 1834–35, first experimented with the light sensitivity of silver salts that allowed him to develop the first contact printing of objects—mostly ferns, leaves, lace and drawings—onto sensitized plates.

Talbot's pictures, which he called *photogenic drawings*, were rediscovered in the 1920s by artists such as Man Ray and László Moholy-Nagy, who further experimented with the photogram technique. During the late nineteenth century a variety of playful encounters with composite photographic portraits developed into a form of entertainment using newspapers. This early form of trick photography became extremely popular—comic postcards, photograph albums, screens, and military mementos all made use of the techniques of cutting out and reassembling photographic images.[2]

The rise of montage as a central element in modern art is, however, in comparison to postcards, less technically motivated; it is rather more understandable as an attempt to develop a new aesthetics that echoed the progressing subjectivization in industrialized cities in the late nineteenth and early twentieth centuries.[3]

The newly introduced form of real montage replaced the concept of linearity with simultaneity, velocity, and multiplicity of sequences of events, suggesting one of the core subjects in the twentieth century avant-garde: the extension of the human sensory apparatus by means of aleatoric and technologically enhanced artistic procedures in search of new areas of experiences, in which the borders between the so-called inner-world and outer-world would eventually dissolve (as depicted for example in Max Ernst's collages). Collage techniques as applied by the Surrealists are encounters between heterogeneous elements, attesting in their entirety to the incompatibility of the two worlds—"as beautiful as the random encounter between an umbrella and a sewing-machine upon a dissecting-table."[4] What unites diverse early modernist avant-garde manifestos is the desire to create an alternative model to the reality of the ordinary everyday to reach a state of absolute power of desire and dream.

Correspondingly, Eisenstein's famous quote "montage is conflict"[5] points to a conflict where new ideas emerge from the collision of the montage sequence (i.e., in synthesis) but where the new emerging ideas are not innate in any of the images of the edited sequence.

Using the example of Italian futurist painter and composer Luigi Russolo, who wrote the manifesto *The Art of Noises* (1916), we can see that the early twentieth century avant-garde challenged the whole faculty of human sensory experience. Russolo argued that the human ear has become accustomed to the speed, energy, and noise of the urban industrial soundscape and thus this new sonic palette requires a new approach to musical instrumentation and composition. He proposed a number of conclusions about how electronics and other technology would allow futurist musicians to "substitute for the limited variety of timbres that the orchestra possesses today the infinite variety of timbres in noises, reproduced with appropriate mechanisms."[6] Nevertheless it was an arduous path for Russolo to design and construct a number of noise-generating devices, and to assemble a noise orchestra to perform with them.

From Russolo's manifesto it took another 30 years, along with the invention of the tape recorder, to separate the sound object (*objet sonore*) from the body of sound (*corps sonore*)—a concept coined by the French composer and theoretician Pierre Schaeffer (1910–95). He is mainly recognized for his accomplishments in electronic and experimental music, notably in his role as the chief developer of an early form of avant-garde music known as *musique concrète*. Other than in classical music, which starts with an abstraction (i.e., musical notation), *musique concrète* refers to the use of sound as a primary compositional resource. Soon after, the core elements of sampling were introduced, such as loops, variable running speed and direction, multitracks, crossfades and cuts.

During the mid-1950s Brion Gysin and William Burroughs used so-called "cut-up techniques"—an aleatory literary technique in which a text is cut up and rearranged to create a new text. The quite obvious Dadaist precedent of this technique can be traced back to Tristan Tzara's generic instructions from the 1920s on how to create poems by shuffling the words of a newspaper article. Yet both Gysin and Burroughs were not so much interested in the individual subconscious than exploring the collective as a kind of parallel and expanded reality or, as Burroughs proposes, "When you cut into the present the future leaks out."[7]

At about the same time, artists experimented with found footage from B-movies, newsreels, and promotional and educational films, whereby *A Movie* (1958) from American beat artist Bruce Conner became one of the aesthetically significant examples in the collage film genre. In his film the tragic and the absurd coexist within the same split-second, whereas the process of selection and combination of horizontal and vertical montage triggers narrative associations.

In contrast to the noncritical relationship between montage and commerce in American pop art, the Situationist International movement (1957–72) proposed the technique of *détournement*, which "turns expressions of the capitalist system and its media culture against itself."[8] In *A User's Guide to Détournement* Guy Debord and Gil Wolman proposed that:

> Any elements, no matter where they are taken from, can be used to make new combinations . . . The mutual interference of two worlds of feeling, or the juxtaposition of two independent expressions, supersedes the original elements and produces a synthetic organization of greater efficacy. Anything can be used.[9]

However, this programmatic take on radical appropriation involved a certain risk of entanglement in the self-imposed logics of artistic subcultures. It was only with the rise of the Internet and the multiplicity of digital information in various media formats that the structural conditions of the prevalent, dominant high culture and market-driven cultural industry were fundamentally altered.

No Man Is an Island

In an attempt to systematize musical borrowing as a pervasive cultural phenomenon over centuries, Peter Burkholder[10] has delineated the field and outlined a tentative typology of procedures for using existing music in new works. In seeking to define and delimit the vast field of musical borrowing, Burkholder defines it broadly as "taking something from an existing piece of music and using it in a new piece." Subsequently, the borrowed and reworked music must be sufficiently individual to be identifiable as coming from a particular work, rather than from a general repertoire.

Yet in order to distinguish the history of musical borrowing from the history of compositional and improvisational practice, Burkholder concludes that it is best to focus on borrowing from specific works and to consider allusion to general repertoires, or even to the styles of individual composers, as closely related but different phenomena. For example, it is impossible to trace every instance of stylistic allusion in Mozart's or Rachmaninoff's work, as it would require writing about virtually every one of his pieces.

Using the example of T. S. Eliot's[11] pertinent lines in his essay about Philip Massinger, a contemporary of William Shakespeare, he comes to the conclusion that, "Immature poets imitate; mature poets steal"—a statement which, ironically, has proven itself in various permutations such as Picasso's "Good artists copy; great artists steal" or Stravinsky's "Lesser artists borrow; great artists steal." Eliot's assertion to obliterate provenience expands as he continues: "A good poet will usually borrow from authors remote in time, or alien in language, or diverse in interest."

Coming back to current remix practices—which, by nature are inclined to these borrowings—Arewa[12] rather succinctly points out that the pervasive nature of borrowing in music suggests that more careful consideration needs to be given to the extent to which copying and borrowing have been, and can be, a source of innovation. Existing copyright frameworks need to recognize and incorporate musical borrowing by developing commercial practices and liability rule-based legal structures for music that uses existing works in its creation.

Individuality to Collective Authorship

Descartes's *cogito ergo sum*—the certainty of one's own thinking as a priori knowledge of the world—emblematically gets to the heart of the bourgeois-liberal concept of subjectivity. Against this background, the philosophical models that emerged from introspection-based creativity subsequently laid the normative basis for the European concept of authors' rights. These notions were popularized by cliché ideas about artistic creation such as the struggle of the author with the blank sheet or the artist in front of the white canvas. No matter what the deconstruction of this everlasting myth has revealed, the cliché prevails, in this case as a crude form that will be shaped by the artist's innermost vision.

In the highly specialized cultural industry (digital media art and business) of the twenty-first century, hardly anyone attempts to speak about the solitary work of the artist. Yet still, the concept of introspection as a source of creativity is maintained through either hierarchical organization or decision-making amalgamated in a single person, as, for example, the film director or producer (especially the film auteur). Precisely because these clichés are deemed inappropriate, cultural industries take advantage of them.

The practice of remix, implicitly or explicitly, pursues a different concept of creativity. It does not foreground the inwardness of the autonomous individual but rather the heterogeneity and excitement of a variety of different stakeholders whose ideas are brought out in synchronous, asynchronous, and serial forms of collaboration.

Synchronous forms of communication, for instance, are utilized by musicians for whom real-time encounters support spontaneous improvisation and dialog. At the beginning of such a process a mere loose framework exists to stimulate a kind of creative leeway eventually leading to an agreeable result. This, however, is no longer attributable to distinguishable contributions, but rather generated through vital interaction among the participants. As a consequence, synchronous modes of communication and collaboration accommodate small groups that are flexible while using ubiquitous technologies. Wikipedia exemplifies an asynchronous form of collaborative communication. The main principle is quite simple: one person edits a media object created by another person, who in return reedits the newly generated version.

At any point in time there is only one version of the media object that is continuously worked upon by the community. The collective work of Wikipedia has become a reliable information resource built on the voluntary work of thousands of individuals whose contributions are reliant on peer review, version tracking, and chronological order.

Serial Collaboration

A widely popular practice in cultural and artistic fields is the serial form of collaboration in which a piece of work emerges from successive elaboration by creative coworkers. This working method essentially differs from the reworking mode of existing media objects, as it foregrounds the creative and transformative process of adding something genuinely new to the existing. Transferring this collaborative form into remix practices enables both the producer of the source material and the remixer to act independently. In this sense collaboration works without spatial or temporal constraints, as the presence of the originator of the source material is no longer required.

Commonly, serial collaboration is less about enhancement of existing work than playful alterations and transformations. Although this operational mode occasionally privileges a distinctive idiosyncratic note of single authorship, the collaborative aspects continue to exist in analysis and dialog with the classics.

One of the first empirical studies on serial collaboration was conducted by Cheliotis and Yew[13] who investigated user behaviors in the ccMixter online community. The community had collectively produced an impressive 7,484 music items at the time of the data collection. This output has been considered quite respectable in regard to the relatively small size of the community and the fact that the production of a music sample or complete piece (even if it is a remix) is generally more time consuming than the taking of an amateur photograph or the creation (or editing) of a Wikipedia entry.

Another finding was that remixing accounts for more than half of the total production volume (3,982 items, or 53 percent), even if about 60 percent of all uploaded original music pieces (2,150 of 3,502) never get remixed. This is suggestive of the central role that reuse can play in digital media production. Interestingly samples that hold a strong degree of remix are less attractive as a base material for new pieces, probably because it is difficult to capture small parts that can be later used as samples. Thus, diverse forms of collaboration constitute an essential element of remix culture inasmuch as individuality is confronted with the collective. As a result, new forms of subjectivity arise. The polarity between predominantly twentieth century thinking of either individuality or collectivity is outdated; instead a single individuality emerges only in relation to other individualities. As an example, the various Wikipedia versions permit much more detailed access to individual entries composing the collectively authored article than acknowledgements in print publications would ever be able to do. Both individuality and collectivity are no longer the opposite: on the contrary, they form the basis of coevolving principles in networking culture.

Everything Is Connected

Potentially everything could become connected with everything. However, the actual connections established and how they evolve need to be empirically demonstrated and they are therefore unpredictable. The reason for this structural openness is that the constituent elements of a remix and the character of the new piece are undetermined. In other words, the new piece is not just the aggregation of individual parts; rather it emerges through the specific characteristics of its components.

In montage theory this feature has not least been established by the film experiments of Lev Kuleshov (1899–1970) in the 1920s. The Russian avant-garde at that time was not solely interested in formal experiments with the potentialities of the film medium but also in search of corresponding artistic forms of expression in parallel with a radical reorganization—a novel montage of society.

Current remix practices, in contrast, are less politically motivated but rather correspond—in many cases probably unknowingly—with theoretical positions of a newly emerging anti-essentialism, represented for example by De Landa's "Assemblage Theory" and Latour's "Actor-Network-Theory."

In particular Latour's quest for a flat ontology is deducible from the trivial fact that all things are objects. By using the example of a command-and-control war room[14]—the place where the commander sits—Latour's principle of irreduction becomes plausible insofar as the commander's strategic view is an illusion because it is constructed for her by various mediators (data analysts, information designers, as well as nonhumans such as the maps, computers, charts, and graphs). Despite their far-reaching impact and the mass of data compiled to give them a strategic view, the generals are part of the system and thus are unable to control it like any other being. This is a state of randomness and heterogeneity suggesting that nothing is reducible to anything else. As soon as you engage with a system, likewise, the representations become part of the system. Hence the map that attempts to represent the territory makes the difference.

De Landa distinguishes between "interiority" and "exteriority" in conceptualizing the components of a thing. Assemblage Theory presupposes that relations among the parts are contingent, and they can be extracted from one whole and inserted into another. As De Landa states:

> These relations imply, first of all, that a component part of an assemblage may be detached from it and plugged into a different assemblage in which its interactions are different. In other words, the exteriority of relations implies a certain autonomy for the terms they relate.[15]

Another key aspect in De Landa's theory is the equal importance of "micro" and "macro," inferring that social reality is "multiscaled," with assemblages existing at every level. With that said, synthesis is privileged over the fragment, provided that its components are in a permanent flux. As for cultural production, this would translate into equations such as synthesis = montage and fragment = remix. In montage techniques the composing elements always remain identifiable and recognizable, such as film cuts, whereas remix pursues granularity and heterogeneity of diverse elements that can be randomly recombined and recontextualized.

S. SONVILLA-WEISS

The Birth of the Prosumer in Social Media

Cultural production in highly specialized modernity was a domain of experts who possessed the essential means of knowledge creation, production, and distribution. Most people were consumers whose cultural productive force was restricted to the private. This caused a natural division between the professional and the widespread amateur culture, along with its accompanying technological, economic, and juridical implications. The montage of early modernism began to confound these cultural norms yet without seriously shaking the societal order as a whole.

Only the mass distribution of networked computers advanced a paradigmatic shift in society. The newly introduced networked practices of distribution and productions, aka remix, suddenly opened up an unknown territory, which was for a long time governed by technological, economic, and juridical restrictions.

In the pursuit of the apparatus, from Freud's "prosthesis god" to McLuhan's "extension of men" to Mann's wearable computers, single user interaction has shifted into multiple user interaction on various platforms with either time-based (e.g., video sharing), image-based (e.g., photo sharing), text-based (e.g., blogs and wikis) or audio-based (e.g., podcasts) media. The driving force behind this global move towards self-expression, authenticity, and community building is rooted equally in human nature's inherent narcissism and the basic desire to belong to a specific group. Both extremes—idiosyncratic exposure and social networking— are phenomena that do not constitute media culture per se, but rather belong to a newly observed phenomenon in current Web 2.0 developments.

A new species, the social networker, has come into being. He/she is a multitasking information producer and manager, a multimedia artist and a homepage designer, an actor and a director of self-made videos, an editor and an author of his/her blog, a moderator and an administrator of a forum, to name only a few of the most prevalent characteristics. Social networkers select and publish their own information and put it straight from other networkers' flows directly into their own communities.

The traditional definition of the "user" thus loses its hitherto determinative character of information consumption and application usage. In this way, content that is created in one place can be dynamically posted and/or updated in multiple locations on the Web; for example photos can be shared from sites like Flickr to social sites like Facebook and MySpace. The interconnectivity of software applications and their users on the Web constitute an online literacy with which most teenagers and prosumers are familiar. Yet the impact of such a remarkable media revolution as that of Web 2.0 on individuals and society at large can only be fully understood in a media-historical context: understanding what and how communication media has transformed within the complex interplay of perceived needs, competitive and political pressures, and social and technological innovations.

Accordingly, two main characteristics drive social media. One dates back to Mark Granovetter's groundbreaking article "The Strength Of The Weak Ties" from 1973. Based on a study of job seekers, he discovered that finding a new position does not come through the strong ties (friends or relatives), but through the extended network of weak ties (in over 80 percent of cases). Similar observations can be made inside "social utility tools" (Facebook) that connect people with friends and others who work, study, and live around them. This so-called "long tail effect" also has implications for the producers of content, especially those whose products could not—for economic reasons—find a place in pre-Internet information distribution channels controlled by book publishers, record companies, movie studios, and television networks. (We will come back to these economic implications shortly.) From the producers' standpoint, the long tail has made possible a flowering of creativity across all fields of human endeavor. One example of this surge can be witnessed on YouTube, where thousands of diverse videos—whose content, production value, or lack of popularity make them inappropriate for traditional television—are easily accessible to a wide range of viewers. From hair and makeup demonstrations to "fail" videos, a user can watch a video in nearly any niche subject area on the video sharing website.

It is exactly this spirit of participation, cooperation and sharing that has fundamentally altered media perception, reception, and production. The shift from implicit (tacit knowledge) to explicit forms of knowledge sharing has paved the way for new forms of collective intelligence, which one pioneer, George Pór, defined as "the capacity of human communities to evolve towards higher order complexity and harmony, through such innovation mechanisms as differentiation and integration, competition and collaboration."[16]

The Rise of the Professional Amateur?

With the advent of mobile technologies, personal and mass communication amalgamated into a single medium, blurring the boundaries of the public and private domains. For example the "blogosphere" covers a broad range of individual and more publicly oriented formats. As a consequence, the hitherto traditional distinction between professional and amateur culture is no longer relevant.

Further, remix culture has unleashed a vast number of cultural producers, resulting in defragmented areas of cultural production. In other words, taking up Shirky's example[17] of car driving, to which he ascribes patterns similar to the social basis of cultural work: a few people do not care about it at all; many drive cars as a daily routine yet more or less unaffiliated; others make their living as bus or taxi drivers; some people consider car driving a highly charged normative issue ("Free driving for free citizens"); and others invest time and money to uplift their social status (veteran car clubs). From occasional drivers to F1 racing drivers, in between exists a wide spectrum of car driving in which professional drivers represent only a small fraction of all passionate ones and those in turn make up only a small subset of actual drivers. Despite the simplicity of learning to drive a car for most people, there are certain situations that require specialization and professionalization. A similar kind of differentiation can be attributed to the production and dissemination of media objects in cultural production. This is not something entirely new, since we all actively reproduce culture —if only in the example of coaffecting the rise and fall of temporary fashions. The essentially new is that all these different forms of cultural production converge in a joint medium, which at least technologically holds the potential for a comparable public and civil engagement.

The Internet brought with it hitherto unknown retail distribution mechanisms, which became popularized as the long tail by Chris Anderson,[18] who refers to Amazon, Apple, and Yahoo as examples of businesses applying this niche strategy. Unlike big box stores that sell large volumes of popular items with little diversity in stock, these online retailers realize significant profit by selling small volumes of hard-to-find items to customers around the world. The total sales of this large number of "nonhit items" is called "the long tail." Long tail strategies will arguably have long-lasting impact on culture and politics.

New technologies, particularly social media, enabled women to participate in the Arab Spring as organizers, journalists, and activists. Protesters used Facebook to mobilize supporters and organize events, and YouTube videos and Flickr photos gave the rest of the world visuals of the events during the uprisings. Twitter functioned as a live newsfeed for other domestic and international activists as well as international media organizations. Mobile phones, especially those with cameras and Internet access, served as a key tool for cyberactivists. One such prominent representative was Lina Ben Mhenni,[19] a blogger and Nobel Prize nominee, whose reporting from Tunisia's rural areas helped drive the revolution and bring it to international attention.

Quite similar tendencies are observable in other areas. At an increasing rate documentaries are made by activists who search for authentic images. This phenomenon is not entirely new—due to cost-effectiveness, the 1980s were under the influence of a "camcorder revolution." Even so, the revolution did not spark off due to limited distribution channels, and inaccessible supply chains clearly pose an obstacle in postproduction.

Concomitant with the disposability of material produced by others along with the resulting remix practices, novel and more complex forms of moviemaking emerged, not least because of easily accessible footage material. *Steal This Film*,[20] a film series (2006–08) produced by the League of Noble Peers, is a major account against intellectual property in favor of peer-to-peer (P2P) file sharing and was first released via the BitTorrent P2P protocol. The first part, made by Swedish activists from The Pirate Bay, Piratbyrån—all of them quite influential for the central European Pirate Party movement—mostly includes interviews about the illegal confiscation of The Pirate Bay's servers by the Swedish police and the political effects of this seizure. This 32-minute film attracted attention for its critical analysis of an alleged regulatory capture attempt performed by Hollywood film lobby groups to leverage economic sanctions by the United States government on Sweden through the World Trade Organization.

The premise of *Steal This Film: Part 2*,[21] which was released at the end of 2007, is that file sharing transforms the basic mechanism of how culture and information is distributed, with consequences as profound as the transformation brought about by the printing press. In an interesting interview taken from a 1972 documentary, Joseph Licklider, who was instrumental in funding the early work on the Arpanet, speaks about the need to invent a better system of information sharing than print because of the physical limitations of moving around paper. Strikingly, Licklider speaks in this small clip about information "sharing," not distribution or the like.

Another documentary on the same subject, *Good Copy, Bad Copy*,[22] released by Danish filmmakers in 2007, takes a global perspective, introducing two major non-Western cultural communities—"tecnobrega" from Brazil and the Nigerian film industry. Looking at Brazil and Nigeria, the movie's core message suggests that whereas technological change might still originate from the West, cultural innovation is distributed much more broadly.

The Pirate's Dilemma[23]

In contrast to linearly organized division of labor in traditional cultural industries, remix culture emanates from intertwined temporal and organizational areas of production, consumption, and distribution. Technically speaking, this is particularly evident in BitTorrent protocols, which inextricably link parallel occurring processes: that of downloading (consumption) and uploading (distribution). As a result, the boundaries between private usage and public distribution blur and clearly affect the distribution infrastructure. Millions of private transactions create—voluntarily or involuntarily—a competitive infrastructure, comparable with the professional versions of the same vendor.

The emergent file sharing scene at the beginning of the new millennium paved— more or less successfully—the way for a variety of global brands. Almost synonymously with the upcoming file sharing subculture, arose an individual using the pseudonym "aXXo"[24] (2005–09). He became popular for releasing commercial DVD movies on the Internet as free downloads. At that time he was public enemy number one for Hollywood executives, and to film fans around the world, he was a modern-day Robin Hood. The fragmentary character of remix unveils a striking analogy with BitTorrent's file sharing principles: pieces of the downloading files are collected by seeking out segments of the film, album or application from every user's computer. This "swarming" character makes downloading faster, as the more users share a particular file, the quicker the downloads will be completed.

Ordinary users may occasionally wonder where all these movies, games, and music come from. It turns out that—against general acceptance—the majority of illicit content available for download is not from consumer-bought entertainment products. On the contrary, film industry insiders, DVD factory workers and retail assistants branch off the forthcoming releases and pass them on to the scene's so-called "release groups"[25] which are at the top of the piracy pyramid. These groups are composed of "rippers" responsible for loss-free file compression and specialization in a certain medium, film, and game genre. Once the copy is released it takes only a few hours to make it available for the average BitTorrent user on The Pirate Bay or Mininova.

Even as cyberculture brought with it early adopters and hackers pushing the envelope to the utmost extent, sooner or later their work was capitalized upon by commercial vendors. Contrarily to the first steps in open source businesses ("Give Away the Razor, Sell Razor Blades"[26]), Matt Mason's euphemistic appraisal of pirates—"what they are actually doing is highlighting a better way for us to do things; they find gaps outside the market, and better ways for society to operate"[27]—quite obviously resembles the deadly embrace in the spider web. The same accounts for hackers who work for both sides, nourishing the economic spiral by means of fierce competition in the global market, something that can be cynically translated into: The only way to fight piracy is to legitimize and legalize new innovations by competing with pirates in the marketplace. As a consequence, originally subversive works and ideas are themselves appropriated by corporate business.

However, beyond the gray-zone of file sharing, the means of production and consumption converge in a very visible way in fan culture. Probably the most significant difference between a fan and consumer is that the identification of the fan with a whole cultural universe makes him/her feel a part of it. In his blog entry from 2007[28] Henry Jenkins points out that the industry overlooks the community aspect of users with their own traditions of participatory culture. In a similar vein, commercial enterprises consider "content" as something commodifiable and thus isolated from the social relations that surround its production and circulation. Fan culture, in contrast, builds on social networks of fans who have their own aesthetics, politics, and genre expectations. Jenkins continues that the noncommercial nature of fan culture is based on a gift economy, and being free of commercial constraints, there is leeway to explore themes or experiment with structures and styles beyond the "mainstream" versions of these worlds.

Reciprocity

The economic model based on existing copyright regulations relies on intertwined control, attribution, and compensation mechanisms that legitimate in great portions the model of cultural industries. Yet this assertion is also disputable, insofar as the widely ramified forms of cultural economy are by nature more comprehensive than the copyright-based industries. One example to back up this argument is the restricted claim of copyright holders on copied material for teaching and research purposes. In that case the authors are granted fees indirectly by collecting societies. However, it should be mentioned that these regulations exert an exceptional regulatory measure that does not question copyright per se, but instead deals with it in a more practical way.

Under the pressure of current remix practices the knot of complex laws and regulations that emerged from copyright slowly but constantly dissolves. That does not necessarily implicate a decline of existing copyright regulations, but in view of the specific needs in the vast arena of cultural production, there is clearly demand for more adaptable and differentiated laws. The widely diffused free licensing practices (Creative Commons, GPL, etc.) have proliferated individual contributions, but at the same time lowered the level of control and perceptibility on individual authorship.

Going back to history, copyright too was a nonissue in the visual arts until recently. In 1921, Kurt Schwitters called his own brand of Dada "Merz," derived from the logo of the German "Commerzbank," which he had used in a collage painting. Artists who would do the equivalent today on the Web are at risk of being sued for copyright and trademark infringement. It is also true that even the best free software and open content license cannot protect you from legal claims of a third party against you. In other words, if you create, like Kurt Schwitters, an art movement called Merz based on the Commerzbank logo and published your Merz logo with an open content license, Commerzbank would still be able to sue you for trademark violation.

One of the advancements of the free software movement was to radically rework the very idea of the user. In sharp contrast to the passive consumer attitude in proprietary systems, the free software model builds on the idea of a user-as-producer. The user-producer is a concept that resonates with the digital experience and the freedom that current digital culture allows for ordinary people to become artists and producers. This model fundamentally challenges the traditional parameters of copyright law by moving away from the concept of "originality" of the work to recognize the value that various users contribute through their modifications and adaptions to an existing work. In this regard it is worth reconsidering the simplistic binary split of the original and the copy as something that does not diminish the value of the original, but instead look at copies as additions to the original.

In their manifesto "right2remix"[29] the promoters assert that "creative copying has become commonplace, the right to remix is a fundamental requirement for freedom of expression and free speech." Consequently, three creative rights are formulated (ibid.):

- The right to change works during usage and to publish the results. (Transformative usage rights with lump-sum compensation, e.g., background music in mobile phone videos.)
- The right to create and to publish remixes of existing works. (Remix rights with lump-sum compensation, e.g., fake trailer for a TV series.)
- The right to commercialize remixes, in exchange for appropriate compensation. (Remix commercialization rights subject to compulsory licensing, e.g., selling music mashups on iTunes).

Among the many petitions and proposals to alter EU and national copyright regulations, the right2remix initiative seeks to redefine the boundaries of free usage, particularly in musical works. Here there is a need for the legalization of samples, which in the case of commercial use could be compensated using compulsory licensing models. Moreover, the "originality" of a work should be assessed independently from the question of whether the inspirational works are still recognizable.

Apart from the creative framework and the rewriting of digital culture via current remix practices, concerns raised about fair compensation are by far the most controversial and apparently unresolvable. On a European scale, there has been an ongoing discussion about the introduction of a "cultural flat rate"[30] (alternative compensating system), which is based on a blank media tax or levy for digital copyright holders. As a quid pro quo, the circulation of digital copies in file sharing networks for private use would then become legal.

One of the major objections against this one-size-fits-all concept is regardless of whether you download anything, you have to pay. More importantly, the number of file sharing activities will be taken as a basis for payouts and is thus prone to manipulation. If you, for example, know that your favorite artist will be paid in proportion to the number of times a song is downloaded, you will soon realize that you can support the artist by repeatedly downloading the same album.

It is often erroneously assumed that file sharing culture has negative impacts on artists' revenues, but, on the contrary, artists are making more, and record companies less, money. Studies[31] on the music business revealed that during a decade when file sharing grew exponentially, revenues increased year by year for the cultural sector as a whole and for each individual segment such as film, music, or computer games. Consumer behavior shows that music fans spend more money going to live concerts and less to buy discs, which leaves more money for the creative people who actually make the music.

In conclusion, the coevolving cultural, economic, and technological implications in cut-copy-paste culture offer several parallel and reciprocal pathways of cultural and economic opportunities—in a process of coevolutionary feedback. Such ventures are embedded in community or culture rather than in business values. At the same time consumer-generated content has carved out new markets and business opportunities. "Web n+1" developments in the broadest sense must be regarded as enabling social technologies supporting the growth of consumer cocreation. Similar to the invention of printing, we are in another evolutionary step in the growth of knowledge, enabling people to cocreate in a "network of networks" which simultaneously holds—following the binary logic of digital culture—promises and risks.

Notes

1 Quote often attributed to Pablo Picasso.

2 See Jennifer Valcke "Static Films and Moving Pictures: Montage in Avant-Garde Photography and Film," PhD thesis (University of Edinburgh, 2009), 11.

3 A good example is the 1929 experimental silent documentary film *Man with a Movie Camera* by Russian director Dziga Vertov.

4 This famous line is from the sixth canto in Comte de Lautréaumont's *The Song of Maldoror* (1868–69).

5 Sergei Eisenstein, from the "Cinematographic Principle and the Ideogram" (1929); trans. Jay Leyda, in Leyda, ed. *Film Form* (New York: Meridian Books, 1957), 37–40.

6 Christoph Cox and Daniel Warner, *Audio Culture: Readings in Modern Music* (London: Continuum International Publishing Group, 2004), 10–14.

7 "Origin and Theory of the Tape Cut-Ups" by William S. Burroughs. "Breakthrough" http://activearchives.org/aaa/media/cache/ubu.artmob.ca/sound/burroughs_william/Break-Through/Burroughs-William-S_01-K-9.mp3/original.mp3 (accessed October 2013).

8 D. Holt, *Cultural Strategy Using Innovative Ideologies to Build Breakthrough Brands* (Oxford: Oxford University Press, 2010), 252.

9 http://www.bopsecrets.org/SI/detourn.htm (accessed July 2014).

10 P. Burkholder (1994) "The uses of existing music: musical borrowing as a field," http://www.thefreelibrary.com/The+uses+of+existing+music%3a+musical+borrowing+as+a+field.-a015109065 (accessed October 2013).

11 T. S. Eliot 'Philip Massinger', in *The Sacred Wood* (1921) http://www.bartleby.com/200/sw11.html (accessed October 2013).

12 O. B. Arewa, "From J. C. Bach to Hip Hop: Musical Borrowing, Copyright and Cultural Context" (*North Carolina Law Review* 84, no. 2, 2006), 547–645.

13 G. Cheliotis and J. Yew, "An Analysis of the Social Structure of Remix Culture," in J. M. Carroll (Ed.), *Proceedings of the Fourth International Conference on Communities and Technologies* (New York: ACM, 2009), 165–174.

14 Bruno Latour, "Why Has Critique Run out of Steam? From Matters of Fact to Matters of Concern," *Critical Inquiry* 30 no. 2 (2003): 225–248.

15 Manuel De Landa, *A New Philosophy of Society: Assemblage Theory and Social Complexity* (London: Continuum, 2006), 10–11.

16 George Pór, "Collective Intelligence and Collective Leadership: Twin Paths to Beyond Chaos," *Sprouts: Working Papers on Information Systems* 8 no. 2, (University of Amsterdam, Netherlands, 2008), 7.

17 Clay Shirky, *Here Comes Everybody: The Power of Organizing Without Organizations* (New York: Penguin, 2008), 57.

18 http://www.wired.com/wired/archive/12.10/tail.html (accessed October 2013).

19 http://www.amazon.com/Tunisian-girl-bloggeuse-révolution-Mhenni/dp/2911939875 (accessed October 2013).

20 http://www.stealthisfilm.com/Part1/ (accessed October 2013).

21 http://www.stealthisfilm.com/Part2/ (accessed October 2013).

22 http://www.goodcopybadcopy.net/ (accessed October 2013).

23 Cf. Matt Mason's eponymous book *The Pirate's Dilemma. How Youth Culture Is Reinventing Capitalism* (New York: Free Press, 2009).

24 https://en.wikipedia.org/wiki/AXXo (accessed October 2013).

25 http://filesharefreak.com/2007/11/22/how-to-identify-tags-on-pirated-releases (accessed October 2013).

26 Cf. Eric S. Raymond's quote in "The Cathedral and the Bazaar," http://www.catb.org/~esr/writings/cathedral-bazaar/magic-cauldron/ar01s09.html#id2762651 (accessed October 2013).

27 http://torrentfreak.com/the-pirates-dilemma-080108/ (accessed October 2013).

28 http://henryjenkins.org/2007/05/transforming_fan_culture_into.html (accessed October 2013).

29 http://right2remix.org (accessed October 2013).

30 See Volker Grassmuck's "Inside Views: The World Is Going Flat(-Rate)," http://www.ip-watch.org/2009/05/11/the-world-is-going-flat-rate/ (accessed October 2013).

31 http://torrentfreak.com/artists-make-more-money-in-file-sharing-age-than-before-100914/ (accessed October 2013).

Bibliography

Anderson, Chris. *The Long Tail: Why the Future of Business is Selling Less of More*. New York: Hyperion, 2006.

Arewa, O. B. "From J. C. Bach to Hip Hop: Musical Borrowing, Copyright and Cultural Context." *North Carolina Law Review* 84, no. 2 (2006): 547–645.

Benkler, Yochai. *The Wealth of Network: How Social Production Transforms Markets and Freedoms*. New Haven, CT: Yale University Press, 2006.

Bourdieu, Pierre. *The Field of Cultural Production: Essays on Art and Literature*. Translated by Randal Johnson. Cambridge: Polity Press, 1993.

Cheliotis, Giorgos, and Jude Yew. "An Analysis of the Social Structure of Remix Culture." In John M. Carroll (Ed.), *Proceedings of the Fourth International Conference on Communities and Technologies*, 165–174. New York: ACM, 2009.

Cox, Christoph, and Daniel Warner. *Audio Culture: Readings in Modern Music*. London: Continuum International Publishing Group, 2004.

De Landa, Manuel. *A New Philosophy of Society: Assemblage Theory and Social Complexity*. London: Continuum, 2006.

Eisenstein, Sergei. "Cinematographic Principle and the Ideogram" (1929). Translated by Jay Leyda, in Jay Leyda, ed., *Film Form*. New York: Meridian Books, 1957.

Holt, D. *Cultural Strategy Using Innovative Ideologies to Build Breakthrough Brands*. Oxford: Oxford University Press, 2010.

Jenkins, Henry. *Convergence Culture: Where Old and New Media Collide*. New York: New York University Press, 2006.

Latour, Bruno. "Why Has Critique Run out of Steam? From Matters of Fact to Matters of Concern," *Critical Inquiry* 30 no. 2 (2003): 225–248.

——. *Reassembling the Social: An Introduction to Actor-Network Theory*. Oxford: Oxford University Press, 2005.

Mason, Matt. *The Pirate's Dilemma. How Youth Culture Is Reinventing Capitalism*. New York: Free Press, 2009.

Navas, Eduardo *Remix Theory. The Aesthetics of Sampling*. Vienna: Springer, 2012.

Pór, George. "Collective Intelligence and Collective Leadership: Twin Paths to Beyond Chaos," *Sprouts: Working Papers on Information Systems* 8 no. 2, University of Amsterdam, Netherlands, 2008.

Shirky, Clay. *Here Comes Everybody: The Power of Organizing Without Organizations*. New York: Penguin, 2008.

Sonvilla-Weiss, Stefan. *Mashup Cultures*. Vienna: Springer, 2010.

Valcke, Jennifer. "Static Films and Moving Pictures: Montage in Avant-Garde Photography and Film." PhD thesis, University of Edinburgh, UK, 2009.

Zittrain, Jonathan. *The Future of the Internet—And How to Stop It*. New Haven, CT: Yale University Press, 2008.

4

TOWARD A REMIX CULTURE

An Existential Perspective

Vito Campanelli

The purpose of this chapter is to frame Vilém Flusser's utopian reflections in relation to the advent of a telematic society in light of a remix culture. In remix culture a work is never completed, it functions rather as a relay that is passed to others so that they can contribute to the process with the production of new works. This dynamic was already obvious in the mid-1980s to Flusser, who argued that in an information society messages are sent to receivers so that they can synthesize them as new messages. With the aid of Flusser's work, and theories by Lévi-Strauss, Tarde and Le Bon, I will frame remix as a pervasive mass phenomenon in which the creation of new information becomes the fundamental criterion for distinguishing between the heterogeneous cultural forms labeled as remix.

Toward a Telematic Society

During his career the media philosopher Vilém Flusser analyzed a number of sociocultural dynamics, in particular those arising from the diffusion of the first computers and their subsequent role in the progression toward a "telematic society" (according to Flusser, this would be the first society that methodically seeks to increase the sum of available information). Some of his reasoning concerning this new form of sociality seemed to be beyond the horizon of possibility during the times in which they were formulated (mid-1980s to early 1990s). Indeed, he anticipated some constitutive aspects of contemporary culture, whose main compositional paradigm appeared to be remix. An in-depth exploration of the distinctive features of a remix culture will be discussed in later sections of this text; at this point it should be clarified that the use of the term "remix" refers to an irreversible process of hybridization of sources, materials, subjectivities, and media ongoing in contemporary society. Focusing on its significant cultural impact we can consider the remix as Manovich defined it, as a metaphor for the generalized amalgamation and digitalization of culture.[1] Manovich argues that today many cultural and lifestyle contexts (music, fashion, design, art, Web applications, user-generated media, food, etc.) are governed by remixes, fusions, collages, and mashups. If postmodernism (Jameson)[2] was a defining paradigm of the 1980s, "during the 1990s remix has gradually emerged as the dominant aesthetics of the era of globalization," therefore we can call it "the cultural logic of networked global capitalism."[3]

A few years before Manovich, Flusser created an interesting parallel between the ways in which "nature" (the world) creates new information and the ways humans create new information. He first notes that because the information "in the world" seems to arise randomly (that is to say beyond any possible intention), the world itself appears as just one of very many chance configurations (*möglichen Zufällswurfen*). From this perspective even the human brain is no longer generated according to some "creative plan" (*schöpferischen Plan*), but by the chance biological development that itself came into being accidentally as the result of chemical processes. Like any information in the world, the human brain is bound to decay, in fact it tends toward disgregation and disinformation (the second principle of thermodynamics is a constant reference for Flusser).

Flusser argues that the way information decays is as important as its production. He contends that information is produced through improbable accidents and decay occurs through probable accidents. If this were true it would be incorrect to argue that we experience an ex nihilo creation constituted of a linear progression from the void toward a predetermined goal ("heat death"). We are not in front of the "universe of linear history" but are actually part of a dull game of dice (*sturen Würfspiel*) in which all improbable cases must happen, sooner or later, and all dice rolls must lead to a plausible situation: the dissolution of information.[4]

According to Flusser, information cannot be produced from nothing; every dialog presupposes the existence of some information stored in memory. To put the point another way it presupposes an earlier discourse that delivered (transmitted) the stored information.[5] Flusser established that all the information is synthesized from previous information (as we shall see later, this assumption is very important from the perspective of the remix); moving from this assumption he states that humans do not create but play with prior information, however—unlike nature which plays by sheer chance (without method)—their play (following the method of dialog) is acted with the purpose of producing information.

Here emerges the first important handhold for supporting the attempt to frame Flusserian insights within the perspective of the remix: For the media philosopher, dialogs are sort of "guided" (*gelenkte*) games of chance, through which information already present in the world is combined (remixed) in all possible ways to construct new information.[6] However it should be clarified that the concept of "intention" cannot refer to "mythical entities" (*Fabelwesen*) as a form of "free spirit" or "eternal soul." We must instead think in the following terms: the so-called "I" is considered as a nexus point in a web comprising streams of information in dialog and, at the same time, a warehouse/ storage (*Lager*) for information that has passed through.[7]

At this nexus point, represented by the "I," unpredictable and improbable computations occur, in other words: new information is made. This new information is experienced as intentional (or as freely produced) because each "I" is a unique nexus point that, by its position and the information it stores, it is distinguished from all other nexus points. Even the telematic society envisioned by Flusser is composed of this unique character. Flusser, who anticipated the informational paradigm of the networked society,[8] suggested that this form of social organization differs from all previous forms because it is "the first to recognize the production of information as society's actual function."[9]

Self-conscious of its actual function, it is also a free society, but one whose freedom has little to do with the tradition of Judeo-Christian anthropology. Here we face a socialization of freedom, that is to say the disappearance of broadcast centers radiating communicative rays out from a center (according to the electric circuitry presiding over a society dominated by unidirectional media). The key point here is the emergence of senders-receivers[10] who, by integrating their decisions in a network with those made by other nodes, give rise to comprehensive decisions as a "cosmic superbrain" (*kosmishes Ubergehirn*). Therefore, in a telematic society the process of information production takes place on a social level, but the single "I," the single node on the network, maintains its singularity. In other words, the socialization of the production of information (of decisions and freedom) does not dissolve the "I" but fully realizes it in comparison with others, to the extent that "'I' is the one to whom someone says 'you'" (*"ich" ist, zu dem jemand "du" sagt*). According to Flusser, the telematic society is a real "information society" in which human beings experience their freedom by playing methodically (utilizing a knowledge base and strategies for play) with information and, in doing so, they give birth to a "rising tide" (*steigernde Flut*) of information capable of opposing entropy.[11]

Flusser underlines that the production of information is "a game of assembling existing information" (*ein Zusammensetzspiel mit bereits vorhandenen Informationen*).[12] Moreover, the reasoning Flusser develops regarding the functioning of chamber music (*Kammermusik*) as a model for the telematic society in general, offers a cue for an interesting analogy with remix practices. He notes that the foundation of this musical practice is an original score, thus a program, but scores take a back seat during the execution as musicians give life to improvisations. These improvisations can be compared to the *variations* that characterize the creative act of Jamaican DJs, who, as we shall see later, are foundational to modern remix culture. According to Flusserian categories chamber music is cybernetic, it is in fact "pure play" staged "by and for the players." Listeners— Flusser writes—are "superfluous and intrusive" as the method of chamber music is the participation (*strategia*) and not the contemplation (*theoria*).

Upon closer investigation, remix culture is also characterized by the prevalence of the participatory over the contemplative. Full immersion in remix culture can only be achieved through participating in the act of remixing. In chamber music and in remix culture each player is both a sender and a receiver of information; in both cases the ultimate goal is to synthesize new information.[13]

Intersubjective Conversations and the Disappearance of all Authorities

Flusser addresses another key issue for a culture dominated by reuse practices—the question of authorship. In the universe of technical (and telematic) images it no longer makes sense to speak of "author" (*Autor*) and "authority" (*Autorität*). Automation of the processes of production, reproduction, and distribution make such terms unnecessary. The creative modes of production of the past were based—as Flusser notes—on an inner dialog (*innerem Dialog*); on the contrary, today most of the information is not produced by individuals but by dialogic groups and, moreover, the statute of the work has been radically changed by the technical possibilities of infinitely reproducing and editing each work. In the telematic society envisioned by Flusser, all information is synthesized through intersubjective conversations and its purpose is to be modified by the receivers and put back into the flow as new information.

More than anything else, the infinite reproducibility of information undermines the Latin myth of the foundation by the "author" (Romulus who founded Rome) and those social structures based on the principle of "authority" (linked with an "author"). Flusser fully comprehends what was to become the foundation of remix culture when he argues that reproducibility and the automatic distribution of messages lead to the disappearance of all authorities. Under the regime of reproducibility "authority" becomes redundant. The romantic myth of the author, the idea that there are "originals" produced by "great people" as a result of inner dialogs must give away in the face of information that waives any claim to originality and realizes the possibility of being automatically everywhere and in a constant state of replicability. Hence social structures are created in which the idea of the individual founder is renounced in order to create a society open to dialog and to its reproducibility (a prelude to "reproducible societies").[14]

For Flusser the outer dialogs, potentially open to participation by all, and intersubjective conversations involving human and artificial memories are far more creative than works created by traditional authors. They also generate "creative enthusiasm" (*schöpferische Begeisterung*) and a widespread consensus with respect to the information society. We can therefore say—with Flusser—that the telematic society does not abolish the concept of "creation" but rather invests it with its real meaning, that of intersubjective activity, directed not toward the creation of works, or of "objects," but toward messages that will appear to other human beings as "challenges" (*Herausforderungen*) to generate eternally reproducible and infinitely synthesizable new information.[15] These last statements ultimately overcome every doubt about the possibility of reading Flusser's reflections on the advent of the telematic society from the perspective of remix culture.

Flusser closes his reasoning on contemporary creativity with a confession that he, too, found himself carried away with the *inebriation* of the game. He expresses the hope that others consider his reflections with the same playful spirit, transmitting and modifying them in turn.[16] Is it possible to imagine a more explicit invitation to remix?

Remix as a Mass Phenomenon

The arguments that Flusser developed about the creativity specific to a utopian telematic society can be connected to the perspective that today we live in a *culture of remix*. He imagined a networked society in which the production of new information can only be conceived in a dialogic game with preexisting information stored in memories, anticipating the general character of remix as a social practice. This approach is crucial to my interpretation of remix, indeed I believe that, rather than facing an artistic (and therefore elitist) practice, we are now encountering a pervasive mass phenomenon. Remix is a game made possible by new technologies (particularly by the development of postproduction techniques) and by the incredible amount of cultural material that the so-called digital revolution has put, literally, in everyone's hands. It is a game perfectly consonant with an era in which "technocodes" based on "technoimages" have replaced the linear code (written texts) as the main model of thought. It is a game that favors the surface and, taking place only at a surface level, is allergic to depth, such as specificity, truth, authenticity, definitivity, and so on.

The act of remixing collocates itself in a gestural *continuum* in which in-depth analysis and a critique of reassembled cultural objects are not entitled to citizenship. Very often we are faced with simple routines in which the materials to be remixed,

> are selected solely for their aesthetic surface, as when images are juxtaposed due to their complementary chromatic scales, regardless of their symbolic value or meaning. Furthermore, machines frequently remix automatically, even if the

primary input is sourced from humans, which further undermines the capacity for critique.[17]

If this is true, it would appear misleading to generalize and overestimate the sporadic remix episodes that are strongly aware of meanings and values connected to each cultural object remixed (remixes made by artists or by other "communication professionals"). These lucky episodes coexist next to billions of cultural objects produced through the same modalities of creative reuse of existing materials and it is possible to argue that, in purely quantitative terms, they represent nothing more than a drop in the ocean of remix.

Analogously, I deem problematic the claim that a remix operates as a transparent surface, in which the reassembled materials remain half in sight. To support this interpretation means considering the practice of remix as a reflective exercise or as a reflection on the elements of the past involved in the practice of the remix and, ultimately, denying any discontinuity between the "original" and the "new."[18]

On the contrary, to consider the remix as something that can (also) lose track of the cultural objects from the past (recontextualized in the present) opens up the possibility of interpreting the remix as a revitalization, entering a new vital life inside sources sclerotized by the passage of time. In the footsteps of Maffesoli, I prefer to think of the remix as an expression of that new form of being-together (that the French sociologist calls "societal") in which modern productivism gives way to a ludic atmosphere. As Abruzzese notes,

> the practices of remix . . . are not only able to act through operations of deconstruction of the existing and of recombination of the emotional and cognitive investment's "objects" derived from such a deconstruction. But, in their accumulating one on the other, they are also interventions of progressive deletion of the normative tracks included in the expressive systems that they incessantly remedied. To the point that in some cases the remix is as effective as much it erases the historical memory, dispelling, for objective or deliberate ignorance, the capital of its traditions and interpretations.[19]

Framed in this manner, remix is seen as a constitutive element of a new cultural reality that disrupts the moral (think of the disruption of copyright) and shared codes and promotes the free gushing of a confused flow of emotions-passions-sufferings able to give back vital effervescence to cultural heritage.[20] In turn, the heritage becomes—thanks to its progressive digitalization—an endless catalog from which remixers can draw with both hands.[21]

A Gigantic Playground

Remix involves all domains of human action and not only because the need to reshuffle the sources of one's own culture is common to all human history, but mostly because it is an evolutionary duty essential to the progress of the human species. Both biological and social evolution takes place by means of minor variations, and then through a repetition of patterns—accordingly the evolutionary model is given by repetition-innovation. Assuming this perspective, one must conclude that when referring to remix, one does not mean that the phenomenon is new: to use fragments of previous works is simply what human beings have always done in arts, in sciences, and in all fields of the intellect. Therefore, if it is true that the attitude to remix has marked every era, we must admit that it is equally true that in recent years we have been witness to phenomena that justifies calling contemporary culture a "culture of remix."

I would like to highlight two significant phenomena: the far-reaching spread of post-production tools (available to almost anyone who has at least a computer) that allow for sampling and the overlapping of sources at a rate that would be simply unthinkable just 30 years ago; and the exponential multiplication (through digital media, especially the Internet) of sources that one can access at virtually anytime and from anywhere. As Flusser writes, in a telematic society all information is at our immediate disposal: "the whole universe awaits me at my terminal as a gigantic playground."[22]

Although it seems reasonable to argue that human beings have always lived in a remix culture, this conviction should not prevent us from delineating the specificity of the present era, a specificity that, in my opinion, is produced by the possibility of reusing cultural material in a way never experienced before.[23] The incredible opportunities to mix and hybridize the amazing amount of digital data to which one has access, simply imposes the act of doing so: "Individuals are forced to think in terms of post-production and remix, if they are to be able to face the everyday overload of digital information" to which their minds and their *machinic appendices* are exposed daily. "Remix is an 'evolutionary duty', arising from every human's innate need to personally transform the materials available to them." If true, this might explain why "the practice of remix is more necessary to the contemporary age than ever before."[24] As Flusser predicted, the information available to human beings has now reached "astronomical dimensions" and is no longer storable by the human mind, hence the need for artificial memories.[25] The digitalization of culture (the tendency to bring all analogically produced human culture into the digital domain) is one of the dynamics that has most encouraged the emergence of a remix culture, to the extent that it is today possible to say that "humans have never had so many materials *in their hands*,"[26] which is to say: *so many materials to remix.*

Another important assumption is that a characteristic of digital media includes one that Lev Manovich defines as *modularity*: the organization of media objects into distinct and separate elements, which can be accessed separately and easily changed and combined with other parts in endless combinations.[27] Digital technologies also play a decisive role, in that they make it possible to work on discontinuous samples (pixels, polygons, fonts, etc.) aggregated in modular structures (new media).

Flusser had already realized that organizing media objects into distinct particles would have a decisive influence on the contemporary game that recognizes images as surfaces. In fact, as sciences dissolve *reality* into punctual elements, the purpose of the contemporary gesture of *Einbildungskraft* (to compute concepts through a peculiar attitude—not to be confused with the traditional concept of imagination) can be nothing other than to give the appearance of surface to points (giving an apparent concreteness to punctual elements) and thereby to return from the most extreme abstraction (scientific theories) to the *representable*, the *conceptualizable*, and the *manageable*. According to Flusser, technical images express the attempt to grasp, through flat surfaces (such as pictures), punctual elements that are all around us (photons, electrons, informational bits, and so on) and to fill in the spaces that open up between them. This gesture can be accomplished only thanks to an apparatus that, through its own interface, makes graspable and manageable punctual elements otherwise intangible for human hands and fingers.[28] In conclusion, modern technology on one hand offers a growing number of increasingly modular media objects (already very suitable for being remixed); on the other hand, it makes selecting, assembling, editing, and publishing elements of the infinite digital data flow simpler than ever before and more cost-effective.[29] All of these elements together (the simplicity of remix operations, the movement toward digital media, and, above all, media modularity) prelude, as noted by Manovich, a progressive hybridization of visual languages and, therefore, a state of "deep remixability" (or *total remixability*), a condition in which *everything* (not just the content of different media but also languages, techniques, metaphors, interfaces, etc.) *can be remixed with everything*.[30]

Do It Yourself

Many authors have reconstructed the history of the liberation of users from a (mostly modernist) condition of passive consumption of cultural objects.[31] Flusser's model of the "discursive society" takes a similar form: Messages are irradiated in a unidirectional way from centers/senders. What these types of theories lack is an account of do it yourself (DIY) as a mass phenomenon; that is, the masses participate rather than only artists. In this sense it is easy to observe that since the 1950s, in response to the progressive massification, specialization, and automation of the production of goods, as well as to the increasing specialization of work duties, the desire to regain possession of a more direct relationship with things spreads in all directions. This is a desire that drives Western workers to perform a series of activities (usually at home) without the aid of professionals, and often without any specialist knowledge.[32] Of course, an in-depth historical perspective of DIY is beyond the scope of this chapter, though I would like to emphasize that no process of gradual erosion of the boundary between producers and consumers has been possible without rooting in society (at least in the West) the attitude of creating things using available materials (overabundant in an era of opulence) and knowledge (easily accessible even before the Internet—consider the popularity of manuals devoted to DIY philosophy). A history that discusses only the avant-garde (or anti-avant-garde) practices of *Do It Yourself* seems profoundly one-sided as an individual who keeps on walking with only one leg.[33] To summarize, without diminishing the decisive contribution of the practices introduced by the avant-garde and counter-avant-garde, it is essential to remember the importance of phenomena that involved Western society in a much more comprehensive way.

The potential for a more widespread DIY culture—including home repair, model-, and prototype-making and many of the heterogeneous activities connected to "hobbies"—has been noted by some philosophers and has become a privileged field of investigation in cultural studies. Beyond this specific research field, it is useful to remember the concept of *bricoleur* (which denotes a way of thinking and working halfway between the concrete and the abstract) at the heart of the reflections of Lévi-Strauss. Although the French anthropologist identified this attitude in non-Western societies,[34] his reflections can be seen to refer to amateurs in general. Framed in this way, they are precious precisely because they mark the distance between the specialized practices of the engineer (a metaphor of the industrial universe) and the way of thinking and working of the *bricoleur*. In Lévi-Strauss's interpretation, the *bricoleur* is someone who works with their hands, someone who uses different tools than those used by professionals. Thus the *bricoleur* behaves primarily as a collector: before any action he/she will browse his/her tools imagining possible uses (the *bricoleur* "interrogates all the heterogeneous objects of which his treasury is composed to discover what each of them could signify").[35] However, the most characteristic here is the addressing of the existent leftovers of human works, in other words, reorganization of the existing *is prevalent in respect* to creating from nothing.

The *bricolage* of the present era uses leftovers of the "'already seen', that which are openly transmitted and displayed in the media universe."[36] They are then reused, reassembled, and put back into circulation as messages (signs) and, in doing so, determining new uses and trajectories, and possibly altering meaning. But—this is the aspect that I want to emphasize most—the act of the *bricoleur* is functional to a system, such as the present one, in which social rooting presupposes the repetition of signs. The contemporary *bricoleur* (the remixer) is part of *the flow* and thus promotes its unstoppable *flowing*.

As mentioned before, the automation of production, as a consequence of the technological innovations of the second half of the twentieth century, ignited in Western workers the desire to regain a more direct relationship with things. This dynamic can be compared to that which nowadays propels the inhabitants of a hyperglobalized world to react to information overload—what Flusser describes as the "flood of (technical) images." Even netizens desire a *more direct relationship with things*, but things have lost their materiality and today appear mainly as information flow.[37] On a closer look, the practice of remix is precisely an answer to this need: remixing a media object (be it content, a *medium*, a language or a thought pattern) means appropriating it, offering a personal version of images, sounds, and whatever else pushes contemporary individuals/remixers to desire (or to the illusion of desiring). In other words, remixing takes the value of *making one's own* the object of desire (despite the ephemeral transience that this gesture assumes in the frame of contemporaneity).

It would appear that the only way to enjoy the infinite flow of information that passes through us at every moment is now a process of selection, editing, and promoting the flow in new contexts or personalized forms. Besides being an evolutionary duty, remix therefore assumes an important specific weight even on an existential plane: in fact, the feeling of appropriating elements of the flow *comforts* the contemporary individual offering, on the one hand, the opportunity to assert his/her social consistency through the dialog with others (the Self that finds him/herself entering a remixing relationship with the Other), on the other, the *inebriation* of having one's own purpose (though it is quite obviously an illusion) to set against the machines' will to program humans to incessantly feed on the flow.

In terms of Flusserian media philosophy *purpose* is a typical conditioning of historical thinking, a kind of ballast that forces the questioning of everything and always prompts a search for underlying reasons. Precisely for this reason, rather than *purpose*, it is preferable to speak of an *engagement* against nature and above all against the inevitable natural decay of information. From this standpoint, the production of new information can be interpreted as an engagement against being forgotten; in fact it is well known that all artificial storage media are subjected to the second law of thermodynamics and, sooner or later, they will decay along with the information stored in them. Electromagnetic information instead, as "pure" information (information that does not require a material *medium*), may, according to Flusser, allow human beings to escape "the curse of being forgotten."[38] With respect to memories, which escape the laws of nature, forgetting becomes an "information strategy" no less important and necessary than learning (that is to say acquiring information).

For Flusser redundant information should be deleted as the informative material should be stored, for this purpose we must learn to differentiate them. One of the main tasks of a telematic society is thus to acquire, through dialog, competency in differentiation (telematics is considered by Flusser a genuine school for freedom: "*Telematik als*

Schule der Freiheit").[39] In the light of these considerations it is possible to rephrase the distinction (absolutely central to Flusser) between the "natural" and the "cultural/human" production of information in the following terms: Natural production is uncertain, it is a "blind play of chance," it decays over time. Cultural/human production is strategic, it is an intentional game set in the opposite direction of the inevitable decay. The intentional aspect of the strategic–dialogic game with "pure" information allows a new way of approaching the question of freedom, which in Flusser's construction becomes "what fights against death" (against being forgotten). Seen from this point of view, only those who are competent at differentiating between redundant information and informative information are free. To use the words of Flusser, freedom is the "human engagement in producing information against entropy, decay, death."[40]

Imitation and the Social: The Foundations of Remix Culture

At this point, to fully understand the true importance of remix culture, it is essential to focus on some ideas that emerged at the end of the nineteenth century when the principle of imitation of an original model was defined in different fields and was considered the common matrix of cultural and social growth. Among the most interesting positions is one created by Gabriel de Tarde, who, in *Les lois de l'imitation* (1890)[41] describes the mechanism of "selective imitation." Tarde identifies two presuppositions: the role of imitation for social life is analogous to the role of heredity in biological life; and every social repetition comes from an innovation. Every human invention (which inaugurates a new kind of imitation) engenders a new series, so that the invention of gunpowder is to social science what the blooming of a new plant species is to biology, or the birth of new matter to chemistry: these "repetitions are also multiplications or self-spreading contagions."[42]

The conception of society proposed by Tarde is based on the rejection of utilitarianism: *Sociality* does not depend on economic (as in the interdependence of needs, mutual assistance, provision of services, and so on) or normative (like the rights established by law, customs, and conventions) relationships, but rather from an imitative relationship. Since society is imitation, and imitation is essentially a phenomenon of contagion of "belief" and "desire,"[43] these "beliefs" and "desires" give shape to society. In fact the stability of social institutions is connected to the unanimous beliefs that they embody, while the revolutionary impetus of the desire constitutes the engine of progress.[44]

Gustav Le Bon, in the footsteps of Tarde, also assigns a pivotal role to contagion in the formation and entrenchment of opinions and beliefs: In addition to determining the intellectual orientation the contagion would also enable the individual to disappear inside the crowd (collective souls whose main feature is the near absolute psychic solidarity of the constituents' minds).[45] A single passage is sufficient to clarify his viewpoint: "Ideas, sentiments, emotions and beliefs possess in crowds a contagious power as intense as that of microbes."[46] The same imitation, which Le Bon also considers decisive in determining the social dynamics of crowds, "is in reality a mere effect of contagion."[47] A proof of Le Bon's statement is the fact that in most cases, imitation is unconscious.[48] As Le Bon describes, a "special atmosphere" for contagion is created, "a general manner of thinking"[49] and opinions and beliefs are propagated "by contagion, but never by reasoning."[50]

Getting back to Tarde, one of the peculiarities of his thought is that imitation and innovation are not presented as logical opposites: the imitative waves follow one another and overlap themselves, crossing each other and outlining a new model to be imitated. He argues that in order for the novelty introduced by innovation to settle, it must be transmitted through imitation. For Tarde, therefore, imitation is the conditio sine qua non of progress, to the point that the initial spark, the original act of imagination of an anthropoid had, as an effect, not only the acts of imitation which have issued directly from it, but also all the acts of imagination that it suggested and which in turn have suggested new ones, and so on indefinitely.[51] This suggests that only the innovations that are imitated assume social relevance.

In this regard, French sociologist and philosopher Bruno Karsenti has given rise to an interesting reinterpretation of the historical opposition between Tarde and Durkheim[52] and writes that:

> considered in the abstract, an imitation is no more than a repetition, an infinite reproduction of the same. Considered in concrete terms, however, imitation becomes pluralized. Multiple flows emerge, within variable relations of composition or substitution. In this context, repetition becomes variation.

Furthermore: "against a background of repetition, differentiation not only can, but indeed must necessarily take place."[53]

Tarde's dynamic characterizes a remix culture. This is already evident in the practice of those Jamaican DJs and producers who, at the end of the 1960s, gave birth to the first modern remix culture by creating new or altered *versions* (revisions) of already existent songs.[54] In Jamaican dub the repetition is never a return to the identical, and, as Tarde stated, repetitions lead to changes. This aspect becomes even more manifest in digital networks, where in order for remix innovation to take root in the networked society it needs to be subsumed into a flow of continuous repetition.[55] Paraphrasing Tarde, who has stated that an idea spreads thanks to the rooting of the languages of communication into conversation[56]—we can suggest that remixes become popular through their rootedness within the aesthetics of repetition. The repetition is the "living environment" in which forms and styles of remix culture are born and spread, and it is almost superfluous to mention that contemporary communication, especially the Internet and more specifically social media, represent the ideal *breeding ground* for the diffusion of ideas, beliefs and trends (memes) which, as with viruses (*virus ideas*), propagate through the network by infecting the minds of those who come in contact with them.[57]

If these assumptions are true, it can be argued that in the contemporary world innovation is possible only within the framework of a practice of remix, in other words, inasmuch as every construction takes the form of reusing and building upon existing materials, it can be deduced that nothing is created out of nothing. Remix culture can therefore be seen as the final destination of that process of disintegration of the modernist myth of originality which, under a series of concentric forces (economic, social, cultural, and technological ones), finds its fulfillment with the global expansion of digital media. If in the artistic avant-gardes of the twentieth century there was still a fundamental ambiguity, concerning the cultivation of the romantic myth of originality (even if their practice contradicted what they professed at a programmatic level), it is in contemporary art that the concept of originality falls into deep crisis and the place of the artwork is ultimately taken over by practices like pastiche, collage, cut-up, quotation, appropriation, and all the grammar of gestures that characterize postmodern art.[58] Nevertheless the system of contemporary art, in its various components (artists, curators, gallery owners, collectors, museums, etc.), is stuck in a paradoxical defense of "originality" (understood as the possibility of attributing the authorship of a work to the solitary genius of an alleged artist). It is therefore only in the remix culture that the originality, in its literal sense of *something that exists from the beginning* or something that is not copied or imitated, finally dies.[59] To use the words of Flusser, the myth of the author succumbs when facing information that, relinquishing any claim to originality, opens the possibility of being *automatically* anywhere, in a state of constant replicability.[60]

Discursive and Dialogic Remixes

Bringing the discourse back to the general Flusserian categories may be useful for distinguishing between two types of activities which may be, in a very broad sense, labeled as remix: the simple copy of a media object (for example sharing on one's own website a picture published in a different context) and the hybridization of two or more sources (for example modifying videos with other media objects, such as background music). First of all, it must be said that there are doubts about the possibility of considering sampling or the simple *copy/paste* a real remix—it is in fact often a mere duplication or displacement of unedited information (except for the different contexts in which they are published). Eduardo Navas claims that such cases cannot be considered remixes, even if they are still important because they demonstrate how the key principles of the logic of remix (in particular sampling) are extended to all media[61] and more generally to contemporary culture as a whole. Aware of this *misuse* I choose to continue to define "remix" as the simple copies of preexisting cultural objects even if my choice is instrumental: Indeed my aim is to demonstrate that these activities, while confirming the initial premise that is the transformation of remix in the compositional paradigm of contemporaneity (one thinks in terms of remix even when not producing real remixes but simple copies), are functional to the diffusion and circulation of information but do not add anything to the cultural fragments transmitted. I therefore propose to call them *discursive remixes* as discourse is the most typical system of information transmission in a society dominated by "unidirectional media." Clearly, the architecture described by Flusser is not reflected in the reality structured by endless *copy and paste* operations: in these cases there are no rays (media channels) that radiate outward from the center (the sender) to reach individual receivers, nevertheless it is possible to maintain the metaphor of the ray as long as one imagines these channels of communication as consisting of a large number of points, or better, from all the nodes (of a network) which retransmit and *copy and paste* the same information. As with broadcast media there is no dialog with the source that issued the original message, sampling is in fact an amplification of the reach of the original message and, at most, a likely (but not obvious) adherence to its content. The situation is however quite different because rays are not mono-directional but technically reversible. The lack of dialog between the original sender and those who copy and retransmit the message is therefore not to be attributed to the technique but to a lack of willingness to communicate or to the prevailing of a new form of dialog—that certainly would not be appreciated by Flusser—in which the *dialogic exchange* is nothing more than a copy to which, in abstract terms and with a huge dose of optimism, one could assign the value of an implicit adherence to the system of values, beliefs, and desires at the base of the copied message.

One element that I wish to emphasize is that we must recognize the full citizenship rights of *discursive remixes* within remix culture. In fact, if it is true that innovation comes from repetition (Tarde) it is just in these infinite chains of *copy and paste* that small differences emerge from the copied model as well as the ability to create new information and escape the natural tendency to entropy.

Of course, in addition to *discursive remixes* there are *dialogical remixes*—those in which the game with information (which we have seen to be the cornerstone of both a remix culture and the utopian telematic society envisioned by Flusser) is fully realized. The *dialogical remixes* are in fact addressed at what Flusser calls "creative receivers": they process them (remix them) giving rise to new information. Here new information is not intended to be "concluded, complete, perfect" but to enrich the information already existing in the world so that others can creatively continue the game.[62] Assuming this perspective, it follows that the *remixer/creative receiver* is not committed to producing something (a work, even if open in the manner of Eco), but to the (creative) process itself.

Dialogical remixes, corresponding to the informative images of Flusser and to the innovations of Tarde, while not escaping the fate of *discursive remixes* (to constantly feed the flow of information required by machines), are the only way to avoid succumbing in the relationship with apparatuses. In order not to be programmed by the apparatuses it is necessary to devote oneself to their reconfiguration and programming, in other words it is necessary to say: "I want to have my program so that I won't be subject to anyone else's."[63]

In a *society dominated by unidirectional media*, senders possess the programs, and we are possessed by them; hence the need to dispossess and to socialize programs. In a fully realized *society of information*, that is to say a society in which centralized senders were overcome, it would no longer make sense to speak of dispossession; one should rather think in terms of dialogical programming and therefore more than using "one's own program" it would be appropriate to use the formula "programs of others." In a *telematic society*, as Flusser points out, there is no longer the need to possess one's own program to reduce the fear of succumbing to someone else's program. What is really fundamental is having the "programs of others" in order to edit, remix, and share, in turn, with others.[64]

Notes

1 Vito Campanelli, *Web Aesthetics: How Digital Media Affect Culture and Society* (Rotterdam: NAi Publishers, 2010), 190.
2 Fredric Jameson, *Postmodernism or, The Cultural Logic of Late Capitalism* (Durham, NC: Duke University Press, 1991).
3 Lev Manovich, *Software Takes Command* (New York: Bloomsbury, 2013), 267.
4 Vilém Flusser, *Ins Universum der technischen Bilder* (Gottingen: European Photography, 1985), trans. *Into the Universe of Technical Images* (Minneapolis, MN: University of Minnesota Press, 2011), 87–90.
5 Vilém Flusser, "Photo Production" (1984), unpublished typescript from a lecture delivered at Ecole Nationale de la Photographie, Arles (France), February 23, 1984. It is available in the Flusser Archive, Berlin.
6 Flusser, *Into the Universe*, 90.
7 It is important to underline that Flusser goes beyond the traditional opposition between Darwin and Lamarck, indeed he applies his reasoning to acquired (Lamarck) as well to inherited information (Darwin).
8 Manuel Castells, *The Rise of the Network Society* (Oxford: Blackwell Publishers, 1996).
9 Flusser, *Into the Universe*, 92.
10 This interpretation of Flusser is partly consistent with the concepts of "demassification" and "prosumer" proposed by Toffler, see Alvin Toffler, *The Third Wave* (New York: Bantam Books, 1981).
11 Flusser, *Into the Universe*, 91–94.

12 Ibid., 95.

13 Ibid., 162–163.

14 Ibid., 95–99.

15 Ibid., 99–103.

16 Ibid., 104.

17 Campanelli, *Web Aesthetics*, 198.

18 For the concept of "reflexive remix," see Eduardo Navas, *Remix Theory: The Aesthetics of Sampling* (Vienna: Springer, 2012). See also Navas, "Regressive and Reflexive Mashups in Sampling Culture," in *Mashup Cultures*, ed. Stefan Sonvilla-Weiss (Vienna: Springer, 2010).

19 Alberto Abruzzese, introduction to *Remix It Yourself* by Vito Campanelli, xi. Unless otherwise noted, all translations are by the author.

20 Michel Maffesoli, *Le temps des tribus. Le déclin de l'individualisme dans les sociétés postmodernes* (Paris: La Table Ronde, 1998), trans. *The Time of the Tribes: The Decline of Individualism in Mass Society* (London: Sage, 1996).

21 Vito Campanelli, *Remix It Yourself. Analisi socio-estetica delle forme comunicative del Web* (Bologna: CLUEB, 2011), 11.

22 Flusser, *Into the Universe*, 126.

23 Campanelli, *Remix*, 15.

24 Campanelli, *Web Aesthetics*, 194.

25 Flusser, *Into the Universe*, 99.

26 Campanelli, *Web Aesthetics*, 194, original emphasis.

27 Manovich, *Software Takes Command*. On the concept of "modularity," see also Manovich, *The Language of New Media* (Cambridge, MA: MIT Press, 2001).

28 Flusser, *Into the Universe*, 15–23.

29 Campanelli, *Remix*, 18.

30 Manovich, *Software Takes Command*, 267–277.

31 Toffler (1981), Lévy (1994), Castells (1996), Bruns (2006), Deuze (2006), Jenkins (2002 and 2006), Lessig (2008), Shirky (2008), Schäfer (2011), *just to quote a few authors*.

32 Campanelli, *Web Aesthetics*, 203.

33 Ibid., 204.

34 Lévi-Strauss relates bricolage to the mythical thinking: it is in fact the method by which primitives organized their myths, their worldview, their language, their society and—ultimately—their thinking and its rules. Claude Lévi-Strauss, *La pensée sauvage* (Paris: Plon, 1962), trans. *The Savage Mind: The Nature of Human Society Series* (Chicago, IL: University of Chicago Press, 1966).

35 Ibid., 7–18.

36 Campanelli, *Web Aesthetics*, 205.

37 According to Flusser, science and technology, "these triumphs of Western civilization" have "eroded the objective world around us into nothingness": "reality" is disintegrated in dimensionless points (quanta) or—as Flusser puts it—"everything is a swarm of points" (Flusser, *Into the Universe*, 38). "What remains are particles without dimension that can be neither grasped nor represented nor understood. They are inaccessible to hands, eyes, or fingers." But they can be calculated and computed by means of computers (Ibid., 10).

38 Ibid., 108.

39 Ibid., 112.

40 Ibid., 105–114.

41 Gabriel de Tarde, *Le lois de l'imitation* (Paris: Félix Alcan, 1890), trans. *The Laws of Imitation* (New York: Henry Holt, 1903).

42 Ibid., 17.

43 These two fundamental poles of Tardian sociology are not referable to feelings (to pure affective states), they are rather mental powers, psychic powers that take a decisive social value by virtue of their measurability, by an identity that endures unchanged while transferring from one individual to another, by the ease with which they are communicated and by their strong contagiousness.

44 Gabriel de Tarde, "Qu'est-ce qu'une société?" *Revue Philosophique*, XVIII (1884), 489–510.

45 Gustav Le Bon, *Psychologie des foules* (Paris: Félix Alcan, 1895), trans. *The Crowd: A Study of the Popular Mind* (New York: Digireads.com, 2008).

46 Ibid., 60.

47 Ibid.

48 Ibid., 66.

49 Gustav Le Bon, *Les lois psychologiques de l'évolution des peoples* (Paris: Félix Alcan, 1895), trans. *The Psychology of Peoples* (New York: Macmillan, 1899) 174.

50 Le Bon, *The Crowd*, 61.

51 Tarde, *The Laws of Imitation*, 43.

52 About the opposition between Tarde and Durkheim see Mike Gane, *On Durkheim's Rules of Sociological Method* (New York: Routledge, 2011), 52–56.

53 Bruno Karsenti, "Imitation: Returning to the Tarde–Durkheim debate," in *The Social after Gabriel Tarde: Debates and Assessments*, ed. Matei Candei (New York: Routledge, 2010), 50.

54 The decisive role of the DJ culture in fostering the emergence of a remix culture is emphasized in: Campanelli, *Web Aesthetics*, and Navas, *Remix Theory*.

55 Campanelli, *Remix*, 44.

56 Gabriel de Tarde, "L'inter-psychologie," *Bulletin de l'Institut Général Psychologique*, 3 (1903), 91–118.

57 Campanelli, *Remix*, 41.

58 Rosalind E. Krauss, *The Originality of the Avant-Garde and Other Modernist Myths* (Cambridge, MA: MIT Press, 1985).

59 Campanelli, *Remix*, 45.

60 Flusser, *Into the Universe*, 95–104.

61 Navas, "Regressive and Reflexive Mashups," 165.

62 Vilém Flusser, *Die Revolution der Bilder. Der Flusser-Reader zu Kommunikation, Medien und Design* (Mannheim: Bollman, 1995), 59–65.

63 Flusser, *Into the Universe*, 155.

64 Ibid.

Bibliography

Abruzzese, Alberto. Introduction to *Remix It Yourself Analisi socio-estetica delle forme comunicative del Web* by Vito Campanelli. Bologna: CLUEB, 2011.

Bruns, Axel. *Blogs, Wikipedia, Second Life and Beyond: From Production to Produsage*. New York: Peter Lang, 2008.

Campanelli, Vito. *Remix It Yourself: Analisi socio-estetica delle forme comunicative del Web*. Bologna: CLUEB, 2011.

———. *Web Aesthetics: How Digital Media Affect Culture and Society*. Rotterdam: NAi Publishers, 2010.

Castells, Manuel. *The Rise of the Network Society*. Oxford: Blackwell Publishers, 1996.

Deuze, Mark. "Participation, Remediation, Bricolage: Considering Principal Components of a Digital Culture." *The Information Society* 22, no. 2 (2006): 63–75.

Flusser, Vilém. *Into the Universe of Technical Images*. Minneapolis, MN: University of Minnesota Press, 2011.

———. *Die Revolution der Bilder. Der Flusser-Reader zu Kommunikation, Medien und Design*. Mannheim: Bollman, 1995.

Gane, Mike, *On Durkheim's Rules of Sociological Method*. New York: Routledge, 2011.

Jameson, Fredric. *Postmodernism or, The Cultural Logic of Late Capitalism*. Durham, NC: Duke University Press, 1991.

Jenkins, Henry. *Hop on Pop: The Politics and Pleasures of Popular Culture*. Durham, NC: Duke University Press, 2002.

———. *Fans, Bloggers, and Gamers: Exploring Participatory Culture*. New York: New York University Press, 2006.

Karsenti, Bruno. "Imitation: Returning to the Tarde–Durkheim debate." In *The Social after Gabriel Tarde: Debates and Assessments*, edited by Matei Candei. New York: Routledge, 2010.

Krauss, Rosalind E. *The Originality of the Avant-Garde and Other Modernist Myths*. Cambridge, MA: MIT Press, 1985.

Le Bon, Gustav. *The Crowd: A Study of the Popular Mind*. New York, NY: Digireads.com, 2008.

———. *The Psychology of Peoples*, New York: Macmillan, 1899.

Lessig, Lawrence. *Remix: Making Art and Commerce Thrive in the Hybrid Economy*. New York: Penguin Press, 2008.

Lévi-Strauss, Claude. *The Savage Mind*, The Nature of Human Society Series. Chicago, IL: University of Chicago Press, 1966.

Lévy, Pierre. *L'intelligence collective. Pour une anthropologie du cyberspace*. Paris: La Découverte, 1994.

Maffesoli, Michel. *The Time of the Tribes: The Decline of Individualism in Mass Society*. London: Sage, 1996.

Manovich, Lev. *Software Takes Command*. New York: Bloomsbury, 2013.

——. *There Is Only Software*, 2011. http://www.manovich.net/DOCS/Manovich.there_is_only_software.pdf (accessed July 10, 2013).

——. *The Language of New Media*. Cambridge, MA: MIT Press, 2001.

Navas, Eduardo. *Remix Theory: The Aesthetics of Sampling*. Vienna: Springer, 2012.

——. "Regressive and Reflexive Mashups in Sampling Culture." In *Mashup Cultures*, edited by Stefan Sonvilla-Weiss. Vienna: Springer, 2010.

Schäfer, Mirko Tobias. *Bastard Culture! How User Participation Transforms Cultural Production*. Amsterdam: Amsterdam University Press, 2008.

Shirky, Clay. *Here Comes Everybody: The Power of Organizing Without Organizations*. New York: Penguin Press, 2008.

Tarde, Gabriel de. *The Laws of Imitation*. New York: Henry Holt, 1903.

——. "L'inter-psychologie," *Bulletin de l'Institut Général Psychologique*. 3 (1903).

——. "Qu'est-ce qu'une société?" *Revue Philosophique*. XVIII (1884): 489–510.

Toffler, Alvin. *The Third Wave*. New York: Bantam Books, 1981.

AN ORAL HISTORY OF SAMPLING

From Turntables to Mashups

Kembrew McLeod

Artists have traditionally borrowed from each other and have been directly inspired by the world that surrounds them. But what happens—ethically, legally, aesthetically—when digital technologies allow for very literal audio quotes to be inserted into new works? Sampling refers to the act of digitally recording pieces of preexisting music and placing those bits in a new song. This appropriation practice can be viewed—with some obvious differences, of course—as an extension of earlier African American musical traditions that valued musical appropriation, such as the blues, jazz, and gospel. Well over a decade before the file sharing controversies—beginning with Napster, in 1999—pushed the topic of copyright to the front pages of newspapers, hip hop artists had already raised similar legal and moral questions when they began using the new audio technology of digital sampling.[1]

During the 1970s, hip hop DJs in the South Bronx reimagined the record player or turntable as a device that could appropriate and create music—by manipulating vinyl records with their hands—rather than simply replaying complete songs. Similarly, hip hop artists in the 1980s embraced the newly developing sampling technology as their own, finding ways to make new music out of old, rare, or sometimes forgotten, sources. As with the sharing of MP3 music files today, many artists and record companies believed that the practice of digital sampling was the equivalent of stealing. Others, like Public Enemy's Chuck D, argued that there should be more freedom to recontextualize found sounds. However, Chuck D and other similar artists lost this particular argument after Gilbert O'Sullivan won the lawsuit he filed against Biz Markie and Warner Brothers Records in 1991 (Markie sampled and looped the hook from the hit "Alone Again (Naturally)").[2] Subsequently, the music industry began to enforce more vigorously copyright law as it related to sampling. The industry developed a cumbersome and expensive "sample clearance" system in which all samples, even the shortest and most unrecognizable, had to be approved and paid for. Since this period, the cost of licensing samples has continued to increase, as have the costs associated with negotiating those licenses.

This made it legally impossible for certain kinds of music to be distributed—such as Public Enemy's early records—because they contained hundreds of fragments of sound, just within one album. Today, it would simply be too expensive to clear copyright licenses for albums such as Public Enemy's *It Takes a Nation of Millions to Hold Us Back*—a record considered so culturally important that *The New York Times* included it on its list of the 25 "most significant albums of the last century"[3] and *Fear of a Black Planet*, which the Library of Congress included it in its 2004 National Recording Registry,[4] alongside the news broadcasts of Edward R. Murrow and the music of John Coltrane. In the interview that follows, Harry Allen stated[5] one would have to sell a record such as *Fear of a Black Planet* for $159 per CD to pay for all the licenses, as opposed to a time before 1991 when not all sound fragments needed to be licensed (and the ones that were licensed did not reach today's astronomical prices—sometimes $100,000 for a single sample). Allen may have been hyperbolic, but there is more than a grain of truth in what he said. In our book *Creative License*, we (Kembrew McLeod and Peter DiCola) conducted an economic analysis of Public Enemy's *Fear of a Black Planet* and the Beastie Boys' *Paul's Boutique*, another "golden age" album that contains hundreds of samples. We determined that it would no longer be viable to release these two albums today.

> In the case of the two records we are examining, the artists pay out more than they receive. Neither album would be commercially practical to release. Each artist, having licensed away more royalties and more publishing than the amount that they would receive on each track of the album, would go further into debt with every copy sold to the public. The prices for all the samples— multiple samples on each track—simply exceed the artist's piece of the recording-revenue pie. Public Enemy would lose an estimated $4.47 per copy sold. The Beastie Boys would lose an estimated $7.87 per copy sold. The total amount of debt incurred for releasing these albums, according to our estimates, would be almost $6.8 million for Public Enemy and would be $19.8 million for the Beastie Boys.[6]

Many artists and critics have argued that this licensing system had a negative impact on the creative potential of this newly emerging African American art form before it had a chance to flower. They allude to the growth of twentieth century jazz music, which would have been similarly stunted if jazz musicians—who regularly "riffed" on others' songs—had been burdened by a similar legal requirement to license and receive permission from music publishers for the use of every "sampled" sonic fragment.[7] The remainder of this chapter is a remix of sampled quotes from a series of interviews with musicians and producers. The oral history form—which relies on interviewees' words to drive the narrative—lends itself nicely to a history of sampling and remixing. Drawing on the knowledge gleaned from over 100 interviews, what follows is the result of hours of crate-digging through transcripts in order to assemble a narrative about the emergence of remix culture and its eventual collision with copyright law.

I have constructed a five-part chronological history (with an introduction and conclusion) that allows those who actively participated in the development of sampling to tell this story. The first is a prehistory of digital sampling, documenting the ways that 1970s hip hop DJs developed an approach to music making that continued into the digital era. The second provides an overview of the impact of digital sampling technologies in the 1980s, which contributed directly to what is often referred to as "the golden age of sampling," roughly from 1986 to 1992. The third offers an account of the copyright infringement lawsuits that exploded in the wake of that golden age, and the fourth explores the ethical—rather than legal—implications of remixing practices. The fifth part brings us into the twenty-first century, discussing the mashup phenomenon before concluding this oral history with some more general observations about sampling from artists, lawyers, and record company owners.

Introduction: Appropriation, Technology, and the Law

Chuck D (Public Enemy): Sampling is playing with sound, or *playing* sound—like it's like an instrument, or a game.

DJ Abilities (Eyedea and Abilities): When I'm sampling, I have all these artists in my band. I've got Wes Montgomery. I've got Art Blakey, he's my drummer.

Chuck D: When those old musicians created magical moments, you had four or five guys that were the best, and they put it *down*. Sampling allowed the best magical moment to be duplicated.

George Clinton (Parliament-Funkadelic): With James Brown, they just sampled "*Yow*" and all that. That was enough for one sample. There was so much personality in the tone, you didn't need to sample much.

Tom Silverman (Tommy Boy Records CEO): The beautiful thing about sampling was it put tools in the hands of people who didn't have the traditional musical training or skills. I would say in the last 20 years the biggest musical contributions have been made by nonmusicians.

Kid 606 (electronic musician): Sampling is like Legos. If you give someone a bunch of Lego blocks and tell them to put something together, then they have something to work with—as opposed to saying, "Here's a bunch of plastic, go mold it and then build it."

Lloyd Dunn (Tape-Beatles): The photocopier was one of those challenges to authorship—also the phonograph, which replaced the traditional artist or musician in many ways.

Mark Hosler (Negativland): I see the computer as the ultimate collage box.

Greg Tate (music journalist): A lot of people look at hip hop sampling as doing what bebop jazz artists did—taking a classic and putting a new melody on top of it.

Shoshana Zisk (entertainment attorney): So that's where people start to wonder, "Why is sampling considered stealing, and jazz isn't considered stealing?" It's hard to say, really.

Harry Allen (music journalist): I've never heard a completely original idea, from anyone. Most musicians will say that the best musicians copy.

Shock G (Digital Underground): How many comedians tell the same joke? Nobody says, "Hey that is my knock-knock joke, or that is my mama joke."

Chuck D:	[Public Enemy] sampling wasn't based on thievery. We used sampling machines as tools and looking at those tools from musician's point of view. We wanted to blend sound. Just as visual artists take yellow and blue and come up with green, we wanted to be able to do that with sound.
DJ Vadim (Electronic Musician):	Think of sampling as being represented by two different painters. One guy takes a photocopy of the Mona Lisa—that's P. Diddy, who just samples the choruses of songs. The other guy takes the same painting, chops it up and it doesn't even look like the Mona Lisa anymore. He's made it into a cow, or a spaceship. That's what sampling can be like.
Harry Allen:	Sampling is like the color red. It's like saying, "Is the color red creative?" Well, it is when you use it *creatively*. It's not when it's just sitting there in a paint can.

I: From Turntables To Samplers

Harry Allen:	The first person to perform hip hop publicly in the South Bronx, and the person that's generally given credit for being the father or godfather of hip hop culture, is DJ Kool Herc. And then of course you had Grandmaster Flash and Afrika Bambaataa.
Greg Tate:	If you've ever had the fortune to see Afrika Bambaataa mix—he can move between bits and pieces of records and create these incredible medleys in a short period of time
DJ Abilities:	The DJing aspect is so complex, and rhythmically challenging. To me, the turntable is the last new instrument of the twentieth century.
Hank Shocklee (Public Enemy):	Sampling came out of the DJ culture. You would have a drumbeat, and you would scratch a horn or a guitar riff on top of it.
Saul Williams (Musician and Poet):	When you think of the beginning of hip hop, you think of breakbeats. You had these extended songs with one section where there would be a drum breakdown.
Qbert (DJ):	The break is the part of the song where it's just the drums.
Chuck D:	Favorite breakbeat of mine? You always have to look at James Brown's catalog—to either the "Funky Drummer" or the "Cold Sweat" breakbeat.
Hank Shocklee:	"Funky Drummer" by James Brown—my favorite. The reason why "Funky Drummer" is so special is because it was the first time James Brown stripped down all his music and he had just a drum beat.
Clyde Stubblefield (James Brown Band):	On "Funky Drummer," I started to play a simple beat and everybody joined in. Next thing I know all the rap artists were sampling it!

George Clinton:	That raw sound appealed to them, the drums and guitar—real flat equalization.
Miho Hatori (Cibo Matto):	James Brown's records sounded so good. The beats have such a fat sound.
Tom Silverman:	In the early days of recorded hip hop, they would just use records and drum machines. There wasn't that much more to it than that.
Hank Shocklee:	I think at the time (in the early 1980s) the only thing that could capture a sample or a recording was in a keyboard called the Synclavier, and that was a $300,000 machine.
Matt Black (Coldcut):	Samplers existed back then, but at the time only rich musicians could afford them. Once they got cheaper, and more people could use them, [this] created an explosion of new music and new ways of making music.
Chuck D:	You had a mad dash of creativity, as far as musicianship and technological innovation was concerned. Those technology companies didn't necessarily have any kind of allegiance to intellectual property owners.
Anthony Berman (entertainment lawyer):	The view on the traditional side was that sampling is a very lazy way of making music, of songwriting.
Shock G:	As far as sampling is concerned, a lot of musicians and artists from the past generation thought that our generation wasn't doing enough work.
Bobbito Garcia (Rock Steady Crew):	If you were sampling Pee Wee Ellis, you know, he was an incredible jazz musician. He was a phenomenal funk musician. I mean, this guy played music for 20 to 30 years, and you're taking his music. You're sampling such a sophisticated level of musicianship.
Harry Allen:	I think for a lot of people who weren't used to sampling, it was almost rude, actually, to say, "I'm going to take this song and sample the drumbeat because I like it."
Clyde Stubblefield:	I never got a "thanks." I never got a "Hello, how are you doing?" or anything from rap artists. The only one who thanked me was Melissa Etheridge.

II: The Golden Age of Sampling (1986–92)

El-P (MC and producer):	During the golden age, you had these records that were these extreme collage records, you know, producers like Prince Paul, who helped create the early De La Soul records.
De La Soul (hip hop group):	We used to sit there with a bunch of records and try to find something to go into a song. That process alone, that's what is so great about it, because we didn't censor ourselves.
Harry Allen:	What you are hearing on those records is true experimentation, unrestrained by suits.

Matt Black:	Public Enemy were iconoclastic, definitely. You'd never heard collage music like that.
El-P:	One song would have five, six, seven, eight layered samples from really famous records, but completely reworked so that it didn't sound like the original sources.
Mr. Len (DJ and producer):	You listen to *It Takes a Nation of Millions*, and you hear the song "Night of the Living Base Heads," if you really listen to that song, it changes so many times.
George Clinton:	They actually did arrangements. They took small parts and had a whole 24-track arrangement that created one song.
Prefuse 73 (electronic musician):	It was just the most powerful onslaught of sound I had experienced. And it all was coming from machines. When you heard it for the first time back then it's just like, "Whoa."
Chuck D:	Public Enemy was manipulating noise, as Hank Shocklee would say.
Hank Shocklee:	Sampling was a very intricate thing for us. We [the Bomb Squad, Public Enemy's production unit] didn't just pick up a record and sample that record because it was funky. It was a collage. We were creating a collage.
Harry Allen:	The Bomb Squad was the association of Chuck D, Hank Shocklee, Keith Shocklee, and Eric Sadler.
Hank Shocklee:	My vision of this group was to almost have a production assembly line where each person had their own particular specialty.
Greg Tate:	The synergy between Chuck, Hank Shocklee and Eric—that really created the Public Enemy sound, because Chuck and Hank *hated* professional musicians who played "correctly." You know what I mean? So they would come out with the most outrageous ideas.
Hank Shocklee:	I'm coming from a DJ's perspective. Eric is coming from a musician's perspective. So together, you know, we started working out different ideas. When we sampled, we'd take a piece from each section of a song. You may get one part of the sound is from the intro, another part of it is from the drum break down, another part of it is from the end, the vamp on the end. So, and all those samples are combined to create one sample.
Chuck D:	We would get into a recording session and all four of us would just be playing. Hank recorded the session, and 95 percent was a mess, and 5 percent of the music was magical. You would listen to this mess and out of that you'd be like, "Whoa, what happened here?" That was the closest thing to a jazz band that you could have, just jamming. Maybe not a conventional jazz band. Maybe someone like Sun Ra [laughs].

Hank Shocklee: When you're talking about sampling, and the kind of sampling that Public Enemy did, we had to comb through thousands of records to come up with maybe five good pieces.

Chuck D: "Fight the Power" has so many different layers of sound. You have musical loops going around with vocals, with vocal samples. And you got the musical loops competing with the words, and the loops are going backwards and forwards. The song contains a great deal of black music history from a 25-year period. You listen to it, and it's like [mock announcer's voice], "This 25-year period black music is brought to you by Public Enemy." From the beginning to the end, it's filled with musical and political history.

Drew Daniel (Matmos): What's exciting about sampling and collage is that it makes sound referential—it's not abstract. Sound contains a specific reference to a specific time and place. That's what's cool about sampling: that it transports the listener, if they're willing, to move in a pathway back to a specific action. It's like an archive of memories of real experiences.

Tom Silverman: There's all these layers of audio archeology, and you can dig down deep enough and find the sampled source.

Miho Hatori: We're just buying records, searching, searching, and we find a record and it's like, "There, *that* bass line." . . . To find the right one or two seconds of sound—that's a lot of work.

Bobbito Garcia: Hip hop has really created a way for artists to take and grab different things around them, including music from past generations.

Chuck D: So you had new generations checking out music from different areas that were not exposed to the history of music, and sampling exposed artists to the new generations. Then those generations became interested in the back catalog of artists like George Clinton.

De La Soul: For someone like George Clinton's Parliament-Funkadelic, you're growing up to their music, and by using this music you make something out of a shared past.

George Clinton: Funk is the DNA of hip hop. It really helped us a lot because people heard it and got to know it and wanted to hear the whole version.

III: Digital Sampling and the Law

Siva Vaidhyanathan (media scholar): In the early 1990s there was a series of lawsuits that made it very clear the entertainment world was going to rein in this practice of unauthorized digital sampling.

Shoshana Zisk:	The other person who was being sampled, of course, their attorneys got up and said, "Well, hey, where's my piece?" That's when all the lawsuits started happening.
De La Soul:	It got to the point when a lot of these older musicians, their grandchildren were telling them, "Yo, you're being sampled," so, you know, that's how they found out.
Mr. Dibbs (DJ):	A Tribe Called Quest's song, "Bonita Applebaum," someone I know, well, his dad performed the beat they sampled. So, when his dad heard that, he's like, "What the *fuck* is that?"
Greg Tate:	I think that everyone woke up after De La Soul's record came out and Turtles sued them.
De La Soul:	For me I felt like, "Wow, we're popular; we're getting sued by someone we don't even know" [laughs].
Tom Silverman:	We would clear samples. The most notable one was *3 Feet High and Rising*, which took forever to clear, and that was back when sampling didn't cost that much.
De La Soul:	The organ and drumbeat was the Turtles' "You Showed Me." We actually told Tommy Boy records, our record company, and they decided not to clear it because it was just a skit.
Tom Silverman:	They never told us there was a sample. We can only clear what we know. And on *3 Feet High and Rising*, they told us what the samples were and we cleared them.
Shoshana Zisk:	The most famous case was Biz Markie, who sampled "Alone Again (Naturally)." The court's opinion began, "Thou shalt not steal" and the judge referred this to the LAPD to be criminally prosecuted. After that, everyone in the industry said, "Okay, we have to change the rules here."
De La Soul:	When it really happened to Biz Markie, [the lawsuits] really took off.
Saul Williams:	You'd start missing albums, like, "Shouldn't Biz Markie have an album out by now?" The album comes out one year late, and the title is *All Samples Cleared* [laughs].
De La Soul:	Things definitely got more complicated. On our fourth album we recorded, we sat down at the beginning of the album with the record company, Tommy Boy, and they went through a list. "Well, George Clinton is in litigation with Westbound so don't mess with his stuff right now, or George Harrison don't like rap, don't mess with him." We actually had a list of people not to touch.
Tom Silverman:	We had great ideas about doing songs that never even went to completion because we knew we wouldn't be able to clear the samples.

DJ Spooky **(electronic musician):**	What happened to Public Enemy in the late 80s and early 90s is they had to change their composition strategy because of lawsuits.
Don Joyce **(Negativland):**	There's a whole industry built up around licensing now, getting clearance rights. Every label has offices that do that, and it has become a big income stream.
Anthony Berman:	It certainly created a big jump in the revenue streams of copyright holders, and it added another layer of bureaucracy to the creative process of making collage-based music.
Tom Silverman:	It's a lot of accounting work. You're having to pay out on 60 different people on one album. It's quite a nightmare actually.
Shoshana Zisk:	When I was working in copyright at Motown, you'd get one song and there'd be 14 people that you had to get permission from. And each one of them is like, "I own 6.2 percent, I own 8.9 percent." There's a pie-graph of a song and everyone has a slice.
Siva Vaidhyanathan:	Sample clearing quickly evolved to the point that it became cheaper to only sample one song per song, for economic reasons. That made sample-based music less creative.
Chuck D:	That's when the sound of hip hop music shifted and people started to only sample one hook, because it was cheaper than paying for 20 or 30 clips in each song— like how we did it.
De La Soul:	That's what's kind of messed up about sampling now. When you create a song you hand it to lawyers and the costs are just so crazy that you can't pay that kind of money.
Michael Hausman **(artist manager):**	You can get some pretty outrageous quotes, and that hasn't helped creativity very much. There has to be some kind of reasonable prices.
Harry Allen:	Those records are kind of artifacts of an earlier time, records that couldn't exist today. They're financially and legally untenable and unworkable records. We can't make those records anymore because you'd have to sell them for, probably, $159 each just to pay all the royalties.
Chuck D:	By 1994, it was impossible to do any type of record we did in the late 1980s, because every second of sound had been cleared. It kind of curtailed creativity.
Dean Garfield **(Former vice** **president of legal** **affairs, RIAA):**	I find it hard to believe that, even with Public Enemy, they couldn't continue doing what they wanted to do because if one person doesn't clear a snippet, they could just use another snippet from someone else who would

clear it. I think Chuck D may say that today because he finds it convenient to say that. But it's not true.

Chuck D: At the end of the day, lawyers never lose money; they gain from both sides going back and forth.

IV: The Ethics of Sampling

Pete Rock (DJ and producer): There's two sides to everything. Some people like to hear their music being sampled, some don't.

Mr. Len: It all depends on what side of the fence you're sitting on. Like, if you're the one infringing someone's copyright, of course, you feel like, "Hey man, this copyright law sucks."

Michael Hausman: The context in which music appears is very important because in my experience artists are very concerned with all aspects of how their art is presented.

Chuck D: If someone else sampled my work without permission, I probably would be mad if my voice was put in a context I don't believe in. If it's put in, for example, some kind of Nazi song, I'd feel offended. Then that'd be a defamation of my character.

De La Soul: I respect anybody who feels an attachment to a song that might be about their mother, and then NWA samples it and says "bitch" over it. It's understandable they don't want that.

Michael Hausman: If the lyrics were sexist, violent, or very profane, they might not want to have anything to do with it. The artists I work with see their creations as an extension of themselves. So I think there is a tremendous desire to control this creation because it is *you*, and you want people to get the best of you that you can put out there.

El-P: I'm empathetic to the other argument, which is that you don't want your music stolen, or taken out of context. I care about my music just as much as anyone else.

Hank Shocklee: I've always been from the school where, you know, from if I'm sampling, who am *I* to attack somebody else from sampling from me?

De La Soul: What happens when we get sampled? Honestly, it's an honor. There's been some things that I've heard that were no good, but I know they sampled it out of appreciation for us.

Mr. Lif (MC and producer): I mean if someone uses my voice, I'm not coming after you. I remember the days when it was an honor to hear someone cut your voice on a chorus. I encourage you to use my voice.

George Clinton: You're supposed to get paid for it, because it's your personality that's in the sample.

Prefuse 73:	If somebody's going to take something of mine, some beat of mine and use it in some different way, do something creative with it, do whatever with it, I'm not going to care.
Shock G:	If it's just a little piece, a little sound bite here, and a sound bite there, use what you like. You like Humpty's voice? Funk with me. Spread it to the world, you know.
Clyde Stubblefield:	Instead of receiving money for sampling, I'd prefer to get my name on the record saying, "This is Clyde playing," to get my name out. Money is not important.
Scanner (electronic musician):	Bjork sampled me for a record called *Post*, which went on to sell something like five million copies. She used about five seconds of a track of mine, which formed the basis of this pop song. I was caught in a boiling pot of lawyers battling while I sat behind them thinking, "What's going on?" I didn't mind it was used for this track because I have also used sounds from other places.
Richard McGuire (Liquid Liquid):	I'm totally for sampling. I think it's just like any other art form. But I feel both ways about it. There should be compensation for the original artist.
De La Soul:	You know, we understand that if you sample someone, you should pay for it. If someone wants to get paid for it, I understand. They made it.
DJ Vadim:	I refuse to pay for sampling. I mean, I've changed the music so I wouldn't have to pay.
Pete Rock:	I've never disguised a sample, I never took the chance doing that. I play by the rules. If you play by the rules, you have to clear the sample—you have to get a license.
Mix Master Mike (DJ):	I can imagine that a few samples I've used I should've cleared—I am not going to name any particular samples. But I kind of reinvented them. Smashed them up.

V: Mashups and Digital Culture

Scanner:	The Internet has liberated the world of mashups. So you can take a Destiny's Child track with a Nirvana track and actually pitch it so it fits perfectly. And you can take two beats that would never ever match and make them match.
Matt Black:	I guess mashups are sampling and mixing for the masses. Because when you use material that audiences are familiar with, they know that something new is being created. It's spelling it out in BIG CAPITAL LETTERS, basically.
Raquel Cepeda (music journalist):	Record companies often release a cappella tracks to DJs so that you can play them over more popular instrumentals, you can mix them.
Drew Daniel (Matmos):	I mean, what's so great about hip hop and R&B is that every single comes with an a cappella on the flipside.

	It's like being given some sort of naked photograph of a celebrity.
Chuck D:	Technology has leveled the playing field. You put a cappella vocals out there and you become 50:50 partners with somebody else who might have come up with an incredible piece of work. It is like a universal network of studios where technology allows people to have studios in bedrooms instead of big expensive studios.
Richard McGuire:	It can just be miraculous how mashups fit together. It just knocks me out. Each time you hear new stuff like that it's like, "Oh, it's so simple, why didn't I think of that?"
Drew Daniel:	But I think that it can reach a banal "stealth oldies" level where it's just sort of oldies by another means. Like, "Oh it's Wham! *and* Van Halen!" It's not actually interesting. It's like, "Wow, you've made another jalapeño mint sandwich and no one wants to eat it."
Michael Hausman:	I personally like Brian [Danger Mouse], and I like *The Grey Album*, but it brings up a lot of ethical issues and I think people have the right to complain about it, you know?
Joanna Demers (Musicologist):	*The Grey Album* was a sort of mashup that was distributed at the end of 2003 by DJ Danger Mouse, who mixed the vocals from Jay-Z's *Black Album* with the Beatles' *White Album*. Soon after it came out, EMI sent out all these cease and desist letters to squelch this album completely, and this got out on the Internet very quickly and galvanized protests in February 2004.
Chuck D:	The Danger Mouse album caused a lot of people to get mad at the fact that more people can be producers and jump to high heights from low places.
Dean Garfield:	Even though I may enjoy *The Grey Album* and may groove to it in my own home, the way *The Grey Album* was released is not the way to go about it. The way to go about it is to get a license.

Conclusion: The Future of Sampling

Chuck D:	Sampling definitely challenged people's conceptions of what music was.
Mix Master Mike:	It's an art to us. We want to recreate stuff from the past and make it new.
George Clinton:	Just like rock 'n' roll in the 1950s and 1960s, it reminded me of that, when people were saying it wasn't music.
El-P:	The musical culture of sampling, way that we do music—that's not going to be embraced, it doesn't fit the bottom line.
Mark Hosler:	What we've seen in the last few decades, because of economic pressure, is more copyright constraints. That,

	I think ultimately, is really bad for the culture. We've moved toward total omnipotent ownership of everything, forever. And that's the death of culture, that's the death of ideas, science, art. It's very shortsighted.
Drew Daniel:	Another danger inherent in all this is the cop in your own head. One of the worst casualties of all this lawyerly stuff is people not doing things because they are afraid maybe someone will sue them in the future.
Lawrence Lessig (Harvard University law professor):	Today, to build on something you need the permission of somebody else. And it's that transformation which has been radical and recent.
Dean Garfield:	The idea that this will result in less creativity is a farce, and it's an excuse not to use your own creative juices to move people. I can suggest an alternative for people who feel stifled by the costs of sampling, which is—*be creative*. There's nothing that compels you to sample someone's work. You can just listen to it and vibe off it and create something new.
Tom Silverman:	I would like to see a level playing field where the smallest guy working in his home studio in the Bronx, or anywhere in the world, could come up with something without censoring himself because he's afraid of being sued. I think it's unfair. I think there are a lot of creators out there who like to work with building blocks that others have created.

Notes

1 Kembrew McLeod, *Freedom of Expression®: Resistance and Repression in the Age of Intellectual Property* (Minneapolis, MN: University of Minnesota Press, 2007), 66.
2 *Grand Upright Music Ltd. v. Warner Brothers Records, Inc.*, 780 F. Supp. 182 (SDNY 1991).
3 http://www.nytimes.com/2000/01/03/arts/critics-choices-albums-as-mileposts-in-a-musical-century.html?src=p,&pagewanted=4 (accessed July 29, 2014).
4 http://www.loc.gov/rr/record/nrpb/registry/nrpb-2004reg.html (accessed July 29, 2014).
5 Kembrew McLeod and Peter DiCola, *Creative License: The Law and Culture of Digital Sampling* (Durham, NC: Duke University Press, 2011), 27.
6 Ibid., 210.
7 Some of the interviews were conducted on camera during the filming of the documentary *Copyright Criminals: This is a Sampling Sport*, produced by Benjamin Franzen and Kembrew McLeod (see bibliography). Others were conducted during research for McLeod's *Freedom of Expression®* and McLeod and DiCola's *Creative License*; all of the interviews were conducted between 1999 and 2011. The answers, in some cases, were edited for clarity.

Bibliography

Franzen, Benjamin and McLeod, Kembrew. *Copyright Criminals*. PBS, 2011.

Grand Upright Music Ltd. v. Warner Brothers Records, Inc. 780 F. Supp. 182, SDNY, 1991.

McLeod, Kembrew. *Freedom of Expression®: Resistance and Repression in the Age of Intellectual Property*. Minneapolis, MN: University of Minnesota Press, 2007.

McLeod, Kembrew and DiCola, Peter. *Creative License: The Law and Culture of Digital Sampling*. Durham, NC: Duke University Press, 2011.

6

CAN I BORROW YOUR PROPER NAME?

Remixing Signatures and the Contemporary Author

Cicero Inacio da Silva

Wills: Are there any nonsigned works, then?
Derrida: No.[1]

The Authorship Culture

The concept of authorship is a mark for the potentialities of the remix in digital culture, in part due to contemporary discussions surrounding identity. There is a need to answer questions posed by authors like Marilyn Randall, who understands the context of authorship as an unquestionable element. Randall:

> define[s] "authorship," provisionally and primarily, as the attribution of a particular set of authorial functions to the agent of the discourse.... Self-consciousness, here, is the presupposition that the speaking position entails the responsibility of assuming the ideas expressed as the writer's own.[2]

Following this argument there is a dependence on authority, which is linked to the foundation of representation.

The French philosopher Jacques Derrida, on the other hand, pointed out that the discourse around the author as a representation attached to a cultural phenomenon lacks a deep discussion on the proper name and the signature. Derrida considers the signature a very delicate and problematic "cultural artifact," with which we are not dealing properly when analyzing the cultural impact in appropriating other people's works to redefine or to create a work of art such as a mashup or music remix, for example. According to Derrida,

> this is not something one can decide: one doesn't disseminate or play with one's name. The very structure of the proper name sets this process in motion. That's what the proper name is for. At work, naturally, in the desire—the apparent

desire—to lose one's name by disarticulating it, disseminating it, is the inverse movement. By disseminating or losing my own name, I make it more and more intrusive; I occupy the whole site, and as a result my name gains more ground. The more I lose, the more I gain.[3]

Derrida's analysis on the proper name deconstructs an established theory of authorship, such as Roland Barthes's famous statement that "the birth of the reader must be at the cost of the death of the Author."[4]

The technological potential to manipulate audio permitted artists to use parts of other people's cultural artifacts in their own artwork during the 1970s and 1980s. Taking these cultural elements into account, Lev Manovich stated that

> Remixing originally had a precise and a narrow meaning that gradually became diffused. Although precedents of remixing can be found earlier, it was the introduction of multi-track mixers that made remixing a standard practice. With each element of a song—vocals, drums, etc.—available for separate manipulation, it became possible to "re-mix" the song: change the volume of some tracks or substitute new tracks for the old ones.[5]

The first artworks that used the technique of remix were also influenced by the introduction of computational procedures in music and video production. These works were also influenced by a theoretical approach following the "death of the author" while manipulating music and video components.

Authorship Origins

The concept of the author is new and recent. It is a complex and broadly stigmatized subject of study with several unfoldings. It has been thought of as a kind of violence against the creative act, linked to the romantic ideas of fury, explosion, and passion.[6] The concept of authorship was gradually created from injunctions that were not very clear and, in certain moments, it was a victim and a villain in debates related to another complex problem of our civilization: property. In several fields linked to culture, economics, politics, and sociology, i.e., all forms of human representation, authorship came to be operated as an unquestionable tool in the formation of private property. In this sense, authorship has been considered a commodity for a long time and the fractures caused by this concept in our culture are still being questioned.

Perhaps we can say that authorship is a symptom of our days, but without forgetting that, like every symptom, it carries out a possibility of symbolic construction, a possibility of representation of what it rejects and a way of thinking of what it retains and displaces. The fact is that authorship was turned into a symbol of creation in contemporary culture. Analyzing how it was affected by the introduction of electronic devices, Richard Grusin reminds us that "This elision of the material and cultural basis of electronic writing seems inconsistent with that aspect of the logic of electronic authorship that foregrounds the causal role of technologies."[7] The article "The Death of the Author" by Roland Barthes was published for the first time in 1967, in *Aspen* magazine, and declared directly that the "author" would be dead and would be something doomed to oblivion. Barthes addressed the subject from his field, literature, and with sagacity he pointed out that in Balzac's text *Sarrasine*, the reader was submitted to a privation of voice on the part of the author, and that such privation caused a vertigo within the sphere of reception, because at a certain moment in Balzac's romance we can't be sure who speaks. Barthes enunciates that the author, at that moment, was absent and the reader became in charge of creating the supplement to the text. "Then, who speaks?" asks Barthes. The author? The reader? The written letter? According to Andrew Bennett:

> His answer is that we cannot know who speaks. The sentence, he suggests, could be spoken by the castrato himself (character of the romance), by Balzac the individual, by Balzac as an author "professing literary ideas," by "universal wisdom," or by an idea of a person proposed by "Romantic Psychology." We cannot know who speaks, Barthes argues, indeed we will never know, because writing involves the "destruction of every voice, of every point of origin."[8]

Barthes's text generated countless discussions and there was rarely a consensus on what could be considered the "end of the author." Barthes saw the author as a producer of a rigid culture, which believed that there was an origin and, in a certain way, such origin guaranteed a series of certainties concerning its own concept. It can be tempting to say that Barthes proposed, through a polemic text, to rethink that the author could give up the position of "property" and "guarantee" of the text, in order to liberate the reader for a demobilized, unaffected reading, if this is possible.

For Barthes, language is treated like a supreme entity, as a founder, as the origin of everything, even of the author. In condemning what he denominated "origin," Barthes ends up creating something more radical: the language unaffected by subjectivity. The object of reading would become an effect of circumstances that would decentralize the movement of the interpretation itself. In effect, when Barthes focuses on the drive that would delimit the reception as a neutral field, he also points in the direction of the letter as a transparent manifestation, like glass, i.e., as an incident, not an object of intentional action.

However, when it comes to remix, the idea of an "original author" can be suspended from the representational scene with an abrupt movement, but in fact the implications created by this intention are not fully known. This is because authorship created a vision that was imposed by the very forms of representation that move around the contemporary conception of private property. And if this notion, conception, or ideology finds a particularity in the author as subject, it seems obvious that this is not a coincidence when a remix becomes popular by using parts of others people creations to produce a "new" interpretation of a cultural artifact. The publication of Barthes's decree that the author is "dead" was, in a certain way, the beginning of a movement to try to destabilize an authority already in question.

The Ends of "the Author"

Martha Woodmansee is concerned about why authorship should be questioned at all. Such concern, according to the author, would come from long ago, in fact from the eighteenth century, when authors like Wordsworth, for example, would also deal with the problem questioning the aspect of power. According to Wordsworth,

> if every great Poet . . . , in the highest exercise of his genius, before he can be thoroughly enjoyed, has to call forth and to communicate power that is, empower his readers to understand his new work, "this service, in a still greater degree, falls upon an original Writer, at his first appearance in the world."[9]

Resuming Barthes's criticism of the author's power, the analysis that Woodmansee shows us refers exactly to a point that we can consider blind when the criticism of the author and authorship is focused on the subject of power, as we will see further with Foucault. It is blind because "power," as we know it, is a reaction to some event, probably created by some reason that should occupy more space in the discussions on the end or the displacement of the theory of author. Woodmansee locates one of the reasons of authorship in the eighteenth century, as something that "establish[es] ownership of the products of their labor so as to justify legal recognition of that ownership in the form of a copyright law."[10] Besides being considered only by the traditionally accepted view of the merchandise that is sold to sustain trade, authorship would be a reason for introducing a control of what is published and a responsibility assumed by an entity or institution.

Around this position, Michel Foucault resumes the idea that the name would be a position accepted according to certain cultural specificity, sometimes occupying the place of the power to speak on behalf of it, or being a mere result of the inherent action of the mark that would establish the supposed condition of the presence of the enunciator, in accepted ways of discourse.[11] In supposing that the subject has been elaborated against a totality, in the Freudian perspective—which would be like elaborating a reason for the emergence of identity beyond the mere classification of the differences—the issue of subjectivity returns to the center of attention, addressing the concept of narcissism. And this is of no interest to Foucault. In a certain way what is demanded by Foucauldian thinking is a premise linked to power, without the subject's social formation being linked, once in a while, to subjectivity. One of the problems not only present in the Foucauldian theory of power and author-function is also absent in the criticism to the capitalist author system. To give up the idea of the "I" is to give up a series of ingrained questions on one's permanence, what is also known as life drive in the Freudian theory, in favor of a self-annulment of perpetuation, what Freud described as death drive. In a certain way, this self-perpetrated disappearance is unbearable in our society based on a fetishist concept of socialization. Foucault calls for the subject's movement beyond its physical configuration, but he is naïve in discarding the basic problem of the idea of humankind, even with the declared apology of its end, linked to the narcissism of permanence, still so cherished by contemporary society.

I Sign, Therefore I Remix

Opposing most of his contemporaries, the French philosopher Jacques Derrida developed an analysis that deconstructed Barthes's and Foucault's arguments, affirming that the signature and the proper name legitimates the cultural artifact at the same time that it is constituted within the object itself. It is worth observing that it is the simple act of signing that gives the author, whoever he/she is, the possibility of committing with what he/she writes and of confirming, in a certain way, what was written. Somehow, the author can affirm that what he/she wrote is what he/she said.

Based on the Derridean notion of authorship, we can infer a series of connotations in the remixes created by music or visual artists since they use parts of the creation of several artists in their own cultural artifacts. The question is whether the artist who signs a remix is the creator of the work or just a representation that creatively assembles cultural manifestations in a different way. Another point to question is: When our culture accepts a remix as a work of art, are we also countersigning this creation? Derrida states that the signature is not to be confused either with the name of the author, with the patronym of the author, or with the type of work, for it is nothing other than the event of the work in itself, inasmuch as it attests in a certain way—here I come back to what I was saying about the body of the author—to the fact that someone did that, and that's what it remains.[12]

At another end of the authorial process, Derrida questions how the fact occurs, or the action of the relation between writing and author, since the performative of the signature is unceasingly external to the text itself, but maintains with it a relation of commitment, being most of the time indispensable for its understanding. What is the influence of such relation? In this case, once there is an understanding of the act of authorship in a society that will recognize it, we will have the author as a concrete possibility. Then the author starts being an effect, even if ephemeral, of such recognition, but

> There needs to be a social "community" that says this thing has been done—we don't even know by whom, we don't know what it means—however, we are going to put it in a museum or in some archive; we are going to consider it as a work of art. Without that political and social countersignature it would not be a work of art; there wouldn't be a signature.[13]

We could continue saying that in all cultural representations there is no author without this possibility of recognition which is external to the very authorial act. In spite of it, we have often observed an unrestricted faith that, to get recognition as a "writer" or as an "author" or even as a personality, an individual has only to dominate the action of the writing and possess the talents required.

According to critics of authorship like Seán Burke, technology also shows us that there is little debate and loss of historicity in terms of what he links in a confused way to "postmodern" theorization.[14] Burke's theory concerning the problem of authorship is between poles that don't appeal to each other and among increasingly wide fissures. On the one hand there is the model of the end of the author and on the other hand there are the defenders of authorship. However, the subjective issues and the political implications must be considered, above all if the thesis of the end of authorship defends the dissolution of subjectivity; and if it is in favor of utopian ideals based on a generalizing metaphysics of the presence and on a constraint of the individual. We know that the system of identity, founded under the stone of separation, exclusion, and autonomy is problematic, but the attempts to invert this system by the violence of state control under the intellectual patrimony and of the individuals' productivity only resulted in a new side of the same coin. Collective authorship that defends the end of the author by means of appropriation and recombination can be read as movements that try to rethink the collectivity by means of the annihilation of self-reference and by questioning the conception of consciousness and identity. In defending appropriation, the end of authorship and the forms derived from this thinking suggest an idea that man is the fruit of nonoriginality and, therefore, has no right to demand something that is not his. This concept originates from the ideas set forth by Foucault and Barthes.

The idea of production without the author is romantic, as well as the declaration of the end of authorship, because the conception that words came before us may indeed be a questioning opposite to the idea of originality and property, but it should be considered that perhaps there is something beyond humans and also that nature or something metaphysical is what guides him, not granting him the right to appropriate something that is not his. If this is taken into account, we can affirm that practically no human system will be original. But if we think that humankind is the creator and the first function of the ideality of what we conceive as "nature," "soul" and "society," among other things, the problem is addressed to the abstract set of human desires. The certainty that we are mere products of something beyond ourselves already demonstrates the origins of ideas concerned with recombination and appropriation, but it is always worth remembering that without what we consider human, probably the sense of what is seen as natural is not logical nor illogical. What the conceptions of collective and recombination propose is the creation of a new origin that wouldn't depend on humanity, but that once again would be thought, commanded and rearranged by humans. Who would be in charge of arranging and defining a nonoriginal real?

In this aspect, we can say that there was little progress in diluting the subject in favor of the crowd and, in several moments, what technologies offer in compensation is still very little in relation to the construction of a possible otherness that thinks itself above the technical apparatus.

What we see nowadays with discourses that defend the breakup of authorial parameters and promulgate the community as paradigm of authorship is the repetition of the history of exclusion of alterity. This structure doesn't allow, in the same way as in the system of identity, that a kind of otherness has a face and a name, but it is organized around an identifying ideal that hopes to exclude identity. The result of this violent autonomy of the end of the name's authority is a constant setup against the presuppositions of the notions that form the subject's particularities and that, in a certain way, lean on imaginary issues of psychic nature stimulated by a supposed encounter with what would configure humanity. Somehow we know that the reasons that take us more and more to dialog with the problem of authority and with the conceptions of the decentralization of the power of authentication are, in some cases, connected to distressing movements related to contemporary humankind's subjective position. What will I be if I am no longer an author? How will I sign? How will I perpetuate what I consider "inherent" to me? The answer is not always easy, taking into account that the phantasmagoric constitution of the proper name will hardly cease to be, at least in contemporary societies like those we live in, taken into account as an element that forms the identity and that, consequently, is connected to some form of perpetuation, be it symbolic or not, of what will remain after us.

The end of authorship and of the author's power can be considered as a complex presupposition and we don't often find people willing to try to reconstitute the tissue linked to the plot of concepts that involve the authorial act. However, the way in which the dialog with the representational forms around power occurs should be reshaped and rethought. Open authorial systems and those without signatures should be relativized.

We can say that we are attached to the concept of identity through the relation to the notion of the self. The switch from an authorial social structure linked to subjectivity to the dissolution of the symbolic, as representing a solution for the impasse on the concentrated power around the author would incur the mistake of instituting another form of authority that would be close to the denial of the act of inscription. Perhaps the most distressing factor in this process is the subjective effacement consolidated by the emergence of the recognition of an alterity through a phantasmagoric representation, which could run the risk of crystallizing in a movement as authoritarian as the contemporary capitalist system that we live in.

Taking into account the field of remix, Derrida's position sustains the fact that the materiality of the production does not matter, but what really counts for the sake of ethics is society's position in the reception and authentication of a cultural representation. This fact can be seen when a video with parts of other people's content receives millions of views on an online video platform and no one complains about the fact that it was made using remix techniques. When remixing, someone is lending another's signature to create a new one. Somehow Jacques Derrida questioned the limits with which the violence of authorship was imposed, but he also tried to present a dialog among the theories to imagine how we could build differentiated forms for the authentication of a representation, as well as for the subjective creation.[15]

It seems, at least when we get in contact with what has been presented by thinkers of the end of authorship, that this concept is on the verge of the end, but what we can conclude is that few of those who make the apology for the end of the author take into account that such an end also presupposes the end of the signature and the recognition of the proper name. And maybe that's the reason why most DJs and VJs use aliases to publicly sign their cultural production.

Notes

1 Peter Brunette and David Wills, "The Spatial Arts: An Interview with Jacques Derrida," in *Deconstruction and the Visual Arts: Arts, Media, Architecture* (Cambridge: Cambridge University Press, 1994), 18.

2 Marilyn Randall, *Pragmatic Plagiarism: Authorship, Profit, and Power* (Toronto: University of Toronto Press, 2001), 58.

3 Jacques Derrida, *The Ear of the Other*, ed. Christie McDonald (Lincoln, NE: University of Nebraska Press, 1988), 76, quoted in Peggy Kamuf, *Signature Pieces: On the Institution of Authorship* (Ithaca, NY: Cornell University Press, 1988), 4.

4 Roland Barthes, "La Mort de l'auteur," in *Le Bruissement de la langue* (Paris, 1984); English translation by Stephen Heath for the collection *Image-Music-Text* (New York: Fontana, 1977), 148.

5 Lev Manovich, "What Comes After Remix?" http://remixtheory.net/?p=169.

6 In my view the "author" in its modern sense is a relatively recent invention. Specifically, it is the product of the rise in the eighteenth century of a new group of individuals: writers who sought to earn their livelihood from the sale of their writings to the new and rapidly expanding reading public.
   Martha Woodmansee, "The Genius and the Copyright: Economic and Legal Conditions of the Emergence of the 'Author'," *Eighteenth-Century Studies* 17, no. 4, Special Issue: The Printed World in the Eighteenth Century (1984), 426.

7 Richard Grusin, "What Is an Electronic Author? Theory and the Technological Fallacy," *Configurations* 2, no. 3 (1994), 482.

8 Andrew Bennett, *The Author* (New York: Routledge, 2005), 13.

9 Paul M. Zall, *Literary Criticism of William Wordsworth* (Lincoln, NE: University of Nebraska Press, 1966), 182, in Martha Woodmansee, "The Genius and the Copyright," 429.

10 Woodmansee, "The Genius and the Copyright," 430.

11 Michel Foucault, "What Is an Author?" in *Twentieth-Century Literary Theory*, eds. Vassilis Lambropoulos and David Neal Miller (Albany, NY: State University of New York Press, 1987).

12 Brunette and Wills, "The Spatial Arts: An Interview With Jacques Derrida," 18.

13 Ibid.

14 Seán Burke, *The Death and Return of the Author: Criticism and Subjectivity in Barthes, Foucault and Derrida* (Edinburgh: Edinburgh University Press 1998), 96.

15 For a more detailed view concerning the concept of collaborative writing, see Lisa Ede and Andrea A. Lunsford, "Collaboration and Concepts of Authorship," *PMLA* 16, no. 2 (2001): 354–369.

Bibliography

Barthes, Roland. "The Death of the Author." In *Image-Music-Text*. Translated and edited by Stephen Heath. New York: Fontana, 1977.

Bennett, Andrew. *The Author*. New York: Routledge, 2005.

Brunette, Peter and David Wills. (Eds). *Deconstruction and the Visual Arts: Arts, Media, Architecture*. Cambridge: Cambridge University Press, 1994.

Burke, Seán. *The Death and Return of the Author: Criticism and Subjectivity in Barthes, Foucault and Derrida*. Edinburgh: Edinburgh University Press, 1998.

Derrida, Jacques. *Of Grammatology*. Translated by Gayatri Chakravorty Spivak. Baltimore, MD: Johns Hopkins University Press, 1976.

Ede, Lisa, and Andrea A. Lunsford. "Collaboration and Concepts of Authorship." *PMLA*, 16, no. 2 (2001): 354–369.

Foucault, Michel. "What Is an Author?" In *Twentieth-Century Literary Theory*, edited by Vassilis Lambropoulos and David Neal Miller. Albany, NY: State University of New York Press, 1987.

Grusin, Richard. "What Is an Electronic Author? Theory and the Technological Fallacy." *Configurations* 2, no. 3 (1994): 469–483.

Kamuf, Peggy. *Signature Pieces: On the Institution of Authorship*. Ithaca, NY: Cornell University Press, 1988.

Manovich, Lev. "What Comes After Remix?" *Remix Theory*, winter 2007. http://remixtheory.net/?p=169 (accessed November 21, 2013).

Navas, Eduardo. *Remix Theory: The Aesthetics of Sampling*. New York: Springer, 2012.

Randall, Marilyn. *Pragmatic Plagiarism: Authorship, Profit, and Power*. Toronto: University of Toronto Press, 2001.

Woodmansee, Martha. "The Genius and the Copyright: Economic and Legal Conditions of the Emergence of the 'Author'," *Eighteenth-Century Studies* 17, no. 4, Special Issue: The Printed World in the Eighteenth Century (1984): 425–448.

7

THE EXTENDED REMIX

Rhetoric and History

Margie Borschke

Many scholars of digital technologies and networks have called "remix" the defining characteristic of digital culture, using it as shorthand for all that is new, digital, and participatory.[1] This chapter offers a critique of such claims by comparing and contrasting the history of remix as an analog cultural practice and artifact with the discourse about remix in digital culture. It considers the use of "remix" in contemporary discourse as a rhetorical strategy and asks whether the assumptions and aspirations that underpin this rhetoric obscure the aesthetic priorities and the political implications of analog copying practices.

During the past half century, the meaning of "remix" changed: What began as a reference to a studio technique, musical form, and a marketing approach is now used metaphorically to describe media made from fragments of extant media.[2] Although early remixes were produced using analog technologies, contemporary discourse tends to associate "remix" and "remix culture" with digital practices and artifacts. As such, remix is now associated with cut/copy/paste technologies,[3] challenges to copyright and intellectual property,[4] participatory media,[5] grassroots social and political empowerment,[6] social networking,[7] user-generated content,[8] and "commons-based peer production."[9] Some see remix as a challenge to the corporate ownership of culture,[10] which either threatens late capitalism, or is just what capitalism needs to flourish in digital ecologies.[11] Remix is used as shorthand for human creativity,[12] an explanatory metaphor that illuminates the connectedness of knowledge and expression (and the problems with romantic conceptions of authorship). Remix can be all-encompassing: it is at once new and old, electronic and natural. Or, as the title of a Web video series put it, "Everything Is a Remix."[13]

Remix is a rhetorical trope in twenty-first century cultural scholarship,[14] a metaphor that attempts to explain and often *defend* creative works (especially those made with digital technologies) as analogous to dance remixes typical of the late twentieth century. Simultaneously, current narratives about remix and its underlying values are at odds with the particular history of remix as a musical practice and artifact. Examining this disjuncture offers insights about digital media technologies and cultural change.

The Shock of the New

Scholarship on remix is closely allied with arguments for copyright reform and, in recent years, with legal scholar Lawrence Lessig's persuasive arguments about the overreach of copyright in an era of digital and network technologies.[15] Lessig's adoption of remix as a description of digital cultural practice is recent—earlier books explored and documented the tensions surrounding intellectual property, corporate control, and personal freedom but they did not employ remix as a metaphor.[16] Given that "remix culture" has come to be so closely associated with Lessig's arguments for copyright reform in the face of expansion, it is essential to tease out his definition of remix from its rhetorical use.[17]

For Lessig, remix is a digital media practice, one that describes a variety of sample-based and digitally manipulated media artifacts, many of which are contested because they violate the copyright of the work they sample. Lessig argues that the regulation of expression was not the intention of copyright law and yet, these laws now criminalize artists like the laptop DJ-producer, known as Girl Talk, who composes music using hundreds of recognizable samples from pop songs.[18] Lessig claims that Girl Talk's "remixes," should be recognized as a *new* form of expression,[19] and as speech.[20] Lessig further argues that remix should also be understood as a participatory mode of creativity, one that marks a return to Jeffersonian ideals of democratic discourse.[21]

Valorizing the "new" as an engine of innovation is characteristic of modernist thinking. Yet, as Charles Acland argues, a preoccupation with the new also "betrays a concern about the past."[22] This dance between past and present is evident in Lessig's characterization of remix. He presents remix as a new form of expression, one made possible by technological progress and enabled by the mass uptake of digital and network technologies at the turn of the twenty-first century.[23] Simultaneously, Lessig claims that this digital-remix culture marks a return to something that was lost in the twentieth century, something "natural" that this new cultural practice has reinvigorated, but copyright laws still threaten. Lessig's conceptualization of remix attempts to naturalize digital expression, to connect it to free speech, while rendering other sorts of mediated expression inauthentic.

Submerged in Lessig's characterization of remix as new is an assumption that technology is inevitable and progressive—an assumption disputed by Friedman,[24] among others. Lessig describes contemporary life as "a world in which technology begs all of us to create and spread creative work differently from how it was created and spread before."[25] In doing so, Lessig grants agency to digital technologies while rendering users of the recent past passive. His technologies have expectations and natural trajectories: they plead with us. Remix is seen as an inevitable consequence of technological change, a position that assumes that technology is progressive, that old technologies are rendered obsolete by newfangled ones.[26] He assumes that if a technology is possible, it is inevitable—and that culture will be pushed forward in its wake. Friedman argues that technological determinism such as this is typical of the libertarian ethic that dominates popular thinking about the Internet, and has become computer culture's "common-sense theory of history,"[27] despite evidence to the contrary.[28] Technological determinists often speculate about the future by ignoring the past,[29] a tendency that is a particular problem for Lessig's understanding of remix as "new" in the face of its own lengthy history.

Schulz argues that determinism "enables the rhetor to make irrefutable prophecies, deflect responsibility when a technology proves deficient, downplay opposing positions and assert their own authority as seers of the future."[30] Friedman's analysis of cyberutopianism offers another insight into how technological determinism functions in an argument such as Lessig's: "Technological determinism actually functions as a cover, authorizing a safe space in which to articulate utopian values."[31] Lessig's understanding of remix as an inevitable consequence of technological progress constructs what

Friedman calls a "utopian sphere: the space in public discourse where, in a society that in so many ways has given up on imagining anything better than multinational capitalism, there's still room to dream of different kinds of futures."[32] The rhetoric of remix shelters Lessig from a key libertarian dilemma, one that copyright seems to bring to the fore: How to simultaneously protect free speech and free markets in the digital sphere?

Falling Down the Analog Hole, or Why We Never Were "Read-Only"

For Lessig, recent improvements to digital and network technologies altered the average person's relationship with both cultural products and media production and caused a shift in "cultures of creativity."[33] Lessig describes this new culture as "Read/Write," in contrast to the "Read-Only" media culture of the twentieth century when the available media technologies prevented the modification of cultural artifacts (e.g., vinyl records, televised broadcasts, etc.).[34] Culture was something that was made by professionals and passively consumed by everyone else. It was the era of the couch potato.[35]

However, remix has a history that predates digital technologies and this history troubles this characterization of the past. The first recordings that were made and sold as "remixes" date to the mid-1970s, in New York City[36] where the new form was closely associated with the ascendance of a new dance culture that used recorded music in tandem with playback technologies to create nonstop dancing.[37] DJs were instrumental in the development of technique and remix aesthetics, building on their understanding of the "dance floor dynamic" to produce the first commercial remixes as 12-inch singles in mid-1976.[38] Not all alternate versions were commissioned and paid for by labels—some DJs were also making unauthorized edits of songs on reel-to-reel and having them pressed on acetate, and this practice would have an impact on the aesthetic. Access and permission are key distinctions between the unauthorized edits and the commissioned remixes.[39] Each producer worked with a different set of sonic possibilities because they had access to different sets of sounds. Edit makers, who were constrained by the mixed sounds of the commercial release, would listen for certain sonic elements in a song such as a drum break. Remixers, on the other hand, had access to the multitrack master recordings and were thus able to isolate and manipulate individual layers in a mix, thereby expanding their sonic options.

Yet it is text rather than music that Lessig cites when explaining his understanding of remix. For him, remix is a new form of quotation, one that can be layered and mixed.[40] As such, referencing via juxtaposition and superimposition, as well as knowledge about the primary source, are crucial to his understanding of remix. The musical practice of remixing, however, is not necessarily dependent on contextual quotation. When a remixer omits vocals, filters the horns, or adds percussion, the tracks that are altered or rearranged aren't being referenced, rather, they are used differently (or not at all).

Lessig's emphasis on the generation of meaning via referencing and his preoccupation with creating conversations between media sources is accompanied by a judgment about what constitutes a "good" remix. He writes, "Remixed media succeed when they show others something new; they fail when they are trite or derivative."[41] In other words, "good" remixes build new meaning by playing with the meaning of old. Dance remixes, however, are derivative by definition. They began as DJ tools, and the aim was to make a song easier for a DJ to use: The remix might make the song more danceable, or more suitable for radio play. A cappellas, dubs, bonus beats, and extended mixes were versions that made it easier for a DJ to mix the record with other records (that is, to play them simultaneously), while other remixes appeal to certain styles or genres of music (e.g., a label might commission a house version and a hip hop mix), or hope for additional attention (and sales) by hiring a well-known remixer. Complicating matters further, there are occasions when only the remix is released or known—some remixes can be seen as attempts to save bad songs from themselves,[42] with no "original" for the listener to reference. My point is not that this technical meaning of remix has priority over the extension of the metaphor (and, of course, the techniques used to remix are indistinguishable from the tools used to mix any number of tracks), but that this extended understanding of remix must also be able to accommodate the technique's origins and continued use.

Lessig's preoccupation with generating meaning over derivations, however, has a specific rhetorical aim related to his desire to reform current copyright regimes. By aligning remix with cultural commentary and the established practice of referencing in art and literature, Lessig leads us toward the notion of fair use in copyright and builds a case that their use is transformative. But is this clever solution also a problem?

In her work on the contradictions in legal debates about the First Amendment and fair use provisions in US copyright law, Rebecca Tushnet draws attention to the emphasis on transformative use and how this potentially devalues copying and overlooks its role in free speech. Tushnet argues, "The rhetoric of transformative use can then be applied in non-transformative cases to devalue pure copying."[43] She explains that emphasis on critical commentary over everyday use might leave many other kinds of speech acts vulnerable. "While using fair use to protect artists from censorship is appealing, other forms of copying are also integral to free speech today."[44] She warns that fair use and free speech are not the same thing:

> Using fair use and free speech as interchangeable concepts thus has a profound and negative narrowing effect on the scope of fair use and in turn threatens First Amendment freedoms, because noncritical uses of copyrighted works have substantial value to society and to freedom of speech.[45]

In Tushnet's opinion, not only does an emphasis on transformative use defend some practices and not others, but it might also play into the hands of the opposition: "An exclusive focus on transformation in thinking about copyright and freedom of speech is likely to support further expansions of copyright."[46]

Copying music was already an important consumption practice in music culture in the analog era,[47] and the networked environment amplifies the role of copies in expression.[48] I do not wish to dispute Lessig's assertion that what technology enables and what the law allows are out of sync, and that difficult policy battles need to be fought. My concern is that the rhetoric of remix distracts us from a deeper understanding of the affordances of copies and fragmentation in general and the particular affordances of digital copies.

Won't Someone Think of the Amateurs?

Remix culture has also come to be associated with the democratization of media production, a shift from the passive consumers of the broadcast era (think couch potatoes) to the active participants of Web 2.0 (think citizen-journalists). Many scholars see remix as a form of empowerment and resistance, a storming of the gates of corporate mass media by "the people formerly known as the audience."[49] For some, this empowerment is an opportunity to forge new business models that sit comfortably in the continuum of late capitalism, while, for others, remix culture represents a wedge against corporate power structures and a challenge to the commodification of culture. The notion of a remix culture is often aligned or associated with Henry Jenkins's conceptualization of a participatory culture.[50] Indeed, Lessig builds much of his argument about remix on the strength of Jenkins's work on convergence and participation.[51] But is this celebration of participation underpinned by an assumption of passive reception? And is this a problem? Does the valorization of production denigrate the cultural worth of consumption?

Lessig looks back to the turn of the twentieth century to argue that "remix culture" can be understood as a return to what was lost when culture became professionalized.[52] Digital remix marks the triumphant (if contested) return of the amateur and the rise of a participatory ethos, one that rouses ordinary folk from their "couch-potato stupor."[53] However, in music culture the division between professionals and amateurs is not always clear-cut nor does it seem that digital technologies are the only ones that encourage participation. Numerous genres and scenes—from rock to electronic dance music—owe their existence to innovations and collaborations among self-trained, untrained, and semi-professional musicians and their "audiences" of listeners, dancers, and hangers-on. Jason Toynbee's research suggests that the advent of the recording industry in the twentieth century increased participation in music culture in part because the mass circulation of recordings were used by amateur musicians to learn their craft.[54] The music industry in the twentieth century is less about the rise of the professional than it is about the commodification of culture—the commercial exploitation of music's objectification. In addition, Paul Théberge argues that the advent of low-cost digital technologies in the early 1980s (e.g., samplers and sequencers) marks a moment in which a "key innovation was the 'production' of musicians as *consumers* of high technology."[55] While Lessig rightly asserts that the tools available today cost a fraction of what they once did, he fails to acknowledge that amateurs and starving professionals did rent studios, that they did buy low-cost samplers when they became available in the late 1980s,[56] that home studios were still within reach in the early 1990s—costing around $1,000[57]—and that many made use of cheaper tape technologies to achieve creative ends. The practice of remixing was forged by these strategies of use and making do with whatever technology was at hand. These strategies support an understanding of consumption practices such as listening, viewing, and reading as active rather than passive and these consumer innovations continue to shape the aesthetic of reuse.

By denying agency and innovation to past users, Lessig obscure an understanding of how their consumption practices shaped ours and how use shapes expression. It is clear that current copyright laws pose threats to creative reuse and present a particular threats for amateur practice[58] (or even to professional practice that does not have deep pockets) but it is problematic to attempt to defend amateur creativity by denying the role of everyday use in shaping the culture of the recent past.

Is Remix Resistance?

In 1977 Jacques Attali theorized that the political economy of music foreshadowed changes elsewhere in society and he hoped that the era of repetition might give way to an era of pure composition citing pirate recordings and illegal radio stations as possible signs of revolution.[59] Is remix a revolutionary form?

Whereas Lessig's argument ultimately sits comfortably within the existing economic and social order, other scholars conceptualize remix as a *resistance* to capitalism and commercial culture.[60] Bernard Schütze, for instance, sees remix not only as a resistance to the status quo, but by definition, as a subversive form.[61] While Lessig views markets as beyond question and copyright as a policy that needs reform, Schütze's understanding of remix is one that challenges these same institutions and structures: He values sharing over ownership, openness over originality, and process over product. Remix, for Schütze, is "an aesthetic of impurity, and an ideology of unrestricted circulation."[62] It is a challenge to existing orders and institutions, a strategy, and a process ("a verb not a noun"),[63] rather than a category or a product.

Schütze distinguishes between remixes he sees as acts of resistance from those that are in bed with the mainstream. He argues, " Remix culture . . . upholds the remix as an open challenge to a culture predicated on exclusive ownership, authorship, and controlled distribution."[64] It's not clear that we can cast aside the music industry's role in the history of remix (or of remakes, in other areas of media) because of political preferences. What if the remake culture Schütze sniffs at and the underground practices he admires have something in common? Schütze and Lessig may have different political agendas, but both value the potential for remixes to offer commentary and criticism. They value narrative or discursive remixes and disparage the nonnarrative (or, in musical terms, musematic) versions as derivative. Valuing narrative over other kinds of expression is not a problem in and of itself, but, in this case, it suppresses an important chapter in the history of remix—that of the musematic, or "repetition at the level of the short figure,"[65] as is common in dance remixing and editing and this preoccupation is a problem for the rhetoric of remix.

In the visual arts, remix is often considered part of a continuum of reuse that had already surfaced in a number of modernist forms—collage, pastiche, bricolage, for example—but is also seen as quintessentially postmodern, a strategy of resistance borrowed from particular cultures of popular music.[66] This flattening of a variety of forms and processes seeks to resurrect an association with the avant-garde at the same time that it declares its impossibility.[67] Resistance is seen as inherent to the process of fragmentation and reuse.

There is an historical problem with the idea that fragmentation is a resistance; that is, the professional aspirations of the various players who contributed to the aesthetic of remix, coupled with the commercial interests that helped to establish social and distribution networks among these players,[68] seem to challenge the view that remix as a form aims to oppose existing hierarchies. The tendency to romanticize the contributions of the amateur over the professional does not entirely mesh with the history of remix in music. Many of the early edits and unauthorized remixes were treated as calling cards by marginalized professionals—DJs—who wanted to join the mainstream industry. While some would come to embrace their status on the margins, many aspired to stardom. However, we also know that unauthorized remixes—appropriations of images, sounds, and so on—have been used as "a tactical assault on commodity culture," as video artist Dan Angeloro suggests.[69] Has appropriation as a tactic merely been appropriated as a consumption practice? Or is the meaning of a form a question of use rather than something inherent in the structure and confines of the form itself? This is not to say that Angeloro and others are incorrect to ascribe "power" to the fragment: Fragmentation is a kind of replication; isolation has aesthetic affordances and possibilities.

The history of fragmentation in music, however, complicates the valorization of remix as resistance—in a way that the history of fragmentation in the visual arts may not. In music, it seems that the aesthetic of remix stems from a number of separate music cultures and processes (dubs in Jamaica, disco and hip hop in New York, *musique concrète*, tape edits, and so on). The role of disco in the foundation of remix is often overlooked and instead the birth of remix is more closely associated with its ascendance in hip hop,[70] thereby associating the metaphor with the political struggles of Black America rather than with the marketing of popular culture and leisure, or with formal experimentation in high art, all of which are part of the history of musical remix. Fragmentation may be a more neutral strategy (or, at least, a more objective one) than the current metaphorical use of remix implies. The outlaw status of sampling as a musical process stems from its relationship to copyright law, not from its status as a fragment. Hence, the assumption that fragmentation has the status of resistance can only be attributed to certain remixes, but not all of them.

Conclusion: Why the History of Remix Matters

Studying remix as rhetoric offers lessons about the interrelationship between consumption, reception, and distribution in the creation of meaning. The vogue for using remix as a metaphor for all creativity obscures the particular history of remix in dance music, and carries with it a number of assumptions about technology and consumption that are problematic. Remix is a fuzzy metaphor, one that is used to defend new modes of participatory digital media engagement, while simultaneously denying agency to users of the recent past.

By foregrounding remix as a rhetorical strategy, I aim to recover these recent histories of use and to highlight the role of copies and copying in these histories.[71] Any theory of contemporary media culture must grapple with the persistence of the copy or fragment as a compositional unit, something that is shared by both analog and digital media. As rhetoric, remix asks us to overlook the copy, to instead focus on notions of transformative use. Though there may be localized legal and political reasons to do so, it fails to provide a rich description of cultural practice. Remix is neither new nor digital. As is true for most artifacts and practices from music culture, the borders between amateurs and professionals, commerce and culture, young and old, performer and audience are poorly defined. If we want to understand the role copies play in contemporary composition, we would do better to think not of their meaning, but of their use.

Acknowledgments

The author would like to thank James Bucknell (University of New South Wales), Kate Crawford (Microsoft Research) and Catharine Lumby (Macquarie University) for discussions and critiques that informed and enriched this work. Some of the material in this chapter appeared in "Rethinking the Rhetoric of Remix." *Media International Australia* 141 (November, 2011): 17–25 and is included with permission.

Notes

1 E.g., Lawrence Lessig, *Remix: Making Art and Commerce Thrive in the Hybrid Economy* (London: Bloomsbury 2008); Lev Manovich, "Remixability and Modularity," October–November 2005, http://manovich.net/index.php/projects/remixability-and-modularity; Bernard Schütze, "Samples from the Heap: Notes on Recycling the Detritus of a Remixed Culture," *Horizon Zero* 8 (2003): http://www.horizonzero.ca/textsite/remix.php?is=8&file=5&tlang=0. For further discussion see Margaret Borschke, "Rethinking the Rhetoric of Remix: Copies and Material Culture in Digital Networks" (PhD dissertation, University of New South Wales, 2012), 80–132.

2 E.g., Manovich, "Remixability and Modularity."

3 E.g., Schütze, "Samples from the Heap."

4 E.g., Lessig, *Remix*.

5 E.g., Henry Jenkins, *Confronting the Challenges of Participatory Culture: Media Education for the 21st Century* (Cambridge, MA: MIT Press, 2009).

6 E.g., Richard L. Edwards and Chuck Tryon, "Political Video Mashups as Allegories of Citizen Empowerment." *First Monday* 14, no. 10 (2009): http://firstmonday.org/htbin/cgiwrap/bin/ojs/index.php/fm/article/view/2617/2305.

7 E.g., Andréa Davis, Suzanne Webb, Dundee Lackey, and Dànielle Nicole DeVoss "Remix, Play, and Remediation: Undertheorized Composing Practices," in *Writing and the Digital Generation: Essays on New Media Rhetoric*, ed. Heather Urbanski (Jefferson, NC: McFarland & Company, 2010), 186–197.

8 E.g., Edward Lee, "Warming Up to User-Generated Content," *Illinois Law Review* 1459 (2008): 1544–1545.

9 Yochai Benkler, *The Wealth of Networks: How Social Production Transforms Markets and Freedom* (New Haven, CT: Yale University Press, 2006), 60.

10 E.g., Schütze, "Samples from the Heap."

11 E.g., Lessig, *Remix*; Matt Mason, *The Pirate's Dilemma: How Youth Culture Is Reinventing Capitalism* (New York: Free Press, 2008).

12 E.g., Eduardo Navas, "Remix: A Critical Analysis of Allegory, Intertexuality, and Sampling in Art, Music, and Media" (PhD dissertation, University of California and San Diego State University, 2009).

13 Kirby Ferguson, "Everything Is a Remix," 2010, http://www.everythingisaremix.info/.

14 This builds on Ted Friedman's interrogation of techno-utopianism (cf. Ted Friedman, *Electric Dreams: Computers in American Culture* (New York: New York University Press, 2005)), and David Paul Schulz's analysis of technological determinism as a rhetorical trope (cf. David Paul Schulz, "The Rhetorical Contours of Technological Determinism" (PhD dissertation, Pennsylvania State University, 2002)).

15 Cf. Lawrence Lessig, The Future of Ideas: *The Fate of the Commons in a Connected World* (New York: Vintage, 2002); Lawrence Lessig, *Free Culture: How Big Media Uses Technology and the Law to Lock Down Culture and Control Creativity* (New York: Penguin, 2004); and Lessig, *Remix*.

16 Cf. Lessig, *The Future of Ideas* and *Free Culture*.

17 As Steven A. Hetcher points out, Lessig never defines the term. Steven A. Hetcher, "Using Social Norms to Regulate Fan Fiction and Remix Culture," *University of Pennsylvania Law Review* 157 (2008): 1871.

18 Lessig, *Remix*.

19 Ibid.

20 Lawrence Lessig, "Lawrence Lessig: Laws that Choke Creativity," *TED*, 2007, http://www.ted.com/talks/larry_lessig_says_the_law_is_strangling_creativity.html.

21 See Lessig, *Remix*, 27.

22 Charles Acland, "Residual Media." in *Residual Media*, ed. Charles Acland (Minneapolis, MN: University of Minnesota Press, 2007), xv.

23 Lessig, *Remix*, 18.

24 Friedman, *Electric Dreams: Computers in American Culture*.

25 Lessig, *Remix*, xviii.

26 Ibid., 30, 39.

27 Friedman, *Electric Dreams: Computers in American Culture*, 27.

28 Ted Friedman, "Electric Dreams: Computer Culture and the Utopian Sphere" (PhD dissertation, Duke University, 1999), 105.

29 Ibid., 14.

30 Schulz, "The Rhetorical Contours of Technological Determinism," 38.

31 Friedman, *Electric Dreams: Computers in American Culture*, 5.

32 Ibid., 4.

33 Ibid., 18.

34 Ibid., 20–31.

35 Ibid., 29.

36 Cf. Tim Lawrence, *Love Saves the Day: A History of American Dance Music Culture, 1970–1979* (Durham, NC: Duke University Press, 2003); and William Straw, "Value and Velocity: The 12-Inch Single as Medium and Artifact," in *Popular Music Studies*, ed. K. Negus and D. Hesmondhalgh (London: Edward Arnold, 2002).

37 There were other commercial precedents: notably 1960s Jamaican dubplates were commissioned by sound systems and labels to create excitement on the dance floor in advance of a record's release and to get customers into the clubs. For a discussion see Jason Toynbee, *Making Popular Music: Musicians, Creativity and Institutions* (London: Arnold, 2000), xvii.

38 Tim Lawrence, *Hold On to Your Dreams: Arthur Russell and the Downtown Music Scene, 1973–1992* (Durham, NC: Duke University Press, 2009), 129.

39 Cf. Margie Borschke, "Disco Edits and their Discontents: The Persistence of the Analog in a Digital Era," *New Media & Society* 13, no. 6 (2011): 929–944; and Borschke, "Rethinking the Rhetoric of Remix," 133–185.

40 Lessig, *Remix*, 69.

41 Ibid., 82.

42 Rob Tannenbaum, "Remix, Rematch, Reprofit. Then Dance." *The New York Times*, August 30, 1992, Factiva.

43 Rebecca Tushnet, "Copy This Essay: How Fair Use Doctrine Harms Free Speech and How Copying Serves It," *Yale Law Journal* 114, no. 3 (2004): 561.

44 Ibid., 545.

45 Ibid., 537.

46 Ibid., 553.

47 Lee Marshall "Infringers," In *Music & Copyright*, ed. L. Marshall and S. Frith (New York: Routledge, 2004), 196.

48 Margie Borschke, "Ad Hoc Archivists: MP3 Blogs and Digital Provenance." *Continuum: Journal of Media & Cultural Studies* 26, no. 1 (2012): 1–10; and "Rethinking the Rhetoric of Remix."

49 Jay Rosen, "The People Formerly Known as the Audience," *PressThink* (blog), posted June 27, 2006. http://archive.pressthink.org/2006/06/27/ppl_frmr.html.

50 Patrik Wikstrom, *The Music Industry: Music in the Cloud* (Cambridge: Polity Press, 2009).

51 Lessig, *Remix*, 28, 78, 81, 94, 206, 207, 212, 276.

52 Ibid., 29.

53 Ibid., 254.

54 Toynbee, *Making Popular Music*, 74.

55 Théberge, Paul, *Any Sound You Can Imagine: Making Music/Consuming Technology, Music/Culture* (Hanover, NH: Wesleyan University Press, 1997): 70–71. See also Toynbee, Making Popular Music.

56 Kembrew McLeod, "How Copyright Law Changed Hip Hop: An Interview with Public Enemy's Chuck D and Hank Shocklee," *Stay Free* 20 (2004): 22–25.

57 E.g., M. Saunders. "Getting Hip to Pop." *Boston Globe*, May 9, 1993, Factiva.

58 Among the problems with the rhetoric of remix is its tendency to avoid examples of digital expression involving straightforward replication. For a discussion of the creative use of copies in MP3 blogs see Borschke, "Ad Hoc Archivists" and "Rethinking the Rhetoric of Remix."

59 Jacques Attali, *Noise: The Political Economy of Music*. Translated by B. Massumi (Minneapolis, MN: University of Minnesota Press, 1985), 5, 20. NB It is worth highlighting that Attali's work was informed by analog recording and broadcast technologies rather than digital ones.

60 E.g., Bart Vautour, "Remix Culture," in *Contemporary Youth Culture: An International Encyclopedia*, ed. S. R. Steinberg, P. Parmar, and B. Richard (Westport, CT: Greenwood Press, 2006): 306; Schütze, "Samples from the Heap."

61 Schütze, "Samples from the Heap."

62 Ibid.

63 Ibid.

64 Ibid.

65 Richard Middleton, "Form," in *Key Terms in Popular Music and Culture*, ed. B. Horner and T. Swiss (Oxford: Blackwell, 1999): 146.

66 Cf. Navas, "Remix: A Critical Analysis."

67 Cf. Rosalind E. Krauss, *The Originality of the Avant-Garde and Other Modernist Myths* (Cambridge, MA: MIT Press, 1985).

68 Straw, "Value and Velocity."

69 Dan Angeloro, "Thoughtware: Contemporary Online Remix Culture," in *SynCity*, ed. Mark Titmarsh (Sydney: dLux Media Arts, 2006): 25.

70 Cf. Lawrence, *Remix*.

71 Borschke, "Rethinking the Rhetoric of Remix."

Bibliography

Acland, Charles. "Residual Media." In *Residual Media*, edited by Charles Acland, xiii–xxvii. Minneapolis, MN: University of Minnesota Press, 2007.

Angeloro, Dan. "Thoughtware: Contemporary Online Remix Culture." In *SynCity*, edited by Mark Titmarsh, 18–25. Sydney: dLux Media Arts, 2006.

Attali, Jacques. *Noise: The Political Economy of Music*. Translated by B. Massumi. Minneapolis, MN: University of Minnesota Press, 1985.

Benkler, Yochai. *The Wealth of Networks: How Social Production Transforms Markets and Freedom*. New Haven, CT: Yale University Press, 2006.

Borschke, Margie. "Disco Edits and their Discontents: The Persistence of the Analog in a Digital Era." *New Media & Society* 13, no. 6 (2011): 929–944.

———. "Rethinking the Rhetoric of Remix." *Media International Australia* 141, November (2011): 17–25.

———. "Ad Hoc Archivists: MP3 Blogs and Digital Provenance." *Continuum: Journal of Media & Cultural Studies* 26, no. 1 (2012): 1–10.

———. "Rethinking the Rhetoric of Remix: Copies and Material Culture in Digital Networks" PhD dissertation, University of New South Wales, Sydney, 2012.

Bruns, Axel. *Blogs, Wikipedia, Second Life, and Beyond: From Production to Produsage*. New York: Peter Lang, 2008.

Burgess, Jean. "Vernacular Creativity, Cultural Participation and New Media Literacy: Photography and the flickr Network." Paper presented at *Internet Research 7.0: Internet Convergences (AoIR)*, Brisbane, September 28–30, 2006.———. "Vernacular Creativity and the New Media." PhD dissertation, Queensland University of Technology, 2007.

Burgess, Jean, and Joshua Green. *YouTube: Online Video and Participatory Culture*. Cambridge: Polity Press, 2009.

Chanan, M. *Repeated Takes: A Short History of Recording and Its Effects on Music*. London: Verso, 1995.

Davis, Andréa, Suzanne Webb, Dundee Lackey, and Dànielle Nicole DeVoss. "Remix, Play, and Remediation: Undertheorized Composing Practices." In *Writing and the Digital Generation: Essays on New Media Rhetoric*, edited by Heather Urbanski, 186–197. Jefferson, NC: McFarland & Company, 2010.

Diakopoulos, N., K. Luther, Y. E. Medynskiy, and I. Essa. "The Evolution of Authorship in a Remix Society." In *Proceedings of the Eighteenth Conference on Hypertext and Hypermedia*. Manchester, UK, 2007: 133–136.

Edwards, R., and C. Tryon. "Political Video Mashups as Allegories of Citizen Empowerment." *First Monday* 14, no. 10 (2009). http://firstmonday.org/htbin/cgiwrap/bin/ojs/index.php/fm/article/view/2617/2305 (accessed July 30, 2014).

Ferguson, K. *Everything is a Remix*, 2010. http://www.everythingisaremix.info/ (accessed July 30, 2014).

Friedman, Ted. "Electric Dreams: Computer Culture and the Utopian Sphere." PhD dissertation, Duke University, 1999.

———. *Electric Dreams: Computers in American Culture*. New York: New York University Press, 2005.

Hennion, A. "Music Lovers: Taste as Performance." *Theory Culture and Society* 18, no. 5 (2001): 1–22.

———. "Listen!" *Music and Arts in Action* 1, no. 1 (2008): 36–45.

Hetcher, Steven. A. "Using Social Norms to Regulate Fan Fiction and Remix Culture." *University of Pennsylvania Law Review* 157 (2008): 1869–1935.

Jenkins, Henry. *Fans, Blogger, and Gamers: Exploring Participatory Culture*. New York: New York University Press, 2006.

———. *Confronting the Challenges of Participatory Culture: Media Education for the 21st Century*. Cambridge, MA: MIT Press, 2009.

Krauss, Rosalind E. *The Originality of the Avant-Garde and Other Modernist Myths*. Cambridge, MA: MIT Press, 1985.

Lawrence, Tim. *Love Saves the Day: A History of American Dance Music Culture, 1970–1979*. Durham, NC: Duke University Press, 2003.

———. "Disco Madness: Walter Gibbons and the Legacy of Turntablism and Remixology." *Journal of Popular Music Studies* 20, no. 3 (2008): 276–329.

———. *Hold On to Your Dreams: Arthur Russell and the Downtown Music Scene, 1973–1992*. Durham, NC: Duke University Press, 2009.

Lee, Edward. "Warming Up to User-Generated Content." *Illinois Law Review* 1459 (2008): 1544–1545.

Lessig, Lawrence. *The Future of Ideas: The Fate of the Commons in a Connected World*. New York: Vintage, 2002.

———. *Free Culture: How Big Media Uses Technology and the Law to Lock Down Culture and Control Creativity*. New York: Penguin, 2004.

———. "The People Own Ideas." *Technology Review*, June 2005. http://www.technologyreview.com/communications/14505/ (accessed July 30, 2014).

———. "Larry Lessig on Laws that Choke Creativity." *TED*, 2007. http://www.ted.com/talks/larry_lessig_says_the_law_is_strangling_creativity.html (accessed July 30, 2014).

———. *Remix: Making Art and Commerce Thrive in the Hybrid Economy*. London: Bloomsbury, 2008.

Manovich, Lev. *The Language of New Media*. Cambridge, MA: MIT Press, 2001.

———. "Remixability and Modularity." October–November, 2005. http://manovich.net/index.php/projects/remixability-and-modularity (accessed July 30, 2014).

Marshall, Lee. "Infringers." In *Music & Copyright*, edited by L. Marshall and S. Frith, 189–207. New York: Routledge, 2004.

Mason, Matt. *The Pirate's Dilemma: How Youth Culture Is Reinventing Capitalism*. New York: Free Press, 2008.

McLeod, Kembrew. "How Copyright Law Changed Hip Hop: An Interview with Public Enemy's Chuck D and Hank Shocklee." *Stay Free* 20 (2004): 22–25.

Middleton, Richard. "In the Groove, or Blowing Your Mind? The Pleasures of Musical Repetition." In *Popular Culture and Social Relations*, edited by T. Bennett, C. Mercer, and J. Woollacott, 159–176. Philadelphia: Open University Press, 1986.

———. "Form." In *Key Terms in Popular Music and Culture*, edited by B. Horner and T. Swiss, 141–155. Oxford: Blackwell, 1999.

Navas, Eduardo. "Remix: A Critical Analysis of Allegory, Intertexuality, and Sampling in Art, Music, and Media." PhD dissertation. University of California and San Diego State University, San Diego, CA, 2009.

———. "Regressive and Reflexive Mashups in Sampling Culture." In *Mashup Cultures*, edited by S. Sonvilla-Weiss, 157–177. New York: Springer, 2010.

Rosen, Jay. "The People Formerly Known as the Audience." *PressThink* (blog). Posted June 27, 2006. http://archive.pressthink.org/2006/06/27/ppl_frmr.html (accessed July 30, 2014).

Saunders, M. "Getting Hip to Pop." *Boston Globe*, May 9, 1993, Factiva.

Schloss, Joseph G. *Making Beats: The Art of Sample-Based Hip-Hop*. Middletown, CT: Wesleyan University Press, 2004.

Schulz, David Paul. "The Rhetorical Contours of Technological Determinism." PhD dissertation, Pennsylvania State University, University Park, PA, 2002.

Schütze, Bernard. "Samples From the Heap: Notes on Recycling the Detritus of a Remixed Culture." *Horizon Zero*, no. 8, 2003, http://www.horizonzero.ca/textsite/remix.php?is=8&file=5&tlang=0 (accessed July 30, 2014).

Straw, William. "Value and Velocity: The 12-Inch Single as Medium and Artifact." In *Popular Music Studies*, edited by K. Negus and D. Hesmondhalgh, 164–177. London: Edward Arnold, 2002.

Tannenbaum, Rob. "Remix, Rematch, Reprofit. Then Dance." *The New York Times*, August 30, 1992, Factiva.

Théberge, Paul. *Any Sound You Can Imagine: Making Music/Consuming Technology, Music/Culture*. Hanover, NH: Wesleyan University Press, 1997.

Toynbee, Jason. *Making Popular Music: Musicians, Creativity and Institutions*. London: Arnold, 2000.

———. "Musicians." In *Music & Copyright*, edited by L. Marshall and S. Frith, 123–138. New York: Routledge, 2004.

Tushnet, Rebecca. "Copy This Essay: How Fair Use Doctrine Harms Free Speech and How Copying Serves It." *Yale Law Journal* 114, no. 3 (2004): 535–592.

Vaidhyanathan, Siva. *Copyrights and Copywrongs: The Rise of Intellectual Property and How It Threatens Creativity*. New York: New York University Press, 2003.

Vautour, Bart "Remix Culture." In *Contemporary Youth Culture: An International Encyclopedia*, edited by S. R. Steinberg, P. Parmar, and B. Richard, 306–310. Westport, CT: Greenwood Press, 2006.

Wikstrom, Patrik. *The Music Industry: Music in the Cloud*. Cambridge: Polity Press, 2009.

8

CULTURE AND REMIX

A Theory on Cultural Sublation

Eduardo Navas

Remix culture is a term increasingly used to explain basic principles of creativity and individual expression since the mid to late 1990s.[1] Given its common usage, the nature of the compound term's dependence on a complex history may not seem obvious. When evaluating the relation of *remix* to *culture* at times one may ask, "What kind of culture are we becoming when we consider remixing an important element in creative production?" And, "What exactly is culture?" In this line of questioning, it becomes evident that in order to understand in depth what role remix plays in culture it is necessary to define with precision the term "culture." This should make possible a discussion about the possibilities and limitations of remix, not only in terms of remix culture, which is a concept in large part informed and shaped by Creative Commons, but also culture in the larger context of history. The following, then, is a brief analysis in which I first define culture to then evaluate its relation to remix. The concept of the avant-garde is presented as a cultural example in which remixing is at play explicitly on two layers that I define as *the framework of culture*.[2] I also analyze how social media relies on the framework of culture to develop a new type of economy. This analysis will expose the reasons why, historically, creative production appears to resist established patterns of production, but eventually is sublated by cultural economies and becomes vital to capital as a whole.

Culture Defined

All cultural critics (as their title implies) have to assume a concise idea of culture. Two cultural critics who have taken the time to define culture at length are Raymond Williams, who published his theories around the 1950s, and Terry Eagleton, who became an authority as a surveyor of culture, due to his focus on the subject particularly in the 1980s. Eagleton defines culture by referencing the definitions of Williams, as well as T. S. Eliot. In Eagleton's definition, one comes away with a sense of culture defined, unapologetically, by the West. He argues that as Western thought has spread throughout the world, it has been able to make claims to a certain way of thinking that affects other cultures that did not hold Western values.[3] Eagleton also points out that culture originates in nature and is defined by labor. Culture is nature modified according to the interests of individuals who perform a specific form of manual work: "We derive our word for the finest of human activities from labour and agriculture, crops and cultivation."[4] Eagleton discusses at some length how culture developed a sense of resistance, especially in the nineteenth century; for him, such resistance has links to the rise of the avant-garde during the same time period.

According to Raymond Williams, the fact that art became a value in and of itself at times separated from everyday life was the result of a preoccupation with cultural changes that started around 1790, and climaxed around 1945. Part of the cultural struggle since the end of World War II, Williams argues, had been to find ways to reintegrate the value of art back into the everyday.[5] Williams divides the separation of art and everyday life into three stages: the first from 1790 to 1870, when industrialism rapidly developed; the second from 1870 to 1914, when specializations started to become the norm; and finally, 1914 to 1945, a time when the specializations of the second period kept developing, but became complicated by the rise of mass media and large corporations.[6]

The stages, as outlined by Williams, trace the history of modernity as it is commonly understood. For Williams, culture came to signify a type of resistance in search of meaning against the rise of capital, where the exile (his own term)—the cultural critic, or the mythologist (as it would come to be renamed by Roland Barthes in the 1960s)[7]—has some critical distance to reflect on the developments of the world. Picking up where Williams left off, Eagleton reflects with certain disappointment on what the term culture meant during modern times:

> The concept of culture grew up as a critique of middle-class society, not as an ally of it. Culture was about value not prices, the moral rather than the material, the high-minded rather than the philistine. . . . It was the rickety shelter where the values and energies which industrial capitalism had no use for could take refuge. . . . From its patrician height, it scorned the shopkeepers and stockbrokers swarming in the commercial badlands below.[8]

In Eagleton's claim we find a clear definition of one type of culture aligned with the aura of the arts and intellectuality. According to critical theorist Andrew Arato, this is the same culture with which previous intellectuals such as the Frankfurt School members identified.[9] Arato argues that this culture is ambiguously complemented by another concept of culture that, at least since the 1790s, went through the same evolution that Williams has outlined. This type of culture consists of shared traditions, institutions, and a wide spectrum of activities that come to define a person's identity.[10] During the beginning of the twenty-first century, this other culture is dependent on mass communication and culminates as abstraction in social media and networked culture. The new technology that made mass communication possible was considered by some cultural critics, such as Theodor Adorno and Max Horkheimer, to push people towards passivity, to become regressive consumers.[11] When such arguments were questioned, it eventually led to postmodern culture.[12] "Cultural resistance," as understood at the time of this writing, is therefore constantly fluctuating between these two notions of culture.

Culture and Postcoloniality

So far culture has been defined through a very specific lens, one that some critics would say leaves out a postcolonial reading. Therefore, another cultural critic must be considered to understand why, as imposing and limiting the views of Eagleton and Williams might appear, they still do help to define the concept of culture during the first decade of the twenty-first century.

According to the Argentine philosopher, Enrique Dussel, modernity as currently recognized is the second of two modern periods. The first was a Hispanic Humanist Renaissance Modernity, which led to discovering the new world in 1492. He argues that in this modernity, the concept of the Other and the equation of center and periphery were defined to privilege Europe. Prior to this period, Europe was by no means the center of culture. The second modernity, which Dussel argues is the only one that is emphasized today, is the Modernity of Anglo-Germanic Europe, which begins with trade in Amsterdam during the sixteenth century. We can note that this is the same modernity that Eagleton and Williams acknowledge. Dussel explains that with the second modernity came a need for simplification, because if this modernity was to become effective it had to invent itself as a world system. This simplification was attained with an equation that favored quantity over quality, and needed to leave out or at least downplay cultural, ethical, political, and even religious values; all quite important for people in Europe during the sixteenth century:

> This simplification of complexity encompasses the totality of the life-world (Lebenswelt), of the relationship with nature (a new technological and ecological position that is no longer teleological), of subjectivity itself (a new self-understanding of subjectivity), and of community (a new intersubjective and political relation). A new economic attitude (practico-productive) will now establish itself: the capitalism.[13]

Once this simplification with the rise of capital takes place, European modernity is able to spread across the world as it is currently experienced in terms of globalization. But there is a space within this framework that, Dussel argues, makes critical reflection possible. Capital's need for simplification as a world system creates demand for subsystems that do not have standards for self-regulation. Some of these subsystems can be "redirected at the service of humanity," Dussel argues.[14] This is what makes any critical analysis possible. Therefore, postcolonial thinking and other methods of questioning the hegemony of European thinking can be considered subsystems within capital proper.

The definitions of culture outlined above are intimate with capitalism, and any critical questioning that takes place has been implemented from within. This is what happens in the rise of dub and the early stages of remix as understood in music culture; disco, hip hop, house, and all other forms of music that followed also function under the same paradigm. From this point of view there is no outside. And if there is no outside, then, perhaps enough subsystems could be developed at the service of humanity, or perhaps not. To evaluate this further, following Dussel's argument, it becomes necessary to take a worldview, and understand that prior to Anglo-Germanic Modernity, Europe was at the periphery. Therefore a worldview could help understand the limitations of the current stage of globalization as informed by capital. Dussel further argues that modernity as it has developed is reaching its limits and understanding what can be redeemed from the current global state is important in developing a "rational management of the world-system." In this system Dussel considers possible the control of domination and exclusion that has made European modernity possible.[15] How this is to take place is not made clear by Dussel, although he does outline three limitations of the simplification of European modernity which point to a shift that globalization itself is making possible.

He cites Noam Chomsky's "system of 500 years" to explain that the limitations include nature as a resource for life, which as capital develops is turned into a hazard with the development of antiecological technology; needless to say that at the moment this limitation has to be desperately reevaluated. The second limit is humanity. Capital can only thrive through labor, and human labor has been reconfigured, made superfluous, as capital finds new ways to optimize itself as a world system. To achieve this, capital developed technology that pushes productivity to an unprecedented level. According to Dussel, with technological development the manual laborer has to live with low wages or unemployment, thus exposing this second limitation with two extreme poles: global wealth and poverty. The third limitation is the inability of capital to effectively assimilate cultures that helped define it as a center. As these cultures develop a global position, they are doing so with an autonomy that does not fully embrace a European model. In sum, as global culture develops, it becomes harder for modernity, as has been defined by Europe, to stand. From this point of view, remix plays and will continue to play a major role in the development of global culture. Remix—while it can be used to promote modernity as a reductive model—can also be used to develop a worldview beyond Eurocentrism. What is also evident in this theoretical framework about culture and modernity is a worldview of culture that demands some form of resistance.

The Meaning of Culture

Based on the previous brief historical definition of culture, it is evident that when the term culture, alone, is mentioned, generally it is understood to imply some abstract form of resistance, or at least, something separate from that which is understood as popular—this is more evident in Eagleton's account. This understanding came to support the separation of culture as high and low, as explained by Arato. Resistance against the popular (watered-down or kitsch) develops due to the fact that popular culture is primarily fueled by capital, whereas "high culture" (what the term culture alone implies) is invested in meaning and issues beyond making a profit. But the reality is that both of these cultures contribute to each other's ongoing development, to the point that at times it is difficult to fully separate the high from the low. This became most evident during the postmodern period.

The conundrum that cultural producers constantly face when engaging this symbiotic relationship is that emerging cultural forms are assimilated with great ease, and this is passed on to remix as a creative binder, which thrives between and is shaped by the high as much as the low. In effect, remix culture is a culture of resistance—almost by default because the very act of taking preexisting, most likely copyright protected, material challenges the way creativity is defined by corporations. When viewed through a historical lens, this process, which if nothing else is certainly a disruption of intellectual property laws, appears to be in the process of sublation, as previous forms and strategies of resistance have been assimilated in the past. One must ask then, can there be *real* changes (in terms of daily life and individual perspective on the world) to this ongoing process of sublation? A possible argument is that by understanding how such a process functions, cultural producers will be able to turn this apparent feedback loop into not only a stronger form of resistance, but also a force of ongoing critical reflection that has the potential to create new possibilities for culture's creative drive. In order to develop a better sense of resistance's potential role in such a process, then, it is worth examining how remix itself functions on a feedback loop, which takes place well within two cultural layers that define culture as understood by those who propose remix as a form of free expression, dissent, and a dematerialized totem for possibilities of a new world.

The Framework of Culture

Now that the term "culture" is defined, it is necessary to consider how it produces value, and how that value becomes prime and rich material for remixing. The framework of culture makes the act of remixing possible. This framework consists of two layers which function on a feedback loop.[16] The first layer takes effect when something is introduced in culture; such an element will likely be different from what is commonly understood. Such an element often is actual research (field work, gathering of data that did not previously exist, the combination of ideas based on field work, lab research, cultural research, and/or gathered data, and day-to-day inquiry into the function of the world, etc.) that needs to be evaluated and therefore its sublation is not immediate. The second layer takes effect when that which is introduced attains cultural value and is appropriated or sampled to be reintroduced in culture. The first layer privileges research and development. Creative practice in the arts, for the most part, functions on the second layer, which is why, more often than not, production consists of appropriation, or at least citation of material with predefined cultural value. The two layers have actually been in place since culture itself came about, but their relation has changed with the growing efficiency in production and communication methods due to the ever-growing speed of technological development. Before we evaluate the implication of this change in creativity and contemporary critical production, we must first understand the relation of the layers.

Some examples from the past include the photo camera, the phonograph, and more recently, the computer. All of these examples were not "original" but rather drastically different amalgamations of ideas, leading to specific technologies that, when first introduced, people had to negotiate by process of sublation into their everyday lives.[17] These are rather modern examples, which were only possible once the loop between the two layers was fast enough to provide feedback at a rate that would make research and development an actual endeavor worthy of capital investment. But this was not always the case.

Before this period, the two layers were separated, or at least there was a great communication lag between them (Figure 8.1). When we think back to the days prior to the Enlightenment, we can see how the development of new forms and technologies took much longer to be produced than in our time. This was in part due to material limitations in combination with social beliefs that perpetrated certain behaviors and attitudes towards the world.

Religion certainly played a major role in how the world was viewed. Prior to the Enlightenment, some people approached nature as a place in which to live, in part because nature was seen as a creation of God, or as though it embodied godly or spiritual powers. But as the Enlightenment took place, the belief that nature could be manipulated for human needs took hold of Western culture.[18] This premise enabled human beings to push for innovation, as we currently understand it. Once humans felt free to bend and shape all things, from nature to ideas, for particular ideological interests, we entered a new era. The speed of innovation became the driving force of what came to be known as modernism (Figure 8.2). Arguably, a recent consequence of this attitude to bend nature to our desires is global warming, and the effects it produces, from hurricanes in the northern hemisphere to the disappearance of glaciers in Antarctica.

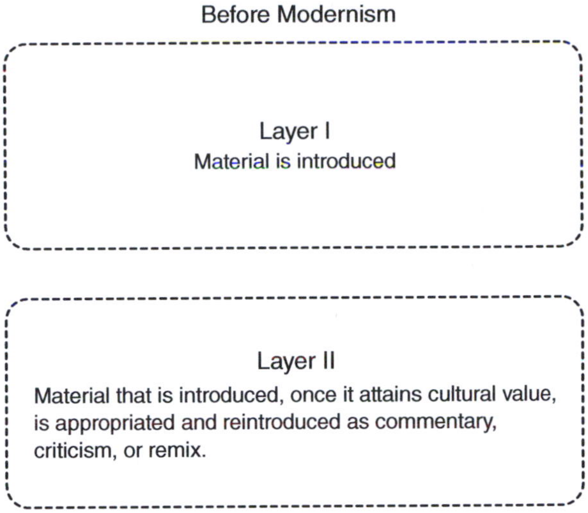

Before Modernism

Layer I
Material is introduced

Layer II
Material that is introduced, once it attains cultural value,
is appropriated and reintroduced as commentary,
criticism, or remix.

Figure 8.1 The framework of culture before modernism (diagrams in this chapter
courtesy of Eduardo Navas)

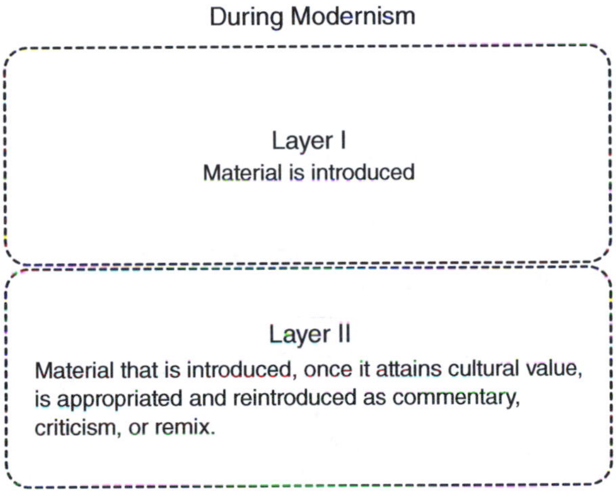

During Modernism

Layer I
Material is introduced

Layer II
Material that is introduced, once it attains cultural value,
is appropriated and reintroduced as commentary,
criticism, or remix.

Figure 8.2 The framework of culture during modernism

As modernism further developed, the efficiency of production led to a streamlined
feedback loop, one which was sensed by cultural critics who came to be associated with
the postmodern period (Figure 8.3). In this case, the feedback loop is not only more
efficient but begins to overlap, albeit with some delay. The questioning of terms such as
originality, uniqueness, and the concept of progress itself, became common subjects for
intellectual debates, and rich source material for mass media to thrive—which then
becomes the subject of resistance by those invested in culture as defined above.

What all this means is that cultural layers have begun to share interests that push the
established critical approaches of the modern and postmodern into a different

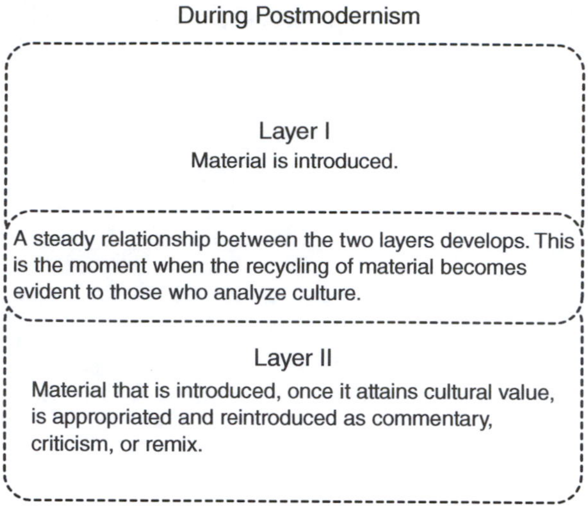

During Postmodernism

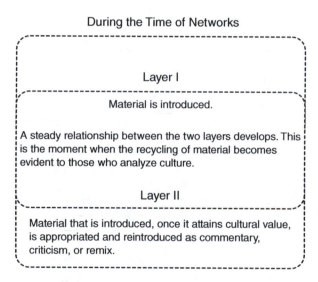

Figure 8.3 The framework of culture during postmodernism

During the Time of Networks

Figure 8.4 The framework of culture during the time of networks (general stage)

relationship; one that we now need to reflect upon. In this case, the loop's efficiency only grew as we entered the times of networked media, and currently the two layers function almost on top of each other (Figure 8.4). The result is a steady relationship between the two layers that form the framework of culture, in terms of recycling the material, leading to an efficient production that is completely dependent on constant communication. This last tendency is best understood in popular terms with the concept of *constant updating*. Just as Twitter remains relevant because people keep tweeting, the two layers have now reached a frenetic level that repositions them in a state of never-ending production; evaluation of that production is immediately relayed back to the producer, and so forth. We can think of our current moment as the dream party of the house DJ, whose ultimate high is to keep the perfect beat going for hours, with an obsession to make the entire mix of multiple songs sound like one single composition in which the dancers can push themselves physically with no other goal than to feel the beat. The perfect loop of beat-blending, then, serves as a decent metaphor for the type of obsession behind the two layers of the framework of culture. The beat-blending eventually turns into a mashup, in which both layers can be acknowledged, much as how in a music mashup two songs are recognized for their respective sound, while also coming together to create a new unique sound. This very tension makes the music mashup a compelling composition, which listeners engage with while understanding the metamessage: the source material has a new role in the service of sounding like one composition. The two layers of the framework of culture function in a similar way once we reach the level of efficiency at play in the beginning of the twenty-first century, due to the ongoing development of computing.

Music, art, and literature function within the overlapping areas of the two layers of the framework of culture, with great dependence on material that is constantly recycled. They consist of appropriating something of cultural value in order to create meaning. This need has long been associated with intertextuality, which in the literary tradition is understood as the act of embedding a text within another text, a conceptual remix of sorts where ideas are cited, but not necessarily the material object or concrete instantiation (which is what the act of remixing achieves in the actual sampling of content). An intertextual work is, in essence, a literary mashup (a direct juxtaposition) of concepts.[19]

Intertextuality plays a pivotal role in critical production. It does so by recycling information between the two layers of the framework. However, for criticality this process functions at a metalevel, in which the material recycled is a source with cultural value, which can be used for both economic interests as well as critical reflection. Such material recycles on metaloops well within the established overlapping of the two layers of the framework of culture (Figure 8.5). These feedback metaloops give way to specializations based on established traditions that have their own metalanguage (specialized

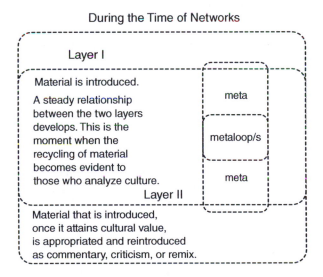

Figure 8.5 The framework of culture during the time of networks (meta stage)

methods and terms that support it as an institution). An example of this type of metaproduction searching for a critical position, that of resistance as defined in relation to culture, is the tradition of the avant-garde in the fine arts. The following sections shows how the framework of culture informs the very concept of the avant-garde, particularly the historical avant-garde and the neo-avant-garde. Both, as will become evident, developed out of cultural resistance, but they were eventually sublated by capital and presented in watered-down form to the mainstream.

Remixing the Avant-Garde

The avant-garde, according to Peter Bürger, can be separated into two major periods: the historical avant-garde and the neo-avant-garde. Bürger, in *Theory of the Avant-Garde*, argues that the historical avant-garde was active during the early part of the twentieth century. In this period he includes the Dadaists, the Futurists, as well as the Constructivists. These groups were historical because they were the first that overtly resisted art as an institution supported by the bourgeoisie, which, paradoxically, legitimized their practice; they not only searched for a "break with the traditional representational system but [also] the total abolition of the institution of art."[20] It was not the historical avant-garde but the neo-avant-garde, which was active after World War II, that attained full autonomy, but only through the negation of the historical avant-garde.[21] This negation was already at play in the historical avant-garde itself, and can be found in the works of Marcel Duchamp, whose signed urinal (*Fountain*) questioned art and negated individual production. This strategy was eventually incorporated as a vital element in art practice—and becomes expected in art production after Duchamp.[22] The avant-garde's negation is vital in the work of the neo-avant-garde, Bürger argues, because it solidified the autonomy that art attained thanks to bourgeois society; an autonomy that separated art from the rest of the world, due to its specialized role as the tool for the bourgeois to exercise self-reflection "that both reveals and obscures an actual historical development."[23]

The historical avant-garde was introduced in the first layer of the framework of culture; once it was absorbed and attained cultural value it became remixed and reintroduced as the neo-avant-garde. But once both terms became familiar, they began to function (as they do to this day) in terms of meta, meaning that both the historical and neo-avant-garde are fully assimilated and legitimated based on cultural value, which contributes to and depends upon Art as an institution. The very concept of the avant-garde, whether historical or neo, at the time of this writing, is no longer an act of resistance in itself—but, through the process of its institutionalization, has become an important account of resistance in history, which informs new forms of critical production. Arguably, if any artists were to call themselves avantgardists, it may sound somewhat romantic and even naïve because the term itself has lost its vernacular power; it now functions primarily as an institutional statement that fully legitimizes Art as both a culture and a market. This is the paradox of cultural production: as it becomes acknowledged, it also dies out, and becomes safe to discuss.

The historical and neo-avant-garde, then, function on a metalevel, in which already introduced material is yet again remixed and goes through various reintroductions and evaluations by art historians and theorists as well as artists, themselves, from the second half of the twentieth century.

Benjamin Buchloh and Hal Foster are particularly interested in the neo-avant-garde, and throughout the 1980s and 1990s revisited Bürger's propositions. Foster, like Bürger, considers the neo-avant-garde to start with postwar culture:

In postwar art to pose the question of repetition is to pose the question of the neo-avant-garde, a loose grouping of North American and Western European artists of the 1950s and 1960s who reprised such avant-garde devices of the 1910s and 1920s as collage and assemblage, the readymade and the grid, mono-chrome painting and constructed sculpture.[24]

Foster goes on to analyze works after the war as repetitions, that at times appear as "ciphers of alienation and reification"[25] which directly quoted the strategies originally tested by the historical avant-garde with almost no originality, complemented by an oedipal drive.

Benjamin Buchloh, on the other hand, considers the neo-avant-garde to start not immediately after World War II but around the 1960s. He sees conceptual art as the first true neo-avant-garde movement. According to Buchloh, art produced between 1968 and the mid-1970s is the first to break away from the paradigm of the historical avant-garde. For him, the neo-avant-garde does not mimic, or merely repeat strategies that were originally introduced by the historical avant-garde. This is the case with the work of Michael Asher and Daniel Buren, Marcel Broodthaers and Hans Haacke, to name a few from his list of artists who developed the strategies of "institutional critique."[26] Regardless of chronological differences, Buchloh, similarly to Foster, openly claims that Bürger places the neo-avant-garde in oedipal fashion in relation to the historical avant-garde.

In the cases of both Buchloh and Foster, the concepts of the historical avant-garde and neo-avant-garde are reevaluated as part of history. This means that the terms enjoy cultural value. The historical and neo-avant-garde, then, are functioning at a metalevel, at play well within established discourse, given that both concepts became contextualized with a specific theory by Bürger; by the time Buchloh and Foster discuss the meaning of the avant-garde, they are doing so as a type of update, which can still be critical and a real contribution to art as an institution, but this is not being done at the edges of the two layers, but well within established paradigms—in other words, material is being remixed in terms of discourse in order to develop a deeper understanding of history. The metaloop, functioning well within the established space of the two layers, does not really allow for much more. Understanding this issue leads people who are critical of scholarly research, but not necessarily reflective of this ongoing process, to call such work an "academic exercise" if the same subject is revisited more or less along the lines of those scholars who are known as experts in the field. This is actually necessary as a process of learning; one which is to be left behind once the knowledge is mastered. However, in part, it is when such repetition is not left behind, but used for career development and not the pursuit of knowledge, that scholarly research develops a stigma for being "academic."

This is a brief reflection on why much of historical criticism, and any critical analysis, becomes sublated once it begins to circulate between the two layers of the framework of culture, not pushing on the edges of either layer, but rather well within areas that are preestablished and are likely to produce material that appears innovative; but in the end is experimenting with source material that is already quite familiar to many people, which is why it has cultural value in the first place. To be clear, there is real value in this recycling, because it offers a space in which people can reevaluate their histories and contributions to the world.

This recycling has no definite end. In effect, the concept of the avant-garde has been revisited many times over and has found its way into new media practice in the writings of a few theorists. Julian Stallabrass, for instance, in his book *Internet Art: The Online Clash of Culture and Commerce*, written in 2003, presents net art as a clear manifestation of the avant-garde. Stallabrass sees net art as a new cultural field that offers real acts of resistance.[27] He contextualizes various works in the tradition of the avant-garde, including the works of the net.art group, that actually claimed an avant-garde position, during the early days of the Internet. Stallabrass notes:

> Many of the actual conditions of avant-gardism are present in online art: its anti-art character, its continual probing of the borders of art, and of art's separation from the rest of life, its challenge to the art institutions, genuine group activity, manifestos and collective programmes, and most of all an idea of forward movement (as opposed to one novelty merely succeeding another).[28]

Stallabrass follows this quote by directly citing Bürger's theory of the avant-garde in relation to net art practice, explaining that the models of the historical avant-garde that Bürger defined are at play once again in net art. Unlike Foster or Bürger, who take on a more or less detached position towards the avant-garde in general, Stallabrass sounds almost celebratory of Internet art throughout his book, as though net artists will achieve what previous avant-garde groups were unable to accomplish: to bring art back into culture at large; a struggle that is of interest to many of the historians who have contemplated the avant-garde.[29]

Stallabrass is also functioning at a metalevel similar to Buchloh and Foster; like them, he is recycling material that is already part of culture; which, as more and more historians and cultural critics write about the historical and neo-avant-garde, increases in cultural value to the point that it eventually supports the very institution both terms question and critique.

The Remix in Remix Culture

How and why the avant-garde is legitimated by a metaloop should be kept in mind in order to understand how this type of recycling also takes place in other areas of cultural production.

Lawrence Lessig, in his various books on remix culture written throughout the first decade of the twenty-first century, argues that during the first stages of the Internet, culture entered an unprecedented level of global creativity that, at the time, appeared to be open for a few years before it would be sublated by corporations who, according to Lessig would try to control it as they did television and radio.[30] Lessig made his most concise case for a read/write culture (his term) in his last book, *Remix: Making Art and Commerce Thrive in the Hybrid Economy*, based on this premise of control by corporations.[31] At the end of a presentation he gave at the 23C3's 2006 conference, one of his colleagues argued that all Lessig and his allies had to do was wait for the "all these guys my age and older" (as he called them) to die in about 20 years, and Lessig responded with excitement that at the time we did not have 20 years, that if we waited that long then the new culture produced with digital technology would effectively be absorbed into the preexisting media models.[32] Lessig argued that, at the time, we had about five years before the possibilities to produce remixes were controlled by corporations.

In this point, Lessig, himself may not be completely correct, for a reason that he himself cited in his book *The Future of Ideas*[33] and further expanded upon in his last book on remix published in 2008.[34] He explains that the exchange of ideas does not impoverish those who have ideas, but rather that ideas thrive when they are contemplated by others.[35] A friction implicit in this exchange is that once an idea is shared, it cannot be taken back (at least not yet, although sci-fi movies have been made about erasing and implanting memories).[36] In this sense the idea of being able to use networked communication creatively as we have been doing for over ten years is unlikely to go away. People will not allow this to happen to them, because they are not about to give up a habit that is part of their daily reality—but this does not mean that people are critical about the situation; as Clement Greenberg once observed about the avant-garde's position in relation to kitsch culture ("watered-down" culture) and totalitarianism:

> Kitsch keeps a dictator in closer contact with the "soul" of the people. Should the official culture be one superior to the general mass level, there would be danger of isolation.
>
> Nevertheless, if the masses were conceivably to ask for avant-garde art and literature, Hitler, Mussolini and Stalin would not hesitate long in attempting to satisfy such demand.[37]

As things have played out since Lessig expressed his concerns, it may not be necessary to take away the means to remix from people. Why culture will not go back to previous forms of communication that were at play before the Internet is because at the moment, the exchange and incessant appropriation of ideas have become part of the global economy itself. If anything, the ability of the consumer to speak up with great efficiency has recently become a ubiquitous tool for corporations' "quality assurance." The main reason why capital is able to thrive no matter what comes its way is because it is able to sublate expediently just about anything with the potential to generate profit.[38] In this sense, Lessig's argument that we have entered a hybrid economy is moot, because capital has always been a hybrid economy since its foundation: it is designed to absorb everything possible; in effect capital is merely assimilating the latest developments in culture at large to keep thriving. Capital is able to redefine itself into new models in order to meet the bottom line and create revenue. It is ruthless in achieving this. Understanding this foundational element of capital is pivotal to having a consistent critical stance as a cultural producer and to be capable of making real changes from within, as Dussel argues in his position in terms of postcoloniality.

Lessig's concern has been well exposed by Douglas Rushkoff in his Frontline documentaries *The Merchants of Cool* (2001) as well as *The Persuaders* (2005). Both documentaries show that during the first decade of the twenty-first century, corporations were always asking for feedback from the consumers.[39] While this might sound like a great thing, Rushkoff shows that corporations, like Viacom, owners of MTV, are not interested in understanding people's concerns. What they want, Rushkoff argues, is to understand what consumers desire in order to give it to them in the products that Viacom and similar corporations produce. The metaloop within the two layers of the framework of culture, previously discussed in relation to the avant-garde, is at play here, but in this case it is not developing a critical reflection; rather it produces a scheme for mass consumerism. Material is recycled primarily not because it is of cultural value (although it may well be), but because it is lucrative.

Both documentaries make evident that consumers are expected to share with corporations what they want via ever-growing forms of feedback. This was actually an early stage of a very efficient economic model which Rushkoff reports on in his latest broadcast documentary *Generation Like* (2014).[40] This documentary makes evident how social media expands the previous economic periods.

Generation Like focuses on Facebook to expose a new type of economy that drives online activity, and turns it into actual revenue for major corporations. Even Google's search engine thrives on this tendency when it records user search queries, and encourages its members to also become part of Google+, its own popular social media platform. The retrieval and analysis of information from these and other online spaces is known as data mining.

The metaloop within the two cultural layers of the framework of culture function, in this case, to produce ideology as the process of sublation leading to the dismissal of the previous form of resistance: to be *cool* was a form of rebelling by young individuals who may not have had critical conscience, or at least reflected self-consciously about what they consumed. Today, kids, tweens, and especially teenagers and young adults do not even know what it means "to sell out" as Rushkoff makes evident in *Generation Like* when he asks teenagers and young adults what the phrase means, and they answer playfully admitting that they do not know. We are clearly living in an environment in which consumers are expected to contribute material in order to consume. This is different from a not so distant period when consumers were expected to be skeptical of what was pitched to them, because they were aware of being manipulated. In *The Merchants of Cool*, Rushkoff shows a focus group of teenagers who express their dismissal of the soft drink Sprite, which around 2001 used sports stars to tell consumers not to drink the very soft drink the stars were advertising. The argument by Sprite, at the time, was that by doing so, the corporation was trying to deconstruct the problem of reaching their target customers (teenagers). This leads to a naturalized state of opining, which is now pivotal to the economy of social media. The twenty-first century user knows that she has the right to speak. However, it is not encouraged for this speaking to be critical, but merely to be expressed so that it can be data-mined for the sake of figuring out what to sell back to the people.

The Feedback Loop and the Future of Culture

The above analysis surveys how elements of resistance are made possible, questioned and eventually sublated via a feedback loop between the first two layers that form the framework of culture. Within this feedback loop are metaloops that allow for cultural and capital value to thrive. Some examples of how these loops function include the historicization of the avant-garde, as well as the development of social media as a new type of economy. These metaloops are so efficient that remixing material, as is commonly known in terms of material sampling, has reached a moment in which we produce almost as fast as we speak. As a result, we are self-aware of how we recycle ideas, information, and material production. The very act of making this observation shows that it is in the materialization of the immaterial—that is, in the careful measurement of the flow of ideas as they are embedded in different forms where there is potential for remix as a form of criticism and creative production to thrive while functioning well within the two layers of the framework of culture. Once individuals invested in cultural production remain critically conscious of this ongoing process of sublation and recycling of material and immaterial elements and objects, and how resistance itself thrives within the loops, it becomes possible to develop a critical position well within the very system being critiqued and challenged. Just as capitalists are well aware of the metaloops within the two layers of the framework of culture, and make the most of them for profit, cultural producers must become self-reflectively aggressive in using and appropriating the very same metaloops for the realization of a future that is rich in cultural production.

Notes

1 An analysis of ngrams of the terms "remix" and "remix culture" gaining major use during the mid to late 1990s can be found in Eduardo Navas, "Remix[ing] Sampling," *Remix Theory: The Aesthetics of Sampling* (Vienna: Springer, 2012), 26–27.

2 This concept was first introduced in my book *Remix Theory*, and has been expanded in various short articles since. For one of the most in-depth analyses on the framework of culture see, Eduardo Navas, "The New Aesthetic and The Framework of Culture," *Media-N Journal* 8, no. 2 (Fall 2012), http://median.newmediacaucus.org/blog/current-issue-fall-2012-v-08-n-02-december-2nd-2012/the-new-aesthetic-and-the-framework-of-culture/ (accessed May 10, 2014).

3 Terry Eagleton, "Versions of Culture" and "Culture in Crisis," *The Idea of Culture* (Oxford: Blackwell Publishing, 2000), 1–50.

4 Ibid., 1.

5 Raymond Williams, *Culture and Society 1780–1950* (New York: Harper, 1958), 296.

6 Ibid., 297.

7 Roland Barthes, "Necessity and Limits of Mythology," *Mythologies* (New York: Hill and Wang, 1972), 156–159.

8 Eagleton, "Versions of Culture," *The Idea of Culture*, 24–25.

9 Andrew Arato, "Esthetic Theory and Cultural Criticism," *The Essential Frankfurt School Reader* (New York: Urizen, 1978), 185.

10 Ibid.

11 Theodor Adorno, *The Culture Industry*, ed. J. M. Bernstein (New York: Routledge, 1991), 61–97.

12 Many books have been written about postmodernism. One of the most influential, arguably, is Fredric Jameson, *The Cultural Logic of Late Capitalism* (Durham, NC: Duke University, 1991).

13 Enrique Dussel, "Beyond Eurocentrism," *The Cultures of Globalization*, ed. Fredric Jameson (Durham, NC: Duke University Press, 1998), 13.

14 Ibid, 17.

15 Ibid, 19.

16 This section of the text is an expanded analysis originally published as part of the essay, Eduardo Navas "The Framework of Culture: Remix in Music, Art, and Literature," *Remix Theory*, http://remixtheory.net/?p=651.

17 This idea is summarized by Kirby Ferguson in his short film series, "Everything Is a Remix," http://www.everythingisaremix.info/watch-the-series/.

18 This is something that is commonly understood in the history of science. For a very basic book see Peter Dear, *Revolutionizing the Sciences: European Knowledge and Its Ambitions, 1500–1700* (Princeton, NJ: Princeton University Press, 2001).

19 See Eduardo Navas, "Regressive and Reflexive Mashups in Sampling Culture," *Remix Theory*, http://remixtheory.net/?p=444.

20 Peter Bürger "Avant-Gardist Work of Art," *Theory of the Avant-Garde*, trans. Michael Shaw (Minneapolis, MN: University of Minnesota Press, 1984), 63.

21 Ibid., 59.

22 Ibid., 51–53.

23 Ibid., 36.

24 Hal Foster, *The Return of the Real* (Cambridge, MA: MIT Press, 1999), 160.

25 Ibid.

26 Benjamin Buchloh, *Neo-Avantgarde and Culture Industry* (Cambridge, MA: MIT Press, 2000), xxiv.

27 Julian Stallabrass, *Internet Art: The Online Clash of Culture and Commerce* (London: Tate Publishing, 2003), 8–9.

28 Ibid., 35.

29 This is certainly the case for Buchloh and Foster. This contention is well exposed in Bürger's thesis; see, "Avant-Garde and Engagement" in *Theory of the Avante-Garde*, 83–94, and "Postscript to the German Edition," ibid., 95–99.

30 See Lawrence Lessig, *Code and Other Laws of Cyberspace* (New York: Penguin, 1999). Lawrence Lessig, *Free Culture* (New York: Penguin, 2004). Lawrence Lessig, *The Future of Ideas and Code 2.0* (New York: Vintage, 2001).

31 Lawrence Lessig, *Remix: Making Art and Commerce Thrive in the Hybrid Economy* (New York: Penguin Press, 2008).

32 Lawrence Lessig "Lawrence Lessig—On Free, and the Differences between Culture and Code (23c3)," presentation at the 23C3, Berlin, December, 2006, particularly at 1:08 and 14:26, https://archive.org/details/LawrenceLessig-OnFreeAndTheDifferencesBetweenCultureAndCode23c3 (accessed July 2014).

33 Lessig, *The Future of Ideas*, 8–11.

34 Lessig, *Remix*, 28–33.

35 Lessig, *The Future of Ideas*, 22–23.

36 Movies like *Total Recall*, TriStar Pictures, 1990, and *Paycheck*, Paramount Pictures, 2003, focus on manipulation of memory, something which is quite possible in the future with the development of cybernetics and nanotechnology.

37 Clement Greenberg, "Avant-Garde and Kitsch," *Clement Greenberg: The Collected Essays and Criticism, Volume 1* (Chicago, IL: University of Chicago, 1988), 20.

38 Terry Eagleton, *After Theory* (New York: Basic Books, 2003), 1–22.

39 Douglas Rushkoff, "The Merchants of Cool," *Frontline*, 2001, http://www.pbs.org/wgbh/pages/frontline/shows/cool. Also, "The Persuaders," *Frontline*, 2005, http://www.pbs.org/wgbh/pages/frontline/shows/.

40 Douglas Rushkoff, "Generation Like," *Frontline*, 2014, http://www.pbs.org/wgbh/pages/frontline/generation-like/.

Bibliography

Adorno, Theodor. *The Culture Industry*, edited by J. M. Bernstein. New York: Routledge, 1991.

Arato, Andrew. "Esthetic Theory and Cultural Criticism." In *The Essential Frankfurt School Reader*, edited by Andrew Arato and Eike Gebhardt. New York: Urizen, 1978.

Barthes, Roland. *Mythologies*. New York: Hill and Wang, 1972.

Buchloh, Benjamin H. D. *Neo-Avantgarde and Culture Industry: Essays on European and American Art from 1955 to 1975*. Cambridge, MA: MIT Press, 2000.

Bürger, Peter. *Theory of the Avant-Garde*. Translated by Michael Shaw. Minneapolis, MN: University of Minnesota Press, 1984.

Dear, Peter. *Revolutionizing the Sciences: European Knowledge and Its Ambitions, 1500–1700*. Princeton, NJ: Princeton University Press, 2001.

Dussel, Enrique. "Beyond Eurocentrism," *The Cultures of Globalization*, edited by Fredric Jameson, 3–32. Durham, NC: Duke University Press, 1998.

Eagleton, Terry. *After Theory*. New York: Basic Books, 2003.

——. *The Idea of Culture*. Oxford: Blackwell Publishing, 2000.

Ferguson, Kirby. "Everything is a Remix." http://www.everythingisaremix.info/watch-the-series/ (accessed May 10, 2014).

Foster, Hal. *The Return of the Real*. Cambridge, MA: MIT Press, 1999.

Greenberg, Clement. *Clement Greenberg: The Collected Essays and Criticism Volume 1*. Chicago, IL: University of Chicago Press, 1988.

Jameson, Fredric. *The Cultural Logic of Late Capitalism*. Durham, NC: Duke University, 1991.

Lessig, Lawrence. *Code and Other Laws of Cyberspace*. New York: Penguin, 1999.

——. *The Future of Ideas and Code 2.0*. New York: Vintage, 2001.

——. *Free Culture*. New York: Penguin, 2004.

——. *Remix: Making Art and Commerce Thrive in the Hybrid Economy*. New York: Penguin Press, 2008.

Navas, Eduardo. *Remix Theory: The Aesthetics of Sampling*. Vienna: Springer, 2012.

——. "The New Aesthetic and The Framework of Culture," *Media-N Journal* 8, no. 2 (Fall 2012): http://median.newmediacaucus.org/blog/current-issue-fall-2012-v-08-n-02-december-2nd-2012/the-new-aesthetic-and-the-framework-of-culture/ (accessed May 10, 2014).

——. "The Framework of Culture: Remix in Music, Art, and Literature." *Remix Theory*. http://remixtheory.net/?p=651 (accessed, May 10, 2014).

——. "Regressive and Reflexive Mashups in Sampling Culture." *Remix Theory*. http://remixtheory.net/?p=444 (accessed May 3, 2014).

Rushkoff, Douglas. "The Merchants of Cool," *Frontline*, 2001. http://www.pbs.org/wgbh/pages/frontline/shows/cool (accessed May 10, 2014).

——. "The Persuaders," *Frontline*, 2005. http://www.pbs.org/wgbh/pages/frontline/shows/persuaders (accessed May 10, 2014).

——. "Generation Like," *Frontline*, 2014. http://www.pbs.org/wgbh/pages/frontline/generation-like/ (accessed May 10, 2014).

Stallabrass, Julian. *Internet Art: The Online Clash of Culture and Commerce*. London: Tate Publishing, 2003.

Williams, Raymond. *Culture and Society 1780–1950*. New York: Harper, 1958.

Part II

AESTHETICS

9

REMIX STRATEGIES IN SOCIAL MEDIA

Lev Manovich

It is always more challenging to think theoretically about the present than the past. But this challenge is what also makes it very exciting. While each major release of Photoshop, Flash, Maya, Flame, and other commonly used applications continues to introduce dozens of new features and improvements of professional media authoring software that were largely shaped in the 1990s, these are incremental improvements rather than new paradigms.

> The author of this chapter refers to some online content that is no longer available or has been expired in newer software versions. However, the points made offer a historical perspective of remix studies that communicate effectively beyond the boundaries of software versions or dead links.

The new paradigms that emerge in the 2000s are not about new types of media software per se. Instead, they are about the exponential expansion of the number media producers—and the new function of the Web as a universal platform for non-professional media circulation. "Social software," "social media," "user-generated content," "Web 2.0," and "read/write Web" are some of the terms coined in this decade to capture these developments.

If visual communication professionals have adopted software-based tools and workflows throughout the 1990s, in the next decade "media consumers" gradually transformed into "media producers." The decline in prices and increase in the media capabilities of consumer electronics combined with the ubiquity of Internet access and with the emergence of new social media platforms have created a new media ecology and dynamic relationship between the media producer and consumer. In retrospect, if 1995 can be designated as the year of the professional media revolution (for example, the release of version 3 of After Effects this year included the ability to import Illustrator and Photoshop layers—enabling authors of motion graphics greater ease and flexibility in their workflows), I would center the consumer media revolution in 2005. During this year, photo and video blogging exploded; the term "user-generated content" (UGC) entered the mainstream; YouTube launched; and both Flickr and

See Chapter 32 for Jonah Brucker-Cohen's discussion of the aesthetics of remix projects.

MySpace were acquired by larger companies (Yahoo and Rupert Murdoch's News Corporation, respectively).

If the professional media revolution of the 1990s can be identified with a small set of software applications, the cultural software which enables new media ecology emerging in the middle of 2000s is much more diverse and heterogeneous. Media and communication software running on cellphones, tablets, and other consumer electronics devices, media sharing sites (Instagram, YouTube), social networking sites (Facebook), Web applications such as Google Docs, APIs of major Web 2.0 companies, blog publishing software (Blogger), microcontent platforms (Twitter), virtual globes (Google Earth, Microsoft Virtual Earth), consumer-level media editing and cataloging software (iPhoto) and, last but not least, search engines are just some of the categories impacting consumers and producers of digital culture. Add to these other software categories which are not directly visible to consumers but which are responsible for the networked-based media universe of sharing, remixing, collaboration, blogging, reblogging, and so on—everything from Web services and client-server architecture to Ajax and social media management dashboards—and the task of tracking cultural software today appears to be daunting. But it is not impossible.

This chapter considers different dimensions of the new paradigm of UGC and media sharing that emerged in the 2000s. My focus is on the relationships between the affordances provided by software interfaces and tools, the aesthetics and structure of media objects created with these tools, and the theoretical impact of software use on the very concept of media. In other words: what is "media" after software (for social networking and media sharing)? One key development is the integration of media production with its consumption: instead of dealing with separate media design applications, we now have to consider social media platforms such as Facebook and Twitter that integrate the functions of creating media, publishing it, remixing other people's media, discussing it, keeping up with friends and interest groups, meeting new people, and so on.

I look at the circulation, editing, and experience of media as components of communication structured by Web interfaces. Given that the term *remix* has already been widely used in discussing social media, I will use it as a starting point. I follow a strategy that helps reveal the parallels and highlight the differences between "remix culture" in general and software-enabled remix operations in particular. (If we don't do this and simply refer to everything today as "remix," we are not really trying to explain things anymore—we are just labeling them.) I discuss interfaces of different Web services to show how they create distinct user experiences, and how seemingly small differences can affect whether a media environment is perceived as a remix. I also investigate an essential condition for the emergence of remix culture from the early 1970s onward—the technological *modularity* of media—in order to explain new types of modularity and, correspondingly, new types of remix operations enabled by software. Finally, this chapter also analyzes another crucial dimension of the social media universe: *mobility*. (Mobility here refers not to the spatial movement of individuals and groups or the ability to access the Web on mobile devices, but to something else: *the new speed and scale of the circulation of media objects between people, devices, and the Web.*)

Remix, Montage, Collage: What's Next?

"Remixing" originally had a precise and narrow meaning limited to music. Although precedents of remixing can be found earlier, it was the introduction of multitrack mixers in 1950s that over next few decades made remixing music a standard practice. With each element of a song—vocals, drums, etc.—available for separate manipulation, it became possible to "re-mix" the song: change the volume of some tracks or substitute new tracks for the old ones. Gradually the term became more and more broad, today referring to any reworking of already existing cultural work(s).

In his book *DJ Culture* Ulf Poschardt singles out different stages in the evolution of remixing practice. In 1972 DJ Tom Moulton made his first disco remixes; as Poschardt points out, they

> show a very chaste treatment of the original song. Moulton sought above all a different weighting of the various soundtracks, and worked the rhythmic elements of the disco songs even more clearly and powerfully . . . Moulton used the various elements of the sixteen or twenty-four track master tapes and remixed them.[1]

By 1987, "DJs started to ask other DJs for remixes" and the treatment of the original material became much more aggressive. For example,

> Coldcut used the vocals from Ofra Hanza's "Im Nin Alu" and contrasted Rakim's ultra-deep bass voice with her provocatively feminine voice. To this were added techno sounds and a house-inspired remix of a rhythm section that loosened the heavy, sliding beat of the rap piece, making it sound lighter and brighter.[2]

The terms "montage" and "collage" come to us from literary and visual modernism of the early twentieth century—think of works by Pablo Picasso, László Moholy-Nagy, Sergey Eisenstein, Hannah Höch, or Raoul Hausmann. They do not always adequately describe contemporary electronic music. Let me note just three differences. First, musical samples are often arranged in loops. Second, the nature of sound allows musicians to mix preexisting sounds in a variety of ways, from clearly differentiating and contrasting individual samples (thus following the traditional modernist aesthetics of montage/collage), to mixing them into an organic and coherent whole. To borrow the terms from Roland Barthes we can say that if modernist collage always involved a "clash" of element, electronic and software collage also allows for "blend."[3] Third, the electronic musicians now often conceive their works beforehand as something that will be remixed, sampled, taken apart and modified. In other words, rather than sampling from mass media to create a unique and final artistic work (as in modernism), contemporary musicians use their own works and works by other artists in further remixes.

The revolution in electronic pop music that took place in the second part of the 1980s was paralleled by similar developments in pop visual culture. The introduction of electronic editing and image-creating equipment such as Switcher, Keyer, Paintbox, and Image Store made remixing and sampling a common practice in video production toward the end of the decade. First pioneered in music videos, it eventually later took over the whole visual culture of TV. Other software tools such as Photoshop (1989) and After Effects (1993) had the same effect on the fields of graphic design, motion graphics, commercial illustration, and photography. And, a few years later, the World Wide Web redefined an electronic document as a mix of other documents. Remix culture has arrived.

The question that at this point is really hard to answer is what comes after remix? Will we get eventually tired of cultural objects—be they dresses by Alexander McQueen, motion graphics by MK12 or songs by Aphex Twin—made from samples of preexisting databases of culture? And if we do, will it be still psychologically possible to create a new aesthetics that does not rely on excessive sampling? When I was emigrating from Russia to the US in 1981, moving from gray and red Communist Moscow to a vibrant and postmodern New York, I felt that the Communist regime would last for at least another 300 years. But within just ten years the Soviet Union ceased to exist. Similarly, in the middle of the 1990s the euphoria unleashed by the Web, the collapse of Communist governments in Eastern Europe and early effects of globalization created an impression that we have left Cold War culture behind—its heavily armed borders, massive spying, and the military-industrial complex. And once again, only ten years later it appeared that we are back in the darkest days of the Cold War—except that now we are being tracked with RFID chips, computer vision surveillance systems, data mining, and other new technologies of the twenty-first century. So it is very possible that remix culture, which right now appears to be so firmly in place that it can't be challenged by any other cultural logic, will morph into something else sooner than we think.

I don't know what comes after remix. But if we now try now to develop a better historical and theoretical understanding of the remix era and the technological platforms that enable it, we will be in a better position to recognize and understand the new era that will inevitably replace it.

The Remix of Things

Given the trends toward ubiquitous computing and "Internet of things," it is inevitable that the remixing paradigm will make its way into physical space as well. Bruce Sterling's brilliant book *Shaping Things* describes a possible future scenario where objects publish detailed information about their history, use, and impact on the environment, and ordinary consumers track this information.[4] I imagine a future RSS reader may give you a choice of billions of objects to track.

For a different take on how a physical space—in this case, a city—can reinvent itself via remix, consider coverage of Buenos Aires by *The*, the journal by "trend and future consultancy" The Future Laboratory.[5] *They* enthusiastically describe the city in remix terms—and while the desire to project a fashionable term on everything in sight is obvious, the result is actually mostly convincing. The copy reads as follows: "Buenos Aires has gone mashup. The porteños are adopting their traditions with some American sauce and European pepper." A local DJ, Villa Diamante, released an album that "mixes electronic music with cumcia, South American peasant music." A clothing brand, 12-na, "mixes flea-market finds with modern materials. And nonprofit publication project Eloisa Cartonea "combines covers painted by kids who collect the city's cardboard with the work of emerging writers and poets."

Remix practices extend beyond particular technologies and areas of culture. *WIRED* magazine devoted its July 2005 issue to the theme "Remix Planet." The introduction boldly stated: "From *Kill Bill* to Gorillaz, from custom Nikes to *Pimp My Ride*, this is the age of the remix."[6] Another top IT trend watcher in the world—the annual O'Reilly Emerging Technology conferences (ETECH) similarly adopted "Remix" as the theme for its 2005 conference. Attending the conference, I watched in amazement how top executives from Microsoft, Yahoo, Amazon, and other leading IT companies not precisely known for their avant-garde aspirations described their recent technologies and research projects using the concept of remix. If I had any doubts that we are living not simply in Remix Culture but in a Remix Era; they disappeared right at that conference.

Communication in a "Cloud"

During 2000s remix gradually moved from being one of the options to being treated as practically a new cultural default. The twentieth century paradigm in which a small number of professional producers sent messages over communication channels that they controlled to a much larger number of users was replaced by a new paradigm.[7] In this model, *a much large number of producers publish content into "a global media cloud"; the users create personalized mixes by choosing from this cloud.*[8] A significant percentage of these producers and users overlap, i.e., they are the same people. Furthermore, a user can also select when and where to view her news—a phenomenon that has come to be known as "timeshifting" and "placeshifting." Another feature of the new paradigm, which I will discuss in detail below, is what I call "media mobility." A message never arrives at some final destination as in a broadcasting/mass publishing model. Instead, a message continues to move between sites, people, and devices. As it moves, it accumulates comments and discussions. Frequently, its parts are extracted and remixed with parts of other messages to create new messages.

The arrival of a new paradigm has been reflected in and supported by a set of new terms. The twentieth century terms "broadcasting," "publishing," and "reception" have been joined (and in many contexts, replaced), by new terms that describe operations now possible in relation to media messages, such as "narrowcasting," "UGC," and "Like." They also include: embed, annotate, comment, respond, syndicate, aggregate, upload, download, rip, and share.

There are a number of interesting things worth noting in relation to this new vocabulary. First, the new terms are more discriminating than the old ones as they now name many specific operations involved in communication. You don't simply "receive" a message; you can also annotate it, comment on it, remix it, etc. Second, most of the new terms describe new types of users' activities which were either not possible with the old media or were strictly marginal (for instance, a marginal practice of "slash" videos made by science fiction fans). Third, if old terms such as "read," "view," and "listen" were media-specific, the new ones are not. For instance, you can "comment" on a blog, a photo, a video, a slide show, a map, etc. Similarly, you can "share" a video, a photo, an article, a map layer, and so on. This media-indifference of the terms indirectly reflects the media-indifference of the underlying software technologies. In effect, the important theme in the development of cultural software has been the development of new information management principles and techniques—such as Doug Englebardt's "view control"—which work in the same way on many types of media. Among these new terms, "remix" (or "mix") occupies a major place. As the user-generated media content (video, photos, music, maps) on the Web exploded in 2005, an important semantic switch took place. The terms "remix" (or "mix") and "mashup" started to be used in contexts where previously the term "editing" had been standard—for instance, when referring to a user editing a video. When in the spring of 2007 Adobe released video editing software for users of the popular media-sharing website Photobucket, it named the software Remix. (The software was actually a stripped down version of one of the earliest video editing applications for PCs called Premiere.[9]) Similarly, Jumpcut, a free video editing and hosting site, does not use the word "edit."[10] Instead, it puts forward "remix" as the core creative operation: "You can create your own movie by remixing someone else's movie." Another popular online open-source video editing service Kaltura also uses the term "remix," or "mashup" instead of "edit" (as of spring 2008).[11]

The new social communication paradigm where millions are publishing "content" into the "cloud" and an individual curates her personal mix of content drawn from this cloud would be impossible without new types of consumer applications, new software features and underlying software standards and technologies such as RSS. To make a parallel with the term "cloud computing," we can call this paradigm "communication in a cloud." If "cloud computing enables users and developers to utilize [IT] services without knowledge of, expertise with, nor control over the technology infrastructure that supports them,"[12] software developments of the 2000s similarly enable content creators and content receivers to communicate without having to deeply understand underlying technologies.

Another reason why a metaphor of a "cloud"—which at first appears vague—may also be better for describing communication patterns in the 2000s than the "Web" has to do with the changes in the patterns of information flow between the original Web and so-called Web 2.0. The lack of a more sophisticated technology for "receiving" the Web in its original format was not an omission on the part of the Web's architect Tim Berners-Lee—it is just that nobody anticipated that the number of websites would explode exponentially.[13]

In the communication model that emerged after 2000, information is becoming more atomized. You can access individual atoms of information without having to read/view the larger packages in which it is enclosed (a TV program, a music CD, a book, a website, etc.). Additionally, information is gradually becoming presentation- and device-independent—it can be received using a variety of software and hardware technologies and stripped from its original format. Thus, while websites continue to flourish, it is no longer necessary to visit each site individually to access their content.

The software technologies used to send information into the cloud are complemented by software that allows people to curate (or "mix") the information sources they are interested in. Software in this category is referred to as newsreaders, feed readers, or aggregators. Examples include separate Web-based feed readers such as Bloglines and Google Reader; all popular Web browsers that also provide functions to read feeds; desktop-based feed readers such as NetNewsWire; and personalized home pages such as live.com and My Yahoo!

Finally, if feed technologies turned the original Web of interlinked Web pages sites into a more heterogeneous and atomized global "cloud" of content, other software developments helped to make this cloud rapidly grow in size.[14] It is not accidental that during the period when "user-generated content" started to grow exponentially, the interfaces of most consumer-level media applications came to prominently feature buttons and options which allow for the upload of new media documents into the "cloud." For example, iPhoto groups functions which allow the user to email photos, or upload them to her blog or website (under a top level "Share" menu). Similarly, Windows Live Photo Gallery includes "Publish" and "E-mail" among its top menu bar choices. Meanwhile, the interfaces of social media sites were given buttons to easily move content around the "cloud," so to speak—emailing it to others, embedding it in one's website or blog, linking it, posting to one's account on other popular social media sites, etc.

Regardless of how easy it is to create one personal mix of information sources—even if it only takes a single click—the practically unlimited number of these sources now available on the "cloud" means that manual ways of selecting among these sources become limited in value. Enter the automation. From the very beginning, computers were used to automate various processes. Over time, everything—factory work, flying planes, financial trading, or cultural processes—is gradually subjected to automation.[15] However, algorithmic automated reasoning on the Web arrived so quickly that it hardly has ever been publically discussed. We take it for granted that Google and other search engines automatically process tremendous amounts of data to deliver search results. We also take it for granted that Google's algorithms automatically insert ads in Web pages by analyzing pages' content. Flickr uses its own algorithm to select the photos it calls "interesting."[16] Pandora, Musicovery, OWL music search, and many other similar Web services automatically create music programs based on the users' musical likes. Digg automatically pushes the stories up based on how many people have voted for them. Amazon and Barnes & Noble use collaborative filtering algorithms to recommend books; Last.fm and iTunes—to recommend music, Netflix—to recommend movies; StumbleUpon—to recommend websites; and so on.[17] In contrast to these systems that provide recommendations by looking at the users that have similar rating patterns, Mufin is fully an automatic recommendation software for music which works by matching songs based on 40 attributes such as tempo, instruments, and percussion.[18]

The use of automation to create mixes from hundreds of millions of information sources is just beginning. (The following examples refer to the state of the art in summer 2008.) One already popular service is the Google News site that algorithmically assembles "news" by remixing material gathered from thousands of news publications. (As it is usually the case with algorithms used by Web companies, when I checked last there was no information on the Google News website about the algorithm used, so we know nothing about its selection criteria or what counts as important and relevant news.) Newspond similarly automatically aggregates news, and it similarly discloses little about the process. According to its website, "Newspond's articles are found and sorted by real-time global popularity, using a fully automated news collection engine."[19] Spotplex assembles news from blogosphere using yet another type of automation: counting most read articles within a particular time frame.[20] Going further, news.ask.com not only automatically selects the news but it also provides BigPicture pages for each news story containing relevant articles, blog posts, images, videos, and diggs.[21] News.ask.com also tells us that it selects news stories based on four factors—breaking, impact, media, and discussion—and it actually shows how each story rates in terms of these factors. Another kind of algorithmic "news remix" is performed by the Web-art application 10×10 by Jonathan Harris. It presents a grid of news images based on the algorithmic analysis of news feeds from *The New York Times*, the BBC, and Reuters.[22]

Remix Versus Collection

Given the wide adoption of the term "remix" to describe many different cultural practices and technologies, do all of them actually qualify as remix? For instance, is the content automatically assembled by Google News, or manually by using an RSS reader actually constituted as a remix? Or shall we more accurately describe it as "collection" achieved through "selection," or perhaps "curation"? After all, it would be a stretch to call one's personal library a "remix" of the bookstore. Or would it?

In order to better differentiate between "selecting" and "remixing," let's compare contemporary online news portals with their predecessors—twentieth century newspapers. Consider a typical front page. To produce this page, the editors and designers did more than simply select a smaller number of content items from a larger set available. They also designed the page. The layout, the choice of photographs and headings, the relative size of the fonts—everything was carefully selected and edited. Just as is the case with any artwork which uses preexisting media content to create a new composition, a newspaper page aims to communicate distinct meanings and emotions by arranging its content in particular ways. For me, it is an example of a remix in the twentieth century meaning of this word.

What is this meaning? A twentieth century "remix" is a particular case of a modern artistic composition (or "work") in general. The key difference is the origin of parts. In a modern(ist) artwork, these parts are created specifically for this composition. In remix, they are selected from a larger, already existing set.

Therefore, we can define remix in this way: a composition that consists of previously existing parts assembled, which is edited to create particular aesthetic, semantic, and/or bodily effects.

Now that I have defined remix, I can formally state *the difference between* "selecting" and "remixing." When confronted with any set of items, no matter what its original purpose and method of production, gestalt psychology holds that a human mind will always try to establish some relationships between these items. For instance, if I have a personal library, I will think of the semantic relationships between the books on my bookshelves. *In the case of a collection, the defining relationships are those between the items that are present and other potential items that are absent.* My bookshelf can hold a limited number of books, so I always wonder about other "must have" books that I did not buy. Similarly, the collection of bookmarks in my browser is a selection from billions of pages on the Web. The collection consists of the pages that are important to me.

To generalize from these examples, we can say that a collection is created by *reduction* of a set of all possible items. Another crucial feature of a collection is that the order between any individual is not important. Think of an Excel spreadsheet which can be sorted by any column. Whatever order you may have defined is relative and can be changed at any time. Similarly, while the categories that I use to organize my bookmarks do matter, the order in which bookmarks appear within a particular folder is usually irrelevant. Thus, a key feature that signals that we are dealing with an artistic composition—the importance of the arrangement of parts—is absent.

In a remix, the defining relations are between the elements that are present. When you listen to a music remix, look at photo-collage, watch a fan video, or use a software mashup, you usually don't wonder about all other songs, photos, videos, or data sources which could have been used. Instead, you are focused on the effect produced by the arrangement of parts that are present.

This analysis, which foregrounds the absent–present dimension, may appear to be identical to the one I provided in *The Language of New Media* when I discussed the differences between a narrative and a database. However, it is different. In a syntagmatic structure such as a sentence or narrative the relationships are between present elements and *similar elements that could have been used in their place.* For instance, in a sentence "I have attended an interesting conference" there are certain other adjectives that can be used instead of "interesting" while maintaining the same grammatical structure and still keeping the statement meaningful. However, a set of items (such as a personal library) does not have an inherent grammatical structure. Consequently, in a collection we have relationships between present items and all other items available. Therefore, a collection is not a syntagm.

In practice, the differences between selecting and remixing are often quite subtle. What this means in practical terms is that we should not make decisions a priori about whole cultural practices being collections or remixes. Instead, we should consider each case individually to decide where it belongs on the spectrum of the collection/remix dimension. For instance, let's compare Google Reader and iGoogle.[23] Google Reader is a Web-based feeds reader; iGoogle is a customized home page that can display feeds along with gadgets (miniapplications which can show weather, currency rates, new emails, etc.). Although both applications have similar functionality, the interface of Google's Reader produces a "collection," while the interface of iGoogle creates a "remix."

Google Reader presents feeds as a linear list. While the user can sort the feeds in a few ways and switch between an expanded view and list view, displaying full posts or displaying only headlines, Reader sticks to its preferred way of organizing information along a single vertical dimension, with the entries displayed one below another. For me this feels like a collection. When I use such interfaces, the relations between what is present and what is absent become quite important—between the feeds which I have subscribed to and all other subscriptions available on the Internet; between the items I have already read and those I did not. And while the ways in which I organize feeds into folders or tag them does affect how I think about them, I'm not creating a new composition based on the original feeds as I am in iGoogle. At any point I can filter this set by using a search box. And since the search allows me to reorganize my set of items in a multitude of ways, whatever higher levels of organization I impose on these items (folders, tags) becomes less relevant. Thus, it is the presence of the search box in a Google Reader interface that ultimately makes the set of feeds in its window a collection rather than a remix. With a search function available, the only two things that are truly relevant are (1) what is the body of information a search can be applied to, and (2) the options the search software provides.

In contrast, I think of the contents in my iGoogle page as a remix. Why? The iGoogle interface allows me to arrange feeds and gadgets over two dimensions of the page—horizontally and vertically. In other words, I can create a composition made from parts. Thus, arranging the elements on iGoogle page is more like arranging objects and furniture in one's room than reading a newspaper or a news ticker (which is what using feed readers often feels like).

Why is arranging elements on an iGoogle page so important in contrast to the Google Reader experience? Because with iGoogle, I can't search the contents of its page (or pages, since iGoogle allows me to organize information over a number of pages linked by tabs). Therefore it really matters where I put the gadgets in relation to each other. The position of each element's frame reflects my habits and how I think about the information available to me. Taken together, the frames on my home page add up to a gestalt—an organized whole which mirrors the structure of my thinking and behavior.

As I mentioned before starting this discussion of the examples of Google Reader and iGoogle, the details of their interfaces are likely to change by the time you read this—of course, you can always use the Way Back Machine to look at the old versions of the websites. However, I hope that the principle, i.e., the distinction between a remix and a collection, will continue to be applicable to new interface designs.

So far I have talked about remix technologies that allow a user to assemble pieces of content from different sources into a single place. What about these pieces themselves? If the old communication paradigm where professionally produced messages moved in linear and finite paths from producers to consumers was replaced by the "communication in a cloud" paradigm, did this also affect the identity of individual messages?

It has indeed. I think that it is legitimate to think of a great deal of "user-generated content" (UGC) as a result of various remix operations. (In other words, the frequent use of "remix" to describe UGC is justified.)

1. The bloggers who commonly republish materials from other sources while adding their own comments are in fact practicing a particular kind remix. In these cases, the modification of the original content—common to all types of remixes—takes the form of commentary.
2. A significant part of UGC available online is produced by users who directly remix media material produced by professionals. For instance, the genre of anime music videos involves creatively combining music ripped from professional music videos and pieces of anime edited together.
3. A common personal blog is a remix of material drawn from other sources and assembled on one site (typically with some comments); this remix is available to others, who in turn may be creating their own remixes. In this respect, it is important that blog software allows for the modularity of each post—facilitating its reuse in other blogs. The same goes for other Web technologies such as "permalink" and the use of "share" buttons on social media sites. The availability of these tools around each piece of media content gives strong encouragement to users to include this content in their own remixes.

Remixability and Modularity

The dramatic increase in the availability of information greatly speeded up by the Web has been accompanied by another fundamental development. Imagine water running down a mountain. If the quantity of water keeps continuously increasing, it will find numerous new paths and these paths will keep getting wider. Something similar is happening as the amount of information keeps growing—except these paths are also all connected to each other and they go in all directions; up, down, sideways. Here are some of these paths, which facilitate the movement of information between people, listed in no particular order: SMS, forward and redirect buttons in email applications, mailing lists, Web links, RSS, blogs, social bookmarking, tagging, publishing (as in publishing one's playlist on a website), peer-to-peer networks, Web services, USB 3.0, Bluetooth. These paths stimulate people to draw information from all kinds of sources into their own space, remix, and make it available to others, and collaborate or at least play on a common information platform (Wikipedia, Flickr). Barb Dybwad introduced a nice term "collaborative remixability'" to talk about this process:

> I think the most interesting aspects of Web 2.0 are new tools that explore the continuum between the personal and the social, and tools that are endowed with a certain flexibility and modularity which enables collaborative remixability—a transformative process in which the information and media we've organized and shared can be recombined and built on to create new forms, concepts, ideas, mashups and services."[24]

If a traditional twentieth century model of cultural communication described the movement of information in one direction from a source to a receiver, now the reception point is just a temporary station on information's path. If we compare information or media objects with a train, then each receiver can be compared to a train station. Information arrives, gets remixed with other information, and then the new package travels to other destination where the process is repeated.

We can find precedents for this "remixability"—for instance, in modern electronic music where remix has become the key method of creation since the 1980s. More generally, most human cultures developed by borrowing and reworking forms and styles from other cultures; the resulting "remixes" were later incorporated into other cultures. Ancient Rome remixed Ancient Greece; Renaissance remixed antiquity; nineteenth century European architecture remixed many historical periods including the Renaissance; and today graphic and fashion designers remix numerous historical and local cultural forms, from Japanese Manga to traditional Indian clothing.

At first glance it may seem that remixability as practiced by designers and other culture professionals is quite different from "vernacular" remixability made possible by the software-based techniques described above. Clearly, a professional designer working on a poster or a professional musician working on a new mix is different from somebody who is writing a blog entry or publishing her bookmarks.

But this is a wrong view. The perceived two kinds of remixability—professional and vernacular—are part of the same continuum, for the designer and musician are equally affected by the same software technologies. Design software and music composition software make the technical operation of remixing very easy; the Web greatly increases the ease of locating and reusing material from other periods, artists, designers, and so on. Even more importantly, since every company and freelance professional in all cultural fields, from motion graphics to architecture to fashion, publish documentation of their projects on their websites, everybody can keep up with what everybody else is doing. Therefore, although the speed with which a new original architectural solution starts showing up in projects of other architects and architectural students is much slower than the speed with which an interesting blog entry gets referenced in other blogs, the difference is quantitative, not qualitative. Similarly, when H&M or Gap can "reverse engineer" the latest fashion collection by a high-end design label in only two weeks, this is an example of the same cultural remixability sped up by software and networked culture. In short, a person simply copying parts of a message into the new email she is writing, and the largest media and consumer company recycling designs of other companies are doing the same thing—they are practicing remixability.

Remixability does not require modularity (i.e., the organization of cultural objects into clearly separable parts)—but it greatly benefits from it. For example, as already discussed above, remixing in music became popular after the introduction of multitrack equipment. With each song element available on its own track, substituting tracks in new compositions becomes commonplace.

In most cultural fields today we have a clear-cut separation between libraries of elements designed to be sampled—stock photos, graphic backgrounds, music, software libraries—and the cultural objects that incorporate these elements. For instance, a design for a corporate report or an ad may use photographs that the designer purchased from a photo stock house. But this fact is not advertised; similarly, the fact that this design (if it is successful) will be inevitably copied and sampled by other designers is not openly acknowledged by the design field. The only fields where sampling and remixing are done openly are music and computer programming, where developers rely on software libraries in writing new software.

Will the separation between libraries of samples and "authentic" cultural works blur in the future? Will the future cultural forms be deliberately made from discrete samples designed to be copied and incorporated into other projects? It is interesting to imagine a cultural ecology where all kinds of cultural objects, regardless of the medium or material, are made from Lego-like building blocks. The blocks come with complete information necessary to easily copy and paste them in a new object—either by a human or machine. A block knows how to couple with other blocks—and it even can modify itself to enable such coupling. The block can also tell the designer and the user about its cultural history—the sequence of historical borrowings which led to the present form. And if the original Lego (or a typical twentieth century housing project) contains only a few kinds of blocks that make all objects one can design with the Lego rather similar in appearance, software can keep track of unlimited number of different blocks.

One popular twentieth century notion of cultural modularity involved artists, designers, or architects making finished works from the small vocabulary of elemental shapes, or other modules. Whether we are talking about the construction industry, Kandinsky's geometric abstraction, or modular furniture systems, the underlying principle is the same. The scenario I am entertaining proposes a very different kind of modularity that may appear like a contradiction in terms. It is modularity without a prior defined vocabulary. In this scenario, any well-defined part of any finished cultural object can automatically become a building block for new objects in the same medium. Parts can even "publish" themselves and other cultural objects can "subscribe" to them the way you subscribe now to RSS feeds or podcasts.

When we think of modularity today, we assume that a number of objects that can be created in a modular system is limited. Indeed, if we are building these objects from a very small set of blocks, there are a limited number of ways in which these blocks can go together. (Although as the relative physical size of the blocks in relation to the finished object get smaller, the number of different objects which can be built increases: think an IKEA modular bookcase versus a Lego set.) However, in my imaginary scenario modularity does not involve any reduction in the number of forms that can be generated. On the contrary, if the blocks themselves are created using one of many already developed software-based design methods (such as parametric design), every time they are used again they can modify themselves automatically to ensure that they look different. In other words, if pre-software-modularity leads to repetition and reduction, post-software-modularity can produce unlimited diversity.

I think that such "real time" or "on demand" modularity can only be imagined today after various large-scale projects created at the turn of the century—online stores such as Amazon, blog indexing services such as Technorati, buildings such as Yokohama International Port Terminal by Foreign Office Architects and Walt Disney Concert Hall in Los Angeles by Frank Gehry—visibly demonstrated that we can develop hardware and software to coordinate massive numbers of cultural objects and their building blocks: books, blog entries, construction parts. Whether we will ever have such a cultural ecology is not important. We often look at the present by placing it within long historical trajectories. But I believe that we can also productively use a different, complementary method. We can imagine what will happen if the contemporary techno-cultural conditions which are already firmly established are pushed to their logical limit. In other words, rather than placing the present in the context of the past, we can look at it in the context of a logically possible future. This "look from the future" approach may illuminate the present in a way not possible if we only "look from the past." The sketch of a logically possible cultural ecology I just made is a little experiment in this method: futurology or science fiction as a method of contemporary cultural analysis.

So what else can we see today if we will look at it from this logically possible future of "total remixability" and universal modularity? If my scenario sketched above looks like a "cultural science fiction," consider the process that is already happening at one end of the remixability continuum. This process is a gradual atomization of information on the Web that we already touched on earlier in this chapter. New software technologies separate content from particular presentation formats, devices, and the larger cultural "packages" where it is enclosed by the producers. (For instance, consider how iTunes and other online music stores changed the unit of music consumption from a record/CD to a single music track.) In particular, the wide adoption and standardization of feed formats allows cultural bits to move around more easily—changing a Web into what I call a "communication cloud." The increased modularity of content allowed for a wide adoption of remix as a preferred way of receiving it (although, as we saw, in many cases it is more appropriate to call the result a collection rather than a true remix).

The Web was invented by the scientists for scientific communication, and at first it was mostly text and "bare-bones" HTML. Like any other markup language, HTML was based on the principle of modularity (in this case, separating content from its presentation). And of course, it also brought a new and very powerful form of modularity: the ability to construct a single document from parts that may reside on different Web servers. During the period of the Web's commercialization (the second part of the 1990s), twentieth century media industries that were used to producing highly structured information packages (books, movies, records, etc.) similarly pushed the Web toward highly coupled and difficult-to-take-apart formats such as those developed for the Shockwave player, first created by Macromedia Flash. However, since approximately 2000, we see a strong move in the opposite direction: from intricately packaged and highly designed "information objects" (or "packages") which are hard to take apart—such as websites made in Flash—to "straight" information: ASCII text files, RSS feeds, blog posts, KML files, SMS messages, and microcontent. As Richard MacManus and Joshua Porter wrote in 2005,

> Enter Web 2.0, a vision of the Web in which information is broken up into "microcontent" units that can be distributed over dozens of domains. The Web of documents has morphed into a Web of data. We are no longer just looking to the same old sources for information. Now we're looking to a new set of tools to aggregate and remix microcontent in new and useful ways.[25]

And it is much easier to "aggregate and remix microcontent" if it is not locked by a design. An ASCII file, a JPEG image, a map, a sound or video file can move around the Web and enter into user-defined remixes such as a set of RSS feed subscriptions; cultural objects where the parts are locked together (such as Flash interface) can't. In short, in the era of Web 2.0, we can state that *information wants to be ASCII.* If we approach the present from the perspective of a potential future of "ultimate modularity/remixability," we can see other incremental steps toward this future which are already occurring.

Creative Commons developed a set of flexible licenses that give the producers of creative work in any field more options than the standard copyright terms. The licenses have been widely used by individuals, nonprofits and companies—from MIT Open Course Initiative and Australian Government to Flickr and blip.tv. The available types include Attribution-ShareAlike (CC BY-SA), which "lets others remix, tweak, and build upon your work even for commercial purposes, as long as they credit you and license their new creations under the identical terms."[26]

In 2005 a team of artists and developers from around the world set out to collaborate on an animated short film *Elephants Dream* using only open-source software;[27] after the film was completed, all production files from the move (3D models, textures, animations, etc.) were published on a DVD along with the film itself.[28]

Flickr offers multiple tools to combine multiple photos (not broken into parts—at least so far) together: tags, sets, groups, Organizr. The Flickr interface thus positions each photo within multiple "mixes." Flickr also offers "notes" which allows the users to assign short notes to individual parts of a photograph. To add a note to a photo posted on Flickr, you draw a rectangle on any part of the phone and then attach some text to it. A number of notes can be attached to the same photo. I read this feature as another sign of the modularity/remixability paradigm, as it encourages users to mentally break a photo into separate parts. In other words, "notes" break a single media object—a photograph—into blocks.

In a similar fashion, the common interface of DVDs breaks a film into chapters. Media players such as iPod and online media stores such as iTunes break music CDs into separate tracks—making a track into a new basic unit of musical culture. In all these examples, what was previously a single coherent cultural object is broken into separate blocks that can be accessed individually. In other words, if "information wants to be ASCII," "content wants to be modular." And culture as a whole? Culture has always been about remixability—but now this remixability is available to all participants of Web culture.

Since the introduction of the first Kodak camera, "users" had tools to create massive amounts of vernacular media. Later they were given amateur film cameras, tape recorders, video recorders . . . But the fact that people had access to "tools of media production" for as long as the professional media creators until recently did not seem to play a big role: the amateur and professional media pools did not mix. Professional photographs traveled between a photographer's darkroom and newspaper editor; private pictures of a wedding traveled between members of the family. But the emergence of multiple and interlinked paths which encourage media objects to easily travel between websites, recording and display devices, hard drives and flash drives, and, most importantly, people changes things. Remixability becomes practically a built-in feature of digital networked media universe. In a nutshell, what may be more important than the introduction of a video iPod (2001), YouTube (2005), the first consumer 3-CCD camera which can record full HD video (HD Everio GZ-HD7, 2007), or yet another exiting new device or service is how easy it is for media objects to travel between all these devices and services—which now all become just temporary stations in media's Brownian motion.

Modularity and the "Culture Industry"

Although we have witnessed a number of important new types of cultural modularity that emerged in the software era, it is important to remember that modularity is something that only applies to RSS, social bookmarking, or Web services. We are talking about the larger cultural logic that extends beyond the Web and digital culture.

Modularity has been the key principle of modern mass production. That is, mass production is possible because of the standardization of parts and how they fit with each other—i.e., modularity. Although there are historical precedents for mass production, until the twentieth century they have been separate historical cases. But after Ford installed the first moving assembly lines at his factory in 1913, others followed.[29] Soon modularity permeated most areas of modern society.

Today we are still living in an era of mass production and mass modularity, and globalization and outsourcing only strengthen this logic. One commonly evoked characteristic of globalization is greater connectivity—places, systems, countries, organizations, etc. becoming connected in more and more ways. Although there are ways to connect things and processes without standardizing and modularizing them—and the further development of such mechanisms is probably essential if we ever want to move beyond all the grim consequences of living in a standardized modular world produced by the twentieth century—for now it appears so much easier just to go ahead and apply the twentieth century logic. Because society is so used to it, it is not even thought of as one option among others.

In November 2005 I was at a Design Brussels event where well-known designer Jerszy Seymour speculated that once Rapid Manufacturing systems become advanced, cheap, and easy, this will give designers in Europe hope for survival. Today, as Seymour pointed out, as soon as some design becomes successful, a company wants to produce it in large quantities—and its production goes to China. He suggested that when Rapid Manufacturing and similar technologies were installed locally, the designers would become their own manufacturers and everything could happen in one place. But obviously this will not happen tomorrow, and it is also not at all certain that Rapid Manufacturing will ever be able to produce complete finished objects without humans being involved in the process.

Of course, modularity principles did not remain unchanged since the beginning of mass production some hundred years ago. Think of just-in-time manufacturing, just-in-time programming or the use of standardized containers for shipment around the world since the 1960s (over 90 percent of all goods in the world today are shipped in these containers). The logic of modularity seems to be permeating more layers of society than ever before, and software—which is great at keeping track of numerous parts and coordinating their movements—only helps this process.

The logic of culture often runs behind the changes in economy (resulting in an uneven development)—so while modularity has been the basis of modern industrial society since the early twentieth century, we have only started to see the modularity principle in cultural production and distribution on a large scale in the last few decades. While Adorno and Horkheimer were writing about the "culture industry" in the early 1940s, it was not then—just as it is not today—a true modern industry.[30] In some areas such as the large-scale production of Hollywood animated features or computer games we see more of the factory logic at work with extensive division of labor. In the case of software engineering, software is put together to a large extent from already available software modules—but this is done by individual programmers or teams who often spend months or years on one project, which is quite different from the Ford production line model that was assembling one identical car after another in rapid succession. In short, today cultural modularity has not reached the systematic character of the industrial standardization circa 1913.

But this does not mean that modularity in contemporary culture simply lags behind industrial modularity. Rather, cultural modularity seems to be governed by a different logic. In terms of packaging and distribution, "mass culture" has indeed achieved complete industrial-type standardization. In other words, all the material carriers of cultural content in the twentieth century have been standardized, just as it was done in the production of all other goods—from the first photo and film formats at the end of the nineteenth century to game cartridges, DVDs, memory cards, interchangeable camera lenses, and so on today. But the actual making of content was never standardized in the same way. In "Culture Industry Reconsidered," Adorno writes:

> The expression 'industry' is not to be taken too literally. It refers to the standardization of the thing itself—such as that of the Western, familiar to every movie-goer—and to the rationalization of distribution techniques, but not strictly to the production process . . . it [culture industry] is industrial more in a sociological sense, in the incorporation of industrial forms of organization even when nothing is manufactured—as in the rationalization of office work—rather than in the sense of anything really and actually produced by technological rationality.[31]

So while culture industries, at their worst, continuously put out seemingly new cultural products (films, television programs, songs, games, etc.) which are created from a limited repertoire of themes, narratives, icons, and other elements using a limited number of conventions, these products are conceived by the teams of human authors on a one-by-one basis—not by software. In other words, while software has been eagerly adopted to help automate and make more efficient lower levels of the cultural production (such as generating in-between frames in an animation or keeping track of all files in a production pipeline), humans continue to control the higher levels, which means that the semiotic modularity of cultural industries' products—i.e., their Lego-like construction from mostly preexistent elements already familiar to consumers—is not something acknowledged or thought about.

The trend toward the reuse of cultural assets in commercial culture, i.e., media franchising—characters, settings, icons which appear not in one but a whole range of cultural products—film sequels, computer games, theme parks, toys, etc.—does not seem to change this basic "preindustrial" logic of the production process. For Adorno, the individual character of each product is part of the ideology of mass culture: "Each product affects an individual air; individuality itself serves to reinforce ideology, in so far as the illusion is conjured up that the completely reified and mediated is a sanctuary from immediacy and life."[32]

Neither the fundamental reorganization of culture industries around software-based production in the 1990s nor the rise of user-generated content and social media paradigms in the 2000s threatened the Romantic ideology of an artist-genius. However, what seems to be happening is that the "users" themselves have been gradually "modularizing" culture. In other words, modularity has been coming into mass culture from the outside, so to speak, rather than being built in, as in industrial production. In the 1980s musicians started sampling already published music; TV fans start sampling their favorite TV series to produce their own "slash films," game fans started creating new game levels and all other kinds of game modifications, or "mods." (Mods "new items, modded weapons, characters, enemies, models, textures, levels, story lines, music, money, armor, life and game modes."[33]) And of course, from the very beginning of mass culture in the early twentieth century, artists immediately starting sampling and remixing mass cultural products—think of collage and photomontage practices that became popular right after World War I among artists in Russia and Germany. This continued throughout the twentieth century with Pop Art, appropriation art, and video art, and beyond in net art and new media practices.

Enter the computer. In *The Language of New Media* I named modularity as one of the trends I saw in a culture undergoing computerization. If before modularity the principle was applied to the packaging of cultural goods and raw media (photo stock, blank videotapes, etc.), computerization modularizes culture on a structural level. Images are broken into pixels; graphic designs, film, and video are broken into layers in Photoshop, After Effects, and other media design software. Hypertext modularizes text. Markup languages such as HTML and media formats such as QuickTime modularize multimedia documents in general. This all already happened by 1999 when I was finishing *The Language of New Media*; as we saw in this chapter, soon thereafter the adoption of Web feed formats such as RSS further modularized media content available on the Web, breaking many types of packaged information into atoms.

Culture has already been modular for a long time. But with a nod to Bruno Latour: "we have never been modular"[34]—which I think is a very good thing.

Notes

1 Ulf Poschardt, *DJ Culture*, trans. Shaun Whiteside (London: Quartet Books Ltd, 1998), 123.

2 Ibid., 271.

3 Roland Barthes, *Image-Music-Text*, translated by Stephen Heath (New York: Hill and Wang, 1977), 146.

4 Bruce Sterling. *Shaping Things* (Cambridge, MA: MIT Press, 2005).

5 Hernando Gomez Salinas, "Buenos Aires," *The*, 1 (September, 2007), p. 8.

6 http://www.wired.com/wired/archive/13.07/intro.html (accessed February 4, 2007).

7 Of course, the twentieth century terms and the paradigm behind them did not disappear overnight. Modern media industries which were established in the nineteenth and twentieth centuries, i.e., before the arrival of the Web—newspapers, television, film industry, book and music publishing, video games—continue with the old paradigm: small number of producers creating content distributed to much larger audiences. ("Small" and "large" are relative numbers. In 2005, 172,000 new titles were published in US alone, while 206,000 were published in the UK. How is that for a "small" number of producers?) However, even for these "going digital" (or, perhaps, "resisting the digital" would be more precise) industries the Web changed the rules of the game. Here traditional large-scale media industries are competing with numerous small-size producers—including individuals—in the same space. And since in comparison to selling physical products like music CDs, the distribution and stocking costs for digital files are tiny while the numbers of customers are much greater, this leads to a so-called "long tail" phenomenon. Now "top 40" items account for only 20 percent of the sales, while the other "nonhits" account for the remaining 80 percent.

8 Thomas Vander Wal, "Understanding the Personal Info Cloud: Using the Model of Attraction," presentation at University of Maryland, June 8, 2004 http://www.vanderwal.net/essays/moa/040608/040608.pdf (accessed February 28, 2008).

9 http://www.webware.com/8301-1_109-9689909-2.html (accessed July 29, 2007).

10 http://jumpcut.com (accessed April 5, 2008).

11 http://www.kaltura.com (accessed April 5, 2008) and http://pixelfish.com (accessed August 25, 2014).

12 Krissi Danielsson, "Distinguishing Cloud Computing from Utility Computing," www.ebizq.net, March 26, 2008. http://www.ebizq.net/blogs/saasweek/2008/03/distinguishing_cloud_computing/.

13 This happened after the first graphical browsers were introduced in 1993. In 1998 First Google index collected 26 million pages; in 2000 it already had one billion; on June 25, 2008, Google engineers announced on Google blog that they collected one trillion unique URLs. http://googleblog.blogspot.co.uk/2008/07/we-knew-web-was-big.html (accessed September 7, 2008).

14 For detailed statistics on the social media usage and growth between 2006 and 2012, see http://dsteven-white.com/2013/02/09/social-media-growth-2006-to-2012/ (accessed August 25, 2014).

15 See Lev Manovich, "Principles of New Media" in *The Language of New Media* (Cambridge, MA: MIT Press, 2001).

16 http://www.flickr.com/explore/interesting/ (accessed March 1, 2008).

17 iTunes calls its automation feature Genius sidebar; it is designed to make "playlists in your song library that go great together" and also to recommend "music from the iTunes Stores that you don't already have." See http://en.wikipedia.org/wiki/Collaborative_filtering.

18 Eliot Van Buskirk, "Signal Patterns: A Socially-Networked Music Personality Test," http://archive.wired.com/business/2008/12/socially-networ/, December 16, 2008 (accessed August 25, 2014).

19 http://www.newspond.com/about/ (accessed March 1, 2008).

20 Formerly available at: http://www.spotplex.com/help (last accessed March 1, 2008).

21 http://en.wikipedia.org/wiki/Ask_BigNews (accessed September 8, 2008).

22 www.tenbyten.org (accessed July 29, 2007).

23 The following discussion refers to the versions available in February 2008, so the interfaces and functionality of both programs may be different by the time you read this.

24 "Approaching a definition of Web 2.0," The Social Software Weblog, formerly available at: socialsoftware.weblogsinc.com (accessed October 28, 2005). For other definitions of Web 2.0, see Tim O'Reilly's article "What is Web 2.0: Design Patterns and Business Models for the Next Generation of Software," September 30, 2005 at http://oreilly.com/web2/archive/what-is-web-20.html (accessed August 25, 2014).

25 "Web 2.0 for Designers," in "Web 2.0 Design: Bootstrapping the Social Web," *Digital Web Magazine*, http://www.digital-web.com/articles/web_2_for_designers/ (accessed October 28, 2005).

26 http://creativecommons.org/licenses/ (accessed August 25, 2014).

27 http://orange.blender.org (accessed September 9, 2008).

28 http://orange.blender.org/production-planning (accessed September 9, 2008).

29 "An assembly line is a manufacturing process (most of the time called a progressive assembly) in which parts (usually interchangeable parts) are added as the semi-finished assembly moves from work station to work station where the parts are added in sequence until the final assembly is produced." http://en.wikipedia.org/wiki/Assembly_line (accessed July 31, 2014).

30 Theodor W. Adorno and Max Horkheimer, "The Culture Industry: Enlightenment as Mass Deception," in *Dialectic of Enlightenment: Philosophical Fragments* (Amsterdam: Querido Verlag,1947).

31 Theodor W. Adorno, "Culture Industry Reconsidered," *New German Critique* 6, Fall 1975, 12–19, https://www.sfu.ca/~andrewf/Culture_industry_reconsidered.shtml.

32 Ibid.

33 http://en.wikipedia.org/wiki/Mod_%28computer_gaming%29 (accessed July 31, 2014).

34 This phrase is an appropriation of Bruno Latour's *We Have Never Been Modern*.

Bibliography

Adorno, Theodor W. "Culture Industry Reconsidered." *New German Critique* 6, Fall 1975: 12–19, https://www.sfu.ca/~andrewf/Culture_industry_reconsidered.shtml (accessed August 25, 2005).

Adorno, Theodor W., and Max Horkheimer. "The Culture Industry: Enlightenment as Mass Deception." In *Dialectic of Enlightenment: Philosophical Fragments*, Amsterdam: Querido Verlag, 1947.

Barthes, Roland. *Image-Music-Text*, translated by Stephen Heath. New York: Hill and Wang, 1977.

Danielsson, Krissi. "Distinguishing Cloud Computing from Utility Computing," www.ebizq.net, March 26, 2008. http://www.ebizq.net/blogs/saasweek/2008/03/distinguishing_cloud_computing/ (accessed September 7, 2008).

Gomez Salinas, Hernando. "Buenos Aires." *The* 1, September, 2007.

Manovich, Lev. *The Language of New Media.* Cambridge, MA: MIT Press, 2001.

Poschardt, Ulf. *DJ Culture,* translated by Shaun Whiteside. London: Quartet Books Ltd, 1998.

Sterling, Bruce. *Shaping Things.* Cambridge, MA: MIT Press, 2005.

Vander Wal, Thomas. "Understanding the Personal Info Cloud: Using the Model of Attraction," presentation at University of Maryland, June 8, 2004. http://www.vanderwal.net/essays/moa/040608/040608.pdf (accessed February 28, 2008).

10

REMIXING MOVIES AND TRAILERS BEFORE AND AFTER THE DIGITAL AGE

Nicola Maria Dusi

Trailers Before Digital Cinema

Trailers of modern and contemporary movies present pathways, previews of upcoming movies. These micronarrations disrupt the space-time order of the plot in a new (fictive) narrative track. This common destructuring provides the film with an opportunistic reconstruction; and a consistent "trailer aesthetic" is often achieved through voice-over or music leitmotiv.[1] According to Genette,[2] the trailer belongs to the "paratext" (or better still the "public epitext" like press books or playbills),[3] and lies in the blurred area not only of "transition," but also "transaction," a communication strategy and practice defined by the presence of the author's (or their financial sponsor's) intention and responsibility. The trailer is a strategic communication that creates hype for the film while drawing the attention of its future audiences. Besides promoting the upcoming movie, paratexts work as reading instructions: they provide potential audiences with an early understanding of the film's genre and theme, and open a cognitive and affective challenge linked to a viewer's curiosity about the film.

An effective trailer is always built from a consistent enunciative choice and a dominant "thematic isotopy."[4] In semiotic terms, this is a guideline, a consistent semantic organization linking together the sequences of the audiovisual text from a discursive point of view. When watching the trailer, the audience acquires a specific "intertextual competence"[5] and will expect to find in the movie some of the prevailing isotopies—more often affective constants—provided by the trailer.

The trailer, like the remake, is at first familiar due to its repetition and then understood as a result of its difference from the related movie. This is not a mere summary, but a targeted synthesis, which takes the new communication purpose into account in the reformulation of the source text for promotional reasons, in order to raise the curiosity and expectations in the audience. In order to interpret the movie in the right way, the trailer should present and outline only part of the narrative, with a focus on thematic, figurative isotopies deemed important for their persuasive elements. Furthermore, trailers produce cognitive and affective attitudes, attraction, and interest for the movie being promoted in terms of, among other things, their expressive and stylistic construction, thus conveying perceptive-sensory experiences and stylistic features from the source text.

In this work I assume that a traditional trailer may be considered a type of *intrasemiotic translation* of its source.[6] A good trailer works like a translation in its attempt to raise in its audience effects of meaning similar to those expected by the movie in its specific text organization. Up to the late 1990s, the primary purpose of the trailer was to give audiences a taste of the pie (the film) in order to encourage them to view the complete feature in the theater. Is this still true for trailers made in the twenty-first century, during the time of the participatory Web? These days, short audiovisual forms have exploded in a myriad of clips for every possible genre and format, disseminated and reinvented innumerable times on video and social sharing websites.

I will discuss some examples of these new practices in movie consumption, exploring the so-called "sweded" short, self-made remakes and some typologies of "remix" trailers. To conclude, I will argue that these new digital trailers of the do-it-yourself (DIY) age deeply transform the meanings and forms of the source film through a *rewriting* operation that still remains an intrasemiotic translation *even if "opened"* through *a composite and creative reformulation.*

The Explosion of Trailers in the Digital Era

In today's medial scenario, some scholars consider the trailer to be one of the winning short forms,[7] which expand its visibility beyond previews in movie theaters and TV screens and invade the Web and new digital platforms. In this trend, the trailer as a paratext is weakened in favor of a new textual and aesthetic autonomy. What remains is the play on the audience's knowledge as they are called upon to fill in gaps or learn more about a film.

With those we could generally dub as *remix trailers* found on the Web, just the opposite is true. In these instances of creative—often amateur—reformulation, the source material is considered well known, and it is precisely on this shared knowledge that the individual variation of "participative audiences" comes about.[8] Producing a remix trailer and posting it on the Web often means mocking the top-down production logics of the audiovisual system, but it also shows the remixer's ability to communicate with an already knowledgeable community of fans. Inevitably this also means increasing the value of the source cultural product.[9]

Prosumers in remix cultures[10] or mashup cultures[11] reverse and expand the areas of value transmission, considering that nowadays the effort to convey values and emotions, topics, and narrative shapes moves from the producer to the audience.

The contemporary digital mediascape—most notably social media websites—offers a great many cases of derived texts that reuse a source text to produce something modified and unexpected. Movie trailers, as stated above, are short audiovisual promotional texts linked to the source material (the film) in an expected way that mixes reformulation and reinterpretation in unexpected ways. Movies and trailers on the Web become a free archive of cultural products to be selected and reopened by users and fans, transformed and reused through a creative DIY or *bricolage*, to develop something new with old materials. According to Jenkins:

A new aesthetic based on remixing and repurposing media content has flowed across the culture—from work done by media professionals in Hollywood or artists working in top museums to teenagers mashing up their favorite anime series on their home computers or hip hop DJs mixing and matching musical elements across different genres.[12]

"Remix" trailers differ from "mashup" trailers: the former use materials from a unique source, or at least a coherent one, such as a movie or a trailer,[13] while the latter use several diverse source texts and involve *selecting and reassembling footage taken from films belonging to different genres, very distant in terms of style and form.*[14]

Both forms of trailers could become a way of subverting the values and the narrative logics of a well-known blockbuster film. They may even create a source text that does not exist, as can be seen in the new trend of fake trailers. For example, on YouTube you can easily find several music videos that remix the credits of *Trainspotting*[15] in order to promote a new song and musician, or one that reuses footage from Fellini's 8½ to promote the rapper Eminem in 8½ *Mile* citing the biopic film 8 *Mile*.[16]

In my view, the most interesting case studies are fake trailers that YouTube users have created for movies like Fellini's *Il viaggio di Mastorna* (*Mastorna's Journey*), which was never actually made, as well as sequels of movies with a tragic ending, such as *Titanic*[17] in which the main character lives a new life in contemporary New York. In *Titanic Two: the Surface* (Figure 10.1),[18] after being found frozen in the deep ocean and resurrected through modern technology, Jack Dawson searches for his love Rose, discovering on TV news that she has just died at the age of 102. This fake trailer, a "reflexive" mashup,[19] cuts and pastes with clever editing some selected scenes of Di Caprio in *Catch Me If You Can*,[20] *Romeo + Juliet*,[21] and *Titanic*. According to Jenkins, these rewriting practices should be analyzed in the light of the social interaction of fans in online fan communities. According

Figure 10.1 Screen shots from Robert Blankenheim's "*Titanic Two: the Surface*" (courtesy of Robert Blankenheim—http://robertblankenheim.com)

to Tryon,[22] these manipulation practices are fueled by the urgency to extend the pleasure of the original cinematic experience. Peverini[23] states that on the Web, many fan communities operate on the closed filmic text by inserting into it a large quantity of fictional tales, discourses and fragments. These expressive forms are linked to the original text but at the same time they demonstrate a certain degree of semiotic autonomy: "the film consequently explodes in a multitude of texts, different for format, genre and editing style. These new texts are interconnected and can trigger debates that involve their own authors and interpretative communities."[24]

In some cases, the pleasure associated with the making and consuming of self-produced texts is indeed triggered by the creative process of reopening the film's sign process. It is something I have tried to define with my co-author Spaziante in 2006, at the very beginning of these phenomena, considering the emerging trend linked to the reiterated pleasure to deconstruct texts, shared by communities and networks, as a widening of the original intertextual connections. In this way these connections can be intended as a big collective game of reinterpretation and enhancement of the "mythopoietic processes."[25]

Sweded Trailers

Anyone who has seen the movie *Be Kind Rewind*[26] will remember the "sweded films," that is, the short "self-remakes" of blockbuster films. They are self-made short movies, low-fi and low budget forms of remix. I consider them as an experimental form of the future remix trailers, namely a first step to better understand the explosion of prosumer trailers self-published on the Web. *Be Kind Rewind* provides some clear examples of the practice of "sweding," something immediately promoted on the film by its director Michel Gondry. Anybody could create a digital short film and post it, and, indeed, many fans of the movie created sweded short features that appear on the film's website.[27] These remakes were ludic reinterpretations, pastiches, and parodies. An example of a home-made remake is the sweded film *The Shining* (2008).[28] In just a few minutes, the clip summarizes the most important moments of Kubrick's 1980 original, using a linear narrative approach. The remix is comically low-fi and its formal solutions are amateurish.

An example is the famous close-up of John's face (Jack Nicholson) glimpsed through the gashes made by his hatchet on the door, when he tries to get to his wife barricaded in the hotel pantry (Figure 10.2). Here, the door and the face shot are recalled through a thin piece of wood torn in two pieces and held with both hands by the protagonist. Another feature of this revisited in an amateur style is the original sound track totally sung (as a cover) by the hoarse voice of the actor. The sweded version of *The Shining* patches together at least three sources: Kubrick's original film, its official trailer composed of short scenes edited in a nonlinear fashion, as well as the under-two-minutes-long teaser trailer, considered by critics and fans one of the best horror trailers in the history of cinema, with its fixed frame of a door inside the hotel, which is suddenly flooded in blood. In the end of the sweded *Shining*, a cardboard model of the hotel doors is washed out with a red liquid by the narrator/protagonist who is nonchalantly humming.

These sweded short remakes exemplify three practices:[29] first, the home-made movie as a form of self-expression; second, the reuse of some key scenes which is the intertextual translation of some *topoi* of the source film; third, the *pastiche* content form of this re-creation. These short remakes reinterpret the dominant guidelines (isotopies) of the source films, alongside a simplification. They are a form of special reworking, holding

Figure 10.2 Screen shots from "The Shining—Sweded" by Paul Hurley (courtesy of Paul Hurley; https://www.youtube.com/watch?v=I2unsGNFdts)

together several sources all from the same movie, thus belonging to the remix family. With their urgency to reprocess the source film rigorously they share, however, the logics of film remake, at least in the rule of maintaining the "affective tonality" of the source film.[30]

Typologies of Remixed Trailers

It is not by chance that I chose the example of the sweded movie, for it is precisely *The Shining* cult movie which was reedited in one of the most famous fake trailers, *The Shining (Spoof Trailer)*—a viral video aired in 2005 in the video sharing websites, and rapidly after that on YouTube.[31] This fake trailer of *The Shining*[32] reprocesses the sound track thus creating a romantic subtext with Peter Gabriel's song "Solsbury Hill." It also recuts the scenes where the characters meet, thus presenting a new narrative plot, all developed in a comedic style. In particular, the exchanges between father and son, before and during their stay in the Overlook Hotel, outline the transformation of their relationship from their distance to a newly found union. The fake trailer stresses the distance between producers and consumers, fans and filmmakers through the use of parody. According to Tryon, it is not only the movie but the trailer itself that is the object of parody, and "the uncanny disjunction between Kubrick's horror film and Ryang's remix enabled the video to find an audience very quickly while spawning a number of imitations and video responses, as others experimented with the fake trailer format."[33]

Tryon's work, from which I quote, presents a systematization of the changing and complex phenomenon of video sharing and movie remixing in the Web. According to Tryon, the participatory culture of digital video makers in the area of DIY is based on the new competences assigned to film audiences starting from the introduction of bonus content in DVDs, as well as on the huge quantity of movies now made available in the digital era. The contemporary redefinition of cinematic text also explodes in the Web 2.0, expanding the possible worlds of films into new transmedia narrative universes,[34] and adds value to the short formats, like the different clips taking pieces from films, through appropriations, sampling and quotations, remixes and mashups.[35] An example of this is the practice of manipulating the source film, like the reediting mentioned by Peverini,[36] in which sequences belonging to the same film are simply taken from the original text and reedited in another order. Or the different operations of fan fictions

> that germinates from the narrative and stylistic construction of the original film and can be connected to it using various strategies and logics: fan-made stories can design a new frame around the original narration, or tell prologues and epilogues, or fill blank spaces in the plot.[37]

The explosion of the trailer format we are talking about in this chapter thus falls within the framework of a larger phenomenon which has brought about a series of new practices in movie consumption, from video-on-demand of pay TV to the downloading of peer-to-peer systems and the Web sharing of personal videos with wide and flexible communities. As Jenkins has stated,[38] this is not the reason why audiences have stopped following festivals or going to the cinema, as instead this has rather multiplied the ways in which they can find access to wanted content.

According to Tryon, while digital cinema is changing the previous forms and practices of watching, as well as of distributing, exhibiting, and promoting movies, it should also be considered that viewings on computer screens, smartphones or tablets are mostly a "means for watching short videos such as trailers or teasers rather than viewing an entire film on a three-inch screen."[39] Marketing strategies in the entertainment industry have come to comprise not only the major media corporations, but also new distribution practices of DIY independent filmmakers, and move in the direction of using the fan practices of digital cinema to expand the consumption of Hollywood films in general, involving at times audiences in the production process of studios,[40] besides tempting audiences to see the upcoming new movie. In the chapter "Hollywood Remixed," Tryon explores amateur activities like the self-production of movie remixes or movie mashups, by fans using the cult movies to reinterpret them, and suggests that, were we to analyze remixed movies and trailers in their entirety, we would find a sort of canon created by fans and film geeks to express their "cinematic sensibilities."[41] Tryon also explains something very interesting for the purposes of our discussion: "The videos constitute not only complex reinterpretations of the remixed films and genres but also of trailers themselves. By exposing the conventions of movie trailers and other promotional shorts, the remixes have the effect of mocking these marketing conventions."[42]

In his exploration of the movie remix and mashup complexity, Tryon suggests focusing on two relevant categories: the *genre remix* and the *compilation video*. In the first, "trailers are recut, often with sound cues from outside the original film, to create the illusion that a film is of a different genre."[43] In this way Stanley Kubrick's *The Shining* becomes a family comedy. But trailers may also be replayed in terms of the relationship between genre and gender, as in *Brokeback trailers*. According to Tryon, after the trailer for Lee's *Brokeback Mountain*[44] many remix trailers recut the film to create the illusion that the movie features a homosexual romance.[45] The case of *compilation videos* is different, as with the "Five-Second Movies" series in which a film is condensed in a few seconds in a mostly parodistic way.[46]

All types of practices and new textualities on the Web are forcibly temporary. What is of interest in Tryon's argument is the effort to reason on transformations in contemporary film culture that are brought to light in remix trailers. The fake trailers, like many parodies of Hollywood film sequences, enable audiences to critically reinterpret genres and their mechanisms intertextually, triggering at times debates and criticism about marketing strategies of Hollywood films and contributing to an increased awareness of popular culture. Political satire has always been one of the reasons for movie remixes, a semiotic way of turning these videos "into a self-conscious form of pop-political commentary."[47] In any case, even criticism ends up by belonging to a much wider promotional culture producing added value, even indirectly.[48]

Peverini[49] presents a map *in progress* of audiovisual changes of movies on the Web based on the case study of a single film in the Batman saga: *The Dark Knight*[50] and the transmedia proliferation of many short forms of remixes. *The Dark Knight* is a successful movie, living in the intertextuality with other languages such as comics and many adaptations, remakes, and videogames. Peverini[51] defines movie remixes as "reworking practices" of intertextual deformation and reprocessing. For example, it happens that social knowledge around the film condenses on a single iconic trait: the smile of the Joker, the antagonist of the superhero, played in this film by Heath Ledger. Fans use this detail as a synecdoche of the entire film and its symbolic apparatus in order to create many reenactments or impressions: short videos in which we may find a reinterpretation of the Joker's monologue by individual performers in front of their webcam. These give proof of acting prowess yet fall within the boundaries of the context, inside a community sharing knowledge and taste for a given film. Peverini argues that it is possible to juxtapose reworking practices, which are instead based on a radical manipulation of the original text, other forms based on an "interpretive effort."[52] In such cases, technical expertise (in particular editing techniques) are used to analyze the semiotic strategies of the work and to suggest a close and critical reading in order to highlight the director's choices, editing solutions, actors' performances, and open a debate that involves fans, critics, and scholars. To the practices of genre remix analyzed by Tryon[53] we could add the peculiar form of cinematic mashup dubbed by Peverini "slipshot movies." A working mashup "linking two films on a narrative level, juxtaposing two scenes and using some fictional elements or props to build an intertextual bridge."[54] In this way, for example, a character can call on the phone another character, answering from another scene in another film with surreal and comic effects, breaking the coherence of a narrative world and sparking off a rereading game. This is a simple and effective technique to build intertextual narrations. It is widely used on the Web in the Shipper's Videos through which fans of the new American TV series hybridize together different TV series. Fans recut characters' actions (for example from *House* and *CSI*) in common narrative contexts as if they were a single narration, thus building a (false) aesthetic of continuity.[55]

The most common forms of filmic reworking and interpretive effort have been selected by Peverini[56] based on the kind of operations made on the source film, from the simple selecting and sharing of scenes to the more challenging mashup. The results of these textual manipulations offer some interesting insights. Some operations redefine the content, with parodistic intention, while others completely change the form (the expression plane) without really transforming the content, as in reenacting and nonparodistic remakes. Peverini[57] recalls the importance of considering the levels of professional and technical competence required by the remix operations, for example in so-called "kinetic typography," where graphics totally substitute images.

The example of kinetic typography remix trailers is particularly interesting: This is a computer-aided animation technique with complex 2D and 3D movements of type letters, initially used for film credits and Web home pages. In the remixed trailer of *The Dark Knight*, for example, the sound track (music, dialog, sounds) is left untouched by "replacing the video track with sequences of words and sentences showing the narrative plane of the original text in an alternative fashion."[58] Taking another example, in the kinetic typography version of the *Trainspotting* trailer, innovative rhythmic effects are created together with a sort of visual poetry animated by the contrast between the moving writing and the voice of the protagonist reciting his initial litany.

Manovich considers the moving graphic applied to typography as a sort of a new "metalanguage" that defines the new contemporary medial aesthetic.[59] The complex textual hybrids promoted by this aesthetic present contents and techniques that mutually collide and transform their practices and meanings. For Manovich this is not merely a *remixing*, but a more general "deep remixability," which is still uncommon now in the videos posted on the Web by amateurs, as it belongs to the supposed professionals of digital media creation. Thanks to postproduction software, digital composition, and computer graphics (like Flash, Adobe After Effects, Final Cut, Softimage XSI, Nuke), techniques that were once separate, like animation and 3D graphics, and music, are now reassembled in films and trailers in a global remix which transforms the textuality of these new cultural products both in terms of content as well as technically and stylistically.[60]

Conclusion

Sweded movies, launched by Gondry's *Be Kind Rewind*, prompt fans to remix film content so as to represent them in a near-caricatural way, showing the power of "bottom-up practices" of reinterpretation.[61] In their low-fi way and with an almost anonymous circulation, sweded films fall within the contemporary aesthetic of postproduction.[62]

With regard to the new forms of remix and mashup of movies and trailers we have briefly outlined, can we still regard them as intrasemiotic translations? If we consider that they open up to the signification of source films (at the content level) with expansions but also with reversals and elisions, we could answer the question affirmatively.

If instead we consider that, at the expression level,[63] they do not just retrieve materials from a single film but mix or remix many different ones, hybridizing and turning them into something new, then we shift to the logics of remix and mashup. Logics which, in semiotic terms, are not exclusively associated with translation and interpretation, aiming to create variants and variations, but also introduce alternatives and "invariants" linked to structural elements.[64] If I change the sound track and the editing of a trailer in order to transform its dominant genre features, I will also be manipulating the overall meaning and textual taste perceived by the film spectator in sensory, affective, stylistic, and discursive terms. I will therefore change something that was an invariant, an essential component for the interpretation of the *intentio operis*[65] of the film or the trailer, and change it into a possible local variant. In other words, I'm building new invariants and deeply transforming meanings through a rewriting operation linked to a new (although short-lived) *intentio lectoris*.[66]

It would be more appropriate to think of these remixes and mashup trailers, and even fake trailers, in terms of reformulations or rewritings[67] of the source texts. By hybridizing and transforming the dominant meanings of the latter, they use the logic of recognizability (repetition of the same) typical of remake and intrasemiotic translation as a means of supporting a logic of transformative and innovative reinterpretation; a reinterpretation which, by working on the forms (connections) and the materials of film expression, but also by replacing them and inventing new ones, creates alternative meanings and tells other stories, with pragmatic purposes different from those of the traditional trailer. It transforms radically the semiotic status of the target text, the movie remix or the trailer remix with respect to films and trailers created by the entertainment industry.

Notes

1 See Nicola Dusi, "Le forme del trailer come manipolazione intrasemiotica," in *Trailer, Spot, Clip, Siti, Banner: Le forme brevi della comunicazione audiovisiva*, ed. Isabella Pezzini (Rome: Meltemi, 2002), 36–41. See Lisa Kernan, *Coming Attractions: Reading American Movie Trailers* (Austin, TX: University of Texas Press, 2004), 6–8.

2 Gérard Genette, *Palimpsestes: La littérature au second degré* (Paris: Seuil, 1982).

3 Robert Stam, Robert Burgoyne, and Sandy Flitterman-Lewis, *New Vocabularies in Film Semiotics: Structuralism, Post-Structuralism and Beyond* (London: Routledge, 1992), 209–210.

4 Algirdas Julien Greimas and Joseph Courtés, eds., *Sémiotique: Dictionnaire raisonné de la théorie du langage* (Paris: Hachette, 1979), 187–188.

5 Umberto Eco, *The Role of the Reader: Exploration in the Semiotics of Texts* (Bloomington, IN: Indiana University Press, 1979), 20–21.

6 The "intralinguistic" translation process uses the same "matters" of the expression of the source text to create different forms of discourse and textual organization. See Roman Jakobson, "On linguistic aspects of translation," in *On Translation*, ed. Robert A. Brower (Cambridge, MA: Harvard University Press, 1959), 232. *Louis Hjelmslev, Prolegomena to a Theory of Language* (Madison, WI: University of Wisconsin Press, 1961), 52–53.

7 See Isabella Pezzini, "Forme brevi, a intelligenza del resto," in *Trailer, Spot, Clip, Siti, Banner: Le forme brevi della comunicazione audiovisiva*, ed. Isabella Pezzini (Rome: Meltemi, 2002), 9–10. Chuck Tryon, *Reinventing Cinema. Movies in the Age of Media Convergence* (New Brunswick, NJ: Rutgers University Press, 2009), 149–154.

8 Henry Jenkins, *Convergence Culture: Where Old and New Media Collide* (New York: New York University Press, 2006), 1–24.

9 Tryon, *Reinventing Cinema*, 155.

10 Lev Manovich, What Comes After Remix? (http://Manovich.net, 2007). Lawrence Lessig, *Remix: Making Art and Commerce Thrive in the Hybrid Economy* (New York: Penguin, 2008), 68–76.

11 Stefan Sonvilla-Weiss, ed., *Mashup Cultures* (Wien: Springer, 2010), 8–10.

12 Henry Jenkins, "Multiculturalism, Appropriation, and the New Media Literacies: Remixing Moby Dick," in *Mashup Cultures*, ed. Stefan Sonvilla-Weiss (Wien: Springer, 2010), 107.

13 Manovich, What Comes After Remix? 3–4.

14 See Paolo Peverini, "Dal bastard pop al mash-up: Mutazioni in corso," *E/C* 1 (2007): 115–116. Eduardo Navas, "Regressive and Reflexive Mashups in Sampling Cultures," in *Mashup Cultures*, ed. Stefan Sonvilla-Weiss (Wien: Springer, 2010), 157.

15 By Danny Boyle (UK, 1996).

16 By Curtis Hanson (USA, 2002).

17 By James Cameron (USA, 1997).

18 By Robert Blankenheim (2010), https://robertblankenheim.com (accessed April, 2014).

19 Navas defines as "reflexive" the mashup that claims autonomy and "challenges the 'spectacular aura' of the original." See Navas, "Regressive and Reflexive Mashups." 159.

20 By Steven Spielberg (USA, 2002).

21 By Baz Luhrmann (USA, 1996).

22 Tryon, *Reinventing Cinema*, 149–150.

23 Paolo Peverini, "La manipolazione filmica come consumo creativo. Soggetti, pratiche, testi," in *Open Cinema: Scenari di visione cinematografica negli anni '10*, eds. Emiliana De Blasio and Paolo Peverini (Rome: Fondazione Ente dello Spettacolo, 2010), 31.

24 Peverini, "La manipolazione filmica come consumo creativo," 32. Translated from the Italian by myself in collaboration with the author.

25 Nicola Dusi and Lucio Spaziante, eds., *Remix-Remake: pratiche di replicabilità* (Rome: Meltemi, 2006), 11.

26 By Michel Gondry (USA, 2008).

27 It is still possible to watch many sweded movies on: http://swededfilms.com/films.html (accessed October, 2013).

28 "The Shining—Sweded" http://www.youtube.com/watch?v=I2unsGNFdts (accessed April, 2014).

29 See Nicola Dusi, "Remaking as a Practice: Some Problems of Transmediality," *Cinéma & Cie XII*, no. 18 (2012): 124.

30 See Augusto Sainati, "Tati's Jour de Fête, il colore progressivo: per una teoria del remake," in *Remix-Remake: pratiche di replicabilità*, eds. Nicola Dusi and Lucio Spaziante (Rome: Meltemi, 2006), 197–200.

31 Tryon, *Reinventing Cinema*, 150.

32 *The Shining (Spoof Trailer)* by Robert Ryang (2005), http://www.youtube.com/watch?v=ca7IHRdy7u4 (accessed April, 2014).

33 Tryon, *Reinventing Cinema*, 150.

34 Jenkins, *Convergence Culture*, 93–168.

35 Manovich, "What Comes After Remix?" 3–4.

36 Peverini, "La manipolazione filmica come consumo creativo," 34.

37 Ibid., 35.

38 Jenkins, *Convergence Culture*, 1–24.

39 Tryon, *Reinventing Cinema*, 7.

40 As in the case of HBO and the online remix *Seven Minute Sopranos*, used to attract new audiences (Tryon, *Reinventing Cinema*, 160).

41 Tryon, *Reinventing Cinema*, 151–152.

42 Ibid., 152.

43 Ibid., 156.

44 Ang Lee (USA, 2005).

45 Tryon, *Reinventing Cinema*, 156.

46 Tryon states that "a high-concept film or film series is boiled down to (approximately) five seconds, thus exposing and playfully mocking the formulaic nature of many Hollywood films" (*Reinventing Cinema*, 156). "Compilation videos," recalls Tryon, could also present the best and worst movie scenes, and encompass a number of different approaches, that can even "include related scenes from multiple films and have been used to parody film culture in some way" (ibid.)

47 Tryon, *Reinventing Cinema*, 157. On the meta-discursive awareness of movie remix see Darren Tofts and Christian McCrea, "What Now? The Imprecise and Disagreeable Aesthetics of Remix," *The Fibreculture Journal* 15 (2009): 1–2.

48 According to Tryon (*Reinventing Cinema*, 155): "whether that value comes from the advertising revenue accumulated by video sharing sites such as YouTube or from the attention directed toward the media texts featured in the parodies."

49 Peverini, "La manipolazione filmica come consumo creativo," 39–71.

50 By Christopher Nolan (USA, 2008).

51 Peverini, "La manipolazione filmica come consumo creativo," 36.

52 Ibid., 36–37.

53 Tryon, *Reinventing Cinema*, 155–156.

54 Peverini, "La manipolazione filmica come consumo creativo," 66.

55 Lev Manovich, The *Language of New Media* (Cambridge MA: MIT Press, 2001), 134–135.

56 Peverini, "La manipolazione filmica come consumo creativo," 34.

57 Ibid.

58 Ibid., 52.

59 Lev Manovich, *Software Takes Command* (London: Bloomsbury Academic, 2013), 254–266.

60 According to Manovich (*Software Takes Command*, 267–276) this is a "stylized" aesthetic, that would previously have been identified as cartoonish, which can be seen in movies such as *The Matrix* trilogy by Wachowsky brothers (USA, 1999–2003); *Sin City* by Robert Rodriguez (USA, 2005); *300* by Zack Snyder (USA, 2006).

61 Michel de Certeau, *L'invention du quotidien. I Arts de faire* (Paris: Gallimard, 1990), 63–84. Or, rather, it is a case of "overinterpretation," according to Umberto Eco, *Interpretation and Overinterpretation* (Cambridge: Cambridge University Press, 1992), 45–66.

62 Nicolas Bourriaud, *Postproduction: Culture as Screenplay—How Art Reprograms the World* (New York: Lukas & Sternberg, 2002), 7–16.

63 "Matters of expression," "matters of content," and the idea of a dynamic "textual strategy" are terms of film semiotics. See Christian Metz, *Language and Cinema* (The Hague: Mouton de Gruyter, 1974), 208–211. Stam et al., *New Vocabularies*, 51.

64 The difference between invariants and variants in languages derives from structural linguistics (Hjelmslev, *Prolegomena to a Theory of Language*, 66): invariants are made by "commutation" (if changing an element of one of the two language planes changes the general meaning, then that is an invariant), while variants are made by the "replacing" of elements without variations in meaning.

65 Umberto Eco, *The Limits of Interpretation* (Bloomington, IN: Indiana University Press, 1990), 44–63.

66 Ibid., 45.

67 Roland Barthes, *S/Z* (New York: Hill & Wang, 1974), 3–11.

Bibliography

Barthes, Roland. *S/Z*. New York: Hill & Wang, 1974.

Bourriaud, Nicolas. *Postproduction: Culture as Screenplay—How Art Reprograms the World*. New York: Lukas & Sternberg, 2002.

Certeau, Michel de. *L'invention du quotidien. I Arts de faire*. Paris: Gallimard, 1990.

Dusi, Nicola. "Le forme del trailer come manipolazione intrasemiotica." In *Trailer, Spot, Clip, Siti, Banner: Le forme brevi della comunicazione audiovisiva*, edited by Isabella Pezzini, 31–66. Rome: Meltemi, 2002 (available on www.ec-aiss.it/biblioteca).

——. "Remaking as a Practice: Some Problems of Transmediality." *Cinéma & Cie* XII, no. 18 (2012): 115–127.

Dusi, Nicola and Lucio Spaziante, Eds. *Remix-Remake: pratiche di replicabilità*. Rome: Meltemi, 2006.

Eco, Umberto. *The Role of the Reader: Exploration in the Semiotics of Texts*. Bloomington, IN: Indiana University Press, 1979.

——. *The Limits of Interpretation*. Bloomington, IN: Indiana University Press, 1990.

——. *Interpretation and Overinterpretation*. Cambridge: Cambridge University Press, 1992.

Genette, Gérard. *Palimpsestes. La littérature au second degré*. Paris: Seuil, 1982.

Greimas, Algirdas Julien and Joseph Courtés, Eds. *Sémiotique. Dictionnaire raisonné de la théorie du langage*. Paris: Hachette, 1979.

Hjelmslev, Louis. *Prolegomena to a Theory of Language*. Madison, WI: University of Wisconsin Press, 1961 (or. ed. 1943).

Jakobson, Roman. "On linguistic aspects of translation." In *On Translation*, edited by Robert A. Brower, 232–239, Cambridge, MA: Harvard University Press, 1959.

Jenkins, Henry. *Convergence Culture: Where Old and New Media Collide*. New York: New York University Press, 2006.

——. "Multiculturalism, Appropriation, and the New Media Literacies: Remixing Moby Dick." In *Mashup Cultures*, edited by Stefan Sonvilla-Weiss, 98–119, Wien: Springer, 2010.

Kernan, Lisa. *Coming Attractions: Reading American Movie Trailers*. Austin, TX: University of Texas Press, 2004.

Lessig, Lawrence. *Remix: Making Art and Commerce Thrive in the Hybrid Economy*. New York: Penguin, 2008.

Manovich, Lev. *The Language of New Media*. Cambridge, MA: MIT Press, 2001.

——. "What Comes After Remix?" http://Manovich.net, 2007 (now in Manovich 2013).

——. "Software Takes Command." http://lab.softwarestudies.com, 2008 (now in Manovich 2013).

——. *Software Takes Command*. London: Bloomsbury Academic, 2013.

Metz, Christian. *Language and Cinema*. The Hague: Mouton de Gruyter, 1974 (or. ed. 1971).

Navas, Eduardo. "Regressive and Reflexive Mashups in Sampling Cultures." In *Mashup Cultures*, edited by Stefan Sonvilla-Weiss, 98–119, Wien: Springer, 2010.

Odin, Roger. *De la Fiction*. Bruxelles: De Boeke, 2000.

Peverini, Paolo. "Dal bastard pop al mash-up. Mutazioni in corso." *E/C* 1 (2007): 115–120.

——. "La manipolazione filmica come consumo creativo. Soggetti, pratiche, testi." In *Open Cinema. Scenari di visione cinematografica negli anni '10*, edited by Emiliana De Blasio and Paolo Peverini, 17–72. Rome: Fondazione Ente dello Spettacolo, 2010.

Pezzini, Isabella. "Forme brevi, a intelligenza del resto." In *Trailer, Spot, Clip, Siti, Banner: Le forme brevi della comunicazione audiovisiva*, edited by Isabella Pezzini, 9–29. Rome: Meltemi, 2002.

Sainati, Augusto. "Tati's Jour de Fête, il colore progressivo: per una teoria del remake." In *Remix-Remake: pratiche di replicabilità*, edited by Nicola Dusi and Lucio Spaziante, 197–208. Rome: Meltemi, 2006.

Sonvilla-Weiss, Stefan, Ed. *Mashup Cultures*. Wien: Springer, 2010.

Stam, Robert, Robert Burgoyne, and Sandy Flitterman-Lewis. *New Vocabularies in Film Semiotics: Structuralism, Post-Structuralism and Beyond*. London: Routledge, 1992.

Tofts, Darren and Christian McCrea. "What Now? The Imprecise and Disagreeable Aesthetics of Remix." *The Fibreculture Journal* 15 (2009): 1–11.

Tryon, Chuck. *Reinventing Cinema: Movies in the Age of Media Convergence*. New Brunswick, NJ: Rutgers University Press, 2009.

11

REMIXING THE PLAGUE OF IMAGES

Video Art from Latin America in a Transnational Context

Erandy Vergara

There has been a strong production of video art in Latin American countries in the last four decades, and an equally strong tradition of appropriation and remixing prerecorded materials, particularly images from popular culture.[1] Remix in video art encompasses reusing, recycling, referencing, and redirecting audiovisual materials toward orientations distinct from the original source. Since the raw materials of many video remixes include imagery that comes from advertising, cinema, magazines, and television, apart from formal experimentation, critiques to those systems of representation are common and bold. The aim of numerous artists is to reevaluate the elements constituting visual culture and to articulate resistance to hegemonic images and discourses in a transnational context.

In contemporary video art from Latin America there is a significant body of work dealing with questions of memory mixing past and present.[2] Other pieces connected to the lineage of the avant-garde in Latin America explore questions of modernity through citations and remix.[3] This chapter focuses on four videos deploying remix strategies as metacommentaries on remix itself.[4] As I will explain, such works cannot be separated from the troubling genesis of the source materials and the wider context of circulation and reception, yet at the same time they function on various levels as self-reflexive cases of the practice of remix.

To be concrete in my argument, I will focus on four case studies which use remix to revise the smooth flowing or the unsteady flickering of the plague of images circulating online and offline on a daily basis.[5] There is the bitter criticism of transnational capitalism and diverse forms of invasion in Ximena Cuevas's *Cinepolis* (2003); the appropriation of images about protection and surveillance in Graciela Fuentes's *To Protect* (2003); the re-vision of 15 years of Colombian television in José Alejandro Restrepo's *Viacrucis* (2004); and the scratching of a speech by Fidel Castro in José Toirac's *Opus* (2005). Despite their differences, these artists complicate remix as a contemporary aesthetic in works privileging contrast and noise to draw attention to the smoothness and/or fragmentation of mainstream media, to reorient the reading of known sounds and images, as well as to expose the relationship between the appropriated elements and what Slavoj Žižek calls the "material traces of ideology."[6]

The Wider Context of Remix: Zapping, Swiping, and Scratching

In his *Máquina e imaginário: o desafio das poéticas tecnológicas*, media scholar Arlindo Machado inserts the zapping effect in the timeline of what he calls the "poetics of remake," a strategy he situates in relation to avant-garde tendencies to reuse materials produced and circulated through mechanical reproduction. Machado links *zapping* and *zipping* to the *scratching* of music and audiovisual material, thereby calling attention to a common thread: users of technologies such as remote controls and VCRs also fragment and rearrange pieces of information.[7] Now with computers and smart phones more cuts can be implemented in the act of swiping, and thus the fragmented reading that Machado traced in zapping and zipping finds yet another vein in computer culture "to crossing spaces and times, and different levels of reality, waving the bandwidths, and shuffling formats and terrains."[8]

At the level of perception actions such as zapping and swiping result in more fragmented reception and hyperattention. N. Katherine Hayles provides insight. In *How We Think: Digital Media and Contemporary Technogenesis*, she advances two forms of fragmented reading and perception. On the one hand, hyper-reading is "a strategic response to an information-intensive environment, aimed to conserve attention by quickly identifying relevant information, so that only relatively few points of a given text are actually read."[9] On the other hand, hyper-reading is related to hyperattention, "a cognitive mode that has low threshold for boredom, alternates flexibly between different information streams, and prefers a high level of stimulation."[10] While economic, political, social, cultural, and racial differences make it impossible to assume that all users who zip, zap, and swipe have a shorter span of attention, it is important to bear in mind that these forms of reception often create a "state of disorder" which determines the fact that contemporary users are familiarized with an aesthetics of fragmentation as in remix. Here is where more "conscious practices" such as *scratching* become relevant.[11]

While zapping and swiping generate ruptures and fragmentation, these actions do not involve a critical rearticulation of the material; the zap and the swipe involve acts of reading, while the scratch involves a process of reinscription or disruption of the material. Hence, the works by scratchers and video artists—particularly self-reflective pieces—dissect images, texts, and sounds but at the same time, they critically engage with the very practice of cutting, pasting, scratching, and remixing. Although the practitioners of scratch video separated themselves from video artists deploying scratching strategies there are two common threads: (1) the literal or symbolic distortion of preexisting elements; (2) the materials and subject of critique are above all advertising, television programming, broadcasting corporations, politicians, and capitalism. In general terms video scratchers and video artists fragment the flow of images as spectators do when zapping or swiping, but in the process of recomposition they scratch the source to appeal to the spectator's imagination and to establish others affective, critical, historical, and political associations.

At the same time, zappers, swipers, and scratchers are also embedded in an aesthetics of continuity as in mainstream cinema. For example, computer-generated characters and locations blend perfectly with live actors in Peter Jackson's *The Lord of the Rings*. What sustains this aesthetics is the contrast-free transition of elements all placed next to each other as if belonging to a seamless world without gaps.

The apparent contradictions between fragmentation and continuity actually coexist, offering a series of ironies that pose a central question: how can contemporary artists use remix to resist the hegemonic discourses that at times would seem to flicker disturbingly in mass media and at other times would seem to flow smoothly? The case studies discussed henceforth target both: while some artists *from* Latin America challenge linear histories and continuity, others aim to expose the gaps. In general, they endeavor to redirect the material toward a critical filter by relying on the zapping effect, by overexposing already overexposed footage, but also by concealing, by slowing down and suspending in time some of the elements they draw from the plague of images.[12]

José Alejandro Restrepo: A Love Story between Religion and Television in Colombia

José Alejandro Restrepo is one of the pioneers of single channel video and video installation in Colombia. Since 1988 he has created more than 20 years of Colombian mass media, cutting and pasting pieces of documentaries, newscasts, and television programs to introduce disorder into the hegemonic order of history, culture, politics, and society. For Restrepo there is no need to produce new images, but rather to create symbolic distortions and interventions on the existing ones and in that sense his cuts and scratches are more than "purely video-graphic" concerns; they foreground hegemonic narratives and systems of practices and sensibilities that support and reproduce mass media messages.[13]

Alluding to the 14 Stations of the Cross which recount the history of Christ from the moment he is condemned to death to his crucifixion, Restrepo constructs a disturbing history of suffering in contemporary Colombia. *Viacrucis, Stations of the Cross* (2004) is a 19 minute 30 second video depicting archival material saturated with scenes of human suffering, torture, and violence. For example, a segment courtesy of Colombian newscast Uninoticias shows the aftermath of a Holy Thursday in Bogotá, where diverse police squads spread out and beat a confused crowd. While the news anchor explains the context of the riot a woman is heard crying: "They are killing us!" Another segment shows a crowd beating a humiliated man in a cloth codpiece with a sign identifying him as a thief; the beating, it seems, is justified. The suffering continues in another scene showing a man about to shoot himself in the head while he cries for his mother. Drama is also embedded on the scenes of Pablo Escobar's funeral depicting a police squad's vain attempt to control the crowd as they shout "Pablo! Pablo!" while they try to reach the open coffin of the Colombian drug lord. More of Colombia's drugs-related news: "Canadian customs agents discover a statue of baby Jesus stuffed with cocaine!" "Drama and human misery overflow these scenes!" The resemblance of these images to Catholic imagery could easily escape the attention of a distracted viewer or a zapper, and yet by cutting and pasting them together Restrepo aims to draw the viewer's attention back to it.

Restrepo's remix is a kind of historical zapping of 15 years of Colombian television bringing forth its religious ties. *Viacrucis* resembles channel surfing performed by a zapper, except that in this case "changing channels" becomes a conceptual tool to expose

Figure 11.1 Stills from *Viacrucis* (*Viacrucis, Stations of the Cross*) José Alejandro Restrepo, 2004, 00:19:30, Colombia, B&W and Color (courtesy of the artist)

the continuous flow of images sadly characterized by similarity. Simultaneously, this video exposes how infamous acts are normalized the minute they are aired. Suffering, sacrifice—there is no difference through the television screen, and in fact the condition for gaining 15 minutes of fame seems to depend on assimilating an event as "holy," as Cuauhtémoc Medina has put it.[14] Yet Restrepo does more than zapping. His desire to carefully examine the images daily flickering on the TV monitor implies "mobilizing the archive" in order to articulate a kind of visual grammar.[15] *Viacrucis* and other works by this Colombian artist thus engage in what Hal Foster describes as the "archival impulse" which deals with physical archival material calling for human interpretation or reinterpretation.[16] But his appropriation and remixing of television images is a creative and also a "political act of re-interpretation" and reordering of history, retrieving images from the near past to rethink the complex entanglement of past, present, and future while underlying the ideological affiliations of the original source.[17] Restrepo cuts fragments to tell another story that begins by bringing back the zap and playing the same images of suffering once more but at a different rhythm, where the Catholic symbols can be heard aloud.

Finally, the mise-en-scène of human misery in television is formed by short pieces that last a few seconds or are repeated; Restrepo recycles them to look at them carefully in a context where the original order is broken down into smaller samples that he brings under the microscope. The same images reinforcing justified, almost natural, suffering tied to Catholicism can be used to symbolically scratch their authority. Viacrucis's multiple stages do flow like the 14 Stations of the Cross, the pieces fit, but as seen in Restrepo's remix they do not lead to salvation. By mobilizing the archive of Colombian television, Viacrucis brings the zapper's attention back to the uniformity within the variety of channels.

A Tale of Invasion, by Ximena Cuevas

For almost three decades Mexican artist Ximena Cuevas has combined deeply personal images and stories with fragments of films, television programs and commercials, magazine clippings, and cut-up songs to explore, among other subjects, gender and sexuality, fiction and reality, and the ongoing construction and negotiation of Mexican culture and society.

During the time the United States invaded Iraq in 2003 and discourses of invasion materialized in complex ways, Cuevas produced *Cinepolis, the Capital of Cinema* (*Cinepolis, La Capital Del Cine*). The title of the work draws from the name and slogan of a Mexican movie theater chain, while the video presents a mix of images associated with cultural, economic, political, and symbolic forms of invasions. In the edition Cuevas plays with audio and visual layers, scratching, slowing down, and playing back some fragments repeatedly as in zapping. Sounds and images, however, are intervened and interspersed with footage of diverse forms of spectatorships. The constant thread is invasion and yet through scratching and remixing the 22-minute video stretches this concept. Although the project begins with images of the Coca-Cola parade in Mexico City and clippings of some key landmark of the city are inserted throughout, the locus of the intrusion is blurry. For example, a segment of a black and white Mexican film shows a group of men talking about a recent meeting where scientists came to the conclusion "that the __ _ invasion has most definitely begun," but Cuevas uses a censor beep sound and the grammatical symbol "_" to conceal the invaders' identity. As the video runs it reveals complex layers of everyday invasion and coexistence of local and imported goods from Mexico and the United States, while the tensions are more explicit on some fragments. For example, behind the scenes of a McDonald's commercial, representing the ultimate symbols of transitional capitalism and Americanization, Cuevas clandestinely recorded a makeup artist for food preparing the burger for the shooting.[18] As she was holding the camera she "encountered" a rather controversial shot: popular singer Pedro Fernández in charro costume sits on a McDonalds restaurant while he receives directions from a male director who sexualizes the burger to spice up the shoot: "You are finally mine! . . . You are so good, oh, so tasty. So good, oh, so tasty," says the man offscreen. The scene is repeated a few times until the director pronounces the final "cut." Fernández then spits out pieces of the hamburger he had previously bitten with pleasure on a McDonald's bag. This part of the video brings to the fore a vast array of complex associations with regards to gender, transnational capitalism, and so forth, however one theme particularly resonates with my discussion of remix. The way in which Cuevas's fragment untangles the *contrasting elements* that in the original ad appears to blend seamlessly. Here I draw from a point recently made by scholar Laura Gutiérrez in order to connect it to other parts of *Cinepolis* that I discuss below. As McDonalds threatened Cuevas with a lawsuit, and the video had to be removed from public screenings in Mexico, Gutiérrez explains that:

> what concerned the television production company executives was not the tainted image that the actor singer Pedro Fernández might have acquired because of this "negative" exposure, but the complex web of signification that they were trying to link in one single moving image: McDonalds's product consumption and *mexicanidad*, or even, *latinidad*[19]

Since the commercial was for a major Spanish-language broadcast network aimed at Latino groups in the United States, the single and coherent image that Univision sought to portray is distorted in Cuevas's *Cinepolis* for the charro—that symbol to which all Latinos are supposed to identify with—does not identify with the food. By using remix strategies, by cutting, scratching, and layering pieces of popular culture Cuevas untangles the "complex web of signification" that mass media aims to connect seamlessly.

This is also the case in another fragment of appropriated images of Big Brother Mexico, as TV host Adela Micha explains that the conflicts among the guests are a

Figure 11.2 Stills from *Cinepolis, La Capital Del Cine* (*Cinepolis, the Film Capital*) Ximena Cuevas, 2003, 00:22:18 Mexico, B&W and Color (courtesy of the artist)

clear example of personal interests, particularly "the kind of interest that you pay on a high price." She continues to reflect: "That is just one tiny cell inside the Big Brother house, which in fact might reflect what is happening in the world tonight. By the way, this was President George Bush's message to the world." Micha then reads the speech she holds in her hands: "The initial phases of defending the world from a great danger have begun. And my commitment is that every effort will be made to protect innocent civilians." As she finishes reading, the host looks back toward the camera and says "And our commitment in Televisa is to always keep you well informed and entertained." Cut: TV commercial where young men and women dance to tropical music. Those kinds of disturbing ruptures running in only one minute of a TV program are Cuevas's source of action. Without any zap the fragments flowing smoothly on the screen pose critical differences: How is Bush's mission similar to a broadcast company's mission to entertain? Or how can the "tiny cell" of Big Brother reflect US president's discourse on military operations in Iraq? Can we dance after Bush's speech? By bringing this fragment to a larger process of conceptual and literal scratching of narratives of invasion, Cuevas exposes the fine layers and subtexts forming these images, and in so doing she challenges the continuity and flattening of the original source (Figure 11.2).

But why is it relevant to challenge continuity at the aesthetic and symbolic levels? Numerous scholars have called attention to how digital technologies support an aesthetics of continuity, the seamless blending of contrasting and sometimes troubling differences. Lev Manovich, for instance, identifies a difference between the 1980s postmodern aesthetics and the 1990s logic of computer-based compositing: in the former "historical references and media quotes are maintained as distinct elements," while in the latter continuity and smoothness predominate. Thus, the traditional cut of montage has been replaced in computer-based media with no cuts.[20] In this context, Manovich and other scholars have argued for the need of "precariousness," "cuts," "opalescence," among other concepts to counter the seamless continuity of mass media.[21] *Cinepolis* deploys cuts, scratches, and juxtapositions to confront the flatness of different formats, media, and realities, and to expose the associational lines of invasion. Further, her cuts are inscribed in the very materials she uses, she overwrites on the Coca-Cola parade, on Big Brother, on films and video clips, to generate a critical order out of the "state of disorder" so familiar to zappers and swipers.

Graciela Fuentes: *To Protect?*

The relationship between discourses of surveillance and protection is investigated by Mexican-born New-York-based artist Graciela Fuentes's remix, *To Protect* (2003). By superimposing political speeches about protection and a movie partially encoded against illegal reproduction, the artwork scratches sound and images to such an extent that the noise obscures an intelligible image.

One of the layers consists of videos appropriated from mass media where different public figures such as George Bush and Dick Cheney speak about protection between 2001 and 2002. Another layer features fragments of Peter Jackson's 1994 *Heavenly Creatures*.[22] The film's scenes and characters, however, are unrecognizable given the encoding that the distribution company used to prevent piracy. Instead, a texture resembling a multilayered chainlike fabric render the moving image a mosaic of textures that keep changing as the film runs, and as it is mixed with images of US politicians. In her remix Fuentes turned the protection of the film into a discursive tool, inverting the protection against itself. On the other hand, Fuentes accentuates an aesthetics of interwoven video signals by pixelating the images, so that the finest details are lost in the larger picture. In addition, Fuentes manipulates the video's tonalities with a green filter in order to make a connection to night vision devices used for protection. The juxtaposition of layers of video in a single image converges in abstract, pixelated, and sped up images of protection.

The audio, on the contrary runs slowly. It consists of the mashup of different audio tracks that cannot be discerned individually, in much the same way as the images. Speeches by George Bush, Dick Cheney, and Colin Powell mix with *Heavenly Creatures'* soundtrack; these two sources of sound change in accordance to segments of video, however only one track is consistent throughout the five-minute duration of the video piece: the voice of George Bush in his post-9/11 speech, specifically as he states the phrase "to protect the American people." In Fuentes's work, only five words of this globally broadcasted speech have been stretched, thus creating an unrecognizable sound track that in the process of editing has lost any meaning. In contrast with the flickering sequencing of images, Bush's phrase sounds like an extreme-slow-scratching of a vinyl record performed by a DJ over five minutes. The low frequency resulting from stretching Bush's phrase sounds calm and guttural, and the vibrations and resonances are almost like a meditation soundtrack, a monk chant, or a long-lasting and distant "hum."

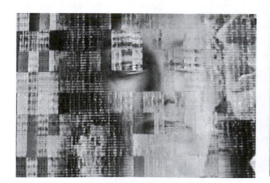

Figure 11.3 Stills from *To Protect*, Graciela Fuentes, 2003, 00:05:30, Mexico/USA, color (courtesy of the artist)

However, both audio and video prevent a clear identification of the source materials, thus *To Protect* also proposes a critique of the circulation and consumption of images in mass media. Fuentes describes her editing as "frenetic and sped up" which according to her "mimics the way televised media attempts to arouse and anesthetize the audience's attention with fragmented information."[23] These fragments and zaps, which are part of our daily life as discussed earlier, are repeated in Fuentes's mix, but unlike images on the newscasts, her mix obstructs a clear vision in order to invite viewers to see beyond the first layer: the realistic representation on the television screen. *To Protect*'s images are pixelated and confusing, they result from a mix which does not blend the differences into a coherent whole. The sequences appropriated by the artist are cut to last only a few seconds as in zapping, but they are also fragmented within the frames so that recognized politicians and Hollywood stars are reduced to ambiguous fragments of bodies and faces that keep changing as though the image is transformed before it can be understood. Further, the protected images of Melanie Lynskey, Kate Winslet, and other cast members of *Heavenly Creatures* mix with images of Bush and other key members of his administration. Hence *To Protect* mixes fiction and reality, blending them in the timeline of a short prewar history that tells itself as the images pass by.

In that sense *To Protect* aligns with the tradition of scratch video to critically target politicians and mass media. In fact, Fuentes's use of the speeches that circulated worldwide during 2001–02 silences the politicians. This might appear as an act of resistance to media overexposure of the September 11 attacks and the subsequent series of events flooding the media stream at a global scale. To that saturation and fragmentation Fuentes responded with a porous image suspended in its own formation. Unlike Restrepo and Cuevas who still retrieve some clear fragments and images, Fuentes's scratches go deeper, turning the material indiscernible. Her five-minute video piece frustrates an affirmative view of faces, words, stories, or something recognizable for the spectator, who is left in a state of expectation. But to say that *To Protect* targets a merely interpretative rearticulation of the source material conceals precisely the political roots of scratching to challenge the power of images.

The Last Composition: Jose Toirac's *Opus*

For many years Cuban artist José Toirac has drawn on strategies such as clipping, cutting, copying, pasting, and quoting material and imagery he appropriates from mass media and popular culture. In his 2005 *Opus*, Toirac appropriates Castro's inaugural discourse of the 2003–04 academic year at the Havana's Revolution Square (Plaza de la Revolución).

Through the editing process the artist cuts all the numbers pronounced by Castro, pasting them one after the other. Starting with a black screen and the title of the work in white font, the video runs in loop and Castro's voice speaks nothing else but numbers: 779; 10,000; 100,000; 4; 1,000; 100,000; 400,000; 2 and so on. Toirac relies on the viewers' recognition of the original source's history; the high-pitched voice of Fidel Castro transformed into a scratch that exposes rather than conceals the artist's manipulation of the material. At times the audio recording appears to cut off and the numbers are clearly separated from the preceding and following words; the context of enunciation that arguably conveys meaning to the overall speech. Thus, Toirac's action of cutting Castro's words is conspicuously audible. In fact, it is not clear whether the cutting and pasting follows the original order in which the numbers were stated or whether the succession is at random. For example, on a fragment of the video Castro states "thirty" seven

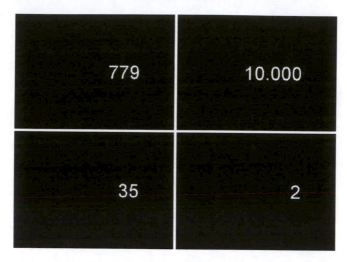

Figure 11.4 The scratching of a speech by Fidel Castro made visible in José Toirac's
Opus (2005) (courtesy of the artist)

continuous times, but his voice sounds different on each utterance; at times it is clear
and strong while at other times the same number sounds rough and harsh. Also, on a
long series the number "one" is inserted between other digits: 1; 42.23; 1; 53.6; 1; 54.7;
1; 55.4; 1; 62.7; 1; 64.6, 1; 66, and so on, exposing Toirac as the author of Castro's speech
recomposition, which sometimes literally sounds like a scratch (Figure 11.4).

Toirac's intervention of Castro's speech plays with the instability of the source material and the truth behind the statistics. Since Castro's words appear cut off, how can we
know whether the artist broke large numbers to form smaller ones or not? Did Castro
really say all those numbers—together they make nearly five minutes of one single
speech? How long was the original speech? What else did Castro say? Did he say anything at all? Cut off from the original source, each number conveys interrogations
exceeding the original source. First, there is no context of enunciation. While Castro's
voice is recognizable he could have been anywhere, not necessarily in Cuba. Second, as
presented in Toirac's remix, Castro's speech resembles the speech of any politician; 11;
12; 13; 1; 150; 81.169; 100; 44.790; the same numbers could have been said by Bush,
Chavez, Chirac, anyone ruling at the time the video was made, before, or afterwards.
This is also because Castro's voice is removed from his body and from his image on the
media. Instead of a medium shot or a close-up of Castro in green army uniform speaking
to the masses, and pointing his finger next to a set of microphones, Toirac's only uses
numbers enunciated strongly, or harshly, or weakly, or raspingly. Lastly there are the
white numbers fading in and out on the black screen; they are slightly positioned toward
the right side of the screen, and from right to left each number morphs into the next
one, so for instance 25 turns into 28, which then turns into 30, and so forth. In these
ways, Toirac's composition oscillates between absence and presence, and in the continuous morphing the absences reveal much more than Castro's speech in itself. Toirac
removes the source material from its context, cutting off the content and emptying its
meaning. By meticulously cutting and pasting just the numbers that Castro pronounced,
he literally scratches the original discourse and pulverizes its very substance, the statistics. Without the mythical and controversial figure of Castro, his numbers convey

nothing about the experience of the people they supposedly represent. In addition, this conceptual video demonstrates how deeply artists can comment upon the culture in which they live by using preexisting material. Toirac creates a new composition of Castro's speech where the formal cut of a series of similar elements contradicts the whole, leaving nothing but a black screen.

Conclusions

The four case studies discussed above show different ways in which contemporary artists from Latin America use remix to aesthetically and symbolically scratch popular culture to resist hegemonic discourses that at times overlap and at other times are not coalesced in mass media. Each case reflects a different pole of remix, from the zapping of channels to the scratch of the smallest components. Most certainly Restrepo, Cuevas, Fuentes, and Toirac share a common concern with the images, ideologies, and the context of circulation and consumption of popular culture, yet on further examination they recognize the potential of extracting pieces from the media stream to reorient the way the audience relates to them. What are those images, what do they want, and what do we do with them apart from glancing at them in different formats? Three of the four pieces discussed in this essay were inspired by the 9/11 media overexposure, a major example of the common stock we share in a transnational context, which functions as overarching framework to reflect on other themes: religion, invasion, protection. But all four cases critically situate the politics of the time, a pre-YouTube era that prepared us for practices of video sharing and social media platforms in which the plague of images spread, reaching "viral" scales. As different as the aesthetic and conceptual deployment of remix strategies by each piece were, they responded to the state of disorder and fragmentation at the core of practices such as zapping, scratching, and swiping with recompositions involving interpretative but particularly material inscriptions and scratches on precisely that plague of images we cannot eliminate. Restrepo's zapping exposes the infinite variety of similar images of suffering. Cuevas accentuates the already existing ruptures offering decomposed pieces of invasion and capitalism. On the other hand, Fuentes and Toirac obstruct the visibility of overexposed public figures and discourses, scratching the material to the smallest components: pixels, textures, numbers, a blank screen. Together, these works form a small sample of remix *from* Latin America, which brings forth local and global issues interwoven on the threads of visual culture. By scratching bodies, pixels, textures, and discourses, these artists aim to bring back the attention of the zapper, the swiper and other scratchers, as well as to critically reflect on the meaning of scratching, for the properties are never granted but rather investigated and instigated; the scratch helps an artist begin to imagine, to interrogate, to resist, to filter, to debunk, to reorient.

Notes

1 Remix strategies have been used by video artists since early experiments with film, TV monitors, and video. Pioneering investigations in Latin America date back to the late 1960s and 1970s in Argentina, Chile, Brazil, and Mexico. For more information on video art from Latin America see: Laura Baigorri, ed. *Video en Latioamérica. Una historia crítica* (Madrid: Brumaria, 2008); and Roberto Moreira Cruz, ed. *Visionários: Audiovisual na América Latina* (São Paulo: Itaucultural, 2008).

2 For example, Chilean Claudia Aravena articulates a critical act of memory by juxtaposing images of the Chilean coup of September 11, 1973, and footage of the September 11, 2001 attacks in the US. Other

artists dealing with issues of memory include Guillermo Cifuentes, Edgar Endress, Sandra De Berduccy, Lotty Rosenfeld, Graciela Taquini, and Carlos Trilnick, among others.

3 The work of Venezuelan Alexander Apóstol is a case in point. In *Documentary* (2005), appropriated documentaries about modern architecture in Venezuela clash with the underdeveloped private space of a construction worker who watches television with his family.

4 Some recent examples include Mauricio Lupini's samba karaoke *Repeat After Reading (Sa Ba Da Ba)* (2011); Jonathan Harker and Donna Conlon's *Drinking Song* (2011); and Alberto Lastreto's *El Prócer* (2008). In addition there are the metacommentaries on remix and issues of copyright in Alfredo Salomón's *No D.R.* (1999) and *Los Rights* (2002).

5 The title of this essay functions as a quotation of Slavoj Žižek's *The Plague of Fantasies* (London: Verso, 2008). I use the notion of "plague" to refer to the epidemic condition of visual materials, to the excess as well as the widespread circulation of images which are advertised, downloaded, shared, remixed, posted, and so forth.

6 Ibid., 4. This term can be best explained with an example provided by Žižek. According to him the colossal figures of an ideal man or a couple installed on top of workplaces and offices during the 1930s' architectural projects of the Soviet Union rendered these public buildings mere pedestals to Stalin's ideology. Ironically, Žižek argues, despite the fact that the monument stood for "an ideological monster which crushes actual living men under his feet," the discourse underneath the design could not have been stated literally, although it was intrinsic to the architecture. This materialization of ideology in a concrete object is for him crucial, for it reveals the antagonisms that the explicit ideological formulation could not recognize. I propose that the profound connections between cultural production and ideology that Žižek summarizes in the aforementioned lines are at the core of the remix by Ximena Cuevas, Graciela Fuentes, José Alejandro Restrepo, and José Toirac.

7 *Zapping* is the act of channel surfing performed by any television spectator with a remote control, though according to Machado we also perform zapping when listening to the radio as we drive. *Zipping* describes the act of fast-forwarding a videotape to avoid commercials on a recorded show. *Scratching* refers to the manual operation of prerecorded materials that leads to its distortion. Arlindo Machado, "O efeito Zapping" in *Máquina e imaginário: o desafio das poéticas tecnológicas* (São Paulo: EDUSP, 1996) 143–164. Unless otherwise noted, all translations are my own.

8 Ibid., 144.

9 N. Katherine Hayles, *How We Think: Digital Media and Contemporary Technogenesis* (Chicago, IL: University of Chicago Press, 2012), 12.

10 Ibid.

11 Scratch video consists of recycled images from broadcasting television that are distorted and reedited through different technical and aesthetics means, but unlike scratching in music, the manipulation of materials does not include the manual operation of scratching the vinyl disc. Machado, "O efeito Zapping," 143–164.

12 My use of the term "art *from* Latin America" draws from Gerardo Mosquera. In order to emphasize a discursive dimension over a geographical location or homogeneous identity, Mosqueta's use of the preposition "from" aims for a subjective, political, and theoretical position rather than representing a particular context or place. Gerardo Mosquera, *Caminar con el diablo: textos sobre arte, internacionalización y culturas* (Madrid: Exit, 2010).

13 José Restrepo, Interview by María A. Iovino, in *Contratextos* (Bogotá: Ministerio de Relaciones Exteriores, 2008), 104.

14 Cuauhtémoc Medina, "De la encarnación como dominio," in *3 Perspectivas: Exposición del Programa de Comisiones CIFO 2007*, ed. María Belén Sáez de Ibarra and José Alejandro Restrepo (Bogotá: Universidad Nacional de Colombia, 2011), 67–72.

15 José Alejandro Restrepo, Interview by Diego Garzón, Casa Daros, Río, 2013. Last modified June 3, 2013. http://vimeo.com/67562953 (accessed August 9, 2014).

16 Hal Foster, "An Archival Impulse," in *October* 110 (Fall 2004) 21.

17 José Alejandro Restrepo, Interview by María A. Iovino, in *Contratextos*, 104.

18 Cuevas recorded the segment of the McDonalds commercial while working for a production company. The fragment lasting 1:33 of a total of 22:18 provoked the rage of both McDonalds's executives and the production company, they threatened Cuevas with a lawsuit as she reveals in her video: *Someone Behind the Door* (2005).

19 Laura Gutiérrez, "Ximena Cuevas's Critical Collages," in *Performing Mexicanidad: Vendidas y Cabareteras on the Transnational Stage* (Austin, TX: University of Texas Press, 2010) 165.

20 Lev Manovich, *The Language of New Media* (Cambridge, MA: MIT Press, 2001), 143.
21 For a discussion of the concept of "precariousness" see: Christine Ross, "Introduction," *Precarious Visualities: New Perspectives on Identification in Contemporary Art and Visual Culture*, eds. Olivier Asselin, Johanne Lamoureux, and Christine Ross (Montreal: McGill-Queen's University Press, 2008). A recent formulation on the "cut" can be found at Sarah Kember and Joanna Zylinska, *Life After New Media: Mediation as a Vital Process* (Cambridge, MA: MIT Press, 2012). With regard to "opalescence" see Margaret Morse, "Nature Morte: Landscape and Narrative in Virtual Environments," in *Immersed in Technology: Art and Virtual Environments*, eds. Mary Anne Moser and Douglas MacLeod (Cambridge, MA: MIT Press, 1996), 195–232.
22 Fuentes also plays with the associations that the film might have with the concepts of protection and reality. For her, *Heavenly Creatures* complicates the mix because the film is based on a book, which at the same time it is supposedly based on facts: two obsessed teenagers decide to commit an act of extreme violence in a moment where according to Fuentes they are "completely disconnected from reality." In the film, the violence is secondary, and yet Fuentes does not suggest a literal connection between military politics in the US and the film's fiction. Fuentes, Graciela. E-mail to the author, August 8, 2013.
23 Graciela Fuentes, *To Protect*, directed by Graciela Fuentes (New York: 2003) DVD.

Bibliography

Baigorri, Laura, Ed. *Video en Latioamérica. Una historia crítica.* Madrid: Brumaria, 2008.

Briceño, Victor, and Rene Naranjo. "Entrevista a Juan Downey." *Catálogo Sexto Festival Franco-Chileno de Video Art.* Santiago: Instituto Chileno-Francés de Cultura, 1986.

Burroughs, William S. "Electronic Revolution." *Ah Pook is Here, and Other Texts: The book of Breeething; Electronic Revolution.* London: Calder, 1979.

Castellanos León, Israel. "José Angel Toirac and Meira Marrero." *Art Nexus* 6, no. 66 (2007): 144–145.

Foster, Hal. "An Archival Impulse." *October* 110 (Fall 2004): 3–22.

García Canclini, Néstor. "Mercosur: la bienal de la desglobalización." *Journal Porto Alegre* 18, no. 31 (2011): 165–167.

Gonzalez, Rita, and Jesse Lerner. *Mexperimental Cinema: 60 Years of Avant-Garde Media Arts from Mexico.* Santa Monica, CA: Smart Art Press, 1998.

Gutiérrez, Laura G. "Ximena Cuevas's Critical Collages." *Performing Mexicanidad: Vendidas y Cabareteras on the Transnational Stage*, 151–166. Austin, TX: University of Texas Press, 2010.

Hall, Doug, and, Sally J. Fifer, Eds. *Illuminating Video: An Essential Guide to Video Art.* New York: Aperture Foundation, 1990.

Hayles, N. Katherine. *How We Think: Digital Media and Contemporary Technogenesis.* Chicago, IL: University of Chicago Press, 2012.

Iovino, María A. *Contratextos.* Bogotá: Ministerio de Relaciones Exteriores, 2008.

Kember, Sarah and Joanna Zylinska. *Life After New Media: Mediation as a Vital Process.* Cambridge, MA: MIT Press, 2012.

La Ferla, Jorge, Ed. *Historia Crítica del Video Argentino.* Buenos Aires: Malba/Telefónica, 2008.

Machado, Arlindo. *Máquina e imaginário: o desafio das poéticas tecnológicas.* São Paulo: EDUSP, 1996.

Manovich, Lev. *The Language of New Media.* Cambridge, MA: MIT Press, 2001.

Medina, Cuauhtémoc. "De la encarnación como dominio." *3 Perspectivas: Exposición del Programa de Comisiones CIFO 2007.* Edited by María Belén Sáez de Ibarra and José Alejandro Restrepo, 67–72. Bogotá: Universidad Nacional de Colombia, 2011.

Mitchell, W. J. T. *What Do Pictures Want? The Lives and Loves of Images.* Chicago, IL: University of Chicago Press, 2005.

Moreira Cruz, Roberto, Ed. *Visionários: Audiovisual na América Latina.* São Paulo: Itaucultural, 2008.

Morse, Margaret. "Nature Morte: Landscape and Narrative in Virtual Environments." In *Immersed in Technology: Art and Virtual Environments.* Edited by Mary Anne Moser and Douglas MacLeod, 195–232. Cambridge, MA: MIT Press, 1996.

Mosquera, Gerardo. *Caminar con el diablo: textos sobre arte, internacionalización y culturas.* Madrid: Exit, 2010.

Navas, Eduardo. *Remix Theory: The Aesthetics of Sampling*. New York: Springer, 2012.

Restrepo, José Alejandro. "Iconomía." In *Arte, Ciencia y Tecnología. Un Panorama Crítico*. Edited by Jorge La Ferla, 161–165. Buenos Aires: Espacio Fundación Telefónica, 2009.

Richard, Nelly. "Contra el pensamiento-teorema: una defensa del video arte en Chile." *Catálogo Sexto Festival Franco-Chileno de Video Arte*. Santiago: Instituto Chileno-Francés de Cultura, 1986.

Ross, Christine. "Introduction." In *Precarious Visualities: New Perspectives on Identification in Contemporary Art and Visual Culture*. Edited by Olivier Asselin, Johanne Lamoureux, and Christine Ross. Montreal: McGill-Queen's University Press, 2008.

Spielmann, Yvonne. *Video: The Reflexive Medium*. Cambridge, MA: MIT Press, 2008.

Žižek, Slavoj. *The Plague of Fantasies*. London: Verso, 2008.

12

RACE AND REMIX

The Aesthetics of Race in the Visual and Performing Arts

Tashima Thomas

Remix is a cultural practice that includes reintroductions of preexisting sources mixed together via the practice of cut/copy and paste. This act of sampling in remix incorporates the fragmentation of various sampled beats vivifying the effect of the composition's style or quality. The remixing and sampling of beats is a strategy popularized in music; however, when considering remix strategies within a visual context, it is possible to theorize how remix operates among visual compositions—including those that deal with race. A discussion of race and remix theory in Latin America challenges the inclination to flatten and marginalize racial and cultural aesthetics and experiences. What follows is a critical reading of the aesthetics of remix in relation to race in the visual and performing arts of Latin America and the Caribbean. This assemblage of visual remix strategies is organized according to three compositional strategies: the Casta Grandmaster Remix, the Banana Remix, and the Monster Mash Remix. Each remix strategy demonstrates a variation of the sampling and reassembling of racialized bodies. The purpose of this research is to create a visual soundtrack, per se, that will illustrate the nuances and complexities of how race, and particularly blackness, is constructed and *remixed* in the cultural imaginary.

I elaborate on the cultural-intertextuality of these remixes as they relate to a visual archive that can be experienced within a cultural space. For example, nineteenth-century Impressionist paintings are often referred to as possessing a kind of "photographic vision," that is having a quality of representing a suspended moment in time. This suggests a connection between paintings conventionally experienced statically with photography which is associated with the temporal experience capturing snatches of time. Kirk Varnedoe dismantles the idea of Impressionist works representing "snapshots" by revealing how the production of photographs contemporary with Impressionist painting have yet to conjure a photo that looks anything like Edgar Degas's painting, *Place de la Concorde* of 1875. Varnedoe observes the nineteenth-century photographic endeavor aspiring to greater control and selectivity while countering with the Impressionists' aspiration to greater spontaneity or receptiveness.[1] He reaffirms the instantaneity of the accidental found in nineteenth-century photography as a kind of meaningless static, saying that, "With structures of time, just as with structures of space, what photographers involuntarily tolerated as eccentricities, these painters independently and aggressively pursued and developed as the basis of a cohesive new reality."[2] What I am suggesting is to consider viewing paintings in a way that belies static attributions, but rather as possessing sequential rhythms enlarging on a temporal experience. This formation of a "cohesive new reality" participates in a variation of remix when considering the aesthetics of individual elements that shifts the spatial reference to the temporal. Thus, the somewhat delimiting sequential experience of music within fragmented time can serve as a larger model for the temporal experience by applying this to how we experience paintings. The precision of selectivity by musicians and painters informs their work by including certain elements and excluding others. This practice of selection assists in the construction of the composition's spatial structure. The remixed projects that follow exhibit some form of selectivity defining their composition.

The Casta Grandmaster Remix

What I refer to as the Casta Grandmaster Remix incorporates *extended* and *selective* remix practices.[3] The *extended* remix is expressed as a longer version of the original song. This particular kind of remix became popular during the mid-1970s when DJs lengthened musical compositions by several minutes, fulfilling a cultural need by creating arrangements that were more danceable. The Casta Grandmaster Remix is a semieponymous reference to one of the pioneers of hip hop, DJing, cutting, and mixing, Grandmaster Flash, who developed innovative techniques that are foundational to the practice of musical remix.[4] Applying the principles of pioneering DJing techniques to visual compositions paves the way to an introduction of cutting and mixing within extended arrangements. Therefore, as a nod to one of the forefathers of remix and hip hop, the debut record on this visual soundtrack is called the "Casta Grandmaster Remix." Visual productions foundational to the study of the aesthetics of race and remix are also found in casta paintings of colonial Mexico.

Casta paintings were a series of images commissioned by the Spanish or creole elite during colonial Mexico. The terms *criollo* and/or creole are used here to describe a person of Spanish decent born in New Spain during the colonial period. The series of casta paintings varied in number to include up to 16 paintings describing the various racial mixtures of the inhabitants. Casta paintings were pseudoscientific family portraits including particular tropes used to identify the population and new racial mixtures. The Spanish did not take very many Spanish women with them at the time of conquest and during the colonial period. The scarcity of Spanish women and the imperialist desire for expansion led to the engagement of Spanish men in interracial relationships with indigenous and African women. Casta paintings offered a visual record of these interracial relationships systematically organized according to the idea of the family unit—the father, mother, and offspring along with some indication of profession or class.

The earliest identified casta paintings began with a series of four works in 1711 attributed to Manuel Arellano. The original four casta paintings were: *Rendition of a Mulatto*, *Rendition of a Mulatto*, *Rendition of a Chichimeca*, and *Rendition of a Chichimeco*.

The first two paintings are of mixed-race subjects with parents of African and Spanish descent. The latter two works are of indigenous subjects. These works are considered to be the prototype for all other casta paintings. As such, I attribute these foundational works to the *extended* remix. *Rendition of a Mulatto* (Figure 12.1), which features a mixed-race woman of African descent, and *Rendition of a Chichimeco* are simplified by only presenting a singular individual in the composition; both paintings include the addition

Figure 12.1 Manuel Arellano, *Rendition of a Mulatto*, 1711, oil on canvas (photo courtesy of Manuel Arellano via Collection of Jan and Frederick Mayer, Denver)

of a young child. The original four casta paintings represent the *extended* remix. They function as expanded versions of the original composition as yet uncomplicated by the adding and deleting of various sounds/images. The original composition would have been the real-life person or imagined personage on whom they are modeled. As the original casta paintings, this set of four works provides a more mixable palette for future artists to remix. These works introduced the idea of the pictorial illustration of racialized bodies, offspring, and an indication of lifestyle or *calidad*, which is a performance of social identity that included variables such as a person's skin color, race, class, occupation, clothing, and social conditions. I elaborate on these locations of performance and identity in further detail when discussing the Banana Remix.

Confirming artistic indebtedness to the original four casta paintings, Ilona Katzew writes, "Modeled after Arellano's series are two sets attributed to Juan Rodríguez Juárez . . . Many of the figures in the complete set strongly rely on Arellano's models"[5] Therefore, the figures in the original casta paintings furnish the racial "types" which operate as solitary beats plucked for insertion and reinsertion into new compositions.

The public accessibility of viewing racial "types" becomes more widespread as casta paintings were presented in quasi-public spaces. As a result of the growing access to casta paintings and the racial stereotypic tropes they represent a second form of remix begins to develop. As noted above, the extension of the original song becomes complicated with the addition of various figures within the composition. This is what is referred to as *selective* remix.

The *selective* remix maintains its relationship to the original while adding and subtracting elements from it. This dependency on recognition of the original composition is captured in the stability of its own specialness. A remix's specialness refers to the idiosyncratic elements of compositions which can be isolated, repeated, and recognized in various reincarnations. Remixes are dependent upon the acknowledgement of the original source material or what I describe as a work's relentless distinctiveness. What happens next is a proliferation of *selective* remixes based on casta painting *extended* remixes. The selectivity of this remix adds and subtracts figures from the original casta paintings, but without diminishing essential distinctive sequences. For example, Miguel Cabrera's *From Spaniard and Mulata, Morisca*, 1763 (Figure 12.2), is painted 52 years after Arellano's *Rendering of a Mulatto*.

Figure 12.2 Miguel Cabrera, *From Spaniard and Mulata, Morisca*, 1763, oil on canvas (photo courtesy Miguel Cabrera via private collection)

Cabrera refers to Arellano's *Rendering of a Mulatto* (Figure 12.1) and cuts/copies and pastes the figure of the *mulata* into a *selective* remix. Cabrera makes three additions by adding a Spanish father, a son, and a daughter. The similarities between Arellano's and Cabrera's *mulata* figure are striking, therefore maintaining or transmitting the special characteristics or relentless distinctiveness from Arellano's composition. Both *mulata* figures are wearing a billowy overblouse called a *manga*, often worn by Afro-Mexicans, over a floral print dress. Both figures have similar honeyed complexions, coiffed hairstyles, facial features, and exhibit the same averted glance. The recognition of the original source material (Arellano's work) is uncompromised and duplicated through the feature of cut/copy and paste and remixed with the additional added figures thereby creating a new work. Although the relentless distinctiveness, or distinguishable characteristics, from Arellano's *mulata* figure remains faithful in racial aesthetic and in attire in Cabrera's work, what makes Cabrera's painting a new remix is the improvisation of additional figures. Like improvising new beats on a popular riff, Cabrera repeats a racial trope that is recognizable, memorable, and recurring.

Casta paintings were attempts to classify the various racial nuances of the rapidly diversifying population and thereby assigned nomenclatures such as "wolf" and "coyote" to identify racially mixed persons. This brand of identity formation was part of a national project in New Spain that functioned to satisfy European curiosity by classifying the Other in an attempt to "enlighten" Spaniards. While other scholars have investigated the process of naming conventions as they relate to power and control, I will focus now on how the endlessness of racial remixing within casta painting relates to the *selective* remix.

As one of the more successful casta painting artists, Cabrera defined the effective treatments of these compositions and was emulated by other artists creating additional remixes. Michele Knobel and Colin Lankshear describe the endless hybridization possibilities for remix, "In the sense that each new mix becomes a meaning-making resource for subsequent remixes, there is no end to remixing. Each remix in principle expands the possibilities for future remixes."[6] The adding and subtracting of various racial mixtures within casta paintings provides multiple possibilities of combinations or remixes. Casta paintings repeated the classification of racial mingling like beats in compositions— repeating the same images through the use of cut/copy and paste. These new compositions or remixes seem inexhaustible in their recombinations of racial mixtures, offspring, and indications of class, trade or *calidad*. Some works focus on labor and have included pastoral countryside scenes, and others include scenes within the city or domestic interior. Some of these remixes also served as propaganda for the industriousness of racial hybridity in the new world, stressing conformance to Bourbon reforms, showcasing natural resources, and as a platform to reconfirm racial stereotypes. It is the familiarity of these racial tropes that operate as a memorable theme and recur in each new remix with infinite possibilities.

The ritualistic sequencing of racialized bodies become enactments of racial mythologies and function as a sociological adhesive uniting a nation under a mythical consciousness. Casta paintings succeeded in the illustration and repetition of perceived racial difference. Although a valid argument can be made about the presentation of class difference in casta paintings, the paintings themselves are titled according to racial taxonomies. For example, typical painting titles include: *Black and Spaniard makes Mulatto* or *Mestizo and Indian makes Coyote*. The interdependence of ritual and myth are opportunities to "perform the world" and the way things ought to be in "conscious tension with the way things are."[7] The *selectivity* of most casta paintings endeavors to organize a recently colonized space and population as part of a much larger national project. The rhythmic sequencing of racial types invokes the myth-and-ritual ontology. The compulsive reiteration of material and visual rhetoric in casta paintings not only provides an endless series of racial remixes, but seeks to "perform the world" in the way the world should be in conscious tension to the way that it is actually experienced.

The Banana Remix

In the 1943 classic film, *The Gang's All Here* (Figure 12.3), Carmen Miranda's bananas and strawberries performance is the acute manifestation of Roland Barthes's masculine and feminine gender assignments to food. Barthes's semiological pioneering interpretations of food constitute a sign system signifying masculinity to bananas and femininity to strawberries. The phallocentric bananas sharing the stage with the ripe strawberries illuminate male sexual desire imposed on the female body. Carmen Miranda's dress is trimmed with red strawberries as she balances a headdress of yellow bananas on her head. Most of Miranda's outfits were specifically modeled after the traditional, colonial dress of the Bahianas (black women from Bahia in the northern region of Brazil). The Bahianas wore long skirts, ruffled blouses, and had baskets on their heads full of fruit to sell in the marketplace. Carmen Miranda's sartorial interpretation of the attire of black women from Bahia would become her most recognized aesthetic.

Figure 12.3 Carmen Miranda in Busby Berkeley's *The Gang's All Here*, 1943

In the documentary, *Carmen Miranda: Bananas Is My Business*, the narrator explains the origins of Carmen Miranda's image saying, "Carmen was our dancing doll; white to disguise the blackness of the music she grew up with; the blackness of most of her musician friends; and of the origins of her outfit."[8] Carmen Miranda's cultural appropriation of blackness through the modeling of her persona after black Bahianas is an active case of remix and sampling. This extended use of cultural sampling becomes remixed through adaptation and allegory while maintaining its relentless distinctiveness. Consequently, Carmen Miranda's image functions as a performative, *reflexive* remix sampling fragments of Brazilian blackness including dress, jewelry, musical traditions, style, and panache. The Banana Remix is a cultural aesthetic capitalizing on recognizable themes of mulattaness, but also challenges the remix's sequencing by manipulating certain notes. This brand of remix allegorizes and extends the aesthetic of sampling, claims autonomy even when carrying the name of the original, and leaves the original tracks largely intact and recognizable.[9]

Carmen Miranda was born on February 9, 1909 in Portugal to parents of Portuguese descent who would later emigrate to Brazil. Although Miranda was a Portuguese-born Brazilian, arguably she symbolized mulatta culture. The aesthetics of her persona was one of a mixed-race woman of African descent, not unlike the Afro-Brazilian women of Bahia. Angela and Onik'a Gilliam discuss the definition of Brazilian mulattaness as being that of a "showgirl" and explain that the term mulatta also may refer to a professional job description: "To dress like a mulata is . . . to put on a long skirt, high-heeled shoes with platform soles . . . It can even be in the daytime, but the mulata is going to put on her heels and arrive very well put together . . . walking around pretty, decorated."[10] The Gilliams further define mulattaness as being shaped by, "the intention of men toward a woman; the woman who is sexualized is thrust into the mulata subject position."[11] Therefore, Carmen Miranda embodies the performativity of the mulatta as she was a professional Brazilian "showgirl," who wore the costume of mulattas, including the platform soles for which she became famous. Her hypersexualized persona as an object of male desire also subscribes to the definition of mulattaness. The opening performance of strawberries and bananas is a cogent witness to the objectification of the mulatta body.

In addition to singing songs like, "Anti-Metropolitan Mulato" and "Back from the Samba," Carmen Miranda also sang a song referencing the black women of Bahia where she inventories what a woman from Bahia has: a silk turban, golden earrings, golden chains, a lace bustier, and golden bracelets. Miranda's cultural Banana Remix appropriates the decorated body of the Bahiana by adopting the silk turban, golden earrings, golden chains, golden bracelets, etc., and yet refashions the memorableness of the Bahiana personification. Miranda allegorizes the magical qualities of the remix's relentless distinctiveness that are most identifiable. She is a symbolic representation of blackness without the blackness. By embodying the personification of Bahiana blackness or mulattaness through sampling the accoutrements of black style she becomes a reflexive remix. However, it is Miranda's whiteness that challenges the distinguishing rhetoric. Miranda's appropriation of blackness in her persona was not unique; however, it may best illustrate how strategies of sampling intersect with the concept of authorship as visited in the work of Roland Barthes and Michel Foucault.

In Roland Barthes's essay, "The Death of the Author" and in Michel Foucault's "What Is an Author?" both discuss the relationships between authorship and readers.[12] Barthes and Foucault investigate through a series of interrogatives, epistemological constructions, and historical analysis the links between the author, the reader, or critic, and the unity of a text. Barthes describes the death of the author as a function of the writing process. Through the recounting of the text the author loses his voice, a gap appears—the author dies and writing commences. Barthes asserts the death of the author is aimed at her identity as a result of the neutering process of writing.[13] Similarly, Miranda's *reflexive* remix challenges the original text of blackness where the author loses her voice, a gap appears, the death of the author ensues and the reader deciphers the text. In other words, the original text of the identity of the black body is lost and the reader deciphers the text as a white identity or body. Remix commences.

At the outset of "What Is an Author?" Foucault explicitly clarifies that in his discussion he is setting aside a sociohistorical analysis of the author as an individual, the cultural status of the author, and other research into authenticities, attributions, and systems of valorization.[14] However, unlike Barthes, Foucault is not suggesting an anni-hilation of the author, but rather a dislocation or decentering of the author in order to lay hold on a greater comprehension of the relationship between the author and the text and as a kind of subversion of the historical privileging of the author. Whereas Barthes applies a reading of the speech-act and examination of linguistics, Foucault investigates the gaps by exploring the use of the "author-function."

Foucault describes how the author-function does not operate uniformly along all dis-courses, but is tied to legal and institutional systems where attributions to texts are required. Foucault goes on to elaborate on this form of investigation that returns to the text itself in order to affect historical discursive analysis. He describes how the complexi-ties of the author-function, "could also reveal the manner in which discourse is articu-lated on the basis of social relationships."[15] As previously stated, Miranda's sampling of black style and presentment was not original, but an editorial power of selection or extended sampling found in the *reflexive* remix. Navas describes how sampling allows for the death of the author and the author-function to take effect in late capitalism, "because 'writing' is no longer seen as something truly original, but as a complex act of resam-pling—as the reinterpretation of material previously introduced."[16] Perhaps this is one of the reasons why the reinterpretation of Miranda's image would come to represent a hybridization of South American identities. Miranda's cultural remix favors the extended sampling of fragmented elements over the whole, which may lead to inaccurate readings and misinterpretations. Miranda would later suffer harsh criticism for this appearance of cultural homogeneity as an aesthetic misrepresentation of Brazilian and Latin American identities. Although she never claimed to represent a singular Latin American identity, her persona was attributed these duties by a system, similar to the casta paintings. Miranda's image serves as a commodified fetish of mulattaness. Interestingly, the *reflexive* remix demands that the viewer question everything that is presented.[17] Even Miranda herself would later question the stereotype of the "Brazilian Bombshell" or the "Latina Spitfire." She began to understand the limitations and damage caused by the extended sampling of hypersexualized blackness.

The repetition of racial types informs mythologized notions of racial identity. In *The Location of Culture*, Homi K. Bhabha states that, "the *same old* stories of the Negro's animality, the Coolie's inscrutability or the stupidity of the Irish *must* be told (compul-sively) again and afresh, and are differently gratifying and terrifying each time."[18] The traditional colonial treatment of the mulatta body is as a fantastical locus of playful exchange. Her image is one of sexual profundity as represented in the many seeded fruits in her headdress and outfit. The poster for the documentary, *Carmen Miranda: Bananas*

Is My Business, says it best: "An explosion of fantasy, energy and playful eroticism." Miranda's remixed hybridization of the mulatta body receives an apotheosis of objectification in this poster. The advertisement capitalizes on the stereotype of the mulatta aesthetic as fantastical, full of inexhaustible sexual energy, and sexually available. The Banana Remix is reauthored with greater public access and profound susceptibility to the repetition of damaging racial stereotypes.

The Monster Mash Remix

The Monster Mash Remix offers a critical reading of the character Tia Dalma/Calypso (Naomie Harris) from Walt Disney's two films, *Pirates of the Caribbean: Dead Man's Chest* (2006) and *At World's End* (2007). Calypso, also known as Tia Dalma in the films, embodies the stereotype of the tragic mulatta figure typical of the colonial desire of the mulatta body. For example, Tia Dalma/Calypso, as the only black character in the films, is rendered as a hypersexualized body and delivers dialog filled with double entendre and mystical divinations. By applying *regenerative* remix theory, it becomes evident that the character of Tia Dalma/Calypso is reiterative of white male, patriarchal desire for the mulatta/Afro-Caribbean body fulfilling the formulaic cinematic stereotype of the tragic mulatta. The image of Calypso is a performative embodiment of remix as an extra-species mashup of mulatta/monster identities.

The *Pirates of the Caribbean* series is a multibillion-dollar franchise in which critics have scarcely read race into the series. If *regenerative* remix takes place in a nonlinear, ahistorical fashion then the fantastical Caribbean of *Pirates* is its own *regenerative* remix. A simulacrum of the Caribbean represented in *Pirates of the Caribbean* is blanketed in whiteness and seldom represents blackness, even though the Caribbean as a paramount center of transatlantic slavery was predominantly canvassed with black bodies. As a utopian paradise of whiteness where one rarely catches a glimpse of blackness (and there is certainly no representation of the transatlantic slave trade), the Caribbean presented in *Pirates* is ahistorical. Although, *Pirates* is written to take place during the seventeenth century, a period concomitant with the height of the triangular trading system, the black body has almost completely disappeared from the landscape—offering a revised history.

Calypso's unrequited love is archetypal of the mulatta as a tragic figure. According to the script Calypso is of Afro-Cuban, mixed-race descent. The mulatta is mythologized as tragic because her body serves as the reminder and the remainder of a perceived illicit sexual encounter between whiteness and blackness. The politics of race are also the politics of sexuality when articulating the tragedy of the mulatta because it is the policing of sexuality that calls her being into question. The figure of the tragic mulatta is denied love and happiness because she is somehow pathologically cursed as a reminder of the tragedy of miscegenation. Francis Galton, the founder of eugenics believed that, "the mulatto was a tragic figure not because he or she was born into a biracist culture that offered no stable position but because he or she 'contaminated' the hereditary pool of (white) racial genius."[19]

In *At World's End*, we discover that Tia Dalma is in a complicated love affair with the pirate Davy Jones (Bill Nighy.) Jones's mortal self was as an Anglo man, but now he has been transformed into the squid-like, humanoid monster covered in squishy tentacles and fitted with a giant crab claw for a left arm. Davy Jones's transformation into the grotesque pirate monster can be read as a retribution for the forbidden love he shared with the mulatta Tia Dalma and therefore reads as a cautionary tale. Jones's grisly mutations are also a reflection of the irreverent combination of Calypso's monstrousness—a mashup of something monster, something evil, and something human. Thus I refer to Tia Dalma/Calypso as a Monster Mash Remix. Davy Jones was charged by Calypso with ferrying the souls of those who died at sea and if he fulfilled this duty he would be allowed to come ashore every ten years and be with the woman he loved—Calypso. After fulfilling his contract and coming ashore after ten years, Calypso was not there waiting for him and therefore violated her end of the contract. Feeling tricked and greatly despondent in being abandoned by Calypso, Jones becomes a menace on the seas exacting his fury. In a scene from *At World's End*, the jailed Calypso is visited by Jones to whom she confides, "It has been torture trapped in this single form; cut off from the sea, from all that I love . . . from you."[20] Jones finally asks Calypso why she wasn't there when he came ashore after ten years of fulfilling his duties ferrying the souls of those who died at sea. Calypso responds, "It's my nature. Would you love me if I was anything but what I am?"[21] This biologizing of race as natural reinforces the stereotype of the mulatta as capricious.

Not long thereafter we find the crucial scene in which Calypso is released from her mortal form of Tia Dalma. Tia Dalma stands bound in heavy ropes on a ship surrounded by pirates beginning the ceremony of her manumission. In releasing Calypso from her human form the pirates hope she will grant them her powers to rule the seas and therefore profit considerably from her talents. Captain Hector Barbosa (Geoffrey Rush) commands, "Calypso! I release you from your human bonds," as he lights the talisman on fire.[22] The incantation was unsuccessful as the spell is only solvent when the words are spoken to Calypso as if to a lover. The wacky-eyed pirate, Ragetti (Mackenzie Cook) whispers sweetly in Calypso's ear, as if to a lover saying, "Calypso, I release you from your human bonds."[23] Calypso inhales the smoke from the fiery talisman and the transformation begins. She begins to tremble and grow exceedingly agitated. William Turner (Orlando Bloom) asks her to identify who it was that betrayed her. She trembles greatly and answers, "Name him!" to which he replies, answering his own question, "Davy Jones."[24] Calypso's manumission from her human form is catapulted as she grows larger and larger in size, bursting the bonds of the ropes binding her. The pirates surrounding Calypso tighten their ropes restraining her body. As she grows larger and larger so do the expanses of bare flesh revealing a partially naked body. The mise-en-scène of a crew of white seamen restraining an enslaved black female body with heavy ropes is powerfully charged, summoning recognition of the cataclysmic violence inflicted upon black bodies during the transatlantic slave trade. Furthermore, the captor's fear of manumission meant the fear of releasing a "monster," as well as the fear of losing wealth and advantage. These fears are played out on a black female body as a performative embodiment of the Monster Mash Remix.

Calypso reaches gargantuan proportions as Captain Barbosa and his crew kneel before her in obeisance. Barbosa begs her favors saying, "Calypso . . . I come before you as but a servant, humble and contrite. I have fulfilled me vow, and now ask your favor . . . Spare meself, me ship, me crew and unleash your fury upon those who dare pretend themselves your masters, or mine."[25] Barbosa hopes to manipulate Calypso's favors and profit financially. He is quoted as stating earlier regarding the potentiality of freeing Calypso, "Imagine all the power of the seas brought to bear against our enemy."[26] Calypso shouts in a manner of speech not clearly understood. After referencing the script, I found Calypso roars in her tirade, "Malfaiteur en Tombeau, Crochir l'Esplanade, Dans l'Fond d'l'eau!" which roughly translates from French to, "Across the deepest waters of the ocean, find the path to he who wrongfully entombed me."[27] Shortly thereafter Calypso has manifested as a terrible maelstrom debilitating the ship of her former lover, Davy Jones, and bringing victory to the ship of Barbosa.

At the height of her harangue, Calypso erupts into an avalanche of crabs which begin to pour from her giant mouth and soon her whole body is transformed into a mountain of crabs flooding the crew. The ship is rocked back and forth as the Calypso crab body/bodies return to the water. The Calypso crab body/black body returning to the waters of the Atlantic is painfully evocative of black bodies committed to the sea by their captors either in hopes of financial gain (insurance claims as with the slave ship, *Zong*), or in the casting overboard of half-dead or dead bodies, and even the frequent suicides of enslaved Africans. This returning of the crab to the waters is also reflected in the trope of the tragic mulatta returning to her black community and rejecting "passing" in white society. Calypso symbolizes the practice of passing because she was secretly a powerful goddess passing as human. She rejects this "passing" and returns to her native state as the goddess Calypso.

LeiLani Nishime discusses the embodiment of mulattaness and monsterness. Nishime argues the correlations between the term "monsters" or cyborgs in the horror/science fiction genre and mulattaness stating, "The good cyborg perfectly replicates the stereotype of the tragic mulatto/a."[28] Nishime refers to the 1982 film *Blade Runner* as a replication of this motif stating, "Often she is shown as caught between two worlds, and since she is obviously the result of an illicit relationship, she suffers from a melancholy of the blood that inevitably leads to tragedy."[29] The Monster Mash Remix operates in a way that adopts elements from at least two distinct sources which are constantly changing while maintaining certain characteristics. The shifting processes of reflexivity are expressed through the constant change of Calypso's body. She is biologically entombed in a physical, female form. This body changes in the process of manumission and she becomes a giant Calypso. However, this giant body changes into multiple crab bodies and returns to the sea. Calypso then changes again into a torrential thunderstorm. Her difference is marked by the constant reflexiveness of biological processes. She is a mashup of mulatta and monster—two distinct individual sources which are a reflection of constant cultural change. This marriage of mulatta and monster is also a cultural commentary on the previously mentioned perceived abominableness of mixed-race offspring. The typical genre of the monster is one in which she must not inhabit the realm of the mainstream. As a familiar trope repeated in Mary Shelley's *Frankenstein*, the monster must die. In *Pirates of the Caribbean*, the monster dies out of her human form and is transformed in a way that positions her within the margins of the action and yet offers a freedom from the constriction of social norms. Calypso is an ahistorical mashup of distinct source material without relying on the memorable theme of previous remixes. She is first a mashup because of her mulattaness and therefore already implicated as monstrous. Her racial in-betweeness is ranked transgressive and carries threats of aberration because she challenges the boundaries between whiteness and blackness. It is a well-established trope among gothic literary genre to integrate the mulatta or "half-breed" with the monstrous as found in Mary Shelley's *Frankenstein*, the vampiric, or the werewolf because of the idea of racial contamination. Furthermore, when the racialized mashup becomes remashed we enter the second order of remix where the human intersects with the nonhuman grotesque, creating a ghoulish resonance of the Monster Mash Remix. Although Calypso's identity favors previously remixed tropes of the mulatta as tragic or hypersexualized, her mashup of mulatta and monster creates a new remix that is constantly updated because of the reiteration of the visual archive reproducing images of the racially mixed as grotesque. The potency of these ideological constructions is enduring because of the repeated gothicizing of blackness as problematic and the emphasizing of the depravity of miscegenation which maintains an ideologically racist archive. H. L. Malchow describes gothicized racial representations as rooted in and reinforcing other areas of prejudice and fear. Malchow describes the use of an "imperial gothic," having elements of atavism, the occult, the grotesque, and the sadistic as being to a large extent racial gothic.[30] Therefore, as an adoption of the "imperial gothic," the mashup of beast-mulatta located in Calypso can be interpreted as a Monster Mash Remix.

Conclusion

By examining remix as a cultural framework for understanding the aesthetics of race in visual representations, we find fragmented bodies that are sampled, reassembled, and repeated like beats producing memorable anthems. Through the use of remix theory as an exploratory strategy it is possible to uncover the ruptures and reassemblages of racialized identities as they relate to national projects, public access, commodified fetishism, and other cultural flows. "Remix means to take cultural artifacts and combine and manipulate them into new kinds of creative blends."[31] These new creative blends may include additions and deletions of various elements that somehow maintain distinctive characteristics exemplifying memorable themes. Remix discourse offers a diversification of instruments and practices for negotiating cultural flows as reflected in the Casta Grandmaster Remix and the Banana Remix. However, as in the case of the Monster Mash Remix, material from two distinct sources combine in ways that are ahistorical, constantly changing, and yet revelatory of the consistency of racialized tropes of blackness.

Notes

1 Kirk Varnedoe. "Artifice of Candor: Impressionism and Photography Reconsidered." *Art in America* 68 (1980), 72.

2 Ibid., 75.

3 See, in addition, regarding the nuances of these terms and their relevant musical and artistic examples, Eduardo Navas, *Remix Theory: The Aesthetics of Sampling* (New York: Springer, 2012), 65–74.

4 Grandmaster Flash, also known as Joseph Saddler, was inducted into the Rock and Roll Hall of Fame in 2007 along with the Furious Five. They were the first rap/hip hop musical artists to receive this honor. Grandmaster Flash is credited for creating the crossfader and experimenting with innovative remixing techniques such as backspin, punch phrasing, and scratching.

5 Ilona Katzew, *Casta Painting: Images of Race in Eighteenth-Century Mexico* (New Haven, CT: Yale University Press, 2004), 15.

6 Michele Knobel and Colin Lankshear, "Remix: The Art and Craft of Endless Hybridization." *Journal of Adolescent & Adult Literacy* 52, no. 1 (September 2008), 26.

7 William G. Doty, *Mythography: The Study of Myths and Rituals* (Tuscaloosa, AL: University of Alabama Press, 2000), 335.

8 *Carmen Miranda: Bananas Is My Business*, Channel Four Films and Riofilme, 1995, filmstrip.

9 Navas, *Remix Theory*, 66.

10 Angela Gilliam and Onik'a Gilliam, "Odyssey: Negotiating the Subjectivity of Mulata Identity in Brazil." *Latin American Perspectives* 106 (1999), 64.

11 Ibid., 66.

12 Eduardo Navas and others have written extensively on Barthes and Foucault describing how remix is informed by poststructural approaches to reading and writing.

13 Roland Barthes, "Death of the Author." *Aspen* 5/6, 1967.

14 Foucault, Michel, "What Is an Author?" *Language, Counter-Memory, Practice: Selected Essays and Interviews by Michel Foucault* (Ithaca, NY: Cornell University Press, 1977), 115.

15 Ibid., 137.

16 Navas, *Remix Theory*, 136.

17 Ibid., 104.
18 Homi K. Bhabha. *The Location of Culture* (London: Routledge Classics, 1994), 111, original emphasis.
19 Shawn Michelle Smith, *American Archives: Gender, Race and Class in Visual Culture* (Princeton, NJ: Princeton University Press), 127.
20 *Pirates of the Caribbean: At World's End* (Walt Disney Pictures/Jerry Bruckheimer Films, 2007), filmstrip.
21 Ibid.
22 Ibid.
23 Ibid.
24 Ibid.
25 Ibid.
26 Ibid.
27 Ibid.
28 LeiLani Nishime. "The Mulatto Cyborg: Imagining a Multiracial Future." *Cinema Journal* 44, no. 2 (2005), 40.
29 Nishime, "The Mulatto Cyborg," 40.
30 H. L. Malchow mines the literary archive in *Gothic Images of Race in Nineteenth-Century Britain* (Stanford, CA: Stanford University Press, 1996) and elaborates on how works such as Robert Louis Stevenson's *Dr. Jekyll and Mr. Hyde*, Bram Stoker's *Dracula*, and H. G. Well's *The Island of Dr. Moreau* operate as cultural studies documenting the relationship between racial anxieties, the imperial realm, and a gothic sensibility. In addition, Maisha L. Wester's *African American Gothic: Screams from Shadowed Places* (New York: Palgrave Macmillan, 2012) explores gothic fiction and racial discourses.
31 Knobel and Lankshear, "Remix: The Art and Craft of Endless Hybridization," 22.

Bibliography

Barthes, Roland. "Death of the Author." *Aspen* 5/6, 1967.
——. *The Rustle of Language*. Berkeley, CA: University of California Press, 1984.
Bhabha, Homi K. *The Location of Culture*. London: Routledge Classics, 1994.
Carmen Miranda: Bananas Is My Business. Channel Four Films and Riofilme, 1995. Filmstrip.
Doty, William G. *Mythography: The Study of Myths and Rituals*. Tuscaloosa, AL: University of Alabama Press, 2000.
Foucault, Michel. "What Is an Author?" *Language, Counter-Memory, Practice: Selected Essays and Interviews by Michel Foucault*, 113–138. Ithaca, NY: Cornell University Press, 1977.
Gilliam, Angela and Onik'a Gilliam, "Odyssey: Negotiating the Subjectivity of *Mulata* Identity in Brazil." *Latin American Perspectives*, 106 (1999): 60–84.
Katzew, Ilona. *Casta Painting: Images of Race in Eighteenth-Century Mexico*. New Haven, CT: Yale University Press, 2004.
Knobel, Michele and Colin Lankshear. "Remix: The Art and Craft of Endless Hybridization." *Journal of Adolescent & Adult Literacy* 52, no. 1 (2008): 22–33.
Malchow, H. L. *Gothic Images of Race in Nineteenth-Century Britain*. Stanford, CA: Stanford University Press, 1996.
Navas, Eduardo. "Regressive and Reflexive Mashups in Sampling Culture." *Mashup Cultures*. New York: Springer, 2010.
——. *Remix Theory: The Aesthetics of Sampling*. New York: Springer, 2012.
Nishime, LeiLani. "The Mulatto Cyborg: Imagining a Multiracial Future." *Cinema Journal* 44, no. 2 (2005): 34–49.
Pirates of the Caribbean: At World's End. Burbank: Walt Disney Pictures/Jerry Bruckheimer Films, 2007. Filmstrip.
Smith, Shawn Michelle. *American Archives: Gender, Race and Class in Visual Culture*. Princeton, NJ: Princeton University Press, 1999.
Varnedoe, Kirk. "Artifice of Candor: Impressionism and Photography Reconsidered." *Art in America* 68 (1980): 66–78.
Wester, Maisha L. *African American Gothic: Screams from Shadowed Places*. New York: Palgrave Macmillan, 2012.

13

DIGITAL POETICS AND REMIX CULTURE

From the Artisanal Image to the Immaterial Image

Monica Tavares

The change in the systems for production of art that result from the use of digital media establishes a modification in the processes for the creation of images. At present, different types of images coexist, distinguishing themselves in view of their ontological principles of material generation. Those are: (1) first generation images, meaning images of artisanal and unique character; (2) second generation images, the technical images of reproducibility: gravure, photography, cinema, video; (3) third generation images, the technological images, made by computer or photonics with the help of numeric or treatment programs and without the help of external references.

In those three logic image production models (i.e., the preindustrial, industrial, and postindustrial), coding processes are identified which sustain the displacement (not the substitution) from analogue to digital. Changes resulting from the use of digital media in the context of art do not imply the elimination of artisanal and mechanical techniques, but rather a change of place for those techniques as they are transcoded to digital information systems. Under this assumption, the computer can be considered a metamedium, which incorporates different kinds of images from the numeric code.[1]

The digital media amplifies the cognitive—sensitive and intelligible—abilities of the creator, therefore characterizing a practice founded on a permanent dialog between individual and collective. New rules are imposed on the artist, demanding that she becomes familiar with techno-scientific models on an interconnection of practices and knowledge (*techné* + *logos*) arranged in interdisciplinary relations.

The contemporary forms of metacreation are supported by the notion of immateriality, considered as a new kind of materiality, which does not mean the absence of matter, but rather should be considered as a form of energy. This immateriality ensures the continuous flow and the instant commutation between codes and languages. The immaterial images are coded in numerical form; therefore, it can be treated, stored, and transmitted through different interfaces, or rather, through distinct forms of materiality, without loss or distortion.

This chapter, then, aims at studying how immaterial potentialities of digital media amplify the artistic processes that are sustained in metacreation procedures—characteristic of remix culture.

First, it will study how digital media potentiates metacreation processes and updates the traditional possibilities of montage, collage, and bricolage, considered in this text as key principles of remix culture.

Second, it will identify what is "new" with the introduction of remix culture in the creative processes, summarizing which differences are introduced in terms of art making and which are the challenges to be faced by the agents of the digital metacreation processes.

Mixing Media, Codes and Languages:
From Intertextuality to Hypertextuality

Since the nineteenth century, the emergence of media, codes, and languages creates interferences among the classic genres (the so-called fine arts), leading them to an interpenetration which results in the erasure of their frontiers, and in the insertion of a text into another, that is, in the use of fragments abstracted from their context and included in different structures.

Based on the principles of intertextuality and dialogism, and on the concept of "strangeness" defined by Russian formalists, the appearance of artistic practices in which the receptor is subtly requested to participate through his or her competence in associating and producing several signs is marked. The visual arts, by prioritizing the vocation for the employment of language therefore highlight, as creative conduct, the relations between procedure and material, which implies overcoming the art of representation. The ideas of art as description and mimesis start to be rejected. The artist begins to promote the exchange with an informed receptor, who is asked to interfere with the choice and articulation of meanings, immanent to the work, brought from distinct references and texts.[2]

From Constructivism, Dadaism, and environmental art, the vocation for the employment of diverse languages makes evident a crisis that affects the materiality of the physical supports in artistic works. In those kinds of experimentations, such as mixture, chance, and casual juxtaposition, the preference for the accumulation of distinct objects is assumed; reinforcing the rupture of the traditional concept of genres, in turn, establishing the emergence of hybrid, impure works. Under this assumption, the use of mixed media becomes a key factor. There is a growing lack of interest for the objects, which consequently implies greater concern for the processes.[3]

Gradually, the participative processes and the use of the mixed media are generalized, anticipating the notion of interaction, in which the artist strives to engender reciprocal exchanges between the work and the viewer, through intelligent technological systems. In this assumption, the formation process of the work becomes relevant and the content of the artwork, many times, turns into nothing more than the communication process itself, sustained by the successive circulation of recoded messages and meanings.

Nevertheless, it was the characteristic of the montage, collage, and bricolage procedures deriving from industrial assembly that inaugurated the reproductive operations of destructuring and restructuring. From those practices, the universes of originals and reproductions, in addition to maintaining parallelism and autonomy, also interpenetrate and semanticize each other. The industrial process, being essentially scientific, analyzes the model in parts aimed at its synthetic reconstitution, therefore allowing us to speak of a language process, in which paradigm and syntagma work together. Thus, the interchange between the parts—montage, collage, and bricolage—is a creative process deriving from the industrial assembly line.[4]

From that moment on, poetics of recoding, or rather of metacreation, introduce a new type of reading which leads to the disappearance of the linearity of the previous text, with a tendency to dissolving the authors, the bases to think on the notions of combination and metamorphosis. By privileging the creation of a new message based on data already known, those poetics operate through intersemiotic translations, under some procedures: embedding one text into another, transposing a significant system to another and correlating artistic (or even extra-artistic) series. To sum up, their forms of operation are the following:[5]

1. As works of transformation and assimilation (montage) of several texts, operating by a centralizing project that holds meaning. The junction and orders are of the author. As historical examples, we should mention: the assembly of cubism, concrete poetry, op art, Valeryan poetry (pure poetry), the works of Mallarmé, of Marcel Breuer (industrial design), of Ludwig Mies van der Rohe (architecture), among others.

2. As works of dissemination of texts in conflict of meanings, as pastiche and/or mixture (patchwork), in short, as collage. It is worth mentioning: surrealism, the collages made by students at their dorms, the works of Dostoyevsky (projection in the romance of juxtaposition between journalism and police narrative), Pollock, etc.

3. As works of continuity, mythopoetic (bricolage), in which we can observe the origin of the text mentioned. Seminal references of such type of procedure are: pop architecture, kitsch, works by Gaudí (architecture), Cage, and Duchamp, among many others.[6]

Thus, the work of transformation and assimilation of the different fragments based on montage (1) suggests, above all, a practice based on the notions of parataxis and paramorphism, being marked by the poetic function of language. On collage (2), the work of transformation is based on the notions of a semantic montage, privileging the idea of conflict. And, on bricolage (3), the organization is structured on the assumption of a pragmatic montage, in which the contiguity universe invades the pole of similarity.[7] Basically, the characteristic of bricolage is to elaborate structured sets, but using residues and fragments of happenings. It creates structures through events.[8] The creations are organized by a new arrangement of elements and the nature of each element is not modified, in view of its final arrangement, acquired in the set. Each fragment brings with it a syntagmatic context, which, when gathered, is reorganized in the form of a narrative.

Therefore, admitting that art also starts to be constituted of intertextual practices means to be able to face it as a work of interpenetration of speeches, in which the "unfinished principle" and the "dialogic opening" give it the mark of existence.

Artistic products constitute, in this sense, as a new order from the repertoire. We start to understand the aesthetic message in a more organized and manipulable way, dismissing with that certain concepts (such as that of genius), loaded with elitist prejudice. The code becomes the preestablished key for structuring and later decoding the message.

However, it is with Eco that the discussion is broadened, by admitting that the creative solution lies within a dialectic between form and opening organized by the creator. In this sense, the participative models are incorporated, naming the receptor as agent of the process.[9] The value of aesthetic experience is not based on purely intuitive fruition, on the posture propagated by romanticism. There is the overcoming of the subjectivist speech of aesthetic; and its model is linked to a new parameter: information. This presupposition allows the perception of aesthetics as an understanding process immersed in the social and cultural system.

Moreover, it is still worth observing that if intertextuality, in principle, incorporates the intrarelations between the same texts, intermedia, by restoring the notions of qualitative montage, is more recently supported by the interrelation between two different forms of language, which develop separately but put in effective correlation a transformation that historically involves the development of a new medium.

The concept of intermedia, coined by Dick Higgins in the 1960s, is then a formal category to define an interrelation among different forms of art that merge to become a new medium, characterizing a kind of "conceptual fusion."[10]

In a similar way, Plaza defines intermedia as the combination of two or more channels from a matrix of invention. An intermediate process results from the montage of several media, from which another medium appears, which result from a qualitative synthesis. Intermedia bear, therefore, the association by similarity of several codes or semiotic systems from a matrix of invention. Consequently, it is the montage of several media leading to the appearance of another which is the qualitative sum of those that constitute it. An unexpected datum is produced, that is, a quality montage.[11]

In addition, such transmutation of messages in multiple supports gives birth to what is called multimedia, also referred to by Plaza as the constitution of a new message based on already-known data. Nonetheless, it results from an association by contiguity of several codes and/or media under the sign of juxtaposition, implying conflict and collage. In other words, it is the superposition of technologies without the sum resolving the conflict (most of the time appearing in advertising, TV, newspapers, social media, shop windows, clips etc.). From this perspective, multimedia is defined as the superposition of several technologies, equivalent to a collage of the media—the qualitative synthesis does not exist in this case.[12]

In summary, both multimedia and intermedia are interdisciplinary categories which, as well as montage or collage (in reference to the previous procedures), call into question forms of production and individual creation and, above all, the notion of authorship. The creation with computers increases the development of those practices, as a form of interrelation and translation. Nowadays, artists benefit from the profusion of media of all types, which lend their differences to expand the creative work, notably through the interfaces.[13]

Thus, in the attempt to better comprehend the unfoldings of the poetics of metacreation in the remix culture, it is still important to understanding how digital media update the possibilities of montage, collage. and bricolage.

The new technological media absorb and incorporate the different language systems, translating them into new supports. Those transcoded languages make collaboration among several meanings, allowing for intersemiotic and creative transit between visual, verbal, acoustic, and tactile.

Digital media, in view of their inherent qualities, behave effectively in the concretization of the so-called translation phenomenon. The signs numerically registered are manipulated in the most diverse forms and, in view of their fluidity as circulating memory, the transit of information becomes viable through different interfaces. The new technological media absorb the most diverse sign systems, allowing for the translation of those several languages into a hybrid product, which reveals itself in a new form, as a technique for creative discovery.

Such hybrid product—seen through the prism of digital media, according to Couchot—is no longer a closed and impenetrable space. The new technologies are pertinent to the notion of immateriality, or rather, the notion of immediate commutation defined by the "Imedia" phenomenon. In that culture of commutation, the interactive manipulation of images, texts, data, installs itself, evidencing a prime interest in the processes of hybridization and metamorphosis. To Couchot, a new germ of temporal aesthetic appears. The frontiers of time and space are destroyed. Image becomes accessible, simultaneously, to different spaces, in a process in which the immediate can be used as quality.[14] Here, I believe, lies the foundation to understand how the digital media sustained the contemporary metacreation processes, as exemplified by mediatic products of remix culture.

The phenomenon of hybridization in the context of digital media potentiates, therefore, the dialogue among several languages, codes, and media. The eminence of an intermediatic space is amplified, dilating into—until then—unthinkable proportions the notion of plurality of discursive instances, of simultaneous voices, of dialogs, in which the complementarity of visions, comprehensions, and sensitivities is incorporated. The capacity to generate and maintain a dialogic, relation-maintaining opening is structurally reinforced.

It is through this immediate transit of information that the teleportation of signs between geographically different locations via telematics is ensured, further increasing the possibilities of exchange, now made available between different receptors.

Thus, the exchange between creator, receptors, and all previous texts contributes to installing recoding processes, as it is seen in the current remix products.

Moreover, digital media, by incorporating the possibilities of combination and permutation, also become viable through the fundamental idea of hypertext which, by using nonlinear computer memories architecture, reverberates the mixture of media, codes, and languages.

Broadening this paradigm, an immaterial image also contemplates the notion of hypermedia,[15] as a permutational, combinatory, and multimedia form. In this case, texts, sounds, images, etc. are connected through probabilistic links which, when diversely combined, may generate different information.

Hypertext and hypermedia are therefore delimitated as a structural potential brought by digital media. When placed in the hands of artists, it may allow for the composition and construction of a polyphonic space, which incorporates new forms of reading and participation. This space is therefore articulated, resulting from the interpenetration between different media and the dialog between distinct languages.

In short, it ensures an intersemiotic flux between the several meanings, made possible by the instant commutation of the immediate, given that the computer is capable of coding, transforming, articulating, and combining all that is inserted into it. Those hypertext and hypermedia dynamics allow the subjects to navigate through such a discontinuous web of information, updated by them at any time, thus characterizing the act of reading as a path, a labyrinth, a process to be constantly redefined in the successive moments of appearance of the image.

Painting, photography, text, newspapers, posters, videos, cinema, music, etc. provide the raw material for the concretization of this hybrid product, or, in other words, of this digital structure. The raw material, coming from different languages in the form of numerical information, circulates among the interfaces, determining a fluid transit of the message, characterized by its condition of pure immateriality. From such conditions the message transmutes itself, and may materialize not necessarily in the same type of support to which it was linked, but in different ones, therefore transcoding itself into other languages.

For its immaterial feature, and by offering endless choices and multimodal alternatives, the digital metacreation can expand the relations of imbrication between different subjects, and between those and the messages produced and, still, between the latter and the previous texts from which they result.

While the possibilities of translation are increased, the conditions for authorship also gain a new focus. Autographic practices are minimized. The creative act is sustained by the field of ideas, of thoughts, of the collective, unquestionably opening itself to the receptors. The artist acquires new functions, emphasizing more the process and less the result.

Such potentialities allow the receptor to assume the author's position, mutually inverting the roles. In view of the contribution of digital technology, intertextual practice nowadays is overstated, ensured by the immediate interaction between production and reception.

Given that something can be updated to endless possibilities, what becomes increasingly important—in the contemporary culture of "availability,"[16] or in remix culture—is that the metacreation is now ensured by the new demand of network circulation and, consequently, the constant recodification of mass media messages.

The results of this are: the acceleration of exchanges, the mixture of disciplines, the remixing of products, and the inversion of roles.

The issue to be discussed in the next section is, therefore, the understanding of how the digital metacreation is used as means of consumption and dissemination of information, seeking to answer what happened to the artistic creation in the dominance of remix processes. In this sense, it becomes essential to understand what supports the paradigms of this new social reality, in which the circulatory operation of the network prevails, having the means of communication and the logic of information consumption as logistic supports.

The Creation of Hybrids in Remix Culture

Making art, in the sphere of remix culture, amplifies the preindustrial and industrial image production models. In the postindustrial period, the artistic practice installs itself in the universe of techno-science. Materials change and processes are renewed, imposing upon the artist dilated forms of creation. The operation with the digital media happens through numerical and conceptual models of objects and materials.

The idea of creation as a reflex of the notable artist becomes increasingly distant, demystifying the creative genius. Creation is based on a collective practice. The creative function broadens its field of operation and incorporates practices inherent to other disciplines. Thus, it absorbs new meanings, acquiring a specificity of its own.

New forms of creation give birth to new forms of reception. The producer/consumer dichotomy is dissolved, mutually inverting the roles. In this context, there is the trend of information to be propagated and disseminated through different flows.

Nonetheless, whatever subliminally sustains such tendencies lies, quoting Rutsky, in the paradox of that technology heading towards the "invisibility," increasingly perceived in the form of data or means of communication. Thus, technology starts to be considered a matter of cultural data, a matter of techno-culture.[17] This contradiction, which sustains the culture of availability and remix processes, stands out from the phenomenon of digitalization.

According to Rutsky, it allows for several cultural products to become easily reappropriated, hybridized, remixed, being retradable and reconsumed. Besides this, it allows the production of completely new information, based on commodities, ranging from computer software to digital communication technologies.[18]

Referring to Brand,[19] Rutsky states that the value of information is not determined as it happens with material goods at its production level, but rather within the sphere of dispersive and reproducible processes by which information is consumed.[20]

From this perspective, the dissemination of information by consumption makes the subjectivity of each one become part of the proliferation of information, of flows of cultural consumption. Consumption is then seen as a means to exercise personal freedom and individual choice. The act of consumption or choice may be seen as the expression of individual identities.

In other words, the consumption of information has become an increasingly important means of asserting an identity and preserving the status of an autonomous and free subject. In this sense, information consumption is less a matter of commodification and fetishization of information than a way of fetishizing individuals themselves. Moreover, Rutsky even says that the consumption of information represents a vicious circle because the more distributors and consumers feel overwhelmed by the proliferation and dispersion that consumption triggers, the more desperately they try to redefine themselves as subjects, so that they may reaffirm their sense of control over consumption.[21]

Rutsky further argues that if we preserve the idea that consumption—and the world of information—reaffirms the perspective of action in terms of a free and autonomous subject, such a subject will remain within that vicious cycle, and will support the premise of the consumption establishing itself simply as a matter of human control. For Rutsky, it is necessary to think of consumption not as an action or a course of action, but as an interaction process in which the individual, sometimes, participates without effectively understanding it.

Based on that assumption, Rutsky believes that the consumption of information has fewer things in common with the direct and linear moves of intelligible information than with the fluid and chaotic spread of "noise,"[22] which features the period referred to in this chapter as the culture of remix or the culture of availability.

Thus, as stated by Rutsky, it is evident that, in the context of information consumption, the representations of the technological life tend to destabilize the distinction between the subject and the object that supports the universalizing conception of the modern subject and his relationship with an equipped world. For Rutsky,[23] if modernity defined the "human being" by the condition of individual (that is, by his alleged mastery in the world), then, the growing acceptance of a notion of autonomous technological agency implies the need to review the assumption in question.[24]

Seen in such light, technology becomes a continuous process of mutation, reproduction, assembly, and generation, which works in terms of its deranged logic of its own mutational aesthetic.[25]

In fact, the mediation of culture by machines of information is evident. It is also patent that the universal language becomes technology, which acts as a widespread translator of all existence[26] increasingly affecting the constitution of contemporary experience and, even more, the constitution of the messages. In logarithmic movement, things, relations, objects etc. mingle, remix, modify, and spread, with no criteria or categories to clearly explain such a change.

Therefore, the remixed products exposed from such context of relations is, above all, a "hybrid," in the notion of "decal of plasticity," which corresponds, in the words of Miranda,[27] "to a zero degree of matter and which, as such, still is 'material'."

By admitting that the situations and experiences resulting from their need, mainly, to be "informed" or, as Flusser asserts,[28] to impose form to matter, the cultural significance that the immaterial image absorbs today becomes evident. In short, whether as interface that feeds the (dis)simulation of possible worlds and images, whether as "method to program the behavior of the employees of the post-industrial society,"[29] or as an informational "hybrid," such a type of image begins to play a central role on the aesthetic and cultural development, as well as a political and social one.

The remixed products consolidate themselves as a vehicle to propose and sediment forms of communication, which usually sustain the consumption of information. Increasingly flexible processes of production, diffusion, distribution, and reception prevail. Information materialized in its most different forms and plasticities becomes a trading currency.

As Hamelink states,[30] the digitalization reinforces a social process in which the production and distribution of information evolve to the most important economic activity of society. Information technology starts to work as the fundamental infrastructure, and information becomes a negotiable commodity on a global scale.

It is in this game—open to everything—that receptors start to explore the field of possibilities available. The image-glorification speeches and the paradigms of the circulatory operation of networks are enhanced, having the means of communication as logistic supports. Everything circulates, from what is in the order of information, which now reaches unsuspected levels of possibilities of combination, remix, blend, arrangement, montage, until that which is in the order of the roles assumed by individuals in the sphere of society.

Nevertheless, the challenge in remix culture starts to be precisely, as Perniola[31] would say, the need of dealing with the experience of contemporary cultural manifestations funded, at the same time, by Kant's aesthetic disinterestedness and by Baudelaire's antiaesthetic overinterestedness. For Perniola, in contemporary society, more and more the disinterestedness is transformed in physical well-being and the overinterestedness is dislocated by the culture of performance or result. Therefore, it is important to verify the existence of a network that sustains remixed actions in contemporary culture, maintained by the production of communicative contents, which emphasizes the interaction of signs, incessant sliding of meanings, flexibility, and superposition of roles and codes.

In remix culture, such dissolution of roles assumed by the agents of the creative act brings premises of a democratization of production and a socialization of reception. However, it is essential not to lose sight of the fact that creative decisions are much more related to and determined by new heteronomies. This demands that visual solutions are, necessarily, governed by the posture and meaning intended by those who invent them, which must imply awareness of language before the media.

Aimed at demystifying the mixtures of roles assumed by individuals, whether as producer or as receptor, it is important to understand that, in arts in general, the biggest problem, as Plaza[32] asserts, refers to the quality of the answer, of the meaning or of the interpretant. Such an important assumption reaffirms the perspective of developing that kind of critical and creative reception; that which is founded on the need to be made concrete by a receptor that knows how to choose the best options (singularly convenient to him), but which anyway updates the proposal then established by the artist. Therefore, a receptor plays the dual role of selecting and being selected.

Such a rare quality is inherent to those few readers, the ones who judge while enjoying and, at the same time, enjoy while judging (Goethe). In this case, as Risério[33] would say, the ideas of disappearance of the figure of the author, as well as the lack of distinction between the author as the one who makes and the receptor as the one who enjoys, become naive assumptions. Thus, according to Risério, we must not forget the need for the artwork to sustain itself on the Barthesian differentiation between the notions of "'intransitive' writer" (*écrivain*) and "'transitive' writer" (*écrivant*).[34] Such a fact suggests an assumption that not all receptors become potential authors. That is, only those who managed to enclose themselves in "how to write" would be authors. In fact, the ones who do that are not many.

Besides such a statement, it is worth saying that there are, of course, intermediatic artworks in remix culture; however, the products mainly express redundant information, which maintains the quantitative and excessive fluxes of quotidian banalities.

The remix processes are considered as a phenomenon of democratic essence; however, we must not forget that its alleged freedom of action, that they propose or allow for, brings with them the articulation of other assumptions emerging from and inherent in the cultural dimension of society; more specifically, those who bring in their foundation the need to maintain information in a constant flow. Without being ingenuous, it is worth recalling that the sphere of art interacts (in a contradictory and nonantagonistic way) with other spheres: those of ideology, knowledge, and technique.[35] In conjunction, art and those three spheres establish and give continuity to the cultural practices, however invisibly maintaining art not as immaculate.

Thus, creation in the context of remix culture sustains and prescribes the continuity of an entire process, nothing more than another and different step, created to ensure the maintenance of illusions. Nevertheless, the metacreation is now involved in a much more general process of digital reproducibility, given that everything can be recombined and replicated.

At last, it is important to highlight that the dominance of the role played by each agent—author, work, and receptor—is maintained by specific ideologies, which, in turn, support in different ways the vicious cycle of consumption of information.

Then, taking the procedures inherent to the metacreation poetics referred to in the previous section, I believe that to each intertextual practice (as monumentality, as dissemination and as continuity, respectively related to montage, collage, and bricolage) corresponds a given relation of dominance: whether of the figure of the author, whether of the work itself as an instrument of mediation, or whether of the figure of the receptor.

Considering that those three spheres are not exclusionary, in the digital metacreation processes inherent to remix culture, there is the dominance of the third one in which the notion of a dilution of authorship between authors and receptors is basically sustained by information consumption. However, in those three typologies of image production, we cannot deny the presence of a communication structure in which both the author-function and the reader-function emerge, overcome by image as strategy and instrument of mediation.

Metacreation in remix culture, undeniably and potentially, brings with itself new forms of intertextuality; however, it updates the traditional relation based on aesthetic and poetic assumptions, which, through history, sustains the artistic problematic of dissemination of authorship.

In the culture of remix, in frighteningly amplified proportions, the condition of dilating and broadening intertextual changes, whether through the flows and reflows of voices—author(s) and receptor(s) or texts—the image and all other texts from which it results, as well as all texts that may result from it. The dialogic resonance is then potentiated in view of the growing emergence of new interfaces, as well as of the possibility, given by the character of digital media, of always showing themselves through the articulation of different forms, of hybrids.

Therefore, the immaterial qualities inherent to digital media impact in divergent ways in the context of remix culture. For some, those potentialities open new meanings and challenges to be incorporated in the sphere of artistic practice, for others, they are seen as destructuring.

Final Remarks

The logical passage of artisanal art to immaterial art allows us to detect the ontological principles of different types of image generations and also to understand what sustains the emergence of digital hybrids which are expressed as a polyphonic space, then built by processes of successive exchanges, which are almost instantaneous and funded by the continuous flow of information between production and reception. The specificities of digital media sustain the construction of a space-time of representation, which can be presented, at the same time, as soft and hard copies.

Not only the technological media ensure the quality of the response in a creation process, but rather the posture and meaning intended by authors and receptors, which must imply awareness of language before the media. In the metacreation processes from remix culture, the boundaries between art and design, creation and reception, and the self and the other show themselves undone. That fact reaffirms the appearance of an increasing number of trivial products that establish as simple entertainment.

The sensation of urgency inherent to the culture of availability separates the individual from himself and places him, in an accelerated and reverted way, sometimes as subject, sometimes as object, sometimes as self and sometimes as other, inserting him into a contingency framework which reflects the hegemonic culture of technology.

If all cultures are made of ideologies and those are revealed through codes, what comes out in the present is, therefore, an ambience supported by a set of ideas and representations that bring to the surface a historic situation sustained by the reverberation of the notion that everything circulates.

In the culture of remix, the maintenance of the relations of continuity between the three agents of the communicative process—author, work, and receptor—is also sustained by a process of superposition of ideologies over ideologies, in which the consumption of information becomes a trading currency. However, we must consider that this entire communicational gear, maintained between these three elements, essentially refers to and amplifies the known concepts of low definition, opening to interpretation, intertextuality, dialogism, and open work.

The pastiche, replication, recombination, proliferation, and remix processes inherent to the logic of the availability are sustained by technology. This logic maintains historical and cultural processes which, nevertheless, potentiate the paradoxical cycle of overcoming the indistinctive borders between formats, areas, and denominations.

Notes

1 Julio Plaza and Monica Tavares, *Processos criativos com os meios eletrônicos: Poéticas digitais* (São Paulo: Hucitec, 1998), 24–25.

2 According to Bense, the text is something that is developed with language. Thus, it is possible to transpose such assumption for the visual and sound languages. See Max Bense, *Pequena estética* (São Paulo: Perspectiva, 1975).

3 Simon Marchan, "Mixed Media," in *Diccionario del arte moderno: Conceptos, ideas, tendencias*, ed. Vicente Aguilera Cerni (Valencia: Fernando Torres Editor, 1979), 336.

4 Plaza and Tavares, *Processos criativos*, 18–19.

5 Ibid., 211.

6 It is worth mentioning that three categories of critical intertextuality—as monumentality, as dissemination and as continuity—proposed by Perrone-Moisés were the key reference to propose the characterization of metacreation procedures presented here. See Leyla Perrone-Moisés, *Texto, crítica, escritura* (São Paulo: Ática, 1993), 217–230.

7 Decio Pignatari, "Semiótica da montagem," *Revista Através* 1 (1987): 169–170.

8 Claude Lévi-Strauss, *O pensamento selvagem* (São Paulo: Ed. Nacional, 1976), 43–48.

9 Umberto Eco, *Obra aberta: Forma e indeterminação nas poéticas contemporâneas* (São Paulo: Perspectiva, 1969).

10 Dick Higgins and Hannah Higgins, "Intermedia," *Leonardo* 34, no. 1 (2001): 49–54.

11 Julio Plaza, *Tradução intersemiótica* (São Paulo: Perspectiva, 1987), 65.

12 Ibid.

13 Ibid., 198.

14 Edmond Couchot, "La fin des medias," in *Art et communication: Actes du colloque*, ed. Robert Allezaud (Paris: Éditions Osiris, 1986), 106.

15 Laufer and Scavetta consider hypermedia as a multimedia hypertext. See Roger Laufer and Domenico Scavetta, *Texte, hypertexte, hypermedia* (Paris: Presses Universitaires de France, 1995), 1–5.

16 Arlindo Machado, *Máquina imaginário: O desafio das poéticas eletrônicas* (São Paulo: Editora da Universidade de São Paulo, 1993), 18.

17 R. L. Rutsky, *High Techné: Art and Technology From the Machine Aesthetic to the Posthuman* (Minneapolis, MN: University of Minnesota Press, 1999), 15.

18 R. L. Rutsky, "Information Wants to Be Consumed," in Sande Cohen and R. L. Rutsky, *Consumption in an Age of Information* (Oxford: Berg, 2005), 67.

19 See Stewart Brand, *The Media Lab: Inventing the Future at M. I. T.* (New York: Viking, 1987).

20 Rutsky, "Information Wants to Be Consumed," 68.

21 Ibid., 72.

22 Ibid., 74.

23 Rutsky, *High Techné*, 19.

24 I think that by following the credulous defense of the posthuman subject, we would be, making a reference to Robins, hiding nothing more than the individual's dissatisfaction with the real world. See Kevin Robins, *Into the Image: Culture and Politics in the Field of Vision* (London: Routledge, 1996), 13.

25 Rutsky, *High Techné*, 20.

26 José A. B. de Miranda, "Introduction" to *Teoria da Cultura* (Lisboa: Século XXI, 2002), http://rae.com.pt/jbm_cultura.htm#Introdu%C3%A7%C3%A3o.

27 José A. B. de Miranda, "O design como problema." *Interact. Revista online arte, cultura e tecnologia* 10 (2004), http://www.interact.com.pt/memory/interact10/ensaio/ensaio3.html.

28 Vilém Flusser, *O mundo codificado: Por uma filosofia do design e da comunicação*, ed. Rafael Cardoso, trans. Raquel Abi-Sâmara (São Paulo: Cosac Naify, 2007), 31.

29 Flusser, *O mundo codificado*, 157.

30 Cees J. Hamelink, *The Ethics of Cyberspace*, 3rd reprint (London: Sage Publications, 2003), 11–12.

31 Mario Perniola, "Cultural Turns in Aesthetics and Anti-Aesthetics," *Filozofski Vestnik* XXVIII, no. 2 (2007), 39–51.

32 Julio Plaza, "Arte e interatividade: Autor-obra-recepção," *Revista ARS* 1, no. 2 (2003): 24.
33 Antonio Riserio, *Ensaio sobre o texto poético em contexto digital* (Salvador: Fundação Casa de Jorge Amado, 1998).
34 For deeper studies, see J. A. Cuddon, *A Dictionary of Literary Terms and Literary Theory*, 5th ed. (Oxford: Wiley-Blackwell, 2013).
35 Robert Henry Srour, *Modos de produção: Elementos da problemática* (Rio de Janeiro: Edições Graal, 1978).

Bibliography

Bense, Max. *Pequena estética*. São Paulo: Perspectiva, 1975.

Brand, Stewart. *The Media Lab: Inventing the Future at M. I. T.* New York: Viking, 1987.

Couchot, Edmond. "La fin des medias." In *Art et Communication: Actes du colloque*. Edited by Robert Allezaud, 101–106. Paris: Éditions Osiris, 1996.

Cuddon, J. A. *A Dictionary of Literary Terms and Literary Theory*. 5th edition. Oxford: Wiley-Blackwell, 2013.

Eco, Umberto. *Obra aberta: Forma e indeterminação nas poéticas contemporâneas*. São Paulo: Perspectiva, 1969.

Flusser, Vilém. *O mundo codificado: Por uma filosofia do design e da comunicação*. Edited by Rafael Cardoso. Translated by Raquel Abi-Sâmara. São Paulo: Cosac Naify, 2007.

Hamelink, Cees J. *The Ethics of Cyberspace*. 3rd reprint. London: Sage Publications, 2003.

Higgins, Dick, and Hannah Higgins. "Intermedia." *Leonardo* 34, no. 1 (2001): 49–54.

Laufer, Roger, and Domenico Scavetta. *Texte, hypertexte, hypermédia*. Paris: Presses Universitaires de France, 1995.

Lévi-Strauss, Claude. *O pensamento selvagem*. São Paulo: Ed. Nacional, 1976.

Machado, Arlindo. *Máquina imaginário: O desafio das poéticas eletrônicas*. São Paulo: Editora da Universidade de São Paulo, 1993.

Marchan, Simon. "Mixed Media." In *Diccionario del arte moderno: Conceptos, ideas, tendencias*. Edited by Vicente Aguilera Cerni, 336. Valencia: Fernando Torres Editor, 1979.

Miranda, José A. B. de. "O design como problema." *Interact. Revista online arte, cultura e tecnologia* 10 (2004). http://www.interact.com.pt/memory/interact10/ensaio/ensaio3.html (accessed April 15, 2014).

——. "Introduction." *Teoria da cultura*. Lisboa: Século XXI, 2002. http://rae.com.pt/jbm_cultura.htm#Introdu%C3%A7%C3%A3o (accessed April 15, 2014).

Perniola, Mario. "Cultural Turns in Aesthetics and Anti-Aesthetics." *Filozofski Vestnik* XXVIII, no. 2 (2007), 39–51.

Perrone-Moisés, Leyla. *Texto, crítica, escritura*. São Paulo: Ática, 1993.

Pignatari, Décio. "Semiótica da montagem." *Revista Através* 1 (1987): 168–172.

Plaza, Julio. *Tradução intersemiótica*. São Paulo: Perspectiva, 1987.

——. "Arte e interatividade: Autor-obra-recepção." *Revista ARS* 1, no. 2 (2003): 8–29.

——, and Monica Tavares. *Processos criativos com os meios eletrônicos: Poéticas digitais*. São Paulo: Hucitec, 1998.

Risério, Antônio. *Ensaio sobre o texto poético em contexto digital*. Salvador: Fundação Casa de Jorge Amado, 1998.

Robins, Kevin. *Into the Image: Culture and Politics in the Field of Vision*. London: Routledge, 1996.

Rutsky, R. L. *High Techné: Art and Technology From the Machine Aesthetic to the Posthuman*. Minneapolis, MN: University of Minnesota Press, 1999.

——. "Information Wants to Be Consumed." In Sande Cohen and R. L. Rutsky. *Consumption in an Age of Information*, 61–75, Oxford: Berg, 2005.

Srour, Robert Henry. *Modos de produção: Elementos da problemática*. Rio de Janeiro: Edições Graal, 1978.

14

THE END OF AN AURA

Nostalgia, Memory, and the Haunting of Hip Hop

Roy Christopher

Individual memories once firmly rooted in places in the past now float free of historical context. Now, we share our memories courtesy of the mass media and its rampant reproduction of artifacts. Technological mediation does a great deal of its work by manipulating context through the replication, reproduction, and circulation of moment-events, what José van Dijck calls "mediated memories."[1] The media of the twenty-first century is rife with references to previous media in a manner unseen in previous eras. Samples, allusions, adaptations, remakes, remixes, copies, are all norms of media and art. Viewing the sampling of the hip hop DJ and the lyrical allusions of the emcee through the lens of Walter Benjamin's "The Work of Art in the Age of Mechanical Reproduction" and the tenets of cyberpunk literature, this chapter aims to illustrate how the mechanical reproduction of mediated memories has created a new nostalgic aura. I will start with a brief overview of these practices, connecting cyberpunk and hip hop to Benjamin's theories, concluding with how advances in technology influence the process.

Welcome to the Terrordome

Looking at images from hip hop's early days feels like peering into the future. The decimated postapocalyptic scene of the South Bronx, the repurposing of outmoded recording technology, wild-style screen-names on every colorfast surface, the gloves, the goggles, the gyrating moves: an entire culture cobbled together from the detritus of past fads and fashions. Add a glimpse of Afrika Bambaataa's Soulsonic Force or Rammellzee's brico-laged battle armor and one might think they were picking up the pieces after a complete global meltdown. The scene evokes a picture of a possible future, and that's not to mention the way it sounds when a booming breakbeat clashes perfectly with just the right horn stab or guitar riff, or when Professor Griff barks, "Armageddon has been in effect! Go get a late pass!" Welcome to the Terrordome.[2]

The sampling of previously recorded slices of sound, at first by repeating them live with two copies of the same record on two turntables, is an example of mechanical reproduction catching up with the cultural practices of hip hop, of technology catching up with what human minds and hands were already doing.[3] With the spread of mechanical reproduction, as well as sampling and referencing as cultural practices, throughout media and technological artifacts, mediated memories are now mass produced, reproduced, and shared, their auras lost, their eras unknown. To most of us though, the sharing of mediated memories, of cultural allusions, bonds us and gives us a sense of belonging. A lot of this togetherness is due to the technological reproduction of media. The digital reproduction of cultural artifacts, images, sounds, events, and moments has rendered authenticity irrelevant. Nostalgia runs rampant through our media. An empty past to fill with greatness unattainable has left context a floating concept.

See John Logie's account of authorship in mashup and remix cultures, in Chapter 21, as he tracks the expanding network of contributors with legally grounded claims to have participated in the authorship of a single, relatively simple mashup.

Atemporal Minded

Though a dialog between social reality and its fictional futures has occurred since we started telling stories, mechanical reproduction has made the exchange easier, wider spread, and more difficult to discern. German critical theorist Walter Benjamin anticipated at least a few of the digital dilemmas we face in the twenty-first century in his landmark 1968 essay, "The Work of Art in the Age of Mechanical Reproduction." Of all forms of art, music seemed to be the least of Benjamin's concerns,[4] but I find it difficult to even read the name of his most famous essay without immediately thinking of hip hop DJs. One seems to evoke the other so directly that such an analysis seems obvious.

"Time moves in one direction, memory in another," cyberpunk author William Gibson writes. "We are that strange species that constructs artifacts intended to counter the natural flow of forgetting."[5] Thanks to recording technology,[6] we live in an era when, as Andreas Huyssen puts it, "the past has become part of the present in ways simply unimaginable in earlier centuries,"[7] and being made up of past bits of recorded music, hip hop is willfully haunted by its own ghosts. Even those apocalyptic visions of the future are specters out of time—they represent what Csiscery-Ronay calls "retrofuturism."[8] The shift from analog to digital production and reproduction only exacerbates the rootlessness of the artifacts produced.

These two forces, futures yet seen and the past reproduced, lift hip hop out of time. It exists in a floating atemporality. The vibe is an example of what Kodwo Eshun describes as a reversal of the avant-garde revolt "against a power structure that relied on control and representation of the historical archive." Instead, "The powerful employ futurists and draw power from the futures they endorse, thereby condemning the disempowered to live in the past. The present moment is stretching, slipping for some into yesterday, reaching for others into tomorrow."[9]

Modern music is inherent to Eshun's Afrofuturism. He continues,

Afrofuturism approaches contemporary music as an intertext of recurring literary quotations that may be cited and used as statements capable of imaginatively reordering chronology and fantasizing history. Social reality and science fiction create feedback between each other within the same phrase.[10]

As mentioned above, Benjamin anticipated these contextual conundrums. According to Benjamin, recording music makes it a commodity and gives it its exchange value. Once recordings become fetishized by collectors, the artifacts accrue their cultic value.[11] The basic argument of Benjamin's essay stems from this shift in value. He writes that an original piece of artwork possesses an aura, a halo of authenticity. Mechanical reproduction, though it democratizes the experience of art, releases this aura.[12] Over time a mechanically reproduced, mediated object evokes nostalgia, a longing for the original and its now-missing aura.[13] I argue that the opposite is happening, that mechanical reproduction—especially digital reproduction—lifts recordings and allusions out of their historical contexts, resulting in a new aura.

For Benjamin, music was also atemporal, and memory and history were the same thing. Chambers calls memory "the skin stretched over the world across which desire, emotions, and expressions flow. Memory evokes the eroticisation of the past." He goes on to say that memory is "sustained and guarded by language, in the record of images, words, and sounds," and "Not only do we recall our past in music, but the very techniques that permit us to return there, recordings, are a form of inscription, of writing."[14] Writing, rewriting, citing, reciting, mixing, remixing—all of these practices involve sampling. Rearranging media into our own stories and memories is as normal as walking down the street.[15] "Actually, of course cut-ups simply make explicit a process that goes on all the time," William Burroughs once said. "When you walk down the street, that's a cut-up—because your stream of consciousness is constantly being cut by random events. Life is a cut-up, by its nature. Every time you look outside the window, you're cutting up."[16] A more normalized and mechanical "cutting-up," such as that found in hip hop, represents a crisis of authenticity for Benjamin, a fragmentation that is "something simply lived through rather than meaningfully experienced."[17] I belabor the point here because this link, between music, memory, and nostalgia, as well as its disconnection with an authentic original are the basis of the new aura.

Cyberpunk and Hip Hop

Like hip hop, the science fiction subgenre of cyberpunk emerged in the 1980s. Also like the names for subgenres of hip hop (e.g., "gangsta" rap, "knowledge" or "conscious" rap, "backpacker" rap, etc.), the term "cyberpunk" came from outside the cipher. It was coined by Gardner Dozois to describe the writing of William Gibson.[18] Writers such as Gibson, Bruce Sterling, Rudy Rucker, John Shirley, Lew Shiner, and Pat Cadigan, among a few others are widely considered the first on this new frontier. Though diverse in its diversions from standard science fiction, cyberpunk responds to a few key themes: the human body (i.e., "meatspace," in contrast to computer network-enabled "cyberspace") melding with or being transformed by technology; the mass media; the subversion of established, conventional wisdom; and globalization.[19] With the release of Gibson's novel, *Neuromancer* (1984), and Ridley Scott's film, *Blade Runner* (1982), cyberpunk was effectively launched into the mass mind.

In 1994, Larry McCaffery wrote an essay exploring the historical ties between punk rock as a cultural movement and cyberpunk as a literary genre entitled, "Cutting Up: Cyberpunk, Punk Music, and Urban Decontextualizations." Reading the piece replacing "punk" with "hip hop" yields many of the same parallels. McCaffery writes,

> What unites all of these artists is what might be called a shared "attitude"—an attitude of defiance towards cultural and aesthetic norms; an attitude of distrust

towards rationalist language and all other forms of discourse required by legal, political, and consumer capitalism, but which ultimately have the effect of distorting the individual's sense of him-or-herself as an individual and as a body made of flesh; (therefore) an attitude that artists need not only to *disrupt* the usual modes of communication but to find means of self-expression that is more "authentic," less tied to abstractions, more tied to the senses and emotions.[20]

Cyberpunk and hip hop have been linked before.[21] In the foreword to his subgenre-defining anthology, *Mirrorshades*, Bruce Sterling defines cyberpunk by its meshing of previously asunder aspects of 1980s culture: "The overlapping of worlds that were formerly separate: the realm of high tech, and the modern pop underground."[22] He continues to reify the connection between cyberpunk and hip hop:

> This integration has become our decade's crucial source of cultural energy. The work of the cyberpunks is paralleled throughout 1980s pop culture: in rock video; in the hacker underground; in the jarring street tech of hip-hop and scratch music; in the synthesizer rock of London and Tokyo. This phenomenon, this dynamic, has a global range; cyberpunk is its literary incarnation.[23]

Mining the past for samples and sounds, hip hop hacks technology for self-expression, and, like cyberpunk, hip hop has a global range. Both are a part of a globalized network culture that decentralizes the human subject's stability in space and time and in which the technologically mediated subject reforms and remixes ideas of body normativity.[24] Christopher R. Weingarten writes,

> Sampling . . . is a uniquely post-modern twist, turning folk heritage into a living being, something that transfers more than just DNA. Through sampling, hip hop producers can literally borrow the song that influenced them, replay it, reuse it, rethink it, repeat it, recontextualize it.[25]

Cybernetics, the science of command-control systems (hence the "cyber" in "cyberpunk"), defines humans as "information-processing systems whose boundaries are determined by the flow of information."[26] Technologically reproduced memories are problematizing more than just body normativity: McLuhan once declared that an individual is a "montage of loosely assembled parts," and furthermore that when "you are on the phone or on the air you have no body."[27] Technology dismembers the body. Our media might be "extensions of ourselves" in McLuhan's terms, but they're also prosthetics, amputating parts as they extend them.

In his book on Public Enemy's undisputed and sample-heavy classic, *It Takes a Nation of Millions to Hold Us Back* (Def Jam, 1987), Weingarten draws a lengthy and effective analogy between records and the body, using samples as organ transplants. Tales of transplanted organs causing their recipients to adopt the tastes and behaviors of their dead donors read like the "meatspace" anxieties of cyberpunk:

> A 68-year-old woman suddenly craves the favorite foods of her 18-year-old heart donor, a 56-year-old professor gets strange flashes of light in his dreams and learns that his donor was a cop who was shot in the face by a drug dealer. Does a sample on a record work the same way? Can the essence of a hip-hop record be found in the motives, emotions and energies of the artists it samples? Is it likely that something an artist intended 20 years ago will reemerge anew?[28]

Hip hop music is an artistic and aesthetic form similar to that of literature, and sampling is a similar practice to that of reference, allusion, and quotation in literature.[29] Regarding European novels, Meyer states that the "charm" of quotation lies "in a unique tension between assimilation and dissimilation: it links itself closely to its new environment, but at the same time detaches itself from it, thus permitting another world to radiate into the self-contained world" of the piece.[30] The use of quoting, or sampling, therefore creates "a new entity greater than any of its constituent parts."[31]

Further conflating sound recording and literature, Peters writes, "The phonograph, as the name suggests, is a means of writing."[32] McLuhan stated that, "the brief and compressed history of the phonograph includes all phases of the written, the printed, and the mechanized word"[33] and Peters points out that the phonograph "is a medium that preserves ghosts that would otherwise be evanescent."[34] Quoting Philip Auslander in their discussion of haunting in music, Shaffer and Gunn argue, "'listeners do not perceive recorded music as disembodied'. Rather, he argues that listeners and performers fashion a 'fictional body' or personae when listening to music, an imaginary corporeality that is ultimately associated with a 'real person'"[35]—living or once living.

The Ghosts of Emcees Passed

The hip hop artist's practice of aural sampling and manipulation generates haunting sounds. Schwartz writes that sampling "ultimately erases the line between the quick and the dead,"[36] and Peters adds that mediated communication via recording "is ultimately indistinguishable from communication with the dead."[37] On September 7, 1996, Tupac Shakur was shot as he waited at a traffic light in the passenger seat of Suge Knight's car on the Las Vegas strip. He died on September 13. Six months later, on March 9, 1997, Christopher Wallace aka Biggie Smalls was gunned down in Los Angeles.[38] The two had been embroiled in a media-abetted, bicoastal battle for hip hop supremacy, dividing the majority of the hip hop nation into two camps: East versus West.[39] On April 15, 2012, Tupac's ghost performed to a packed crowd at the Coachella Music Festival in Indio, California. The appearance of this apparition stunned and delighted those in attendance.[40]

Hip hop is haunted by a number of dead performers (e.g., Jam Master Jay, Guru, Ol' Dirty Bastard, Big L, Big Pun, Eazy-E, Adam Yauch, Proof, Pimp C, et al.). Their ghosts continue to release records, do duets with living acts, and appear on magazine covers. Over a decade later, Biggie Smalls and Tupac Shakur are the two most prominent of these ghosts. They are deities subsequent emcees must pay homage to by mentioning them, performing posthumous duets with them, or aspiring to become them (of course, having done a record with one or both before their deaths is the most respected position). At the end of the music video for his song "99 Problems," Jay-Z is gunned down on the streets of New York City. The song is from his *Black Album* (2003), which was supposed to be his last release. Preparing to retire from the hustle of recording and performing, Jay-Z simulated his own death, imitating the high profile and unsolved slayings of Tupac Shakur and Biggie Smalls—two of his contemporaries. On the unreleased track, "Most Kings," Jay-Z raps, "Hov got flow though he's no Big and Pac, but he's close / How I'm supposed to win? They got me fighting ghosts."[41] Much as Malcolm X had at the end of his autobiography, Tupac and Biggie anticipated their own deaths in many of their songs.[42] Unlike Malcolm, dead emcees live on in the recordings of those songs.

Derrida calls our obsession with recording "archive fever," writing, "The archivization produces as much as it records the event."[43] Nowhere is our feverish archiving of things for the future more powerful than in digital recordings. As Robin Rimbaud aka electronic artist Scanner puts it,

> Capturing these moments, storing them, and redirecting them back into the public stream enables one to construct an archeology of loss, pathos, and missed connections, assembling a momentary forgotten past in our digital future. It is a form of found futurism.[44]

Sound studies scholar Jonathan Sterne adds that the advent of sound recording maintains the promise of future archeology, writing, "sound recording is understood as an extension of the art of oratory—a set of practices that depended heavily on the persona and style of the speaker and relations between the speaker and audience."[45] Sterne's analogy to oratory resonates with the emcee in hip hop. Indeed, George Lipsitz calls rap songs, "repositories of social memory,"[46] but whose memories are they?

Inauthentic Memories

Nostalgia is often considered the longing for a time that never existed, the unconscious filling in of an empty memory with something better than now.[47] These false memories poison progress in what Gibson calls the "corrosion of nostalgia."[48] Grainge points out an important distinction between nostalgia as a *commercial mode* and nostalgia as a social or *collective mood*.[49] The former—what Benjamin referred to as an artifact's "exchange" value—is often enabled by the latter—Benjamin's "cult" value—as fans drool over reissues of long-lost demo tapes or posthumous tracks as well as reunion-tour tickets. With that said, the nostalgia that sometimes plagues hip hop is more about the fans than the music, what Boym calls "reflective nostalgia."[50] "A modern nostalgic can be both homesick and sick of home," she writes.[51] We want to go back to a time that never existed, to relive times we never actually experienced, what Torlasco calls "tertiary memory." Infinitely repeatable recordings leave us with nothing but "the indexical trace" of themselves.[52] "By replicating the work many times over," writes Benjamin, "it substitutes a mass existence for a unique existence. And in permitting the reproduction to reach the recipient in his or her own situation, it actualizes that which is reproduced."[53] Benjamin argued that the reproduction of art democratizes its experience, but also that it loses its aura in the process. Others are more radical.

In his 1999 book *Culture Jam*, *Adbusters Magazine* founder Kalle Lasn describes the commodification of personal interaction in a scene in which two people who embark on a road trip speak to each other using only movie quotations. Others have argued that our lived experience has been increasingly slipping into technological mediation and representation. Based on this idea and the rampant branding and advertising covering any surface, he argues that our culture has inducted us into a cult. "By consensus, cult members speak a kind of corporate Esperanto: words and ideas sucked up from TV and advertising." Indeed, we quote television shows, allude to fictional characters and situations, and repeat song lyrics and slogans in everyday conversations. Lasn argues, "We have been recruited into roles and behavior patterns we did not consciously choose."[54]

Lasn writes about this scenario as if it is a nightmare, but to many individuals, this sounds not only familiar, but fun. Cultural allusions invoke game play. They create a quizzical situation: To understand the reference is to be in on the gag. Our media is so saturated with allusions that we scarcely think about them as such. A viewing of any single episode of popular television shows *Family Guy*, *South Park*, or *Robot Chicken* yields references to any number of artifacts and cultural detritus past. Their humor relies in large part on the catching and interpreting of allusive references, on their audience sharing the same cultural memories. Hip hop, with its rife repurposing of sounds via sampling and lyrical allusions, is a culture built on appropriating cultural artifacts and recognizing shared memories. "That's what's cool about sampling," claims Drew Daniel of the sample-heavy, electronic duo Matmos, "It transports the listener, if they're willing, to move in that pathway back to a specific moment in time. So, it's sort of like an archive of memories, of real experiences."[55]

"The past is not the issue at all," writes Klein, "it serves merely as a 'rosy' container for the anxieties of the present."[56] Lasn argues that this makes us victims of the corporate commodification of culture. For many, the sharing of memories and cultural allusions is a bonding agent, providing a platform for heightening a sense of belonging. A lot of this togetherness is due to the technological reproduction of media. As Benjamin writes,

> technical reproduction can put the copy of the original into situations which would be out of reach for the original itself. Above all, it enables the original to meet the beholder halfway, be it in the form of a photograph or a phonograph record.[57]

Where such photographs and phonograph records are reproductions of scenes and sounds, respectively, those forms have given way to digital reproductions of both. Another layer removed lies in the manipulation of the digital to replicate its previous analog form. Their remediation represents a crisis of context when filters on digital photos make them look old and digital effects make recordings sound like scratched vinyl.[58] The results is not only longing, it is evidence of the undermining of that longing.

Like Lasn, Benjamin also questioned whether mass culture is a site of exploitation or emancipation.[59] He was equally concerned with authenticity. "The presence of the original is the prerequisite to the concept of authenticity,"[60] he writes. The empty nostalgia of our mediated memories holds no original and no original context.[61] Benjamin continues,

> The whole sphere of authenticity is outside technical—and, of course, not only technical—reproducibility. Confronted with its manual reproduction, which was usually branded as a forgery, the original preserved all its authority; not so *vis à vis* technical reproduction.[62]

Simon Reynolds, who calls our obsession with reproductions of the past "retromania," draws a parallel between nostalgic record collecting and finance, "a hipster stock market based around trading in pasts, not futures," in which a crash is inevitable: "The world economy was brought down by derivatives and bad debt; music has been depleted of meaning through derivatives and indebtedness."[63] It's hard to be a purist when nothing is pure.

Allusions work by mapping one context to another. By translating something from one context to another, a new meaning is brought to bear.[64] As Siva Vaidhyanathan writes, "It gives the song another level of meaning, another plane of communication among the artist, previous artists, and the audience."[65] All meaning is in some way mediated by a mapping as such.[66] The new meaning is dependent, however, on recognizing both the original and new contexts. Trow writes of television, "The work of television is to establish false contexts and to chronicle the unraveling of existing contexts; finally, to establish the context of no-context and to chronicle it."[67] Debord said the same about mass media, that it had no historical context, no stable memory.[68] Now media has gone not only digital but also global via the Internet, the Web, and mobile technologies of all kinds.

Below the surface of these new media, distinguishing context is even more dodgy. As Clay Shirky writes, "Since all the data is digital (expressed as numbers), there is no such thing as a copy anymore. Every piece of data . . . is identical to every other version of the same piece of data."[69] Unlike most analog media, there is no such thing as an original in the digital.[70] With this in mind, Abby Smith emphasizes,

> the need for preservation experts to develop a keen understanding of the context in which non-object based information is used, in order to ensure capture of all the vital data necessary to meaningful retrieval. When all data are recorded as 0's and 1's, there is, essentially, no object that exists outside of the act of retrieval. The demand for access creates the "object," that is, the act of retrieval precipitates the temporary reassembling of 0's and 1's into a meaningful sequence that can be decoded by software and hardware. A digital art-exhibition catalog, digital comic books, or digital pornography all present themselves as the same, all are literally indistinguishable one from another during storage, unlike, say, a book on a shelf.[71]

Analog media show their wear through patina of use. Books show "shelf-wear." Vinyl records—even compact discs—display gouges and scratches. Scrapes, scars, stretches, tears, marks, and grooves: These are analog concepts. Digital artifacts black-box their wear, hiding their story and its context from us. Benjamin's argument suggests that once mechanical reproduction gives way to the digital, art is entirely without aura. However, his argument is based on the artifact's cult value rather than its exchange value.[72] Benjamin writes,

> In the case of the art object, a most sensitive nucleus—namely, its authenticity—is interfered with whereas no natural object is vulnerable on that score. The authenticity of a thing is the essence of all that is transmissible from its beginning, ranging from its substantive duration to its testimony to the history it has experienced.[73]

Benjamin was thinking within the bounds of ritual and tradition, which have less and less of a hold on culture in the digital age.[74] The central lesson of the ruminations of cyberpunk: Technology is the opposite of ritual.

Conclusion

Viewing hip hop through cyberpunk illuminates its obsession with memories, its nostalgia for a time that never existed, its openness to the themes of modern science fiction. As Ted Swedenberg writes,

It's a kind of soundscape version of the dystopian images purveyed in William Gibson's cyberpunk novels and sci-fi films like *The Terminator* and *Robocop*. But this bad future is now, as if the atom bomb or toxic catastrophe had hit the South Bronx or Compton.[75]

From the musical samples, lyrical references, recorded memories, and now rapping revenants, the haunting of hip hop seems endless. If our art and artifacts are to have aura without nostalgia, if we care at all about authentic experiences, we have to be more mindful of the contexts floating in the media around us. Being able to translate data into meaning requires our attention on the banks it bridges. Authenticity comes from the moment we live in, from our experience, not from the objects we buy or their proximity to "the original work."[76] Like the Afrofuturistic feedback loop between social reality and science fiction,[77] another exists between cultural artifacts and our mediated memories. José van Dijck writes, "Mediated memory objects never stay put once and for all: on the contrary, the deposits themselves are *agents* in an ongoing process of memory (re)construction, motivated by desire."[78] One should resist the longing for an original when none exists. Of all the things anticipated and invented in the South Bronx so long ago, a crippling nostalgia was not one of them.

Notes

1 José van Dijck, *Mediated Memories in the Digital Age* (Stanford, CA: Stanford University Press, 2007), xii.

2 "Welcome to the Terrordome" is a song from Public Enemy's 1990 LP, *Fear of a Black Planet* (Def Jam/Columbia), which AllMusic.com writer John Bush described as "a complete sonic apocalypse." Professor Griff is Public Enemy's Minister of Information.

3 Bill Brewster and Frank Broughton, *Last Night a DJ Saved My Life: The History of the Disc Jockey* (London: Headline, 2006), 267.

4 See Rajeev S. Patke, "Benjamin on Art and Reproducibility: The Case of Music," in Andrew Benjamin, ed., *Walter Benjamin and Art* (New York: Continuum Books, 2005), 185–208.

5 William Gibson, *Distrust That Particular Flavor* (New York: Penguin, 2012), 51.

6 See Keren Tenenboim-Weinblatt, "Bridging Collective Memories and Public Agendas: Toward a Theory of Mediated Prospective Memory." *Communication Theory* 23 (2013): 91–111.

7 Andreas Huyssen, *Present Pasts: Urban Palimpsests and the Politics of Memory* (Stanford, CA: Stanford University Press, 2003), 1.

8 Istvan Csiscery-Ronay, "Futuristic Flu, or, the Revenge of the Future," in *Fiction 2000: Cyberpunk and the Future of Narrative*, eds. George Slusser and Tom Shippey (Athens, GA: University of Georgia Press, 1992), 33.

9 Kodwo Eshun, "Further Considerations on Afrofuturism." *CR: The New Centennial Review* 3, no. 2 (Summer 2003), 289.

10 Ibid., 299.

11 Patke, "Benjamin on Art," 192.

12 Walter Benjamin, "The Work of Art in the Age of Mechanical Reproduction." *Illuminations* (London: Fontana, 1968), 217–252.

13 See van Dijck, *Mediated Memories*, 2007.

14 Iain Chambers, "Maps, Movies, Musics and Memory." In David B. Clarke, ed., *The Cinematic City* (New York: Routledge, 1997), 234.

15 Some equate the two activities even further. See Michel de Certeau's *The Practice of Everyday Life* (Berkeley, CA: The University of California Press, 1984), especially "Part III: Spatial Practices," 91–130.

16 Quoted in Allen Hibbard, ed., *Conversations with William S. Burroughs* (Jackson, MS: University Press of Mississippi, 2000), 92–93.

17 Richard Shusterman, *Performing Live: Aesthetic Alternatives for the Ends of Art* (Ithaca, NY: Cornell University Press, 2000), 18.

18 Rudy Rucker, "What is Cyberpunk?" in Rudy Rucker, ed., *Seek!* (New York: Four Walls Eight Windows, 1999), 315.

19 See James Patrick Kelly and John Kessel, "Hacking Cyberpunk: Introduction." In *Rewired: The Post-Cyberpunk Anthology*, eds. James Patrick Kelly and John Kessel (San Francisco, CA: Tachyon, 2007), vii–xv; and Rucker, *Seek!*

20 Larry McCaffery, "Cutting Up: Cyberpunk, Punk Music, and Urban Decontextualizations." In Larry McCaffery, ed., *Storming the Reality Studio: A Casebook of Cyberpunk and Postmodern Science Fiction* (Durham, NC: Duke University Press, 1994), 288.

21 See Mark Dery, "Black to the Future: Interviews with Samuel R. Delaney, Greg Tate, and Tricia Rose." In Mark Dery, ed., *Flame Wars: The Discourse of Cyberculture* (Durham, NC: Duke University Press, 1994), 179–222; and Kodwo Eshun, *More Brilliant Than the Sun* (London: Quartet, 1998) for two early examples.

22 Bruce Sterling, "Preface." In Bruce Sterling, ed., *Mirrorshades: The Cyberpunk Anthology* (Westminster, MD: Arbor House, 1986), xi.

23 Ibid.

24 See Rosi Braidotti, *The Posthuman* (Cambridge: Polity Press, 2013).

25 Christopher R. Weingarten, *Public Enemy: It Takes a Nation of Millions to Hold Us Back (33⅓)* (New York: Continuum Books, 2010), 38.

26 N. Katherine Hayles, *How We Became Posthuman: Virtual Bodies in Cybernetics, Literature, and Informatics* (Chicago, IL: University of Chicago Press, 1999), 113.

27 Marshall McLuhan, *The Gutenberg Galaxy: The Making of Typographic Man* (Toronto: University of Toronto Press, 1962), xxix.

28 Weingarten, *Nation of Millions*, 37.

29 See Richard Schusterman, "Challenging Conventions in the Fine Art of Rap." In *That's the Joint! The Hip-Hop Studies Reader*, eds. Murray Forman and Mark Anthony Neal (New York: Routledge, 2004).

30 Herman Meyer, *The Poetics of Quotation in the European Novel* (Princeton, NJ: Princeton University Press, 1968), 6.

31 E. E. Kellette, *Literary Quotation and Allusion* (Cambridge: Heffer, 1933), 13–14.

32 John Durham Peters, *Speaking into the Air: A History of the Idea of Communication* (Chicago, IL: University of Chicago Press, 1999), 160.

33 Marshall McLuhan, *Understanding Media: The Extensions of Man* (New York: McGraw-Hill, 1964), 277.

34 Peters, *Speaking into the Air*, 160.

35 Tracy Stephenson Shaffer and Joshua Gunn, "'A Change is Gonna Come': On the Haunting of Music and Whiteness in Performance Studies." *Theatre Annual* 59 (2006): 44.

36 Hillel Schwartz, *The Culture of the Copy: Striking Likenesses, Unreasonable Facsimiles* (New York: Zone Books, 1996), 311.

37 Peters, *Speaking into the Air*, 276.

38 Joy Bennett Kinnon, "Does Rap Have a Future?" *Ebony* 52, no. 9, June 1997, 76.

39 See Jeff Chang, *Can't Stop, Won't Stop: A History of the Hip-Hop Generation* (New York: St. Martin's Press, 2005).

40 Hayley Tsukayama, "How the Tupac 'Hologram' Works," http://www.washingtonpost.com/business/technology/how-the-tupac-hologram-works/2012/04/18/gIQA1ZVyQT_story.html.

41 Shawn Carter, *Decoded* (New York: Spiegel & Grau, 2010), 98.

42 Mickey Hess, *Is Hip-Hop Dead? The Past, Present, and Future of America's Most Wanted Music* (Westport, CT: Praeger, 2007), 8.

43 Jacques Derrida, *Archive Fever: A Freudian Impression*, trans. Eric Prenowitz (Chicago, IL: University of Chicago Press, 1995), 16–17.

44 Scanner aka Robin Rimbaud, "The Ghost Outside the Machine," in Paul D. Miller, ed., *Sound Unbound: Sampling Digital Music and Culture* (Cambridge, MA: MIT Press, 2008), 134.

45 Jonathan Sterne, *The Audible Past: Cultural Origins of Sound Reproduction* (Durham, NC: Duke University Press, 2003), 308.

46 Lipsitz, George, "The Hip Hop Hearings: Censorship, Social Memory, and Intergenerational Tensions among African Americans," in *Generations of Youth: Youth Cultures and History in Twentieth-Century America*, eds. Joe Austin and Michael Nevin Willard (New York: New York University Press, 1998), 405.

47 See Norman M. Klein, *The History of Forgetting: Los Angeles and the Erasure of Memory* (New York: Verso, 1997).

48 William Gibson, "The Recombinant City: A Foreword," in Samuel R. Delaney, *Dhalgren: A Novel* (New York: Vintage, 2001), xiii.

49 See Paul Grainge, *Monochrome Memories: Nostalgia and Style in Retro America* (Westport, CT: Praeger, 2002).

50 Svetlana Boym, *The Future of Nostalgia* (New York: Basic Books, 2001), 49.

51 Ibid., 50.

52 Domietta Torlasco, *The Heretical Archive: Digital Memory at the End of Film* (Minneapolis, MN: University of Minnesota Press, 2013), 92.

53 Benjamin, "Art in the Age," 221.

54 Kalle Lasn, *Culture Jam: The Uncooling of America* (New York: William Morrow, 1999), 53.

55 Quoted in Kembrew McLeod and Peter DiCola, *Creative License: The Law and Culture of Digital Sampling* (Durham, NC: Duke University Press, 2011), 99.

56 Klein, *The History of Forgetting*, 11.

57 Benjamin, "Art in the Age," 220–221.

58 See Mark Katz, *Capturing Sound: How Technology Has Changed Music* (Berkeley, CA: University of California Press, 2004).

59 See Paddy Scannell, "Benjamin Contextualized: On 'The Work of Art in the Age of Mechanical Reproduction,'" in *Canonical Texts in Media Research*, eds. Elihu Katz et al. (Cambridge: Polity Press, 2003), 74–89.

60 Benjamin, "Art in the Age," 220.

61 See Eleanor Heartney, "Appropriation and the Loss of Authenticity," *New Art Examiner* (1985, March), 26–30.

62 Benjamin, "Art in the Age," 220.

63 Simon Reynolds, *Retromania: Pop Culture's Addiction to Its Own Past* (New York: Faber and Faber, 2011), 419–420.

64 See Gary Saul Morrison, *The Words of Others: From Quotations to Culture* (New Haven, CT: Yale University Press, 2011).

65 Siva Vaidhyanathan, *Copyrights and Copywrongs: The Rise of Intellectual Property and How It Threatens Creativity* (New York: New York University Press, 2001), 138.

66 See Douglas Hofstadter, *I Am a Strange Loop* (New York: Basic Books, 2007).

67 George W. S. Trow, *Within the Context of No Context* (New York: Atlantic Monthly Press, 1980), 82.

68 See Guy Debord, *The Society of the Spectacle* (New York: Zone Books, 1994).

69 Clay Shirky, *Coginitive Surplus: Creativity and Generosity in a Connected Age* (New York: Penguin, 2010), 54.

70 See Michael Betancourt, "1000 Days of Theory: The Aura of the Digital," http://ctheory.net/articles.aspx?id=519 and The RZA, *The Tao of Wu* (New York: Penguin, 2009).

71 Abby Smith, "Preservation in the Future Tense." *CLIR Issues*, 3 (1998, May/June), 6.

72 Betancourt, "1000 Days of Theory."

73 Benjamin, "Art in the Age," 221.

74 Betancourt, "1000 Days of Theory."

75 Ted Swedenberg, "Homies in the Hood: Rap's Commodification of Insubordination." In *That's the Joint! The Hip-Hop Studies Reader*, eds. Murray Forman and Mark Anthony Neal (New York: Routledge, 2004), 581–582.

76 Mickey Hess, "The Rap Career." In *That's the Joint! The Hip-Hop Studies Reader*, eds. Murray Forman and Mark Anthony Neal (New York, NY: Routledge 2012), 644.

77 See Eshun, "Afrofuturism."

78 van Dijck, *Mediated Memories*, 37–38.

Bibliography

Benjamin, Walter. "The Work of Art in the Age of Mechanical Reproduction." *Illuminations*, 217–252 London: Fontana, 1968.

Betancourt, Michael. "1000 Days of Theory: The Aura of the Digital." from http://ctehory.net/articles.aspx?id=519 (accessed March 30, 2013).

Boym, Svetlana. *The Future of Nostalgia*. New York: Basic Books, 2001.

Braidotti, Rosi. *The Posthuman*. Cambridge: Polity Press, 2013.

Brewster, Bill and Frank Broughton. *Last Night a DJ Saved My Life: The History of the Disc Jockey*. London: Headline, 2006.

Carter, Shawn. *Decoded*. New York: Spiegel & Grau, 2010.

Chambers, Iain. "Maps, Movies, Musics and Memory." In *The Cinematic City*, edited by David B. Clarke, 230–240. New York: Routledge, 1997.

Chang, Jeff. *Can't Stop, Won't Stop: A History of the Hip-Hop Generation*. New York: St. Martin's Press, 2005.

Csiscery-Ronay, Istvan. "Futuristic Flu, or, the Revenge of the Future." In *Fiction 2000: Cyberpunk and the Future of Narrative*, edited by George Slusser and Tom Shippey, 26–45. Athens, GA: University of Georgia Press, 1992.

de Certeau, Michael. *The Practice of Everyday Life*. Berkeley, CA: The University of California Press, 1984.

Debord, Guy. *The Society of the Spectacle*. New York: Zone Books, 1994.

Derrida, Jacques. *Archive Fever: A Freudian Impression*. Translated by Eric Prenowitz. Chicago, IL: University of Chicago Press, 1995.

Dery, Mark. "Black to the Future: Interviews with Samuel R. Delaney, Greg Tate, and Tricia Rose." In *Flame Wars: The Discourse of Cyberculture*, edited by Mark Dery, 179–222. Durham, NC: Duke University Press, 1994.

Eshun, Kodwo. *More Brilliant Than the Sun: Adventures in Sonic Fiction*. London: Quartet Books, 1998.

——. "Further Considerations on Afrofuturism." *CR: The New Centennial Review* 3, no. 2 (Summer 2003): 287–302.

Gibson, William. "The Recombinant City: A Foreword." In Samuel R. Delaney, *Dhalgren: A Novel*, xi–xiii. New York: Vintage, 2001.

——. *Distrust That Particular Flavor*. New York: Penguin, 2012.

Grainge, Paul. *Monochrome Memories: Nostalgia and Style in Retro America*. Westport, CT: Praeger, 2002.

Hayles, N. Katherine. *How We Became Posthuman: Virtual Bodies in Cybernetics, Literature, and Informatics*. Chicago, IL: University of Chicago Press, 1999.

Heartney, Eleanor. "Appropriation and the Loss of Authenticity." *New Art Examiner* (1985, March), 26–30.

Hess, Mickey. *Is Hip-Hop Dead? The Past, Present, and Future of America's Most Wanted Music*. Westport, CT: Praeger, 2007.

——. "The Rap Career." In *That's the Joint! The Hip-Hop Studies Reader*, edited by Murray Forman and Mark Anthony Neal, 635–654. New York: Routledge, 2012.

Hibbard, Allen, ed., *Conversations with William S. Burroughs*. Jackson, MS: University Press of Mississippi, 2000.

Hofstadter, Douglas. *I Am a Strange Loop*. New York: Basic Books, 2007.

Huyssen, Andreas. *Present Pasts: Urban Palimpsests and the Politics of Memory*. Stanford, CA: Stanford University Press, 2003.

Katz, Mark. *Capturing Sound: How Technology Has Changed Music*. Berkeley, CA: University of California Press, 2004.

Kellette, E. E. Literary Quotation and Allusion. Cambridge: Heffer, 1933.

Kelly, James Patrick, and John Kessel. "Hacking Cyberpunk: Introduction." In J. P. Kelly and J. Kessel, eds., *Rewired: The Post-Cyberpunk Anthology*, vii–xv. San Francisco, CA: Tachyon, 2007.

Kinnon, Joy Bennett. "Does Rap Have a Future?" *Ebony* 52 no. 8 (June 1997): 76–79.

Klein, Norman M. *The History of Forgetting: Los Angeles and the Erasure of Memory*. New York: Verso, 1997.

Lasn, Kalle. *Culture Jam: The Uncooling of America*. New York: William Morrow, 1999.

Lipsitz, George. "The Hip Hop Hearings: Censorship, Social Memory, and Intergenerational Tensions among African Americans." In *Generations of Youth: Youth Cultures and History in Twentieth-Century America*, edited by Joe Austin and Michael Nevin Willard, New York: New York University Press, 1998.

McCaffery, Larry. "Cutting up: Cyberpunk, Punk Music, and Urban Decontextualizations." In *Storming the Reality Studio: A Casebook of Cyberpunk and Postmodern Science Fiction*, edited by L. McCaffery, 286–307. Durham, NC: Duke University Press, 1994.

McLeod, Kembrew, and Peter DiCola. *Creative License: The Law and Culture of Digital Sampling*. Durham, NC: Duke University Press, 2011.

McLuhan, Marshall. *The Gutenberg Galaxy: The Making of Typographic Man*. Toronto: University of Toronto Press, 1962.

———. *Understanding Media: The Extensions of Man*. New York: McGraw-Hill, 1964.

Meyer, Herman. *The Poetics of Quotation in the European Novel*. Princeton, NJ: Princeton University Press, 1968.

Morrison, Gary Saul. *The Words of Others: From Quotations to Culture*. New Haven, CT: Yale University Press, 2011.

Patke, Rajeev S. "Benjamin on Art and Reproducibility: The Case of Music." In *Walter Benjamin and Art*, edited by Andrew Benjamin, 185–208. New York: Continuum Books, 2005.

Peters, John Durham. *Speaking into the Air: A History of the Idea of Communication*. Chicago, IL: University of Chicago Press, 1999.

Reynolds, Simon. *Retromania: Pop Culture's Addiction to Its Own Past*. New York: Faber and Faber, 2011.

Rimbaud, Robin. "The Ghost Outside the Machine." In *Sound Unbound: Sampling Digital Music and Culture*, edited by Paul D. Miller, 131–134. Cambridge, MA: MIT Press, 2008.

Rucker, Rudy. "What is Cyberpunk?" In *Seek!* edited by Rudy Rucker, 315–322. New York: Four Walls Eight Windows, 1999.

Scannell, Paddy. "Benjamin Contextualized: On 'The Work of Art in the Age of Mechanical Reproduction.'" In Elihu Katz, John Durham Peters, Tamar Liebes, and Avril Orloff, eds., *Canonical Texts in Media Research*, 74–89. Cambridge: Polity Press, 2003.

Schwartz, Hillel. *The Culture of the Copy: Striking Likenesses, Unreasonable Facsimiles*. New York: Zone Books, 1996.

Shaffer, Tracy Stephenson, and Joshua Gunn. "'A Change is Gonna Come': On the Haunting of Music and Whiteness in Performance Studies." *Theatre Annual* 59 (2006): 39–62.

Shirky, C. *Coginitive Surplus: Creativity and Generosity in a Connected Age*. New York: Penguin, 2010.

Shusterman, Richard. *Performing Live: Aesthetic Alternatives for the Ends of Art*. Ithaca, NY: Cornell University Press, 2000.

———. "Challenging Conventions in the Fine Art of Rap." In *That's the Joint! The Hip-hop Studies Reader*, edited by Murray Forman and Mark Anthony Neal, 459–479. New York: Routledge, 2004.

Smith, Abby. "Preservation in the Future Tense." *CLIR Issues* 3 (1998, May/June), art. 1.

Sterling, Bruce. "Preface." In *Mirrorshades: The Cyberpunk Anthology*, edited by Bruce Sterling, ix–xv. Westminster, MD: Arbor House, 1986.

Sterne, Jonathan. *The Audible Past: Cultural Origins of Sound Reproduction*. Durham, NC: Duke University Press, 2003.

Swedenberg, Ted. "Homies in the Hood: Rap's Commodification of Insubordination." In *That's the Joint! The Hip-Hop Studies Reader*, edited by Murray Forman and Mark Anthony Neal, 579–591. New York: Routledge, 2004.

Tenenboim-Weinblatt, Keren. "Bridging Collective Memories and Public Agendas: Toward a Theory of Mediated Prospective Memory." *Communication Theory* 23 (2013), 91–111.

The RZA. *The Tao of Wu*. New York: Penguin, 2009.

Torlasco, Domietta. *The Heretical Archive: Digital Memory at the End of Film*. Minneapolis, MN: University of Minnesota Press, 2013.

Trow, George W. S. *In the Context of No Context*. New York: Atlantic Monthly Press, 1980.

Tsukayama, Hayley. "How the Tupac 'Hologram' Works." http://www.washingtonpost.com/business/technology/how-the-tupac-hologram-works/2012/04/18/gIQA1ZVyQT_story.html (accessed April 18, 2012).

Vaidhyanathan, Siva. *Copyrights and Copywrongs: The Rise of Intellectual Property and How It Threatens Creativity*. New York: New York University Press, 2001.

van Dijck, José. *Mediated Memories in the Digital Age*. Stanford, CA: Stanford University Press, 2007.

Weingarten, Christopher. R. *Public Enemy: It Takes a Nation of Millions to Hold Us Back (33¹/₃)*. New York: Continuum Books, 2010.

Williams, J. A. *Rhymin' and Stealin': Musical Borrowing in Hip-Hop*. Ann Arbor, MI: University of Michigan Press, 2013.

Williams, T. C. *Losing My Cool: How a Father's Love and 15,000 Books Beat Hip-Hop Culture*. New York: Penguin, 2010.

15

APPROPRIATION IS ACTIVISM

Byron Russell

It is imperative to those of us who see the true value of remix to articulate its fundamental importance. Avenues of self-expression such as remix are an absolute necessity for an inclusive, healthy society. Remix is an expression of who we are today and the world in which we live. It is up to our community to claim this validity, to defend remix against its detractors and to put forth a vision for a world inclusive of remixing practices and cultures.

In their most basic form, remixes are simply media created in part or in full from pre-existing media made to be recognizably distinct from their sources.[1] A remix is therefore something new, an original creation expressing the ideas and perspectives of its accredited creator. The self-evident nature of this authorship engages critical perspectives the remixer may employ. Such critical remixes express a spirit that is fundamental to remixing and its validity as creative practice. Critical remix is thus a metagenre of remix that includes all remixes demonstrating a critical perspective, whether that critical eye is focused on the source or elsewhere.[2] Activist artists and remixing cultures have demonstrated the limitless possibilities and potential that this form has, contributing to the creative and critical dialogs of our culture and validating remix as a meaningful practice.

Remix in the Media Landscape

Even as audiences fracture, mainstream media continues to dominate the media landscape as individuals find the same content through multiplying outlets and content providers. Moreover, mainstream media outlets still incite hysteria using the same symbolic languages, tropes, archetypes, and patterns of communication relied on throughout the last century.[3] These highly coded and controlled messages are also promulgated through means previously unavailable, such as Web links, affiliated channels, and social media to create a self-reinforcing narrative and worldview. Corporate media code their symbols, tropes, and archetypes to suggest values and priorities and to convey legitimacy to specific messages and messengers while denying the same to others.

> See Chapter 28 for Nadine Wanono's extensive discussion on détournement.

See Chapter 30 for Tom Tenney's discussion of fusing a read-only culture.

Remix responds in various ways to this onslaught of propaganda.[4] Corporate media convey their messages in highly predictable and recognizable ways, allowing remixers to play into or against these tropes, archetypes, and patterns. Remixers imitate such practices to momentarily masquerade as the dominant media, setting up a moment of insight as the illusion becomes transparent. As the syntax of media is unwrapped, deconstructed, and reconstituted, détournement can occur.[5] The powerful images and associations used by corporations and governments are no less powerful when wielded to deconstruct their messages. In this way, a remixer can point to a trope, harness its power, reverse the message, and stimulate a moment of insight, all in a single action. Remix can momentarily equalize, or even gain the upper hand temporarily in the struggle with a source for control of a given message. Explosive critical and popular results can thus be achieved by remixers from a position of relative weakness and obscurity.

Increasing access to information and outlets for finding an audience has fueled this empowerment. Remix embodies the ethic that all people deserve a culture that is read-write and should refuse one that is merely read-only,[6] to lift ourselves from passive reception to active reception.[7] This is a kind of cultural resistance, in the words of Fatimah Tobing Rony, "a refusal to accept the passive status of spectator."[8] Remix, as a quotidian cultural practice is a way to decode and understand popular media and their modes of communication for both the remixer and the viewer. It can be a direct response to mainstream media[9] and to their sponsors, methods, and assumptions.

However, the validity of remixes remains to be recognized broadly and video remixing practices face particular scrutiny from content providers, governments, and a still-skeptical public. Misinformation and other obstacles obscure how creative, valuable, and justified such practices really are. Overcoming these obstacles is necessary to foment a reality wherein copying practices such as remixing can be truly validated as legitimate creative activities and vehicles for expression and criticism.

A common misconception is that any work based wholly or in part on existing material is essentially derivative, and therefore devoid of creativity. Without experiencing remixes, one might overlook their value and meaning to the larger culture. Media may be viewed solely as products to consume, rather than as an integrated part of the cultural context in which we all exist and therefore have rights to. In this context, content creators and owners feel that losing control of an original creation to remix devalues it and weakens their brand. Misconceptions and false premises such as these must be addressed to build a lasting foundation for remix in the cultural canon of society. Asserting basic principles that can build a lasting appreciation for remix practices must become a part of this foundation.

Central among these principles must be the idea that remixes express not only the ideas of the sources used, but also those of their creators. Beyond this, remixes contribute valuable and necessary reflection and reimagination to existing works, providing new insight and deepening our understanding of them. Viewed in this way, even a highly critical remix burnishes and validates the original material as relevant to the greater culture, securing its place and enhancing its financial and cultural value. Copying for creating is valid practice and remixers must have a way to profit from their creations.[10] Without the right and ability to access existing media, a remix cannot be created. Finally, communities and cultural institutions must recognize remix.[11] The Right2Remix.

org website articulates and asserts many of these ideas in a succinct manifesto focused on issues of copyright and intellectual property as they relate to remix.[12]

Remix and Authorship

Whether a remix is nuanced social critique with a pointed argument,[13] or an apparent non sequitur,[14] it is clear that the remix author is engaged in a dialog with the original material. Remixes thus exhibit authorship, critical or otherwise. Remixes can create an illusionary reality that temporarily disguises authorship by masquerading as the visual language of the source. Since the play between the source material and the remix necessitates the inclusion of original footage, a remix ultimately reveals itself in places where it contrasts with the source. By way of editing, the perspective of the remixer becomes apparent.

Once this authorship is recognized, it follows naturally that a remix represents a form of personal expression of the type described as a perspective, what Virginia Kuhn describes as a "digital argument,"[15] and therefore an expression of media literacy.[16] As with literary practices, the creator of a remix may operate in any style or format, address any subject matter and do so from any perspective. A remix may or may not express an opinion of its source or direct a critique at any subject, but inevitably expresses a perspective representative of its creator.[17] Paul Booth suggests that, "if we look at remixes as decidedly pointed activities rather than just as objects or collections of samples, then we can form a more robust understanding of the cultural value of contemporary remix theory."[18]

Remixers combine multiple sources, editing techniques, themes, and approaches, often in combination to achieve unique multiplicity of meaning and perspective. As Martin Leduc suggests, "Affective and critical relationship with mass media do not have to cancel each other out but can be leveraged in each other's favor."[19] Remixes often contain literal messages and stories to create a kind of premise on which to place content displayed for a different purpose. There can be strong juxtapositions, ironies, paradoxes, and even outright contradictions between contexts and narratives presented. Tangential or unrelated messages and confections may be inserted. References to other remixes, media, comparative constructions, and even self-referencing may occur. This variant multiplicity depends heavily on viewer awareness of the author, which is naturally and conveniently self-evident in the remix, as Paul Booth suggests: "it takes the activity of the audience to intertextually reference deeper meanings of the texts to construct a mashup in all its complexity."[20]

This awareness assists the viewer to consider the context of remixed media and to hold onto and allow multiple realities, and perspectives throughout.[21] With its constant communication of authorship, remix is uniquely well suited for this multidimensionality, able to speak concurrently with literal meanings, cultural contexts, and diametrical viewpoints. Breaking the codes and context of consumption, remix possesses a critical dimension, constantly reminding the viewer of its unique perspective and engaging creative and social perspectives.

Defining Critical Remix

Remixes that directly engage this critical potential, "critical remixes," are particularly relevant to the validation of remixing practices in general as they exemplify the spirit of remix and highlight the authorship all remixes possess.[22] Rather than belonging to a subculture or movement, critical remixes share a common identity defined according to their basic nature. Critical remix thus includes works created by any individual or group,[23] those intended for "high art" audiences, works that received permission from sources[24], works in any format,[25] and works that comment on any subject.[26]

To communicate in this way is to assert one's claim to self-expression as described in *Rip: A Remix Manifesto* by Brett Gaylor.[27] Critical remixes engage the ideas and values our world presents to us in their original form. The power and purpose of remix can be seen in greatest relief embodied by the activist artist, waging a war of ideas against an overwhelming opponent, using the power of media to redress injustice, intolerance, and hegemony of discourse.

Critical remixes are a manifestation of this ethic and an embodiment of the value of a "read-write" society.[28] It follows that those remixes that directly invoke this critiquing nature would be uniquely potent as they address the very nature of media.

Critical Remix and the Activist Artist

Critical remix can be endlessly fascinating in the hands of an activist artist, an individual motivated to deconstruct the assumptions, propositions, codes, and conventions wrapped up in the mainstream media to which we are all exposed on a daily basis. A typical political remix video, for example, distills a vicious détournement by placing the greatest emphasis on contradiction between source and message: in the words of Eisenstein, "Degree of incongruence determines intensity of impression."[29] Critical remixes addressing the injustices of media itself are naturally powerful and abundant among this diverse landscape. Corporate and government power structures and their manufactured media identities created through advertising, official statements, and the cooption of news media by the powerful are frequent targets. Such practices may address gender issues in advertising,[30] political hypocrisy, attempts by Hollywood to make a scapegoat of religious or ethnic groups,[31] or the right of individuals to create and reuse media.[32]

As remix has faced so many existential threats in its short existence as a practice,[33] it is natural that critical remixers would have strong opinions, both politically and in regard to what or who might be included or excluded from the conversation. Nevertheless, critical remixes of all perspectives share a common identity as an embodiment of self-expression and the unique critical perspectives they contribute to our culture.

See Chapter 40 for Jesse Drew's discussion on creating his political remix video, *Manifestoon*.

Remix Cultures and Futures

Access to remixing communities, and the growing body of theory and criticism fertilizes the evolution of remix.[34] The more one observes remix production, the more it becomes apparent that remix cultures and practices hold the potential for infinite diversity in limitless combination, potential that transcends both art and advocacy, offering the promise of limitlessly fertile cross-pollination.[35] Regardless of how or by whom various categories of remix may be divided, a common identity spans across genres and media types validating the sense of community and purpose that remixers share as well as affirming the works and perspectives of diverse groups and individuals.[36]

The relatively anonymous environment of online communities also enables creativity and risk-taking. Remixing ecologies foster successive treatments of a subject, resulting in a more fully realized exploration of a subject or theme than individuals working in isolation might achieve and in a much shorter time frame, as described by Kathleen Amy Williams.[37] Remix can become a virtual hall of mirrors regressing infinitely, reflecting our collective desire for an impossible totality of knowledge and self-awareness, the ultimate meta-meta-awareness.[38]

Remixing practices and cultures can be expected to continue to multiply and diversify throughout digital culture and remix will be at times familiar and at times wholly unfamiliar and unpredictable in nature, defying attempts to proscribe its potential. Remix is utterly fascinating, creative and open-ended. In particular, people with a fresh perspective will continue to find a voice through critical remixing. By hacking the messages of corporate media, critical remixes illuminate the power of technology and activism to give individuals a voice in the media landscape.

Critical remixes will continue to flourish and evolve as they embody a universal urge to express ourselves and to respond to the messages we are exposed to, striving to assert our freedom of expression. As corporations and governments possess money and power, their messages and media are omnipresent in our world. To respond in a meaningful and effectual way, we as individuals strive to match the medium and coding that they employ. If Marshall McLuhan was right that "The Medium is the Message,"[39] then the medium must be the response as well.

Notes

1 Eduardo Navas, "We Really Need to Rethink Intellectual Property," http://right2remix.org/remixer-28-eduardo-navas-we-really-need-to-rethink-intellectual-property/, (accessed August 5, 2014).

2 Ibid.

3 Berthold Brecht, "Der Rundfunk als Kommunikationsapparat" (The Radio as an Apparatus of Communication), *Bjiter des Hessichen Landestheaters Darmstadt* 16 (July, 1932).

4 Richard L. Edwards and Chuck Tryon, "Political Video Mashups as Allegories of Citizen Empowerment," *First Monday* 14, no. 10, 2009. http://firstmonday.org/ojs/index.php/fm/article/view/2617/2305.

5 Guy Debord and Gil J. Wolman, "Mode d'emploi du détournement," *Les Lèvres Nues* 8 (May, 1956). ["A User's Guide to Détournement," translation by Ken Knabb from the *Situationist International Anthology*, revised and expanded edition, 2006. http://www.bopsecrets.org/SI/detourn.htm.]

6 Lawrence Lessig, *Remix: Making Art and Commerce Thrive in the Hybrid Economy* (New York; Penguin Press, 2008), 28.

7 Eli Horwatt, "A Taxonomy of Digital Video Remixing: Contemporary Found Footage Practice on the Internet," in *Cultural Borrowings: Appropriation, Reworking, Transformation*, ed. Iain Robert Smith, Nottingham: Scope, 2009, e-book. http://www.academia.edu/207383/Cultural_Borrowings_Appropriation_Reworking_Transformation.

8 Horwatt, "A Taxonomy of Digital Video Remixing," 84.

9 Eclectic Method—The Colbert Report—Remix feat. Lawrence Lessig, 2009, YouTube video, http://www.youtube.com/watch?v=CvvhDngERXo (accessed August 5, 2014).

10 Navas, "We Really Need to Rethink Intellectual Property."

11 http://www.guggenheim.org/new-york/interact/participate/youtube-play (accessed August 5, 2014).

12 www.right2remix.org (accessed August 5, 2014).

13 Jay Sandler, "Star Trek on Why the US should Withdraw from Iraq and Afghanistan," 2009, YouTube video, http://www.youtube.com/watch?v=pea8wZqPKi8 (accessed August 5, 2014).

14 HowMagnetsWork, "Miracles (Magnets Remix)—Insane Clown Posse," 2010, YouTube video, http://www.youtube.com/watch?v=ItrG8zFNPhQ (accessed August 5, 2014).

15 Virginia Kuhn, "The Rhetoric of Remix," in *Transformative Works and Cultures* 9, special issue, Fan/Remix Video, edited by Francesca Coppa and Julie Levin Russo, 2012. doi:10.3983/twc.2012.0358. http://journal.transformativeworks.org/index.php/twc/article/view/358.

16 Kim Middleton, "Remix Video and the Crisis of the Humanities." In *Transformative Works and Cultures* 9, special issue, Fan/Remix Video, edited by Francesca Coppa and Julie Levin Russo, 2012. http://journal. transformativeworks.org/index.php/twc/article/view/349.

17 John D. Boswell, "Carl Sagan—'A Glorious Dawn' ft Stephen Hawking (Symphony of Science)," 2009, YouTube video, http://www.youtube.com/watch?v=zSgiXGELjbc&list=PL77363C37932243A1.

18 Paul J. Booth, "Mashup as Temporal Amalgam: Time, Taste, and Textuality." In *Transformative Works and Cultures* 9, special issue, Fan/Remix Video, edited by Francesca Coppa and Julie Levin Russo, 2012. http:// journal.transformativeworks.org/index.php/twc/article/view/297.

19 Martin Leduc, "The Two-Source Illusion: How Vidding Practices Changed Jonathan McIntosh's Political Remix Videos," special issue, Fan/Remix Video, edited by Francesca Coppa and Julie Levin Russo, 2012. http://journal.transformativeworks.org/index.php/twc/article/view/379/274.

20 Booth, "Mashup as Temporal Amalgam."

21 Ibid.

22 Diran Lyons and Byron Russell. "It's Critical: Ethical Foundations for Critical Remix Practice and Theory" for the 2010 Open Video Conference Theory of Remix Panel, 2010, YouTube video, http://www. youtube.com/watch?v=9F-zxvjgE7M.

23 Teamcoco, "Harrison Ford Angrily Points At Stuff' Supercut," 2013, YouTube video, YouTube video, http://www.youtube.com/watch?v=K4Rqx9TvtlM (accessed August 5, 2014).

24 John Boswell, "Mister Rogers Remixed—Garden of Your Mind," 2012, YouTube video, http://www.you-tube.com/watch?v=OFzXaFbxDcM (accessed August 5, 2014).

25 Matt Williams, KQED Education, "The Personal is Political: Remix Video," 2012, YouTube video, http:// www.youtube.com/watch?v=rHzWglZ79E4 (accessed August 5, 2014).

26 KTN Kenya, "Political Remix," 2013, YouTube video, http://www.youtube.com/watch?v=uiwi9RMFphA (accessed August 5, 2014).

27 Brett Gaylor, *Rip: A Remix Manifesto*, The Disinformation Company, 2009, DVD. http://ripremix.com.

28 Lessig, *Remix: Making Art and Commerce Thrive in the Hybrid Economy*, 28.

29 Sergei Eisenstein, *Film Form* (New York: Harcourt, Brace & World, Inc., 1949), 9.

30 Jonathan McIntosh, "The Reel Grrls Remix Gendered Toy Ads," http://www.politicalremixvideo. com/2010/03/21/reel-grrls-remixed-ads/, 2009; and more recently, in 2012, "The HTML5 Gendered LEGO Advertising Remixer," http://www.genderremixer.com/lego/ (both accessed August 5, 2014).

31 Jackie Salloum, "Planet of the Arabs." 2006, YouTube video, http://www.youtube.com/ watch?v=Mi1ZNEjEarw (accessed August 5, 2014).

32 Eric Faden, "A Fair(y) Use Tale," Center for Internet and Society Blog at Stanford Law School, 2007. http://cyberlaw.stanford.edu/blog/2007/03/fairy-use-tale (accessed August 5, 2014).

33 "Good Copy Bad Copy," Andreas Johnsen, Ralf Christensen, and Henrik Moltke, 2007. A documentary about the current state of copyright and culture, YouTube video, http://www.youtube.com/ watch?v=WEKl5I_Q044 (accessed August 5, 2014).

34 www.remixstudies.org, Seminar Series 11 (accessed August 5, 2014).

35 Kuhn, "The Rhetoric of Remix."

36 Ibid.

37 Kathleen Amy Williams, "Fake and Fan Film Trailers as Incarnations of Audience Anticipation and Desire," in *Transformative Works and Cultures* 9, special issue, Fan/Remix Video, edited by Francesca Coppa and Julie Levin Russo, 2012. doi:10.3983/twc.2012.0360. http://journal.transformativeworks.org/ index.php/twc/article/view/360/284.

38 SuperYoshi, "Sango REMIX REMIX REMIX," 2008, YouTube video, http://www.youtube.com/ watch?v=3GCU0vXCyWY (accessed August 5, 2014).

39 Marshall McCluhan and Quentin Fiore, *The Medium is the Message* (New York: Random House, 1967).

Bibliography

Benjamin, Walter. *The Work of Art in the Age of Mechanical Reproduction*. New York: Prism Press, 2010 [1936].

Booth, Paul J. "Mashup as Temporal Amalgam: Time, Taste, and Textuality." In *Transformative Works and Cultures* 9, special issue, Fan/Remix Video, edited by Francesca Coppa and Julie Levin Russo, 2012. http://journal.transformativeworks.org/index.php/twc/article/view/297 (accessed August 5, 2014).

Brecht, Bertolt. "Der Rundfunk als Kommunikationsapparat" (The Radio as an Apparatus of Communication), *Bjiter des Hessichen Landestheaters Darmstadt* 16 (July, 1932): 259–263.

Coppa, Francesca. "Women, *Star Trek*, and the Early Development of Fannish Vidding." *Transformative Works and Cultures* 1 (2008). http://journal.transformativeworks.org/index.php/twc/article/view/44 (accessed August 5, 2014).

Debord, Guy, and Gil J. Wolman. "Mode d'emploi du détournement." *Les Lèvres Nues* 8 (May, 1956). ["A User's Guide to Détournement," translation by Ken Knabb from the *Situationist International Anthology*, revised and expanded edition, 2006. http://www.bopsecrets.org/SI/detourn.htm, accessed August 5, 2014.]

Edwards, Richard L., and Chuck Tryon. "Political Video Mashups as Allegories of Citizen Empowerment." *First Monday* 14, no. 10 (2009). http://firstmonday.org/ojs/index.php/fm/article/view/2617/2305 (accessed August 5, 2014).

Eisenstein, Sergei. *Film Form*. New York: Harcourt, Brace & World, Inc., 1949.

Gaylor, Brett. *Rip: A Remix Manifesto*. The Disinformation Company, 2009. DVD. http://ripremix.com (accessed August 5, 2014).

Horwatt, Eli. "A Taxonomy of Digital Video Remixing: Contemporary Found Footage Practice on the Internet." In *Cultural Borrowings: Appropriation, Reworking, Transformation*, edited by Iain Robert Smith, Nottingham: Scope, 2009. http://www.academia.edu/207383/Cultural_Borrowings_Appropriation_Reworking_Transformation (accessed August 5, 2014).

——. "Remix and the Roulles of Media Production." *New Media and Networked Art History*. August, 2010. http://wiki.networkedbook.org/index.php/Remix_and_the_Rouelles_of_Media_Production (accessed August 5, 2014).

Kuhn, Virginia. "The Rhetoric of Remix." In *Transformative Works and Cultures* 9, special issue, Fan/Remix Video, edited by Francesca Coppa and Julie Levin Russo, 2012. http://journal.transformativeworks.org/index.php/twc/article/view/358 (accessed August 5, 2014).

Leduc, Martin. "The Two-Source Illusion: How Vidding Practices Changed Jonathan McIntosh's Political Remix Videos," special issue, Fan/Remix Video, edited by Francesca Coppa and Julie Levin Russo, 2012. http://journal.transformativeworks.org/index.php/twc/article/view/379/274 (accessed August 5, 2014).

Lessig, Lawrence. *Free Culture: The Nature and Future of Creativity*. New York: Penguin Press, 2004.

——. *Remix: Making Art and Commerce Thrive in the Hybrid Economy*. New York: Penguin Press, 2008

Lyons, Diran, and Byron Russell. "It's Critical: Ethical Foundations for Critical Remix Practice and Theory" for the 2010 Open Video Conference Theory of Remix Panel, 2010. http://www.youtube.com/watch?v=9F-zxvjgE7M (accessed August 5, 2014).

McLuhan, Marshall, and Quentin Fiore. *The Medium Is the Message*. New York: Random House, 1967.

Middleton, Kim. "Remix Video and the Crisis of the Humanities." In *Transformative Works and Cultures* 9, special issue, Fan/Remix Video, edited by Francesca Coppa and Julie Levin Russo, 2012. http://journal.transformativeworks.org/index.php/twc/article/view/349 (accessed August 5, 2014).

Navas, Eduardo. "We Really Need to Rethink Intellectual Property," http://right2remix.org/remixer-28-eduardo-navas-we-really-need-to-rethink-intellectual-property/, 2013 (accessed August 5, 2014).

——. "Remix Defined." *Remix Theory*. http://remixtheory.net/?page_id=3, nd (accessed August 5, 2014).

Rony, Fatimah Tobing. 2003. "The Quick and the Dead: Surrealism and the Found Ethnographic Footage Films of Bontoc Eulogy and Mother Dao: The Turtlelike." *Camera Obscura* 18, no. 1 52: 129–155.

Williams, Kathleen Amy. "Fake and Fan Film Trailers as Incarnations of Audience Anticipation and Desire." In *Transformative Works and Cultures* 9, special issue, Fan/Remix Video, edited by Francesca Coppa and Julie Levin Russo, 2012. doi:10.3983/twc.2012.0360 (accessed August 5, 2014).

Part III

ETHICS

16

THE EMERGING ETHICS OF NETWORKED CULTURE

Aram Sinnreich

One of the central themes of this book, and indeed of most research that focuses on emerging digital cultural practices and forms, is *ambiguity*. The sociotechnical regimes of the twentieth century, often discussed under the conveniently broad rubric of "mass media," have broken down—undermining traditional institutions and economies and changing the discursive paradigm of mediated communication itself. When confronted with an anonymously produced, animated GIF combining the structure of a popular meme with recent footage of a celebrity dance routine and textual elements discussing the shortcomings of the latest smartphone release, posted to the comments section of an online video embedded on a social media page beneath an observational-critical comment expressed via emoji, how can we possibly reduce its significance to Lasswell's[1] famous dictum that communication can be summarized in terms of "Who says what in which channel to whom with what effect?"

This discursive slipperiness is immediately evident when we survey the range of theoretical lenses that have been applied to the effort to make sense of such cultural practices. Leaving aside the "nothing has changed" and "everything is different" extremists, most scholars have attempted to describe the emerging field in terms of its own ambiguity. Yet, even on this front, there is little consensus. Some theorists base their terminology on the observation that the classifications defining traditional cultural *forms* have blurred, and that these forms themselves are now amalgams of other media. Lessig's "remix culture"[2] and Sonvilla-Weiss's "mashup cultures"[3] are two such examples. Others focus instead on the fact that the cultural *actors* themselves no longer occupy fixed roles, but now fall somewhere in the gray area between our traditionally understood polarities of "producer" and "consumer." Tapscott and Williams's concept of "prosumption"[4] and Bruns's term "produsage"[5] both share this vantage point. Finally, some theorists try to capture both of these dynamics in one pithy term; Jenkins's "convergence culture"[6] and my own "configurable culture"[7] both walk this line.

The consequences of these ambiguities for social institutions such as the marketplace and intellectual property law have been thoroughly explored by scholars ranging from Vaidhyanathan[8] to Lessig[9] to Benkler[10] to O'Reilly[11] (though consensus has hardly been achieved here, either). A less frequently examined dimension of these changes, however, is the role that *ethical systems* play in defining and regulating emerging cultural practices. Part of the challenge, as Boon has observed, is that the discursive ambiguity itself means that "there seems to be an almost total lack of context for understanding what it means to copy, what a copy is, [and] what the uses of copying are."[12] A related problem is that the digital cultural landscape is hardly fixed, and continues to change at a rate that outstrips the pace of academic publication. Thus, Church observes that "remix" as a broad field is "a nuanced and evolving phenomenon,"[13] and Campanelli argues that as a result, "ethical principles governing online communities are also in constant evolution."[14]

Because of these challenges, it is difficult even to know where to begin establishing the basis for an ethics of configurability.[15] It would be optimistic at best and more likely fruitless to begin with traditional media ethics and attempt to mold them to the shifting forms and practices at issue in this research. A far more effective course, as Boon argues, is to recognize that "practice has its own ethics—and this ethics is worked out in the configuration of practice itself, and in relation to other practices and practitioners."[16] In other words, ethics can be observed in the way that people engage with and discuss digitally mediated communication, rather than seen as an a priori framework against which such behaviors may be evaluated.

So what are people actually doing, and what can we learn about their ethics from their practices? Several scholars have made observations along these lines. Church argues that *aesthetic* concerns trump traditional ethical considerations in the case of mashups: "the fragment of music that sounds the best with another is the one that gets sampled, irrespective of ownership or ethical issues with its appropriation."[17] Yet he also acknowledges a separate value, "larger than whether a mashup is aesthetically beautiful," tied to the "rhetoric of inventional choices . . . that are embedded in the very idea of the Western liberal tradition."[18] In short, self-actualization through *self-expression* is the paramount value in configurable culture.

Other scholars have identified additional considerations at work in the context of remixing. Lessig emphasizes the importance of *innovation* within underground Japanese *doujinshi* comic art: "the artist must make a contribution to the art he copies, by transforming it either subtly or significantly."[19] Similarly, in her discussion of "borrowing" in both hip hop and academic writing, Chanbonpin observes that "the ethical and professional danger inherent in this type of production is that one who borrows too freely from the past may be merely copying instead of interpreting or innovating."[20]

Another ethical value observed within these communities of practice is *labor*, or the amount of work applied to a given project. Discussing computer hackers, for instance, Lessig observes that they "like to challenge themselves and others with increasingly difficult tasks. There's a certain respect that goes with the talent to hack well. There's a well-deserved respect that goes with the talent to hack ethically."[21] In other words, the amount of skill and effort applied to the process of transformation is itself an index of whether the transformation in question is ethical. Something as easy as pressing a single button wouldn't make the grade, but an elegant hack involving a novel or clever application of code to materials would.

Finally, some scholars have observed that traditional markers of media ethics, including *market behavior* and *legal compliance*, continue to play a role in the ethical calculi applied to configurability, though the traditional *power relations* are often inverted. Grimmelmann argues that "the default ethical vision" of copyright occurs when "authors and audiences respect each other and meet in the marketplace."[22] In that context, he says, open licenses such as Creative Commons can be seen as "a challenge to the default ethical vision of copyright itself, not merely a critique of authorial behavior made from within that vision."[23] That is, configurable practitioners don't simply ignore traditional ethics, they seek to displace and revise them. Trammell provides a context for these challenges, observing that video game modders and fan fiction authors explicitly recognize intellectual property laws as an instrument of "exploitation of fan labor in the service of branded community," and face potential liability for infringement out of resilience and resolution rather than mere ignorance.[24] Along similar lines, West and Coad interpret "the resistance to both the introduction and the policing of copyright law in China" as the expression of a fundamentally Eastern ethic of individuality and authorship, and a philosophical rejection of the Western liberal ideal.[25]

To summarize, then, a range of scholars have observed a variety of different ethical considerations brought to bear by various communities of practice on the configurable cultural forms they produce and reproduce. These include aesthetic beauty, self-expression, innovation, labor, commercial valence, legality, and power relations. As I will argue later in this chapter, these and a handful of other ethical criteria are consistently invoked by the general public in their own efforts to develop a workable ethical framework for engagement with digital media and communications.

To return for a moment to the subject I introduced at the outset of this chapter, I propose that the fundamental ambiguities at the heart of configurable culture demand resolution, and that, in the absence of a legal regulatory system suited to the realities of networked media, individuals and communities have begun to develop their own ethical frameworks to distinguish between permissible and impermissible conduct, between good copying and bad copying. Consequently, much of my research in this field has been devoted to discovering and cataloging these new frameworks, and to understanding who adopts them, in what context, and for what reason.

The Ethics of Configurability: Survey Data

Though I addressed many of the ethical issues surrounding configurable culture in the course of extended ethnographic interviews with DJs and music industry executives,[26] it is my aim here to share the results of two more systematic studies my coauthors and I conducted on the population at large, using a series of surveys. The first[27] was fielded to 1,779 American adults in mid-2006, and the second[28] was fielded to 3,055 English-speaking adults around the globe in late 2010. In addition to fixed-choice questions geared toward quantitative analysis, the surveys asked participants to answer open-ended questions regarding their general opinions of configurable cultural practices. These write-in responses were examined for the underlying ethical frameworks deployed by respondents to establish the legitimacy or illegitimacy of such practices, and then coded individually using an emergent open coding scheme.

In our first survey, seven ethical themes emerged from the responses, and these reappeared in the second survey, joined by four additional themes, which are marked by asterisks in Table 16.1. The data present these themes, selected examples of quotes from respondents that span the poles of each ethical category, and demographic profiles of the respondent subgroups who employed these themes.

The first ethical criterion that emerged from our data was *commercial* in nature. Thirty-eight of our respondents to the 2010 survey indicated that profiting from appropriated content (without paying for its use) is unethical. This emerging ethic diverges from the letter of copyright law, which considers most unauthorized appropriations of content to constitute infringement, irrespective of a for-profit or nonprofit intention or effect. Selected examples are:[29]

Table 16.1 Ethical dimensions for configurable culture

Unethical	Criterion	Ethical
For-profit	*Commercial*	Nonprofit
Unpermissioned	*Legal*	Permissioned
Pretension	*Authenticity*	Referenced
Unoriginal	*Innovation*	Original
Easy	*Labor*	Hard work
Bastardization	*Moral*	Homage
Rupture	*Continuity*	Evolution
Useless/harmful	*Use Value**	Fun/beneficial
Ugly	*Aesthetic**	Beautiful
Undermining	*Power Relations**	Empowering
Meaningless	*Self-Expression**	Expressive

- "if the remixes are intended for profit, they should need licenses . . . if it's just for fun, then the artists should appreciate having fans out there who enjoy their music, and enjoy using it."
- "I think that if you're profiting from other people's creations then it should be treated as theft. Otherwise, I think it's fine to use other people's work."
- "As soon as the creator of the mash-up makes a penny having used someone elses materials as the basis for the mash-up they are stealing . . . even if what is created is 'original' and possibly eligible for it's own protection." [all *sic*]

Who are the respondents using this criterion, and how do they differ from the population at large? A comparison of the means for the entire survey population and the means for respondents for this category (Figure 16.1) indicates a relatively small gender gap (106.8 percent male compared to baseline); slightly better education (103.8 percent); lower-than-average income (75.3 percent); low representation by African-Americans (84.2 percent); and high representation by Asian-Americans (150.8 percent). This was also the only category overrepresented by US citizens/residents (108.7 percent).[30]

The second ethical criterion that emerged from our write-in responses was adherence to *legal* regulations—specifically the notion, expressed by 118 respondents to the 2010 survey, that permission from the owner or originator of a piece of content is a requisite element for the ethical reuse of that content. Note that some respondents actively acknowledged the functional limitations of copyright law, and identified open licenses as a viable solution to the mismatch between old systems of permission and new modes of cultural expression. Selected examples of such responses are:

- "I strongly feel that unauthorized use of remixes and mash-ups are illegal and should be reported immediately."
- "doing without permission from the original owner is wrong."
- "I'm not personally a fan, but I can understand the appeal, at least from a creation point of view. I agree that the copyright issues need clearing up, and welcome the development of Creative Commons licenses, etc. to facilitate legitimate use." [all *sic*]

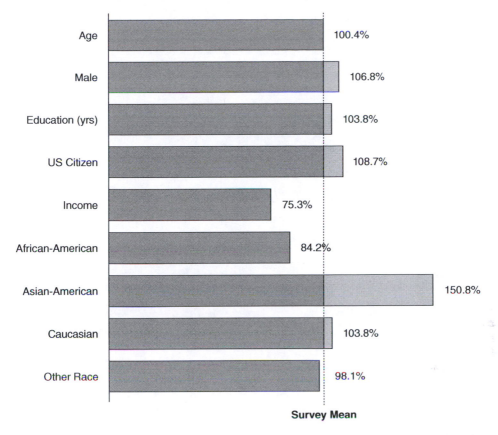

Figure 16.1 Survey response means for commercial criterion (all graphics in this chapter courtesy of the author)

The respondents who embraced this ethical framework were the most similar demographically to the general survey base (Figure 16.2). Compared to the base means, the respondents employing the legal category were the oldest subgroup (105.5 percent), the second-least male biased (105.1 percent), more educated than average (104.7 percent), of moderately low US citizenship (65.8 percent), and they had the second-highest income of any subgroup (88.5 percent). The ethnic breakdown for these respondents hewed close to the general survey base except for "Other" (137.7 percent).

A third ethical criterion that emerged from our survey responses was the notion of *authenticity*. A remix or mashup was deemed legitimate by these respondents if its creator acknowledged the influence of, or debt to, his or her source materials. Yet if a remix pretends to ex nihilo authenticity, it can be seen as illegitimate. Examples are:

- "They can be dangerous when the viewer isn't privy to the original referenced work."
- "Remixes and mash-up should be allowed with due acknowledgement to the original work and author."
- "About remixes and mashups, as long as you acknowledge the original creator of item and do justice to his work I think remixes and mashups should be acceptable." [all *sic*]

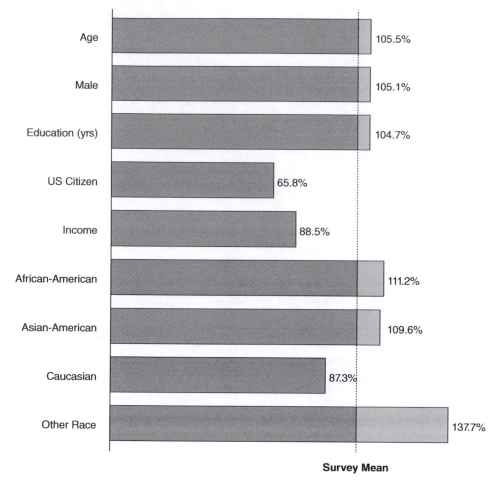

Figure 16.2 Survey response means for legal criterion

Compared to the general survey population, Figure 16.3 shows that the 23 respondents using the authenticity criterion in 2010 represented the second-highest percentage of male respondents of any category (117.6 percent male), were slightly more educated (103.6 percent), and were far less likely to be US citizens/residents, even compared to other categories (54.8 percent). This group also had the lowest mean income of any category (70 percent), and a relatively high proportion of African-Americans (137.9 percent) and Asian-Americans (148.1 percent).

The next ethical value to emerge from our survey responses was *innovation*. Some respondents perceived configurable cultural practices as unoriginal and derivative and therefore illegitimate, while others viewed them as something new and "original," and therefore legitimate. For many respondents, the premise of "original" authorship retained a prior, and therefore hierarchically superior, position relative to creative reappropriation. Selected examples include:

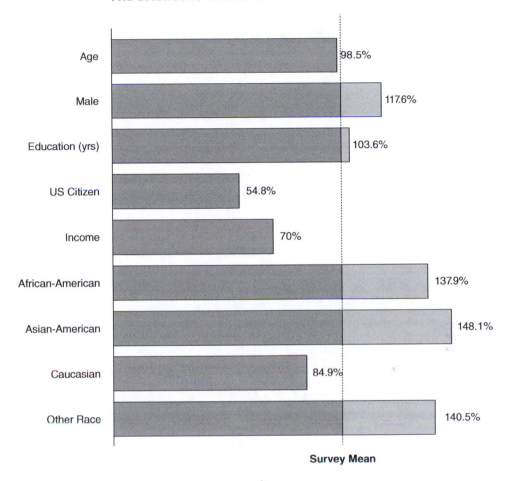

Figure 16.3 Survey response means for authenticity criterion

- "This should be considered theft because it is not an orginal work especially if he was using someone else's music/voice and selling it."
- "i like remixes and mash ups less than the origanl songs."
- "Remixes and mash-ups are so cool! People with the ability to take a song or video that already exists and turn it into art are very inspirational." [all *sic*]

The large group (118 of our 2010 survey respondents) that used innovation-based ethical criteria was predominantly male (111.7 percent compared to the baseline), more educated than average (104.3 percent), moderately low in US citizenship (68.5 percent), and had the highest mean income of any subgroup (especially given the significant non-US representation (89.5 percent)). Furthermore, Figure 16.4 shows that respondents were exceptionally likely to be African-Americans (189.4 percent) or self-described "Other Race" (181.3 percent), and unlikely to be Caucasians (69.8 percent).

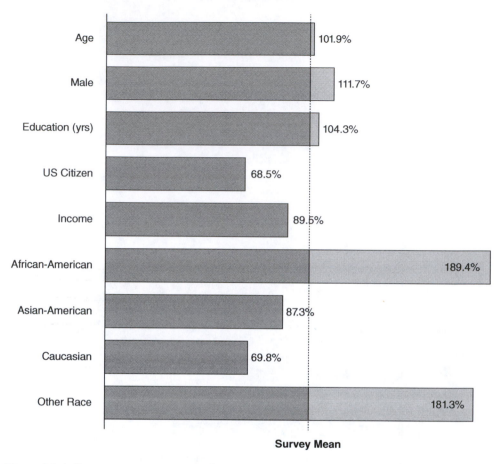

Figure 16.4 Survey response means for innovation criterion

Another ethical criterion that appeared in both the 2006 and 2010 survey responses was *morality*, defined as the relationship between configurable content and its sources. A work that pays homage or does justice to its source may be perceived as legitimate, whereas one that disrespects, insults, or bastardizes the original may be seen as illegitimate. Some specific examples are below:

- "REMIXES & MASH-UPS ARE ACCEPTABLE AS LONG AS THEY DO NOT SPOIL THE FLAVOR OF THE ORIGINAL."
- "Sense of ownership is important. Acknowledging where the remixes and/or mash-ups originated must be practiced at all times. It signifies respect."
- "Remixing is basically building on a creative work. But the one making them should always pay respect to the creator by acknowledgements." [all *sic*]

The 39 respondents to our 2010 survey employing moral criteria (Figure 16.4) tended to be younger (95.2 percent of baseline age) and, unlike every other subgroup, skewed female relative to the general survey population (110.6 percent female). They had the

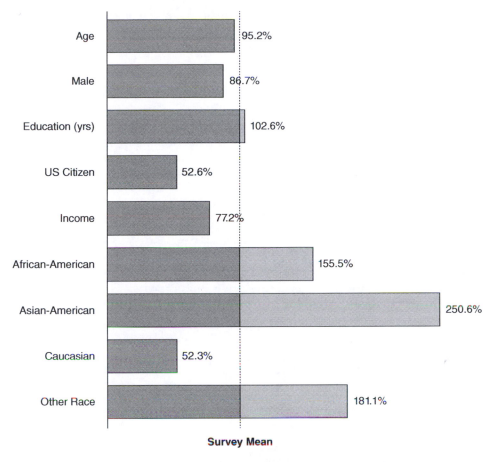

Figure 16.5 Survey response means for morality criterion

second-lowest US citizenship/residency rate (52.6 percent), were relatively low income (77.2 percent), had a high representation of African-Americans (155.5 percent) and individuals identifying as "Other Race" (181.1 percent), and had the highest representation of Asian-Americans (250.6 percent) and the lowest representation of Caucasians (52.3 percent) of any subgroup.

Some respondents (34 in the 2010 survey) also reacted to the idea of configurable cultural practices within a larger historical context, using a criterion my coauthors and I call *continuity* (Figure 16.5). The relative novelty of these practices was either bemoaned by some as an unwelcome break from established tradition (and therefore illegitimate) and viewed by others as part of an evolution of past practices (and therefore legitimate). Examples of these responses include:

- "The remixes and mash ups are the good idea looking at the changing world but as a mother and very devoted hindu, has drifted my kids away from the meaningful world. I love changes but not to forget or lose my origin."
- "Remix songs, at least in my opinion be extremely important opportunities for young people to know the old songs."

- "Personally I really enjoy myself listening to mash-ups and remixes, simply because they give a complete breath of fresh air (if made successfully) in things we've already heard or seen." [all *sic*]

The respondents deploying the continuity ethical category in 2010 skewed male (112.7 percent compared to baseline data), were the most educated subgroup (106.8 percent), were far less likely to be US citizens/residents, even compared to most other subgroups (57.6 percent), and had relatively high income (84.9 percent), especially considering the high non-US representation. Figure 16.6 also shows that this group had exceptionally high representation by African-Americans (189.4 percent) and "Other Race" (234.6 percent), the lowest representation of Asian-Americans (67.9 percent), and the second-lowest representation of Caucasians (58.4 percent).

Another ethical category that emerged from both surveys was the notion (discussed in reference to Lessig,[31] above) that *labor* may determine whether an act of creative reappropriation is ethical or not. Specifically, easier mixes, mashes and hacks are insufficiently original to be accorded respect, while more challenging or taxing appropriations may achieve legitimacy. Because only four respondents to the 2010 survey embraced this criterion, we did not perform a demographic analysis of the group. Some examples of relevant write-in responses are:

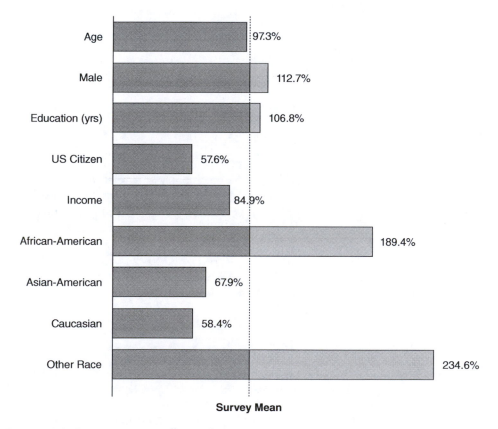

Figure 16.6 Survey response means for continuity criterion

- "I think lazy is a word that covers their work. Like adding one letter in a scrabble game to profit from someone else's ideas"
- "Derivative works only become original creative content in their own right when a decent amount of work goes into producing something new"
- "it is easy to copy someone else's work or ideas when you have no talent or are too lazy to do it yourself." [all *sic*]

The seven ethical criteria outlined above emerged from our survey responses in both 2006 and 2010. In the later survey, an additional four categories emerged. One such criterion was the perceived social or psychological *use value* of a given configurable cultural practice or form. Specifically, those deemed fun, entertaining, and useful were seen as legitimate while those deemed boring or damaging were seen as illegitimate. Some examples are as follows:

- "usually they don't hurt anyone so that's when I think its okay. only if it was being used in a harmful way would it be not okay to use the copyrighted original work."
- "Remixes must be done for good cause of the society."
- "remixes and mash-ups should be used only for entertainment purposes." [all *sic*]

The 86 respondents citing use value as an ethical consideration (Figure 16.7) represented the second-youngest subgroup (92.9 percent of baseline age), showed near gender parity (106.1 percent male) and a very low US citizenship/residency rate (55.3 percent), and had a relatively low mean income (78.2 percent). The group had a very high representation of Asian-Americans (162.9 percent) and "Other Race" (160 percent), and a fairly low representation of African-Americans (75.8 percent) and Caucasians (68 percent).

Some respondents in 2010 used *aesthetic* considerations as an ethical standard for configurable cultural practices, though aesthetics were entirely absent in the 2006 survey responses (Figure 16.8). Artistic, beautiful, and melodious configurable forms were deemed legitimate, while those that sound bad and/or ruin their source materials were seen as illegitimate. Examples include:

- "Sometimes the remixes are awful and if I would be original artist, I would not want my material sounds awful."
- "remix and mash up should be melodious and pleasant."
- "Remixes ruin whatever it is they are trying to redo." [all *sic*]

These 18 respondents represented the greatest gender gap (118.6 percent male), were slightly better educated (103.9 percent), had a relatively high US citizenship/residency rate compared to other categories (76.8 percent), and were somewhat low income (79.2 percent). As Figure 16.8 shows, this group had no African-American representation (0 percent), very high representation of Asian-Americans (191.6 percent), and relatively high representation of Caucasians compared to other categories (80 percent).

Respondents in 2010 were also concerned with the *power relations* that surround the use and regulation of emerging cultural forms—a consideration absent in the 2006 survey data (Figure 16.9). Those who understood configurable culture to embody functions such as commentary, parody, and satire saw these practices as legitimate. Others elicited concern that such practices could undermine community or individual agency. Some examples are:

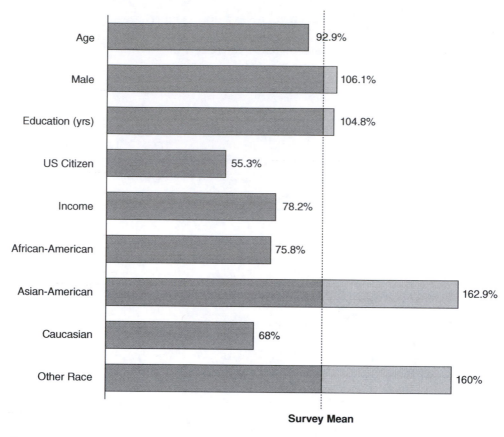

Figure 16.7 Survey response means for use value criterion

- "it was a good experience to see political parodies and local satires because that is what changes our world view and our thoughts. it gets the politican more conscience about our feelings and tries to hone in our concerns more appropriately."
- "It should not be created to hurt any community or any person's personal life and his/her privacy."
- "Knowlegde is power and should be shared together." [all *sic*]

This group of 30 respondents was the second oldest subgroup (105.1 percent), exhibited a significant gender gap (112.7 percent male), and was slightly more educated (103.9 percent) than general survey respondents (Figure 16.9). This group also had the highest US citizenship/residency rate—the only category to exceed the baseline (110.9 percent). It also earned the highest income—the only category to exceed baseline (113.9 percent). The ethnic makeup of this subgroup hewed close to the overall survey—except for very low Asian-American representation (37.4 percent) and moderately high 'Other Race' (137 percent).

The final new ethical category to emerge from the 2010 survey results was based on the premise that configurable cultural practices enable *self-expression*, and therefore carry an inherent ethical legitimacy (Figure 16.10). Conversely, respondents who saw these

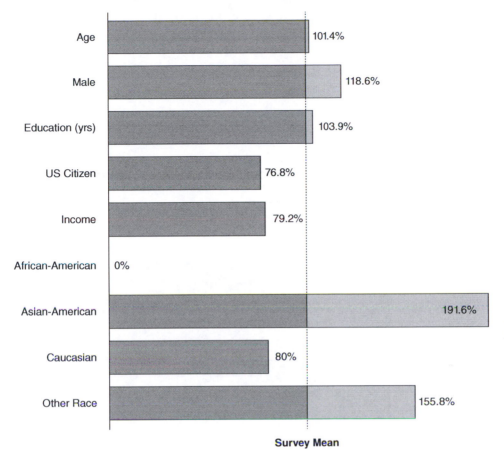

Figure 16.8 Survey response means for aesthetic criterion

emerging forms as meaningless or unexpressive had reservations about their legitimacy. Examples of both perspectives are included:

- "Remixes and mash-ups sound like something that people with way too much time on their hands would do."
- "i think remixes and mash ups are an idea, for people who don't know how to make music, to make music, but if the goal of a remix or a mash up is to make a point about a subject than i consider it to be important."
- "It's a great way to express yourself and your individuality." [all *sic*]

Compared to the baseline survey averages, this subgroup (Figure 16.10) was the youngest by far (76 percent), had the greatest gender parity of any subgroup (102.5 percent male), had the lowest US citizenship/residency rate by far (46.1 percent), and earned the second-lowest income of any category (73.5 percent). The group had an extremely high representation of African-Americans (275.5 percent) and "Other Race" (240.8 percent), as well as the lowest representation of Caucasians of any category (41.2 percent) (Figure 16.10).

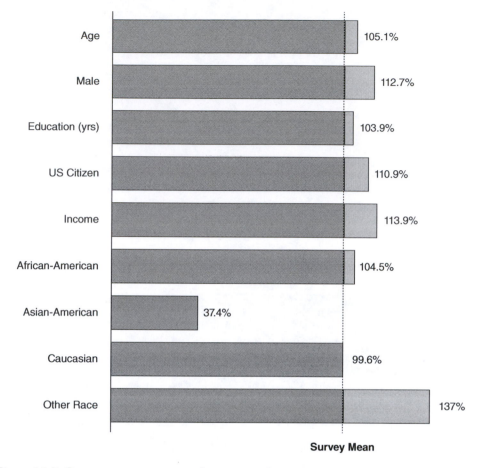

Figure 16.9 Survey response means for power relation criterion

Old Laws, New Ethics

Two decades after the development of the World Wide Web and the resulting emergence of the Internet as a global platform for the creation and dissemination of new, configurable cultural forms and practices, our legal and regulatory apparatuses are still hopelessly mired in the expectations, economics, and ethical frameworks of the mass media era.[32] This disjuncture has arguably hindered cultural innovation; as Kafai, et al. argue, lack of participation in online communities "may very well be tied to the ethical issues associated with the remixing process so commonly used to create content" in such communities.[33] Yet, despite (or because of) these institutional inadequacies and the social problems they may engender, people who are not lawyers are developing their own ethical frameworks to distinguish between legitimate and illegitimate uses of reappropriated work in their cultural environments.

These emerging ethical criteria draw in part on preexisting cultural premises from a range of social, economic, and moral systems, which potentially lessens the relative importance of an ethical framework rooted in copyright law per se. That said, legality

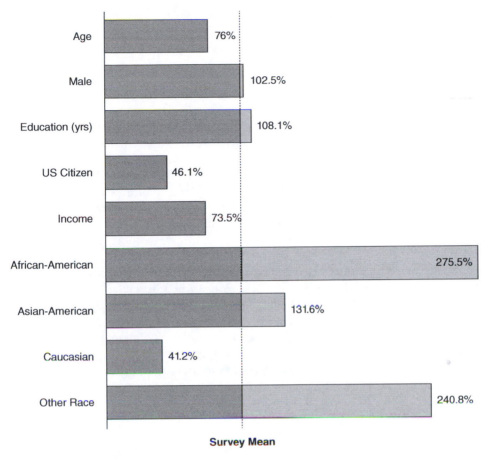

Figure 16.10 Survey response means for self-expression criterion

remains a central element of respondents' overall ethical calculus; permission-based criteria, which are closest to the letter of copyright law, were among the most frequently cited. Similarly, moral rights, which exist in several non-US copyright systems (as discussed by Geller,[34] Kwall,[35] and Smiers and van Schijndel[36]), were far more likely to be cited by non-US citizens than by Americans.

While much has been written about the distinctions between "digital natives," who have been acculturated to information communication technologies (ICTs) and networked culture, and their elders and less fortunate contemporaries who have not (see, for instance, Palfrey and Gasser[37] or Prensky[38]), our analyses suggest that age is only one of many factors influencing ethics and attitudes about digital culture—and that it plays a far less significant role than either ethnicity or nationality. This point has significant policy implications. As the total population of Internet users continues to age, any reflexive assumption of a correlation between youth culture and digital culture, or the expectation that youth "lead the way" in the adoption and cultural assimilation of ICTs, may risk obscuring other, more important socioeconomic factors and may contribute to policies and investments that are biased against older users.

Though age is a factor in awareness, practices, and even attitudes regarding the overall legitimacy of configurable practices, there were no considerable age distinctions between most ethical categories. In fact, the average age of the categories typically hovered very close to the average age of all survey respondents (~40 years). This indicates that the different emerging ethical frameworks are not cohort-based, but rather are rooted in geographic and ethnic communities—in other words, preexisting ethical systems from around the world are being applied, in different ways, to this common emerging set of cultural practices. This finding is important because configurable culture is a global, and globalizing, phenomenon. Of course, the commonalities of these global practices do not erase demographic differences altogether.

Indeed, the survey research indicates that national differences are important in this context. For instance, the fact that US citizens represent a far greater percentage of commercial and power relations evaluators relative to other ethical frameworks (by a ratio of more than two to one with respect to authenticity, morality, and self-expression) reflects the differing models for broader cultural legitimacy in the United States and elsewhere.

The recent appearance of power relations as an ethical category in 2010, after being absent in 2006, is also significant. It shows, as Lessig[39] and others have argued, that the rapid propertization of culture is beginning to provoke mainstream backlash and awareness of the inadequacies and inequities of copyright law in its current form. This is exacerbated by the rapid expansion of configurable culture, which makes those inadequacies and inequities far more evident because of their immunity to traditional categorization. The fact that this ethical category skews most toward US citizens conforms to this analysis, as the United States is the epicenter of cultural propertization and the engine of most maximalist copyright policy around the globe.[40]

The ethnic differences between respondents in different categories are also very telling. Like the national differences, they suggest that preexisting ethical systems tied to networks based on religion, heritage, and other ethnically skewed factors play a large role in determining how people make sense of the ethics of configurability—in short, that old networks help to determine the rules of engagement on new networks.

Finally, the self-expression criterion, which is a new addition in the 2010 survey data, is the greatest anomaly. It skews very young, international, and nonwhite. This suggests the spirit of global youth at work, and perhaps even the development of a new, global vision of networked individuality, augmenting and supplanting the Western liberal ideal. These data may indicate that we are coming to see configurable cultural participation as a fundamental civil liberty—in the words of Boon, that "the right to copy, and to transform ourselves and our environment through copying, is a political issue in ways that go far beyond intellectual-property law."[41]

It is not my aim to advocate for the superiority or legitimacy of one of these ethical frameworks compared to another, or to suggest that each demographic group be allowed to pick and choose its own laws, but rather to observe that these frameworks have arisen in the absence of a robust and adaptive legal regulatory apparatus, and often in contradistinction to the letter of copyright law itself. If intellectual property can be amended to suit the new cultural realities of a digital, networked, globalized media environment, careful examination of these emerging frameworks will be a necessary first step in ensuring that norms, laws, and ethics are effectively reconciled, and that cultural innovation can proceed without the categorical criminalization of mainstream cultural participation.

One particular element of our current intellectual property landscape that bears special scrutiny in this context is the recent move toward "harmonization" of intellectual property laws and regulations across national boundaries (see Benkler,[42] Brown,[43] Crews,[44] Long,[45] and Sinnreich[46]). As the survey responses suggest, this process obscures very real differences in the attitudes of different nationalities and ethnicities regarding the appropriate borderline between legitimate and illegitimate uses of cultural property, as well as the variant methods by which this line is established. To suggest, as the logic of harmonization does, that one legal framework is equally optimal in all countries and contexts is to risk introducing a form of bias into cultural regulation that privileges the needs and attitudes of some demographics and nationalities over those of others. Specifically, the existing legal apparatus most closely fits ethical frameworks disproportionately embraced by white Americans, and may therefore be critiqued as an instrument of hegemonic power.

Thus, we must view today's battles over intellectual property on the Internet, and the broader range of debates over the scope of "Internet freedom," as a collective effort to reconcile our disparate and emerging ethical systems with the regulatory legacy of a bygone technological, social, and political era. The methods we employ to address these concerns and to rectify these disjunctures will serve as both an indicator and an instrument of evolving cultural power relations around the globe.

Notes

1 Harold D. Lasswell. "The Structure and Function of Communication in Society." In *The Communication of Ideas*, ed. Lyman Bryson (New York: Harper, 1948), 37.
2 Lawrence Lessig. *Remix: Making Art and Commerce Thrive in the Hybrid Economy* (New York: Penguin, 2008).
3 Stefan Sonvilla-Weiss, ed. *Mashup Cultures* (New York: Springer, 2010).
4 Don Tapscott and Anthony D. Williams. *Wikinomics: How Mass Collaboration Changes Everything* (New York: Penguin, 2006).
5 Axel Bruns. *Blogs, Wikipedia, Second Life and Beyond: From Production to Produsage* (New York: Peter Lang).
6 Henry Jenkins. *Convergence Culture: Where Old and New Media Collide* (New York: New York University Press, 2006).
7 Aram Sinnreich. *Mashed Up: Music, Technology and the Rise of Configurable Culture* (Amherst, MA: University of Massachusetts Press, 2010).
8 Siva Vaidhyanathan. *Copyrights and Copywrongs: The Rise of Intellectual Property and How It Threatens Creativity* (New York: New York University Press, 2001).
9 Lawrence Lessig *Free Culture: How Big Media Uses Technology and the Law to Lock Down Creativity* (New York: Penguin Press, 2004).
10 Yochai Benkler. *The Wealth of Networks: How Social Production Transforms Markets and Freedom* (New Haven, CT: Yale University Press, 2006).
11 Tim O'Reilly. *What is Web 2.0? Design Patterns and Business Models for the Next Generation of Software* (Cambridge, MA: O'Reilly Media, 2009).
12 Marcus Boon. *In Praise of Copying* (Cambridge, MA: Harvard University Press), 6.
13 Scott H. Church. "All Living Things are DJs: Rhetoric, Aesthetics, and Remix Culture." (PhD dissertation, University of Nebraska, 2013), 68.
14 Vito Campanelli. "Remix Ethics." *International Review of Information Ethics* 15 (2011): 26.
15 Per the above discussion regarding nomenclature, I will continue to use the "configurable culture" framework I outlined in previous publications.
16 Boon, *In Praise of Copying*, 247.
17 Church, "All Living Things," 86.
18 Ibid., 143.
19 Lessig, *Free Culture*, 25–26.

20 Kim D. Chanbonpin. "Legal Writing, the Remix: Plagiarism and Hip Hop Ethics." *Mercer Law Review* 63 (2011): 598.

21 Lessig, *Free Culture*, 154.

22 James Grimmelmann. "Ethical Visions of Copyright Law." *The Fordham Law Review* 77, no. 5 (2009), 2014.

23 Grimmelmann, "Ethical Visions," 2035.

24 Aaron Trammell. "Magic Modders: Alter Art, Ambiguity, and the Ethics of Prosumption." *Journal for Virtual Worlds Research* 6 (2013), 5.

25 Patrick Leslie West and Cher Coad. "Drawing the Line: Chinese Calligraphy, Cultural Materialisms and the 'Remixing of Remix.'" *M/C Journal* 16 (2013).

26 Sinnreich, *Mashed Up*.

27 Aram Sinnreich, Mark Latonero, and Marissa Gluck. "Ethics Reconfigured: How Today's Media Consumers Evaluate the Role of Creative Reappropriation." *Information, Communication & Society* 12 (2009), 1242–1260.

28 Mark Latonero and Aram Sinnreich. "The Hidden Demography of New Media Ethics." *Information, Communication & Society* 17, no. 4 (2014): 572–593.

29 I have declined to correct the spelling and grammatical errors in the original data, in order to provide as transparent a representation of respondents' communications as possible.

30 It is important to point out that, on the whole, the base of respondents who reported using any ethical criteria at all in the 2010 survey were less likely to be US citizens, lower-income, better educated, and more likely to be male than the overall survey population. Given this general trend, there was still significant variation between the populations embracing each ethical framework.

31 Lessig, *Free Culture*.

32 This is a subject I examine at great length in my book *The Piracy Crusade*.

33 Yasmin B. Kafai, William Q. Burke, and Deborah A. Fields. "What Videogame Making Can Teach Us About Access and Ethics in Participatory Culture." In *Breaking New Ground: Innovation in Games, Play, Practice and Theory* (Proceedings of DiGRA), 2009, 8.

34 Paul Geller. "Copyright History and the Future: What's Culture Got to Do With It?" *Journal of the Copyright Society of the USA* 47 (2000), 209.

35 Roberta Rosenthal Kwall. *The Soul of Creativity: Forging a Moral Rights Law for the United States* (Stanford, CA: Stanford University Press 2010).

36 Joost Smiers and Marieke van Schijndel. *Imagine There Is No Copyright and No Cultural Conglomerate Too* (Amsterdam: Institute of Network Cultures, 2009).

37 John Gorham Palfrey and Urs Gasser. *Born Digital: Understanding the First Generation of Digital Natives* (New York: Basic Books, 2008).

38 Marc Prensky. "Digital Natives, Digital Immigrants." in *Cross Currents: Cultures, Communities, Technologies*, ed. Kris Blair, Robin Murphy, and Jen Almjeld (Boston, MA: Wadsworth, 2014), 45–51.

39 Lessig, *Free Culture*.

40 Peter Drahos and John Braithwaite, *Information Feudalism: Who Owns the Knowledge Economy?* (London: Earthscan Publications, 2002).

41 Boon, *In Praise of Copying*, 104.

42 Benkler, *Wealth of Networks*.

43 Michael F. Brown. "Can Culture Be Copyrighted?" *Current Anthropology* 39 (1998), 193–222.

44 Kenneth D. Crews. "Harmonization and the Goals of Copyright: Property Rights or Cultural Progress?" *Indiana Journal of Global Legal Studies* 6 (1998), 117–138.

45 Doris E. Long. "Dissonant Harmonization: Limitations on 'Cash n' Carry' Creativity," *Albany Law Review* 70 (2007), 1163–1205.

46 Aram Sinnreich. *The Piracy Crusade: How the Music Industry's War on Sharing Destroys Markets and Erodes Civil Liberties* (Amherst, MA: University of Massachusetts Press, 2013).

Bibliography

Benkler, Yochai. *The Wealth of Networks: How Social Production Transforms Markets and Freedom.* New Haven, CT: Yale University Press, 2006.

Boon, Marcus. *In Praise of Copying.* Cambridge, MA: Harvard University Press, 2010.

Brown, Michael F. "Can Culture Be Copyrighted?" *Current Anthropology* 39 (1998): 193–222.

Bruns, Axel. *Blogs, Wikipedia, Second Life, and Beyond: From Production to Produsage.* New York: Peter Lang, 2008.

Campanelli, Vito. "Remix Ethics." *International Review of Information Ethics* 15 (2011): 24–32.

Chanbonpin, Kim. D. "Legal Writing, the Remix: Plagiarism and Hip Hop Ethics." *Mercer Law Review* 63 (2011): 597–638.

Church, Scott H. "All Living Things Are DJs: Rhetoric, Aesthetics, and Remix Culture." PhD dissertation, University of Nebraska, 2013.

Crews, Kenneth D. "Harmonization and the Goals of Copyright: Property Rights or Cultural Progress?" *Indiana Journal of Global Legal Studies* 6 (1998): 117–138.

Drahos, Peter, and John Braithwaite. *Information Feudalism: Who Owns the Knowledge Economy?* London: Earthscan Publications, 2002.

Geller, Paul. "Copyright History and the Future: What's Culture Got to Do with It?" *Journal of the Copyright Society of the USA* 47 (2000): 209–264.

Grimmelmann, James. "Ethical Visions of Copyright Law," *Fordham Law Review* 77, no. 5 (2009): 2005–2037.

Jenkins, Henry. *Convergence Culture: Where Old and New Media Collide*. New York: New York University: Press, 2006.

Kafai, Yasmine. B., William Q. Burke, and Deborah A. Fields. "What Videogame Making Can Teach Us About Access and Ethics in Participatory Culture." *Breaking New Ground: Innovation in Games, Play, Practice and Theory*. Proceedings of DiGRA (2009).

Kwall, Roberta Rostenthal. *The Soul of Creativity: Forging a Moral Rights Law for the United States.* Stanford, CA: Stanford Law Books, 2009.

Lasswell, Harold D. "The Structure and Function of Communication in Society." In *The Communication of Ideas*, edited by Lyman Bryson. New York: Harper, 1948.

Latonero, Mark, and Aram Sinnreich. "The Hidden Demography of New Media Ethics." *Information, Communication & Society* 17, no. 4 (2014): 572–593.

Lessig, Lawrence. *Free Culture: How Big Media Uses Technology and the Law to Lock Down Creativity.* New York: Penguin Press, 2004.

——. *Remix: Making Art and Commerce Thrive in the Hybrid Economy.* New York: Penguin, 2008.

Long, Doris. E. "Dissonant Harmonization: Limitations on 'Cash N' Carry' Creativity." *Albany Law Review* 70 (2007): 1163–1205.

O'Reilly, Tim. *What is Web 2.0? Design Patterns and Business Models for the Next Generation of Software.* Cambridge, MA: O'Reilly Media, 2009.

Palfrey, John, and Urs Gasser. *Born Digital: Understanding the First Generation of Digital Natives.* New York: Basic Books, 2008.

Prensky, Marc. "Digital Natives, Digital Immigrants." In *Cross Currents: Cultures, Communities, Technologies*, edited by Kris Blair, Robin Murphy, and Jen Almjeld, 45–51. Boston, MA: Wadsworth, 2014.

Sinnreich, Aram. *Mashed Up: Music, Technology, and the Rise of Configurable Culture*. Amherst, MA: University of Massachusetts Press, 2010.

——. *The Piracy Crusade: How the Music Industry's War on Sharing Erodes Markets and Undermines Civil Liberties.* Amherst, MA: University of Massachusetts Press, 2013.

——, Mark Latonero, and Marissa Gluck. "Ethics Reconfigured: How Today's Media Consumers Evaluate the Role of Creative Reappropriation." *Information, Communication & Society* 12 (2009): 1242–1260.

Smiers, Joost, and Marieke van Schijndel. *Imagine There Is No Copyright and No Cultural Conglomerate Too.* Amsterdam: Institute of Network Cultures, 2009.

Sonvilla-Weiss, Stefan, ed. *Mashup Cultures*. New York: Springer, 2010.

Tapscott, Don and Anthony D. Williams. *Wikinomics: How Mass Collaboration Changes Everything.* New York: Penguin, 2006.

Trammell, Aaron. "Magic Modders: Alter Art, Ambiguity, and the Ethics of Prosumption." *Journal of Virtual Worlds Research* 6 (2013): 1–14.

Vaidhyanathan, Siva. *Copyrights And Copywrongs: The Rise of Intellectual Property and How It Threatens Creativity.* New York: New York University Press, 2001.

West, Patrick Leslie, and Cher Coad. "Drawing the Line: Chinese Calligraphy, Cultural Materialisms and the 'Remixing of Remix.'" *M/C Journal* 16 (2013).

17

THE PANOPTICON OF ETHICAL VIDEO REMIX PRACTICE

Mette Birk

Ethical practice is generally supported by our radar of common sense, as well as a framework of laws and regulations, but when it comes to online practices and user-created content such as video remixing, the law fails to provide this framework. Creating remix videos of copyrighted intellectual property is not an illegal practice per se, but "in general, no one may use another's property without permission of the owner"[1] and the act of taking a piece of copyrighted material and using it for remixing is a form of trespassing.[2] There are major gray zones in law, but it does not keep creative people from making and distributing remix videos. The question I will address here is, therefore, what is the current situation of ethical practice within video remixing communities? Some may ask if we are left with anarchy or normless chaos when remixers may need to operate outside of reasonable normative standards of law; albeit, a more reasonable question would be which mechanisms are used to establish and maintain subcultural norms[3] when the framework of law does not supply proper guidelines.

In spring 2012, I distributed a survey encompassing 108 responses from video remixers across the globe with the purpose of clarifying these questions. Each remixer was asked to evaluate a number of ethical focal points. The idea of each focal point was to decipher ethical principles which in a general perspective would be anything "that causes the growth of human beings (and) would be judged good or primarily moral"[4] and principles, which video remixers in particular would consider as "defining the fundamental terms of their association."[5]

The results showed a heterogeneous culture in which some ethical focal points could largely be agreed upon while the majority of ethical focal points yielded more debate. However, there appeared to be a tendency for the majority of respondents to support a somewhat limited framework of ethical practice rather than total autonomy. On the other hand, the respondents were opposed to having rules and restrictions enforced upon them. Instead it seemed that each participant created an individualized set of norms, which were motivated by self-observation and discipline. To make sense of this research, this chapter considers the disciplining principles of panopticism, by French philosopher and social theorist Michel Foucault, in order to elaborate on the emergence of self-discipline in the absence of a defined framework of the proper. Remixers are in many ways empowered in what could be called a "do-ocratic panopticon," ruled by daily practice and no need for restrictions. This will be taken into consideration with reflections upon ethical perspectives of YouTube's Content ID tracking.

Before we dive deeper into the research it is important to emphasize that the intention behind this article is not to propose a set of "best practices for video remixing." For this purpose, the survey responses, let alone the general motivations for engaging in remix practices, are simply too diverse. While we may never be able to say anything about a common ethical standard, because such a thing simply does not exist, it is possible to point toward certain tendencies from this study.

Evaluation of Ethical Focal Points

The study includes responses from five continents and practitioners of 13 different video remix genres, reaching 108 respondents from 18 different countries. Some respondents were producing countless remix videos, some were producing less; some had motivations of monetizing, some produced them for the sheer joy of sharing their vision and videos; some were engaged in online communities and some were not. The survey was distributed among video remixers, who were further asked to share the survey with their peers.

Regarding the so-called snowballing method—asking peers to share with their peers—a paradox of studying online cultures appeared. Respondents in communities are more likely to share an online survey like this with other remixers over remixers who do not regard themselves as a part of a community. This will obviously provide a community-biased sample and possibly not reflect the true picture of the many individual video remixers. Of course it would be ideal to have used a classic demographically representative sample, but the incidence rate of video remixers would be far too low, and thus the study would be economically unfeasible. Sinnreich also acknowledges the flaws of snowballing[6] and like him I have chosen to use snowballing regardless—not to generalize on the total population of video remixers, but to explore the various facets of ideal ethics within video remix culture.

The central part of the survey was built upon evaluations of seven selected ethical focal points, which were formulated and inspired by the study of Aram Sinnreich et al. on media consumers' evaluation of remix practices.[7] For the purpose of evaluating common ethics among video remixers, the response to four selected focal points showed interesting results: (1) acknowledgement of original creators; (2) degree of creativity; (3) transformativeness of the original content used in a remix video; and finally (4) whether remixers should be able to profit from their work.

The respondents were presented with a statement in relation to each focal point and they were asked to respond on a four-point scale. Transformativeness and creativity both resemble aesthetic perspectives and here respondents answered to what degree they believed each focal point should be visible in a remix video on a scale from (1) "Not necessarily to any degree" to (4) "To a high degree." Likewise, respondents were asked if remixers could/should profit as well as acknowledge their sources on a scale from "Absolutely NOT" to "Absolutely YES." A delimiting answer is understood by whatever creates the most limits to ethical practice. So in the instance of transformativeness it would be most delimiting to answer that transformativeness should be visible in a remix video "to a high degree," because that would imply certain demands for how the remix should be executed. The liberal answer would be "not necessarily to any degree" because this leaves the remixer with full autonomy to publish anything, including copies of media that may be protected by copyright laws. A delimiting answer to profiting would

Attitudes Towards Ethical Focal Points

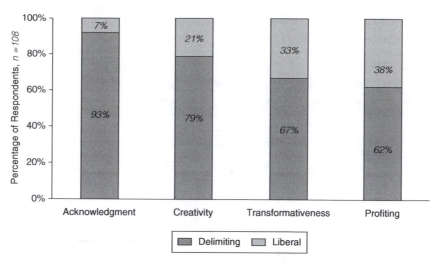

Figure 17.1 Attitudes toward ethical focal points (graph courtesy of Mette Birk)

be a respondent saying that remixers can "absolutely not" profit, and so on. Further, the respondents were asked how important it is to discuss the respective matters and they had an opportunity to comment on each question.

For the four focal points, the distribution of answers showed a tendency toward more delimiting evaluations (Figure 17.1). We see this especially with regards to *acknowledgement* and *creativity*. Hence, any presumptions about video remixers as anarchistic or lawless rebels have—not surprisingly—been proven wrong.

It is difficult to draw conclusions with regards to transformativeness and especially profiting. Some remixers were liberal in their evaluation while almost two-thirds were in favor of a delimiting framework regarding these two focal points. The perspectives of each of the four focal points are presented in the following sections.

Acknowledgement

The results on acknowledgement were very clear. Remixers generally think they should credit their sources. But this is not saying that they always do so, as a respondent explained in the comment section:

> Crediting sources is a huge pain, and sometimes it's impossible. In an ideal world, everyone gets credited, but most of my farmed material I have no idea where it comes from.
>
> (Respondent A)

In other words, there is a discrepancy between the ideal ethical behavior and the actual behavior. If we take a look at actual practice, it is unlikely that 93 percent of all remix videos show a full credit list of all used material. This is of course a well-known problem within most audience and behavioral research—the difference between claimed and actual practice. But, as stated above, the purpose of this study was not to decipher actual practice. It was to decipher the understanding of ideal ethics within the culture. And the ideal thing to do as a remixer is clearly to credit one's sources.

None of the respondents chose the most liberal answer to the question of acknowledgement. And only 7 percent chose to answer that remixers should "probably not" have to credit their sources. The distribution of answers between the two remaining and delimiting options on the four-point scale, seemed to differ when looking separately at community-engaged and non-community-engaged remixers. It was a clear tendency that the group of respondents involved in a remix community were more strictly delimiting than those who were not, as they displayed a higher rate of responding "Absolutely YES" instead of "Probably YES." Both groups favored crediting the sources used in remix videos but not with the same idealistic passion.

Creativity

Ranking number two in degree of delimitation was creativity. For this focal point, the answers were a little more scattered than for acknowledgement, and we begin to see more diverse opinions within the heterogeneous group. The quotations reflect the disagreements of creativity; they make evident a rather delimiting demand for creativity, as supported by the majority of respondents, and a very liberal attitude to remix practice on the other hand.

> If you're going to use somebody else's copyrighted work, at least have the decency to make it look good and be entertaining.
>
> (Respondent B)

> On a non-commercial level, if a person wishes to use copyrighted material to express their creativity, however limited or poorly-executed, no law should stop this. It would be like taking Lego from a child because they mixed them up with Mega Bloks
>
> (Respondent C)

Creativity, in short, is a topic that can go both ways, although the majority prefers a certain degree of it. And again the tendency was that respondents not engaged in a community by comparison to those in a community were a little more liberal about requirements of creativity. But the majority of the respondents found that creativity should be visible to a certain degree, and it is a focal point that is nevertheless important to discuss.

Transformativeness

The degree of transformativeness was regarded as a less important ethical focal point, and the average of delimiting responses was lower than for creativity and acknowledgement. However, the respondents seemed to agree more about degrees of transformativeness than for examples of creativity, by primarily choosing the two intermediate and more inexplicit answering options.

The degree of transformativeness relates to matters of plagiarism and piracy, of which most remixers dread being accused. Several respondents distanced themselves from piracy in their written comments. While a certain degree of transformation of original content is anticipated, what really mattered seemed to be the presence of an "original" concept behind the remix.

The original work (video anyway) SHOULD be changed and to a pretty large degree . . . What really matters is that the concept or idea is fairly original and that the artist has completed his/her goal with that concept.

(Respondent D)

Again, the respondents did not all agree. But two-thirds versus one-third indicated some sort of preference for remix videos to be transformative to a certain degree.

Profiting

Profit, like transformativeness, was a topic that received more diverse responses. Some thought it was primarily unethical to use third party content in order to profit. Others again did not want to be restricted by any means. Nevertheless, the number of respondents in favor of nonprofiting was remarkably higher than the number of more liberal responses. Some even used an exceptionally delimiting discourse about it:

Making money off remixing is illegal and simply immoral. You're using somebody else's work already—at least have the decency not to make money off of it.

(Respondent B)

Few respondents claimed that they earn money producing remix videos. Only four respondents implied that they do so. Of course this number was affected by the distribution method[8] but it is fairly clear that video remixing is, for the most part, not about monetary profit. It is about practicing one's skills, living one's fandom, making political statements, and possibly showing one's creative skills to the world. And if luck strikes, one may be hired as an editor or offered other opportunities to make money, like this respondent:

I find the question about profit the hardest. In my corner of fandom, this is considered concretely wrong and against the law by most people. But I think it really depends on what kind of remix we're talking about, and in what way the profit happens. For instance, receiving payment for having your work displayed in an art gallery . . . feels different than, say, charging money for people to download a vid or something like that.

(Respondent E)

Profiting—to my surprise—was, on average, regarded the least important focal point to discuss in relation to remix culture. Considering the varying perspectives of profiting as seen in this quotation, it is understandable. We may say that nonprofit does not seem to be a requirement for producing remix videos. But we sense a more specific expectation of not charging users for watching videos.

An Average of Delimiting Attitudes to Ethical Remix Practice

Overall, the focal points above imply a tendency to a more delimiting attitude to ethical remix practice. But this should not be said without emphasizing the fact that within especially two of the four ethical focal points there were contradicting opinions of right and wrong. Aside from moral ideals, however, there seemed to be a general discomfort about rules of how to remix ethically. When asked for a final comment, this respondent made it very clear that rules were not welcomed:

> I don't think there should be rules and "have tos" concerning what you do with remixing, as if intellectual property concerns did not exist. If you have access to the files, it's part of culture and we all own it, and have the same right to mash the fucking shit up however we see fit.
>
> (Respondent A)

The point being, here—there should be no legal or ethical restrictions. But ethics on individual levels are still relevant. Another respondent also rejects rules while further emphasizing that individual remixers can have their own framework of ethical remix practice.

> I have little interest in how remixers "should" be creating. I have personal opinions about attribution, profit, etc., but I think that the world of video remix is diverse and I know that my ethics are not universally held, nor would I necessarily want them to be.
>
> (Respondent F)

It is the combination of each individual ethical evaluation that gives us an idea of the structure of ethics within remix culture. With the results and quotations such as these, it is clear that there can be no collective fundamental terms of remixers' association[9] but it does not mean that all remixers support total autonomy of remix practice. From the results we saw a very united voice on the matter of acknowledgement, as well as certain expectations of creativity; that is, we see that video remixers in their distancing from regulations are individually empowered navigators and even manipulators of the strategies of corporate measures.

Staying Close to the Existing Rules

It should be clear by now that digital technologies for content production and distribution have made it possible for anyone to be visible to everyone. Furthermore, the current framework of law does not properly support the remixers' pursuits of ethically appropriate behavior. This is the case because remixing is not always accepted by IP regulations. From the results we see that video remixers tend to support practices such as: acknowledging their sources, transforming the original material to a certain degree, and using a minimum degree of artistic skills in order to create "original" remixes from original content without charging people for watching them. Now, consider this for a moment. And consider fair use and, for example, what is called for in European countries' regulations of fair quotation practices.

In the United States, the Limitation on Exclusive Rights deals with the amount and character of the portion of the original work, as well as the purpose of the work—whether it is commercial or nonprofit[10]. In Danish law it is stressed that "The author of a work shall have the right to be identified by name as the author in accordance with the requirements of proper usage."[11]

The generalized picture of ethical evaluations of these 108 respondents is very close to such legal propositions. The survey data revealed different tactics of how to operate closely to the legal discourses. Vidders, for example, often distribute videos with full-length musical scores to support the visuals, and if these scores are not public domain, the vidders are essentially breaking the law. All the while, vidders fervently advocate fair practices that pay tribute to the original creator and they support a noncommercial video remix culture. Other remixers may have a more liberal attitude to profiting, but most of them are then delimiting to the degree of transformativeness. This is the case with remixers producing music video remixes, as they tend to use video remixing for more professional purposes, having high standards of quality.

In other words, there is a need to stay as close to the framework of existing law as possible, which I believe can be more properly unfolded through the concept of the panopticon in the next section.

The Panoptic Principle and Its Contemporary Reconstruction

In general, our everyday behavior is supported by a framework of rules and expectations and an inherent compulsion to stay within this framework. Several social theorists have described this, but here I will illustrate it through the analogy of British philosopher Jeremy Bentham's Panopticon. *Pan-* meaning all, and *-opticon* meaning to observe, the panopticon is a type of building, created to expose its inhabitants.[12] It is a circular building—a prison—of several stories with a tower for observation placed in the center of the circle. All cells were placed in the periphery of the circle and installed with inner and outer windows so the inmates were fully exposed to an observer who might, or might not, be observing at any given moment from the tower in the center. In this sense, the panopticon conveyed a sentiment of an invisible omniscience[13] that encouraged inhabitants to monitor their own behavior.

Panopticism as a societal analogy is concerned with surveillance and hierarchy. A minority would possess total knowledge and the masses would only know what was communicated to them by this minority.[14] Further, the minority—with or without trained skills and power—could monitor the masses from the panoptic tower. Regardless, the prisoner would feel a sentiment of an invisible omniscience: "He is seen, but he does not see; he is the object of information, never a subject in communication."[15]

Therefore, the panopticon should be understood as a system in which laws and rules are applied to society in a way that encourages self-discipline. With today's opportunities to communicate from peer-to-peer (P2P) and to share and produce content, the communicative and inherently disciplining structure of the panopticon is falling apart. Michel Bauwens argues that panopticism is strongly challenged in the new media landscape due to the fact that knowledge is no longer assigned to a small elite.[16] The exclusive minority has instead transformed into a majority and the tower of the panopticon—guarding laws and rules—is breaking down because of the P2P flow of communication and knowledge. To extend the analogy to the contemporary network society,[17] the prisoner has gained sight while also becoming a subject in communication.

Considering video remix practice, the tower of the panopticon loses its raison d'être as it is no longer the only source of communication (remixers communicate directly with each other), nor does it hold a fair framework of rules for remixers to operate within, taking the major gray zones in the law into consideration. It does not mean, however, as we saw from the survey results, that the disciplining function—the sentiment of an invisible omniscience—has been lost. But the power relations, and thus the origins of norms, have definitely changed.

In Foucault's opinion, the strategies of the minority in power are a way of manipulating the majority of people into acting in the best interest of the system.[18] According to French philosopher and historian Michel de Certeau, manipulation is something everyday people do to the space that is created for them.[19] And researching ethics in remix culture, this dual perception of manipulation is important to keep in mind, as the results reflect a certain empowerment and autonomy among remixers, as we saw in the results. On one hand remixers engage in a system that is designed to manipulate their behavior (e.g., through law), while on the other they are the ones manipulating the framework around them.

So while the societal analogy, formulated by Foucault and challenged by Certeau, is reformed by new ways of communication, it does not mean that it loses its relevance. The panopticon has its rationale in the invisible omniscience and physical partition of cells. A video remixer is most likely to be physically parted from other remixers, although she remains virtually visible through her content. We can therefore use Foucault to understand how a certain disciplinary approach—a framework for ethical behavior—is upheld in video remix culture.

Self-Discipline through the Sentiment of Visibility

Michel de Certeau would have considered what we saw from the data results to be common logic—remixers seem to stick to the expected path for as long as this path does not intervene with their personal objective. In several comments above we also observed a general discomfort with rules and regulations. That is, video remixers try to follow the discourse of fair use regulations but they do not want to be restricted by them. As Foucault would argue, "Visibility is a trap"[20] and operating within the visual range of others may create an inherent self-reflection of one's practices and ultimately guarantee a minimum of behavioral order. In particular, the respondents engaged in communities support more delimiting ethical ideals when it comes to acknowledgement, creativity, profiting, and transformativeness. The more the respondents are engaged within—and visible to—a community, the closer to legal regulations they seek to operate.[21]

In other words, the panopticon of a minority projecting rules over the masses while leaving them with a sentiment of an invisible omniscience is breaking down in its principle. But it may actually be less of a breakdown and more of a restructuring of power. The power is transferred from the tower in the center of the panopticon and spread out to all other "cells in the prison." In other words, there are a large number of fans, users who stumble upon a video, remixers in the community, and to some degree also legal stakeholders, who can all assess and have expectations of a video. I believe this indicates that the sentiment of an invisible omniscience still exists in remix culture, but the omniscience is decentralized and legal stakeholders are far from the core of it. The visibility available to other remixers followed by the induced self-discipline leads to the rather delimiting tendency we saw in the results for ethical remix practices.

A Do-ocratic Order

The allegory of the panopticon, chosen for this study, of course has its limitations. It is important to emphasize that the sentiment of an invisible omniscience should not be understood as anxious self-control because *Big Brother is watching you*. Instead it is a subconscious action—as in when city-goers instinctively find the most decent way to behave in a crowded urban space. Video remixers produce videos—if not instinctively, then without the need for greater analysis of consequences. Remixing can be an every-day practice and a synergy of a community. We know from the survey that remixers often look to each other for inspiration and sometimes also for friendly competition:

> The community thrives on building off of each other. It's the entire premise of the remixing movement. It's more of a culture than a community, in that there is no barrier to entry, except for creating content that builds on other content instead of duplicating previous work.
>
> (Respondent G)

Certeau would call this "building off of" each other's work a mere tactic. A tactic to navigate through everyday restrictions of place, time, and law.[22] Meanwhile, popular culture has proposed a more concise term to explain this practice.

In July 2012 *WIRED* magazine published an article about the hacking collective known as Anonymous. It was not the in-depth description of Anonymous that caught my attention as much as the term the undercover journalist Quinn Norton used to describe the structure of the collective: a *do-ocracy*, "that means rule by sheer doing: Individuals propose actions, others join in (or not) . . . . There's no one to grant permission, no promise of praise or credit, so every action must be its own reward."[23]

Katherine Chen was the first to introduce the term in her book on the countercultural festival Burning Man.[24] Here, do-ocracy was used to describe a phase of the festival's development. Before it became structured and organized Burning Man was an inspiring self-forming order without rules of procedure imposed by an officialdom—it was a do-ocracy.

Having worked through the process of deciphering ethical values in video remix culture, I have seen a clear parallel between the organizational structure of remix culture and do-ocracy. When I started this project, I imagined that there would be specific norms of remixing within remix culture. Instead I discovered the tendency that video remixers are delimiting in regard to certain perspectives (acknowledgement and transformativeness) although I found no collective fundamental terms. But the panopticon still guards the principles that "cause growth" within remix culture—in the essence of Lévy's delineation of ethics.[25] In other words: Video remix culture has a do-ocratic structure, which is kept in some sort of order through the sentiment of visibility to other remixers. The remixers are mainly liberated from organized structures and empowered to find their own individual path of ethical practice.

Do-ocracy was the admirable strength of Burning Man and it is the current force of Anonymous. Likewise, video remix culture is a market place of doings and it thrives off of the chaotic and unstructured actions of individuals. Burning Man lost value as it was structured through the strategies of organized power relations, and one might fear that video remix culture will lose its strength if larger media organizations were to get involved—even if it is merely to greet the video remix culture.

Greeting Video Remix

Historically it is rare that video remixers have been sentenced or heavily fined for violations of copyright, although inconsequential takedowns of videos are quite common. Several respondents object to cases of rather hostile treatment from media corporations:

I have the same frustration as others who are forced to hide their work because they are being pursued by corporate entities with no understanding whatsoever of fanmixing, only of piracy (which in many cases isn't even involved).

(Respondent H)

Now, with the majority of remixers supporting ethical ideals close to those proposed by law, one might ask why some media conglomerates are still trying to make video remixers' lives harder. It has already become clear to some parts of the modern media industry that the fight against remixers is not a fight that can be won. YouTube has taken the consequence of this and implemented a system, which enables the IP rights holders to either block, track, or make money in cases of undeclared usage of third party material. They do so through the Content ID system.[26] Content providers send audio or video files to YouTube and every uploaded video is then compared to a database of reference files. In cases where a match is made, the content owner can choose between making the video nonviewable; keeping the video viewable and tracking statistics of views and usage of content; or making money from ads that will appear in conjunction with the video.

More than 200 million videos have been claimed by Content ID so far.[27] The system has the advantage of letting its users interact with, and maybe even remix, the content while not demolishing the lucrative incentive for content producers to produce new content. On the other hand, remix videos may still be unreasonably blocked even though they meet all fair use requirements.

Not making restrictions for video remixers but rather possibilities for content owners could be a step in the right direction. But the downside of the Content ID system may be that it reenables an elite to monitor the actions within the panopticon through the use of huge servers and masses of data. To use the terminology of Certeau,[28] it is a way for media corporations to implement and exercise strategies to control the tactics of the users. And in reference to Foucault's perception, Content ID can be thought of as an invisible omniscience, it allows an elite to possess knowledge to which the rest of the panopticon has no access.[29] In the end this could be the emergence of a new panoptic tower.

Conclusion

Everyday practice within the remixing panopticon is—for video remixers—an activity with no defined fundamental terms of their association. There are, however, a few fundamental terms, which primarily can be agreed to be of good practice. For example it is good practice always to credit the owners of the original content and to treat creatively the materials in use. A less distinct majority supports a certain degree of transformation of original content as well as a noncommercial remix culture. In this sense the video remixers often support a degree of delimitation, which also seems to make them operate as close to law as legal obstacles will allow.

The panopticon with the missing tower is an analogy of the tendencies of normative behavior in remix culture—a behavior that emerges through the structure of what we may call a do-ocracy. Norms simply come into existence through the everyday and individual actions of participants of the community and not through rules enforced by a selected minority. Video remixers are panoptic inhabitants who have gained sight and have become subjects in communication. That is, remixers do not sit up and listen to a minority of lawmen and displeased content owners; instead they can be held account-able to the entire Internet population. Mostly this encourages self-discipline of ethical behavior such as the aforementioned acknowledgement of sources. But it does not call for further regulations. On the contrary regulations are not well received.

With the described self-discipline, IP rights holders should worry less about adverse abuse and more about supporting a regulation-free space for remixers to operate within. But first and foremost we should advocate a remixing panopticon free of the panoptic tower. A culture where people "build off of" each other with no other restrictions other than their own self-consciousness.

Notes

1 Robert Cooter and Thomas Ulen. *Law and Economics*, 6th ed. (Boston, MA: Prentice Hall, 2012), 158.
2 Ibid.
3 The theoretical difference of norms, ethics, and morals are important to some. But here they shall be used relatively interchangeably. This is because of the fact that respondents of the survey also did so.
4 Pierre Lévy. *Collective Intelligence: Mankind's Emerging World in Cyberspace* (New York: Plenum Trade, 1997), 28.
5 John Rawls. *A Theory of Justice* (Cambridge, MA: Belknap Press, 1999), 10.
6 Aram Sinnreich. *Mashed Up: Music, Technology, and the Rise of Configurable Culture* (Amherst, MA: University of Massachusetts Press, 2010).
7 Aram Sinnreich, Mark Latonero, and Marissa Gluck. "Ethics reconfigured," *Information, Communication & Society* 12, no. 8 (2009).
8 Snowballing gained more resonance in established communities, such as vidding and other fandom communities, which rarely accommodate professionals who would make money from distributing remix videos.
9 Rawls, *A Theory of Justice*.
10 "U.S. Code—Title 17 § 107—Limitations on Exclusive Rights: Fair Use," in 17, ed. Legal Information Institute (1992), http://www.law.cornell.edu/uscode/text/17/107?qt-us_code_tabs=1#qt-us_code_tabs.
11 "Consolidated Act on Copyright," in *Consolidated Act No. 202*, ed. Kulturministeriet, http://www.kum.dk/Documents/English%20website/Copyright/Consolidated%20Act%20on%20Copyright%202010%5B1%5D.pdf.
12 John McAuley, Joanne Duberley, and Phil Johnson. *Organization Theory: Challenges and Perspectives* (Harlow, UK: Prentice Hall/Financial Times, 2007); Michel Foucault, *Discipline and Punish: The Birth of the Prison* (New York: Penguin Books, 1991 [1975]).
13 Foucault, *Discipline and Punish*.
14 Michel Bauwens. "The Poltical Economy of Peer Production," *1000 Days of Theory*, 2005, http://www.ctheory.net/articles.aspx?id=499.
15 Foucault, *Discipline and Punish*, 200.
16 Bauwens, "The Political Economy of Peer Production."
17 Manuel Castells. *The Rise of the Network Society*, 2nd ed., The Information Age: Economy, Society, and Culture, vol. 1 (Chichester, UK: Wiley-Blackwell, 2010 [1997]).
18 Willem Frijhoff. "Foucault Reformed by Certeau: Historical Strategies of Discipline and Everyday Tactics of Appropriation," in *Cultural History after Foucault*, ed. John Neubauer (New York: Aldine de Gruyter, 1999).
19 Michel de Certeau. *The Practice of Everyday Life* (Berkeley, CA: University of California Press, 1984).
20 Foucault, *Discipline and Punish*, 200.
21 Mette Birk. "Remixers in the Panopticon—An empirical study of ethics and communities within video remix culture" (master's thesis, University of Copenhagen, 2012).
22 Certeau, *The Practice of Everyday Life*.
23 Quinn Norton. "How Anonymous Picks Targets, Launches Attacks, and Takes Powerful Organizations Down," *WIRED* July 2012.
24 Katherine K. Chen. *Enabling Creative Chaos: The Organization Behind the Burning Man Event* (Chicago, IL: University of Chicago Press, 2009).
25 Lévy, *Collective Intelligence*, definition in Chapter 1.

26 YouTube.com, "Content ID," http://www.youtube.com/t/contentid.
27 YouTube.com, "Statistics," http://www.youtube.com/yt/press/statistics.html.
28 Certeau, *The Practice of Everyday Life*.
29 Foucault, *Discipline and Punish*.

Bibliography

Bauwens, Michel. "The Poltical Economy of Peer Production." In *1000 Days of Theory*, January 12, 2005, http://www.ctheory.net/articles.aspx?id=499 (accessed May 1, 2014).

Birk, Mette. "Remixers in the Panopticon: An Empirical Study of Ethics and Communities within Video Remix Culture." Master's thesis, University of Copenhagen, 2012.

Castells, Manuel. *The Rise of the Network Society. The Information Age: Economy, Society, and Culture*, vol. 1, 2nd ed. Chichester, UK: Wiley-Blackwell, 2010 [1997].

Certeau, Michel de. *The Practice of Everyday Life*. Berkeley, CA: University of California Press, 1984.

Chen, Katherine K. *Enabling Creative Chaos: The Organization Behind the Burning Man Event*. Chicago, IL: University of Chicago Press, 2009.

"Consolidated Act on Copyright." In *Consolidated Act No. 202*, edited by Kulturministeriet, 35, 2010, http://www.kum.dk/Documents/English%20website/Copyright/Consolidated%20Act%20on%20Copyright%202010%5B1%5D.pdf (accessed May 1, 2014).

Cooter, Robert, and Thomas Ulen. *Law and Economics*. 6th ed. Boston, MA: Prentice Hall, 2012.

Foucault, Michel. *Discipline and Punish: The Birth of the Prison*. New York: Penguin Books, 1991 [1975].

Frijhoff, Willem. "Foucault Reformed by Certeau: Historical Strategies of Discipline and Everyday Tactics of Appropriation." In *Cultural History after Foucault*, edited by John Neubauer. New York: Aldine de Gruyter, 1999.

Lévy, Pierre. *Collective Intelligence: Mankind's Emerging World in Cyberspace*. New York: Plenum Trade, 1997.

McAuley, John, Joanne Duberley, and Phil Johnson. *Organization Theory: Challenges and Perspectives*. Harlow, UK: Prentice Hall/Financial Times, 2007.

Norton, Quinn. "How Anonymous Picks Targets, Launches Attacks, and Takes Powerful Organizations Down." *WIRED* July 2012.

Rawls, John. *A Theory of Justice*. Cambridge, MA: Belknap Press, 1999.

Sandvik, Kjetil. "Magt, Oplevelseøkonomi Og Web 2.0-En Forandringsfortælling." *Ordet #47/Magt* no. 47 (2007).

Sinnreich, Aram. *Mashed Up: Music, Technology, and the Rise of Configurable Culture*. Amherst, MA: University of Massachusetts Press, 2010.

Sinnreich, Aram, Mark Latonero, and Marissa Gluck. "Ethics Reconfigured." *Information, Communication & Society* 12, no. 8 (2009): 1242–1260.

"U.S. Code—Title 17 § 107—Limitations on Exclusive Rights: Fair Use." In *17*, edited by Legal Information Institute, 1992. http://www.law.cornell.edu/uscode/text/17/107?qt-us_code_tabs=1#qt-us_code_tabs (accessed August 6, 2014).

YouTube.com. "Content ID." http://www.youtube.com/t/contentid (accessed August 6, 2014).

———. "Statistics." http://www.youtube.com/yt/press/statistics.html (accessed May 1, 2014).

18

CUTTING SCHOLARSHIP TOGETHER/APART

Rethinking the Political Economy of Scholarly Book Publishing

Janneke Adema

So as we flow across the page in the here and now, and as you process the words as you read them, remember this: they process you as well.[1]

The act of cutting media and the concept of "the cut" form an essential aspect of remix theory and remix practice. Remix can be seen as being "supported by the practice of cut/copy and paste."[2] Yet, on a larger scale, cutting can also be understood as an essential aspect of the way reality is structured and defined. The first part of this chapter will provide an analysis of the way the cut and the practice of cutting have been theorized in remix studies, mostly from within a *representationalist* framework. This analysis will then be juxtaposed and entangled with a diffractive[3] reading of a selection of critical theory, feminist new materialist, and media studies texts. These specifically focus on the act of cutting from a *performative* perspective, from which I will explore what a posthumanist vision of remix and the cut might look like.

In the second part, I will examine how the potential of the cut and related to that, how the politics inherent in the act of cutting, can affirmatively be applied to scholarly book publishing.[4] How can we account for our own ethical entanglements as scholars in the becoming of the book? After analyzing how the book functions as an apparatus, a material-discursive formation or assemblage which enacts cuts, I will explore two publishing projects—*Living Books about Life* and *remixthebook*—that have tried to rethink and reperform the apparatus. Both projects specifically take responsibility for the cuts they make in an effort to "cut well."[5] How have these projects established an alternative politics and ethics of the cut that is open to change, and what are their potential shortcomings?

This chapter thus explores how remix and the cut can be used as part of a posthumanist performative framework to question issues of quality, fixity, and authorship/authority—essentialist and inherently humanist notions on which a great deal of the print-based academic institution continues to be based. As I will argue, remix, as a form of "differential cutting," can be a means to intervene in and rethink humanities knowledge production—with respect to the political economy of book publishing and the commodification of scholarship into knowledge objects—opening up and enabling a potential alternative politics of the book. Based on Foucault's concept of "the apparatus," as well as on Barad's posthumanist expansion of this concept,[6] it will be argued that the scholarly book functions as an apparatus that cuts the processes of scholarly creation and becoming into authors, scholarly objects, and a separate observed world. Drawing attention to the processual and unstable nature of the book instead, this contribution will focus on the book's critical and political potential to question these cuts and to disturb existing scholarly practices and institutions.

By engaging in a diffractive reading, this chapter should be read as a "performative text." It is not only a piece of writing on the topic of remix and on "cutting things together and apart," but through its methodology it also remixes a variety of theories from seemingly disparate fields, locations, times, and contexts.[7]

The Material-discursive Cut within a Performative Framework

Remix theorist Eduardo Navas has written extensively about cut/copy/paste as a practice and concept within (remixed) music and art. For Navas, remix is deeply embedded in a cultural and linguistic framework, where it is a form of discourse at play across culture.[8] This focus on remix as a *cultural variable* or as a form of cultural *representation* seems to be the dominant mode of analysis within remix studies as a field.[9] Based on his discursive framework of remix as representation and repetition (following Jacques Attali) Navas, for instance, makes a distinction between copying and cutting. He sees cutting (into something physical) as materially altering the world, whereas copying (a specific form of cutting), keeps the integrity of the original intact. Navas explores how the concept of sampling was altered under the influence of changes in mechanical reproduction, where sampling as a term started to take on the meaning of copying as the act of taking not from the world, but from an archive of representations of the world. Sampling thus came to be understood culturally as a meta-activity.[10] In this sense Navas distinguishes between material sampling from the world (which is disturbing) and sampling from representations (which is a form of metarepresentation that keeps the original intact). The latter is a form of cultural citation—where one cites in terms of discourse—and this citation is strictly conceptual.[11]

To go beyond such a distinction between a materialist and a representationalist vision of remix, the insights of new materialist theorists will be beneficial. They will aid in exploring what a "material-discursive" and performative vision of cutting and the cut will be able to contribute to the idea of remix as a critical affirmative *doing*. Here remix is extended beyond a *cultural* logic operating at the level of *representations*, seeing it as always already a *material* practice disturbing and intervening in the world. Karen Barad for instance moves beyond the binary distinction between reality and representation by replacing representationalism with a theory of posthumanist performativity, when she states: "the move toward performative alternatives to representationalism shifts the focus from questions of correspondence between descriptions and reality (e.g., do they mirror nature or culture?) to matters of practices/doings/actions."[12] Here remixes as representations are not just mirrors or allegories *of* the world but direct interventions *in* the world. In this respect, *both* copying and cutting are performative, in the sense that they change the world, they alter and disturb it. Following this reasoning, copying is not ontologically distinct from cutting, as there is no distinction between discourse and the real world: language and matter are entangled (they are ongoing material (re)configurings of the world), where matter is already discursive and vice versa.[13]

Barad's form of realism is not about representing an independent reality outside of us, but about performatively intervening, intra-acting with and as part of the world.[14] For her intentions are attributable to complex networks of agencies, both human and nonhuman, functioning within a certain context of material conditions.[15] Where in reality agencies and "differences" are entangled phenomena, what Barad calls "agential cuts" cleave things together and apart, creating subjects and objects by enacting determinate boundaries, properties, and meanings. The separations that people make signify that they create inclusions and exclusions through their specific focus. We need to take responsibility for these cuts, Barad argues, as we are accountable for the entanglements of self and other that we weave, as well as for the cuts and separations, and the exclusions that we create.[16] Although not enacted directly by us, but by the larger material arrangement of which we are a part (cuts are made from the inside), we are still accountable to the cuts that we help enact: there are new possibilities and ethical obligations to act (cut) at every moment.[17] In this sense "cuts do violence but also open up and rework the agential conditions of possibility."[18] It matters which cuts are enacted, where different cuts enact different materialized becomings. As Barad states: "It's all a matter of where we place the cut. . . . what is at stake is accountability to marks on bodies in their specificity by attending to how different cuts produce differences that matter."[19]

Cutting Well

Media theorists Sarah Kember and Joanna Zylinska explore the notion of the cut as an inevitable conceptual and material interruption in the process of mediation, focusing specifically on *where* to cut in as far as it relates to *how to cut well*. They argue that the cut is both a technique and an ethical imperative, where cutting is a necessary act to create meaning, to be able to say something about things.[20] On a more ontological level they argue that "cutting is fundamental to our emergence in the world, as well as our differentiation from it."[21] Here they see a similarity with Derrida's notion of *différance*, a term that functions as a cut, where it stabilizes the flow of mediation into things, objects, and subjects.[22] Through the act of cutting we shape our temporally stabilized selves (we become individuated) as well as actively forming the world we are part of and the matter surrounding us.[23] Kember and Zylinska are specifically interested in the ethics of the cut. If we have to inevitably cut in the process of becoming (to shape it and give it meaning) how is it that we can cut well? How can we engage with a process of, as they call it, "differential cutting," enabling space for the vitality of becoming?[24] To enable a "productive engagement with the cut," Kember and Zylinska are interested in performative and affirmative acts of cutting. They use the example of photography to explore the necessity to make cuts while still enabling the duration of things.[25] Cutting becomes a technique not of rendering or representing the world, but of managing, ordering, and creating it, of giving it meaning. The act of cutting is crucial, Kember and Zylinska argue, to our "becoming-with and becoming-different from the world," by shaping the universe and shaping ourselves in it.[26] Through cutting, they state, we enact both separation and relationality where an "incision" becomes an ethical imperative, a "decision," one which is not made by a humanist, liberal subject but by agentic processes. For Kember and

Zylinska a vitalist and affirmative way of cutting well thus leaves space for duration, it does not close down life's creative impulse.[27]

The Affirmative Cut in Remix

To further investigate the imperative to cut well, I want to return to remix theory and practice, where the potential of the cut and of remix as a subversive and affirmative logic, and of appropriation as a political tool and a form of critical production, has been extensively explored. Here I want to examine what a performative vision on and of remix might look like. In what sense do remix theory and practice function, in the words of Barad, as "specific agential practices/intra-actions/performances through which specific exclusionary boundaries are enacted?"[28] Navas, for instance, conceptualizes remix as a vitalism: a formless force, capable of taking on any form and medium. In this vitalism lies the power of remix to create something new out of something already existing, by reconfiguring it. In this sense as Navas states, "to remix is to compose." But remix, through these reconfiguring and juxtaposing gestures, also has the potential to question and critique, becoming an act that interrogates "authorship, creativity, originality, and the economics that supported the discourse behind these terms as stable cultural forms."[29] However, Navas warns for the potential of remix to be both what he calls "regressive and reflexive," where the openness of its politics entails that it can also be easily co-opted, where "sampling and principles of Remix . . . have been turned into the preferred tools for consumer culture."[30] A regressive remix then is a form of regression: a recombination of something that is already familiar and has proven to be successful for the commercial market. A reflexive remix on the other hand is regenerative, as it allows for constant change.[31] Here we can find the potential seeds of resistance in remix, where, as a type of intervention, Navas states it has the potential to question conventions, "to rupture the norm in order to open spaces of expression for marginalized communities," and, if implemented well, it can become a tool of autonomy.[32]

One of the realms of remix practice in which an affirmative position of critique and politics has been explored in depth, while taking clear responsibility for the material-discursive entanglements it enacts, is in feminist remix culture, most specifically in vidding and political remix video. Francesca Coppa defines vidding as "a grassroots art form in which fans re-edit television or film into music videos called 'vids' or 'fan-vids.'"[33] By cutting and selecting certain bits and juxtaposing them with others, the practice of vidding, beyond or as part of a celebratory fan work, has the potential to become a critical textual engagement as well as a recutting and recomposing (cutting-together) of the world differently. As Kristina Busse and Alexis Lothian state, vidding practically deconstructs "the ideological frameworks of film and TV by unmaking those frameworks technologically."[34] Coppa sees vidding as an act of both bringing together and taking apart, to receive the desired image. Here Coppa argues we need to pay attention to what gets cut out too.[35] The act of cutting is empowering and gives agency to vidders in Coppa's vision, where "she who cuts," is better than "she who is cut into pieces."[36]

Video artist Elisa Kreisinger, who makes queer video remixes of TV series such as *Sex and the City* and *Mad Men*, states that political remix videos harbor more of an element of critique, to correct

Elisa Kreisinger writes about her remixes in Chapter 37 Remixing the Remix.

certain elements (such as gender norms) in media works, without necessarily having to be fan works. As Kreisinger states, "I see remixing as the rebuilding and reclaiming of once-oppressive images into a positive vision of just society."[37] As Renee Slajda argues with respect to Kreisinger's remix videos, critique is not about deconstructing images "without constructing something new in its place." Slajda sees this as a feminist move beyond criticism, where she is interested in how remix artists turn critical consciousness into a creative practice to "reshape the media—and the world—as they would like to see it."[38] For Kreisinger too, political remix video is not only about deconstructing and creating "more diverse and affirming narratives of representation."[39] It has the potential to effect actual change (although, as Navas, she is aware that remix is also co-opted by corporations to reinforce stereotypes). Remix challenges dominant notions of ownership and copyright as well as the author/reader and owner/user binaries supporting these notions. By challenging these, remix videos also challenge the production and political economy of media.[40] As video artist Martin Leduc argues, "we may find that remix can offer a means not only of responding to the commercial media industry, but of replacing it."[41]

The Agentic Cut in Remix

Next to providing important affirmative contributions to the imperative to cut well, and to reconfigure boundaries, remix has also been implemental in rethinking and reperforming agency and authorship in art and academia, critiquing the liberal human-ist subject that is the author, while exploring more posthumanist, entangled forms of agency in the form of agentic processes, in which agency is more distributed. Paul Miller, aka DJ Spooky, writes about flows and cuts in his artist's book *Rhythm Science*. For Miller, sampling is a doing, a creating with found objects, but this also means that we need to take responsibility for its genealogy, for he or she "who speaks through you."[42] Miller's practical and critical engagement with remix and the cut is especially interesting when it comes to his conceptualizing of identity, where—as in the new materialist thinking of Barad—he does not presuppose an identity or a self, but states that our identity comes about *through* our cuts, where the act of cutting shapes and creates our selves. "The collage becomes my identity," he states.[43] For Miller, agency is thus not related to our identity as creators or artists, but to the flow or becoming, which always comes first. We are so immersed in and defined by the data that sur-rounds us on a daily basis, that, Miller argues, "we are entering an era of multiplex consciousness."[44]

Miller writes about creating different personae as shareware, while Mark Amerika is interested in the concept of performing theory and critiquing individuality and the self through concepts such as "flux personae," establishing the self as an "artist-medium" and a "post-production medium."[45] Amerika sees performing theory as a creative process in which pluralities of conceptual personae are created that explore their becoming. Through these various personae, Amerika critiques the unity of the self.[46] In this vision the artist becomes a medium through which language, in the form of prior inhabited data, flows. When the artist writes his words they don't feel like his own words but like an assemblage of sampled material from his cocreators and collaborators. By becoming an artist-medium, Amerika argues, "the self per se disappears in a sea of source mate-rial."[47] By exploring this idea of the networked author concept or of the writer as an artist-medium, Amerika contemplates what could be a new (posthuman) author function for the digital age, with the artist as a postproduction medium "becoming instrument" and "becoming electronics."[48]

Recutting the Scholarly Apparatus

What can we take away from this transversal reading of feminist new materialism, critical and media theory, and remix studies, with respect to cutting as an affirmative material-discursive practice? Through this reading I will analyze alternatives to the political economy of book publishing with its focus on ownership and copyright and the book as a consumer object. How can remix and the cut performatively critique established (humanist) notions such as authorship, authority, quality, and fixity underlying scholarly book publishing? This (re)reading might pose potential problems for our idea of critique and ethics when notions of stability, objectivity, and distance tend to disappear. So, how can we make ethical, critical cuts in our scholarship while simultaneously promoting a politics of the book that is open and responsible to change, difference, and exclusions?

To explore this, we need to analyze the way the book functions as an apparatus. The concept of *dispositif* or "apparatus," originates from Foucault's later work.[49] As a concept, it went beyond "discursive formation" connecting discourse more closely with material practices.[50] The apparatus is the system of relations that can be established between these disparate elements. However, an apparatus for Foucault is not a stable and solid thing but a shifting set of relations inscribed in a play of power that is strategic and responds to an urgent need, a need to control.[51] Deleuze's fluid outlook sees it as an assemblage capable of escaping attempts of subversion and control. He is interested in the new, the variable creativity which arises out of *dispositifs* (in their actuality), or in the ability of the apparatus to transform itself, where we as human beings belong to *dispositifs* and act within them.[52] Barad connects the notion of the cut to her posthuman Bohrian concept of the apparatus. As part of our intra-actions, apparatuses, in the form of certain material arrangements or practices, effect an agential cut between subject and object, which are not separate but come into being through intra-actions.[53] Apparatuses for Barad are open-ended and dynamic material-discursive practices, articulating concepts and things.[54]

In what way has the apparatus of the book—consisting of an entanglement of relationships between amongst others authors, books, the outside world, readers, the material production and political economy of book publishing and the discursive formation of scholarship—executed its power relations through cutting in a certain way? As I will argue, it has mostly operated via a logic of the cut that favors neat separations between books and authors (as human creators) and readers; that cuts out fixed scholarly book objects of an established quality and originality; and that pastes this system together via a system of strict ownership and copyright rules. How and where the apparatus of the book cuts at the present moment does not take into full consideration the inherent fluid nature of the book and authorship,[55] nor the increased possibilities for collaboration, updates, versionings, and multimedia enhancements in the digital environment. It enforces a political economy that keeps books and scholarship closed off from the majority of the world's potential readers, functioning in an increasingly commercial environment (fueled by public money), which makes it very difficult to publish specialized scholarship lacking commercial promise. It also does not take into consideration how the humanist discourse on authorship, quality, and originality that continues to underlie the humanities, perpetuates this publishing system in a material sense, nor how likewise the specific print-based materiality of the book and the publishing institutions that have grown around it have been incremental in shaping the discursive formation of the humanities and scholarship as a whole.

Following this essay's diffractively collected insights on remix and the cut, I want to underscore the need to see and understand the book as a process of becoming, as an entanglement of plural (human and nonhuman) agencies. The separations or cuts that have been forced out of these entanglements by specific material-discursive practices have created inclusions and exclusions, book objects and author subjects, controlling subject and object positions.[56] Books as apparatuses are thus performative, they are reality shaping. As I will argue, not enough responsibility is taken for the cuts that are enacted with and through the book as an apparatus. There is a lack of acknowledgement of our own roles as scholars in shaping the way we publish research. Next to that our approved, dominant scholarly practices—which include the (printed) book—are simultaneously affecting us as scholars and the way we act in and describe the world and/or our object of study. It is important to acknowledge our entangled nature in all this, where scholars need to take more responsibility for the practices they enact and enforce, and the cuts that they make—especially in their own book-publishing practices.

Open-Ended Scholarly Recutting

Living Books about Life and *remixthebook* are two book-publishing projects that have explored the potential of the cut and remix for an affirmative politics of publishing. In what sense have they, through their specific cuts, promoted an open-ended politics of the book, which enables duration and difference?

Mark Amerika, author/curator of the *remixthebook* project, states it is not a traditional form of (book) scholarship, but a hybrid performance platform.[57] *Remixthebook* is a collection of multimedia writings that explore remix as a cultural phenomenon by themselves referencing and mashing up curated selections of earlier theory, avant-garde and art writings on remix. It consists of a printed book and an accompanying website that functions as a platform for a collaboration between artists and theorists exploring practice-based research.[58] Amerika tries to evade the bound nature of the printed book, and its fixity and authority, by bringing together this community of people to remix, perform, and discuss the theories and texts presented in the book via video, audio, and text-based remixes published on the website—opening the book and its source material up for continuous multimedia recutting. Amerika also challenges dominant ideas of authorship by playing with personae and by drawing on a variety of remixed source material in his book, as well as by directly involving his remix community as collaborators on the project.

However a discrepancy remains visible between Amerika's aim to create a commons of renewable source material along with a platform for everyone to use, and the specific choices/cuts he has made with respect to the outlets he chose to fulfill this aim. *Remixthebook* is still published as a traditional printed book which hasn't been made available on an open-access basis to more fully enable remix and reuse. The website is also not openly available for everyone to contribute to as the contributors have been selected or curated by Amerika and cocurator Rick Silva. The remixes on the website are also not available for remixing, as they are licensed under an all-rights-reserved copyright. Furthermore, Amerika is still acting as the "traditional" humanist author of both his book, and of the (curated) collection of material on the website, by using his name on the cover of the book and as part of the copyright license, which in the scholarly and artistic realm still function as signs of attribution and crediting. It is this issue of human-ist authorship that the *Living Books about Life* project actively tried to challenge.

Living Books about Life is a series of open-access books about life published by Open Humanities Press, providing a bridge between the humanities and the sciences. All the books repackage existing open-access science-related research, supplementing this with an original editorial essay to unify the collection. They also provide additional multime-dia material, from videos to podcasts to whole books. The books have been published online in an open source wiki platform, meaning the books are "open on a read/write basis for users to help compose, edit, annotate, translate and remix."[59] As Gary Hall, one of the initiators of the project has argued, this project challenges the physical and con-ceptual limitations of the traditional codex by including multimedia and whole books, but also by emphasizing its duration by publishing in a wiki. Thus it "rethinks 'the book' itself as a living, collaborative endeavor."[60] Hall argues that wikis offer a potential to question and critically engage issues of authorship, work and stability. They can offer increased accessibility and induce participation from contributors from the periphery. As he states, "wiki-communication can enable us to produce a multiplicitous academic and publishing network, one with a far more complex, fluid, antagonistic, distributed, and decentered structure, with a variety of singular and plural, human and non-human actants and agents."[61] One of the drawbacks of wikis, however, is that they are envisaged and structured in such a way that authorship and clear attribution/respon-sibility, as well as version control, remain an essential part of their functioning. The structure behind a wiki is still based on an identifiable author and a version history, giving access to changes and modifications. In reality, the authority of the author is not challenged. Furthermore, the books in the series also include a "frozen version" and are published not as common wikis, but as books with covers and clearly defined authors and editors. Mirroring the physical materiality of the book in such a way also reproduces the aura of the book, including the discourse of scholarship this brings with it. This might explain why the user interaction with the books in the series has been limited in comparison to other wikis. Here the choice to recut the collected information as a book, as part of rethinking and reperforming the book as concept and form, might paradoxi-cally have been both the success and the failure of the project.

Conclusion

This text too, in all its conceptual performativity, falls prey to many of the above criti-cisms: it is published in a closed-access paperbound book by a reputable press with a clearly distinguishable set of editors and authors. Nevertheless, just as the projects men-tioned above, it has attempted to rethink (through its diffractive methodology) how we might start to cut differently where it comes to our research and publication practices. Cutting and stabilizing still needs to be accomplished. The politics of the book itself can be helpful in this respect, where, as Gary Hall and I have argued elsewhere, "if it is to continue to be able to serve 'new ends' as a medium through which politics itself can be rethought . . . then the material and cultural constitution of the book needs to be con-tinually reviewed, re-evaluated and reconceived."[62] The book itself can thus be a medium with the critical and political potential to question specific cuts and to disturb existing scholarly practices and institutions. Books are always a process of becoming (albeit one that is continuously interrupted and disturbed). Books are entanglements of different agencies that cannot be discerned beforehand. In the cuts that we make to untangle them we create specific material book objects, but in these specific cuts, the book has always already redeveloped; it has been remixed. It has mutated and moved on. The book is thus a processual, contextualized entity, which we can use as a means to critique our established practices and institutions, both through its forms (and the cuts we make to create these forms) and its metaphors, and through the practices that accompany it.

Notes

1 Paul D. Miller, *Rhythm Science* (Cambridge, MA: MIT Press, 2004), 9.

2 Eduardo Navas, *Remix Theory: The Aesthetics of Sampling* (New York: Springer, 2012), 65.

3 Donna Haraway first introduced the practice and concept of reading diffractively. Her approach was extended by Karen Barad, who argues that as a methodology, diffraction "provides a way of attending to entanglements in reading important insights and approaches through one another." Iris van der Tuin defines it as a reading that "breaks through the academic habit of criticism and works along affirmative lines." In this sense it is not based on a comparison between philosophies as closed, isolated entities, but on "affirming links between . . . schools of thoughts." Karen Barad, *Meeting the Universe Halfway: Quantum Physics and the Entanglement of Matter and Meaning* (Durham, NC: Duke University Press, 2007), 30. Iris van der Tuin, "'A Different Starting Point, a Different Metaphysics': Reading Bergson and Barad Diffractively," *Hypatia* 26, no. 1 (February 2011), 22, 27.

4 With affirmative politics I want to focus on the potential of power as a form of empowerment (potentia), where negative, reactionary politics can be operationalized into affirmative alternative practices. As Rosi Braidotti has argued, this does not mean a distancing from critical theory. Rosi Braidotti, "On Putting the Active Back into Activism," *New Formations* 68, no. 1 (2010), 42–57.

5 Sarah Kember and Joanna Zylinska, *Life after New Media: Mediation as a Vital Process* (Cambridge, MA: MIT Press, 2012).

6 In which apparatuses are conceptualized as specific material configurations that effect an agential cut between, and hence produce, subject and object. Barad, *Meeting the Universe Halfway*, 148.

7 This is akin to what net artist Mark Amerika calls "performing theory." As a "remixologist," Amerika sees data as a renewable energy source, where ideas, theories, and samples become his source material. By creating and performing remixes of this source material, which is again based on a mashup of other source material, a collaborative interweaving of different texts, thinkers, and artists emerges, one that celebrates and highlights the communal aspect of creativity in art and academia. Mark Amerika, *remixthebook* (Minneapolis, MN: University of Minnesota Press, 2011).

8 Navas, *Remix Theory*, 3.

9 Lawrence Lessig and Henry Jenkins, for instance, talk about, respectively, remix as a read/write culture and as part of convergence cultures, although both see remix as embedded in technology and encapsulated by powers of material-economic production. Elisabeth Nesheim on the other hand—although still starting from a position of human agency—goes beyond remix as a cultural concept and explores principles of remix in nature, analyzing bioengineering as a form of genetic remixing and investigating bioartists who remix nature/culture as a form of critique and reflection. Lawrence Lessig, *Remix: Making Art and Commerce Thrive in the Hybrid Economy* (New York: Penguin Press, 2008); Henry Jenkins, *Convergence Culture: Where Old and New Media Collide* (New York: New York University Press, 2008); Elisabeth Nesheim, "Remixed Culture/Nature: Is Our Current Remix Culture Giving Way to a Remixed Nature?" presented at UIB: DIKULT 303 Remix Culture, November 2009.

10 Navas, *Remix Theory*, 12.

11 Ibid., 11–16.

12 Karen Barad, "Posthumanist Performativity: Toward an Understanding of How Matter Comes to Matter," *Signs* 28, no. 3 (1 March 2003): 802.

13 I am talking here about the fact that there is no onto-epistemological distinction between cutting and copying. From an ethical perspective, however, one might argue, as Navas has done extensively, that making a distinction between referencing ideas in conceptual and material form, might help us in our aid toward copyright reform. Eduardo Navas, "Notes on Everything Is a Remix, Part 1, 2, and 3," *Remix Theory*, September 3, 2011, http://remixtheory.net/?p=480.

14 Barad, *Meeting the Universe Halfway*, 37.

15 Ibid., 23.

16 Ibid., 393.

17 Ibid., 178–179.

18 Rick Dolphijn and Iris van der Tuin, *New Materialism: Interviews & Cartographies* (Ann Arbor, MI: Open Humanities Press, 2012), 52, http://hdl.handle.net/2027/spo.11515701.0001.001.

19 Barad, *Meeting the Universe Halfway*, 348.

20 Kember and Zylinska, *Life After New Media*, 27.

21 Ibid., 168.

22 Ibid., xvi.

23 Ibid., 168.

24 Ibid., 81.

25 Ibid., 81.

26 Ibid., 75.

27 Ibid., 82.

28 Karen Barad, "Posthumanist Performativity: Towards an Understanding of How Matter Comes to Matter," in *Material Feminisms*, ed. Stacy Alaimo (Bloomington, IN: Indiana University Press, 2008), 816.

29 Navas, *Remix Theory*, 61.

30 Ibid., 160.

31 Ibid., 92–93.

32 Ibid., 109.

33 Francesca Coppa, "An Editing Room of One's Own: Vidding as Women's Work," *Camera Obscura* 26, no. 2 77 (January 1, 2011): 123.

34 Kristina Busse and Alexis Lothian, "Scholarly Critiques and Critiques of Scholarship: The Uses of Remix Video," *Camera Obscura* 26, no. 2 77 (January 1, 2011): 141.

35 Coppa, "An Editing Room of One's Own," 124.

36 Ibid., 128.

37 Francesca Coppa, "Interview with Elisa Kreisinger," *Transformative Works and Cultures* 5 (July 15, 2010), doi:10.3983/twc.v5i0.234.

38 Renee Slajda, "'Don't Blame the Media, Become the Media': Feminist Remix as Utopian Practice," *Barnard Centre for Research on Women Blog*, May 30, 2013.

39 Elisa Kreisinger, "Queer Video Remix and LGBTQ Online Communities," *Transformative Works and Cultures* 9 (September 30, 2011), doi:10.3983/twc.v9i0.395.

40 Ibid.

41 Martin Leduc, "The Two-source Illusion: How Vidding Practices Changed Jonathan McIntosh's Political Remix Videos," *Transformative Works and Cultures* 9 (September 30, 2011), doi:10.3983/twc.v9i0.379.

42 Miller, *Rhythm Science*, 37.

43 Ibid., 24.

44 Ibid., 61.

45 Amerika, *remixthebook*, 26.

46 Ibid., 28.

47 Ibid., 47.

48 Ibid., 58.

49 It first appeared as a concept in Foucault's *History of Sexuality* (1976). Michel Foucault, *The History of Sexuality: The Will to Knowledge* (New York: Penguin Books, 2008).

50 Michel Foucault, *Power/Knowledge: Selected Interviews and Other Writings, 1972–1977*, ed. Colin Gordon, 1st American ed. (New York: Vintage, 1980), 194–195.

51 Ibid., 196. In Agamben's vision the apparatus is an all-oppressive formation, one from which human beings stand outside. Here he creates new binaries between inside/outside and material/discursive that might not be helpful for the posthuman vision of the apparatus. See, Giorgio Agamben, *What Is an Apparatus? And Other Essays* (Stanford, CA: Stanford University Press, 2009), 14.

52 Gilles Deleuze, "What Is a Dispositif?" in Michel Foucault, *Philosopher: Essays*, ed. Timothy J. Armstrong (Chichester, UK: Harvester Wheatsheaf, 1992).

53 Barad, *Meeting the Universe Halfway*, 141–142.

54 Ibid., 334.

55 John Bryant, *The Fluid Text: A Theory of Revision and Editing for Book and Screen* (Ann Arbor, MI: University of Michigan Press, 2002).

56 Look for example at the way the PhD student as a discoursing subject is being (re)produced by the dissertation and by the dominant discourses and practices that accompany it. Janneke Adema, "Practise What You Preach: Engaging in Humanities Research through Critical Praxis," *International Journal of Cultural Studies* 16, no. 5 (September 1, 2013): 491–505.

57 Amerika, *remixthebook*, xi.

58 Ibid., xiv–xv.

59 Gary Hall, "Better Living through Sharing: Living Books About Life and Other Open Media Projects," *Media Gifts*, June 17, 2012, http://garyhall.squarespace.com/journal/2012/6/17/better-living-through-sharing-living-books-about-life-and-ot.html.

60 Ibid.

61 Gary Hall, "Fluid Notes on Liquid Books," in *Putting Knowledge to Work and Letting Information Play: The Center for Digital Discourse and Culture,* edited by Timothy W. Luke and Jeremy Hunsinger (Blacksburg, VA: The Center for Digital Discourse and Culture, 2009), 43.

62 Janneke Adema and Gary Hall, "The Political Nature of the Book: On Artists' Books and Radical Open Access," *New Formations* 78, no. 1 (2013), 138.

Bibliography

Adema, Janneke. "Practise What You Preach: Engaging in Humanities Research through Critical Praxis." *International Journal of Cultural Studies* 16, no. 5 (1 September 2013): 491–505.

——, and Gary Hall. "The Political Nature of the Book: On Artists' Books and Radical Open Access." *New Formations* 78, no. 1 (2013): 138–156.

Agamben, Giorgio. *What Is an Apparatus? And Other Essays.* Stanford, CA: Stanford University Press, 2009.

Amerika, Mark. *remixthebook.* Minneapolis, MN: University of Minnesota Press, 2011.

Barad, Karen. *Meeting the Universe Halfway: Quantum Physics and the Entanglement of Matter and Meaning.* Durham, NC: Duke University Press, 2007.

——. "Posthumanist Performativity: Toward an Understanding of How Matter Comes to Matter." *Signs* 28, no. 3 (1 March 2003): 801–831.

——. "Posthumanist Performativity. Towards an Understanding of How Matter Comes to Matter." In *Material Feminisms,* edited by Stacy Alaimo. Bloomington, IN: Indiana University Press, 2008.

Braidotti, Rosi. "On Putting the Active Back into Activism." *New Formations* 68, no. 1 (2010): 42–57.

Bryant, John. *The Fluid Text: A Theory of Revision and Editing for Book and Screen.* Ann Arbor, MI: University of Michigan Press, 2002.

Busse, Kristina, and Alexis Lothian. "Scholarly Critiques and Critiques of Scholarship: The Uses of Remix Video." *Camera Obscura* 26, no. 2 77 (1 January 2011): 139–146.

Coppa, Francesca. "An Editing Room of One's Own: Vidding as Women's Work." *Camera Obscura* 26, no. 2 77 (1 January 2011): 123–130.

——. "Interview with Elisa Kreisinger." *Transformative Works and Cultures* 5 (15 July 2010). doi:10.3983/twc.v5i0.234.

Deleuze, Gilles. "What Is a Dispositif?" In *Michel Foucault, Philosopher: Essays,* edited by Timothy J. Armstrong. Chichester, UK: Harvester Wheatsheaf, 1992.

Dolphijn, Rick, and Iris van der Tuin. *New Materialism: Interviews & Cartographies* (Ann Arbor, MI: Open Humanities Press, 2012), http://hdl.handle.net/2027/spo.11515701.0001.001 (accessed August 6, 2014).

Foucault, Michel. *The History of Sexuality: The Will to Knowledge.* New York: Penguin Books, 2008.

——. *Power/Knowledge: Selected Interviews and Other Writings, 1972–1977.* Edited by Colin Gordon, 1st American edition. New York: Vintage, 1980.

Hall, Gary. "Better Living through Sharing: Living Books about Life and Other Open Media Projects." *Media Gifts,* 17 June 2012. http://garyhall.squarespace.com/journal/2012/6/17/better-living-through-sharing-living-books-about-life-and-ot.html (accessed August 6, 2014).

———. "Fluid Notes on Liquid Books." In *Putting Knowledge to Work and Letting Information Play: The Center for Digital Discourse and Culture* edited by Timothy W. Luke and Jeremy Hunsinger. Blacksburg, VA: The Center for Digital Discourse and Culture, 2009.

Jenkins, Henry. *Convergence Culture: Where Old and New Media Collide.* New York: New York University Press, 2008.

Kember, Sarah, and Joanna Zylinska. *Life after New Media: Mediation as a Vital Process.* Cambridge, MA: MIT Press, 2012.

Kreisinger, Elisa. "Queer Video Remix and LGBTQ Online Communities." *Transformative Works and Cultures* 9 (30 September 2011). doi:10.3983/twc.v9i0.395.

Leduc, Martin. "The Two-Source Illusion: How Vidding Practices Changed Jonathan McIntosh's Political Remix Videos." *Transformative Works and Cultures* 9 (30 September 2011). doi:10.3983/twc.v9i0.379.

Lessig, Lawrence. *Remix: Making Art and Commerce Thrive in the Hybrid Economy.* New York: Penguin Press, 2008.

Miller, Paul D. *Rhythm Science.* Cambridge, MA: MIT Press, 2004.

Navas, Eduardo. "Notes on Everything Is a Remix, Part 1, 2, and 3." *Remix Theory*, September 3, 2011. http://remixtheory.net/?p=480 (accessed August 6, 2014).

———. *Remix Theory: The Aesthetics of Sampling.* New York: Springer, 2012.

Nesheim, Elisabeth. "Remixed Culture/Nature: Is Our Current Remix Culture Giving Way to a Remixed Nature?" presented at UIB: DIKULT 303 Remix Culture, November 2009.

Slajda, Renee. "'Don't Blame the Media, Become the Media': Feminist Remix as Utopian Practice." *Barnard Centre for Research on Women Blog*, 30 May 2013. http://bcrw.barnard.edu/blog/dont-blame-the-media-become-the-media-feminist-remix-as-utopian-practice/ (accessed August 6, 2014).

Van der Tuin, Iris. "'A Different Starting Point, a Different Metaphysics': Reading Bergson and Barad Diffractively." *Hypatia* 26, no. 1 (February 2011): 22–42.

19

COPYRIGHT AND FAIR USE IN REMIX

From Alarmism to Action

Patricia Aufderheide

Video remixing has grown rapidly from a semiexpert act to a broadly participatory one infusing daily life. Its growth has been pervaded with a discourse of criminality, with practitioners who proudly call themselves pirates, showcases with names like "Illegal Art," endless listserv discussions of often-bogus copyright lore, and meaningless but well-intentioned placatory messages on YouTube denying any intent to infringe. This has been accompanied by corporate alarmism around piracy, takedown notices online that do not distinguish between legal and illegal uses of unlicensed material, inappropriate cease-and-desist letters, overreaching terms of service, and sometimes-confusing and categorical warnings against copying.[1]

In the same time period, the importance of fair use (and, in other nations, exceptions such as fair dealing and right to quotation) has been ever more recognized in courts and in legal scholarship. Much of what is being produced in remix video has a good case for fair use, particularly since so many uses echo long-standing artistic practices in other media.

Despite endemic alarmism, there is an extremely low level of litigation around remixing. There are no instances of copyright holders suing reusers of copyrighted material on YouTube after a takedown incident, even after a creator responded to the takedown by asserting fair use rights. Two lawsuits regarding YouTube were initiated by reusers themselves: journalist and home-video maker Stephanie Lenz[2] and legal scholar Lawrence Lessig,[3] asserting that stakeholders wantonly overreached their rights in issuing a takedown notice without first having a human being check to see if the use was legitimate. In nations where "three strikes" or other punitive legislation was tried,[4] it has either been withdrawn, as in France[5] or simply has not been effective.[6]

ContentID matches (Google's preemptive search for copyrighted materials independently of copyright holders) and takedowns (copyright holder-initiated complaints to Google) of copyright-protected material on YouTube, which are constant, result from robotic acts triggered by algorithms. They can be easily challenged, with work reinstated promptly, by asserting fair use rights. Users who knew they had the right to do so would also be in a position to work together, either as consumers confronting providers who refuse to employ human intelligence to discern fair use, or challenging lawmakers to affect policy, such as the Digital Millennium Copyright Act (DMCA), more friendly to the creation of culture.

But people would have to know that they have fair use rights, and that those rights can be exercised without unacceptable risk. The most common reason that users find it difficult to assert their fair use rights is that they are unsure how to interpret the law. Even when they are familiar enough with fair use to employ it in remix, when they are challenged with a takedown notice, most makers do not challenge with a counter-take-down after seeing a forbidding legal notice that makes them wonder if they were right. Further, as Peter Decherney has noted, wrangling between corporate entities such as Google and Viacom over financial arrangements has made things worse: "the mixed signals sent out by media companies have introduced confusion into fair use communities that had long-standing traditions of using copyrighted material."[7]

This problem with exercising rights under the law is ignored at the peril of the future of culture. Earlier research with other communities of practice demonstrates the power of self-censorship to limit the creative possibilities of a field of action.[8] The self-criminalization of remix video makers, however glamorous in the short term, constrains expression today and crimps its future. This realization was an impetus for legal scholar Rebecca Tushnet to form, with film studies professor Francesca Coppa and others, the Organization for Transformative Works (OTW),[9] to assert the fair use rights of people who make fan fiction and other work. It is also a motivation for the nonprofit organization, Public Knowledge, with its focus on remix in its annual World's Fair Use Day.[10]

This chapter describes how some remixers have been able to strengthen their understanding of the law and increase legal exercise of their rights, without impairing their monopoly rights under copyright, or those of others.

Fair Use

Copyright law is national, and the nation in which work is created is the nation whose law applies. Whatever the national regime, copyright law always puts limits on copyright monopoly holders' rights, although the logic by which policies limit them differs from country to country. By limiting the monopoly rights of copyright holders, such limitations and exceptions effectively protect freedom of speech. As the writers of the American constitution noticed, they limit the private censorship capacity of copyright holders, who otherwise could forbid anyone to use their material without their permission.[11] Exceptions have become ever more important as the limits on copyright brought by the need to register, by the traditional short length of copyright monopolies, and by limits on derivative rights have gradually fallen away.

The benefits of copyright law have, especially in the last decades, been dramatically tilted in most Northern nations toward copyright holders.[12] Copyright is typically the default status for anything now created in tangible form; terms are extremely long (70–90 years after the death of the author) and derivative rights apply. So, almost everything in the culture is effectively copyrighted forever, in practical terms. Specific exceptions and limitations become the escape hatch from owners' private censorship, and have come under renewed scrutiny by creators needing access to copyrighted material.

The US fair use provision is often the default exception internationally for business, since it is widely assumed that if work is seen as fair use in the US, it will not be contested elsewhere. Fair use also exists in the Philippines and Israel, and has been highly regarded in copyright reform discussion elsewhere. Canadian copyright reform has resulted in a redefinition of fair dealing to be, if anything, even more flexible than fair use.[13] Australian reform discussion currently features the option of fair use prominently. In the UK, Prime Minister David Cameron has suggested that incorporating fair use into British law would be crucial for innovation.[14] The 2011 Hargreaves report, while eventually advising against it, recommended measures that would do substantially the same thing.[15] In Scandinavia, as in South Africa, the right of quotation appears unchallenged as an avenue to access unlicensed copyrighted material.[16] European scholars Hugenholtz and Senftleben have proposed copyright reform that would incorporate some of the flexibilities of US-style fair use at a European Union-wide level.[17]

Fair use is both flexible and powerful in its design. Section 107 of the US Copyright Act broadly asserts the right to use copyrighted material if the benefit to society (e.g., the creation of new culture) is greater than the private loss. Considerations include the nature of the original work, the nature of the new work, the amount taken, and the effect on the market (beyond mere loss of a licensing fee). The application of fair use, like many exceptions, is on a case-by-case basis. In practice, given recent case law, fair use involves two simple questions: (1) is the use transformative, or different from the original material? and (2) was the appropriate amount taken to match the new use—not too much or too little?[18]

Fair Use and Remix Video

Fair use is enormously valuable to remixers of all kinds. People who want to create something new will, whether they want to or not, sample (literally or abstractly) from their cultural surroundings. And when a digital work can freely and visibly circulate, authors need to be made aware, with an even greater urgency than in the analog era, of their rights to use material without permission.

Remixers often participate in a culture that typifies itself as novel, innovative, even revolutionary. Remixers herald the novel affordances of digital creation and transmission tools. And indeed those affordances dramatically change opportunities and the scale of those opportunities. But the uses to which remixers put existing material often conform to time-honored creative practices, recognized in law as appropriate for unlicensed use under fair use.[19] This was demonstrated in the area of online video, in a 2008 American University study analyzing hundreds of online videos on YouTube and other video sites, which found many familiar transformative purposes for reuse of copyrighted material in remix (as well as other transformative purposes in videos that were not remixes).[20]

Satire and Parody

Parodies and satires in remix video spoof popular mass media in ways that demonstrate makers' power over the material. In *Lord of the Rings Was Too Long*,[21] for instance, interpolated scenes rewrite a key moment in the story (Figure 19.1). In this version, the men refuse to listen to the sensible suggestions of a young woman and doom themselves to a long, tortuous adventure rather than resolving the ring problem efficiently. In other cases, parodies and satires sometimes make political comments. In *Bush vs. the Zombies*,[22] video footage of President Bush at a press conference is reedited with added comments from a fake journalist, to make it seem as though Bush is talking about zombies instead of terrorists. *If Dick Cheney Was Scarface*[23] combines Cheney press conference news

Figure 19.1 "Lord of the Rings Was Too Long" makes a funny feminist critique of Tolkien (courtesy of Oren Brimer on YouTube)

footage with the voice and images from the mouth of Al Pacino, in order to satirize the vice president as a criminal.

Negative or Critical Commentary

Whatever the form of commentary, use of unauthorized copyrighted material for this purpose has long-standing legal recognition as fair use. We found video commonly quoted in critique, whether political or cultural. For instance, a Daily Kos entry, *Fox News: Oil and Adventure in the Arctic!*[24] includes embedded videos in its criticism of the Fox News coverage of the melting ice caps (Figure 19.2). The blog post excoriates Fox News for its current and past coverage of climate change. Another common form of critique is the mashup that quotes copyrighted works in order to create a metacommentary. For instance, in *Clint Eastwood's The Office*,[25] clips from the TV show *The Office* and the movie *Evan Almighty* are used to show (and thus make a snarky comment about Eastwood), in the movie preview format, what *The Office* would be like if it had been directed by Clint Eastwood. Less pointedly, in *Re-Inventing Culture*,[26] video artist Mark Cantwell juxtaposes clips from 24 artists' music and hundreds of images drawn from popular culture sources—such as classic films, music videos, television performances,

Figure 19.2 A remixer critiques biased coverage of climate change (source: Page van der Linden for Daily Kos)

scientific films, and advertisements—to make a comment about popular culture and its creative capacities.

Positive Commentary

Unauthorized quotation of copyrighted material for celebratory purposes may be just as defensible under fair use as it has been in analog environments, depending most importantly on its transformativeness. This kind of work, including fan tributes, shows the flip side of negative or parodic impulses toward popular commercial culture, while evincing the same desire to participate, contribute, and make one's mark upon it. *Internet People*[27] is a celebration of online video creations themselves. The celebrated *7 Minute Sopranos*[28] by Paul Gulyas and Joe Sabia (eventually blessed by HBO, which also hired Sabia to work in new media) provides a punchy, condensed version of the dark, twisted plot lines of the TV series.

Illustration or Example

Such uses are widely eligible for fair use, and such use was pervasive in all kinds of videos in our study. In some cases, quotation for illustration was at the core of the

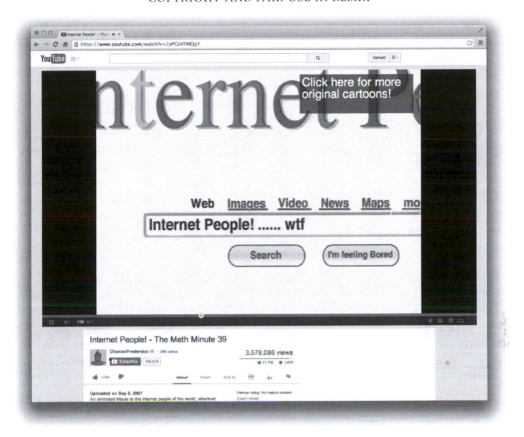

Figure 19.3 "Internet People" celebrates online video (courtesy of ChannelFrederator on YouTube)

video's meaning. *Evolution of Dance*[29] quotes popular music from a succession of fads, matching them with dance styles of that moment. All the quoted music in *Evolution* is quoted as illustration of the maker's point about the evolution of popular music over time. In other cases, images and video are used to illustrate independent arguments of some kind. For instance, one man's rant against Oprah Winfrey's choice of other online video makers (rather than himself or his favorites) to feature on her television show, *What the Buck—to Oprah with Love*,[30] includes photographs of Oprah, other celebrities, and related images captured from YouTube to illustrate his remarks.

Incidental Use

Merely incidental use is available for fair use consideration. This is common, indeed seemingly unavoidable, in uses of copyrighted material, which often contains other copyrighted content. Copyrighted material sometimes appears in online videos that record something else—for instance, the Lenz video referenced in the Fair Use section

See Chapter 34 for xtine burrough and Emily Erickson's
discussion on using Lenz's
Let's Go Crazy video as an
opportunity to teach remix,
fair use, and appropriation in
the classroom.

of this chapter, *Let's Go Crazy #1*,[31] is a video of
an 18-month-old child dancing to Prince's song
Let's Go Crazy. The online environment abounds
with the incidental use of the copyrighted song
Happy Birthday, as families celebrate the occasion. When this material gets remixed, the copyrighted content is inevitably carried along,
although it was never affirmatively selected.

Pastiche or Collage

Collage and pastiche are time-honored practices, evident in remix culture as well, which
are eligible for fair use to the extent that there is transformative and appropriate use of
the copyrighted material. Although all remix juxtaposes preexisting media to create new
meaning, some is done without any clear intent to comment on the original (which
would make it fall into one of the categories of satire, parody, criticism, or celebration).
Instead, makers express their own identities by advertising their frames of cultural reference and affinity. Many online memes share this characteristic. In some mashups, music
and sound effects are freely quoted in order to create or enhance meaning. For instance
in one of the most widely viewed online mashups, the five-second *Dramatic Chipmunk*[32]
video of a prairie dog (itself appropriated from a children's television program) is accompanied by horror movie music to create an audiovisual joke. The meme *Downfall/Hitler
Reacts*[33] has served to make jokes about everything from office politics to fair use.

Codes of Best Practices

In many fields, codes of best practices establish an outline of what is acceptable fair
use to peers, and thus lower perceived risk in situations where some degree of risk is
unavoidable.[34] Such codes, also called statements or sets of principles, have had enormous impact in the creative work and lives of the professionals who use them, and
have changed business practices. For the professional communities that have created
them, codes of best practices provide the norm-setting standard for individual
practitioners.

The value of such codes rests in their mode of creation. They are not expert dicta, but
genuine expressions of professional communities' shared values, which have linked the
terms of the law to the requirements of the profession's mission. This is valuable because,
as legal scholar Michael Madison has meticulously demonstrated,[35] courts inevitably
must, explicitly or implicitly, refer to a community's practice to understand the implications of a cultural activity. Unlike a set of (typically negotiated) fair use guidelines,
which have been shown to have a constraining effect,[36] a code of best practices is created
in a bottom-up process by the field itself, and without asking permission from major
copyright holding interests that affect the field.

This process has become fairly standard since documentary filmmakers became the
first professional community to make the attempt, by beginning to create what became
their "Statement of Best Practices in Fair Use" in 2004, with the sponsorship of five
national organizations in the field. The process was designed and facilitated by Peter
Jaszi and myself. It typically begins with research on community practices, conducted by
survey or interview of practitioners; convening of practitioners to discuss common

scenarios in which fair use is eligible, to discover mission-related purposes and limitations on use; formation of a code of best practices by facilitators; review by a legal advisory team and national associations; and release. All codes of best practices are organized by situation. They describe common situations in which fair use is relevant to the mission and activities of a particular field, articulate the principle justifying fair use, and describe the limitations on such use.

There have been measureable results from the creation of such codes. In documentary filmmaking, where obtaining errors and omissions insurance is the filmmaker's responsibility, filmmakers had long been unable to obtain such insurance for fair use claims. Within a year of issuing the "Documentary Filmmakers' Statement of Best Practices in Fair Use,"[37] they found that every insurer of documentaries in the US accepted fair use claims within the general terms of the policy. One can now obtain such insurance with no incremental cost, thus showing that insurers value the risk taken by accepting claims within the bounds of the filmmakers' code to be effectively zero.

Filmmakers have been able to circulate works that rely heavily upon fair use, such as Kirby Dick's feature documentary *This Film Is Not Yet Rated*,[38] which includes 134 clips, none of which are accompanied by clearances, of major motion pictures in its critique of the Motion Picture Association of America's (MPAA) ratings system. They have been able to do their work in ways they might not have previously attempted; *The Interrupters*,[39] for instance, a Kartemquin Films feature documentary by Steve James, employs excerpts from a wide range of media in its story about grassroots antiviolence efforts in Chicago, and Barbara Kopple's documentary *Gun Fight*,[40] about the gun control debate, features thoughtful use of popular culture imagery.

After poets and scholars created their codes, individual authors used the codes in discussions with publishers. Among the publishers who have changed their approach to fair use, from a default-permissions policy to a fair-use-is-possible approach, are Cambridge University Press and Oxford University Press. Blackwell's, an international academic publisher, issues a policy statement to its authors that it assumes uncleared material is being used under fair use or the exemption standard in the Commonwealth, fair dealing. The University of Chicago Press has become markedly more fair-use friendly. One recent scholarly book, Geoff Kaplan's *Power to the People: The Graphic Design of the Radical Press and the Rise of the Counter-Culture, 1964–1974*, heavily depends upon fair use.

Open courseware began at the Massachusetts Institute of Technology (MIT), where the creators decided not to fight copyright battles at the outset. They only published educational materials that were either original or cleared, and all of it is available on the Web. Creators found that this excluded many courses, since professors routinely used copyrighted material for purposes ranging from illustration to demonstration and often encountered it incidentally. Many courses ended up as "skeletons"—mere outlines—because of these limitations. Others, creators said in the sessions I cofacilitated, looked like "Swiss cheese" making it impossible for students to learn. Once they created their code of best practices, at MIT alone 31 new courses were uploaded within the first year. The course designers also established a visual convention to identify all fair use material, which was properly sourced with a warning to users that this content was not covered under the university's Creative Commons licensing, which applied to the rest of the course.

In English classrooms across the US, students who had long been told that they could not send their video work out for national student competitions unless all third-party work was cleared, are now employing the "Code of Best Practices in Fair Use for Media Literacy Education"[41] to make their own decisions, with their mentors, on the nature of their use. They are able to post their work online, show it at school events, and apply to competitions, all of which were previously off-limit activities.

Code of Best Practices for Fair Use in Online Video

The burgeoning of remix video, accompanied by a plethora of takedowns on YouTube, led to the formation of a project in 2008, led by myself and Peter Jaszi, to create a "Code of Best Practices in Fair Use for Online Video."[42] An earlier convening of lawyers, legal scholars, and industry actors at the American University had resulted in strong recommendations for such a code.[43] Research into common uses of copyrighted material for uses clearly eligible for fair use consideration, discussed above, further reinforced the logic of creating such a code. Remix in online video was not, however, a professional practice—far from it. It was diffused throughout the culture. There was no national association of remixers. There was no dominant professional body of practice that nicely represented the sprawling creative energy evident on YouTube. There was no business model.

As a result of consultation with professionals who had been involved in the study and in earlier projects, a high-level interdisciplinary committee of experts in two areas was formed: popular culture and copyright law. The scholars of popular culture understood firsthand both the kind of work being created in this participatory environment and the motivations behind it—and often sympathized passionately with new media makers. Legal scholars (with one entertainment industry lawyer, Michael Donaldson) understood the recent history of fair use practice and litigation, and the historical arguments justifying fair use in an analog, professional, media environment. No one in the group had a direct market investment in the outcome.

The group met both via conference calls and email, using the common Web platform, Basecamp, over a period of four months. Initially, some of the lawyers struggled to fully grasp the new media environment. In this situation, finding analogies with more traditional media became important. Differences arose between cultural studies experts and legal experts over how the law might accommodate contemporary practices that—often on the Darknet (closed, private Internet sites)—went beyond conventional, established interpretations of fair use. In some cases, the group eventually agreed that such practices might fall beyond a code of best practices, although not necessarily beyond the doctrine of fair use.

"The Code of Best Practices in Fair Use for Online Video"[44] described fair use reasoning, stressed the importance of demonstrating good faith (for instance by attribution), and organized the presentation according to situations in which fair use questions typically emerge in current practice. These situations were drawn from the previous report analyzing common uses of copyrighted material in remix work. They resulted in six situations:

- commenting on or critiquing of copyrighted material;
- using copyrighted material for illustration or example;
- capturing copyrighted material incidentally or accidentally;
- reproducing, reposting, or quoting in order to memorialize, preserve, or rescue an experience, an event, or a cultural phenomenon;

- copying, reposting, and recirculating a work or part of a work for purposes of launching a discussion; and
- quoting in order to recombine elements to make a new work that depends for its meaning on (often unlikely) relationships between the elements.

Each category was described—preferentially in traditional language, referencing analog creative practices—and provided with a general fair use principle with appropriate limitations. Thus, users could apply the doctrine of fair use within a practice context.

Results

"The Code of Best Practices in Fair Use for Online Video" was downloaded tens of thousands of times within the first two months of its publication, and was referenced on a variety of websites.[45] The Code was brought to the attention of lawyers at Google as well. This contact resulted in Google funding the production of a video about the code: "Remix Culture: Fair Use Is Your Friend."[46] There have been no industry critiques of the Code, other than a nonlawyer's disparagement of it on the website of the Copyright Alliance (funded by large copyright holders).[47]

Alan Watts wrote, "We seldom realize, for example that our most private thoughts and emotions are not actually our own. For we think in terms of languages and images which we did not invent, but which were given to us by our society."[48] Understanding fair use rights is an important part of the creative toolkit for those engaging in remix culture, and for those who think in terms of "languages and images which we did not invent." Other approaches to expanding access to useable material—Creative Commons licenses, for example, which permit makers to share work more freely; the creation of digital databases of public domain material (mostly pre-1923); more efficient licensing and microlicensing practices—will also facilitate remix. But fair use is the tool that allows the legitimate, legal, and unlicensed use of material still under copyright, owned by someone who is not necessarily interested in sharing, and either unavailable or not willing to license it for that purpose. It enables culture to continue to grow, adapt, and change, and for innovation to flourish. Remix video is just one of the many ways in which fair use encourages cultural creation.

Notes

1 Tarleton Gillespie, "Characterizing Copyright in the Classroom: The Cultural Work of Antipiracy Campaigns," *Communication, Culture & Critique* 2, no. 3 (2009); William Patry, *Moral Panics and the Copyright Wars* (New York: Oxford University Press, 2009); Jason Mazzone, *Copyfraud and Other Abuses of Intellectual Property Law* (Stanford, CA: Stanford Law Books, 2011); Joshua Fairfield, "Anti-Social Contracts: The Contractual Governance of Virtual Worlds," *McGill Law Journal* 53, no. 3 (2008); Aram Sinnreich, Mark Latonero, and Marissa Gluck, "Ethics Reconfigured," *Information, Communication & Society* 12, no. 8 (2009); Henry Jenkins, Sam Ford, and Joshua Green, *Spreadable Media: Creating Value and Meaning in a Networked Culture* (New York: New York University Press, 2013).
2 "Lenz v. Universal" Electronic Frontier Foundation, https://www.eff.org/cases/lenz-v-universal (accessed February 28, 2014).
3 "Lawrence Lessig Settles Fair Use Lawsuit Over Phoenix Music Snippets, Electronic Frontier Foundation," https://www.eff.org/press/releases/lawrence-lessig-settles-fair-use-lawsuit-over-phoenix-music-snippets (accessed March 6, 2014).
4 Eldar Haber, "The French Revolution 2.0: Copyright and the Three Strikes Policy," *Harvard Journal of Sports & Entertainment Law* 2, no. 2 (2011).

5 Ben Challis et al., "Third Strike Out," *The 1709 Blog*, July 9, 2013 http://the1709blog.blogspot.fr/2013/07/third-strike-struck-out.html (accessed August 7, 2014).

6 Rebecca Giblin, "Evaluating Graduated Response," *Columbia Journal of Law & the Arts* 37 (2014).

7 Peter Decherney, *Hollywood's Copyright Wars: From Edison to the Internet* (New York: Columbia University Press, 2012), 227.

8 Patricia Aufderheide, Renee Hobbs, and Peter Jaszi, "The Cost of Copyright Confusion for Media Literacy" (Center for Social Media, School of Communication, American University, 2007); Patricia Aufderheide and Peter Jaszi, "The Good, the Bad and the Confusing: User-Generated Video Creators on Copyright" (Washington, DC: Center for Social Media, School of Communication, American University, 2007); Peter DiCola and Kembrew McLeod, *Creative License: The Law and Culture of Digital Sampling* (Durham, NC: Duke University Press, 2011).

9 Organization for Transformative Works, http://transformativeworks.org/ (accessed February 28, 2014).

10 World's Fair Use Day, http://worldsfairuseday.org/ (accessed on February 28, 2014).

11 Benjamin Kaplan, *An Unhurried View of Copyright, Republished (and with Contributions from Friends)* (Newark, NJ: LexisNexis Matthew Bender, 2005); Lewis Hyde, *Common as Air: Revolution, Art, and Ownership* (New York: Farrar, Straus and Giroux, 2010).

12 James Boyle, *The Public Domain: Enclosing the Commons of the Mind* (New Haven, CT: Yale University Press, 2008); Kembrew McLeod, *Freedom of Expression: Overzealous Copyright Bozos and Other Enemies of Creativity* (New York: Doubleday, 2005); David Bollier, *Silent Theft: The Private Plunder of Our Common Wealth* (New York: Routledge, 2002); P. Bernt Hugenholtz, "Copyright, Contract and Code: What Will Remain of the Public Domain?" *Brooklyn Journal of International Law* 78 (2000).

13 Ariel Katz, "Fair Use 2.0: The Rebirth of Fair Dealing in Canada," in *The Copyright Pentalogy: How the Supreme Court of Canada Shook the Foundations of Canadian Copyright Law*, ed. Michael A. Geist (Ottawa: Ottawa University Press, 2013).

14 "UK Copyright Laws to be Reviewed, Announces Cameron," BBC News, last modified November 4, 2010, http://www.bbc.co.uk/news/uk-politics-11695416 (accessed August 7, 2014).

15 Ian Hargreaves, *Digital Opportunity: A Review of Intellectual Property and Growth* (London: Intellectual Property Office, 2011).

16 Sean Flynn and Peter Jaszi, "Untold Stories in South Africa: Creative Consequences of the Rights Clearance Culture for Documentary Filmmakers" (American University, WCL Research Paper No. 2010-23, Washington, DC: Program on Intellectual Property and the Public Interest, Washington College of Law, American University, 2010); Leif Ove Larsen and Torgeir Uberg Nærland, "Documentary in a Culture of Clearance: A Study of Knowledge of and Attitudes toward Copyright and Fair Use among Norwegian Documentary Makers," *Popular Communication* 8, no. 1 (2010).

17 P. Bernt Hugenholtz and Martin R. F. Senftleben, "Fair Use in Europe: In Search of Flexibilities," SSRN eLibrary (2011), http://dx.doi.org/10.2139/ssrn.1959554.

18 Patricia Aufderheide and Peter Jaszi, *Reclaiming Fair Use: How to Put Balance Back in Copyright* (Chicago, IL: University of Chicago Press, 2011); Neil Netanel, "Making Sense of Fair Use," *Lewis & Clark Law Review* 15, no. 3 (2011); Michael J. Madison, "A Pattern-Oriented Approach to Fair Use," *William and Mary Law Review* 45 (2004); Barton Beebe, "An Empirical Study of U.S. Copyright Fair Use Opinions, 1978–2005," *University of Pennsylvania Law Review* 156, no. 3 (2008).

19 Sinnreich, Latonero, and Gluck, "Ethics Reconfigured."

20 Patricia Aufderheide and Peter Jaszi, "Recut, Reframe, Recycle: Quoting Copyrighted Material in User-Generated Video" (Washington, DC: Center for Social Media, School of Communication, American University, 2008).

21 https://www.youtube.com/watch?v=CJb9UV_HUWA (accessed August 7, 2014).

22 https://www.youtube.com/watch?v=IoXgRtDysLY (accessed August 7, 2014).

23 https://www.youtube.com/watch?v=2nPUjIW7i7k (accessed August 7, 2014).

24 http://www.dailykos.com/story/2007/10/08/395509/-Fox-News-Oil-and-Adventure-in-the-Arctic# (accessed August 7, 2014).

25 http://www.youtube.com/watch?v=gPwmG3VuO_E (accessed August 7, 2014).

26 http://labs.divx.com/node/4390 and http://www.letztechance.org/read-21-2957.html?Re-Inventing%20Culture%20-%20Mark%20Cantwell (accessed August 7, 2014).

27 http://www.youtube.com/watch?v=2pPCkhYMQgY (accessed August 7, 2014).

28 http://www.youtube.com/watch?v=Tz_Ees_-kE4 (accessed August 7, 2014).

29 http://www.youtube.com/watch?v=dMH0bHeiRNg (accessed August 7, 2014).

30 http://www.youtube.com/watch?v=K3UQ0OuQLhs (accessed August 7, 2014).

31 http://www.youtube.com/watch?v=N1KfJHFWlhQ (accessed August 7, 2014).

32 http://www.youtube.com/watch?v=Af-ezch1L4c (accessed August 7, 2014).

33 https://www.youtube.com/watch?v=WDKaO-2eur4 (accessed August 7, 2014).

34 Aufderheide and Jaszi, *Reclaiming Fair Use*; http://cmsimpact.org/fair-use.

35 Madison, "A Pattern-Oriented Approach to Fair Use."

36 Kenneth Crews, "The Law of Fair Use and the Illusion of Fair-Use Guidelines," *Ohio State Law Journal* 62 (2001).

37 "Documentary Filmmakers' Statement of Best Practices in Fair Use," Center for Media and Social Impact, http://www.cmsimpact.org/sites/default/files/fair_use_final.pdf (accessed August 7, 2014).

38 http://www.youtube.com/watch?v=UTL3XMDwY0c (accessed August 7, 2014).

39 https://www.youtube.com/watch?v=sXmm0MZLGxY (accessed August 7, 2014).

40 "Interview with Barbara Kopple," HBO Documentaries, http://www.hbo.com/documentaries/gun-fight#/ (accessed on February 28, 2014).

41 "The Code of Best Practices in Media Literacy Education," Center for Media and Social Impact, http://www.cmsimpact.org/fair-use/related-materials/codes/code-best-practices-fair-use-media-literacy-education (accessed August 7, 2014).

42 "The Code of Best Practices in Fair Use for Online Video," Center for Media and Social Impact, http://www.cmsimpact.org/sites/default/files/online_best_practices_in_fair_use.pdf (accessed August 7, 2014).

43 Patricia Aufderheide, "Unauthorized: The Copyright Conundrum in Participatory Video" (Washington, DC: Center for Social Media, School of Communication, American University, 2007).

44 http://cmsimpact.org/fair-use/related-materials/codes/fair-use-and-online-video (accessed August 7, 2014).

45 Including Revver, Boing Boing, and Jonathan McIntosh.

46 http://www.cmsimpact.org/fair-use/video/remix-culture-fair-use-your-friend and http://www.youtube.com/watch?v=tCpBhU16TzI (accessed August 7, 2014).

47 July 7, 2008, formerly available at: http://blog.copyrightalliance.org/2008/07/the-remix-culture/. Google lawyer William Patry responded acerbically, critiquing Ross's ignorance and bravado as "chutzpah": http://williampatry.blogspot.com/2008/07/patrick-ross-and-fair-use.html (accessed August 7, 2014).

48 Alan Watts, *The Book on the Taboo Against Knowing Who You Are* (New York: Vintage, 1989), 53–54.

Bibliography

Aufderheide, Patricia. "Unauthorized: The Copyright Conundrum in Participatory Video." Washington, DC: Center for Social Media, School of Communication, American University, 2007.

Aufderheide, Patricia, and Peter Jaszi. "Recut, Reframe, Recycle: Quoting Copyrighted Material in User-Generated Video." Washington, DC: Center for Social Media, School of Communication, American University, 2008.

——. *Reclaiming Fair Use: How to Put Balance Back in Copyright.* Chicago, IL: University of Chicago Press, 2011.

——. "The Good, the Bad and the Confusing: User-Generated Video Creators on Copyright." Washington, DC: Center for Social Media, School of Communication, American University, 2007.

Aufderheide, Patricia, Renee Hobbs, and Peter Jaszi. "The Cost of Copyright Confusion for Media Literacy." Center for Social Media, School of Communication, American University, 2007.

Aufderheide, Patricia, Peter Jaszi, Tijana Milosevic, and Bryan Bello. "Copyright, Permissions, and Fair Use among Visual Artists and the Academic and Museum Visual Arts Communities: An Issue Report." New York: College Art Association, 2014.

Beebe, Barton. "An Empirical Study of U.S. Copyright Fair Use Opinions, 1978–2005." *University of Pennsylvania Law Review* 156, no. 3 (2008): 549–624.

Bollier, David. *Silent Theft: The Private Plunder of Our Common Wealth.* New York: Routledge, 2002.

Boyle, James. *The Public Domain: Enclosing the Commons of the Mind.* New Haven, CT: Yale University Press, 2008.

Crews, Kenneth. "The Law of Fair Use and the Illusion of Fair-Use Guidelines." *Ohio State Law Journal* 62 (2001): 98.

Decherney, Peter. *Hollywood's Copyright Wars: From Edison to the Internet*. New York: Columbia University Press, 2012.

DiCola, Peter, and Kembrew McLeod. *Creative License: The Law and Culture of Digital Sampling*. Durham, NC: Duke University Press, 2011.

Donaldson, Michael. "Fair Use: What a Difference a Decade Makes." *Journal of the Copyright Society of the U.S.A.* 57, no. 3 (2010): 331–335.

Fairfield, Joshua. "Anti-Social Contracts: The Contractual Governance of Virtual Worlds." *McGill Law Journal* 53, no. 3 (2008): 427–476.

Falzone, Anthony, and Jennifer Urban. "Demystifying Fair Use: The Gift of the Center for Social Media Statements of Best Practices." *Journal of the Copyright Society of the U.S.A.* 57, no. 3 (2010): 337–350.

Flynn, Sean, and Peter Jaszi. "Untold Stories in South Africa: Creative Consequences of the Rights Clearance Culture for Documentary Filmmakers." American University, WCL Research Paper No. 2010-23. Washington, DC: Program on Intellectual Property and the Public Interest, Washington College of Law, American University, 2010.

Giblin, Rebecca. "Evaluating Graduated Response." *Columbia Journal of Law & the Arts* 37 (2014): 147–209.

Gillespie, Tarleton. "Characterizing Copyright in the Classroom: The Cultural Work of Antipiracy Campaigns." *Communication, Culture & Critique* 2, no. 3 (2009): 274–318.

Haber, Eldar. "The French Revolution 2.0: Copyright and the Three Strikes Policy." *Harvard Journal of Sports & Entertainment Law* 2, no. 2 (2011): 297–339.

Hargreaves, Ian. *Digital Opportunity: A Review of Intellectual Property and Growth*. London: Intellectual Property Office, 2011.

Hugenholtz, P. Bernt. "Copyright, Contract and Code: What Will Remain of the Public Domain?" *Brooklyn Journal of International Law* 78 (2000): 77–90.

Hugenholtz, P. Bernt, and Martin R. F. Senftleben, "Fair Use in Europe: In Search of Flexibilities," SSRN eLibrary, 2011, http://dx.doi.org/10.2139/ssrn.1959554.

Hyde, Lewis. *Common as Air: Revolution, Art, and Ownership*. New York: Farrar, Straus and Giroux, 2010.

Jenkins, Henry, Sam Ford, and Joshua Green. *Spreadable Media: Creating Value and Meaning in a Networked Culture*. New York: New York University Press, 2013.

Kaplan, Benjamin. *An Unhurried View of Copyright, Republished (and with Contributions from Friends)*. Newark, NJ: LexisNexis Matthew Bender, 2005.

Katz, Ariel. "Fair Use 2.0: The Rebirth of Fair Dealing in Canada." In *The Copyright Pentalogy: How the Supreme Court of Canada Shook the Foundations of Canadian Copyright Law*, edited by Michael A. Geist, 93–156. Ottawa: Ottawa University Press, 2013.

Larsen, Leif Ove, and Torgeir Uberg Nærland. "Documentary in a Culture of Clearance: A Study of Knowledge of and Attitudes toward Copyright and Fair Use among Norwegian Documentary Makers." *Popular Communication* 8, no. 1 (2010): 46–60.

Madison, Michael J. "A Pattern-Oriented Approach to Fair Use." *William and Mary Law Review* 45 (2004): 1525.

Mazzone, Jason. *Copyfraud and Other Abuses of Intellectual Property Law*. Stanford, CA: Stanford Law Books, 2011.

McLeod, Kembrew. *Freedom of Expression: Overzealous Copyright Bozos and Other Enemies of Creativity*. New York: Doubleday, 2005.

Netanel, Neil. "Making Sense of Fair Use." *Lewis & Clark Law Review* 15, no. 3 (2011): 715–772.

Patry, William. *Moral Panics and the Copyright Wars*. New York: Oxford University Press, 2009.

Sinnreich, Aram, Mark Latonero, and Marissa Gluck. "Ethics Reconfigured." *Information, Communication & Society* 12, no. 8 (2009): 1242–1260.

Watts, Alan. *The Book on the Taboo Against Knowing Who You Are*. New York: Vintage, 1989.

20

I THOUGHT I MADE A VID, BUT THEN YOU TOLD ME THAT I DIDN'T

Aesthetics and Boundary Work in the Fan-Vidding Community

Katharina Freund

Holy crap, vids are serious business.

Anonymous LiveJournal user, on Fail
Fandom Anon, LiveJournal community, 2010

After attending VividCon, the holy grail of fan-vidding conventions held in Chicago in 2009, I returned home to Australia with a grin on my face. I had been enthralled by the friendliness and enthusiasm of the vidders I met, and felt like I had become part of a unique online community. Exhausted after many hours of vid-watching, panel discussions, dance parties, and interviews, I was shocked to discover that the online community of vidders on LiveJournal had erupted into discord during my travels home. Arguments and retractions, comments and private messages had flown around discussing the changing nature of the vidding community. Due to the egocentric organization of LiveJournal,[1] I only had access to sections of this debate: much of it occurred behind members-only discussions or in private messages or emails. But the debate swirled around the changing aesthetics of vids, and the changing membership of the vidding community in an event that later became known on LiveJournal as "Vid Fail 2009."[2]

This chapter explores the complex community negotiations which occurred as a result of this event. Based on two years of ethnographic research conducted in the online and face-to-face spaces of the vidders, it discusses how this community orients itself around the perception of a shared history and shared aesthetic traditions.

Introduction to Vidding Practices

Technically speaking, a fan video (or vid) is a type of remix that takes footage from film or television and edits it to music in order to tell a story about that film or television text. Many vids focus on romantic narratives about two characters from a particular text, such as Harry and Hermione from *Harry Potter* or Bella and either Jacob or Edward (or both) from *Twilight*. A common subset of the theme, known as slash, involves homoerotic romances such as Kirk and Spock from *Star Trek*. Type any of those sets of names into YouTube and a bevy of videos will appear, all of which match the above description.

The act of vidding, however, is a lot more complex for the vidders I studied. There is a negotiation at play in the vidding community about who gets to be "in" and what types of videos fit their understanding of what makes a vid. These boundaries between what is and is not a vid, and who is and is not a vidder, reveal the complex social and artistic arguments occurring beneath the surface of a productive group of remixers. In the case of the vidding community, relying mostly on the social-networking and blogging site Livejournal.com, these community boundaries are based along aesthetic, historical, and gendered lines. According to my research conducted from 2009 to 2011, more than 90 percent of vidders on LiveJournal identify as female.

When I asked long-time vidder and "big name fan" Laura Shapiro to explain how anyone becomes a member of the vidding community, she detailed the multiplicity of vidding communities:

> First of all, I don't believe there is *the* vidding community, I believe that there are many vidding communities, most of which I probably have no idea about. I think it's a big mistake to refer to *the* vidding community, I think when people say that they're speaking from within a vidding community that I am a member of that is where vidding began, the community that grew out of vidding's origins with Kandy Fong and out of slash fandom.[3] What I'd call the traditional vidding community, and its offshoots. But even within *this* community, that people call *the* vidding community, that I call the traditional vidding community, there are many, many communities. And so defining—definitions are hard.[4]

Definitions are indeed difficult: The vidders themselves certainly cannot agree on what constitutes the core identity of this group. As noted by Bell, the term "community" functions as a descriptor, but it is also a normative and ideological term that carries a lot of baggage.[5] The early cyber-enthusiast Howard Rheingold is most commonly quoted for his definition of online communities as "social aggregations that emerge from the Net when enough people carry on those public discussions long enough, with sufficient feeling, to form webs of personal relationships in cyberspace."[6] Later critiques of Rheingold often denounced online communities as inauthentic, compensatory, and somehow lacking: sure "community" could not be so easily applied to digital groups, as they were so vastly different from face-to-face, "authentic" communities.[7]

Raymond Williams notes that the term "community" is particularly problematic: Unlike other terms for social organization such as "nation" or "society," it is rarely used unfavorably and carries "warmly persuasive" connotations.[8] The positive associations are noted by Baym who chose to use it precisely for its "warm, emotional resonance."[9] According to Marshall, "The vagueness of the term is part of its power. It can unify because it is imprecise. Different people using the term may have different expectations, but they can all appear to be talking similarly."[10] As the term "community" represents an idea, its use to groups is obvious: It evokes commonality, support, and friendship, and it erases difference. The debates among vidders about just what constitutes their community and the powerful arguments supporting different viewpoints take advantage of these positive-yet-vague elements of the term.

For the purpose of this chapter, I am not interested in what "community" may mean, but rather what it means to the vidders. Following Marshall again, I believe "it is fruitless to search for the essence of community, but it is useful to see what enables a particular group to be so classified by its members."[11]

Consider the following quotes from a questionnaire I conducted with the vidders during my ethnographic research:

Q: Please add any comments you'd like to make on the vidding community, your online and offline friendships, or anything else you'd like to share here.

R1: I have found the best friends of my adult life through vidding and fandom.

R2: YouTube quality is crap. *pukes* If a vid is posted on YouTube, I most likely will NOT watch it. I've made great friends online that I could never have met offline and those friendships mean the world to me.

R3: Vidders who care about quality and learning and constantly getting better are the only people I care about. The 12 year olds on YouTube are generally not in my orbit, and people who just throw crappy clips together and call it a vid or steal clips are not part of the vidding community I hang out in. I miss the days when it was smaller.

R4: There's a strong sense of community I don't see elsewhere.

Several of these respondents (R2, R3) define the vidding community in exclusionary and normative ways: by highlighting aspects of other, inferior vidding groups (namely, those on YouTube), the superiority of their vidding group is established. YouTubers are derided as young, frivolous, and unconcerned with quality, thereby setting up the LiveJournal (LJ) vidding community as mature, thoughtful, and serious about aesthetics and narrative standards.

This tension was obvious to many vidders, such as Australian vidder Boppy:

These are "centres" for vidding and people that "hang" in any of those places are members of the vidding community. However, I find these centres limiting as well. The truth is that many, many people vid completely separately—either on their own or in other communities online—and to pretend that the vidding community has clearly defined boundaries would be a lie.

After her LiveJournal page became the focal point of an argument about inclusion in the vidding community during Vid Fail 2009, Boppy reflected about where the boundaries lie and how she felt her work and the work of many of her friends was excluded by more traditional members:

I had fans who do not have me friended, probably have never even heard of me before, show up and throw their weight around about what "is" and "isn't" vidding. I honestly don't think they could see how their behavior came across but it's exactly this sort of thing that makes people feel excluded—whether it's because they're a guy and people are going on and on about vidding being a "female" tradition, or whether it's because they've made a vid that is reverential rather than "commenting on" the source and here are these famous, long-term fans telling them that that is "not vidding."

Figure 20.1 "I thought I made a vid, but then you told me I didn't" Internet meme

While the LiveJournal vidding community claims the term "vidding" as their own, Boppy and many of the commenters on her post pointed out that YouTubers and other remix artists commonly use the term to describe their own work. The message seen in Figure 20.1 was shared privately among many vidders and vid-fans during this debate.

When I used the terms "remix" and "new media" to define vidding on my LiveJournal, it caused significant disagreement in the comments. Traditional vidders argued that if the definition of the term was expanded to include other types of remixes made by other communities, it would constitute an erasure of the female-centered history. One such comment read:

> I think that it is not just the traditional/old school vidders who would object to "new media form"—you don't have to experience it first-hand to be proud and protective of vidding's long history. "Remix" is not only a word not used by vidders, it's a word that is going to make vidding seem much younger than its 30+ years.[12]

At the vidding conventions I attended, I was approached by several individuals who quizzed me on my knowledge of vidding history. I was taken aside, along with several other first-time convention attendees, and shown some of the oldest vids that still existed, and was taught about the "grandmothers" of vidding in hotel rooms and hallways.

The Origins of Vidding

To a large extent, the origins of vidding have become mythologized by the community through their own efforts to document the history of their practice. VividCon (VVC), the central face-to-face social event of the vidding community, opens every year ritualistically with a "Genealogy of Vidding" vid show, which Coppa refers to as "an annual recitation of our history" for everyone at the convention.[13] While there are usually two tracks of parallel programming at VVC, nothing is scheduled concurrently with the history vid show so that all the con-goers are able to attend. This event is one of self-conscious community building, where the vidders come together to recount their origins and introduce newer vidders and vid watchers to the mythic origins.

According to the canonized version of fan-vidding history, vidding was created in 1975 when a *Star Trek* fan named Kandy Fong converted footage from her favorite series into 35mm slides, and used a slide carousel to click through the images in time to music. These proto-vid slideshows were shown live at conventions and in fan club meetings around the United States during the course of several years. "Fong began to videotape her results, partly because [*Star Trek* creator Gene] Roddenberry wanted copies and partly because Fong herself became interested in creating records of fannish art."[14] Few of these slideshow vids are now accessible, although Fong's very popular vid *Both Sides Now* (first shown in 1980 and recorded in 1986) is often shown at conventions even today. It is probably the only slideshow vid that newer vidders are able to view because it has been made available online.[15]

These slideshow presentations inspired other fans to make similar works, so they turned to the VCR technology of the mid-1980s. As mentioned above, these early vids were often heavily influenced by slash fandom (such as Kirk/Spock in this period). This early VCR vidding period is covered extensively by Jenkins[16] and Bacon-Smith[17] and the vidders profiled in those works are now revered as the founders of contemporary vidding aesthetics. The members of the community during this time were mostly women. Many vids during the 1980s and 1990s were made by large groups of editors known as collectives, due to the high cost of VCR editing decks and the complexity of the technology. The process was incredibly time-consuming and required several people: stopwatches and log books were used to keep track of the timing of clips needed in relation to the song used, as the VCR numerical counter rarely corresponded to an actual amount of time.

Despite the trouble, VCR vidder Gwyn fondly recalled her experiences vidding together with her collective:

> So when you're vidding with VCRs, basically someone would sit in front of the TV and the editing decks and push all the buttons, and we would all sit on the couch and give thumbs up or thumbs down to the clip choices, and stuff our faces full of junk food, drink copious amounts of soda . . . It was a group activity, and we had these monthly bashes where we would do stuff other than vidding, just hang out . . . We were all very close-knit.

The VCR vidders are highly regarded for their tenacity in creating vids using such intricate methods, and these "good ol' days" are also romanticized through such narratives. Tales of this camaraderie are often told in the convention spaces where the VCR and newer, digital vidders come into contact to highlight the differences between them.

VCR vidding was a friendly and communal creative practice, totally unlike that of modern vidders who work alone on computers that automatically process many of the elements that were formerly painstaking processes of manual labor.

By the time computer-aided vidding arrived in the late 1990s, VCR vidding was an established part of fandom culture, and had its own distinct discourse of aesthetics, analysis, and criticism (as explained in detail below). Despite the significant advantages digital vidding held over analog, the arrival of digital vids was not initially embraced. According to Melina, who was an early digital vidder:

> Doing things with computers that you couldn't do with a VCR was seen as flashy, and frequently unnecessarily flashy. It didn't serve the vid, you were just showing off that you had a computer. Some of this I think was valid, but obviously lots of it was not.

Throughout the early and mid-2000s, vidding began to expand as the community shifted to communicating primarily through mailing lists on the Web. As vids were now shared online and more easily accessible, it became common for people to stumble across a vid posted on the Internet without already being a member of fandom. More and more vidders from outside the United States began to appear: unable to attend the US-based conventions, these "feral" vidders interacted with each other solely online and were unaware of the accepted history of the community. It is interesting to consider the use of the term "feral": somewhat disparaging, it indicates that these new vidders were seen as uncivilized and wild by traditional vidders. Gwyn was, and indeed still is, apprehensive about these "newbie vidders":

Q: Who are these newbie vidders, when did they arrive?
Gwyn: [laughs] Well, it's anyone who started vidding on computer! It was YouTube—YouTube really didn't exist four years ago, and now it's taken over the world! And then there were all these people who were coming in to vidding who had no idea there was this culture, there was this history. They thought they had invented it.

The arrival of YouTube in 2005 popularized and mainstreamed the practice of watching streaming video on the Web.[18] New genres of remix, which also appropriated copyrighted media, appeared quickly throughout this period, such as machinima (films made using video game engines), trailer mashups (creating a parody movie trailer by altering the genre), political remix videos, and many more. The closest relative of the vid, the anime music video (AMV) also migrated on to YouTube while maintaining its own domain, animemusicvideos.org. And some of these remix videos looked just like the vids made by vidders: new editors were cutting clips of television footage to music and posting it on YouTube, entirely unaware of·the existence of a vidding community which claimed a 30-year history. Many of these new editors were from different countries, backgrounds, and age groups than the traditional vidding community. There were also more men now creating remix videos they called "vids," and the vids themselves also began to change as the influx brought new music, new aesthetic concerns, and also new types of edited imagery.

A tug-of-war between the established "vidding aesthetic" and these new forms began. This tension is played out through vidding reviews and commentary, both online and face-to-face at the vid review sessions during fan conventions. Most of the stylistic traits of LiveJournal vidding are flexible to an extent in the name of innovation and play. However, if a vid is seen to stray too far from the accepted traits, or includes faux-pas elements, then it is often critiqued as a "bad vid" or "not a vid."

The source text is usually, but not always, science-fiction, fantasy, or a cult television series: *Star Trek*, *The X-Files*, *Highlander*, *Buffy the Vampire Slayer*, *Supernatural*, and *Doctor Who* have all been heavily vidded, for example. Generally speaking, a traditional type of vid focuses on a relationship from the text (which can be part of the "canon" of the text, or constructed by fans) or on a particular character and their motivations and back story; these are the shipper vid and character study, respectively. Many vidders see this focus on characters and relationships as a particularly female way of understanding media texts, and as part of what makes vidding different from other types of remix videos. While some effects can be used, they should generally be in service of the story the vid is telling rather than just demonstrating a new visual technique.

There are certain traits, which vidders agree are important to a good vid, such as "going somewhere" with the story or telling a narrative, saying something new about a character, relationship, or storyline from the television show, or recontextualizing a well-known song through interesting juxtaposition with the televisual source.

The vid *Displaced* by Canadian vidder Milly is a good example of a classic type of vid. Using footage from *Heroes*,[19] the vid explores the actions and motivations of the character Claire, and alludes to self-harm in Claire's ability to heal from any wound. The vidder uses sparing special effects such as those shown in the frames represented by Figure 20.2, and the emphasis is on the character's development throughout the series.

The traits of a "bad vid" are much more concrete, but also less well-known, particularly by newer vidders. For example, including black screen in the vid or showing the characters lips moving without dialog (known as "talky-face") are agreed to be the hallmarks of a "bad vid." Including too many flashy special effects, such as tinting the footage with a monochrome hue like orange or purple, are seen as unnecessary. This particular stylistic concern hearkens back to the earliest days of digital vidding, where VCR vidders were skeptical of effects that could not be accomplished via the VCR, and were thus not part of the accepted aesthetic style of vidding at the time.

The vidder jescaflowne, who came to vidding from the closely related AMV community, took these gaffes to the limit in the vid *Another Sunday* (Figures 20.3 and 20.4). Using footage from *Stargate: Atlantis*[20] set to Jefferson Starship, jescaflowne uses every filter, cheesy effect, and slow-motion trick available. The vid was a surprise hit on the convention circuits for its over-the-top take on the source material.

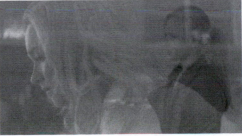

Figure 20.2 Screenshots of *Displaced* by Milly (courtesy of Milly)

Figure 20.3 Ronon Dex (Jason Momoa) sparkles in this screenshot from *Another Sunday* by jescaflowne (courtesy of jescaflowne)

Figure 20.4 The original shot of Teyla Emmagan (Rachel Luttrell) in *Another Sunday* is overlaid with a green color wash (courtesy of jescaflowne)

Interestingly, the fan-written wiki, Fanlore, points to the vidder's origins in AMV editing as part of the reason as to why it is different from traditional vids:

> *Another Sunday* is also representative of the anime music video [amv] aesthetic as applied to live action vidding; . . . Jescaflowne comes to live action by way of amvs, and brings a fast-cutting, highly spectacular, colorful and almost cartoon-ish style to live action footage.[21]

While the vid was wildly popular when it premiered, it is remembered for toeing the line between what is acceptable for vids and what is more common in other remix video communities.

Many newer vidders expressed confusion at the feedback they received in reviews, as the aesthetic rules they were breaking were not clear to them. For example, Keerawa premiered one of her first vids at VividCon in Chicago, and was surprised at the negative reaction to the inclusion of a voiceover she had recorded at the beginning and end of the vid: "I think I'm breaking some really big rule that I didn't even know existed." This was echoed by several other vidders, including Vinny who similarly felt like she was violating a rule that she had never heard of when she used the black screen in her first vid premiere at VividCon:

> I'm still struggling to get to know more about the genre, about the history of it. During the critique, one of the mentions was that apparently using lots of black footage is like breaking wind in an elevator! [laughs] Before this I had no idea that was a faux pas, I mean I'd read stuff in comments [on LJ] saying you shouldn't use lots of white flashes but I guess this is just telling me I still have a ton to learn.

One vidder known for pushing the boundaries of what is acceptable commented, "It's been said that I'm fearless, which is kind of true. But it's more that I don't realize when I should be fearful or resist."[22]

A long-time vidder, who had previously worked in the AMV community, pointed out that the vids that get roundly panned at the vid review panel at the conventions tend to be those that include aesthetic elements that the community is not familiar with:

> Chloe: I wouldn't say it's reluctant to change, because I don't think it is at all, it changes all the time, but it's a community that's very wide in ages, so you have those really young people who are probably exploring more and trying new things, and the community that's in a really safe place, where it doesn't really want to—I mean, it knows what it wants to do and it's willing to evolve in that line, but it takes a little probing to send them exploring.

This is also at work in the vidding community: I heard much discussion as to the differences between LiveJournal and YouTube vidders, and between LiveJournal vidders and AMV editors as well. In these discussions, vidding was said to be older, more critical, thoughtful, and less focused on special effects. In his work on the free software movement, David Berry analyzed the specific discourses that were being employed by different groups.[23] The use of terms such as "we" and "they" help the different software groups define their boundaries between the in-group and the out-group. When reading the material published by these groups, he notes, "These subject positions are treated as a dichotomy and the reader is assumed to be supportive of the FSF [Free Software Foundation] objectives, a friend and colleague—or if not, an enemy."[24] He also points out that these groups spend a great deal of time explaining how they are different from other open source advocacy groups, even though they are quite similar and overlap in their membership. By defining themselves as the "first" remix video community, particularly as the first female remix video community, vidders are able to legitimize themselves as the most authentic, and therefore best type, of video remix in the face of newer, male-dominated ones.

With the rise of other forms of remix on YouTube in the beginning of the twenty-first century, vidding practices that had existed since 1975 found themselves in danger of "being written out of the history of remix," according to Francesca Coppa in her presentation at the DIY Video Summit in 2008.[25] She continued: "[The popular conception is] that guys have been remixing mass media since 1994, or 1991 if you're talking about machinima, so we really want to say, no, women have been remixing mass media since 1975."[26] This history of vidding is explicitly gendered. It is extremely important to the identity of this community to identify their origins as older than the other forms of remix, and specifically to point out that this is a *women's* practice.

As Gwyn explains:

> We [women] don't get to see the stories we want to see. Most TV and certainly movies are done for a male audience, eighteen to thirty-four . . . and they are not making the entertainments we necessarily want to see. We see all these other texts inside these things. So we have to take what is given to us and instead show the world how we see it; I'm going to make what I want to see.

Vidders resisted making broad generalizations about "women's vidding" and "men's vidding" and were quick to explain that vidding doesn't mean that the participants are only interested in romance. Gwyn herself pointed out that she likes making violent, action vids. But the emphasis on characters and relationships in vids, prominent vidder Laura Shapiro explained to me at VividCon, "are values associated with femaleness." In interviews, vidders commonly described their practices as a method of writing back, or against, the televisual source material as a way to critique or rewrite the text against the intentions of the (male) creators and writers. An increase in the number of male participants in the community has also led to fears that the women's space of fan-vidding conventions and LiveJournal circles may be changing.

Conclusion

There have been several calls out to the community to encourage more inclusivity in defining the anatomy of a vid, and characteristics of a vidder. In response to a convention panel entitled *What Do We Want From Vids Now?* one vidder wrote:

> The discussion had such a subtext of anxiety at certain points, a sense that we were in danger of losing something or losing control of something as vids become less an orphan art and expand out to meet a world of new media that is also rushing in to meet us. At least two people said, and said sincerely, that they were "not interested in policing the boundary between what is and isn't a

vid," but I felt that there was a lot of repressed desire in the room to do so . . . I really wanted to ask: What is it we are anxious about? . . . Because change is coming to us whether or not we go out to meet it.

So what is it that vids that push the envelope make us fear? Loss of definition as an artform, as a community, when we can no longer clearly say what is a vid and what isn't? Invasion by hostile forces that don't understand (boys!) or that simply outnumber us, so that we get swamped and lost, when the boundaries between fanvidder and other new media artist blur?[27]

Most of the comments on this post were supportive of other new media forms of remix, but simultaneously protective of their particular community as a female-dominated and critical response to media texts. Or, as Australian vidder Boppy put it, "The LiveJournal—slash—female-dominated vidding community does not have a monopoly on vidding and the sooner they realize that the better."

Vidders are now more visible as they communicate online, and media participation through remix and editing has become a much more common practice. The appropriative elements of fan culture have spread with the development and dissemination of interactive, Web 2.0 technologies and platforms.[28] The community has also moved more into the open, and begun sharing vids using more public platforms such as YouTube, Tumblr, and Vimeo. These new spaces bring them into more and more contact with new types of vids. Despite many efforts to preserve traditional vidding styles, the genre changes every day and many contemporary vids would be unrecognizable to the early VCR vidders.

While vidding is a comparatively small fan practice, this study of amateur video producers has provided historical and cultural context of a community engaged in practices that are currently at the forefront of public attention in light of recent copyright battles between governments, media industries, users, and Web 2.0 service providers.

Vidders provide valuable insight into the historical origins of remix culture, and demonstrate that there has not been a paradigm shift in the role of the audience with the advent of digital media and participatory culture. Rather, new media formats, such as the remix video, did not arise unbidden, but represent the long-standing desire for audiences to participate in and personalize their media.

Notes

1 danah boyd, "Friends, Friendsters, and Top 8: Writing Community into Being on Social Network Sites," *First Monday* 11, no. 12 (2006).

2 The event changed from a straightforward debate about these topics to a "fail" after the debate turned to argument, and often became personal attacks which left the community in turmoil.

3 Kandy Fong and the origins of vidding in slash fandom will be discussed further below.

4 Unless otherwise indicated, all quotations from vidders or other communities members are based on personal interviews with the author conducted during ethnographic fieldwork.

5 David Bell, *An Introduction to Cybercultures* (London: Routledge, 2001), 93.

6 Howard Rheingold, *The Virtual Community: Homesteading on the Electronic Frontier* (Reading, MA: Addison-Wesley Publishing Co., 1993), 5.

7 Kevin Robins, "Cyberspace and the World We Live In," in *The Cybercultures Reader*, ed. David Bell and Barbara M. Kennedy (London: Routledge, 2000).

8 Raymond Williams, *Keywords: A Vocabulary of Culture and Society* (Oxford: Oxford University Press, 1976).

9 Nancy K. Baym, *Tune In, Log On: Soaps, Fandom, and Online Community* (Thousand Oaks, CA: Sage Publications, 2000), 2.

10 John Paul Marshall, *Living on Cybermind: Categories, Communication, and Control*, vol. 24, New Literacies and Digital Epistemologies (New York: Peter Lang, 2007), 214.

11 Marshall, *Living on Cybermind*, 275

12 This comment was collected anonymously during online ethnographic data collection.

13 USC School of Cinematic Arts, "Genealogy of Vidding with Francesca Coppa—'24/7 a DIY Video Summit'" (University of Southern California, 2009).

14 Francesca Coppa, "Women, *Star Trek*, and the Early Development of Fannish Vidding," *Transformative Works and Cultures* 1 (2008): para. 3.3.

15 Francesca Coppa, "Celebrating Kandy Fong: Founder of the Fannish Music Video," in *In Media Res*, 2007, http://mediacommons.futureofthebook.org/imr/2007/11/19/celebrating-kandy-fong-founder-of-fannish-music-video.

16 Henry Jenkins, *Textual Poachers: Television Fans and Participatory Culture* (New York: Routledge, 1992).

17 Camille Bacon-Smith, *Enterprising Women: Television Fandom and the Creation of Popular Myth* (Philadelphia: University of Pennsylvania Press, 1992).

18 Jean Burgess and Joshua Green, *YouTube: Online Video and Participatory Culture* (Cambridge, MA: Polity Press, 2009).

19 *Heroes*, created by Tim Kring. NBC, 2006–10.

20 *Stargate: Atlantis*, created by Robert C. Cooper and Brad Wright, Sci-Fi Channel, 2004–09.

21 Fanlore, *Another Sunday*, http://fanlore.org/wiki/Another_Sunday.

22 This individual preferred to remain anonymous.

23 David M. Berry, *Copy, Rip, Burn: The Politics of Copyleft and Open Source* (London: Pluto Press, 2008).

24 Ibid., 167.

25 As a point of interest, Coppa is also a founding board member of the Organization for Transformative Works.

26 USC School of Cinematic Arts. "Genealogy of Vidding with Francesca Coppa—'24/7 a DIY Video Summit.'" University of Southern California, 2009.

27 The location of this post has been kept anonymous to protect the identity of the poster.

28 Henry Jenkins, *Convergence Culture: Where Old and New Media Collide* (New York: New York University Press, 2006).

Bibliography

Bacon-Smith, Camille. *Enterprising Women: Television Fandom and the Creation of Popular Myth*. Philadelphia: University of Pennsylvania Press, 1992.

Baym, Nancy K. *Tune In, Log On: Soaps, Fandom, and Online Community*. Thousand Oaks, CA: Sage Publications, 2000.

Bell, David. *An Introduction to Cybercultures*. London: Routledge, 2001.

Berry, David M. *Copy, Rip, Burn: The Politics of Copyleft and Open Source*. London: Pluto Press, 2008.

boyd, danah. "Friends, Friendsters, and Top 8: Writing Community into Being on Social Network Sites." *First Monday* 11, no. 12 (2006).

Burgess, Jean, and Joshua Green. *YouTube: Online Video and Participatory Culture*. Cambridge, MA: Polity Press, 2009.

Coppa, Francesca. "Celebrating Kandy Fong: Founder of the Fannish Music Video." In *In Media Res*, 2007, http://mediacommons.futureofthebook.org/imr/2007/11/19/celebrating-kandy-fong-founder-of-fannish-music-video (accessed August 10, 2014).

———. "Women, *Star Trek*, and the Early Development of Fannish Vidding." *Transformative Works and Cultures* 1 (2008).

Fanlore. "Another Sunday." http://fanlore.org/wiki/Another_Sunday (accessed May 1, 2014).

Jenkins, Henry. *Textual Poachers: Television Fans and Participatory Culture*. New York: Routledge, 1992.

———. *Convergence Culture: Where Old and New Media Collide*. New York: New York University Press, 2006.

Marshall, John Paul. *Living on Cybermind: Categories, Communication, and Control*. Vol. 24, New Literacies and Digital Epistemologies. New York: Peter Lang, 2007.

Rheingold, Howard. *The Virtual Community: Homesteading on the Electronic Frontier*. Reading, MA: Addison-Wesley Publishing Co., 1993.

Robins, Kevin. "Cyberspace and the World We Live In." In *The Cybercultures Reader*, edited by David Bell and Barbara M. Kennedy, 77–95. London: Routledge, 2000.

USC School of Cinematic Arts. "Genealogy of Vidding with Francesca Coppa—'24/7 a DIY Video Summit.'" University of Southern California, 2009. YouTube video. http://www.youtube.com/watch?v=aYdllH7jZxg (accessed August 8, 2014).

Williams, Raymond. *Keywords: A Vocabulary of Culture and Society*. Oxford: Oxford University Press, 1976.

21

PEELING THE LAYERS OF THE ONION

Authorship in Mashup and Remix Cultures

John Logie

In this chapter I seek to illustrate the degree to which digital composition strategies—and in particular remix and mashup—dramatically complicate the task of ascribing authorship, and throw into relief the degree to which inherently collaborative compositions (like most recorded music and *all* films) defy ready mapping onto the "author/work" model that typically serves as the default model for the creative process. The author/work model also is foundational in the development of most copyright laws and especially US copyright law, which is rooted in a clause in the US Constitution calling for "securing limited rights" for "authors" in their "writings." All subsequent expansions of US copyright build upon this foundation, even though many contemporary composers of texts—whether written, musical, cinematic, and/or digital—bear little resemblance to the solitary author invoked in this clause.[1]

To underscore the complexities of digitally facilitated mashup and remix composition, my method will be a full accounting of the creative processes that culminate in a fairly straightforward "A vs. B" mashup of two popular songs (or "versus" mashup for short). The "versus" subgenre of mashup typically strips the vocals from one track and lays those vocals over the instrumental bed from a second track. The resulting composition initially seems a work of tripartite authorship, with the composers of song A and song B each retaining authorship for their parts of the mashup, and the mashup artist(s) claiming an overarching layer of authorship (or curatorship, at least) grounded in determining where and how parts of song A and B can be brought into conversation with one another. But a full reckoning of the creative processes involved in the construction of a "versus" mashup—arguably the simplest type of mashup—brings us to a realization that theories of authorship grounded in solitary authors producing written compositions are not able to fully account for the networks of citation, quotation, and influence that lie at the heart of mashup, remix, and associated modes of digital composition.

See Chapter 31 for Gustavo Romano's first-person account of curating an exhibit in which the author/work model is challenged.

The very term "authorship" carries with it a considerable amount of inertia. For most of the last half millennium, questions of authorship were perceived as straightforward. Those wishing to establish or clarify authorship needed merely to locate the acknowledged composer of a given text (or cultural artifact), briefly consider whether that composer was the prime (or, ideally, exclusive) mover in the construction of that text, and then double-check to ensure that the text was "original" enough to merit ascription to that composer. This approach has been especially pronounced from roughly the period of the Romantics up to and through the continental critique of authorship, anchored by Roland Barthes's 1967 artistic manifesto in essay form, "The Death of the Author,"[2] and Michel Foucault's 1969 lecture "What Is an Author?"[3] Taken together Barthes's and Foucault's challenges to authorship-as-usual served to emphasize the roles readers and cultures played in *constructing* both the text and the figure of the author. But, as the title (and core argument) of Seán Burke's 1992 monograph, *The Death and Return of the Author: Criticism and Subjectivity in Barthes, Foucault and Derrida* testifies, Barthes's report of the author's death proved *à la* Twain to be an exaggeration.[4] Even as Barthes and Foucault critiqued the phenomenon of authorship, their alternative models involved similarly weighted figures (Barthes's "reader" and Foucault's "author-function").

The advent of digital composition productively complicated questions of authorship. Even before the widespread adoption of Internet technologies, George Landow (among other scholars) noted "how complex decisions about authorship can be in a hypertext environment."[5] Landow's argument was grounded in a sense that even nonnetworked hypertext writing environments were already offering a substantial realization of less author-centered composing models suggested by continental critique of authorship. Indeed, this quote is drawn from a 1991 monograph titled: *Hypertext: The Convergence of Contemporary Critical Theory and Technology*: "Even though print technology is not entirely or even largely responsible for current attitudes in the humanities toward authorship and collaboration, a shift to hypertext systems would change them by emphasizing elements of collaboration."[6]

Landow was rightly underscoring the degree to which digital media could facilitate collaborative composing strategies that were difficult, if not impossible, in analog composing spaces. But Landow's heavy orientation toward the digital as the key facilitator of these nontraditional modes of composition was grounded in an apparent lack of awareness of the full range of composing strategies already apparent in analog media at the time of his writing. Consider Landow's 1991 discussion of "analogue recording":

> Whereas analogue recording of sound and visual information requires serial, linear processing, digital technology removes the need for sequence by permitting one to go directly to a particular bit of information. Thus if one wishes to find a particular passage in a Bach sonata on a tape cassette, one must scan through the cassette sequentially, though modern tape decks permit one to speed the process by skipping from space to space between sections of music. In contrast, if one wishes to locate a passage in digitally recorded music, one can instantly travel to that passage, note it for future reference, and manipulate it in ways impossible with analogue technologies—for example, one can instantly replay passages without having to scroll back through them.[7]

What Landow does not acknowledge here is that—at the time of his writing—an entire genre of music had, for over a decade, been building compositions through the *alinear* processing of analog information. I am, of course, referring specifically to the first wave of rap and hip hop, and in particular the DJ-centered compositions built around scratching, punch phrasing, breaks, and other remix strategies that can be traced to street parties in the boroughs of New York City in the late 1970s.

Indeed, the creative practices of hip hop DJs largely anticipate the cut-and-paste aesthetics of contemporary digital culture. The goals of "prevent[ing], block[ing], and bypass[ing] linearity and binarity" had certainly been achieved by even early DJs armed with little more than turntables, rudimentary mixers, and well-curated stacks of vinyl records. Compositions like "The Adventures of Grandmaster Flash on the Wheels of Steel"—which was released in 1981—showcase aesthetic strategies centered on the selective disassembly and reassembly of songs. These strategies, when paired with affordable sampling tools, prompted an explosion of compositional creativity with arguably high water marks in the production work of Hank Shocklee and The Bomb Squad on the first three Public Enemy records (1987–90); and The Dust Brothers' and Beastie Boys' production work on the 1989 album *Paul's Boutique*.[8]

But the success (and attendant public awareness) of these works also prompted a shift in the interpretation of United States copyright laws that made similarly sample-rich productions functionally impossible, at least as commercial products. The breaking point was the Judge Kevin Thomas Duffy's December 17, 1991 decision in *Grand Upright vs. Warner* in which rapper Biz Markie's parodic treatment of Gilbert O'Sullivan's "Alone Again (Naturally)" was found so egregiously in violation of copyright as to expose both Biz Markie and his label to potential criminal liability.[9] In this case, Judge Duffy largely confined his investigation to the question of whether O'Sullivan had properly transferred copyright to Grand Upright Music Ltd. Duffy's opinion makes abundantly clear that he understands O'Sullivan's authorship rights—though transferred to Grand Upright—as *absolute*. Duffy's opinion infamously opens with "Thou Shalt Not Steal," carefully footnoted to the Book of Exodus. Duffy describes Gilbert O'Sullivan as "the acknowledged writer of the composition 'Alone Again (Naturally)' and the performer who is featured on the master recording pirated by the defendants" thereby establishing that—for Duffy—the only question on the table in the *Grand Upright* decision is whether the transfer of rights from O'Sullivan to Grand Upright is verifiable (it was). Warner Brothers, arguing on behalf of Biz Markie, chose to focus on this ownership question instead of focusing on Biz Markie's likely right to compose a parody and his possible fair use right to build a composition around a brief sample from a previous song, if the new work was substantially *transformative* in nature. The *Grand Upright* decision ushered in the era of "clearance" in which—at least as far as major labels were concerned—all samples incorporated into new compositions had to be either expressly permitted or licensed by copyright holders. For productions like *Paul's Boutique* in which a typical song was constructed by a dozen or more samples that were woven together in a dynamic creative process, the *Grand Upright* decision was both an administrative and financial death knell. In its wake, copyright owners were free to charge whatever they thought the market would bear, or, more troublingly, simply refuse permission for derivative works altogether.

And so, for the most part, samples have gone underground. To the extent that a segment of a song—however brief—is processed in the wake of *Grand Upright* as an "authored work," all samples are subject to legal and administrative processes that can be expensive, time-consuming, and arbitrary. And yet, because of the ever-broadening reach of digital tools, more and more composers are exploring the possibilities of remix and mashup composing strategies. Most commonly they do so on the fringes of mainstream commercial culture, and without participating in the conventional revenue structures for musical compositions. Indeed, the legacy of the *Grand Upright* decision is occasional licensing fees drawn from the most deep-pocketed composers and labels. It should be noted, though, that while the clause in the US Constitution that serves as the basis for US copyright law suggests that copyright will *"promote the progress of useful arts"* by securing limited monopoly rights for "authors," the *Grand Upright* case is typical in that the litigant is not the "author," but the entity that purchased the rights *from* the author.[10]

While the mashup composing strategies of DJs like Greg Gillis (better known as Girl Talk)—in which dozens and dozens of samples are tweaked, transformed, and interwoven—tend to dominate public perceptions of mashup as a genre, this essay will focus on a superficially simpler mashup titled simply "No Fun/Push It," released in 2002 and attributed to "2 Many DJs." While the records of how all of the contributing works ultimately participating in this mashup were composed are imperfect and patched together (from sometimes contrasting accounts) my hope is that by taking the time to "peel the onion" of this relatively simple mashup composition, we will not only understand each layer more fully, we will arrive at its center with a newfound understanding of the significance of the mashup's collective construction and its implications for understanding twenty-first century digital composing practices.

As its title suggests, this mashup consists of a roughly 50:50 blend of portions of The Stooges' song "No Fun" with portions of Salt-n-Pepa's song "Push It." The mashup was first commercially available as part of a massive "suite" of interwoven mashups on 2 Many DJs' album *As Heard on Radio Soulwax Pt. 2*. At first the track seems fairly straightforward. The aggressive vocals from Salt-n-Pepa are laid over the grinding instrumental bed from the Stooges' track. The balance shifts slightly after a minute, with Iggy Pop's vocal exhortations carefully interwoven with Salt-n-Pepa's rap. That said, the mashup is largely The Stooges' instruments overlaid with Salt-n-Pepa's vocals.

Too often, academic discussions of music and jokes find ways to spoil the fun of the artifact under examination. I'm confident that this particular mashup will withstand my process of analysis in the following pages. This is in no small part due to the power of its constituent songs. The Stooges' foundationally and emblematically proto-punk track composed in 1969 still has the capacity to roar out from speakers and rattle the listener, if played with sufficient volume. 1987's "Push It" teeters on a knife's edge between an aggressively feminist statement on one side, and engagingly forthright smut on the other. Each of these songs arguably deserves an article-length examination, but for the purposes of this chapter, the focus will be limited to the specific modes of composition involved in the songs and the eventual mashup.

"No Fun" is the first track on The Stooges' self-titled debut album. This song, like all of the others on the album, is credited to the four members of the band at that time: Dave Alexander, Ron Asheton, Scott Asheton, and Iggy Stooge (aka Iggy Pop, with both of these as pseudonyms for James Osterberg). The studio recordings on the album stabilized what—in live performance—were almost certainly highly variable presentations with improvised lyrics and relatively free-form musical passages. Iggy Pop describes the band's composing process at the time in the following terms:

Stooges rehearsals never lasted too much more than 20 minutes. During them, I was writing, putting together the riffs and pieces of music so they would add up to songs, finishing words madly before we went to New York [to record the album]. We had four songs ready and we thought that was going to be our album. This was "1969," "I Wanna Be Your Dog," "No Fun" and "Anne." Each of the songs was meant to have a 7 to 15 minute instrumental after the conclusion of the song format. The good news was the song parts were good and the improv was good up to about a minute. The bad news was that after that, we hadn't put the homework into making an improv stand up as a listening experience.[11]

Sonic Youth guitarist Thurston Moore wrote of the original Stooges line-up: "Their music was total high-energy blues with the contemporary freakout of Jimi Hendrix and the free-jazz spirit of John Coltrane."[12] Notably, each of Moore's points of comparison foregrounds improvisation as a creative strategy. So while it is tempting to begin and end the question of the authorship of "No Fun" with the four members of the band, it seems clear that those responsible for wrangling The Stooges in the studio bear some significant responsibility for what listeners hear when they listen to the track as presented on *The Stooges* (Figure 21.1).

Figure 21.1 The Stooges record cover (photo courtesy of the author)

300

The Stooges' debut LP was produced by John Cale, who, in 1969, had just left the Velvet Underground. He was charged with the responsibility of helping to shape the record into a less improvisational and more traditionally verse-and-chorus presentation by Elektra Records label head Jac Holzman, who—according to Pop—said the record "didn't have enough songs." Holzman later intervened in the record directly, having rejected Cale's initial mix. Holzman's mixdown of the tracks is the one that was heard on the initial 1969 release of *The Stooges*.

So, in the case of the song "No Fun" we have—at minimum—six actively contributing creative people (the four Stooges, Cale, and Holzman) all of whom can reasonably claim significant and direct influence over the final sound of the record. While both convention and common sense invite us to place Iggy Pop (as lyricist as well as singer) and The Stooges in the primary position of composers, it is also reasonable to observe that the song might have neither its final shape nor its final sound without the interventions of Cale and Holzman.

The question of accountability for the specifics of Salt-n-Pepa's 1987 "Push It" single is substantially more complicated than that of "No Fun." On the most recent pressings of Salt-n-Pepa's debut album, the songwriting credit for "Push It" is split between Hurby "Luv Bug" Azor, primarily known as Salt-n-Pepa's producer, and Raymond Douglas Davies, better known as Ray Davies, the principal songwriter for the legendary British band The Kinks. Azor is generally recognized as the principal lyricist for the song, though some accounts of the song's construction suggest that the vocalists improvised (or "freestyled") throughout the recording. It is also likely that Azor was the person who made most of the production decisions on "Push It," as this account illustrates:

> James and Azor recorded ["Push It"] in a bathroom, in the house of his friend Fresh Gordon. (They liked the echo the bathroom tiles made.) Azor had written the lyrics, which were fairly mundane. Then Gordon had played a string line on his synthesizer—it was so corny he considered it a joke. But Azor, who has an ear for this sort of thing, cried "Play that!"[13]

The cover for the 12-inch single charmingly summarizes Azor's role in "Push It" as follows: "Hyped up by HURB—the Supa Def Dope Produsa," and indeed he appears to have been the prime mover in the construction and lyrical content of the song (Figure 21.2).

The split writing credit, then, is attributable to a passage in "Push It" wherein the vocalists rap "Boy, you really got me going/You got me so I don't know what I'm doing." These two lines flip the gender of lyrics from The Kinks' 1964 hit "You Really Got Me" and the rhythm of the vocal delivery is rhythmically (but *not* melodically) patterned after The Kinks' song, but The Kinks' familiar power guitar chords are nowhere in the mix. That Davies somehow received this split credit for a brief, adulterated lyric quotation, testifies to the expansiveness of current interpretations of copyright laws. Indeed, Davies was neither present in this creative process nor aware of his now-credited contribution until after the record's release. Nevertheless, he is recognized under US law as a co-composer of "Push It" because of a lyrical borrowing that may have been a spur-of-the-moment improvisation as the track was recorded. But this is by no means the only borrowed element within the Salt-n-Pepa track.

Figure 21.2 "Push It" record cover (photo courtesy of the author)

Interestingly, the initial pressings of "Push It" actually feature *no songwriting credit at all* (Figure 21.3). This is perhaps due to the track's significant reliance on the distinctive "Ahhhh . . . Push It!" intonation that is clearly modeled after a similar vocal turn from a deeply obscure track titled "Keep on Pushin' by the 1970s St. Louis funk and soul band Coalkitchen (and distinct from the similarly named track by The

Figure 21.3 Salt-n-Pepa record (photo courtesy of the author)

Impressions). The "corny" synthesizer line that became the hook for the Salt-n-Pepa track also sounds like a simplified version of the groove from the Coalkitchen track. The 45 rpm single of "Keep on Pushin' lists lead singer Pauli Carman, keyboard player/producer/engineer Michael Day, and guitarist/vocalist Rob Newhouse as the songwriters for the track. In addition to the Coalkitchen borrowings, Salt-n-Pepa's vocal incorporates the distinctive call to "Pick up on this!" from James Brown's "Greedy Man" (cocredited to Brown and Charles Bobbitt, Brown's longtime road manager); an "Ow! There it is!" from James Brown's "There It Is" (credited to Brown and saxophonist St. Clair Pinckney) and a lengthy invitation for "Just the sexy people" to start dancing, modeled after a section of The Time's "The Bird," a song formally credited to Jamie Starr (a pseudonym for Prince), Time lead singer Morris Day, and Time guitarist Jesse Johnson.

All of this said, lyrically there isn't much to "Push It." Like The Kinks' "You Really Got Me" before it, "Push It" succeeds due to the combination of the emotive force and attitude of the singers' delivery and the power of the song's instrumental hooks.

Interestingly, the core beats in the hit version of the song are not attributable to Azor, but to the remixing skills of San Francisco DJ and producer, Cameron Paul, who heard the original version of "Push It" in the context of his work as a club DJ and went to work:

I brought it into my studio and I started playing around with it . . . I started playing with my keyboards and I . . . I just wanted to do a remix for my remix record label (Nikfit). And I started playing around with the bassline . . . and then I started playing around with a melody line on another keyboard on my Emax I think it was, and some sampling . . . you know stuff like that. And I just . . . I did it, I overlaid all these tracks and mixed it down . . . and I did a radio edit for KMU . . . So they added that version to their playlist and the record label is going "What is going on?" They didn't even know "Push It" existed practically, the record label and now all of a sudden they're hearing all of this stuff from the Bay Area about "Push It" and so the program director told them they were playing my remix, so they contacted me, the record label contacted me and they asked if they could buy my remix and I said "yes" and they released it on 12-inch on the album, and that was the version that they did the video to, and, y'know, that's what happened. It ended up going platinum. I got a platinum record out of it.[14]

So, in multiple ways, "Push It" is a work of *distributed* collaborative composition, with many of the co-composers (Davies and Paul in particular) being both geographically and personally distant from Azor, Fresh Gordon, Salt, and Pepa when they recorded the vocal and keyboard elements of the song.

Nevertheless, US copyright law effectively encourages us to seek out composers whose contributions can be roughly mapped onto the author/work model. And in the case of "Push It," there are at least 14 co-composers who contributed at least as much as (and in several cases *much*, much more than) credited "cowriter" Ray Davies: Azor and Gordon; the three Coalkitchen cowriters; James Brown and his cowriters (Charles Bobbitt, and St. Clair Pinkney); The Time's team of Starr, Day, and Johnson; DJ Cameron Paul, and, of course, Salt and Pepa (neither of the two women who have been known professionally as DJ Spinderella contributed to the composition). In the counts included above, we are limiting the scope of participation to lyricists, vocalists, credited composer/musicians, producers, mixers, and remixers. For "No Fun" and "Push It" combined, the available records point to at least 21 hands-on participants, triple the number of group members (seven: the four Stooges, Salt, Pepa, and the second DJ Spinderella) on the record covers for the albums housing the two songs. Notable in the descriptions of the creative processes of both songs is a general acknowledgment that improvisation and spur-of-the-moment decisions played a large part in the eventual shape of each track's sound. And in the case of "Push It" the network of contributors and sites of production stretches from: IBC Studios in London in 1964; through Nashville, Tennessee in 1971 (the site of Starday-King Studios used by James Brown); to "Sunday Studios" (likely in the US Midwest where Coalkitchen recorded); up to First Avenue in downtown Minneapolis, Minnesota (where The Time recorded a live version of "The Bird"); to Fresh Gordon's house in Brooklyn, New York City; and finally to Cameron Paul's San Francisco studio in 1987.

The 2002 2 Many DJs' mashup of "No Fun" and "Push It" finds Stephen and David Dewaele in their studio in Ghent, Belgium selectively blending the by-products of the "Push It" and "No Fun" networks with one another, bringing the aggregated total of identifiable composers for their mashup to 23, and resulting in a musical composition that has—if all of its compositional elements and sites of production are taken into account—literally crossed the Atlantic *twice*.

The effect of the "No Fun/Push It" mashup depends entirely on the listener's familiarity with both songs and, to a degree, with the cultural contexts that produced both songs.

Without putting too fine a point on it, the disaffected Dionysian stance that Iggy manifested in 1969 was a clear response to the apparent broken promises of the Summer of Love. Salt-n-Pepa were pioneers in rap, being the first all-female group to have chart success (in 1987) in what was an almost exclusively male-dominated genre. The two acts come from distinct cultural moments and distinct subcultures, and neither group was initially welcome on mainstream commercial radio. But despite the deck being stacked against this occurrence, each act found its way to a substantial number of listeners' ears.

The Dewaele Brothers' composition leverages their intended audiences' familiarity with both songs. Indeed, the mashup's effect hinges on the implicit challenge that the Dewaele Brothers have accepted. Because the default perception of The Stooges and Salt-n-Pepa at the time was that they hailed from fairly polarized spaced on the spectrum of musical possibilities, the mashup is and should be understood as—among other things—a political statement. The Dewaele Brothers' composition invites listeners to understand The Stooges and Salt-n-Pepa in terms of one another. Indeed, the Dewaele Brothers' near-seamless integration of the two songs calls into question the then-commonplace compartmentalization of the songs according to race, gender, genre, or some combination of all three.

Nevertheless, in a 2011 interview, Stephen Dewaele downplays this aspect of the composition:

> Interviewer: Your popularity went through the roof after your mixtape *As Heard on Radio Soulwax Pt. 2.* It mashed up things that nobody had thought of putting together before, from Salt 'N' Pepa's "Push It" to Stooges' "No Fun," and Destiny's Child's "Independent Woman" over 10cc's "Dreadlock Holiday" to Dolly Parton's "Nine to Five." Are you proud of that?
>
> Dewaele: I don't look at it like that. I'm not proud that we managed to bring together such different styles. That's not what we're about. We like the attitude of the music most of all. I think in our heads there's no difference between a really old Chicago house track and hardcore punk—they have the same fuck you in the music. That's the reason why we'll mash something.[15]

But this account of the team's process is at odds with some of the choices the team has made elsewhere. There really is precious little (if any) "fuck you" to be had in 10cc's sappy "Dreadlock Holiday" so there was clearly some other reason for the team mashing it with Destiny's Child.

Neil Strauss's 2002 *New York Times* article, which introduced mashups to the *Times*' readership, found David Dewaele articulating a different rationale:

> From the opening track of their album, there is a distinct style and aesthetic at work. Often, the songs are cut up by computer, so that an introduction can be shortened, a verse removed or a section repeated to maintain the set's fast pace. "It has to be something that has some sort of edge to it, something weird that makes you go, 'What is this!'" said David Dewaele.[16]

Whatever their ultimate motivation, the Dewaele Brothers' expert blending of "No Fun" and "Push It" results in an artifact that does not (and indeed *cannot*) travel through culture with the traditional trappings of authorship. For starters, the Dewaele Brothers'

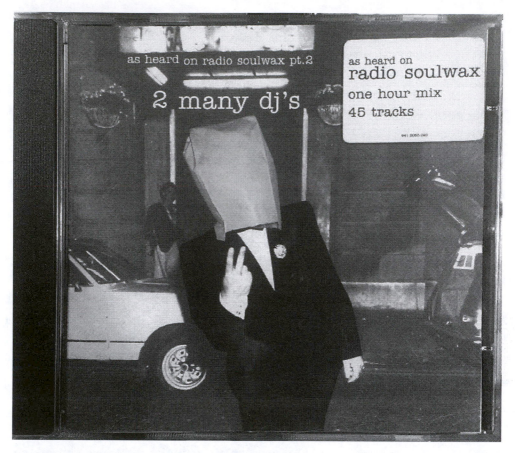

Figure 21.4 2 Many DJ's album cover (photo courtesy of the author)

aggregation of pseudonyms speaks to their refusal to fully occupy the position of "author" with respect to their mashup compositions. While initially known professionally as The Fucking Dewaele Brothers (or Flying Dewaele Brothers for politer company) the Dewaele name is nowhere to be found on the CD containing this mashup (Figure 21.4). Rather, it is credited to 2 Many DJs and, confusingly, titled *As Heard on Radio Soulwax Pt. 2* with the Dewaeles' names never listed.

The mashups on *As Heard on Radio Soulwax Pt. 2* are unusual for the mashup genre, in that they were painstakingly licensed and cleared:

> It's been almost three years in the making. It took one record company employee more than six months of hard labour, 865 e-mails, 160 faxes and hundreds of phone calls to contact over 45 major and independent record companies, a total amount of 187 different tracks were involved from which 114 got approved, 62 refused and 11 were un-trackable. It caused massive headaches and sweaty palms to employees of "clearance centers" and record companies all over the world. But it's finally here. It's about 62 minutes long and there's 45 (or is that 46?) tracks on it. It took seven long days and nights to cut, edit, mix and re-edit it all together and it fucking rocks![17]

Because of this painstaking process, *As Heard on Radio Soulwax Pt. 2* was legally released in Europe, but not in the United States, where permissions issues proved intractable. Indeed, in the wake of the *Grand Upright* decision, the Dewaele Brothers were arguably wise to conceal their roles as composers of the album, to create at least a mild roadblock for United States-based litigants pursuing copyright claims. As with many other mashup compositions, the Dewaele Brothers' work cannot circulate commercially in the United States. Were they to attempt to sell their album—wherein the "No Fun/Push It" mashup is only one of 45 songs, each of which likely has its own set of 21 (or so) composers with a potential copyright claim, the Dewaele Brothers would be potentially exposing themselves to a continuing series of micro-reenactments of the interminable Jarndyce case at the heart of Charles Dickens's *Bleak House*.[18]

Even the most basic mashup speaks to the complexities of composition in networked digital spaces. Whether authorized or not, twenty-first century networked digital composers have levels of access to extant works that greatly exceed those of all previous generations combined, with copyright laws being the only significant barrier to the use and appropriation of these works. Further, digital tools readily facilitate the disassembly and reassembly of these works. Contemporary composers and curators also have substantial opportunities to consider extant works *in part* as well as *in toto*. Opportunities to isolate sections of a given text, artifact, or composition—whether present in the original presentation or not—offer contemporary composers a wide array of opportunities to reexamine, reconsider, and recontextualize those works.

Contemporary musical compositions routinely arrive as the by-products of complex networks of distributed authorship. While practices of remix, mashup, and recomposition have gained increasing traction in popular culture (examples include the so-called "mashups" performed on the TV program *Glee*, and Anna Kendrick's portrayal of a remix/mashup DJ in the film *Pitch Perfect*) the same studios that circulate these (licensed) mashups are exercising profound influence over how and whether others might play with their "intellectual property." Over the past two decades, the Recording Industry Association of America (RIAA) and the Motion Picture Association of America (MPAA) have relentlessly lobbied the United States Congress to pass laws (many of them overly drawn) that reinscribe the notion of the author as *owner* of a given work. This makes business sense. These industries depend upon the opportunity to cleanly and efficiently purchase copyrights from composers. But as a practical matter, these organizations represent the companies whose core artifacts—recorded music and motion pictures—are among the *least* amenable to being understood as the products of anything resembling the traditional author/work composing model. They are, rather, the by-products of layered collaboration. Indeed, as the above-cited examples illustrate, it takes many hands to compose and produce even a stripped down punk anthem. It takes *many* more to produce a representative hip hop track. And when these kinds of tracks become participants in larger remix projects, the process of sorting out authorship and ownership becomes maddeningly complex.

Mashup and remix compositions are grounded in a notion of play with respect to the concept of authorship. These compositions celebrate curation, connection, collaboration, and critique (whether conscious or not). As such, they are at odds with US copyright law's foundational organization around an author/work model that has been the subject of continuous theoretical challenges since at least Barthes's 1967 essay positing "The Death of the Author." But the Barthesian move of supplanting the author with the reader is inadequate to the task of understanding the dynamic layers of collaboration, connection, curation, and criticism that produce compositions like the "No Fun/Push It" mashup. Indeed, mashups like these make evident the degree to which authorship and ownership have been intermingled both conceptually and in laws addressing creativity. There is clearly too little cultural space for those who wish to occupy the role of composer/curator/critic—and not (at least primarily) "originator."

Foucault's closing suggestion that we might rediscover a time when texts could circulate "in the anonymity of a murmur"[19] pulls us closer to the practical reality of contemporary mashup cultures in which authorship is often both convoluted and suppressed. The first of these qualities is due to the very nature of the composing tasks involved. The second, by contrast, is likely a response to current law. In the absence of a copyright regime that requires authors not only for the purposes of streamlined sales of compositions, but also for purposes of legal accountability, most mashup composers have opted out of both composition and credit, allowing pseudonyms to stand in for their names. Mashup composers are, in our current legal landscape, often *strategically anonymous*, but we can easily envision revisions to laws addressing creativity that would open up spaces for the overtly dependent creativity of mashup and remix artists. The problem is ultimately not one of credit so much as it is one of compensation. And those questions are, by contrast, maddeningly complex, and further complicated by existing infrastructures for the purchase and compensation of creative work that have—at best—a mixed record with respect to adequately rewarding composers for their work.

While scholars and theorists have been building toward nuanced understandings of these complex modes of composition for decades, when US law is presented with a work like the "No Fun/Push It" mashup, its response is to ask first, "Who wrote this?" and then, failing that, to ask, "Who are the composers who most resemble authors?" This search for authorship is—in effect—an attempt to assign legal ownership as expeditiously as possible. This is needed for commerce even when it is not needed by the composers or the cultures they are addressing. And because *any* of the many legal "authors" who contributed to a mashup (or their heirs, or the purchasers of their copyrights) might be ceded not only credit and compensation, but also *control* over the circulation of the mashup (including, potentially, the right to suppress it altogether) current United States law actively discourages mashup and remix modes of composition. And that, among other things, is *no fun*.

Notes

1 U.S. Copyright Office "Copyright Law: Preface." *Copyright Law of the United States of America*, http://www.copyright.gov/title17/92preface.html.
2 Roland Barthes, "The Death of the Author." *Aspen* 5/6, art. 3 (1967), http://www.ubu.com/aspen/aspen-5and6/threeEssays.html#barthes.
3 Michel Foucault, "What Is an Author?" In *Language, Counter-Memory, Practice*, ed. Donald F. Bouchard (Ithaca, NY: Cornell University Press, 1977), 124–127.
4 Séan Burke, *The Death and Return of the Author: Criticism and Subjectivity in Barthes, Foucault and Derrida* (Edinburgh: Edinburgh University Press, 1992).
5 George P. Landow, *Hypertext: The Convergence of Contemporary Critical Theory and Technology* (Baltimore, MD: Johns Hopkins University Press, 1992), 98.
6 Ibid., 94.
7 Ibid., 21.
8 *Paul's Boutique*, Beastie Boys album, published July 25, 1989 by Capital Records.
9 *Grand Upright v. Warner*, 780 F. Supp. 182 (SDNY 1991).
10 U.S. Copyright Office "Copyright Law: Preface."

11 Jaan Uhelszki, "Iggy Pop—Album By Album." *Uncut*, http://www.uncut.co.uk/iggy-pop/iggy-pop-album-by-album-feature#wDVKDfEwtoUf7t58.99.

12 Thurston Moore, "100 Greatest Artists: 78, The Stooges," *RollingStone.com*, http://www.rollingstone.com/music/lists/100-greatest-artists-of-all-time-19691231/the-stooges-20110420.

13 Dinitia Smith, "Straight Outta Queens: How Salt-N-Pepa Turned Rap on Its Head," *New York*, January 17, 1994. Google Books.

14 Jarrell Mason, "Cameron Paul Interview—Part 2," YouTube, May 27, 2007, http://www.youtube.com/watch?v=C0a00PXuZ3A.

15 "'All We Are Doing Is Playing Other People's Records': 2 Many DJs Interview," *Skiddle.com*, December 20, 2011, http://www.skiddle.com/news/all/All-we-are-doing-is-playing-other-peoples-records-2manyDJs-Interview/11042/.

16 Neil Strauss, "Spreading by the Web, Pop's Bootleg Remix," *The New York Times*, May 9, 2002, http://www.nytimes.com/2002/05/09/business/spreading-by-the-web-pop-s-bootleg-remix.html?pagewanted=all&src=pm.

17 Kevinen Joyce, "*As Heard on Radio Soulwax Pt 2*," kevinenjoyce.com, September 13, 2013, http://www.kevinenjoyce.com/soulwax/disco.php?idgr=47Gr2ac961017.

18 The characters in *Bleak House* anxiously await the resolution of an estate case involving multiple conflicting wills. As the novel concludes, the entire estate has been consumed by legal fees. The novel is thought to be—at least in part—a roman à clef, based on Dickens' own experiences as a litigant attempting to pursue enforcement of his copyrights.

19 Foucault, "What Is an Author?" 127.

Bibliography

'All We Are Doing Is Playing Other People's Records': 2 Many DJs Interview." *Skiddle.com*, December 20, 2011. http://www.skiddle.com/news/all/All-we-are-doing-is-playing-other-peoples-records-2manyDJs-Interview/11042/ (accessed August 11, 2014).

Barthes, Roland. "The Death of the Author." *Aspen* 5/6, art. 3 1967. http://www.ubu.com/aspen/aspen5and6/threeEssays.html#barthes (accessed August 11, 2014).

Burke, Seán. *The Death and Return of the Author: Criticism and Subjectivity in Barthes, Foucault and Derrida*. Edinburgh: Edinburgh University Press, 1992.

Foucault, Michel. "What Is an Author?" In *Language, Counter-Memory, Practice*, edited by Donald F. Bouchard, 124–127. Ithaca, NY: Cornell University Press, 1977.

Grand Upright v. Warner, 780 F. Supp. 182 (SDNY 1991).

Joyce, Kevinen. "As Heard on Radio Soulwax Pt 2." kevinenjoyce.com, http://www.kevinenjoyce.com/soulwax/disco.php?idgr=47Gr2ac961017 (accessed August 11, 2014).

Landow, George P. *Hypertext: The Convergence of Contemporary Critical Theory and Technology*. Baltimore, MD: Johns Hopkins University Press, 1992, 98.

Mason, Jarrell. "Cameron Paul Interview—Part 2." YouTube, May 27, 2007. YouTube video. http://www.youtube.com/watch?v=C0a00PXuZ3A (accessed August 11, 2014).

Moore, Thurston. "100 Greatest Artists: 78, The Stooges." *RollingStone.com*. http://www.rollingstone.com/music/lists/100-greatest-artists-of-all-time-19691231/the-stooges-20110420 (accessed November 5, 2013).

Smith, Dinitia. "Straight Outta Queens: How Salt-N-Pepa Turned Rap on Its Head." *New York*, January 17, 1994. http://books.google.com/books?id=xbcBAAAAMBAJ&pg=PA32&dq=Straight+Outta+Queens:+How+Salt-N-Pepa+Turned+Rap+on+Its+Head.%E2%80%9D&hl=en&sa=X&ei=QgtOU9XXA7DfsASHlYBI&ved=0CC0Q6AEwAA#v=onepage&q&f=false (accessed August 11, 2014).

Strauss, Neil. "Spreading by the Web, Pop's Bootleg Remix." *The New York Times*, May 9, 2002. http://www.nytimes.com/2002/05/09/business/spreading-by-the-web-pop-s-bootleg-remix.html?pagewanted=all&src=pm (accessed August 11, 2014).

Uhelszki, Jaan. "Iggy Pop—Album By Album." *Uncut*. May, 2013. http://www.uncut.co.uk/iggy-pop/iggy-pop-album-by-album-feature#wDVKDfEwtoUf7t58.99 (accessed S).

U.S. Copyright Office. "Copyright Law: Preface." *Copyright Law of the United States of America*. http://www.copyright.gov/title17/92preface.html (accessed August 11, 2014).

22
REMIXTHECONTEXT (A THEORETICAL FICTION)

Mark Amerika

At the Café Merz, an assemblage of software copyleftists, ostracized academics, para-professional adjunct curators, #NewAesthetic glitch artists, media archaeologists, digital humanities grad students, creative commoners, and Facebook *flâneurs* are congregating at a long table drinking cups of fresh Bella Aurora Nicaraguan coffee roasted by the pros over at Coava Coffee Roasters where sourcing single origin coffee is definitely part of the eco-ethical mix . . .

—What are you working on? (asks Saul, a colleague from the English department).

—I'm writing an essay for a new collection of academic essays on remix culture.

—Really? Are remix and academia even compatible terms in the same sentence?

—Sure, how do you think I got promoted to full?

—By being a remix artist?

—Sort of. Maybe it's because I figured out how to mashup my creative skills as a professor of remixology with my practical skills as a context provider. I mean, how many times can you remix the same thing over and over again while staying true to Ezra Pound's dictum to always "make it new"? My strategy has always been to remix the context, right? Remixing the context is remixing me, Mark Amerika, as a kind of *thoughtographical* font that I transmit through different media formats. Different scenes of writing.

—For example?

—Well, there was this one cool online journal that wanted an essay from me on remix, appropriation, copyright/copyleft, and literary cut-ups.

—Peer-reviewed?

—Absolutely, but that's not why I did it. I don't care about the brownie points.

—*Really?*

—Yeah, because if you focus on the brownie points then you have always already sold out to an outmoded reward system that tends to mostly benefit the academic publishing mafia that exploits the networked intelligentsia by transferring their well-wrought intellectual labor into the publisher's own intellectual property.

—What do you mean?

—I mean you spend months researching and writing your essays and, if you're "lucky" enough to get it accepted for publication with a reputable academic press, then most of them will send you contracts that are clearly situating you, the artist, the scholarly writer, the applied remixologist—whatever role you take on—as a kind of work-for-hire knowledge worker-drone.

—You mean they take your copyright?

—Pretty much that's the case a lot of the time now. But they act like they're seriously doing you a favor—and they even promise you one whole copy of the book or journal your work will appear in. Plus, if you treat them nicely, they'll let you publish that piece you wrote—but that they now own—in your own collection.

—But you're, like, Professor Remix, right? Your blog is even titled *Professor VJ*! You are always taking source material and manipulating it into an experiential and contextual field of *différance*. And you tend to distribute it for free over the Internet, no? This giving away of your copyright to the academic publishing mafia goes against everything your practice-based research is focused on.

—Of course, and this is what I was getting at. Not only do I usually distribute it for free over the Net, "it" is always a remix of prior works—both mine and other things that I happen to be sampling from at any given moment in time. It's kind of how my brain works. Vannevar Bush, the physicist who founded the MIT Media Lab, wrote an essay in 1945 called "As We May Think," where he makes the case that we all think associatively and that our practice-based research is all about thinking as linking. He writes about the need to invent technology that makes this linking easier and suggests that once that source material—he calls it data—becomes more available through advanced networked and mobile media communication systems, we will create a networked intelligentsia capable of manipulating all of this data for our own research purposes without the need for profiteering middlemen. Of course, today we just think of that remixological thought process as a kind of hypertextual consciousness. Welcome to the World Wide Web.

—So, really, what you're saying is that most contemporary thinking is being transmitted via a larger networked intelligentsia that is constantly remixing different iterations of contemporary thought. Maybe it's something like cite-specific versioning.

—Yes, and if Ted Nelson, the computer scientist who invented the term and ideas behind *hypertext* had had his way, we would also be able to virtually republish bits and pieces of writing from all around the Web however we choose to collage them into our own version. He saw us doing this the same way we can virtually republish a GIF or JPEG by plugging its image source location into the HTML code. So, yes, it's a bit different given the networked media apparatus we have at our disposal right now, but basically you can create cite-specific versions of your own thinking by linking to the different work that you remix over time. Case in point: that essay-article I was referring to just a moment ago. I wrote it for *Media-N: Journal for the New Media Caucus* and the opening scene of that story took place in a café very similar to the one we're in right now.

—Cool. You call it a story. So if I understand your position on this, you see this larger networked intelligentsia as a kind of public domain narrative environment for the various social media performance artists to remix their personae in, yes? The idea is to easily cut and paste one's shifting new media presence into different scenes of writing, right? I get it. So for this *Media-N* story, what happened in *that* café?

—Well, it had a few of my students in it, talking about my remix culture course.

—I was in it. (One of the students that's been listening to this dialog pipes up.)

—Yeah, Pink was in it. What were you talking about? Do you remember?

311

—Yeah, I was saying how in your course we have to write weekly blog assignments that respond to the readings but that also remixologically inhabit the styles, the voices, the structural rhythms, and the syntactical media agenda of the artists we bring into the mix, and that basically what we're being graded on is how well we perform our roles as parasites.

—And that's not all. Every grad student who works with me has to exhibit or otherwise perform their practice-based research outcomes in a public context. My goal is to get them to participate in the local visual, literary, and performance arts communities. They are also required to collaboratively and collectively publish notes on their creative work and research process in an online format as well as contribute to email lists that stimulate dialog around all of these subjects we're covering.

—Like what?

—Well, copyleft versus copyright for one.

—What's your take on that?

—In my heart of hearts, I'm against intellectual property. Having said that, I'm even more against someone owning my intellectual property and not paying for it. Like the academic publishing mafia who try to leverage the fact that tenure-track and would-be/wannabe professors need to publish with established presses and use that brownie point system to club them into submission until they agree to hand over all or most of the rights to their work! They really do act as if they are The Untouchables.

—As if the Internet never really happened.

—Exactly. My first collection of artist writings was over 400 pages and most of the writing was previously published on the Internet where it was given away for free. I intentionally wanted to situate the work in what we think of as the gift economy. But MIT Press, the publisher, now owns the copyright to all of that material. Fortunately, for the avid information hunter and gatherer, almost all of that work is still available on the Net for free.

—Still, it must be weird to give the rights away.

—Totally out of character, really. It's like, as Ken Wark says, a vast social movement has arisen that intuits the significance of digital information as a social fact, right? And in its more public and self-conscious forms, this social movement includes Creative Commons, the Open Source and Free Software Movement, the student Free Culture movement, etc. But this is just the tip of the iceberg. Submerged out of sight is a vast culture of freewheeling digital remixologists who, without even really thinking about the implications of what they are doing, are participating in what you might tag *digitally distributed transgressive shareability* (to rephrase a line from the artist-theorist Bracha Ettinger). Like me, Wark also came up against similar issues with the publication of his *Hacker Manifesto* with Harvard University Press. He too saw how this private, pervasive new economy—a gift economy in which the artifact is nothing and its digital information everything—might be an even more significant part of this social movement than its more publicly declared aspects. Meanwhile, there are these death-defying corporate interests that use the institutionalized academic marketplace as their territory, right? It's like, what else can we own as a way to further control the flow of information through these outmoded supply chains.

—Right. So you do all the research, all the writing, all the branding, all the networking, all the clever social media marketing by way of your online presence as a kind of pop-intellectual performance artist establishing presence in the reputation economy—and then they come in at the end and swoop up your data and demand that you let them own it so that they can control its flow in perpetuity.

—Something like that, yes. Not all of them are this way. My last publisher was a pleasure to work with and MIT, it should be said, have a great reputation and have essentially taken responsibility for keeping the work archived in print and digital libraries where some of your audience is bound to find it. But at what point does this process produce overreach? At what point is it not in the academic or artist's best interest to participate in this proprietary overkill?

—I think that's totally relevant (Saul says—he seems stimulated by the source material). Lately, I've been wondering, why would I, as a so-called digital humanist who is focused on media archaeology, spend all of my productive work time writing books— books that most, but not all of the reputable academic publishers want to own for their own profit? So I can then get promoted to Super-Full Professor? Extra-Special Beyond Belief Professor? What's the incentive here?

—Sure, that's easy for you to say (says usually silent Tex-Mex, the MFA bodybuilder). What about those of us who are hungry for jobs? Everybody has to play the game.

—That's true, and so now Saul and I have to try and change the way the game is played. It's up to me and the other fully full-of-themselves full professors to start making a stink over this process. The system is too gamed. I mean, I am interested in game culture, game theory, game studies—but is this ancient model of tenure and promotion that's so codependent on "publish or perish" really the only way? This is why I am looking at practice-based research outcomes—exhibitions, performances, software creation, transmedia publications, and the like, as one possible alternative. I guess if I can get those kinds of outcomes to count as legit criteria for evaluation, *get it in writing* as part of the institutional bylaws, then that will be part of my legacy too.

—How else do you plan on changing the game?

—Through incremental steps, like the way I'm intentionally sampling and remixing prior published writing into this dialog, here, in Café Merz, for the purpose of questioning how much I can playfully appropriate myself, claim the work to be "original," and to mix up the issue of what it means to own copyright to something that is really just shop talk. What if I were to cut and paste large chunks of this text into an e-book that I self-publish as part of an exhibition of my conceptual art work whose theme is the slow death of reputable print publishers? Or what if someone else were to take my idea and do the same, but in a completely different language? As far as I'm concerned, anyone can sample any of the language being performed in this remix and manipulate it for their own transmedia purposes. Hell, I'm doing it too.

—So basically what you're saying is that your ongoing practice-based research into networked and mobile media forms of creativity is partly about the act of remixing yourself and nobody can own that, not even you?

—Sure, you could say that. Raymond Federman referred to it is as *playgiarism*. Get it? Play+giarism.

—It sounds familiar. Where would I have heard of that before?

—You probably read it in one of my books or at my remixthebook.com website. I use Federman a lot. Basically, for Federman, *playgiarism* refers to the intentional, conceptual, and playful reuse of existing source material. In Federman's own use of playgiarism, he specifically remixes the different versions of his own personal narrative that he rewrites in book form over and over again. He terms this creative method playgiarism writing that it should be viewed as a *playful self-appropriation*. Federman tells us that we are either born a playgiarizer or we are not. It's as simple as that. He says that the laws of playgiarism are unwritten, that it's a *taboo* and that like incest, it cannot be legalized. The great playgiarizers of all time, Homer, Shakespeare, Rabelais, Diderot, Rimbaud, Proust, Beckett, and Federman have never pretended to do anything else than playgiarizing. Inferior writers deny that they playgiarize because they confuse plagiarism with playgiarism. These are not the same. The difference is enormous, but no one has ever been able to articulate it as well as I'd like.

—Well, I like that it's unapologetic.

—It must be. We must be, or else we lose the game. This is why we must, out of necessity, make fun of what playgiarism does while doing it ourselves. To playgiarize is to perform with and/or playfully manipulate existing source material (thus the playful use of the letter "y" as in "play").

—You wrote about playgiarism in that other essay you recently published, although it was in a more cryptic, fictional style. What were you saying again? About how your Professor VJ persona is developing some kind of new audiovisual program for his live multimedia writing performances?

—Yes, you remember! Do you want to come to my studio and check out this new patch I've just developed?

—You mean for that software program you've been poking away at? What's it called again? Oh, wait, it's *The Playgiarizer*?

—Exactly.

—Sure. Now I know why we're on this subject again. Let's just cut and paste ourselves into that prior scene and see how this new context creates a measurable *différance*.
[CUT]
[PASTE]

—So you're really going to do this? Go back on the road this summer and perform as the writerly VJ?

—Yep, my nom de plume will be The Playgiarist.

—The Playgiarist who plays the Playgiarizer.

—Something like that.

—So tell me how it works.

—Actually, I can just show you. What I've done is I've mashed up voice recognition software with this typographic glitch randomizer. Here I'll speak into the mic and you watch what happens to the words on the screen as I speak, OK?

—Cool.

—OK, watch the screen.

—Got it.

—Every decision a person makes stems from the person's values and goals.

—That's cool. The screen looks like typographic rain.

—Nice description. Here's another line I plan on reading in my live set: Software to be written vs. codes to be corrupted vs. publishing protocols to be cracked open vs. systems to be hacked.

—Wow, that looks great. Radical typographimania.

—Yeah, now watch this: Programs that look at you vs. programs that read you vs. programs that write you vs. programs that seduce you into touching them back.

—Huh. I've never seen anything like that before. I'm not even sure how you could visualize that in a book.

—Here's another one: Programs that are living vs. programs that are dead vs. crunching numbers vs. drowning in a vat of involuntary secretions.

—Did you see that glitch? Do it again.

—Programs that stimulate a body's thought process vs. programs that bring you to a creative climax vs. the programmatic stealing of an entire historical era's intellectual labor.

—That was weird.

—The disappearing unified subject vs. personae as shareware vs. a textually inhabited series of social media art performances under duress.

—Did you see that?! It was as if James Joyce himself had invented augmented reality.

—Biting the hand that feeds you vs. eating the entire arm attached to the hand that feeds you vs. opening your mouth so wide you eat yourself vs. excreting yourself on the page that authorizes your presence.

—Your presence *in academia*, no doubt. Can I try it?

—Sure.

—Programs that read your mind vs. programs that undress you vs. programs that undress yourself vs. programs that just rip their codes off.

—Again.

—Programs that produce counterfeit paracurrencies vs. programs that show disdain for human authenticity vs. programs that leak aesthetic information vs. programs that have no taste.

—One more.

—Programs that run in auto-affect mode vs. programs that transform the networked intelligentsia into a monopolized niche market vs. programs that auto-shift reality and trigger novelty.

Professor VJ bid his colleague adieu and rushed upstairs where one quick administrative detail required his attention, and then he went back down into the basement lab where his digital seminar room was squeezed with grad students awaiting him.

—OK, I want to start the session by throwing out some quotes and random phrasings as more open source just to see what we can do with them today. Take your thinking caps off and rev up your remixological engines. Let's just go straight to the unconscious readiness potential that keeps the creative spirit alive and role-play our intersubjective agency as ancient remixologists dressed in the latest technological fashion, OK? This is what it means to be present, right? Or maybe you feel like a ghost today? Do you guys know who once wrote that "a guest + a host = a ghost?"

—Duchamp.

—Yeah, great, exactly, how did you know?

—You told us last week.

—Oh, did I? Maybe I'm my own ghost remixologically inhabiting the spirit of my presence from last week?

—A new refutation of time.

—Who wrote this? "If it's true that we're all born remixers who unconsciously manipulate the data of everyday life as part of our ongoing social media or performance art practice—and I think we are—then remixology is the study of how we do that and the ways we turn this daily, even ritualized remix practice into emergent forms of personal expression."

—You did.

—Correct.

—Thank you for cutting and pasting it into the seminar scene too.

—You're very welcome. The idea, of course, is to get us to start thinking about some of the context this language of remix theory manifests itself in. It's not necessarily something you will encounter at a live audiovisual performance, right?

—Unless it's your performance.

—Correct again. But let's introduce the concept of transmedia narrative as well.

—Can you explain what that term really means?

—Well, meaning is subject to remix just like everything else, so perhaps we should ask ourselves what is transmedia narrative in the Wikipedia sense of the term, and what value does it have for contemporary artists? The traditional art and entertainment industries would have us believe that transmedia is a powerful marketing concept that uses new media technologies to aggregate fragmented audiences by delivering story information across multiple media platforms. But as a remix artist who is investigating these "ways of filtering"—and here I am remixing Jon Berger's idea of "ways of seeing"—and who experiments with his conceptual language art practice in the fields of digital distribution as well as in relation to social media performance, I am hoping to—if you will—reclaim the term "transmedia narrative" for my own uses as I try to imagine how fragmented stories being told by amateur-auteurs resist what the commercially minded academics call "convergence." In fact, the idea of convergence doesn't really match up well when discussed in relation to audience or even story fragmentation. It's part of a very old-fashioned modernist agenda that gets theorized by industry-friendly academics where we are asked to buy into the idea that everything will magically come together in this technologically sophisticated utopia. To me, this seems so anachronistic given how distributed and personalized social media networking feels to me (think Hakim Bey's *Temporary Autonomous Zones*) especially in these times of faux prosperity and real-world, dystopian financial ruin. It is my hope that new media artists, many of whom identify with the historical avant-garde, can now expand the forms of transmedia narrative to foreground this *antidisciplinary* approach to encompass both contemporary practice and theory.

—Can you remind us what you mean by "antidisciplinary"?

—Sure. What does it take for networked scenes of artists who employ strategic remix methodologies to produce—or, in my version, *perpetually postproduce*—novel forms of togetherness? How would we want to start measuring the value of the aesthetic traces remix artists leave while proactively navigating our practices through these antidisciplinary spaces we happen to *occupy-when-making*. The terms are intentionally loaded—"antidisciplinary" suggesting a mashup of antiauthoritarian and interdisciplinary—and the idea of "occupying" as remixologically inhabiting—something absolutely connected to the global occupy performances that were initially started by the magazine collective associated with *Adbusters*, a culture jamming remix crew if ever there was one.

—Is your artwork, *Immobilité* a transmedia narrative?

—You're about two steps ahead of me. But, yes, let's talk about *Immobilité* as a quick case study. You guys know where to find that, right? It's at immobilite.com. OK, so in the US, we call films from other countries "foreign films." Now, when I was a teenager, watching foreign films, which none of my friends wanted to do, changed who I was. It turned me on to this alternative way of processing narrative. First of all, since I only spoke English, I had to *read* the films every step of the way. This means that my favorite films, the ones that changed my life, are always films that I have had to read. But by reading, I am operating on many different conscious, subconscious and/or unconscious levels, because I am also seeing and listening and even moving, too. I'm filtering. For me, movies, or motion pictures, have always been about moving, the art of riding with or *on* someone else's rhythm, and learning to process those rhythms and layer them or remix them into my own ever-shifting rhythms. In *remixthebook*, I refer to this process of embodying rhythms as moving-remixing and I must say, sampling and remixing foreign movements have completely altered both my style and my life's story. Moving with Antonioni is different than moving with Bergman is different than moving with Marker is different than moving with Varda is different than moving with Cassavetes. And here is where I really disturb the commercial theories and premises of so-called transmedia narrative: for me, this moving-remixing of different rhythms—these always-live postproduction sets I am intersubjectively navigating while reading other narratives—is what informs the ongoing distribution of my own transmedia narrative over the networked and mobile media environments I circulate in. And so the phrase "foreign film" can now, for me, be applied to much more than film per se. I can apply it to this investigation of—for example—choreographing the way we mobilize our states of presence over the network . . . and if I were to put a footnote here, which I'm not, but if I *were* to put a footnote here I would also reference the concept of *choragraphy* in relation to the Internet theories of Gregory Ulmer who tells us that choragraphy is a state of mind, or a state of anticipatory consciousness where invention takes place—and here I am reminded of Mallarme's notion of *nothing having taken place but the place*. This is like saying that nothing will have been remixed but the remix process itself, except in this case, and throughout *remixthebook*, we find that it's the unconscious readiness potential of the postproduction artist who creates novel forms of togetherness that ultimately triggers this performative gesture.

—So remix is both part of the production and postproduction methods? I guess they kind of blur.

—Yes, you could say that. While in Cornwall, the cast and crew would magically convene via a localized social networking scene and the time limit for research and production was something like five–six weeks. Kate Southworth and the team she directed in iRES, the Interactive Art and Design Research Cluster, were incredibly generous and agreed to my proposition. A then brand new, just released Nokia N95 mobile phone with a first generation mobile-phone ready Carl Zeiss lens and something like video recording technology was purchased and waiting for me upon my arrival. Once I was there, I was literally on location and in production.

But this is where I want to get a little philosophical with you and suggest that being "in production" is a ruse because, in fact, we are all always already *in postproduction*. The digitally born avant-garde remixer is *always* in postproduction. In fact, they must—out of necessity—acquire an elaborate skills-set focused at the interface of *electracy*—what Ulmer sees as electricity + literacy—so that they may constantly manipulate the data of everyday life. This is when transmedia narrative becomes a work-in-progress distributed across the networked and mobile media environments ones social practice unfolds in. For me, this is what being creative is becoming all about. *Becoming all about.* Think of that phrase for a moment. The creative act, as Duchamp called it, is embedded in our unconscious readiness potential—and by that I mean it's something that is quite naturally triggered when we find ourselves caught in the heat of the remixological moment—the simultaneous and continuous fusion of moments that comprise the artfulness of what it means to always be *in postproduction*, to become an intuitive medium engaged with digital media while caught in the heat of the creative act.

—This doesn't sound like your typical film production.

—No, far from it. To give you a behind-the-scenes idea of what it's like to make an artwork like *Immobilité*, let me start by saying that *Immobilité* self-consciously remixes the rhythms and styles of European art-house directors such as Bergman, Antonioni, Varda, Cassavetes, Marker, and Ackerman, but also the underground film work of artists like Andy Warhol, Carolee Schneemann, Stan Brakhage, Maya Deren, and others . . . and here it should be noted that during our making of the work, in the summer of 2007, one very late night that went into early morning, we found out that both Bergman and Antonioni died on the same day, and this unquestionable fact also fed into our collective and collaborative conversations and mood as we continued socializing the project as an always in-process performance art event. What would these deaths do to us? How would they tweak our collective social filters as we collaboratively postproduced our feelings while making the "foreign film?"

—Why foreign film?

—This idea of a "foreign film" as part of a new series of feature-length works is related to what Atom Egoyan once wrote. In the introduction to a book titled *Subtitles*, Egoyan writes, "Every film is a foreign film." This concept of the "foreign film" relates to my initial impulse to mashup the DIY amateurism of mobile phone video performers playing with the aesthetics of YouTube-styled vernacular video with the predominantly European art-house auteur cinema that as an undergraduate film student at UCLA radically altered my vision of the world. My sense was that this was an area ripe for discovery. Now, as an artwork, *Immobilité* remixes other media besides film. The work not only remixes the stylistic tendencies or rhythms of filmmakers. As I mentioned, the work was shot on location in Cornwall and the wild and beachy landscapes appear throughout. I shot the scenes with this early version of mobile phone video recording technology, in my case the Nokia N95, and really wanted to see what was possible regarding experimental hand-held techniques and very self-consciously used this small device that I could hold in the palm of my hand as a kind of lens-brush, if you will, one that I could manipulate through all kinds of hand-held gestural moves that I would improvisationally choreograph with the actor-players as part of our collaborative spatial and social practice. This ended up involving the gradual building of a small network of actors and crew members who basically just hang out together and make the work by sharing their stories, their books, their websites, their music, their food, and their movement through the project as it develops. I'm sure many low-budget independent films and underground art rock bands have created new work in this kind of environment as well.

—The landscapes are beautiful.

—Thanks. The landscapes are also clever remixes of paintings but involve the experimental use of the mobile phone video technology. In fact, the look and feel of many of the experimental landscape shots are absolutely informed by the painterly rhythms of the post-World War II British Abstract Expressionists who, for the most part, resided in Cornwall, along with Surrealist refugees from the European continent who were themselves escaping their war-torn countries but were also, like all artists who eventually come to learn once they live in Cornwall, dramatically affected by the light. It ends up that the lineage of painterly light artists, from the naïve fishermen of the late nineteenth century, to the British Abstract Expressionists and temporary Surrealist residents, directly inform many of the abstract landscape imagery found throughout *Immobilité*. And then there are all of the writerly remixes as well, and here I specifically mean the subtitles, 90 percent of which are sampled and remixed from other films, novels, poems, and philosophical tracts that were circulating within our social network during the making of the film.

—So this feature-length foreign film operates on a number of simultaneous levels or layers of remixological inhabitation.

—Precisely. But you could have read all of this in my blog. *The one I give away for free over the Internet.* This is just my live performance version of it. I remixed certain elements for consistency.

—So does that mean we can go now?

—No, not yet. I would like us to go together to the immobilite.com website and look at it as well as listen to some of the video and audio remixes. I think once we leave this page behind us you'll get a better sense of what I've been talking about.

Bibliography (Source Material)

Amerika, Mark. *Remixology (A Theoretical Fiction)*. http://median.s151960.gridserver.com/?page_id=99 (accessed December 5, 2013).

———. *remixthebook*. http://www.remixthebook.com (accessed December 5, 2013).

Bey, Hakim. *Temporary Autonomous Zones*. http://hermetic.com/bey/taz_cont.html (accessed December 5, 2013).

Bush, Vannevar. "As We May Think." *The Atlantic*. http://www.theatlantic.com/magazine/archive/1945/07/as-we-may-think/303881/ (accessed December 5, 2013).

Federman, Raymond. *PLAJEU*. http://epc.buffalo.edu/authors/federman/shoes/plajeu.htm (accessed December 5, 2013).

Professor VJ. *Professor VJ*. http://professorvj.blogspot.com (accessed December 5, 2013).

Ulmer, Gregory. *The Chora Collaborations*. http://www.rhizomes.net/issue18/ulmer/ (accessed December 5, 2013)

———. *Choragraphy (A Map)*. http://ensemble.va.com.au/enslogic/text/ulm_lct.htm (accessed December 5, 2013)

Wark, McKenzie. *Copyright, Copyleft, Copygift*. http://www.skor.nl/_files/Files/OPEN12_P22-29%281%29.pdf (accessed December 5, 2013).

Part IV

POLITICS

23

A CAPITAL REMIX

Rachel O'Dwyer

In May 2012, Harry Rodrigues, aka DJ Baauer, released a sampled dance track called "Harlem Shake."[1] Initially little known, the song developed into a pandemic Internet meme in Spring 2013. An initial video by George Miller of friends dancing to the track went viral.[2] Versions of Baauer's "Harlem Shake" circulated on YouTube, with countless amateurs making and uploading interpretations. Amateur and professional musicians released sanctioned and unauthorized remixes of the track.[3] For a short time, the "Shake" was lauded for highlighting the grassroots nature of media organization and the significant role of amateur and user-generated content in shaping contemporary culture.

Such enthusiasm was short lived. A number of theorists argued that this Internet meme—far from being a spontaneous, bottom-up phenomenon—was engineered by corporations who stood to benefit from the circulation of content.[4] Shortly after the first video was uploaded, Time Warner subsidiary Maker Studios, who specialize in extracting revenue from YouTube videos, produced an imitation dance video and promoted it extensively through their social media channels.[5] Consequently the meme produced value for Google (the proprietor of YouTube), who extracted advertising revenue from its circulation. Further revenue went to entertainment conglomerate Warner Bros. and its subsidiary Time Warner for the distribution rights to the track and to corporations such as Volkswagen and Pepsi Max, who used the meme in a Super Bowl commercial in February 2013.[6] Interestingly, DJ Baauer allegedly did not profit from the track's success due to legal issues surrounding the clearance of samples used in the song.[7]

"Harlem Shake" highlights many conflicts concerning the production and distribution of remix in contemporary culture. Remix culture is thought to cultivate a more critical and democratic culture driven by users as opposed to corporations. So too, as an activity that thrives on social production and the free exchange of culture, remix disrupts an economy that extracts value from the enclosure of intellectual and cultural products, threatening the monopoly of corporations who have succeeded in privatizing these goods. As the "Harlem Shake" meme demonstrates, however, transformations to the cultural industries mean that the nonmarket potential of remix is now contested. Forms of attention, spontaneous creativity and bottom-up circulation are among the main sources of value in the contemporary economy.

Elaborating on these competing perspectives and their situation within a political economy of Internet culture, this chapter will rethink the practice of remix and the accumulation of value from remix in light of significant transformations to creative work and to the cultural industries. This involves first looking at the ways in which remix is presented as a nonmarket and often anticommercial practice, before examining the transformations that situate remix at the center of an economy where cultural content is now a primary driver of wealth.

Remix and Free Culture

Both the products and practices of remix are frequently understood as nonmarket and nonproprietary. They fall within the broader remit of what is sometimes called "free culture," referring to the social production of information and culture over digitally networked media.[8] Progressing alongside the countercultural and hacker movements of the 1980s through to present-day collaborative production in Web 2.0, free culture has emerged as a countercapitalist ideology. Free culture builds on interrelated claims regarding the economic nature of cultural goods, the nature of creative work, and the technological affordances of digital networks. These claims underpin an ideology of remix as a noncommercial practice and as an anticapitalist practice. They require further elaboration.

First of all, the outputs of cultural production are thought to resist commercial enclosure and marketization. The kinds of goods commonly produced through networked media platforms such as information, software, images, music, and cultural texts, are classified as "immaterial" or "intangible."[9] Material and tangible goods like food and shelter are to different degrees "rival" goods, meaning their use or consumption by one individual prevents or inhibits consumption by others. Where such goods are in demand they are typically consolidated in property relations and provisioned by a pricing system. Immaterial goods, on the other hand, are by nature "nonrival," meaning they are shared easily and with little cost. As a result such goods are socially provisioned and equally they are not easily absorbed into a market or corralled as private property.[10] Consequently, immaterial goods such as those produced through remix are candidates for substantial nonmarket production. In order to make culture profitable within a market, various forms of artificial scarcity in the shape of intellectual property or licensing have to be produced to effect economic competition.

Second, not only are these goods not easily enclosed, the "work" they require to produce—creative and collaborative practices—isn't easily managed by organized labor or wages. Instead free culture generally describes outputs that are voluntarily produced outside of work hours and often given away for free without the expectation of future economic returns. So too, the "work" required for the production of these cultural goods also requires the purest expression of the self; it primarily stems from passion, enthusiasm, a desire for social connection, and a hedonistic pursuit of creativity and knowledge.[11]

Third, the technological affordances of digitally networked media are thought to support not only new forms of production and distribution of content, but also new systems of peer production and decentralized organization conducive to nonmarket cooperation. Free culture is premised on a consumer electronics culture that places the means of production (and reproduction) in the hands of the majority of individuals in developed societies. However, not only the ubiquity of these communications media, but also their technical organization, is significant to fostering free culture. There are topological and legislative dimensions to cooperation outside of market signals or managerial command and the decentralized and nonhierarchical organization of digital networks is thought to facilitate these.[12]

Remix Is Anticapitalist

Remix has a privileged position in free culture as its practices and outputs not only encourage the nonmarket reproduction and distribution of cultural texts, they actively contest the commercial industries that threaten the commonality of culture. Many people who write about remix take the view that culture is produced by the whole of society and should not belong to any single individual or corporation.[13] Practices that flout copyright present a threat to corporations that rely on the production of artificial scarcity and proprietary constraints over goods in order to make a profit. In this way remix presents a direct sabotage to the cultural industries with its own instruments. As a cultural expression that relies on the multiplicity of texts, remix disrupts the dynamics of those collusive media corporations that have succeeded in privatizing cultural goods. So, too, as a practice largely concerned with quotation and circulation, in economic terms, remix does not produce any new object, but instead is parasitical to the cultural industries. It strategically utilizes techniques for networked appropriation, reproduction, and circulation to contest the commercial expropriation of forms of symbolic and cultural value.

Furthermore, we can argue that digital content is often produced in the spirit of nonmarket communality, and this is particularly so with remixes, mashups, and recuts of all kinds. Not only are these works often produced without any expectation of financial remuneration, they often eschew notions of authorship and subsequently origins, property, and their associated restrictions to use, abuse, profit, and transfer. As a practice, remix rejects the commodity status associated with symbolic and cultural products. Even where a certain fetishism pervades the outputs of earlier DJ cultures, this is less often the case with digitally networked forms of remix. Instead the contemporary mashup is thought to emerge as less of a homage and more of a backlash against the cultural authority and administrative perspectives of professionalized cultural practitioners and against the commodity fetishism of the cultural object more generally.[14]

Remix as Discourse

Alongside its substantially nonmarket origins, a number of theorists argue that remix also allows for the expression of anticapitalist and political viewpoints.[15] If historically a particular linguistic capital was required for entry into a political or public sphere,[16] the tools of remix cultivate another kind of political vocabulary, migrating from the manipulation of language to the manipulation of rich media content.

Remix often involves the adoption of cultural memes, tropes, and popular references both to situate and to dramatize contemporary political discourses. Familiar images, melodies and popular references are reflected, recombined, and recontextualized to produce the remix as a vehicle for communicating and expressing political opinion. Thus, remix is a rich discourse that communicates through the troubling and defamiliarization of shared associations. Take, for example, the "Occupy Gotham" montages that circulated around the Occupy movement's highlight of wealth inequality, or the ubiquitous "Pepper Spray Cop" meme that followed on alleged excessive force in student demonstrations in University of California, Davis.

Eduardo Navas[17] and Henry Jenkins[18] have both separately argued that remix constitutes a form of discourse, because its communicative effect relies on its broader position within a system of signs, dependent on its conceptual association and historical position in relation to other cultural texts. In *Remix Theory*, Navas describes this as a modular repetition, in which the remix draws on and extends an archive of shared knowledge and culture, building on tropes and imaginaries, at times referencing and at other times disrupting tacit understandings and literacies.[19] If shared language is one kind of cultural commons—something we can't really imagine being privatized or "owned"—then understanding remix as a discourse also points to the totality of a society's cultural outputs as another kind of commons, with a vitality that is excessive to any commercial or proprietary claim made by a single corporation or individual. This drives home the idea that making and remaking culture is a social and collective activity that cannot and should not be corralled as property.

Remix Is Central to the Economy

Like much of the ideology of free culture, however, the emancipatory potential of remix is arguably contested and at best, overstated. Following on a series of transformations to the relations of production, the technical composition of labor and the property regimes under which labor produces, we can no longer think of remix as operating in fundamental opposition to the market or indeed as fundamentally anticapitalist. Today symbolic and cultural value is central to the economy, work has aligned itself with artistic and cultural production and the tools and platforms underpinning that work, while superficially accessible, are substantially owned and controlled by corporations.

Today the process of wealth accumulation extends beyond material goods to include informational and cultural goods of all kinds.[20] This doesn't mean that industrial production disappears; rather, the value of material goods—cars, trainers, consumer electronics—is increasingly subordinate to immaterial factors, contingent on all kinds of symbolic, cultural, aesthetic, and social outputs that are produced by the whole of society. Consequently, a number of theorists argue that the primary driver of wealth in society now comes from cultural attributes.[21] The value of software conglomerates and social media networks capitalize on user-generated content; urban real estate and tourist destinations often derive much of their value from local cultural injections; and consumer brands feed on the tastes and distinction of youth cultures and subcultural groups to name just a few examples.[22] Remix arguably has a significant role to play in this economy.

The conditions under which informational and cultural capital is produced also involve transformations to labor. Work is requalified and recomposed in such a way that the activities associated with remix culture are now productive to the economy. Forms of human attention, creativity, and bottom-up circulation are now the main sources of value for software companies, advertising agencies, and crowd-sourcing marketplaces. Artistic and cultural production, the formation of norms and public opinion, the fixing of tastes, the development of relations of trust and cooperation, and the circulation of desire are now part and parcel of the contemporary composition of labor.

From this perspective the outputs and productivity of remix are extremely valuable to contemporary capitalism. Furthermore, the figure of the "remixer" as an artist, fan, or playful individual engaged is the ideal laboring subject for the contemporary economy, as a worker that does not recognize subjugation in their labor, who often does not even expect to be paid, but instead associates their practice with freedom, play, and creative expression, even as these activities—making, responding to and circulating remixes—produce economic value for others.

Remix and Value Capture

Let's look more closely at some of the ways that the work of remix can be said to produce economic value. When capital expropriates informational and cultural products, value capture relies, not on direct intervention, but on the production of a strategic position with respect to forms of free cultural production. This system of accumulation isn't so much about paying a wage for labor that produces surplus value that is subsequently reinvested in production. Instead it becomes about using the ownership of some resource—cultural products or digital networks or real estate for example—to extract value from a position external to creative production. Even as it functions as a rejection of the commodity status of the object, therefore, the remix constitutes an extended and developed investment in forms of cultural and "subcultural" value that can be extracted, translated, and reinvested into commercial goods. There are a number of different ways in which this comes about.

A straightforward instance is where the cultural currency of remix is used directly to market commodities, harvesting the cool factor associated with a niche or subculture. For example, the anticapitalist and antiproprietary character of remix can actually be utilized to produce revenue at a remove, conferring symbolic value to commercial products it comes to be associated with.[23] This produces a cultural value that can be converted and reinvested in the sale of commodities. This might be in a direct form, where remix is channeled into related venue promotion or legitimate record sales. Or it might be used indirectly in the sale of mass-produced commodity goods such as cars or high-street fashion.

If remix subcultures are commercialized to confer status to a commercial good, advertisements targeting fans of music and video remixes are also inserted into noncommercial remixes on media platforms. Instead of working on the cultural cachet of the remix to sell products, this approach also relies on the creative work of the remixer, who produces something other people want to pay attention to, as well as the work of the remix audience, who are obliged to respond to and distribute commercial messages to their peer group in order to access a remix.

This approach can be identified in YouTube's revenue model. Since its development as a video platform, YouTube has been home to remix distribution of all kinds, and platform owners and individual producers alike have encountered difficulties hosting and circulating remixes that appropriate material from copyrighted sources in the public domain. In the past this has often led to the removal of content deemed to infringe copyright on behalf of powerful industry conglomerates. More recently however, the distribution platform has adopted a different approach to the management and monetization of remix in a way that is commercially productive for the platform owner and for the holder of the distribution rights to media content. Rather than expressly forbidding and removing content that is deemed to infringe on intellectual property, using CopyID software developed by Google, YouTube now identifies contributions that draw on copyrighted material and inserts advertisements into these. Following the logic of Google's Adsense algorithm—an advertising system that monetizes a user's attention (clicks) to commercial messages—these advertisements subsequently produce value that accrues to the video platform and to the license holder.[24] This extracts value from the work of the remix artist and from the work of his or her audience, who are obliged to attend to commercial content in exchange for access to the cultural product. The remix as tune, idea, catch phrase, fashion, or meme becomes a consumer object.

We can also consider remix in terms of a broader corporate philosophy of open innovation and codesign that expands the sphere of production to the extent that the consumer now becomes an active producer of value. As Read argues: "Our culture is obsessed with remixing content and showing individuality."[25] Brands should look to embrace this by creating content and messages that can be remixed and easily passed on.[26]

In this sense we can identify the remix as a labor and innovation model central to many industries today, redolent of the increased role of codesign and collaborative production in a variety of industries and the rise of open innovation models in corporate R&D and design. Nike, as a core example, has opened up its designs to consumers, allowing them to "remix" their trainers with NIKEiD.[27] So too, many software companies have opened aspects of their software, websites, or APIs to third party developers for innovation, mashup, and improvement, where the risks of innovation are socialized while the substantial market benefits are privatized under a powerful corporation or brand.

These examples of the ways that remix is economically productive also force us to reconsider the role of remix as a discursive practice. Theorist Jodi Dean has argued that networked communication technologies transform the political content of "messages" into mere circulatory contributions to cognitive capitalism.[28] The exchange value of a message obfuscates its use value; contributions need not be understood or responded to, only repeated, reproduced, and forwarded in an endless economy of circulation. The content of the message and subsequently its discursive potential are subordinate to the act of circulation; the only thing of significance is its network value: where it has travelled to, how many people have seen it, and how it illustrates connections between individuals, commercial tastes, and habits of consumption. In this light the remix becomes less of a discourse and more of a circulation of different perspectives robbed of any political potential.[29]

Critical and Reflexive Remix

From this perspective, the "sabotage" potentiated by the remix is more symbolic than material. While the remix might appear to challenge some aspect of the market economy (most typically intellectual property), it normally does not engage the broader conditions structuring cultural production in networked environments. These include the vertical integration of large media and software companies; the ownership of creative tools, platforms, and network infrastructure; and the various algorithmic and codified systems of value accumulation surrounding user-generated content. While cultivating a critical practice is important, therefore, it is also necessary to consider how issues of control and ownership extend beyond the text or file to inflect channels for content production and distribution. I would like to conclude by attending to remix practices that not only contest intellectual property and artificial scarcity, but also the dynamics of value accumulation in contemporary networks.

A classic definition of remix refers to rich media texts composed of samples drawn from popular culture. But there is also an expanded understanding of remix that alludes to the critical recomposition of two or more sources of digital content. The former is principally aesthetic work that relies on cultural literacy for legitimacy and meaning; the latter approaches the assembly of sources in ways that use aspects of the remix, such as scraping, aggregating, and juxtaposing informational content, to engage the underlying mechanisms of networked media and value extraction.

Navas refers to this second practice as "reflexive" and uses the term "regenerative remix" to designate the dynamic and real-time aspects of this practice.[30] This form of remix is particularly common in software mashups, utilized by commercial media forms such as the video platform, search engine, and social media platform as well as by everyday individuals in the development of live feeds, interactive maps, and mobile applications. This practice is not only reflexive in the sense that it reflects on cultural texts and cultural production. In the context of a political economy of remix, the most interesting works mirror the economic, financial, and political concatenations of cultural value and expropriation in the networks the work operates within. This is more about producing tactics that are parasitical to the systems of accumulation operating over remix culture than attempting to produce content that is somehow autonomous or authentic. Here remix intersects with politicized practices such as hactivism[31] and tactical media.[32] Furthermore, the work produced is not a static cultural object but a generative process that relies on dynamic streams of information and the future interventions of users to build upon what is produced. Where political and economic questions are concerned this approach has much to offer.

For example, much of the hactivist work produced by Alessandro Ludovico and Paolo Cirio as part of the *Hacking Monopolism Trilogy* can be characterized as a form of reflexive remix. *Amazon Noir* (2006) used an algorithm coded by Cirio to extract the content of Amazon Books through the online "Search Inside" preview function. These were reconstructed as PDFs and distributed free of charge on a dedicated website. As the work appropriates and arranges samples of copyrighted texts, the artist's narrative presentation of the book "heist" also appropriates and remixes the familiar tropes of film noir and detective fiction, where the artist team present themselves as the "bad guys" operating against the "good guy" image of the Amazon Corporation, who are eventually victorious in their battle against book theft.[33] The third in the trilogy, *Face-to-Facebook* (2011), provocatively scraped one million user profiles from the social media site and used the profile content to develop a custom dating website (lovely-faces.com) sorted by the facial expression characteristics of its involuntary members.[34]

In 2012 Golan Levin circulated a toolkit that allows users to reassemble everyday objects. Levin's *Free Universal Construction Kit* (a purposeful acronym) is a matrix of 3D printable blocks that enable interoperability between popular children's construction toys. This work uses digitally networked media tools to facilitate the remix of physical objects. The kit comprises a set of downloadable digital design files for two-way adapter pieces that can be used to interface between toys such as Bristle Blocks, LEGO, Duplo, Fischertechnik, and K'Nex. These adapters open a previously closed system of objects, allowing elements to assemble in playful, unprecedented ways, "enabling radically hybrid constructive play, the creation of previously impossible designs, and ultimately, more creative opportunities for kids."[35] As remix, the *Free Universal Construction Kit* gestures to and challenges the systems of production and the property relations around which commercial artifacts are traditionally fabricated. It also uses the tools that are so successful in the remix of digital files to extend into material cultures. While the transformative potential of 3D printing is still in question, conceptually this project allows us to think about remix as a potential challenge to our everyday material cultures and built environment.

Conclusion

This chapter explores two alternative perspectives on the political economy of remix: first as part of the broader ideology of free culture, contributing to noncommercial and critical culture and second as a practice that is implicated in the broader valorization of networked cultural products, where the work of the remix artist and the remix audience produce value for the owners of media content, networked platforms, and network infrastructure. In the development of remix culture these two perspectives are highly conflictive; it is not always clear when a cultural object mixes with systems of circulation, appropriation, and reappropriation whether the outcome contests or reproduces the commercial regime. It is clear that we need to think critically about not only the formal content of the remix but attend to the underlying platforms and tools used for culture production and distribution of network media. This includes recognizing not only how the ownership of content but also the ownership of network infrastructure and platforms plays a significant role in the commercial expropriation of remix culture. In turn we also need to give further consideration to the development of a remix toolkit for mining and scraping data, for the peer-to-peer distribution of content, for hacking digital rights management systems and disrupting the artificial scarcity of common cultural goods.

Notes

1 The song featured samples from a 2001 Plastic Little track, "Miller Time."

2 Jason Notte, "Harlem Shake Was One Big Google Commercial," April 1, 2013, http://money.msn.com/now/post.aspx?post=f60d7312-f99d-4ab8-ba55-a9723ad8f69e.

3 Remixes were produced by: Dave Silcox, Azealia Banks, Filthy Disco, Rob Luna, Manish Law, Kid Womp. Harlem Shaker "Top Ten Harlem Shake Remix," June 10, 2013, http://harlemshakeoriginal.com/top-10-harlem-shake-remix/ (accessed August 11, 2014).

4 Kevin Ashton, "You Didn't Make the Harlem Shake Go Viral—Corporations Did" March 28, 2013, http://qz.com/67991/you-didnt-make-the-harlem-shake-go-viral-corporations-did/; Notte, "Harlem Shake"; Kim Peterson, "How 'Harlem Shake' Became a No. 1 Song," February 2, 2013, http://money.msn.com/now/how-harlem-shake-became-a-no-1-song.

5 Ashton, "You Didn't Make the Harlem Shake go Viral."

6 http://www.youtube.com/watch?v=e83YtSzGHC8 (accessed August 11, 2014).

7 David McCormack, "Harlem Shake DJ Baauer Made NOTHING from Global Hit Due to Legal Loophole," *Daily Mail* August 20, 2013.

8 Lawrence Lessig, *Free Culture: How Big Media Uses Technology and the Law to Lock Down Culture and Control Creativity* (London: Penguin, 2004).

9 This refers to a product or a good whose use and/or exchange value resides in "informational and cultural content" rather than in some tangible form. Maurizio Lazzarato, "Immaterial Labor," in *Radical Thought in Italy: A Potential Politics*, ed. Paolo Virno and Michael Hardy (Minneapolis, MN: University of Minnesota Press 1996): 133–147; Yann Moulier Boutang, *Cognitive Capitalism* (Cambridge: Polity, 2012).

10 Michel Bauwens, "The Political Economy of Peer Production," CTheory 1 (2005); Yochai Benkler, *The Wealth of Networks: How Social Production Transforms Markets and Freedom* (New Haven, CT: Yale University Press, 2006); James Boyle, "The Second Enclosure Movement and the Construction of the Public Domain," *Law and Contemporary Problems* 66, no. 1/2 (2003): 33–74.

11 Moulier Boutang, *Cognitive Capitalism*, 88–89.

12 Francois Bar, Walter Baer, Sharham Ghanderharizadeh and Fernando Ordonez "Infrastructure: Network Neutrality and Network Futures," in *Networked Publics*, ed. Kazys Varnelis (London: MIT Press, 2008), 109–144.

13 See, for example, the work of Cory Doctorow, Henry Jenkins, and Lawrence Lessig: Cory Doctorow, *Pirate Cinema* (CorDoc-Co, Ltd (UK), 2012); Henry Jenkins, "Multiculturalism, Appropriation, and the New Media Literacies: Remixing Moby Dick," in *Mashup Cultures*, ed. Stefan Sonvilla-Weiss (New York: Springer, 2010); Lawrence Lessig, *Free Culture: How Big Media Uses Technology and the Law to Lock Down*

Culture and Control Creativity (London: Penguin, 2004); and Lawrence Lessig, *Remix: Making Art and Commerce Thrive in the Hybrid Economy* (London: Penguin, 2008).

14 John Shiga, "Copy-and-Persist: The Logic of Mash-Up Culture," *Critical Studies in Media Communication* 24, no. 2 (2007): 107.

15 See Richard L. Edwards and Chuck Tryon, "Political Video Mashups as Allegories of Citizen Empowerment" *First Monday* 14, no. 10 (2009) http://firstmonday.org/ojs/index.php/fm/article/view/2617/2305; and Jenkins, "Multiculturalism."

16 Jürgen Habermas, *The Structural Transformation of the Public Sphere: An Inquiry into a Category of Bourgeois Society* (London: MIT Press, 1991).

17 Eduardo Navas, "Regressive and Reflexive Mashups in Sampling Culture," in *Mashup Cultures* ed. Stefan Sonvilla-Weiss (New York: Springer, 2010).

18 Henry Jenkins, "Multiculturalism." In conversation with Jonathan McIntosh, November 17, 2010. Jenkins also alluded to the relations between remix and discourse in a keynote address at the 2012 Technology Conference in UCLA in January 2012.

19 Eduardo Navas, *Remix Theory: The Aesthetics of Sampling* (New York: Springer, 2012), 30–31.

20 Slavoj Žižek, "The Revolt of the Salaried Bourgeoisie," *London Review of Books* 34, no. 2 (2012).

21 Maurizio Lazzarato, "Immaterial Labor"; Christian Marazzi, *The Violence of Financial Capitalism* (Los Angeles, CA: Semiotext(e), 2011).

22 As Terranova has argued "[n]urtured by the consumption of earlier cultural moments, subcultures have provided the look, style and sounds that sell clothes, CDs, video games, films and advertising slots on television." Tiziana Terranova, *Network Culture: Politics for the Information Age* (New York: Pluto Press, 2004), 80.

23 In his analysis of digital mashup cultures, Shiga gestures to some of ways in which the cachet of illegality or a certain DIY aesthetic produces a mark of distinction precisely through its performance of criticality and its seeming rejection of mass culture. Shiga, "Copy-and-Persist."

24 Katie Allen, "GMT Google Seeks to Turn a Profit from YouTube Copyright Clashes," theguardian.com, November 1, 2009, http://www.theguardian.com/technology/2009/nov/01/google-youtube-monetise-content; Shawn Hess "YouTube Strikes Deal to Monetize User Videos Featuring Copyrighted Material," June 6, 2013, http://www.webpronews.com/youtube-strikes-deal-to-monetize-user-videos-featuring-copyrighted-material-2012-06; Greg Sandoval, "YouTube's Filters Help Copyright Owners Profit from Pirated Videos" August 7, 2013, http://news.cnet.com/8301-1023_3-10027509-93.html.

25 Ashley Read, "An Introduction to how Remix Culture is Changing Marketing," https://medium.com/digital-advertising/a684801cd8a3.

26 As an illustration of good practice, Read describes the Old Spice Muscle Music campaign launched in August 2012. This features actor and NFL player Terry Crews wired to electrodes and playing a variety of musical instruments by flexing his muscles. The advertisement includes a video of the actor performing but also a recordable player that initiates after the video finishes and allows users to record their own music video by pressing different keys to animate Crews. The advertisement, at the time of this writing, has ten million views and 18,400 likes on the Vimeo platform. http://vimeo.com/47875656.

27 Ibid.

28 Jodi Dean, "Communicative Capitalism: Circulation and the Foreclosure of Politics." *Cultural Politics* 1, no. 1 (2005): 51–74.

29 Ibid., 55.

30 Navas, *Remix Theory*, 73.

31 A portmanteau of hack and activism that describes the use of networked media in political intervention and social movements.

32 A term developed by Geert Lovink to designate forms of media activism by groups or individuals operating outside of positions of power that privilege temporary interventions and guerrilla media tactics.

33 Paolo Cirio and Alessandro Ludovico, *Amazon Noir* (2006), http://www.amazon-noir.com/.

34 Paolo Cirio and Alessandro Ludovico, *Face-to-Facebook* (2011), http://www.face-to-facebook.net/.

35 Golan Levin, *The Free Universal Construction Kit* (2012), http://fffff.at/free-universal-construction-kit/.

Bibliography

Allen, Katie. "GMT Google Seeks to Turn a Profit from YouTube Copyright Clashes." *theguardian.com*. November 1, 2009, http://www.theguardian.com/technology/2009/nov/01/google-youtube-monetise-content (accessed May 3, 2014).

Ashton, Kevin. "You Didn't Make the Harlem Shake Go Viral—Corporations Did" March 28, 2013, http://qz.com/67991/you-didnt-make-the-harlem-shake-go-viral-corporations-did/ (accessed August 12, 2014).

Bar, Francois, Walter Baer, Sharham Ghanderharizadeh, and Fernando Ordonez. "Infrastructure: Network Neutrality and Network Futures." In *Networked Publics* edited by Kazys Varnelis, 109–144. London: MIT Press, 2008.

Bauwens, Michel. "The Political Economy of Peer Production." *CTheory* no. 1 (2005).

Benkler, Yochai. *The Wealth of Networks: How Social Production Transforms Markets and Freedom*. New Haven, CT: Yale University Press, 2006.

Boyle, James. "The Second Enclosure Movement and the Construction of the Public Domain." *Law and Contemporary Problems* 66, no. 1/2 (2003): 33–74.

Cirio, Paolo, and Alessandro Ludovico, *Amazon Noir*. 2006. http://www.amazon-noir.com/ (accessed May 3, 2014).

———. *Face-to-Facebook*. 2011. http://www.face-to-facebook.net/ (accessed May 3, 2014).

Dean, Jodi, "Communicative Capitalism: Circulation and the Foreclosure of Politics." *Cultural Politics* 1, no. 1 (2005): 51–74.

Doctorow, Cory. *Pirate Cinema*. CorDoc-Co, Ltd (UK), 2012.

Edwards, Richard L., and Chuck Tryon. "Political Video Mashups as Allegories of Citizen Empowerment" *First Monday* 14, no. 10 (2009) http://firstmonday.org/ojs/index.php/fm/article/view/2617/2305 (accessed May 3 2014).

Habermas, Jürgen. *The Structural Transformation of the Public Sphere: An Inquiry into a Category of Bourgeois Society*. London: MIT Press, 1991.

Hess, Shawn "YouTube Strikes Deal to Monetize User Videos Featuring Copyrighted Material." June 6, 2013, http://www.webpronews.com/youtube-strikes-deal-to-monetize-user-videos-featuring-copyrighted-material-2012-06 (accessed May 3, 2014).

Jenkins, Henry. "Multiculturalism, Appropriation, and the New Media Literacies: Remixing Moby Dick." In *Mashup Cultures* edited by Stefan Sonvilla-Weiss, 98–119. New York: Springer, 2010.

Lazzarato, Maurizio. "Immaterial Labor." In *Radical Thought in Italy: A Potential Politics* edited by Paolo Virno and Michael Hardy (Minneapolis, MN: University of Minnesota Press, 1996): 133–147.

Lessig, Lawrence. *Free Culture: How Big Media Uses Technology and the Law to Lock Down Culture and Control Creativity*. London: Penguin, 2004.

———. *Remix: Making Art and Commerce Thrive in the Hybrid Economy*. London: Penguin, 2008.

Levin, Golan, *The Free Universal Construction Kit*. 2012. http://fffff.at/free-universal-construction-kit/ (accessed May 3, 2014).

Marazzi, Christian. *The Violence of Financial Capitalism*. Los Angeles, CA: Semiotext(e) (2011).

McCormack, David "Harlem Shake DJ Baauer Made NOTHING from Global Hit Due to Legal Loophole." *Daily Mail*, August 20, 2013.

Moulier Boutang, Yann. *Cognitive Capitalism*. Cambridge: Polity, 2012.

Navas, Eduardo. "Regressive and Reflexive Mashups in Sampling Culture." In *Mashup Cultures* edited by Stefan Sonvilla-Weiss, 157–177. New York: Springer, 2010.

———. *Remix Theory: The Aesthetics of Sampling*. New York: Springer, 2012.

Notte, Jason. "Harlem Shake Was One Big Google Commercial," April 1, 2013, http://money.msn.com/now/post.aspx?post=f60d7312-f99d-4ab8-ba55-a9723ad8f69e (accessed May 3, 2014).

Peterson, Kim. "How Harlem Shake Became a no. 1 song" February 2, 2013, http://money.msn.com/now/how-harlem-shake-became-a-no-1-song (accessed May 3, 2014).

Read, Ashley. "An Introduction to How Remix Culture is Changing Marketing." https://medium.com/digital-advertising/a684801cd8a3 (accessed May 18, 2014).

Sandoval, Greg. "YouTube's Filters Help Copyright Owners Profit from Pirated Videos" August 7, 2013, http://news.cnet.com/8301-1023_3-10027509-93.html (accessed May 3, 2014).

Shiga, John. "Copy-and-Persist: The Logic of Mash-Up Culture." *Critical Studies in Media Communication* 24, no. 2 (2007): 93–114.

Terranova, Tiziana. *Network Culture: Politics for the Information Age*. New York: Pluto Press, 2004.

Žižek, Slavoj. "The Revolt of the Salaried Bourgeoisie." *London Review of Books* 34, no. 2 (2012): 9–10.

24
REMIX PRACTICES AND ACTIVISM

A Semiotic Analysis of Creative Dissent

Paolo Peverini

Even though remix practices are a very complex phenomenon and their impact on media genres and audiences is undeniable, it is only recently that scholars tried to legitimate transformative works as a serious area of study. In this chapter I focus on remixes intended as texts, privileging a semiotic approach. In particular I argue that the analysis of sign processes and systems of communication is very useful, both on a theoretical and on a methodological level, to deepen comprehension of hybrid texts.

The chapter concentrates on audiovisual remixes, precisely on tactics and strategies planned by activists to involve public opinion with respect to issues like environmental protection or freedom of expression.

The hypothesis is that the effectiveness of some of the most radical and innovative creative protests is based on the ability to recognize and manage remixes intended as techno-political tools, even though in digital media the most original campaigns are rapidly assimilated by unconventional marketing strategies, triggering a process of progressive standardization. Through the analysis of some exemplary campaigns planned by Greenpeace and Wikileaks I aim to demonstrate that an emerging trend consists in a gradual stratification of texts used to address the receivers. The aim is to provoke a reaction while entertaining the audience, remixing in an ironic way consists of various intertextual and interdiscursive references.

The first part of the chapter delves into the matter of a semiotics of remix, the second section focuses on its use in subversive advertisement, typical of culture jamming, and the conclusion examines how activists combine remix with camouflage tactics concealing at first sight the very objective of their discourse and renegotiating the fiduciary contract with their audiences.

Remix: A Semiotic Phenomenon

Any articulate reflection on the rapid spreading of remix and mashup practices in the context of digital media cannot but take into consideration the fact that these forms of rewriting are based on a semiotic logic performed with a combined set of actions consisting of the selection, decomposition, hybridization, and rewriting of (pre)existing texts. In other words: actions based on a metalinguistic competence which permits the subject to produce signification repurposing preexisting meaning.

As Eduardo Navas affirms:

> The remix is in the end a re-mix—that is, a rearrangement of something already recognizable; it functions on a meta-level. This implies that the originality of the remix is non-existent; therefore it must acknowledge its source of validation self-reflexively. The remix when extended as a cultural practice, as a form of discourse, is a second mix of something pre-existent. The material that is mixed at least for a second time must be recognized, otherwise it could be misunderstood as something new and it would become plagiarism.[1]

Significantly, one of the distinctive features of any remix, here understood as being a composite set of semiotic practices, is that it goes beyond the borders of any particular discourse genre, avoiding any attempt to construct effective and exhaustive taxonomies. From this point of view, the expressive potential of remix should instead be set within the context of a more general theory of culture, since any work involving the manipulation of preexisting texts is always based on the selection and reelaboration of "pre-stressed blocks of meaning,"[2] cultural resources on which the enunciative praxis of a "bricoleur" subject is concentrated. As Jean Marie Floch stated:

> As with other enunciative practices, bricolage means calling upon a number of already established forms. However, the enunciative activity involved in bricolage does not lead to the production of merely stereotyped discourse. Rather, in this case, the selection and exploitation of the facts of usage and the products of history lead to a kind of creativity that constitutes the originality of bricolage as an enunciative praxis. We can, in fact, think of this as a double creativity. For, on the one hand, bricolage leads to statements that qualify as independent entities; while, on the other hand, any such statement will give substance, and hence identity, to an enunciating subject.[3]

From the perspective of a semiotic theory of culture, texts are not to be intended as isolated entities; on the contrary, their identity is constantly renegotiated, due to the endless translation with other texts that are connected with them: new texts assimilate them or rework the initial structure, in a process of hybridization and reworking that foster cross-cultural connections. Following this train of thought, the manifold practices and forms of the remix are not merely a "surface phenomenon" of cultures, but should be gauged within the set of all logics of translation between texts that fuel the "life cycle" of a culture. In other words, as remix practices and forms spread, they produce an impact on transformations that guarantee the functioning of the so-called semiosphere.[4]

As Nicola Dusi remarks,

in the production of culture, all texts are supported by something else; they are produced, distributed, and absorbed, circulating in a culture always alongside other products, other texts that receive them, associate with them, use them, cite them, and contaminate them. We agree with the anthropologist James Clifford, who claims that "the pure products go crazy" (Clifford, 1998). A swarm of texts, or rather, a web of references in endless translation with one another. As Yuri Lotman (1984) would argue, translation constructs and at the same time dynamizes cultural universes.[5]

The effectiveness of any form of remix does not stem merely from the skill used in selecting a set of cultural resources on the paradigmatic plane and then recombining them in a relatively original and creative fashion on the syntagmatic plane. This kind of enunciative praxis is instead based on the enunciator's strategic capacity to recognize and handle the know-how possessed by the interlocutor, in other words planning his/her moves according to the interpretative competences of the receiver.

Given that this peculiar form of metatext is marked by the presence of a strategic rationality that can contribute to renegotiating the interaction between the subjects participating in a discourse, at the same time soliciting their critical sensibility, remix proves to be one of the practices best suited to political protest.

Remix as a Form of Creative Political Protest

Remix can be conceived as a political act in itself: This is more relevant from a semiotic perspective, because whenever a text is sampled, its meaning is always renegotiated and reopened. Patently political remix videos gradually emerge as a popular genre of media texts characterized by some specific elements.[6] Transformative works use preexisting audiovisual source texts, privileging pop culture materials (music videos, trailers, commercials, news fragments) and ignoring copyright laws. The reworking practices appropriate content, reopen their structure, commenting on narratives, ideological assumptions, and stereotypes with the aim of criticizing and/or highlighting original meanings. These works are DIY materials and since 2005 their massive circulation increasingly relies on video-sharing websites such as YouTube.

Undeniably, the ambit of political debate is therefore one of the discursive areas that is most congenial to forms of remix, as evidenced by the steadily increasing number of videos created with this technique for a variety of distinct subjects: citizens, political parties, associations, nongovernmental organizations, and the nonprofit sector in general.

With reference to the transformations that involve activist practices in the social media scenario, DIY remixes can be used to increase civic engagement or to motivate participation in political debates and decisions providing subjects with very limited financial resources an alternative mean to reach wide audiences.

From this point of view, the growing popularity of remix practices cannot but be seen in relation to the increasingly marked interconnection between media convergence, digital networking, and the emergence of a sociosemiotic logic, defined by Richard L. Edwards and Chuck Tryon[7] as "critical digital intertextuality," which typifies the use of remix as one of the most effective techno-political tools of protest. In other words: as one of the most popular methods of media activism.

However, one of the consequences of the growing diffusion and sharing of remix forms in the digital media scenario is a rapid process of standardization that affects not only the choice of materials to be remixed but also the sequences of combinations which, as a whole, form the text's structure. What we see, therefore, is the emergence of a progressive codification of remixes, where the protest gradually loses its meaning, a process that is linked to the operating logics of participatory cultures.

This is why, in the most interesting cases, the potentially most effective forms of protest start with a general rethinking process about how the remix itself works, with the aim of fine-tuning texts that are increasingly stratified, complex, rich in references to other texts and discourses designed to solicit, ever more intensely, the competence of the receiver.

As mentioned previously, when tackling the theme of using remix as a communicative form of protest, we refer almost exclusively to the scenario of user-generated content, which is undoubtedly extremely wide-ranging and in constant evolution, yet we fail to consider that there are myriads of subjects of enunciation committed to shaping the discourse of dissent, and that the goals they set themselves are extremely diversified.

In this sense, it should be noted how, over the past few years, an increasing number of social guerrilla campaigns, planned by the most well-known international nonprofit organizations, have focused on remix and mashup practices, with the aim of experimenting with new expressive solutions, designed to attract a public that is increasingly used to the explicit portrayal of pain.[8]

The most innovative forms of campaign by nonprofit organizations are characterized by constant research on new remix practices that will affect the audience, aiming to stimulate engagement with the social cause.

Disruptive media actions such as those organized by the Adbusters collective or the Billboard Liberation Front have been progressively reproduced and used for various goals by the same subjects who were initially targeted by the protest actions, and have now been largely assimilated into the repertoire of tactics and techniques that make up so-called guerrilla marketing.

How do activists react to the fact that their own "weapons," their guerrilla strategies, have become part of brand communication? Significantly, we are facing a progressive "aestheticization" of the protest, whose effectiveness relates to an enunciative praxis. Some of the most interesting social campaigns aim to solicit public opinion by shifting from the "transparency" of the content plane to the display of a fictitious metadiscourse based on heterogeneous processes of recombination and recomposition, on complex intrasemiotic and intersemiotic operations.

In other words, the semiotics of creative dissent is increasingly based on remix intended as a discursive practice or, more precisely, a political discourse. In any case, the effectiveness of the most provocative protest cannot be conceived of as simply a matter of creative and heterogeneous techniques but, on the contrary, its effectiveness is based on a subtle strategic competence that consists of first detecting characteristic features in the discourses made by activists, so as then to plan alternative and unpredictable communicative actions. Activists display the setup of their discourse, the stratification of their provocative protest, pointing out, in other words, the opacity of the meaning displayed.

To strengthen the message, three very common discursive strategies in civic media (warning, suggestion, and condemnation) are being continually redefined using *irony* and *paradoxes*, often sparking passionate public debate about the ethics of portraying a serious situation in a humorous manner. In the most relevant examples, the impact of an innovative protest is based on a metadiscursive approach to dissent, tending to reopen texts, manipulate signification processes, "inoculate" paradoxes within the original message. In other words, the effectiveness of such protests depends on the ability shown by an enunciator in distorting the semantic coherence of some preexisting materials, that are often, as we will see, very distant from the discursive genre of dissent.

Activists try to bypass the indifference of audiences by moving beyond the idea that exhibiting the realistic effects of an emergency is enough to obtain the attention of public opinion. Some signs of a significant variation in the semiotics of dissent are therefore gradually emerging: the explication of the subject of enunciation becomes increasingly relevant. As a result, the strategic enunciative contract between activists and their followers takes on new forms and the soundness of the protest is often staged through a professedly fictional mise-en-scène.

The activists' denouncement is expected to be more incisive, more apparently incongruous, stratified, oblique. Accordingly, whereas the effectiveness of nonprofit organizations' most innovative campaigns relies on the ability to avoid some narrative rules and stereotypes regarding the representation of dramatic issues, with regard to mechanisms that reveal the enunciation process within the text, the strategy consists of using remix practices to enhance the *reflexive opacity more than the transparency of texts*.[9]

Activists increasingly resort to complex resemantization practices, in order to reiterate the transparency and soundness of their denouncement. The strategic use of remix therefore consists of planning targeted use of intertextuality and interdiscursivity, at first sight camouflaging the true semiotic nature of the protest campaign, with the aim of bypassing the public's inurement to the canonical forms of political discourse. Social guerrilla action often develops in this way, starting from a two-fold operation entailing selection-simulation of features that are characteristic to commercials, amateur user-generated content and social networking platforms. With the aim of soliciting public support for issues such as environmental protection, (abolition of) the death penalty, or the rights of children, the practice of remix is used in numerous campaigns to make the protest message even more effective when it is based on the veridictive logic of *secrecy*, defined by Greimas and Courtés[10] as a combination of being + not-seeming.

Further expanding the perspective of the analysis, the frequent use of remix in innovative forms of media activism is made even more meaningful by the fact that the potential for social criticism which typifies this kind of rewriting is often expressed in a playful way. In particular, when planning increasingly stratified forms of dissent that are, at the same time, expressed through a variety of media, the protest takes on the guise of *entertainment*, a reworking of texts that aim to amuse the receiver and, at the same time, provoke a reaction on a cognitive, passional, and pragmatic plane.

The Entertaining Use of Political Remix Videos

From this point of view, one of the names in activism that stands out for its ability to plan, prepare, and manage communicative protest actions that successfully arouse the interest of the media is certainly Greenpeace. Their social guerrilla campaign against Volkswagen, accused of promoting their commitment to environmental protection (greenwashing) in a misleading way, is characterized by an exemplary use of remix, explicitly intended as a political tool. The disruptive action effected by this environmental movement was conceived as a refined, intertextual, and intermedial strategy, using as its starting point the official commercial produced by Volkswagen for the market launch of the Passat, consisting of an advertising campaign entitled "The Force," likewise based on a series of quotations from the cult sci-fi saga: *Star Wars*.

The Greenpeace narrative reverses the communicative strategies of the adversary (VW) in a stratified metastrategy that applies forms of reworking, typical of fandom communities.[11] In a subverting campaign,[12] eco-activists on the VWdarkside.com website compared the German automaker's logo to the Death Star, transforming the famous pay off "Das Auto" with "Dark Side" while reserving the role of Rebel Alliance for themselves.

Greenpeace's strategy is based on a complex metacommunication project, which consists of a website, two Web videos, and some guerrilla actions staged in London and Brussels. In this true masking strategy, the videos created by Greenpeace for the Web are particularly interesting because simulating typical features of amateur films self-produced by the fans of that science fiction saga (user-generated content) are used to rewrite the ending of Volkswagen's official commercial. In the videos,[13] the role of defenders of nature is entrusted to children wearing the masks and costumes of the main *Star Wars'* characters and, by defeating the fake Darth Vader, the protagonist of VW's advertising campaign, they convince the automobile giant to abandon the dark sides of force and wed the cause of ecology. The unconventionality of the discourse about nature consists here in shifting the conflict between proponents and detractors of the social cause onto an explicitly fictional level. By keeping the soundtrack from the original motion picture in the parody video, eco-activists demonstrate the stratification of their discourse, thereby indicating the intricacy of the meaning displayed.

The remarkable diffusion obtained by these videos is therefore based on the skill shown by a subject of enunciation (the nongovernmental organization) in recognizing the polemic potential of forms of rewriting, collocating the discourse according to a media scenario that is increasingly typified by a proliferation of complex intertextual references. In other words, the strategic competence that initially guides this kind of communicative action is based on the idea that remix is not merely a phenomenon found on the edges of a culture, intended as a semiotic space,[14] but rather testifies to the

Figure 24.1 "VW: The Dark Side," Greenpeace (courtesy of http://youtu.be/ nXndQuvOacU)

fact that social circulation of any text whatsoever within a culture is fueled by constant renegotiation of its borders.

The effectiveness of the most interesting rewriting actions, highly rewarded on the Web with massive diffusion (often superficially referred to as "viral"), is never actually achieved through indiscriminate deformation of a text, but rather by the ability to "read" its different levels, the internal links to the source story, which then subsequently creates a controlled transformation. In this sense, only the number and quality of a text's rewritings, of its remakes, of its translations can testify to the rich significance of a text within a culture.

Expanding our horizons from the texts to the overall scenario of social media, an important aspect that should be highlighted concerns the correlation between the increasing use of remix as a playful protest tool and the practices of manipulating preexisting content (in most cases protected by copyright laws) that lie at the base of the growing phenomenon of user-generated content (UGC). In the UGC scenario, the enunciation process is never purely individual but always open, potentially collective, temporary, evolving.

The marked flexibility shown in forms of appropriation and reelaboration of content on the Web clearly reflects the dynamism typical of differing *prosumer* figures in terms of skills and practices. Following this reflective train of thought, the actions of reopening and manipulating texts on the Internet that typify forms of remix (with particular reference to audiovisual language) escape all calculation or control, and, as far as enunciation is concerned, creative rewriting practices fuel a process whose boundaries are at the very least blurred. In this sense, playful forms of protest should always be analyzed from a diachronic standpoint, taking into consideration the entirety of the reactions that they fuel, all the communicative moves and countermoves that they contribute to trigger.

From this point of view, there is a particularly significant second stage in the planned strategy of dissent by Greenpeace activists against Volkswagen, following the 2012 promotional campaign for the launch of the New Beetle (sequel of the 2010 commercial based on *Star Wars*), entitled "The Dog Strikes Back: 2012 Volkswagen Game Day Commercial." The countermove chosen by the environmental organization to denounce the carmaker's boycott of European legislation on reducing CO_2 levels in the atmosphere, consisted in its invitation to its supporters, and in general to fandom groups dedicated to the science fiction saga, to unite in common protest against the German brand, using remixes and mashups as truly semiotic guerrilla tools.[15] This represents a significant shift in terms of planning forms of protest, since the principal organization for environmentalism on an international scale not only directly used forms of rewriting to deliver their political message, but also recognized the potential of creative consumer forms conceived by fans, inviting them to take part in a collective remix process that blatantly violated copyright laws. Furthermore, it is particularly relevant that Greenpeace did not stop merely at inviting and encouraging the creative reaction of fans, but also indicated how they could make the remix result even more visible (and so potentially more effective) on social networks, suggesting they tag videos with titles similar to that of Volkswagen's official commercial, so as to optimize their content in Google's search results.

The role of remixes as support tools for protest actions and, more generally, for raising public awareness emerges explicitly in the announcement posted on Greenpeace UK's official blog:

VW has launched its latest advert ahead of the US Super Bowl this weekend.

The advert is a follow-up to last year's Little Darth one which we lampooned to reveal the Dark Side of VW's environmental claims. It still riffs on a *Star Wars* theme and throws in a cute dog for good measure, but is there any mention of supporting ambitious climate laws?

Any room for a mention of radical efficiency improvements across VW's range? Or just generally living up to VW's ambitious claims of being the greenest car company on the planet?

Sadly not, but I think it's a missed opportunity. The Super Bowl is one of the biggest television events in the world so why not use it to announce some brave green measures?

That got me thinking: how could this advert be changed to show the real VW? The one that's lobbying against new laws to reduce emissions from vehicles in Europe. The one that won't meet with our campaign team for a chat. How about improving VW's advert? Download the video and give it a make-over. Then post it on our Facebook page. Drop in some new footage, add some subtitles, or revoice the guys propping up the cantina bar. Feel free to use clips from any Greenpeace films.[16]

As mentioned in the introduction, addressing the issue of the effectiveness of forms of remix on the pragmatic level, i.e., as communicative actions that can trigger real change in the political sphere, means first of all recognizing that the practice of so-called *adbusting* has long spread far beyond the borders of protest discourse, to the point of being widely used by the very same corporations against which they were initially directed.

According to this viewpoint, the ongoing stratification of communicative protest action is a response (provisional since it is subject to the constant dialectic relationship between activists and corporations) to the rapid assimilation of remix practices, to the recourse by a growing number of people to the semiotic logic on which the effectiveness of any form of rewriting within the digital media landscape is based: critical digital intertextuality.

A prime case in demonstrating to what extent remixes have become an established practice, both in fine-tuning the most original forms of activism and in constructing a complex marketing strategy, is undoubtedly the "Dove Onslaught(er)" campaign,[17] an exemplary action by Greenpeace, both in terms of the extraordinary interest aroused on the Web, and from the viewpoint of the pressure exerted against a corporation that had been committed to a vast program of corporate social responsibility for years.

In 2007, this well-known company, manufacturer of body care products, a brand of the Unilever group, launched an initiative dedicated to raising the awareness of consumers (in particular women) to the issue of the repercussions on an ethical plane of stereotyped patterns of beauty promoted by the cosmetics industry: "Campaign for real beauty."[18] Significantly, the structure of the film created to spread Dove's social message, which rapidly became one of the most successful on the Web, reproduced a consolidated form of enunciative bricolage typical of many DIY remixes, i.e., a recutting of preexisting images taken from TV news programs, advertising, covers of fashion magazines, that was then backed by the soundtrack taken from a preexisting song ("La Breeze" by Simian) which here aimed to raise a point of view that was explicitly critical of the spectacularization of women's bodies. Dove's message of social denouncement was made explicit by contrasting the images of sleek bodies, shaped by cosmetic surgery, with the

Figure 24.2 "Dove Onslaught(er)," I, Greenpeace (courtesy of http://youtu.be/odI7pQFyjso)

close-up of a little girl coming out of school, accompanied by the campaign slogan: "Talk to your daughter before the beauty industry does" (Figure 24.2).

In response to this initiative, Greenpeace planned a counterinformation campaign in 2008 to denounce to the public (and particularly to consumers of Dove products) the responsibilities of the Unilever Group, the largest global purchaser of palm oil, in the destruction of rainforests in southeast Asia. The video and the exposure initiative as a whole created one of the most successful cases for the environmental organization which, in just two weeks, thanks to huge support from tens of thousands of people who directly supported the campaign by sending emails of protest directly to Unilever, forced the multinational to accept a moratorium on the indiscriminate exploitation of endangered ecosystems.

The strategy chosen to create the film clip (which obtained over a million views in only a few days, visibility far higher than Dove's official commercial) combined spoof tactics with the practice of remix. The images of women's bodies were replaced by a series of photographs and video excerpts that portrayed the destruction of Indonesian forests and the killing of endangered animals for commercial purposes. The same song chosen for the Dove campaign was kept as a soundtrack but the words were changed to explain the ecologist cause's issue. The end result, produced by the band, Ohm Square, was therefore a "new" song called "There They Go" (referring to tree felling) and, at the same time, a parodic reference to Dove's communicative work. The social guerrilla operation was then completed by maintaining and simultaneously manipulating the opening and closing sequences of the video, substituting the image of the girl leaving school with the face of a young Indonesian woman, on whose scared face the camera focuses for a few seconds, accompanied by the protest's slogan: "98% of Indonesia's lowland forest will be gone by the time Azizah is 25. Most is destroyed to make palm oil, which is used in Dove products. Talk to Dove before it's too late" (Figures 24.3 and 24.4).

Figure 24.3 "Dove Onslaught(er)," II, Greenpeace (courtesy of http://youtu.be/odl7pQFyjso)

Figure 24.4 "Dove Onslaught(er)," III, Greenpeace (courtesy of http://youtu.be/odl7pQFyjso)

A last aspect that should be taken into consideration when analyzing the forms of political remix videos is that of the dialectical relationship established between the brands targeted by the protest and the logos that define the identity of the activists. The impact of the communicative attack never consists of merely deforming the hallmarks of a brand that is considered an "enemy" to their social cause. Increasingly, manipulation of the antagonist's signs is in fact framed within a wider discourse, a narrative organized into a myriad distinctly separate yet simultaneously interconnected texts that greatly expand the boundaries of traditional forms of protest.

In this sense, a particularly significant example was the social guerrilla campaign organized in 2011 by Wikileaks against Visa Europe, MasterCard, and American Express, which the previous year had blocked financial transactions in support of Julian Assange's cause.[19]

The video, which was at the center of an immense protest action against the major international credit cards, not only manipulated the MasterCard logo, remixing it with the image of Earth, but then gradually made the logo disappear, as the "winning" brand, Wikileaks, steadily advanced. This subvertising operation actually proved to be even more refined, for MasterCard's entire television advertising campaign was manipulated by using extremely precise camouflage, in which the soundtrack, the choice of shots, the photography, and the timbre of the narrator's voice-off reproduced the style of the official commercial in an absolutely believable way.

One can therefore see a further shift in the evolution of remix forms as tools of dissent. The polemic rewriting of texts not only deforms the narrative structure of adversaries' materials or brands, but also faithfully reproduces the overall style of their discourse. In this way, by assimilating the slick style of their opponent's television campaign, activists denounce even more dramatically the artificiality of their adversary's message and the soundness of their own protest.

In the professionalization of dissent, the practice of remix renews itself yet again by flaunting (with the sole aim of then overthrowing) the signs of that quintessential glossy discourse: advertising.

Conclusions

Even though the subversive use of remix is not a recent phenomenon, since its history is related to the very beginning of the moving picture, undoubtedly in the digital media composite milieu the ease of access to an unlimited archive of contents, combined with the more and more relevant role of postproduction tools in redefining the complex scenario of user-generated content, contribute to foster the popularity of this kind of media text and thereby the spreading of stratified hybridization processes.

An important parameter to keep in consideration in studying forms of reappropriation concerns the planes of text involved in manipulations. The effectiveness of the most interesting rewriting forms is not built on an indiscriminate deformation of the source text, but on authors' ability to select narrative, thematic, figurative, and enunciative elements that can be used to provoke a *controlled audiovisual manipulation*.

Hence, referring to the distinction between use and interpretation of texts,[20] we must admit that these heterogeneous and subtle manipulation practices should not be simply and briefly described as mere recreational deconstruction of texts because, as many cases demonstrate, they rely on complex interpretive cooperation semiotic processes.

From this perspective, the growth of political remix videos represents a remarkable phenomenon since the effectiveness of these transformative works relies undeniably on the enunciator's ability to address the audience, to select and manage the complex intricacy of intertextual and interdiscursive references. In this very broad category some of the most innovative forms of remix regard the creative strategies planned by media activists involved in nonprofit sector.

If on one side remix proves to be one of the most common techno-political tools of protest, on the other, the life cycle of any successful campaign is constantly conditioned by the increasing number of variants conceived by competitors and, more generally, by the constant dialectic between cultural rebellion and corporate co-optation.

To contain the progressive standardization of remix practices, the most creative strategies planned by activists consist in highlighting the stratification of the discourse, often resorting to camouflage tactics that emphasize the apparent extraneousness of the text to the political protest frame. Creative protest becomes a marketing weapon that fosters a sort of cultural loop, a battle between activists and brands where both sides compete and manipulate each other's signs, tactics, and strategies.

Notes

1 Eduardo Navas, "Regressive and Reflexive Mashups in Sampling Culture" in *Mashup Cultures*, ed. Stefan Sonvilla-Weiss (Wien: Springer, 2010), 161.
2 Claude Lévi-Strauss, *La Pensée Sauvage* (Paris: Plon, 1962).
3 Jean Marie Floch, *Visual Identities* (London: Continuum, 2000), 5.
4 Yuri M. Lotman, *Universe of the Mind: A Semiotic Theory of Culture*, trans. Ann Shukman (London: I. B. Tauris & Co Ltd, 1990).
5 Nicola Dusi "Translating, Adapting, Transposing," ASSA—Applied Semiotics, *Sémiotique Appliquée*, 24 (2010): 82–83.
6 See Jonathan McIntosh, "A History of Subversive Remix Video before YouTube: Thirty Political Video Mashups Made between World War II and 2005," *Transformative Works and Cultures* 9 (2012): 1–25.
7 Richard L. Edwards and Chuck Tryon, "Political Video Mashups as Allegories of Citizen Empowerment," *First Monday* 14 (2009): 1–11, http://firstmonday.org/ojs/index.php/fm/article/view/2617/2305.
8 See Luc Boltanski, *La souffrance à distance: morale humanitaire, médias et politique* (Paris: Editions Métailié, 1993); Susan Sontag, *Regarding the Pain of Others* (New York: Farrar, Straus and Giroux, 2003).
9 Louis Marin, *De la représentation* (Paris: Seuil/Gallimard, 1994).
10 Algirdas Julien Greimas and Joseph Courtés, *Sémiotique. Dictionnaire raisonné de la théorie du langage* (Paris: Hachette, 1979).
11 Henry Jenkins, *Fans, Bloggers, and Gamers: Exploring Participatory Culture* (New York: New York University Press, 2006).
12 Subvertising is a subversive advertisement common to culture jamming.
13 http://www.youtube.com/watch?v=eZ_vvDtv8lA (accessed May 3, 2014).
14 Lotman, *Universe of the Mind*.
15 Paolo Peverini, "Environmental Issues in Unconventional Social Advertising: Semiotic Perspective." *Semiotica: Journal of the International Association for Semiotic Studies*, 199 (2014): 219–246.
16 "VW's New Advert Misses a Trick, So Remix Your Own Version," http://www.greenpeace.org.uk/blog/climate/vws-new-advert-misses-trick-so-remix-your-own-version-20120202 (accessed May 3, 2014).
17 https://www.youtube.com/watch?v=HWaekMdpDDE (accessed May 3, 2014).
18 https://www.youtube.com/watch?v=Ei6JvK0W60I (accessed May 3, 2014).
19 https://www.youtube.com/watch?v=jzMN2c24Y1s (accessed May 3, 2014).
20 Umberto Eco, *The Limits of Interpretation* (Bloomington, IN: Indiana University Press, 1990).

Bibliography

Boltanski, Luc. *La souffrance à distance: morale humanitaire, médias et politique*. Paris: Editions Métailié, 1993.

Coppa, Francesca and Julie Levin Russo. "Fan/Remix video" special issue, *Transformative Works and Cultures* (2012), doi:10.3983/twc.2012.0371 (accessed May 2, 2014).

Dusi, Nicola. "Translating, Adapting, Transposing." ASSA—Applied Semiotics, *Sémiotique Appliquée* 24 (2010): 82–83.

Dusi, Nicola, and Lucio Spaziante, eds. *Remix-remake. Pratiche di replicabilità*. Roma: Meltemi, 2006.

Eco, Umberto. *The Limits of Interpretation*. Bloomington, IN: Indiana University Press, 1990.

Edwards, Richard L., and Chuck Tryon. "Political Video Mashups as Allegories of Citizen Empowerment." *First Monday* 14 (2009): 1–11. http://firstmonday.org/ojs/index.php/fm/article/view/2617/2305 (accessed May 2, 2014).

Eugeni, Ruggero. *Semiotica dei media. Le forme dell'esperienza.* Rome: Carocci, 2010.

Floch, Jean-Marie. *Visual Identities.* London: Continuum, 2000.

Gramigna, Remo. "Between Cultural Studies and Semiotics of Culture: The Case of Culture Jamming." *Lexia. Rivista di semiotica* 13/14 (2013): 61–99.

Greimas Algirdas Julien, and Joseph Courtés. *Sémiotique. Dictionnaire raisonné de la théorie du langage.* Paris: Hachette, 1979.

Jenkins, Henry. *Fans, Bloggers, and Gamers: Exploring Participatory Culture.* New York, NY: New York University Press, 2006.

Lasn, Kalle. *Culture Jam. How to Reverse America's Suicidal Consumer Binge—And Why We Must.* New York, NY: HarperCollins, 1999.

Lasn, Kalle, ed. *Meme Wars. The creative destruction of neoclassical economics.* New York, NY: Seven Stories Press, 2012.

Leone, Massimo, ed. "Protesta/Protest." *Lexia. Rivista di semiotica* 13/14 (2013).

Lévi-Strauss, Claude. *La pensée sauvage.* Paris: Plon, 1962.

Lotman, Yuri M. *Universe of the Mind: A Semiotic Theory of Culture.* London: I. B. Tauris & Co Ltd, 1990.

Marin, Louis. *De la représentation.* Paris: Seuil/Gallimard, 1994.

McIntosh, Jonathan. "A History of Subversive Remix Video before YouTube: Thirty Political Video Mashups Made between World War II and 2005." *Transformative Works and Cultures* 9 (2012): 1–25 doi:10.3983/twc.2012.0371.

Navas, Eduardo. "Regressive and Reflexive Mashups in Sampling Culture." In *Mashup Cultures,* edited by Stefan Sonvilla-Weiss, 157–177. Wien: Springer, 2010.

Peverini, Paolo "La manipolazione filmica come consumo creativo. Soggetti, pratiche, testi." In *Open Cinema: Scenari di visione cinematografica negli anni '10,* edited by Emiliana De Blasio and Paolo Peverini, 17–71. Roma: Edizioni Fondazione Ente dello Spettacolo, 2010.

——. "Eco-Images and Environmental Activism: A Sociosemiotic Analysis," in "Eco-Images. Historical views and political strategies," edited by Gisela Parak, special issue, *Rachel Carson Center Perspectives* 1 (2013): 73–85.

——. "Environmental Issues in Unconventional Social Advertising: A Semiotic Perspective." *Semiotica: Journal of the International Association for Semiotic Studies* 199 (2014): 219–246.

Pezzini, Isabella and Veruska Sabucco. "Praticare il testo. Oltre l'interpretazione, gli usi." In *Forme della testualità. Teorie, modelli, storia e prospettive,* edited by Paolo Bertetti and Giovanni Manetti, 331–343. Torino: Testo & Immagine, 2001.

Smith, Iain R. ed. "Cultural Borrowings: Appropriation, Reworking, Transformation" special issue and e-book, Scope (2009), https://www.academia.edu/207383/Cultural_Borrowings_Appropriation_Reworking_Transformation (accessed May 2, 2014).

Sontag, Susan. *Regarding the Pain of Others.* New York, NY: Farrar, Straus and Giroux, 2003.

Tryon, Chuck "Pop Politics: Online Parody Videos, Intertextuality, and Political Participation." *Popular Communication: The International Journal of Media and Culture* 6 (2008): 209–213.

25

POLITICAL REMIX VIDEO AS A VERNACULAR DISCOURSE

Olivia Conti

Remix processes in the contemporary media environment are responsible for objects of tremendous entertainment, aesthetic, and cultural value. Video remix, in particular, ranges from surrealist absurdity to sharp cultural critique, working with the ever-malleable materials of video, sound, and text to craft nuanced messages. Within the spectrum of video remix, political remix video (PRV) stands out for a number of reasons. PRV is: "a genre of transformative DIY media production whereby creators critique power structures, deconstruct social myths and challenge dominate [sic] media messages through re-cutting and re-framing fragments of mainstream media and the popular culture."[1]

In presenting explicitly political messages using solely bits of dominant mainstream discourse, the form is as fraught as it is full of subversive potential. It is this tension within the form that I will explore in this chapter. According to the *Political Remix Video* blog, maintained by remixer Jonathan McIntosh (most well known for his "Buffy vs. Edward" remix as well as his Donald Duck and Glenn Beck remix, "Right Wing Radio Duck")[2] political remix videos have three common traits. First, they present political messages, a term used loosely to refer to all manner of cultural and social issues. Second, they are guerilla insofar as the material that they use is copyright-protected. Third, they "utilize and embrace dominant media forms," meaning that they make use of the formal characteristics of their sources.[3] Through this process of reworking the familiar images and sounds of the media landscape, PRV encourages viewers to interrogate dominant ideologies.

While many previous discussions of remix have classified it in relation to art or music, some recent studies have focused on remix as an argument.[4] Continuing in this vein, my goal in this chapter is to describe the ways in which PRV functions discursively. I argue that political remix represents a vernacular discourse that affirms marginalized communities by calling up and subverting institutional texts. Ono and Sloop define vernacular discourses as those that "emerge from discussions between members of self-identified smaller communities within the larger civic community."[5] In remixing institutional texts in ways that resonate with these vernacular communities, PRV creators have the potential to affirm identity and strengthen community bonds. However, because the vernacular asserts itself both within and against the larger civic community, a continual oscillation between institutional and vernacular discourses is created, which produces tension within remix texts as well as at the sites of their reception.

In what follows, I first establish PRV as a vernacular discourse and then, through examples from the works of Elisa Kreisinger (with whom I worked during the summer of 2011) and Corey Ogilvie, I illustrate how PRV affirms vernacular community through the deployment of institutional source texts. I then analyze more deeply the remixes themselves to illustrate the points of friction between PRV's source material and its constructed messages. In so doing, I hope to illustrate how remix, by calling upon ideologically fraught sources for its arguments, represents a powerful site for critique and a site where rhetorical negotiation must be carefully undertaken.

Vernacular Discourse and its Relation to Political Remix Video

With the critical turn in rhetoric in the 1980s arose a desire on the part of scholars to focus not just on texts emanating from within cultural institutions, but rather on everyday—vernacular—discourses. Focusing on the vernacular has allowed scholars to uncover and analyze the speech of localized and marginalized communities so often denied access to mainstream discursive avenues.[6] The vernacular emerged as a rich point of study because it does not always maintain a consistent relationship to dominant discourse. Despite my emphasis on the vernacular, I think it serves digital scholars well to acknowledge that remix is such a deeply embedded cultural practice that there is certainly no definitive way to talk about it. Our understanding of remix is highly contextual—we understand it within the framework of our knowledge of the source, our views on intellectual property and originality, and our own disciplines. Vernacular discourse, like all other critical lenses, has its limitations. However, I believe that it is one of many potentially fruitful angles from which scholars can approach remix as discourse.

Ono and Sloop's framework for understanding vernacular discourse relies on two characteristics: cultural syncretism and pastiche. Cultural syncretism describes the manner in which the vernacular "affirms cultural expressions while at the same time protesting against dominant cultural ideology."[7] This is accomplished through pastiche, the way in which institutional discourses are appropriated and recycled in order to affirm the localized, community-based character of the vernacular. Ono and Sloop write that pastiche is embodied and ever-changing, "reconstituting discourses within specific racial, cultural, gendered, and ethnic communities."[8] In this way, pastiche can also describe the remixing process. For example, Guo and Lee explore pastiche through Jason Wu, an Asian American video blogger who uses pop culture representations of Asian stereotypes to bolster his critiques.[9] Appropriating these images affirms Wu's audience and inspires critical reflection. Seen in this way, a critical consideration of remix as vernacular discourse must take into account the interplay between appropriated bits of mainstream discourse and the constructed messages of smaller, more localized communities.

As Ono and Sloop note, critical studies of the vernacular must attend to the inherent hybridity of the form, and attempt to destabilize essentialized representations of marginalized communities.[10] Hybridity, reinvigorated by Homi Bhabha in the 1990s, is a useful, if complicated, analytical lens. Theories of hybridity can become locked into either pluralism or dualism, neither of which captures the essence of a truly hybrid form.[11] In the words of Guo and Lee, hybridity blurs and complicates rather than clarifies.[12] With this in mind, interrogating the hybridity of online vernacular discourses is important. However, as Leonard has observed, viewing a discourse as solely hybrid risks destabilizing marginalized groups.[13] As such, it is important to have a framework by which we may analyze vernacular discourses that takes their hybridity into account without relegating them to the realm of unknowable obscurity. Towards this end, Robert Glenn Howard has theorized a "dialectical vernacular" discourse that continually oscillates between top-down, mass-produced messages and grassroots, everyday discourses. The goal of this framework is not so much to create a new, third classification, but rather to acknowledge that discourse from within everyday communities must contain the institutional to establish its difference.[14] In turn, discourse producers are constituted as hybrid agents, simultaneously invoking vernacular and institutional authority. This is especially applicable to participatory media platforms such as Facebook, YouTube, and blogging platforms (which actively encourage sharing, user interaction, and the creation of new content) in that users continually assert themselves both within everyday online communities through the work they create, but also as institutional agents due to their use of large, commercial sites. Considered alongside cultural syncretism and pastiche, the dialectical vernacular permits a deep exploration of hybridity in PRV.

An analysis of PRV also invites a consideration of art versus discourse, a tension that exists both in vernacular and remix scholarship. Ono and Sloop note that vernacular discourse is both the speech resonating from and within localized communities, but also the culture of these communities, particularly, their artistic, musical, and architectural productions.[15] Since these cultural productions are discursive in and of themselves, a broader theoretical lens can help locate the vernacular. Kuhn explores this in her article as well, noting that analyzing political remix as an argument occurring across various registers (verbal, aural, and visual) requires a flexible theoretical focus.[16] This rhetorical and discursive view of remix represents a departure from many prior studies which have attempted to classify remix with regard to particular sorts of cultural production. For example, Eli Horwatt placed PRV in a lineage alongside Situationist *détournement* and other forms of culture jamming and appropriation art.[17] Similarly, Eduardo Navas defined contemporary remix practice as a historical trajectory emanating from practices in music communities, dividing the types of remix into extended, selective, and reflexive. These first two types refer mostly to music, however a reflexive remix is that in which "the remixed version challenges the aura of the original and claims autonomy," a designation applicable to video remixes including PRV.[18] While these are useful classifications for studying remix, it seems that there is a need for more rhetorical scholarship on remix as discourse and argument. As Kuhn notes, an analysis of remix as argument provides greater opportunity to destabilize the amateur/professional boundary by analyzing aesthetically and technically sophisticated videos that are constructed within (and often for) everyday communities, in order to express a desire for social change.[19]

Common to both vernacular discourse and remix is the necessity of a community affirmed by the reception of a mutually understood text. As Howard notes, the "celebratory insertion" of vernacular discourse into the institutional is read as subversive because the viewing audience sees the vernacular as alternate from the institutional.[20] In this way, the dialectical vernacular has the potential to affirm community identities and bonds and also to make a political argument. Similarly, Kuhn links the understanding of remix as a digital speech act to the affirmation of community, writing that "speech absolutely depends on a shared lexicon and the intent to communicate."[21] As such, remix emerges as a communicative form beyond entertainment or art—remix videos are often made for and within online communities, and communicated through a shared vocabulary. In recutting and reframing bits of this discourse—news broadcasts, popular television and radio programs, iconic cartoons and figures—remixers bolster their arguments while simultaneously setting themselves apart from the dominant normative discourse.

The Vernacularity of Political Remix Video

Elisa Kreisinger's *Queer Carrie* remix series is a prominent example of the subversive potential of PRV, having been widely shared online and also explored by remix scholars. The project takes the form of three video remixes that invoke the formal qualities of the *Sex and the City* episode as well as the season preview, wherein narrative arcs are conveyed through quick cuts. The remixes recast the show's protagonist, Carrie Bradshaw, as a queer woman navigating the vicissitudes of dating in New York. Alongside Carrie, friends Miranda, Samantha, and Charlotte have queer experiences of their own, from three-somes to blind dates with women. Kreisinger crafts these narratives using a number of different techniques, including reediting voiceovers, removing heteronormative language, and recontextualizing homosocial utterances in order to enhance romantic storylines, all while retaining aspects of the original show such as the theme song and Carrie's ubiquitous voiceovers.

> See Chapter 37 for Elisa Kreisinger's discussion on creating the remixes referenced here.

The source, *Sex and the City*, is one of the most popular entertainment franchises in the United States, having received 50 Emmy nominations and inspired two feature films.[22] After attracting initial acclaim for its willingness to tackle taboo issues and expose the "real world" of Manhattan dating, the series ended with all of the characters happily paired with members of the opposite sex, eliding any consideration of the true diversity of sexual orientation. The show also celebrated conspicuous consumption, frequently featuring designers and highlighting characters' consumer obsessions (Manolo Blahnik shoes, for instance).[23] *Sex and the City* became established as institutional through both its status as an entertainment franchise as well as its deployment of hegemonic Western ideals of consumerism and compulsory heterosexuality.

In contrast to its source, *Queer Carrie* embodies the hybridity of vernacular discourse both in its message as well as its means of production. Far from creating a "third text" that is entirely outside of *Sex and the City* or queer discourses, the remix calls up the source while simultaneously affirming a community that the original ignored and tokenized. Ono and Sloop note that vernacular discourse, via pastiche,

> can combine elements of popular culture in such a way as to create a unique form that implicitly and often explicitly challenges mainstream discourse, while at the same time affirming and creating the community and culture that produce vernacular discourse.[24]

Nuanced use of pastiche such as Kreisinger's does just this. The formal elements of the remix—the season preview format, the retention of Carrie's voiceovers and the show theme song—illustrate the oscillation inherent in the dialectical vernacular, for these aspects of the original call to mind the institutional affiliation of the source while the narrative and argument affirm a queer viewing community. By mimicking the standard *Sex and the City* format they call upon a community who have a familiarity with the source, while at the same time affirming queer and feminist viewers who objected to the original show's erasures of various identities.

Another example of political remix video used to reach a vernacular community is Corey Ogilvie's powerful Occupy Wall Street remix, *I Am Not Moving*. Ogilvie is a director whose first feature length documentary, *Think Peace: Portrait of a 21st Century Movement* debuted in 2008, and who has received Leo nominations for other documentaries and short films.[25] *I Am Not Moving* debuted on YouTube on October 11, 2011 and within a month had garnered over one million views.[26] In this video, samples of addresses by President Barack Obama and then-Secretary of State Hillary Clinton on 2011's Arab Spring revolutions are juxtaposed with street footage from protests in Libya, Egypt, and the Occupy Wall Street protests in New York City, as well as with historical footage from the civil rights movement. Overall, the juxtaposition of news footage with street footage in New York serves to highlight the perceived hypocrisy of the US government: while the footage of Obama and Clinton shows world leaders espousing the right of the people to peacefully protest their government and have a say in its policies, the footage from Occupy Wall Street shows ostensibly peaceful protesters at the mercy of armed police officers. In turn, the juxtaposition of protest footage from the Middle East with protest footage from New York shows striking similarities between a government derided by Obama for using "brutal suppression" and US law enforcement.

In juxtaposing these sources, Ogilvie makes a powerful argument about the US government and its perspective on dissent at home and abroad. In drawing parallels between the Occupy and Arab Spring protesters, the remix affirms Occupy Wall Street and its supporters—a large vernacular collective. Additionally, those who disagree with the remix are positioned as very much other-than the community it speaks to, even on the level of the title: *I am not moving* (a quote from one of the protesters), which encourages viewers to identify with the vernacular "I" or the institutional "you." *I Am Not Moving* also serves to highlight the versatility of the remix argument. As Kuhn writes, remix has the ability to "subvert the dominant discursive field and its reified genres: Hollywood film, broadcast television, documentary, journalism, ethnography. Remix lays bare the constructed nature of the original and often calls attention to its own construction."[27] The juxtaposition of widely broadcast addresses made both by contemporary political figures as well as historical civil rights heroes such as Martin Luther King Jr. with user-shot video of police brutality calls attention to the ways in which protest is reconfigured in the news cycle and throughout history to suit various political agendas and narratives. The shots from Egypt and Libya are not, on their surface, all too different from the shots from New York, yet the way they were translated for the deeply institutional venues of the political speech and the news broadcast express vastly different views of the two protests. Thus, the remix simultaneously proffers a critical view of US government and news media, while also elevating the Occupy Wall Street protests to the level of the Arab Spring revolutions through juxtaposition. While this claim may seem dubious to some, there is no doubt that Ogilvie's argument powerfully affirms the Occupy Wall Street collective and sharply critiques US policy.

With these examples in mind, it's clear that PRV can be held as an example of online vernacular discourse. In constructing arguments from preexisting texts (and the ideologies attending such texts), remixers call upon viewers to recognize their own vernacular community and to interrogate the primacy of hegemonic discourses. This mode of argument constitutes the remix as both a rhetorical and a vernacular text, for it makes an argument that resonates with its intended other-than-institutional audience. However, institutional sources are a volatile substance, arriving to the viewer rife with associations and affiliations. A skillfully executed remix, witnessed by its intended audience, will likely be well received. However, given the ease with which remix videos are published and shared, as well as the delicate work of constructing an argument from preexisting texts, the impact of a remix cannot always be predicted.

The Frictions of Vernacular Remix

In this section, I will discuss the areas of friction that remix causes and encounters online. Ono and Sloop note that it is essential to any critical consideration of the vernacular that we do not require it to always be counterhegemonic, for "even if the vernacular is concerned with local conditions these concerns can at times be more hegemonic than not."[28] When applied to Internet discourse, these "local conditions" expand outward to include vast, institutionalized practices, the types of prejudice that are woven into the fabric of everyday life and encoded into source texts used by remixers. My primary concern is that occasionally these discourses "tag along" with remixed source footage, meaning that, regardless of a remixer's intent to argue, their remixes can be read as implicitly or explicitly institutional. Here, there also exists a second issue regarding vernacular expressions online: the "spreadability" of online video in combination with participatory media such as YouTube, social media sites, and blogs. "Spreadability," coined by Henry Jenkins, refers to "the potential—both technical and cultural—for audiences to share content for their own purposes."[29] The permeable boundaries between communities and the spreadability of vernacular expressions actively challenge the notion of online "localization" and often lead to remixes being misunderstood. Beyond these tensions, questions also persist about remix as art given the professional and polished nature of many popular remixes.

One of the most interesting facets of Kreisinger's *Queer Carrie* is that it stays thematically consistent with its source—it is about women consumed by their romantic relationships and their consumer obsessions. This simultaneously contributes to the remix's vernacular nature, for it is what makes the queer narrative stand out, but it also rearticulates problematic values that are inseparable from the source itself. For instance, in one episode, Carrie's jealousy and insecurity about her ex-boyfriend's new partner (Natasha) are transformed, via remix, into romantic jitters. Carrie is shown having lunch with Charlotte and discussing the outfit that she plans to wear to an upcoming event where Natasha will be in attendance. She describes how her "Natasha-specific obsession" will be put to rest once she is seen in a pair of recently purchased shoes and a dress that will cost her a month's rent.[30] Charlotte's response to this is a reassurance that Carrie is "stunning" and "intelligent" and that she will impress Natasha regardless of what she wears.[31] While the situation is recontextualized to describe Carrie's complicated feelings about a romantic relationship with Natasha, the show's consumer values and romantic obsession are untouched—Carrie believes that her worth is conferred upon her by her choice of footwear rather than her qualities as a woman. Thus, *Queer Carrie* still reflects

351

the original show's problematic relations between gender, sexual desirability, and conspicuous consumption. Guo and Lee echo this concern when discussing Asian American video producers' use of Asian stereotypes to produce a humorous response. While among their target audience (fellow Asians/Asian Americans) this may be read as humorous rather than offensive or alienating, Guo and Lee note that using these stereotypes even in a parodic manner risks perpetuating them.[32] With this in mind, it is important to interrogate whether the reproduction of these consumer and romantic obsessions has the potential to perpetuate hegemonies that would be best deconstructed by other means.

This potential of remix to be read as unwittingly institutional also calls up questions of how it is read as it circulates throughout online venues. Virginia Kuhn emphasizes the importance of a "common lexicon" when she writes about her initial ambivalent response to *Queer Carrie* and her process of attempting to better understand the remix. Kuhn's initial impression resulted from the fact that the remixed characters only choose women after being disappointed by men, a retelling that reinforced gender inequality and heteronormativity.[33] However, after discussing the remix with Kreisinger herself, Kuhn rewatched it, attending to the manner in which toxic homosocial competition and jealousy are transformed via remix into fulfilling same-sex relationships, ultimately concluding that her initial "flawed" reading was due to her expectation that the remix referred to life rather than to its source.[34] It is worth noting that the average viewer is neither as charitable nor as proactive as Kuhn, a remix scholar who sought out the video's creator to discuss the work. Thus, while its relation to the source may be read as ironic or subversive, the complex dissection of the argument's many registers may not happen on first glance for many viewers. Indeed, as Kreisinger acknowledges, the more queer remixes are shared among general audiences, the greater the potential for them to be read incorrectly due to audiences' lack of familiarity with the "discursive community" from which they arise.[35] Yet, this spreadability is part and parcel of the current media environment, and an important factor in building community online.

Participatory media (blogs, social media, and so on) represent a complex site of negotiation, for remixed texts, the sites on which they are shared, and to some extent the remixers themselves are tenuously balancing between vernacular and institutional, something acknowledged by Howard.[36] As Howard writes, vernacular authority at these discursive nodes is "accessible to everyone through the webs of structured discourse."[37] For instance, websites where Kreisinger's remix videos are posted—their "web of structured discourse"—generally cater to at least one of her target audiences. Commenters representing this cross-section of the Internet appear across venues—members of the political remix video community, or figures in the feminist and queer blogospheres. However, given the complex relationships of each commenting agent, vernacular authority takes vastly different shapes at each discursive node in the network. While Kreisinger's remixes are celebrated on her own website, on YouTube, and in original posts by other bloggers, as they move further and further away from this nucleus of familiarity—where viewers know what to expect and have a fairly comprehensive understanding of what political remix video is all about—the receptiveness of Kreisinger's audience seems to decrease.

To be precise, the perceived decline in audience receptivity becomes apparent when we note that Kreisinger's work rarely appears on her own blog or elsewhere without the inclusion of either an interview or a quote taken from her website about the mission of PRV. For this reason, her remixes rarely appear as "entertainment-only" texts, if such texts can be said to exist. On her blog and also on YouTube, the commenters show a willingness to engage with Kreisinger on PRV as well as her intended argument, asking questions and posting their own thoughts. On YouTube, many users expressed their admiration for the remix and their desire for more queer storylines, though a number of comments also focused on the attractiveness of the same-sex pairings (this unprecedented level of civility could be due to the fact that Kreisinger admits to deleting offensive comments).[38] However, when *Queer Men* (a queer remix of *Mad Men*) appeared on feminist blog *Jezebel* and *The Atlantic*'s entertainment section, each alongside interviews with or statements by Kreisinger, it met with some resistance from the commenting bodies at each site, despite being well contextualized within PRV as a whole. *Jezebel* users (again) focused on the hotness of the Don and Roger pairing and generally did not engage with Kreisinger's goals for the remix, though some made critical comments about her artist statement, for instance criticizing her use of the word "patriarchy" rather than "status quo."[39] Users on *The Atlantic* entertainment website mostly poked fun at the idea of a remix, suggesting, for instance, queering the *700 Club* or saying that "with enough footage, you can make 3 minutes of anything."[40] Almost no user comments (on both websites) responded to the argument of the remix or any of Kreisinger's statements regarding her work.

These differing responses seem to relate to differing communicative expectations. As Kuhn notes, a speech act depends on a "shared lexicon and intent to communicate," and a remix's criticality should be judged by its "participation in a discourse community."[41] While Kreisinger is positioned as a member of the communities where her work is posted—a feminist, an entertainment critic—the audiences at a number of these discursive nodes challenge this vernacular authority. Additionally, they do not seem to see the remix as a speech act but rather as an entertainment object, despite the fact that the original posts do deal with the remix as a political argument. In the case of *The Atlantic*, Kreisinger's remix seems to disrupt some sort of expected norm, perhaps due to the YouTube video being foregrounded in the post (which may signal frivolity or entertainment) or the fact that it was included in the site's "entertainment" section. In the case of *Jezebel*, the remix is misunderstood as an entertainment object or challenged outright due to Kreisinger's failure to use the desired vocabulary ("patriarchy" versus "status quo"). When the videos are embedded in locations that have different expectations for communication than Kreisinger's more immediate circle, the remixes do not show any sort of community resonance. This reception across discursive nodes extends notions of the dialectical vernacular because the vernacular expression does not change (i.e., the video remains the same), but the community that it evokes (or fails to evoke) takes a different form wherever the video is shared. Thus, even though the audience may be familiar with the original show, they fail to see the remix as an argument due to the context in which it is placed.

Professional remix techniques are another contested issue raised by some PRV. Remixes like Kreisinger's and Ogilvie's, as well as many other celebrated remixes like Jonathan McIntosh's "Right Wing Radio Duck" or Diran Lyons's "99 Problems," exhibit a tremendous degree of technical skill, and in many cases these creators have credentials and experience in the realm of media production. Vernacular discourse, generally speaking, refers to the everyday creations of communities. However, in the case of remix, a certain amount of creative and technical skill seems to be required to make a successful video. While there are many amateur remixes, the ones that generally end up achieving viral status demonstrate professional or quasi-professional levels of technological proficiency, as evidenced by the wide circulation of the above-mentioned videos. Eli Horwatt notes (of trailer remixing) that "a successful remix is predicated on a highly media literate creator who can deconstruct and recreate the nuances and technical devices employed by the film preview."[42] These media and technical literacies undoubtedly place the remixer in a relatively privileged position in comparison to many in their audience, who may not have the media awareness, time, or skills to create remixes themselves, though they may be able to recognize the cleverness of the remix. This, again, invokes a discussion of remix as art versus remix as argument. As Kuhn notes, understanding remix as art risks reinforcing the amateur/professional binary.[43] While these two categories are by no means diametrically opposed, the frames of analysis and assessment for each are different. While this does not hinder the ability of remix to argue, I am concerned that the polish and professionalism of some largely successful remixes may potentially distance viewers, or further encourage the analysis of remix through artistic rather than rhetorical frameworks. In turn, this may weaken the remix's ability to affirm vernacular communities by positioning the act of remixing as something outside of the capabilities of the viewer. Thus, while viewers may engage in discourse *around* the video (by sharing and commenting) they may be less inclined to make their own remixes.

Given the immense variety of vernacular communities online and the tremendous mobility afforded vernacular expressions by networked technologies, there is no definitive way to assess whether a particular PRV was received as intended. Indeed, it seems that the most likely answer is that a remix's effect depends largely on its context. This reinforces preexisting notions of the vernacular in that the successful affirmation of a vernacular community takes place in certain localized areas (for instance, Kreisinger was best received on her own blog). These areas of friction also illustrate the nuances of hybridity, and do away with any notion of a hybrid as a third form by highlighting the continuing oscillation between vernacular, community-focused discourses and dominant institutional ones. Both the online venue where a remix is placed as well as the viewer's own perspective and understanding of the remix upon first viewing determine the manner in which it is interpreted. In looking at these areas of friction we can come to understand that any given PRV, while itself presenting a complex argument, is also necessarily involved in a give-and-take with its audience, its venue, and various other contextual factors. This demonstrates the importance of viewing remix with a critical eye both as scholars and as laypeople.

Conclusion

In this chapter, I've introduced the idea of PRV as a hybrid vernacular form, a notion that extends previous studies of the rhetoric of remix by situating PRV as an expression that evokes smaller, often marginalized groups of the larger civic community. This grants PRV tremendous potential to affirm community bonds, however as many vernacular scholars note, being vernacular does not immediately grant liberatory or counterhegemonic potential.[44] Nonetheless, in remixing mainstream discourses, remixers offer sharp critiques of the world in which we live and draw their viewing communities together. I have also suggested that the spreadability of remix can present a challenge to notions of the vernacular due to the fact that different communities take shape wherever the remix is shared. In turn, I have posited that the reproduction of problematic discourses via remix may not always serve a subversive potential for this same reason.

PRV is a new media phenomenon that merits study from a variety of perspectives. It sits at the nexus of image, discourse, and technology, and it is this hybrid status that makes remix such a useful vehicle for expression and critique, but also what imbues it with tension. As a rhetorical scholar interested in remix as argument, I have been drawn to the vernacular as a lens through which to view remix because it highlights how remix functions, how it occasionally fails to function, and also where the vernacular lens itself fails. Understanding PRV as a vernacular discourse involves interrogating how remix serves to affirm marginalized communities, but also how it is forever hybrid, incorporating institutional texts into vernacular messages and broadcasting them (most often) in institutional venues. With this hybridity comes complication, for the institutional is saturated with hegemony and oppression, and so too is remix forever grappling with these issues.

Notes

1 "About Political Remix Video," Political Remix Video, http://www.politicalremixvideo.com/what-is-political-remix/.
2 Jonathan McIntosh, "Buffy vs. Edward: Twilight Remixed," *rebelliouspixels*, http://www.rebelliouspixels.com/2009/buffy-vs-edward-twilight-remixed; "Right Wing Radio Duck," *rebelliouspixels*, http://www.rebelliouspixels.com/2010/right-wing-radio-duck-donald-discovers-glenn-beck.
3 Ibid.
4 Virginia Kuhn, "The Rhetoric of Remix," *Transformative Works and Cultures* 9 (2012). doi:10.3983/twc.2012.0358.
5 Kent A. Ono and John M. Sloop, "The Critique of Vernacular Discourse," *Communication Monographs* 62 (1995): 23.
6 Ibid., 19.
7 Ibid., 22.
8 Ibid., 23.
9 Lei Guo and Lorin Lee, "The Critique of YouTube-based Vernacular Discourse: A Case Study of YouTube's Asian Community," *Critical Studies in Media Communication* 30, no. 5 (2013): 10, doi:10.1080/1529503.2012.755048.
10 Ono and Sloop, "The Critique of Vernacular Discourse," 34.
11 Marwan Kraidy, *Hybridity, or the Cultural Logic of Globalization* (Philadelphia, PA: Temple University Press, 2005): 5.
12 Guo and Lee, "The Critique of YouTube-based Vernacular Discourse," 5.
13 Philip Leonard, *Nationality between Poststructuralism and Postcolonial Theory: A New Cosmopolitanism* (Basingstoke: Palgrave Macmillan, 2005): 150.
14 Robert Glenn Howard, "Electronic Hybridity: The Persistent Processes of the Vernacular Web," *Journal of American Folklore* 121 (2008): 204.
15 Ono and Sloop, "The Critique of Vernacular Discourse," 20.
16 Kuhn, "The Rhetoric of Remix," 1.5.
17 Eli Horwatt, "A Taxonomy of Digital Video Remixing: Contemporary Found Footage Practice on the Internet," Cultural Borrowings: Appropriation, Reworking, Transformation, *Scope: An Online Journal of Film and Television Studies*, http://www.scope.nottingham.ac.uk/cultborr/Cultural_Borrowings_Final.pdf#page=88.
18 Eduardo Navas, "Remix Defined," *Remix Theory* (n.d.). http://remixtheory.net/?page_id=3.
19 Kuhn, "The Rhetoric of Remix," 1.7.
20 Howard, "Electronic Hybridity," 205.
21 Kuhn, "The Rhetoric of Remix," 1.7.
22 "About The Show," HBO, http://www.hbo.com/sex-and-the-city/index.html#/sex-and-the-city/about/index.html.
23 Elisa Kreisinger, interview by Koa Beck, *Daily Brink*, http://www.dailybrink.com/?p=762.
24 Ono and Sloop, "The Critique of Vernacular Discourse," 23.
25 Corey Ogilvie, "About," OgilvieFilm.com, http://www.ogilviefilm.com/about.html

26 Corey Ogilvie, "News," OgilvieFilm.com, http://www.ogilviefilm.com/news.html

27 Kuhn, "The Rhetoric of Remix," 5.4.

28 Ono and Sloop, "The Critique of Vernacular Discourse," 34.

29 Henry Jenkins, Sam Ford, and Joshua Green, *Spreadable Media: Creating Value and Meaning in a Networked Culture* (New York, NY: New York University Press, 2013): 3.

30 Elisa Kreisinger, *Sex and the Remix (Queering Sex and the City) Season 2*, YouTube video, January 11, 2010, http://www.YouTube.com/watch?v=JVWWQF2jcsg.

31 Elisa Kreisinger, *Sex and the Remix (QueerCarrie Project: Queering Sex and the City) Seasons 3–6*, YouTube video, May 26, 2010, http://www.youtube.com/watch?v=f1QfWRD7qfA.

32 Guo and Lee, "The Critique of YouTube-based Vernacular Discourse,"13.

33 Kuhn, "The Rhetoric of Remix," 4.4.

34 Ibid., 4.6.

35 Elisa Kreisinger, "Queer Video Remix and LGBTQ Online Communities," *Transformative Works and Cultures* 9 (2012): 1.1.

36 Robert Glenn Howard, "The Vernacular Web of Participatory Media," *Critical Studies in Media Communication* 25, no. 5 (2008): 497.

37 Ibid.

38 Elisa Kreisinger, e-mail message to author, April 9, 2012.

39 Dodai Stewart, "What if Don Draper Was Deeply in Love with Roger Sterling?" Jezebel. March 15, 2012. http://jezebel.com/5893622.

40 Kasia Cieplak-Mayr von Baldegg, "Sex, Lies, and Video Remixes: Critiquing 'Mad Men' in Its Own Words." *The Atlantic*, March 22, 2012. http://www.theatlantic.com/entertainment/archive/2012/03/sex-lies-and-video-remixes-critiquing-mad-men-in-its-own-words/254912/.

41 Kuhn, "The Rhetoric of Remix," 1.7.

42 Horwatt, "A Taxonomy of Digital Video Remixing."

43 Kuhn, "The Rhetoric of Remix," 1.7.

44 Ono and Sloop, "The Critique of Vernacular Discourse," 40.

Bibliography

"About Political Remix Video," *Political Remix Video*, http://politicalremixvideo.net (accessed August 13, 2014).

Cieplak-Mayr von Baldegg, Kasia. "Sex, Lies, and Video Remixes: Critiquing 'Mad Men' in Its Own Words." *The Atlantic*. March 22, 2012. http://www.theatlantic.com/entertainment/archive/2012/03/sex-lies-and-video-remixes-critiquing-mad-men-in-its-own-words/254912/ (accessed August 13, 2014).

Guo, Lei and Lorin Lee. "The Critique of YouTube-based Vernacular Discourse: A Case Study of YouTube's Asian Community." *Critical Studies in Media Communication* 30, no. 5 (2013): 1–16. doi 10.1080/15295036.2012.755048.

"HBO: Sex and the City: Homepage." *HBO*. http://www.hbo.com/sex-and-the-city/index.html (accessed August 13, 2014).

Horwatt, Eli. "A Taxonomy of Digital Video Remixing: Contemporary Found Footage Practice on the Internet." Cultural Borrowings: Appropriation, Reworking, Transformation. *Scope: An Online Journal of Film and Television Studies*. PDF e-book.

Howard, Robert Glenn. "Electronic Hybridity: The Persistent Processes of the Vernacular Web," *Journal of American Folklore* 121 (2008): 192–218.

——. "The Vernacular Web of Participatory Media," *Critical Studies in Media Communication* 25, no. 5 (2008): 490–513.

——. "Toward a Theory of the World Wide Web Vernacular: The Case for Pet Cloning," *Journal of Folklore Research* 42, no. 3 (2005): 323–360.

Jenkins, Henry, Sam Ford, and Joshua Green. *Spreadable Media: Creating Value and Meaning in a Networked Culture*. New York, NY: New York University Press, 2013. Kindle e-book.

Kraidy, Marwan. *Hybridity, or the Cultural Logic of Globalization*. Philadelphia: Temple University Press, 2005.

Kreisinger, Elisa, e-mail message to author, April 9, 2012.

——. Interview by Koa Beck, *Daily Brink*. http://www.dailybrink.com/?p=762 (accessed August 13, 2014).

——. *Pop Culture Pirate*, http://www.popculturepirate.com (accessed August 13, 2014).

——. *Sex and the Remix (Queering Sex and the City) Season 1*. YouTube video. 5:44. October 14, 2009. http://www.YouTube.com/watch?v=Wn_WHLTK3qI (accessed August 13, 2014).

——. *Sex and the Remix (Queering Sex and the City) Season 2*. YouTube video. 4:04. January 11, 2010. http://www.YouTube.com/watch?v=JVWWQF2jcsg (accessed August 13, 2014).

——. *Sex and the Remix (QueerCarrie Project: Queering Sex and the City) Seasons 3–6*. YouTube video. 4:22. May 26, 2010. http://www.youtube.com/watch?v=f1QfWRD7qfA May 26, 2010.

——. *QueerMen: Don Loves Roger Mad Men Remix*. Vimeo video. 5:36. March 11, 2012. http://vimeo.com/38342068 (accessed August 13, 2014).

——. "Queer Video Remix and LGBTQ Online Communities." *Transformative Works and Cultures* 9 (2012). doi:10.3983/twc.2012.0395.

Kuhn, Virginia. "The Rhetoric of Remix." *Transformative Works and Cultures* 9 (2012). doi:10.3983/twc.2012.0358.

Leonard, Philip. *Nationality between Poststructuralism and Postcolonial Theory: A New Cosmopolitanism*. Basingstoke: Palgrave Macmillan, 2005.

Navas, Eduardo. "Remix Defined," *Remix Theory* (n.d.). http://remixtheory.net/?page_id=3 (accessed August 13, 2014).

Ogilvie, Corey. *OgilvieFilm.com*. http://www.ogilviefilm.com/index.html (accessed August 13, 2014).

Ono, Kent. A and John M. Sloop. "The Critique of Vernacular Discourse," *Communication Monographs* 62 (1995): 19–46.

——. *Shifting Borders: Rhetoric, Immigration and California's Proposition 187*. Philadelphia: Temple University Press, 2002.

Stewart, Dodai. "What if Don Draper Was Deeply in Love with Roger Sterling?" *Jezebel*. March 15 2012. http://jezebel.com/5893622 (accessed August 13, 2014).

26
LOCATIVE MEDIA AS REMIX

Conor McGarrigle

While data-driven art is not new, recent developments in technical, artistic, and social spheres have coalesced to produce new opportunities for artists and activists who remix data with space and place to form locationally specific political critiques of great power and flexibility.

These opportunities arise from multiple factors including the wide availability of smartphones and other mobile devices, their location awareness and "always-on" network connectivity combined with an increased computational power. These location-aware devices are capable of running complex apps that employ locational data to provide context-specific information. This location awareness is not new—it has been available in various forms since the early 2000s when unrestricted access to the Global Positioning System (GPS) was made available with the ending of selective availability.[1] What is new is the ubiquity of these devices, their increased computational power, improved imaging systems, and the capability to add geolocation data to images and videos. Greatly improved hybrid positioning techniques have overcome the limitations of relying on GPS for position, particularly in urban settings,[2] which in turn have enabled an extensive infrastructure of social media applications that encourage users to share their location.

This places the individual as not only the author or producer of an extensive data trail but one which can be tracked in time and space, and one for which there is no longer a reasonable expectation of privacy.[3] Preexisting concerns about data privacy, particularly for information held by the Internet big five (Google, Amazon, Facebook, Microsoft, and Apple), reached a crisis point in the wake of Edward Snowden's 2013 revelations about the NSA's PRISM program[4] when the scale of possible surveillance of these data shadows was revealed to be significantly more comprehensive than previously thought. The purpose here is not to dwell on the implications of the lack of locational privacy immanent in location-aware networked devices, which have been well exercised in the media, but instead to lay out the landscape in order to examine methods for intervening in these areas and to identify the opportunities to work within (and against) the affordances of these systems.

These developments have led to the increased ability of networked location-aware devices to effectively deliver real-time, location-specific, contextual remix. This builds on the idea of the mashup, familiar from Web applications such as the ubiquitous Google Maps mashup, that incorporates constantly updated information or data sampled directly from a variety of database sources. For example a map displaying train station locations pulled from a static database mashed up with live timetable information from a live data feed. In considering locative media as remix, however, I suggest there is more at work than this familiar scenario of combining related information into a single interface with the objective of increasing the information's utility for the user. It is important to differentiate these first-order mashups, which combine data sources but essentially leave these sources untouched, from a locative media remix which operates at multiple levels, beginning with data. Data is in essence a text and can be remixed as such, this can be done statically or dynamically through algorithmic processes which extract, sample, and combine multiple data sources in real time to form new data sets that are shaped by the logic of the remix expressed through the action of algorithms. For example the database of the *NAMAland* case study had its origins in multiple sources such as corporate annual reports and business news reports processed multiple times to produce a data set with a substantially different meaning and form than its base material.

Locative media remix thus goes further than a simple overlayering of information at specific locations, rather through its application of contextual artistic and activist data (itself already a remix) it offers a competing understanding of location. This draws on Lefebvrian ideas of spatial production that see space as a social product, defined by a complex set of interrelationships, resulting in a multiplicity of interconnected, overlapping and competing spaces which influence, and are influenced by, each other.[5] Locative media remix then operates at a number of levels; at the data level with data sampled from many sources and combined to produce a data set which owes more to the objective and logic of the remix than to the original source, and at the level of critical spatial practice[6] through the introduction of competing spatialities which cause social space to be understood and produced differently. The final level of remix is the potential for user practices generated through these approaches to shape emergent location-aware technologies opening them to a broader constituency of users and expanding the range of normalized applications as the technologies stabilize.

These capabilities have come together with a burgeoning open data infrastructure, which provides the raw material for the remix. Open data initiatives in the United States, Western Europe, and, increasingly, in the developing world, make available vast swaths of data, often at no cost, about all aspects of city and government operations. Much of this comprehensive data is geotagged and supplied in formats that lend themselves to remix. In parallel with open data developments, more and more locational data is available from geotagged social media data such as tweets and shared images. Many of these social media services offer API[7] access to their data and for those who do not, data-scraping techniques can usually be used to access this information.

Together, these represent accessible sources of large data sets about many aspects of urban life and its social practices which, when remixed with location-aware platforms such as mobile augmented reality (AR) browsers, present opportunities to overlayer urban space with data-powered critique, activist interventions, and powerful visualizations, providing new methods for understanding and engaging with the space of our cities. To consider how this works, the methods to be used, and the potential for remix to generate alternative knowledge I want to turn to early locative media art practice, which demonstrated an engagement with GPS that had a profound impact on this emergent technology and, I argue, our understanding and application of location-aware technologies.

Locative Media as an Art Practice

Thomas McDonough described the Situationists as being engaged in "an attempt to change the meaning of the city through changing the way it was inhabited."[8] This could equally be applied to emergent locative media art practitioners, who attempted to change the meaning of locative technologies by changing the ways in which they are employed. When consumer level GPS technologies first became widely available in the early 2000s, the dominant view of location, one perhaps intrinsic to the GPS system, was Cartesian—it described position as a point in Cartesian space which could be uniquely identified by coordinates of longitude and latitude. Locative media practitioners, while working within the affordances of the GPS system, brought an expanded understanding through their introduction of new user practices, which ran counter to this prevailing view. This came from a desire to provide alternatives to existing views, which were seen as "unnecessarily impoverished."[9] Central to this understanding was the belief that as locational technology became available to a broader constituency it opened up previously unavailable opportunities, and allowed individuals and communities to augment space[10] with context-sensitive annotations. In the words of Ben Russell's prescient *Headmap Manifesto*, "what was once the sole preserve of builders, architects and engineers falls into the hands of everyone: the ability to shape and organize the real world and the real space."[11]

The term "locative media" is widely accepted to have been first coined by Karlis Kalnins[12] at the "Locative Media Workshop: Mapping the Zone" event, which took place in an abandoned Soviet-era military base in Karosta, Latvia from July 16 to July 26, 2003.[13] The term was originally employed to distinguish between the questioning of artistic uses of locative technologies from their instrumentalized commercial and military uses. The proposition was that locative technologies, which had at this point (2003) only recently become widely available for civilian use, represented a fundamental, perhaps even paradigmatic, shift (or the means to bring about such a shift) in our perception of geographic location. It was further proposed that the artistic uses of these technologies not only represented a new artistic medium, but had an important role to play in the opening up of the possibilities of the medium to everyone. In thinking about locative media and its influence on the unfolding and understanding of location-aware technologies, it is important to position it as an aleatory product of the GPS system. This places it in a very specific context as a practice only possible due to a multibillion-dollar US military initiated space-based navigation, positioning, and timing system.[14] The essential enabling component of most locative work at this time was GPS, consisting of a constellation of 24 orbiting satellites and an extensive network of earth tracking and control stations—a system that was developed at a cost of over $10 billion,[15] with an annual $400 million maintenance bill, operated by the US Department of Defense to provide "navigation, position location, and precision timing services to users worldwide." This acknowledges that the "culture of location-awareness"[16] from which locative media and its associated art practices spring, is a direct result of the military envisaging, design, and implementation of a satellite-based location system. On the other hand, it establishes it as a practice seeking to discover, in the words of Lisa Parks, "how might Western controlled satellite technologies be appropriated and used in the interests of a wider range of social formations?"[17]

Yet, locative media is a parasitic practice, one that, while working within the GPS infrastructure, introduced spatial practices, which owe more to Henri Lefebvre's concept of "lived space" than to what has been seen as the innate Cartesian translation of the GPS system. This distinction in approach, I suggest, comes down to the difference between understandings of "position" and "location." "Position" is a point on a Cartesian grid identified by coordinates of longitude and latitude; for example, as I write this, my position can be uniquely identified by coordinates of longitude and latitude, which is very useful information if I was lost at sea, or to be targeted by a proximity marketing campaign, or a Predator drone, but provides no information about the nature of this place, its history, and the layers of association that constitute my relationship with it. This key differentiation is at the heart of locative media; the distinction between position as instrumentalized localization of space as points in a Cartesian grid, to be tracked and targeted with locative technologies, and of "location" as an "existential, inhabited, experienced and lived place,"[18] the space of individuals and communities replete with histories, narratives, and layers of association, which imbue location with meaning that can be revealed and made visible through the application of locative technologies.

In this way, locative media draw together a number of practices, technologies, and techniques to produce critical work, which augment real space with contextual layers of information enabled through the affordances of the technologies. Once this ability of the individual to locate herself (or to be located) in space and to access multiple layers of context-sensitive information exists, it opens up the possibility of new spatialities, from panoptical control space to spaces of radical transparency. Locative media artists operate within this window, establishing practices, which are sometimes experimental and other times eminently practical. In so doing, they establish a mode of operating for new location-aware technologies which, if successful, remain permanently inscribed. In this way, the pervasive games of *Pac Manhattan*[19] or Brighton's Blast Theory[20] collective established location-aware mobile devices as tools for transforming the city into a playful space, whereas pioneering locative media projects such as Urban Tapestries,[21] adopted a grassroots approach, where local communities tell their own stories, locating them in real space, to be accessed through location-aware technologies so that the technology becomes an enabling tool for creation rather than a broadcast channel.

With the increasing availability of contextual data sources, from the location-specific data sets of open data initiatives, to scraping geotagged social media and closed or proprietary Web resources, new options are becoming available that follow in the tradition of these early locative media works, while augmenting them with extensive data-driven overlays. Before discussing these trends in more detail it is important to situate them within a history of data-driven art, a tradition which, I argue, informs recent work and provides an art historical perspective when considering location and data remixing.

Data in Art

The use of data as a tool of political critique within an art context has an established tradition,[22] one in which the convergence of data and physical space of locational remix follows. I will trace this tradition through the work of three artists, Hans Haacke, with his seminal *Shapolsky et al. Manhattan Real Estate Holdings, A Real Time Social System, as of May 1, 1971*; Mark Lombardi and his data-based drawings and Josh On's *They Rule*. The case of *Shapolsky et al.* is of particular interest, as it was a data-rich installation detailing ownership of 142 (mostly tenement) properties and sites in New York City in the ownership or effective control of the Shapolsky family. The work was based on data derived from publicly available records assembled and refined, in the case of obfuscated records designed to conceal effective ownership, by the artist. The work reveals the city as a real estate system, uncovering its complex structure and demonstrating the ways in which the physical fabric of the city, and the arcane financial dealings designed to maximize the value of real estate holdings, are imbricated. It expands the idea of site beyond physical location to include its associated data space. This serves to activate these sites through remixing location with data to provide a sociopolitical narrative, transforming individual buildings by augmenting them with data and situating them within a complex network of property and financial transactions, with far-reaching consequences, both for the space of the city and for the everyday lives of the people living in these tenements. The work was slated for exhibition in the Guggenheim Museum, but was controversially canceled before its opening in April 1971. In her treatment of this infamous case, Rosalyn Deutsche identifies the specificity of the work as the principal reason given by the museum director, who held that social issues should be addressed "artistically only through symbolism, generalization and metaphor."[23] That the work was suppressed due to the specificity of its data-based critique demonstrates the potential of such an approach to deliver location-based critique of great impact.

The artist Mark Lombardi is known for his large-scale data-based drawings or "narrative structures," which detail the networks of power and money involved in various political financial scandals, such as the collapse of the Bank of Credit and Commerce International detailed in *BCCI-ICIC-FAB, c. 1972–1991 (4th Version)*, 1996–2000. For each drawing, Lombardi built a custom database culled from published information sources and assembled onto cross-referenced index cards.[24] The painter Greg Stone recounts the reaction of a friend, a reporter at *The Wall Street Journal*, who on seeing Lombardi's *George W. Bush, Harken Energy and Jackson Stephens* drawing, although familiar with the characters in the narrative, said he "hadn't fully understood the implications until he saw it all laid out that way."[25] Lombardi's work illustrates thus how data-driven visual messages can have a greater impact on a viewer's ability to understand relationships in large-scale happenings.

Josh On's Web-based work, *They Rule*,[26] pursues a similar mission of making connections between networks of powerful individuals connected though corporate directorships, once again drawing from publicly available databases (Figure 26.1). *They Rule* provides a front-end interface to its underlying data, allowing users to make their own connections and share them with others. As a work of art, it presents a framework to interface with the data, inviting its users to provide the narrative structure and coconstruct the meaning. Originally powered from a custom database of directorships of the top 100 companies in the US, it now employs the database of LittleSis, a "free database of who-knows-who at the heights of business and government."[27] *They Rule*'s move from a custom database, which represented a very significant research commitment on the part of the artist (as did Haacke's *Shapolsky et al.*) to LittleSis, which collates and makes this information freely available and accessible, is significant as it demonstrates the power of newly available data resources to supply raw material for remixing for a wide range of applications.

These projects illustrate that the power of data art lies in its ability to re-present and remix information to reveal the underlying structures and patterns. How then can ubiquitous networked location awareness of mobile devices and emergent AR add to this tradition, in an era where data and its use has assumed a greater importance than ever

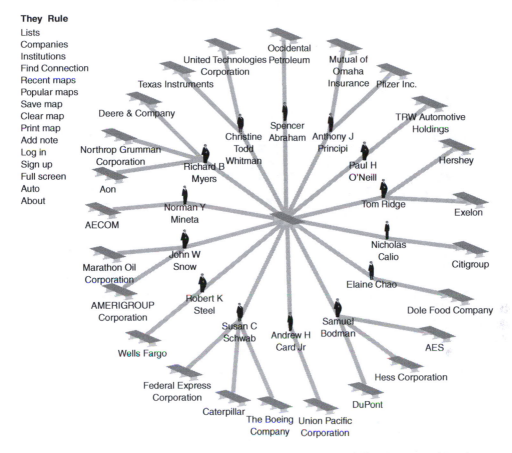

Figure 26.1 They Rule, Josh On, website screenshot, 2004 (all images in this chapter courtesy Conor McGarrigle)

before what can art practice contribute to this burgeoning field? At this point I will introduce a case study of a recent work, which follows in the tradition of data art. It is a work that does not claim any technical innovation, that was created for an existing platform and built using free and open source software, but it offers a powerful example of the ways in which data can politically activate sites and, I suggest, a model for remixing data space and physical space to create an activated hybrid space.

NAMAland

NAMAland[28] is an augmented reality artwork, built on the Layar platform, which remixes a custom data set with location and AR techniques to visualize and critique aspects of the Irish financial collapse, through an overlayering of the city of Dublin with a database-driven data layer, which identifies properties under the control of the National Assets Management Agency (NAMA) (Figure 26.2).

NAMA is an Irish government agency established in December 2009 to acquire bad property loans from Irish banks with the aim of removing them from the banks' balance sheets as a bailout mechanism. The agency, which was controversial from

Figure 26.2 NAMAland, Conor McGarrigle, augmented reality app, 2010

the start, acquired properties worth approximately €40 billion, but failed in its stated aim of bailing out the banks, culminating in Ireland entering an IMF/EU bailout program in November 2010 due to the imminent collapse of the banking system. Despite (or perhaps because of) its central role in the financial collapse, NAMA was secretive in its workings. Legally exempted from freedom of information requirements, the agency was intent on shielding its property portfolio, and the individuals and corporations involved, from public scrutiny under the guise of "commercial sensitivity."

Building on Hans Haacke's treatment of the Shapolsky real estate holdings and New York City, it was obvious that mapping out NAMA's property holdings was essential to gain an understanding of the organization and the events that led to its creation, in order to open it to scrutiny and critique. After some research I was able to identify an alternative, activist source of information on NAMA properties on the anonymous website NAMA Wine Lake.[29] Maintained as a Google Doc, the spreadsheet was compiled from multiple published sources of information connecting property developers known to be in NAMA, their directorships of companies and properties controlled by these companies. Each entry was well-documented with links to the original published sources, important in a litigious climate. This data was, however, locationally vague. Street names were typically included with vague descriptors such as "site on Mayor St.," but lacked sufficient detail to automatically geotag. With further research it was possible to initially manually geotag approximately 120 Dublin properties through visually identifying the sites in person and tagging them with a handheld GPS device. For legal reasons the database had to be confined to properties that could be located with a high degree of certainty and for which sufficient documentary evidence of their ownership could be provided. This data was then used to create a geotagged MySQL database, which became the data source for *NAMAland*.

The application was built in October 2010 and has been updated on a regular basis since. It employs the Layar platform, which provides a development environment and software platform to create AR applications that run on the Layar App for Apple iOS and Android devices. Layar provides a standardized user interface, with limited options for modification, and supplies a set of standard AR methods upon which Layars can be built. It was selected for two reasons; the first was ease of use—it imports a database effectively and is a working, reasonably robust, AR app, which can be deployed with a minimum of development. The data that drives the Layar is contained in a self-hosted open source MySQL database, which can be updated regularly without recourse to Layar's approval and without need to update the app to get the latest information. Second, it provided a method of publishing a politically sensitive work on the iPhone (at the time the most popular smartphone platform in Ireland) as Layars are submitted to Layar's own approval process and publishing through the Layar iPhone app, effectively evading Apple's app store gatekeeping, essential for a politically sensitive app working with gray, unofficial data.

The *NAMAland* Layar in operation takes the location of the user's phone and compares it to this database of geotagged properties of NAMA properties within certain defined ranges (Figure 26.3). An overlay of properties within the specified range is then created which can be further interrogated for ownership details (the majority of properties in NAMA are associated with a small number of individuals with vast property holdings and billions in defaulted loans). The location of each response is indicated by an overlay of a cartoon Monopoly Man figure over NAMA properties in the camera-view of the user's device. It also generates a real-time map of localized NAMA properties, along with a list of nearby properties and their locations. *NAMAland* thus visualizes

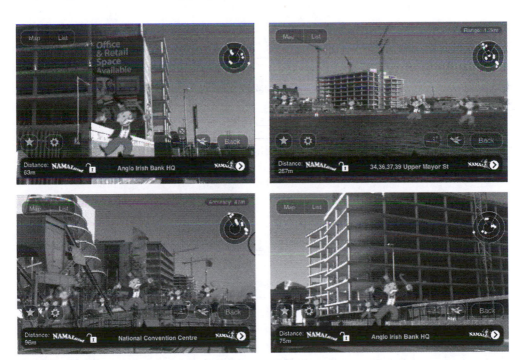

Figure 26.3 NAMAland, Conor McGarrigle, screen capture from mobile app, 2010

the extent of NAMA property ownership, allowing users to identify nearby properties and interrogate specific regions of the city for NAMA connections. As the first mapping of NAMA properties available *NAMAland* succeeded in capturing the popular imagination in Ireland.

It was widely reported in the mainstream media, including an interview and report on the Nine O'Clock News on RTE (the Irish national broadcaster), and it has been featured numerous times on national radio and in national and international print media on many occasions. The title, *NAMAland,* has even entered common usage as a descriptor for the post-IMF bailout situation. The project has, more importantly, succeeded in focusing attention on its subject matter where more traditional approaches failed. It overcame official attempts to limit information and discussion on the subject, and has acted as a conduit through which concerns over the lack of transparency inherent in NAMA could be expressed. On one level it operated as a mobile app, a ready-to-hand source of information locating NAMA properties, as a myriad of other apps locate coffee shops and restaurants. However as an intervention, particularly one with political aspirations, it was not sufficient to remain as a "virtual" intervention; it needed to operate in conjunction with physical actions to be effective. In this respect it was vital that the project was expanded to include real world events such as walking tours, situated public discussion forums, public speaking engagements, media coverage, and individual interventions, with the work itself being an amalgam of all its constituent components.

Peripatetic Activism

The most significant activities were a series of walks, informed by the mobile app, which took place in Dublin City Center and Tallaght, two areas characterized by a high concentration of NAMA properties. These were public, as with the *NAMA-Rama* event in conjunction with Market Studios, the *In These Troubled Times* event with RuaRed Arts Centre and *Ireland after NAMA* with The Exchange Arts Centre, and private activities, such as the guided walks for RTE News and Channel Four News TV crews. In this way the project bridged the gap between the abstract data set hosted in an online database and the real space of the city, the walking interventions, in effect, acting as a locational remix. The location-aware mobile app first takes the user's position, placing her on a point on a Cartesian grid. Position is then transformed into location (in the locative media sense) as the app remixes location with an activist database of NAMA connections creating invisible, but readily accessible, annotations, which attach to familiar buildings and public spaces. This creates a remixed narrative that presents the spaces of the city within the network of financial and property transactions and light-touch government regulation, which had far-reaching implications. This establishes the conditions, through a spatialization of the data, for a walking forum, airing the NAMA debates at the sites where NAMA and its role in austerity politics of the bailout are concretized.

Walking is essential for the *NAMAland* project—it is necessary to deploy it on the street for it to operate at all. The guided walks, through careful selection of routes, were able to maximize this impact by proceeding through areas of the highest concentration of landmark buildings and, as participatory events, functioned as walking forums facilitating participants by discussing the issues represented by NAMA and its property portfolio (Figure 26.4). NAMA represents a complex system of abstract financial dealings, transactions that have become disconnected from everyday understanding, but yet have

Figure 26.4 Participatory *NAMAland* walk in Dublin

significant and very real consequences. The project and its walks attempt to counter this growing abstraction of space—they operate in hybrid space,[30] that is, "a convergence of geographic space and data space"[31] where the distinctions between Manuel Castell's space of place (physical space) and the space of flows (informational space)[32] collapse with the overlayering of context-sensitive data. Whereas the narrative of NAMA was the narrative of the property market, international finance, and IMF bailouts, *NAMAland* reconnected these issues to real spaces in order to expose their interconnectedness and consequences.

These activities were all supported and enabled through the remix of a locationally specific data layer, the affordances of location-aware smartphones and the application of AR technology. They offered multiple points of entry and modes of engagement with the project, which were not necessarily technologically dependent and remained open to as broad a constituency as possible, even those without access to smartphones. Indeed, as the project disseminated, it became clear that many of the people who spoke to me of the project were not actually users, as they didn't have a phone capable of running the application. Their experience of the project was second hand, passed to them as a story which resonated as a tale of resistance. Somebody had used mobile technology to reveal a list of NAMA properties despite efforts to keep this information from the public. It wasn't even necessary to see it in operation, it seemed to be enough to know that it had been done. The walking artist Francis Alÿs speaks of his work as myth making; he sets out to "keep the plot of a project as simple as possible, so that it can be told as a story, an anecdote, something that can be transmitted orally without the need to have access to images."[33] *NAMAland* similarly has a simple narrative that can be told as a story, which means that even without access to the requisite technology, the project still succeeds at some level. Not only does *NAMAland* recount a story about NAMA and its consequences, but from the point of view of AR it speaks of the technology and its uses. This ability to rethink and recontextualize technologies is at the heart of the remix, and is of particular significance for emergent technologies, as it is through practice that functions and usage modes of technologies come to light and their relative value and importance is revealed. At another level *NAMAland* acted as a catalyst, facilitating a range of conversations, debates, and activities as part of a wide-ranging critique of NAMA and the sequence of events that led to it. The project crossed boundaries from art to geography, urbanism, activism, open data, economics, and politics as one would expect from work that engages critically with the space of the city, international finance, and IMF bailouts. As the project became known through publicity and word of mouth, another side was revealed from the diversity of the discussions, from the Occupy Dublin camp one day, to city-sponsored seminars on open data and the smart economy the next; this was its ability to function as a conduit that reconnected NAMA with the space of the city, a connection which had been deliberately severed, to preserve the idea of the government agency as a by-product of obscure international financial dealings. What *NAMAland* contributed was not only an opening up of previously unavailable data, but a reconnecting of this data with the fabric of the city itself. This served to add specificity in place of generalization, fueling debate through the provision of an infrastructure on which specific spatial critiques could be structured, supplying a point of entry hitherto unavailable. *NAMAland* data was opened to other interested groups, unconnected to this author, resulting in a series of direct actions such as the *Occupy NAMA* and *Welcome to NAMAland* (Figure 26.5) interventions made possible by the availability of accurate data. This is the power of the locational data remix and with the unprecedented availability of data from both open data initiatives and though social media APIs, the

Figure 26.5 Welcome to *NAMAland* intervention in Dublin

potential is considerable, yet because it is reliant on data sources over which it has no control, it is also a precarious practice.

Precariousness of Data

The growth in open data has seen a considerable increase in the availability of high-quality data sets from governmental and city sources. Data.gov,[34] the clearing-house for US governmental open data, lists in excess of 64,000 available sets, and this increase is reflected internationally. Other important sources of data are social media platforms such as Twitter, Facebook, Google+, Flickr, and Foursquare, whose APIs offer access to their data. While this data is currently available, it is tied to problematic models, which could potentially could lead to access restrictions in the future. Twitter has imposed strict rate limits on access to its data while offering commercial access through reseller companies.[35] The open data model is driven by the rhetoric of the smart economy and a desire for transparent public services, with a view toward increasing efficiency. For example Dublinked, the Dublin City open data initiative launched in November 2011, seeks to "encourage the next generation of jobs and companies in the area of urban solutions, by enabling data-driven innovation and promoting Dublin as a world-leader in developing and trialing new urban solutions."[36] With the European Commission estimating the value of the European open data market at €27 billion,[37] initiatives such as those underway in Dublin aim to secure a portion of that market. This view of open data as driver of the smart economy places a monetary value on data, which potentially could lead to a commercialization of this valuable raw material, with the current phase a transitory "gold rush" of free access to high-value data sets. These trends are already evident with Twitter's API changes restricting access to Twitter big data to paying customers,[38] reflecting the realization that for social media platforms like Facebook their product is user data.[39]

However, in tandem with these developments, we have seen the emergence of a range of data-scraping techniques and tools, which allow researchers, activists, and artists to access restricted data. Art works such as Paolo Cirio and Alessandro Ludovico's *Face to Facebook*,[40] which scraped one million Facebook profiles and remixed the data as *Lovelyfaces.com*, a fake dating site matching the stolen profiles using facial recognition techniques, demonstrate a hacktivist response to these trends, which seeks alternate methods to access and deploy this data. While data scraping, until recently, required a high degree of coding skills with many scrapers written in the Python language, newer services are becoming available which allow nonprogrammers to scrape data. Scraperwiki.com, one of the longest established data scraping and storage services, recently overhauled the system allowing users to scrape a limited range of data sources without writing a line of code. Importi.io offers a beta point-and-click tool, which promises to allow a range of Web scraping features without needing to resort to the detailed source code parsing typically required. In the way that OpenStreetMap emerged in response to the restrictions of Google Maps to build an open source digital map of the world that rivals its commercial competitors in scope, it can be expected that these trends will continue, enabling continued access to data, even in the face of a commercially driven data lock-down.

Conclusion

I have argued elsewhere[41] that artistic practices, which engage with emergent technologies, are involved in a process of shifting the understanding of these technologies.

As Richard Coyne writes "technologies do not conform politely to predetermined or intended functions"[42] rather it is through use that functions and usage modes come to light and their relative value and importance is revealed. AR, as it stands, is being promoted as a marketing technology, with the principal AR browsers developing corporate tie-ins using image recognition to replace QR codes[43] in conjunction with location-based AR applications. The technology is being thus presented and developed as a method of connecting companies with their customers in real space. While these applications will be a feature of the mature practice of AR, they are, to invoke the developers of the Urban Tapestries public authoring project, "unnecessarily impoverished."

Art practices have a role to play in broadening the understanding and application of technologies through expanding their range of applications and permitted usages. *NAMAland* demonstrates one such application, but the potential for these tools is only limited by the data sets that can be accessed and the desire of artists and activists to engage with them as part of their practice. At an everyday level this might take the form of locative technology enabling a retailer to combine data and location to deliver location-aware special offers and deals to a customer's phone. However, this coexists alongside the ability of the user to interrogate the retailer's history on a range of issues from health and safety to their environmental record, or simply customer satisfaction. This is not necessarily to privilege one over the other. Both have their place but what is of prime importance is that multiple options coexist as aids to informed decision-making, where the user can offset, for example, say a welcome reduction in the price of a cup of coffee earned by checking-in against a company's antiunion policies.

NAMAland is an application that remixed data and location at multiple levels, enabled through the affordances of AR technology, to deliver a political critique and catalyze a range of interventions, in the process reaching a wide audience through usage, mainstream media accounts, and word of mouth. This success establishes AR as a tool of political critique, which can reveal and situate information and data of political significance. When connected to the burgeoning open data movement, AR has an even more significant role to play in the realm of political criticism. Open data seeks to make freely available data collected by government and city authorities both in the interests of transparent government and as an impetus to the smart economy. As new sources of data become available there are opportunities for artists and activists to go beyond the rhetoric of the smart economy and develop critical narratives based on remixing this newly liberated data. This emergent practice has the power to expand the range of practices and strengthen locative technologies as tools for enhancing and critiquing everyday life with the addition of data. This, I suggest, can be achieved through practices that resonate with their audiences, assimilating themselves into the technology by establishing meaningful connections to the everyday, expanding the logic of the remix into locational data.

Notes

1 Selective availability is an intentional degradation of the accuracy of GPS for nonmilitary receivers, see GPS.gov. http://www.gps.gov/systems/gps/modernization/sa/ (accessed September 9, 2013).
2 Hybrid positioning involves a mixture of positioning techniques including cell tower location, Wi-Fi signals as well as GPS to get a faster and more accurate location fix.
3 Dominic Rush, "Google: Don't Expect Privacy When Sending to Gmail," *The Guardian*, August 15, 2013, http://www.theguardian.com/technology/2013/aug/14/google-gmail-users-privacy-email-lawsuit.
4 Glenn Greenwald and Ewen MacAskill, "NSA Prism Program Taps in to User Data of Apple, Google and Others," *The Guardian*, June 6, 2013, http://www.theguardian.com/world/2013/jun/06/us-tech-giants-nsa-data.

5 Henri Lefebvre, *The Production of Space* (Oxford: Blackwell, 1991), 86–87.

6 Jane Rendell, "Critical Spatial Practice" (2008), http://www.janerendell.co.uk/chapters/critical-spatial-practices-a-feminist-sketch-of-some-modes-and-what-matters.

7 An application programming interface (API) is a method for developers to programmatically access selected functions and data of a platform for other applications.

8 Thomas F. McDonough, "Situationist Space," *October* 67, Winter (1994): 77.

9 Alice Angus et al. "Urban Social Tapestries," *IEEE Pervasive Computing* 7, no. 4 (2008).

10 Lev Manovich, "The Poetics of Augmented Space," *Visual Communication* 5, no. 2 (2006).

11 Ben Russell. "The Headmap Manifesto" (1999) http://technoccult.net/technoccult-library/headmap/.

12 Marc Tuters and Kazys Varnelis, "Beyond Locative Media: Giving Shape to the Internet of Things," *Leonardo* 39, no. 4 (2006).

13 See http://locative.x-i.net/ for the original workshop Web page (accessed September 9, 2013).

14 USAF Space Command Global Positioning Systems Wing, http://www.losangeles.af.mil/library/factsheets/factsheet.asp?id=5311 (accessed September 9, 2013).

15 Scott Pace et al., *The Global Positioning System: Assessing National Policies*, RAND Corporation (1995), http://www.rand.org/pubs/monograph_reports/MR614.html.

16 Julian Bleecker and Jeff Knowlton, "Locative Media: A Brief Bibliography and Taxonomy of GPS-Enabled Locative Media," *Leonardo Electronic Almanac* 14, no. 3 (2006).

17 Lisa Parks, *Cultures in Orbit: Satellites and the Televisual* (Durham NC: Duke University Press, 2005).

18 Ibid.

19 *Pac Manhattan* was a 2004 urban game developed by the Interactive Telecommunications program at NYU that enacted the computer game *Pacman* on the streets of Manhattan, http://pacmanhattan.com/ (accessed March 3, 2014).

20 Blast Theory is group of artists who have created mixed reality urban games and performances since 1991, http://www.blasttheory.co.uk/ (accessed March 3, 2014).

21 Urban Tapestries was a pioneering public authoring research and development project developed by Proboscis between 2002 and 2004, http://urbantapestries.net/ (accessed March 3, 2014).

22 A tradition which can be traced to Jack Burnham's articulation of Systems Art in the 1960s see, Jack Burnham, "System Esthetics," *Artforum* (September, 1968); reprinted in *Open Systems: Rethinking Art c. 1970* ed. Donna De Salvo (London: Tate, 2005), 166–169.

23 Rosalyn Deutsche, *Evictions Art and Spatial Politics* (Cambridge, MA: MIT Press, 1996), 169–181.

24 Deven Golden, "Mark Lombardi," *Art Critical*, November 1, 2003, http://www.artcritical.com/2003/11/01/mark-lombardi.

25 Frances Richard, "'Obsessive—Generous' Toward a Diagram of Mark Lombardi" (2002), http://www.wburg.com/0202/arts/lombardi.html.

26 *They Rule*, theyrule.net (accessed September 9 2013).

27 *LittleSis*, Littlesis.org (accessed September 9 2013).

28 *NAMAland*, http://www.conormcgarrigle.com/namaland.html (accessed September 9 2013).

29 NAMA Wine lake, http://namawinelake.wordpress.com (accessed September 9 2013).

30 See Steve Harrison and Paul Dourish. "Re-place-ing Space: The Roles of Place and Space in Collaborative Systems," in *Proceedings of the 1996 ACM Conference on Computer Supported Cooperative Work*, 7: 67–76 (ACM, 1996) http://portal.acm.org/citation.cfm?id=240193; and Eric Kluitenberg. "The Network of Waves: Living and Acting in a Hybrid Space," *Open* 11 (2006): 6–16.

31 Drew Hemment, "Locative Arts," *Leonardo* 39, no. 4 (2006): 348–355.

32 Manuel Castells, *The Rise of the Network Society* (Malden, MA: Wiley-Blackwell, 2000).

33 Mark Godfrey, *Francis Alÿs: A Story of Deception* (London: Tate Publishing, 2010).

34 Data.gov/metric (accessed September 9, 2013).

35 Twitter introduced restrictions on API access in August 2012 while offering packaged data for sale through licensed companies Gnip and Datasift, see http://blog.twitter.com/2012/changes-coming-to-twitter-api (accessed March 6, 2014).

36 Dublinked.com (accessed September 9, 2013).

37 *Re-Use of Public Sector Information—Review of Directive 2003/98/EC*, Communication from the Commission to the European Parliament, the Council, the European Economic and Social Committee and the Committee of the Regions, http://eurlex.europa.eu/LexUriServ/LexUriServ.do?uri=COM:2009:0212:FIN:EN:PDF.

38 Dick Wisdom, "How Twitter Gets In The Way Of Knowledge," *Buzzfeed*, January 4, 2013, http://www.buzzfeed.com/nostrich/how-twitter-gets-in-the-way-of-research.

39 Elizabeth Dwoskin, "Facebook Reminds Users: All Your Data Is Fair Game," *The Wall Street Journal*, August 29, 2013.
40 See http://www.face-to-facebook.net/ (accessed March 6 2014).
41 Conor McGarrigle, "The Construction of Locative Situations," PhD, Dublin Institute of Technology, 2012.
42 Richard Coyne, *The Tuning of Place: Sociable Spaces and Pervasive Digital Media* (Cambridge, MA: MIT Press, 2010).
43 QR codes are square barcodes that connect to a URL when scanned with a mobile device.

Bibliography

Angus, Alice, Dikaios Papadogkonas, George Papamarkos, George Roussos, Giles Lane, Karen Martin, Nick West, Sarah Thelwall, Zoetanya Sujon, and Roger Silverstone. "Urban Social Tapestries." *IEEE Pervasive Computing* 7, no. 4 (2008): 44–51. doi:10.1109/MPRV.2008.84.

Bleecker, Julian, and Jeff Knowlton. "Locative Media: A Brief Bibliography and Taxonomy of GPS-Enabled Locative Media." *Leonardo Electronic Almanac* 14, no. 3 (2006).

Burnham, Jack. "Systems Esthetics." In *Open Systems: Rethinking Art c. 1970*, edited by Donna De Salvo, 166–169. London: Tate Publishing, 2005.

Castells, Manuel. *The Rise of the Network Society*. Malden, MA: Wiley-Blackwell, 2000.

Coyne, Richard. *The Tuning of Place : Sociable Spaces and Pervasive Digital Media*. Cambridge, MA: MIT Press, 2010.

Deutsche, Rosalyn. *Evictions Art and Spatial Politics*. Cambridge, MA: MIT Press, 1996.

Dwoskin, Elizabeth. "Facebook Reminds Users: All Your Data Is Fair Game." *The Wall Street Journal*, August 29, 2013.

Frances, Richard. "'Obsessive—Generous' Toward a Diagram of Mark Lombardi." *Wburg.com*, 2002. http://www.wburg.com/0202/arts/lombardi.html (accessed August 13, 2014).

Godfrey, Mark. *Francis Alÿs: A Story of Deception*. London: Tate Publishing, 2010.

Golden, Deven. "Mark Lombardi." *Art Critical*, November 1, 2003. http://www.artcritical.com/2003/11/01/mark-lombardi (accessed September 9, 2013).

Greenwald, Glenn, and Ewen MacAskill. "NSA Prism Program Taps in to User Data of Apple, Google and Others." *The Guardian*, June 6, 2013. http://www.theguardian.com/world/2013/jun/06/us-tech-giants-nsa-data.

Harrison, Steve, and Dourish, Paul. "Re-Place-Ing Space: The Roles of Place and Space in Collaborative Systems." In *Proceedings of the 1996 ACM Conference on Computer Supported Cooperative Work*, 7: 67–76. ACM, 1996. http://portal.acm.org/citation.cfm?id=240193 (accessed August 13, 2014).

Hemment, Drew. "Locative Arts." *Leonardo* 39, no. 4 (2006): 348–355.

Kluitenberg, Eric. "The Network of Waves: Living and Acting in a Hybrid Space." *Open* 11 (2006): 6–16.

Lefebvre, Henri. *The Production of Space*. Oxford: Blackwell, 1991.

Manovich, Lev. "The Poetics of Augmented Space." *Visual Communication* 5, no. 2 (June 2006): 219–240. doi:10.1177/1470357206065527.

McDonough, Thomas F. "Situationist Space." *October* 67, Winter (1994): 58–77.

McGarrigle, Conor. "The Construction of Locative Situations." PhD, Dublin Institute of technology, 2012.

Pace, Scott, Gerald P. Frost, Irving Lachow, David R. Frelinger, Donna Fossum, Don Wassem, and Monica M. Pinto. *The Global Positioning System: Assessing National Policies*. RAND Corporation, 1995. http://www.rand.org/pubs/monograph_reports/MR614.html (accessed August 13, 2014).

Parks, Lisa. *Cultures in Orbit: Satellites and the Televisual*. Durham, NC: Duke University Press, 2005.

Rendell, Jane. "Critical Spatial Practice," 2008. http://www.janerendell.co.uk/chapters/critical-spatial-practices-a-feminist-sketch-of-some-modes-and-what-matters (accessed August 13, 2014).

Re-Use of Public Sector Information—Review of Directive 2003/98/EC. Communication from the Commission to the European Parliament, the Council, the European Economic and Social Committee and the Committee of the Regions. http://eurlex.europa.eu/LexUriServ/LexUriServ.do?uri=COM:2009:0212:FIN:EN:PDF (accessed September 9, 2013).

Rush, Dominic. "Google: Don't Expect Privacy When Sending to Gmail." *The Guardian.* August 15, 2013. http://www.theguardian.com/technology/2013/aug/14/google-gmail-users-privacy-email-lawsuit (accessed August 13, 2014).

Russell, Ben. "The Headmap Manifesto," 1999. http://technoccult.net/technoccult-library/headmap/ (accessed August 13, 2014).

Tuters, Marc, and Kazys Varnelis. "Beyond Locative Media: Giving Shape to the Internet of Things." *Leonardo* 39, no. 4 (2006): 357–363. doi:10.1162/leon.2006.39.4.357.

Wegener, Mareike. *Mark Lombardi—Death Defying Acts of Art and Conspiracy.* Documentary, 2011.

Wisdom, Dick. "How Twitter Gets In The Way Of Knowledge." *Buzzfeed*, January 4, 2013. http://www.buzzfeed.com/nostrich/how-twitter-gets-in-the-way-of-research (accessed September 8, 2013).

27

THE POLITICS OF JOHN LENNON'S "IMAGINE"

Contextualizing the Roles of Mashups and New Media in Political Protest

J. Meryl Krieger

Remix and mashup are mechanisms of recycling or transforming materials from other media creators with the aim of producing new content. As distinct from remixing, mashups not only reuse older materials but retain the references that often provide cultural contextualization for the mashup audience. Remixes often attempt to blend these materials to the point where original authorship or identifiers can be lost. Mashups are also often used conceptually as a metaphor or trope for cultural change while incorporating techniques of remixing. This essay explores remix and mashup as cultural processes of transformation and re-creation. I focus attention specifically on the mashup and remix by CalTV and WaxAudio, "Imagine This," released in 2005/2006 to demonstrate my case. My goal is to address a lack of scholarly attention to the intersection of remix and mashup as they intersect with protest movements.

In what follows, I examine the role of remix and mashup through the metaphors and tropes generated from the work of singer-songwriter John Lennon with particular focus on his 1971 song "Imagine," and its ongoing use in enactments of political protest across the globe. I begin by historically situating Lennon himself within the genre of protest music, and the widespread dissemination of music videos through the Internet became feasible due to rapid expansion of computer technologies, particularly access through the increase of bandwidth in the first decade of the twenty-first century. My analysis includes an interview conducted with Irish filmmaker John Callahan, who uses the professional name of CalTV, who created the "Imagine This" video mashup based on WaxAudio's remix. This interview with Callahan, allows me to add the thread of professional filmmaking to the scholarly discussions of the place of video mashups in contemporary society during this formative period of social media sharing. I further explore the place of "Imagine This" as a text around which a protest public could engage in discourse furthering its cause. I conclude by considering some of the theoretical and analytical implications the example of "Imagine This" provide for the study of music video remix and mashup in protest communities in online research, engaging with ideas from Bloodgood and Deane (2005), Berger

(2009) and Warner (2002). Finally, I selectively review the role that social media play in communities of protest, with particular emphasis on the place of YouTube during the mid-2000s period when "Imagine This" was first released on the Internet.

> See Chapter 38 for Eric S. Faden's discussion on creating a remixed video that cleverly protests the restrictive nature of traditional copyright laws.

Historically, protest as a political consideration receives scholarly attention from political scientists, sociologists, anthropologists, and others, while mashup and remix get limited attention as vehicles for those protest statements. Instead, they are frequently treated as static objects rather than creative processes that are part of public discourse surrounding an ongoing social or political concern. This latter approach is the essential, underlying assumption embedded in my approach to this essay.

The attention remix and mashup get is most often embedded in research addressing specific regions or countries, with some limited attention to the role (particularly) remix plays in politics. There have been increases in the remix and mashup dissemination of spoken and music video, mostly from the DIY, "bedroom filmmaker" community. CalTV and WaxAudio's mashup "Imagine This" occurred at a unique juncture of events and practices where professional video and audio production intersected with a global anti-war sentiment that developed around the United States' incursion into Iraq. The confluence of factors include the roles of then President George W. Bush, anti- and prowar sentiment regarding the US-led invasion of Iraq, and the place of John Lennon as a political, particularly left-wing, antiwar figure. These occurred during a time when the explosion of commercially available Internet bandwidth gave rise to social media sharing sites, notably YouTube, in 2005, from which UGC (user-generated content) politically charged media objects could be disseminated, shared, and dissected. John Lennon here can be understood in contrast with Bob Geldof, a musician who uses music and music performance as a vehicle for encouraging awareness about social issues, such as the first globalized presentation of musicians working to highlight and educate the Western world about starvation in Africa during the first Live Aid concert in the early 1980s. It is clear that having a public figure consistently identified with that political ideology allows communities to coalesce, creating a nexus point for public expression and education.

John Lennon's "Imagine," Remix, and Protest Music

In the 1960s, political protest in the United States could be recognized in forms that looked remarkably like protest communities anywhere in the world of its time or from generations before: groups of individuals congregating in a particular place to make a statement against political policies that were objectionable in some fashion, most notably those regarding the Civil Rights Movement and the Vietnam War. At that time there was already a long history of musical involvement in countercultural political statements.[1]

Mainstream, mass culture has co-opted many vehicles formerly used by such countercultural movements, and the American public in particular is jaded into ignoring all but the most sensational aspects of political statement in any form. Such vehicles have not vanished, but have instead transformed themselves through new mass communication technologies into collectives that would be almost unrecognizable in generations past.

Online communities have evolved to take on the leadership role in such social move-ments in contemporary culture, ranging from groups like MoveOn.org on the liberal end of the spectrum, to the conservative groups, gopusa.com and conservativeusa.org.

One place where these changes have been evident is YouTube.com, one of the most common public websites hosting user-generated videos. YouTube launched in 2005 as a site where:

> everyone can watch videos . . . People can see first-hand accounts of current events, find videos about their hobbies and interests, and discover the quirky and unusual. As more people capture special moments on video, YouTube is empowering them to become the broadcasters of tomorrow.[2]

This transformation of protest community from predominantly live and synchronous to predominantly online and asynchronous has happened so naturally and rapidly, within the span of a decade, that it seems useful to step back and look at how this transforma-tion took place.

During its early years, YouTube described itself as a community that supports and encourages dialog and interaction. In reality, from its beginnings YouTube has oper-ated more as a space in which the public comes together to dialog, interact, and focus cultural objects or texts that appeal to different communities and different individuals for highly divergent reasons. These cultural objects, whether spoken or music videos, appeal to different communities whose concerns range from dialog and interaction to purely commercial. Because these cultural objects can be read in a variety of ways, they can become the focus for an aspect of community action—in this case the inter-national protest movement against military intervention in Iraq by the United States and its allies. YouTube as a space for collective dialog as a public space engages with the DIY sensibility of UGC. Many new media scholars consider YouTube to have been an outgrowth of the DIY approach to media and file sharing of fan-based creative work that dates back to the 1970s. Some of the restrictions placed on uploading have been generally targeted toward limiting the spread of pirated copies of commercially pro-duced media.[3]

Similarly, remix as a musical practice gets less attention from music scholars. In his discussion to contextualize what he terms the "remix era," Manovich argues that this lack of recognition of remix as musical practice comes from its related absence from music industry discourse—it is tied to copyright violation and is consequently labeled "stealing." This emphasis on identifying remix as theft, consequently delegitimizing it as a cultural text, is a basic element in the conflict of interest between the artistic and commercial goals of members of the music community.[4] While Manovich brings the case into the twenty-first century, as Porcello notes, the debate over the ethics of digital music sampling had long been the subject of debate among audio recording engineers.[5]

Despite the ongoing public discourse about YouTube as an online site for amateur production during this period, those video products that got widespread distribution fall into two basic categories—productions aspiring to or following professional standards of commercial video/audio production, and productions that are unabashedly amateur that appeal to a temporary public interest or fad. Burgess and Green address the tensions between these two—user-generated, or expressions of "vernacular creativity" and "tra-ditional media."[6] Purcell brings the data up to the time of this writing, specific to the US market, noting that the number of (US-based) American users who upload and share content on social media sites like YouTube, and more recently Vimeo, have steadily increased:

> The introduction of video-sharing site YouTube in 2005, and later other video-sharing sites like Vimeo, has been the driving force in the increasing percentage of online adults who post, watch and download videos. [Between 2006 and 2013] . . . the percent of online adults using video-sharing sites has grown from 33% to the current figure of 72%.[7]

Since 2001, a number of social movements have engendered protest community expression, heavily using social media and other online sources for community identification and expression. Ethnomusicologists and cultural studies scholars focusing on particular communities have engaged in ethnographic research exploring the behaviors of those communities[8] but they have not specifically addressed the roles that new media technologies play in those protest communities. Historically there has been something of a "blind eye" to technology in the ethnographic study of community behaviors; the role of remix is a similar instance, for example, to that of the role of technology in recording music performance. This is something of a curious anomaly since technology is fundamental to the discipline of ethnomusicology, but it was not until Louise Meintjes's important 1990 study of Paul Simon's *Graceland* (1986) that ethnomusicological scholarship began to formally problematize the technologies that record performance, exploring the role of racialized apartheid politics in the production and performance of recorded music.[9] Ethnographic research into media technologies has expanded through the two decades since Meintjes's study into the study of the impact of recording technologies themselves,[10] though it is more often carried out through media studies, sociological research, and other social science disciplines.

Political Activism in the Americas: The Move from Live to Mass Mediated

Activism through popular music has a long history. In the United States, Woody Guthrie and Pete Seeger became central figures in the union and civil rights movements from the 1930s through the 1960s. By the end of this period, a number of popular culture figures emerged in connection with counterculture protest. Bob Dylan had taken on, in one fashion or another, the mantle of Woody Guthrie, and The Beatles' John Lennon became politicized by the late 1960s and was actively involved with nonviolent antiwar protesting with his second wife, artist Yoko Ono. Lennon's death in 1980 cemented his place as an icon to antiwar protests.[11] Similarly, from the early days of the digital age there has been a clear trend in the use of popular artistic and cultural figures to clarify and articulate the vision of political and social movements.

In the 1980s a sense of the possibilities of such public attention joined with new technological capabilities in communication. This new movement in pop figure public social engagement signaled a change in the kinds of authority required to get the attention of large parts of the public. A clear case demonstrating this new potential came in the (Western) worldwide production of Live Aid, produced by Boomtown Rats singer Bob Geldof, and Ultravox leader Midge Ure, first as a single in 1984 by a "supergroup" of British pop musicians ("Do They Know Its Christmas") and then as a live, international fundraising event in 1985:

[t]he event was tagged as a music event like none the world had ever seen, but even the advance hype couldn't accurately portray the momentousness of the occasion. After all, no one had ever tried to coordinate two massive concerts on two continents with the world's biggest music stars, and make the whole thing a sufficiently slick TV event to encourage the kind of donations Geldof had in mind.[12]

Geldof's feat inspired others, from "We Are the World" copenned by Michael Jackson to Hands Across America, Farm Aid, Comic Relief, and others. While these efforts continue into the twenty-first century, they get less notice, partly due to fundraising exhaustion, often called "donor fatigue,"[13] but also because of the decentralization of media and the proliferation of outlets.[14] Indeed, the tool kit necessary to bring together the elements needed to run a Live Aid in the current millennium would be nearly lost in the background noise of contemporary media. In 2005 Geldof organized Live 8, similar to Live Aid except that the focus was social justice rather than charity. While the event itself was a great success, it engaged in a whole other sphere of international activity, namely the relationship between politics and social change. Burkeman notes that Geldof, for all his abilities as an organizer and his vision to make a difference in the world, lacked the political skills and credentials to successfully navigate this arena, often proceeding with what he describes as an "utopian" worldview rather than what he describes as the "messy pragmatism" necessary to create actual change.[15]

While some political activists can successfully navigate political terrain, most do this in dialog with publics with whom they have common ground. Geldof engaged with the political elite of the British government, then-British Prime Minister Tony Blair, coming away tarnished. Burkeman connects Geldof's ideas with internationally critiqued American President George W. Bush, who at this same point in time was being criticized for his poor response to Hurricane Katrina's aftermath in New Orleans, Louisiana.[16]

The tools of political activism had changed by 2005. Since then the target audience has become as important as the message it conveys. "Imagine This," a 2006 mashup video by CalTV, aka Irish filmmaker and image artist John Callahan, built on the WaxAudio remix by Australian Tom Compagnoni, was released July, 2005 on the digital album *Mediacracy*.[17] Like Geldof's Live Aid, "Imagine This" became influential for its imitators' use of found footage and music already associated with political protest messages. "Imagine This," first posted to YouTube in March, 2006, itself played on WaxAudio's use of President George W. Bush's public image (among his detractors), as Callahan commented, as the "village idiot," with subsequent mashups that used similarly politicized themes including rx2008's mashup of the U2 song "Sunday Bloody Sunday" in 2006 which, like "Imagine This," uses publicly accessed footage of President George W. Bush in its creation.[18] Both these videos use politically charged musical materials to protest military intervention, a common theme in political protest music that has been connected with American military actions since the 1960s.

Protest Icons: "Imagine" and John Lennon

Callahan's and WaxAudio's "Imagine This" is part of a continuous legacy of John Lennon and his song "Imagine" as icons of popular song and antiwar protest. Lennon first became involved with the antiwar protests after his marriage to Yoko Ono in 1969, with their first "Bed for Peace" protest in March, 1969; it was during this period of his career, in 1971, when the album *Imagine* and its title song were released. The construction of Lennon as a working-class hero and antiwar icon began with the peace vigil surrounding his death in 1980 and continues to the present day.

Contemporary sources problematize Lennon as a person, but his image remains in use as an icon of peace, leftist politics, and antiwar movements across the world.[19] The song "Imagine" appears regularly, performed in a variety of places around the world by professional and amateur performers as part of protest events. In 2010 the *New Statesman* published the top 20 protest songs, as compiled by the Political Science Association. "Imagine" is ranked eighteenth.[20] By 2011 John Lennon had become an institutionalized symbol for political protest that he is included in educational curricula as a pop culture icon, peace movement activist, and poet.[21] In 2013 and 2014 "Imagine" has been performed by famous performers and amateurs across the globe, continuing to build on this representation.[22]

CalTV on "Imagine This," Remix, and Political Protest

On being asked why he created the "Imagine This" mashup, filmmaker John Callahan comments:

> The video was a reaction to the song . . . I was doing a masters at the time and was working on a project for that . . . I heard the WaxAudio track on BBC radio and it stopped me in my tracks, I was amazed at the work that went into finding the G[eorge] W. Bush samples, and I instantly thought, wouldn't it be funny if I could find all the exact same video and match them up, but . . . "surely someone has done that already," so I checked and nobody had. . . . I contacted the creator of the song and asked him if he had extracted the audio from video. My initial plan was to match it up to that, but he had extracted everything from audio clips so I had to start from scratch.
>
> At the time, as like most people, I was against the Iraq war . . . in a way it politicised me slightly . . . The main goal was to replicate the mood of the audio, which basically poked fun at G[eorge] W. Bush by playing on his image of the village idiot, whilst making an important point at the same time.[23]

Callahan uses video mashups as a way of expressing a personal statement and of his own developing politicization. For Callahan, this mashup expresses his view by using tools at his disposal to express his opposition to the US-led war in Iraq and his interest in how audiences understand the content he uses. As Stavans notes, art can be a way to either explore the human condition or "blow off steam."[24] Callahan, as a professional filmmaker, used his film and video skills as an expression of individual creativity, and only second as political statement.

> I was originally drawn to mashups for two reasons. I think, one, they were "easy" to make, I didn't need to shoot anything and I could usually rip the footage from somewhere online, the other was because of the work that was being done by people like Hexstatic, Ninja Tune, DJ Food etc. in the mid-2000s, they were doing very inventive mashups using audio that worked particularly well in a live "dancefloor" setting at music festivals etc. . . . it added an extra dimension to live performances of "mashup" music, which I think is needed, because as a genre it can become a bit repetitive, the video side adds another element of craft and skill to it, and also humour which I think is really important, and really I work in music video rather than film, and that's what was turning me on at the time.[25]

Later, when asked about why he didn't stay with mashups as a creative tool he notes: "I didn't stick with mashups as find them a bit limiting and repetitive . . . Aesthetically they are a little unappealing also. It was just a case of the correct tool/medium to match the song/audio."[26]

Despite the early appeal of creative, dance music mashups as a technique for his own creative agenda, mashup proved less productive as a sustained tool for his aesthetic goals compared to production techniques Callahan had access to as a professional filmmaker. Two additional points are very striking. First, the series of technological confluences that allowed his mashup to be widely distributed to a disparate public. Second, the new, increased availability of video footage from George W. Bush's presidency marks the beginnings of an era when online access to video footage of a major chief of state was at an unprecedented level for its time. The possibilities for a dissection of political move-ments or materials for political commentary are certainly something that could be addressed in further research.

Callahan comments that the timing of "Imagine This" was part of the key to its success and impact:

> the reaction was unexpected but in some ways the timing was important; it was released around the start of YouTube and caught the first wave of people's inter-est in that . . . Media and film festivals also were interested as it was part of the first wave of "bedroom filmmakers," and they like that aspect of it as a pointer toward the future and as a way of showing anti-Iraq war sentiment in art.[27]

Fan works and "bedroom filmmakers" are common and the most popular media on YouTube involve music, though US audiences are also highly interested in videos with political content.[28]

Mashup and Remix as Texts for Protest Publics

Warner's concept of publics is central to understanding remixing and mashup as texts, or cultural objects, that helped spread a wider appreciation for the protest movement against the US invasion of Iraq. This correlates with the global anti-American, and anti-George W. Bush, sentiment that crystallized in 2004–06 as part of the DIY culture in public online forums. As Warner notes, where a public comes into being only in relation to a text and its circulation,[29] the possibilities of mediated performance and interaction take on the emergent possibilities in DIY media production; something that clearly emerged around Callahan's "Imagine This." Bloodgood and Deane note that protest songs being used in the early twenty-first century are more often than not recycled older songs, and that few new ones are being written, particularly in genres strongly associated with protest music of the past, such as folk music in the 1960s, or rap and hip hop in the 1980s and 1990s.[30] Protest songs from the past thus become a metaphor for successful activism and political protest. Lennon's songs "Imagine" and "Give Peace a Chance" are layered texts upon which Callahan's creative statement of protest against George W. Bush and the US invasion of Iraq could be presented in sound and image.

John Lennon's iconic status with online protest communities and their ties to our ideas of community, public, audience, text, and performance becomes key to understand the success of the mashup, and its ongoing relevance and impact on video audiences.

Such performances can be indexed to specific events that took place during Lennon's life, and to the events identified in the mashup.

Warner's articulation of a public as a grouping that can coalesce around a text allows us to understand why CalTV and WaxAudio's "Imagine This" were important when it was released in 2006.[31] As Manovich notes, 2006 was a period where rapid technological changes were happening in new media platforms and technology, leading many creative professionals and amateurs to experiment with creating and sharing ideas that were, in one fashion or another, "remixed".[32] These texts interacted with one another—one posted video was put up in response to its predecessor—or curators and other creators (Purcell) might respond through comments attached to the video.[33] Given the DIY nature of YouTube, it is only to be expected that some of these texts would be responding to international affairs, more specifically the Bush Administration's war in Iraq, which was opposed by a number of communities and groups across the globe. "Imagine This" had a strong influence on mashup videos responding to political issues that continue into the current era, though the topic has unsurprisingly shifted from President George W. Bush to President Barack Obama and other contemporary political figures. These videos similarly span the gamut of support for each public figure.[34]

Mashups and remixing can be quite successful at articulating specific issues and/or addressing particular constituencies as they are repurposed by professionals who channel the views of the protest community. One might question, based on publicly available mashup lists on YouTube and SoundCloud, to what extent mashups function as creative, rather than political texts; Callahan's one conclusion was to move away from the mashup format because he found it limiting. It is notable that productions like Callahan's, as such visible means of political statement by a professional filmmaker, can be seen in only a small number of cases and then primarily during this mid-2000s period. While they are still being developed professionally, most music remixes seem to be grounded in the world of dance music—either in electronica or in generic variants of hip hop. Political elements can be frequently found in mashups and remix but the dominant issues are local/national, rather than international, and personal to the artist involved in each case. The use of John Lennon as an icon here fits the antiwar sentiments that Callahan and those who gravitated to his video by means of their agreement with his political agenda and/or their personal veneration of Lennon the activist.

Conclusion: Remix as Practice and Metaphor for Public Expression and Protest

Remix, without a doubt, functions as part of the discourse of protest community discourse. Political remixing as a professional audio and video practice may have a limited range of public viability. However, an experiment I conducted during the summer of 2013 on Facebook provides an example of the ways that mass culture is remixing protest music as a metaphor I describe earlier, using Bloodgood and Deane's description.[35] While in the final stages of writing this chapter, I decided to informally poll my own network with a public post[36] requesting friends' favorite political remix or mashup videos. While not one of my respondents could come up with a remix audio or video that matched the classification of political—other than the example of "Imagine This," which I provided when asked for an example, all came up with parodies that spoke to political or politicized issues, that themselves remix elements of popular culture in a music video format. My expectation was that respondents would mention rap remixed videos produced in North Africa, or the

"Sunday Bloody Sunday" remix that came out immediately after CalTV and WaxAudio's "Imagine This." What my audience was doing was interpreting mashup and remix through the filter of the mass media they regularly consume. In short, they were translating remix into a metaphor of cultural expressions. This experiment allows us to reframe the paradigm for how we understood remix and the place remixes hold in contemporary online culture from strictly practical to metaphorical, reflecting the ways cultural practice has integrated other physical practices into digital cultural and metaphor.[37]

One compelling element of "Imagine This" is how it illuminates the period in which the mashup itself was released, during that first wave of "bedroom film production" dominating the early period of YouTube in 2005 and 2006. A combination of forces were at work—an international community who were protesting the war in Iraq and President George W. Bush's policies that led to this engagement, the new accessibility at the consumer level for posting remix, and the lack of other, more user-friendly, technologies. Callahan comments that, in terms of protest media, "people will just go where the audience is. I can't see specific [protest] tools being developed, people will just use whatever is easiest and most widely available: Twitter, YouTube, etc."[38] While Callahan may not himself recognize his impact, the stylistic components of "Imagine This" has had a strong impact on subsequent video remixes, and the professionalization of political remix can be seen in those that came after him. YouTube has not remained the only site of distribution, but its impact on the artistic production of political statements has been vast and will remain one tool of many for the foreseeable future. Geldof's move of political activism to mass media still creates ripples in the ways that political activism is expressed by music makers and filmmakers. Remixes and mashups are invaluable tools for creative expression for "bedroom filmmakers." With the lack of support from the mainstream music industry for professional protest songs and events, protest statements have returned to the reuse of traditional materials, allowing remixers to use commonly understood tropes of social commentary, and icons of political protest to be remixed into new contexts and new causes.

Notes

1 Bloodgood and Deane (2005) trace this history in the United States. Additional instances can also be identified through the nationalist movements across Europe and Latin American from the late nineteenth through the mid-twentieth centuries. Elizabeth Bloodgood and Shelley M. Deane, "Where Have All the Protest Songs Gone? Social Movements' Message and Their Voice in Politics," presented at the Annual Meeting of the American Political Science Association, September 2, 2005, 10. Used with permission of the authors.
2 http://youtube.com/t/about (accessed September 30, 2007).
3 Upload limits in 2006 when CalTV uploaded "Imagine This" were ten minutes in length and 1GB in file size; a demonstration of the increase in capacity for video in social media sharing can be seen in the hugely expanded capacity: by 2013 videos from any user have a time limit of 15 minutes, but users with a "channel" can upload videos of unlimited length (http://en.wikipedia.org/wiki/YouTube).
4 Lev Manovich, "What Comes After Remix?" (2007) http://manovich.net/index.php/projects/what-comes-after-remix.
5 Thomas Porcello, "The Ethics of Digital Audio-Sampling: Engineers' Discourse," *Popular Music* 10, no. 1 (1991), 69–84.
6 Jean Burgess and Joshua Green, *YouTube Online Video and Participatory Culture* (Cambridge: Polity Press, 2009), 26, 41–44.
7 Kirsten Purcell, "Online Video 2013." Pew Research Institute Internet and American Life Project, October 10, 2013, Washington, DC. http://www.pewinternet.org/files/old-media//Files/Reports/2013/PIP_Online%20Video%202013.pdf

8 Examples come from the #Idlenomore and #Occupy protest communities that can be seen in the follow-ing: Idle No More Flash Mob dancing in Portland, or at http://youtu.be/3xVvE8Ymrpw; Round Dance Flash Mob Calgary at http://youtu.be/HGCD8B9RPDg; and J11Action's "#J11: Idle No More Global Day of Action—January 11, 2013" at http://youtu.be/-mKefAbUbCs (all accessed July 16, 2013).

9 Louise Meintjes, "Paul Simon's Graceland, South Africa, and the Mediation of Musical Meaning," *Ethnomusicology* 34, no. 1 (1990).

10 See, for example, Leslie C. Gay, Jr. and René T. A. Lysloff, eds., *Music and Technoculture* (Middletown, CN: Wesleyan University Press, 2003); Louise Meintjes, *Sounds of Africa! Making Music Zulu in a South African Studio* (Durham, NC: Duke University Press, 2003); Paul D. Greene and Thomas Porcello, eds., *Wired for Sound: Engineering and Technologies in Sonic Cultures* (Middletown, CN: Wesleyan University Press, 2005); and J. Meryl Krieger, "Rough to the Board: Creating Performance in American Recording Studios" (PhD dissertation, Indiana University, 2009).

11 The understood position of Lennon's iconic status is evident from the kinds of essays found consistently about him on the Internet. They follow some combination of the following three patterns. They either laud Lennon as an icon of antiwar protest, or attempt to dismantle his iconic status as a cultural icon, or finally they assume his status as a cultural icon of antiwar protest and attempt to analyze one facet or another of his artistic and political expression. Some examples of these include: *New Statesman's* "Top 20 Political Songs: Imagine/John Lennon/1971" (http://www.newstatesman.com/music/2010/03/lennon-imagine-political) and *Rolling Stone's* "John Lennon: Biography" (http://www.rollingstone.com/music/artists/john-lennon/biography#ixzz2T2qQrXNw) (both accessed May 11, 2013).

12 Gil Kaufman, "Live Aid: A Look Back at a Concert that Actually Changed the World," MTV.com, June 29, 2005, http://www.mtv.com/news/articles/1504968/live-aid-look-back.jhtml.

13 Donor fatigue is a generally understood phenomenon among charitable organizations. See, for example, Tim Sarrantonio "A Few Ways to Avoid Donor Fatigue" NEON CRM http://www.z2systems.com/neon-crm/blog/few-ways-avoid-donor-fatigue (accessed May 9, 2014).

14 Donor fatigue has also been compared with the compassion fatigue experienced by caregivers for chronically and terminally ill patients. Controlling media exposure is one common technique to avoiding this problem: David Porter "Charity and Compassion Fatigue is Wearing Down Fundraising" The Compassion Fatigue Awareness Project. http://www.compassionfatigue.org/pages/davidporter.pdf (accessed January 15, 2012).

15 Oliver Burkeman, "Three Months Ago Bob Geldof Declared Live 8 Had Achieved Its Aim. But What Really Happened Next?" *The Guardian*, September 12, 2005, http://www.theguardian.com/world/2005/sep/12/hearafrica05.development.

16 Ibid.

17 http://www.waxaudio.com.au/audio/political-eps-mashed-media-trilogy/mediacracy (accessed August 14, 2014).

18 https://www.youtube.com/watch?v=PXnO_FxmHes (accessed August 14, 2014).

19 Seth Mullins, "John Lennon and the Peace Movement: Cutting through the Political Rhetoric and Jargon that Keeps People in the Dark" (2007), formerly available at: http://voices.yahoo.com/john-len-non-peace-movement-185959.html.

20 *New Statesman* "Top 20 Protest Songs."

21 "John Lennon Lesson Plan—Anniversary of his birth—October 9th;—anniversary of his death—December 8th." Developing Teachers.com 2012 lesson plan, http://www.developingteachers.com/plans/lennonpf.htm 9/2/2013.

22 Joan Baez—live performance in Turkey—June 17, 2013: http://www.ibtimes.co.uk/folk-legend-joan-baez-sings-imagine-turkish-480170 (accessed August 19, 2014); Eddie Vedder in Meco, Portugal, responding to violence between Israel and Palestinians: Kory Grow, "Eddie Vedder Plays 'Imagine' at Concert, Reinforces Anti-War Stance," *Rolling Stone*, July 21, 2014, http://www.rollingstone.com/music/news/eddie-vedder-reinforces-anti-war-stance-plays-imagine-at-concert-20140721; and responding to the December 16, 2012 gang rape of a 23-year-old student on a bus in New Delhi, India, 600 guitarists attempt to set a world record by performing 'Imagine' live at the Darjeeling Tea and Tourism Festival: http://www.huffingtonpost.co.uk/2013/01/03/india-gang-rape-victim-john-lennon_n_2402287.html, with video footage at http://youtu.be/njz6ztJzxOE (both accessed August 19, 2014).

23 John Callahan, personal interview, July 18, 2013.

24 Ilan Stavans, *Art and Anger: Essays on Politics and the Imagination* (New York, NY: Palgrave, 2001).

25 John Callahan, personal interview. July 26, 2013.

26 John Callahan, personal interview, August 6, 2013.

27 Ibid.

28 Sysomos, Inc., "Inside YouTube Videos: Exploring YouTube Videos and Their Use in Blogosphere—Michael Jackson and Health Care Dominate" (2010) (http://www.sysomos.com/reports/youtube/).

29 Michael Warner, *Publics and Counterpublics* (New York, NY: Zone Books, 2002), 66.

30 Bloodgood and Deane, "Where Have All the Protest Songs Gone?" 10.

31 A discussion of the contrast in the ways publics can be understood here can be found in Cody (2011), who contrasts Warner's position on publics with those of Habermas and Anderson. Francis Cody, "Publics and Politics," *Annual Review of Anthropology* 40 (2011): 37–52.

32 Lev Manovich, "The Practice of Everyday (Media) Life," in *Video Vortex Reader: Responses to YouTube*, ed. Geert Lovink and Sabine Niederer (Amsterdam: Institute of Network Cultures, 2008), 33–44.

33 Purcell, "Online Video 2013."

34 Many examples demonstrate this: "99 Problems" at http://www.youtube.com/watch?v=2C22wBf2h5k; and probably the most clearly connected to CalTV's "Imagine This," "Obama State of the Union Remix" at http://www.youtube.com/watch?v=WVmq5A4m1fU; "Bachmania! 'Countdown's Michele Bachmann Remix" at http://www.youtube.com/watch?v=wytKBIC_ZNA; and "You Be Da Man! Michelle Bachmann Soils Herself in Public While Michael Steele Cringes" at http://www.youtube.com/watch?v=h-DQANalAe0, among many others (all accessed August 14, 2014).

35 Bloodgood and Deane. Ibid. 10.

36 My own Facebook network consists of about 750 persons, who can generally be classed as active participants in social media and online culture. I am not accounting for Facebook's algorithm, which has a strong impact on who sees these posts.

37 Indeed, I am not suggesting something new. Manovich (2005 and 2007) projected and recognized this move to remix as a metaphor for public cultural expression. Lev Manovich, "Remixability" (2005) http://www.manovich.net/DOCS/Remix_modular.doc and Lev Manovich, "What Comes after Remix?" (2007) http://manovich.net/index.php/projects/what-comes-after-remix.

38 John Callahan, personal interview. August 7, 2013.

Bibliography

BBC.com. "1985: Live Aid Makes Millions for Africa." July 13, 2008. http://news.bbc.co.uk/onthisday/hi/dates/stories/july/13/newsid_2502000/2502735.stm (accessed July 21, 2013).

Berger, Harris M. *Stance: Ideas about Emotion, Style, and Meaning for the Study of Expressive Culture.* Middletown, CT: Wesleyan University Press, 2009.

Bloodgood, Elizabeth and Shelley Deane. "Where Have All the Protest Songs Gone? Social Movements' Message and Their Voice in Politics." Presented at the Annual Meeting of the American Political Science Association in Washington, DC, September 2, 2005 (with permission of the author, granted July 11, 2013).

Burgess, Jean, and Joshua Green. *YouTube: Online Video and Participatory Culture—Digital Media and Society.* Cambridge: Polity Press, 2009.

Burkeman, Oliver. "Three Months Ago Bob Geldof Declared Live 8 Had Achieved Its Aim. But What Really Happened Next?" *The Guardian*, September 12, 2005. http://www.theguardian.com/world/2005/sep/12/hearafrica05.development (accessed July 21, 2013).

Cody, Francis. "Publics and Politics." *Annual Review of Anthropology* 40 (2011): 37–52.

Edwards, Richard, and Tryon, Chuck. "Political Video Mashups as Allegories of Citizen Empowerment" *First Monday* 14 no. 10 (2009).

Gay, Leslie C., Jr., and René T. A. Lysloff, eds. *Music and Technoculture.* Middletown, CN: Wesleyan University Press, 2003.

Geldof, Bob. "Live 8: What's It All About." http://www.live8live.com/whatsitabout/ (accessed July 21, 2013).

Greene, Paul D., and Thomas Porcello, eds. *Wired for Sound: Engineering and Technologies in Sonic Cultures.* Middletown, CN: Wesleyan University Press, 2005.

Grobelny, Joseph. "Mashups, Sampling, and Authorship: A Mashupsampliography." *Music Reference Services Quarterly* 11, no. 3/4 (2008): 229–239. doi:10.1080/10588160802570375.

Grow, Kory. "Eddie Vedder Plays 'Imagine' at Concert, Reinforces Anti-War Stance." *Rolling Stone*, July 21, 2014. http://www.rollingstone.com/music/news/eddie-vedder-reinforces-anti-war-stance-plays-imagine-at-concert-20140721 (accessed August 19, 2014).

Howard-Spink, Sam. "Grey Tuesday, Online Cultural Activism and the Mash-up of Music and Politics." *First Monday* 9, no. 10 (2004). http://firstmonday.org/htbin/cgiwrap/bin/ojs/index.php/fm/article/view/1180/1100 (accessed August 14, 2014).

"John Lennon Lesson Plan—Anniversary of his birth—October 9th;—anniversary of his death—December 8th." Developing Teachers.com 2012 lesson plan. http://www.developingteachers.com/plans/lennonpf.htm (accessed September 2, 2013).

Kaufman, Gil "Live Aid: A Look Back at a Concert that Actually Changed the World," MTV.com. June 29, 2005. http://www.mtv.com/news/articles/1504968/live-aid-look-back.jhtml (accessed July 21, 2013).

Krieger, J. Meryl. "Rough to the Board: Creating Performance in American Recording Studios." PhD dissertation, Indiana University, 2009.

———. Interview with John Callahan/CalTV. June–August, 2013.

Leaf, David, and John Scheinfeld, producers. 2006. *The U.S. vs. John Lennon*. Lionsgate and VH1: Santa Monica, CA. Documentary film.

Lessig, Lawrence. *Remix: Making Art and Commerce Thrive in the Hybrid Economy*. New York: Penguin, 2008.

"Live Aid." http://www.bobgeldof.com/content.asp?section=31 (accessed June 22, 2013).

Lovink, Geertz, and Sabine Niederer, eds. *Video Vortex Reader Responses to YouTube*. INC Reader #4. Amsterdam: Institute of Network Cultures, 2008.

Lovink, Geertz, and Miriam Rasch, eds. *Unlike Us Reader: Social Media Monopolies and Their Alternatives*. INC Reader #8. Amsterdam: Institute of Network Cultures, 2013.

Manovich, Lev. "Remixability and Modularity." 2005. http://manovich.net/index.php/projects/remixability-and-modularity (accessed August 14, 2014).

———. "What Comes after Remix?" 2007. http://manovich.net/index.php/projects/what-comes-after-remix (accessed August 14, 2014).

———. "The Practice of Everyday (Media) Life." In *Video Vortex Reader: Responses to YouTube*, edited by Geert Lovink and Sabine Niederer, 33–44. Amsterdam: Institute of Network Cultures, 2008.

Meintjes, Louise. "Paul Simon's Graceland, South Africa, and the Mediation of Musical Meaning." *Ethnomusicology* 34, no. 1 (1990): 37–73.

———. *Sounds of Africa! Making Music Zulu in a South African Studio*. Durham, NC: Duke University Press, 2003.

Mullins, Seth. "John Lennon and the Peace Movement: Cutting through the Political Rhetoric and Jargon that Keeps People in the Dark," (2007) formerly available at: http://voices.yahoo.com/john-lennon-peace-movement-185959.html (last accessed May 11, 2013).

Porcello, Thomas. "The Ethics of Digital Audio-Sampling: Engineers' Discourse." *Popular Music* 10, no. 1 (1991): 69–84.

Postill, John. "Digital Politics and Political Engagement." In *Digital Anthropology*, edited by Heather A. Horst and Daniel Miller, 165–184. London: Berg, 2012.

Purcell, Kristen. "Online Video 2013." Pew Research Center's Internet and American Life Project, Washington, DC, 2013. http://www.pewinternet.org/files/old-media//Files/Reports/2013/PIP_Online%20Video%202013.pdf (accessed May 9, 2014).

Shiga, John. "Copy-and-Persist: The Logic of Mash-up Culture." *Critical Studies in Media Communication* 24 no. 2 (2007): 93–114. doi:10.1080/07393180701262685.

Simons, Jan. "Between iPhone and YouTube: Movies on the Move?" In *Video Vortex Reader 2: Moving Images Beyond YouTube*, edited by Geert Lovink and Rachel Somers Miles. INC Reader #6. Amsterdam: Institute of Network Cultures, 2011.

Stavans, Ilan. *Art and Anger: Essays on Politics and the Imagination*. New York: Palgrave, 2001.

Sysomos. "Inside YouTube Videos: Exploring YouTube videos and their use in blogosphere—Michael Jackson and health care dominate." 2010 http://www.sysomos.com/reports/youtube/ (accessed October 1, 2013).

Tacchi, Jo. "Digital Engagement: Voice and Participation in Development." In *Digital Anthropology*, edited by Heather A. Horst and Daniel Miller, 225–241. London: Berg, 2012.

Warner, Michael. *Publics and Counterpublics*. New York: Zone Books, 2002.

"YouTube." http://en.wikipedia.org/wiki/Youtube (accessed September 5, 2013).

28

DÉTOURNEMENT AS A PREMISE OF THE REMIX FROM POLITICAL, AESTHETIC, AND TECHNICAL PERSPECTIVES

Nadine Wanono

In the late 1950s the French revolutionary artists' group the Situationist International (SI) formed to fight against, and destabilize, capitalist society by creating visual representations, objects, and situations that would question the spectators, invite them to reconsider their own position toward society, and increase their international consciousness. Guy Debord and Constant Nieuwenhuys articulate the SI initiative, as "The situationists must take every opportunity to oppose retrograde forces and ideologies, in the culture and wherever the question of the meaning of life arises."[1]

An example of their actions and modalities is an attack made by the SI during the International Assembly of Art Critics in Belgium. They disrupted the press conference by handing out a flyer signed "In the name of the Algerian, Belgian, French, German, Italian and Scandinavian sections of the SI, by Khatib, Korun, Debord, Platschek, Pinot-Gallizio and Jorn."[2] It was a tactic that had served them well as the Lettrist International when they disrupted a Charlie Chaplin press conference,[3] or when one member, dressed as a priest, denounced God and the church from the pulpit of Notre Dame cathedral.

To reach international audiences, they supported acts of defiance such as the Los Angeles Watts race riots of 1965. They wrote and asked for support from artists and intellectuals in Europe to sign the *Declaration on the Right to Insubordination in the Algerian War* and published it in September 1960. Within their home nation of France, they made assaults on cyberneticians at Strasbourg University in 1966 and against sociologists at Nanterre University. These violent actions were a prelude to the events of May '68, the first wildcat strike in history and the largest general strike to stop the economic functioning of an industrial capitalist society. In a speech about the aftermath in June

1968, Charles de Gaulle declared "this explosion was provoked by groups rebelling against modern consumer and technical society, whether it be the communism of the East or the capitalism of the West."[4]

The ramifications of this movement in different cultural contexts are interesting enough to warrant a specific study of its history, its goals, and its various means of expression.

The transmission of these powerful political and aesthetic moments were part of my training initiated with Jean Rouch; and were rooted in the dynamic of *détournement*[5] a word that is nearly impossible to translate into English. Ken Knabb who translated into English most of the texts of the Situationist movement explained "The French word *détournement* means deflection, diversion, rerouting, distortion, misuse, misappropriation, hijacking, or otherwise turning something aside from its normal course or purpose."[6]

A look back on Rouch's transmission process, regularly referring to these ideas, could be a useful tool allowing us to fully understand the ways such ideas and values can be transmitted in an academic context. Jean Rouch, ethnologist, engineer and internationally famous filmmaker, questioned our relationship to the so-called "real," our ways of perceiving differences in cultural expression, and our means of understanding phenomena classified as invisible.

After a brief historical overview of the SI and their political agenda based on *détournement*, I will explore some of the work produced by Jean Rouch as a connecting factor between the SI and the remix movement to recall some of the different forms taken by the remixer in the visual arts and in music production, and then examine how the *détournement*, in correlation with the programming language, affected remix and influenced it in regard to its different political, aesthetic, and technical dimensions.

History

To fully understand the dynamic and theoretical position of the SI, we should keep in mind that since 1940, aesthetic production was fully transformed into a commodity, as Walter Benjamin outlined in his work.[7]

On July 27, 1952, in Italy, a collective of avant-garde artists, members of several movements and associations such as Cobra for Copenhagen, Brussels, Amsterdam, the Lettrist movement, the International Movement for an *imaginiste* Bauhaus of Asger Jorn and the London Committee, founded the Situationist International (SI). One of its prominent thinkers and most powerful personalities was Guy Debord.

We can detect three main periods in the development of the Situationists. The Lettrists formed an experimental avant-garde movement, which became emblematic through a text by Ivan Chtcheglov, "Formulary for a New Urbanism,"[8] which became part of the new direction of the International Lettrists and also part of the archives of the SI. The text exemplifies the position of the Surrealists who focused on "forgotten desires" in the city. The act of *déambulation* in the city, without self-consciousness, echoing the "cadavre exquis" technique based on the random juxtaposition of words—these personal meanderings were part of a process to rediscover visual meanings inscribed in the city which conveyed negation, rebellion and eccentricity.

The second period, 1958–62, gave rise to an experimental form of expression: the imposition of additional or altered speech, bubbles on preexisting photo-comics, promotion of guerrilla tactics in the mass media, production of situationist films and comic strips. Later, from 1963 to 1968, the SI developed the theory and practice of the Exemplary Act. In "Our Goals and Methods in the Strasbourg Scandal," members of the SI wrote, "In fact, we want ideas to become dangerous again. We cannot be accepted with the spinelessness of a false eclectic interest, as if we were Sartre's, Althusser's, Aragon's or Godard's."[9] They developed an incisive and coherent critique of Western capitalism and Eastern bureaucratic capitalism. Their singular position toward political classification took them to the edge, navigating between socially or morally unacceptable positions, revolutionary discourse, and exhortations to protest. To describe themselves at the time, the SI wrote that their movement "can be seen as an artistic avant-garde, as an experimental investigation of possible ways to freely construct everyday life, and as a contribution to the theoretical and practical development of a new revolutionary protest."[10]

In 1956 Guy Debord and Gil J. Wolman published a user's guide to *détournement* defining the different kinds of *détournement*: the minor one based on "an element which has no importance in itself . . . a press clipping, a commonplace photograph . . . " and "the deceptive one, based on an intrinsically significant element, which derives a different scope from the new context."[11]

Extensively *détournés* works are a composition of several deceptive and minor *détournements*.

The Movement's members formulated different laws for *détournement*. Without describing all these laws, such a specific and precise classification alludes to the necessity for the SI to organize their actions against the bourgeoisie and intellectuals at large by proposing a list of commitments and clear methodologies to reach their goals.

Debord, in his user's guide to *détournement*, explains each of these laws. We can refer to the first one as an example. "*It is the most distant detourned element which contributes most sharply to the overall impression, and not the elements that directly determine the nature of this impression.*"[12] For example, in a metagraph[13] relating to the Spanish Civil War the phrase with the most distinctly revolutionary sense is a fragment from a lipstick ad: "Pretty lips are red."

On the other hand, this precise ontology of methods and possibilities to destabilize entrenched society raises the question of exclusion. The SI were too often excluding themselves in order to protect themselves from being bought out, exploited, and weakened by any form of misinterpretation. It is most likely the *ultra-détournement* operating in everyday social life, the construction of situations and the nature of the ultimate goal of the SI's activities that gave rise to aggressive exclusion. In fact, over the course of its history, there were approximately 70 members. However, due to the frequent expulsions, only 10 to 20 members were part of the movement at any one time. In 1972, the SI movement had only two remaining members: Gianfranco Sanguinetti and Guy Debord. The political situation in the aftermath of May '68 in France, and the state of political upheaval in Italy led Debord to officially dissolve the SI. This dissolution was less the consequence of its internal disputes than of its external failure.

> The political, artistic and personal position of an "assault on bourgeois culture," an assault which is invariably both superficially scandalous and notoriously superficial, condemns itself to the anonymity of peripheral opposition. It was this precarious condition involving alternate forms of paralysis which the SI both described and fell victim to.[14]

Dissemination of the *Détournement*

Even if this political and artistic movement failed to reach its goals, we should not underestimate the international repercussions it had in different cultural areas, withstanding the test of time. One of the most famous documentary filmmakers, Jean Rouch, had been influenced by the Surrealist movement and the SI and disseminated their anarchist ideas in his teaching all over the world. In the field of visual anthropology, he took a prominent role by questioning the relationship between fiction and documentary as two complementary approaches. He introduced a poetic slant to a descriptive technique to convey the realities of the otherness. Within this methodology he promoted the production of "worrying object:"[15] or genre-breaking film, neither part of the fiction register nor the documentary style. It was his way to force students and scholars to redefine their own position toward the observed group of people filmed and toward the discipline with its implicit rules.

In fact, as the SI would suggest, having fun, enjoying oneself and laughing or even deriding everyday situations, were part of the everyday agenda of these practitioners. Based on these beliefs, one of Jean Rouch's pleasures, in his role as an educator, was to transmit his knowledge and experience while creating a situation in which laughing was the first priority when faced with a new or complex situation. He disseminated this pedagogical agenda around the world—in the United States, Japan, Mexico, and in France, where he founded a PhD in visual anthropology. This courageous and revolutionary approach (for instance, including filmic elements in a doctoral anthropology course around 1975) was rooted in the idea of democratizing the power of creation, introducing students to sensible forms of the appropriation of knowledge, and to view and discover the real by recreating it. Rouch always referred to *détournement* as an everyday basic activity, and as a way of seeing. Students should be aware of their capacities to produce queer objects[16] as he did, by producing films questioning traditional academic classifications. The goal was to blur the boundaries between disciplines and subjects in order to question the act of creation and to put into circulation objects strange enough never to be truly classifiable. One example Rouch provided was the scandal provoked by the screening of his film *Mad Masters* at the Museum of Man in 1955. This documentary about Hauka possession dances portrayed the undermining colonialist power, the political domination, and the violence it exerted on the population. After Marcel Griaule asked Rouch in public to destroy the film, the only one who took to his defense was Luc de Heusch, also named Luc Zangrie, who took part in Cobra activities, as a writer and filmmaker. He openly defended Rouch's film for its singular vision and its powerful statement about society. It's likely that Luc de Heusch had quickly understood the persuasive discourse and the necessity of really questioning the repercussions and consequences of colonialism, and the need to position them within an artistic answer. *Mad Masters* received a prize at the Mostra of Venice in 1957.

By recalling the links between activist movements and academic activities, I underline the fact that *détournement* became a mindset, a dynamic, a loyalty to a revolutionary dimension outside of any political movement.

Rouch, inspired by this dynamic based on controversial activities claimed to be an anarchist and this dimension was crucial to him. He often told his students that he never took part in a vote. He felt that this strong position was rooted not in an artistic desire or in intellectual aesthetics but in his own childhood experiences, his relationship with his mother and also his experiences of the war: "He speaks of his memories in the womb using the image of a lover's separation, a carnal separation, a separation that would structure the rest of his life . . . 24 years of heaven between two bouts of Hell."[17] Or as he also said,

> We were witnesses to the defeat, to the landslide of the French army, which was supposed to be the best in the world. At this moment, something happened in my life: I couldn't believe in anything, either in my father, or my professors, in God, in Freud, in Marx . . . Nothing. It was the end . . . I was no longer answerable to my society . . . that's how it all began on a beautiful day in May . . . [18]

These declarations were part of our training; the spirit of our work was imbued with the values and methods of the SI. Rouch, by his permanent questioning, has most of the time been a source of mistrust for his colleagues. If we recall the political and social environment of this period in France, inviting people to employ the *détournement* as a pertinent reaction toward the system, was still at the margin of society and perceived as a kind of violence against the official mise-en-scène of the political realm.

At the Margins of *La Société du Spectacle?*

For SI, "there is no Situationist art, only Situationist uses of art"[19] The SI used *détournement* in films, art, and graphics for their journal and in posters that "hijacked" comics during the events of May '68. Plagiarism was both the source and the meaning of the original work, which was subverted to create a new work. The ideas behind the concept, the methodology, the actions, which were part of the *détournement*, drove people to denounce directly The Society of the Spectacle. Debord wrote extensively on this theme in a book published in 1967 and in a film, *La Société du Spectacle*, released in 1973. Both declared:

> The spectacle presents itself simultaneously as society itself, as a part of society, and as a *means of unification*. As a part of society, it is ostensibly the focal point of all vision and all consciousness. But due to the very fact that this sector is *separate*, it is in reality the domain of delusion and false consciousness: the unification it achieves is nothing but an official language of universal separation.
>
> The spectacle is not a collection of images; it is a social relation between people that is mediated by images.[20]

The inspirational values and revolutionary visual messages found everywhere from the walls of May '68 to the Internet have become part of a global culture. SI might have said, "our ideas are now commonplace, in all of our minds."[21] After May '68, this revolutionary attitude fighting against political consensus with artistic means spread all over the world and particularly in Europe with the punk movement. We choose to analyze this moment through the Sex Pistols who took advantage of the *détournement* methodology to reach their goals in conservative English society in the 1970s.

It is probably in the punk movement that we find the most obvious public connection with the SI. In the aftermath of May '68, the Sex Pistols was one of the first punk bands to fully take advantage of society's political and sociological weaknesses. In the lyrics to the song "Anarchy in the UK," the band refers explicitly to the *Mouvement Populaire de*

Libération de l'Angola, the Ulster Defence Association and the Irish Republican Army. For the younger generation, these lyrics introduced revolutionary ideas as the product of revolutionary political movements. By giving them a voice the group reintroduced the challenges of these struggles: leaving the peripheral to become part of the central sphere. Interestingly enough was the commercial success of the songs, and the album *Never Mind the Bollocks, Here's The Sex Pistols*.[22] Jamie Reid designed this famous LP. Graphically, his cut-and-paste collage style clearly referred to an aesthetic *détournement* process as it obviously reveals the edges of juxtaposed images, and uses the official portrait of the Queen with a safety pin on her mouth, as if to repossess her as a symbol for the punk movement. His work was quite provocative from an aesthetic point of view in opposition to the more harmonious codes prevailing in graphic design at the time, but also from a political point of view.[23] If for the Situationists commercialization was not part of the agenda, for this band the financial aspect and the commercialization of their albums were integral to their success. Even if traditional English society was heavily critical of their lyrics, the album, banned from the official distribution circuit, was widely sold in alternative distribution networks. For the Situationists, the links between the proletariat and students were crucial to their political struggles, for the Sex Pistols their controversial positions, their public "offenses" (for instance, on TV shows) urged the workers in the vinyl pressing plant to go on strike, refusing to create their records for "moral reasons."[24]

"Anarchy in the UK" opened the door to a type of protest holding radical and provocative positions in Thatcher's Britain. They pursued their destabilization of the prevailing values of English society by asserting, in "God Save the Queen," "that the function of sacred thought has been taken over by ideology; and by challenging in "Pretty Vacant," the cult of the image; and finally, in "Holidays in the Sun," by demanding the right to 'make history now'."[25] If one can believe their manager Malcolm McLaren, who once told *Melody Maker* that "it's wonderful to use situationism in rock 'n' roll," the connection between the Sex Pistols and the SI is solidified.[26]

The questions we could raise after the comparison of this musical phenomena in regard to The Society of the Spectacle and the power of *détournement* is: Where are the margins in a time of digital globalization? If for the SI the confrontation within society was crucial as they always reinvented new forms of contestation, what could be the characteristics of a marginal opposition now? The CopyLeft movement, the Hackers' strategies are, on some level, part of the global arena as dub or remix are part of the media industry and The Society of the Spectacle. Since we cannot step out of the digital universe and go back to the analog system in order to protect and locate our creation as an outsider to prolong the *détournement* process, we must focus on our capacities to create and produce detourned objects, thus questioning and challenging the politics in our respective domains, and specifically in the academic system.

The Remix as *Détournement*

The idea of *détournement*, has played an important role since 1970 in music, media, arts, and the creative industries overall.

Creating and disseminating songs, lyrics, and pictures that condemn The Society of the Spectacle is commonplace, and the artists referring to the movement and philosophy are numerous—Hackers, Free Software and Adbusters, among others. The complexity of the situation is not to define whether the references to the SI or *détournement* are true, honest, or accurate but to underline how the globalization process and the media industry are now exploiting all these elements, which originally came from the counterculture. The question raised by these creative industries focus on the role and place of such dissident production. If for the SI their productions should produce a confrontation or even a destabilization between the marginal artistic forms of expression and the mainstream art production, how then can this opposition be reframed in a digital age where margins are quickly mainstreamed through the cultural jamming that gained traction in a saturated media environment?

As a student, trained within this *détournement* spirit, I realized progressively that the films I produced were part of The Society of the Spectacle[27] and I was invited to fight against this from the early days of my training with Rouch. In order to keep this heritage alive and to favor the transmission of this important spirit, I decided to conduct research on digital technologies and more specifically on programming languages to see how we could keep control of the singularity observed on the field without being trapped by the standardization process. As Rouch might have put it, "there is no such thing as an arbitrary objective."[28]

During this research, I realized how remix could refer to the SI as a source of inspiration, with its own rules, its specific political agenda, and its own means of expression. One of the first people I read on this subject was Lev Manovich, with his book *The Language of New Media*.[29]

By trying to explain and to analyze the definition and function of new media in early 2001, Manovich took his inspiration from Dziga Vertov, one of Jean Rouch's totemic ancestors,[30] and his film *Man with a Movie Camera*. Manovich explained the different types of values upheld in his editing technique: for instance, one linked to the process with a temporal aspect, whereas another utilized superimposition of different images or multiple screens. He pursues his reasoning by presenting Vertov as the filmmaker who conceived the first database of city life in 1920, a database of film techniques, and a database of new operations of visual epistemology. "Film can overcome its indexical nature, by presenting the viewer with objects that never existed in reality . . . . It is also a database of new interface operations which together aim to go beyond simple human navigation through a physical space."[31]

As soon as I captured the capacities of the language of programming, I realized this new language could be a powerful *détournement* tool as well as a creative language, once we had mastered it. It was clear that programming languages could also be the best method and the most effective system for the standardization of representations and their rapid dissemination.

Marcos Novak, a digital artist creating "liquid architecture" environments, explained how to create, to shape reasoning as Da Vinci might have done. He would say, "If your reasoning is right then you can shape it."[32] He was inspired by Garcia Lorca's concept of the *duende*, and he invited his students to create and to put into circulation what could be called "queer objects." In this programming language class, far away from the French Surrealist movement, far away from any documentary film questions, there was the same spirit, the same motivation as with Rouch almost 20 years earlier.

Novak quickly concluded that creation was not the main purpose or even the goal of the training and production. The dynamic was to prolong what had been done: the focus was on the action not the author, students didn't invest in posing as creators or artists with an inspirational spirit, nor to build a career as the creators of a new form—the goal was to focus on the interpretation, understanding, conception, and all other elements pertaining to producing and shaping lines of inquiry, becoming more conscious of the multiplicity of realities. The strength had to be in creating new forms from preexisting elements. In this way the students abandoned their private dreams of conceiving personal creations, in favor of investing in the idea of repetition, recreation, and transformation. Progressively, Marcos Novak invited his students to slip into the world of remix, on the border between the actualization of the SI and the achievement of The Society of the Spectacle.

These examples show how the notion of *détournement* linked different political situations, cultural surroundings, social productions, and technical systems in a very subtle way.

As we said and probably for the SI themselves, the question of the original versus the copy is not the challenge we are faced with anymore. The most important question is the topology of these expressions in the field of the *détournement* and the counterculture in a time of the World Wide Web. If on one hand the digital technologies favor the links between the SI, the *détournement* and the remix by permitting individuals living in countries connected to the Internet to produce creative and personal accounts and enhance their individual creativity and reactivity or consciousness, on the other hand we should accept that most of the production issued from these manipulations with a social context—Facebook, Twitter, YouTube or with media context like Photoshop and After Effects—encourage the standardization of the message. "The shift to digital enables the development of media software—but it does not constrain the directions in which it already evolved and continues to evolve."[33]

In fact, the *détournement* and the remix have also largely been detourned by the advertising industry or the newspaper business as an effective commercial technic, losing its political dimension.

As Manovich explains in *Software Takes Command* interview:

> We are much more aware of the multiplicity of societies and subcultures, and how the same technologies are used very differently in different places by different people. Think of all uses of Internet, from selling things and collecting data about consumers to organizing resistance and protests, to acting as the only publishing outlet for academics in many countries that do not have academic publishing houses.[34]

In order to capture the *détournement* spirit in times when software takes command we can refer to the work of Jenkins who, like Manovich, has an optimistic approach of the new landscape created by a young generation of active producers and skilled manipulators of program meanings, as nomadic poachers constructing their own culture from borrowed materials, as an alternative social community defined through its cultural preferences and consumption practices. Jenkins, in his book, *Textual Poachers*,[35] proposed an ethnographic account of the media fan community, its interpretive strategies, its social institutions and cultural practices, and its troubled relationship to the mass media and consumer capitalism.

In *The Practice of Everyday Life*, Michel de Certeau[36] demonstrates how mass media uses tactics and strategies to poach upon the marketability of consumable goods. This in turn encourages practices of *détournement*, tricking consumers with false promises.

In our societies, where media, economy, and social relations all run on software, any investigation of code, software architectures, or interfaces is only valuable if it helps us to understand how these technologies are reshaping societies and individuals, and how our imaginations could *détourne* it in order to keep control of our creative capacities.

Notes

1 Constant Nieuwenhuys and Guy Debord, "The Amsterdam Declaration 1958," trans. Paul Hammond, *Internationale Situationniste* bulletin no. 2, http://www.cddc.vt.edu/sionline/si/is2.html (accessed March 24, 2014).

2 Here is an excerpt of the text signed by Khatib, Korun, Debord, Platschek, Pinot-Gallizio and Jorn:

> Vanish, art critics, partial, incoherent and divided imbeciles! In vain do you stage the spectacle of a fake encounter. You have nothing in common but a role to cling to; you are only in this market to parade one of the aspects of Western commerce: your confused and empty babble about a decomposed culture. History has depreciated you. Even your audacities belong to a past now forever closed. Disperse, fragments of art critics, critics of fragments of art. The Situationist International is now organizing the integral artistic activity of the future. You have nothing more to say. The Situationist International will leave no place for you. We will starve you out.
>
> *Internationale Situationniste* bulletin no. 1 Paris, June 1958, trans. Ken Knabb,
> http://www.cddc.vt.edu/sionline/si/action.html (accessed March 24, 2014)

3 Text entitled "No More Flat Feet!"

> Sub Mack Sennett director, sub-Max Linder actor, Stavisky of the tears of unwed mothers and the little orphans of Auteuil, you are Chaplin, emotional blackmailer, master-singer of misfortune.
>
> The cameraman needed his Delly. It's only to him that you've given your works, and your good works: your charities.
>
> Because you've identified yourself with the weak and the oppressed, to attack you has been to attack the weak and oppressed—but in the shadow of your rattan cane some could already see the nightstick of a cop.
>
> You are "he-who-turns-the-other-cheek"—the other cheek of the buttock—but for us, the young and beautiful, the only answer to suffering is revolution.
>
> We don't buy the "absurd persecutions" that make you out as the victim, you flat-footed Max de Veuzit. In France the Immigration Service calls itself the Advertising Agency. The sort of press conference you gave at Cherbourg could offer no more than a piece of tripe. You have nothing to fear from the success of Limelight.
>
> Go to sleep, you fascist insect. Rake in the dough. Make it with high society (we loved it when you crawled on your stomach in front of little Elizabeth). Have a quick death: we promise you a first-class funeral.
>
> We pray that your latest film will truly be your last.
>
> The fires of the kleig lights have melted the makeup of the so-called brilliant mime—and exposed the sinister and compromised old man.
>
> Go home, Mister Chaplin.

Internationale Lettriste: Serge Berna, Jean-L. Brau, Guy-Ernest Debord, Gil J. Wolman
  Internationale Lettriste # 1 (Paris, November 1952). Trans. Sophie Rosenberg http://www.cddc.vt.edu/sionline/presitu/flatfeet.html (accessed March 24, 2014).

4 http://fresques.ina.fr/de-gaulle/fiche-media/Gaulle00143/entretien-avec-michel-droit.html (accessed August 14, 2014).

5 If we go back to the original definitions as the SI did in 1959, in the *Internationale Situationniste* bulletin:

> DÉTOURNEMENT: the re-use of pre-existing artistic elements in a new ensemble, has been a constantly present tendency of the contemporary avant-garde, both before and since the formation of the SI. The two fundamental laws of détournement are the loss of importance of each "detourned" autonomous element—which may go so far as to completely lose its original meaning—and at the same time the organization of another meaningful ensemble that confers on each element its new scope and effect. This combination of parody and seriousness reflects the contradictions of an era in which we find ourselves confronted with both the urgent necessity and the near impossibility of initiating and carrying out a totally innovative collective action.
>
> *Internationale Situationniste* bulletin no. 3 (Paris, December 1959),
> http://www.cddc.vt.edu/sionline/si/detournement.html (accessed August 14, 2014).

6 Ken Knabb's Bureau of Public Secrets, note 1 to Guy Debord and Gil J. Wolman "A User's Guide to *Détournement*," 1956, ed. and trans. Ken Knabb, http://www.bopsecrets.org/SI/detourn.htm (accessed August 26, 2014).

7 Walter Benjamin, "The Work of Art in the Age of Mechanical Reproduction," *Illuminations* (London: Fontana, 1968 [1936]), 214–218.

8 "Formulary for a New Urbanism," October 1953. http://www.cddc.vt.edu/sionline/presitu/formulary.html (accessed August 14, 2014).

9 "Our Goals and Methods in the Strasbourg Scandal," *Internationale Situationniste* #11, October, 1967, trans. Ken Knabb, http://www.cddc.vt.edu/sionline/si/strasbourg.html (accessed August 26, 2014).

10 "The Situationists and the New Forms of Action in Art and Politics," June 1963, http://www.cddc.vt.edu/sionline/si/newforms.html (accessed August 14, 2014).

11 *Les Lèvres Nues* #8 (May 1956), Revue trimestrielle Bruxelles no. 10–12 (September 1958) Rédactio Marcel Mariën Editeur responsable Marcel Mariën, translated by Ken Knabb from the *Situationist International Anthology* (Revised and Expanded Edition, 2006) http://www.cddc.vt.edu/sionline/presitu/usersguide.html (accessed August 26, 2014).

12 Ibid.

13 The "metagraph," a genre developed by the Lettrists, is a sort of collage with largely textual elements.

14 David Jacobs and Christophe Winks, *At Dusk: The Situationist Movement in Historical Perspective* (Berkeley, CA: Perspectives, 1975). http://libcom.org/files/At%20Dusk%20The%20Situationist%20Movement%20In%20Historical%20Perspective%201975.pdf.

15 *Objets inquiétants*, an expression commonly employed by Rouch during his teaching either at Ecole Pratique des Hautes Etudes or at the Cinémathèque Française.

16 Christopher Thomson, *L'Autre et le sacrée: Surréalisme, cinéma, ethnologie* (Paris: l'Harmattan, 1995 [in French, my translation]), 284. I conceived creative modelization inspired from my fieldwork in Mali. Completely aware of the queer movement and its importance in the US, I decided to employ this word to underline the possibilities to produce representation characterized by their appurtenances to different registers: media art, film, experimental cinema, algorithm, experimental visual anthropology. It was a way for me to affirm the importance of representation referring to unthought classification by Western society.

17 Ibid., 285.

18 Ibid.

19 *Internationale situationniste* #7, Paris (April 1962), 27. Central bulletin published by the sections of the Situationist International, trans. Reuben Keehan, http://www.cddc.vt.edu/sionline/si/is7.html (accessed August 20, 2014).

20 Definition 3 and 4 from *The Society of the Spectacle* by Guy Dubord, trans. Donald Nicholson Smith (New York: Zone Books, 1994), 5.

21 "Our ideas are on everyone's minds" particularly those exploring the constant threat of boredom and commodification. *Enragés et situationnistes dans le mouvement des occupations* (Paris: Gallimard, 1968), 45.

22 Producers: Chris Thomas and Bill Price, label: Virgin Records, Barclay, 1977.

23 His work came in at number two in a *Rolling Stone* magazine poll of the best rock album sleeves of all time.

24 George Gimarc, *Punk Diary, 1970–1979: The Ultimate Complete Day-By-Day Reference Guide to Punk* (New York: St. Martin's Press, 1994), 70; Jon Savage, *England Dreaming* (London: Faber and Faber, 2005 [1991]), 349.

25 Notbored.org, "Review of Exhibit of Works by Jamie Reid," http://www.notbored.org/reid.html (accessed August 14, 2014).

26 Bill Brown, *Not Bored! Anthology 1983–2000* (New York: Colossal Books, 2011), 265.

27 The spectacle presents itself simultaneously as society itself, as a part of society, and as a means of unification. As a part of society, it is ostensibly the focal point of all vision and all consciousness. But due to the very fact that this sector is separate, it is in reality the domain of delusion and false consciousness: the unification it achieves is nothing but an official language of universal separation. **4** The spectacle is not a collection of images; it is a social relation between people that is mediated by images. **5** The spectacle cannot be understood as a mere visual excess produced by mass-media technologies. It is a worldview that has actually been materialized, that has become an objective reality.

Guy-Ernest Debord, *The Society of the Spectacle*, Chapter 1,
http://library.nothingness.org/articles/SI/en/pub_contents/4 (accessed August 14, 2014).

28 It is a well-known expression often quoted by Rouch to underline his approach and belief. He employed it on a regular basis during his teaching at La Cinémathèque Française, where he taught more than 20 years, every Saturday morning.

29 Lev Manovich, *The Language of New Media* (Cambridge, MA: MIT Press, 2001).

30 In *Principles of Visual Anthropology*, Rouch wrote an article entitled "Our Totemic Ancestors and Crazed Masters." Paul Hockings, ed. *Principles of Visual Anthropology*, 3rd edition (Berlin: De Gruyter, 2003), 217–234.

31 Manovich, "Prologue: Vertov's Dataset," *The Language of New Media*, captions to Figures 149 and 243.

32 Media Art and Technology class, University of California at Santa Barbara.

33 "*Software Takes Command*: An Interview with New Media Theorist Lev Manovich, Part 1," by Illya Szilak, December 16, 2013, *HuffPost, The Blog*, http://www.huffingtonpost.com/illya-szilak/software-takes-command-an_b_4449999.html (accessed August 14, 2014).

34 Ibid.

35 Henry Jenkins, *Textual Poachers: Television Fans and Participatory Culture*, updated twentieth anniversary edition (New York: Routledge, 2013).

36 De Certeau, Michel *The Practice of Everyday Life*, trans. Steven Rendall (Berkeley, CA: University of California Press, 1984).

Bibliography

Atkins, Guy, with Troels Andersen. *Asger Jorn: The Crucial Years, 1954–1964*. New York: Wittenborn Art Books, 1977.

Benjamin, Walter. *Illuminations*. London: Fontana, 1968 [1936].

Brown, Bill. *Not Bored! Anthology 1983–2000*. New York: Colossal Books, 2011.

Cutler, Carol. "Paris: The Lettrist Movement." *Art in America* 58 (1970): 117–119.

Debray, Régis. "Remarks on the Spectacle." Translated by Eric Rauth. *New Left Review* 214 (1995): 134–141.

Ford, Simon. *The Realization and Suppression of the Situationist International: An Annotated Bibliography 1972–1992*. San Francisco, CA: AK Press, 1995.

——. *Situationist International: A User's Guide*, London: Black Dog Publishing, 2004.

Gimarc, George. *Punk Diary, 1970–1979: The Ultimate Complete Day-By-Day Reference Guide to Punk*. New York: St. Martin's Press, 1994.

Hockings, Paul, ed. *Principles of Visual Anthropology*, 3rd edition. Berlin: De Gruyter, 2003.

Home, Stewart, ed. *What is Situationism? A Reader*. Edinburgh: AK Press, 1993.

Jacobs, David, and Christopher Winks. *At Dusk: The Situationist Movement in Historical Perspective*. Berkeley, CA: Perspectives, 1975, http://libcom.org/files/At%20Dusk%20The%20Situationist%20Movement%20In%20Historical%20Perspective%201975.pdf (accessed August 14, 2014).

Jenkins, Henry. *Textual Poachers: Television Fans and Participatory Culture*, updated twentieth anniversary edition. New York: Routledge, 2013.

Lefebvre, Henri. "Lefebvre on the Situationists: An Interview." With Kristin Ross *October* 79 (1997): 69–83.

Manovich, Lev. *The Language of New Media*. Cambridge, MA: MIT Press, 2001.

Savage, Jon. *England Dreaming*. London: Faber and Faber, 2005 [1991].

Thomson, Christopher. *L'Autre et le sacrée: Surréalisme, cinéma, ethnologie*. Paris: l'Harmattan, 1995.

29

THE NEW POLYMATH (REMIXING KNOWLEDGE)

Rachel Falconer

The innovators of the future will be the DJs of Thought, sampling, mixing, and spinning all existing ideas and thought-objects into ever-new structures. They will remix what we know into what we could know. They will show the Academy how to dance.[1]

Discipline-hopping is often the default strategy employed when negotiating the complex sociotechnical topics related to protocol. This boundary raiding was the natural modus operandi of the classical figure of the Renaissance Man, and continues to be so for the new polymath in the digital age. In this chapter, the polymath[2]—traditionally defined retrospectively as a particularly gifted individual who excelled in a number of disciplines—is recast as subversive remixer as she navigates the camouflaged control systems of networked knowledge production.

In this chapter, the new polymath is placed at the epicenter of the digital informational storm and her political traction is gauged through her positioning as the archetypal figure within remix culture, in which the agency of the act of remix—an integral part of contemporary knowledge production—is tested. Taking a cue from Certeau's[3] championing of the subversive agency of the user in everyday practices, I position the polymath as "DJ of Thought."[4] As the informational remixer approaches the decks, the spaces within which the new polymath might operate are examined.

With the advent of creative and social capital, there has been an exponential increase in public participation in knowledge production and consumption. There is, however, a clear disconnect between traditional, hierarchical systems of information distribution and the emergent rhizomatic networks of flattened digital data flow. These conflicts are most evident within cultures of knowledge production. The mass dissemination and production of online knowledge endemic to the digital age marks a paradigmatic leveling of the status of those who claim to be "in the know."

The veneer of the utopian vision of the democratization of the elitist channels of knowledge transference by the early Internet pioneers, and the championing of the "participation society"[5] is increasingly showing fracture lines. The stronghold of the historical institutions on the artifacts of knowledge is still very much in force, and is poignantly evidenced in the case of Aaron Swartz and JSTOR.[6] This episode serves to emphasize the gaping disparity between popular open knowledge rhetoric and the harsh reality of the gatekeeping and control systems at play on the Internet. In this ambiguous and unstable arena, the polymath must transgress the networked cognitive control systems at play. In the following sections, a brief overview of the figure of the polymath will be given in relation to remix culture and the various operational spaces of her activity will be probed and tested.

The Polymath

According to popular history, the polymath came to prominence during the Renaissance and was associated with the related figure of the—predominantly male—genius.[7] During the eighteenth and nineteenth centuries the idea of what constituted knowledge was determined by the development of systems of academic study and education. These systems were a way of measuring and quantifying knowledge, and guaranteed the polymath's prowess. However, as more expansive historical narratives emerge,[8] the figures included in this exclusive club broaden out to include Ada Lovelace, Sir Jagadish Chandra Bose, Cyrill Collard and Maria Gaetana Agnesi.

See Chapter 36 for Owen Gallagher's discussion on creating a critical remix video (CRV) that challenges utopic visions, and was inspired by a confluence of global political events, including the Arab Spring across the Middle East, and the Occupy movement in the US and Europe.

Nonetheless, the classical polymath remains fixed in a vacuum of prestige—his superhuman qualities seemingly impervious to our retrospective gaze. Today, the new polymath is an increasingly maverick creature as her agency is inextricably linked to her relationship with digital knowledge production and distribution and the operational systems that control its flux and flow. Consequently, in order for the connection between the new polymath and the remixer to be made, the defining features of knowledge in the digital age need to be acknowledged.

The seismic informational shift generated by the digital revolution and emergent convergence culture,[9] has changed the way we think about knowledge ecologies. This is seen in the proliferation of technologies providing platforms for the homogenous dissemination of data and information and the phenomenon of the "hive mind." In "Out of Control,"[10] Kevin Kelly defines the nonhierarchical nature of the hive mind: "The marvel of 'hive mind' is that no one is in control, and yet an invisible hand governs, a hand that emerges from very dumb members."[11] The hive mind is associated with the rise of decentralized technologies such as peer-to-peer, Web services, and wireless networks that facilitate the exploding channels of user-generated content on the Web.[12] Wikipedia is often cited as the epitome of these systems of flattened knowledge exchange by hive mind skeptics.[13] This swarm of networked collective intelligence forms the cognitive landscape in which the new polymath must resonate.

The idea that knowledge production takes place exclusively in the head of the individual is further challenged by the theories of "collective intelligence" by Donna Haraway[14] and in N. Katherine Hayles's conception of the "cognisphere."[15] In this updated version of the de Chardinian noösphere,[16] Hayles positions the sphere of the mind as having "expanded to include not only the Internet but also networked and programmable systems that feed into it."[17] The meme is a clear example of such an expansive cognitive system,[18] and Richard Dawkins argues that the meme has hijacked the very concept of an original idea. Internet memes are deliberately choreographed by human creativity,[19] he says, and it is in this act of cognitive modification that the new polymath's agency resides.

This is symptomatic of the more general cognitive environment in which the new polymath operates—*networked knowledge*. David Weinberger defines this as knowledge that has shifted from the minds of individuals to become the "property of the network."[20] This signals a change in the infrastructure of knowledge itself as it becomes more unstable, but increasingly transparent.[21] Furthermore this shift directly challenges the old idea that universal knowledge is achievable and, as Weinberger suggests, this transformation is a straightforward acknowledgment of one basic truth we've always known "but that our paper-based system of knowledge simply couldn't accommodate: The world is far, far too big to know."[22] This places the figure of the *Uomo Universale*,[23] in crisis, and the expectations placed on the new polymath need to be reassessed.

The crucial point to emphasize here in repositioning the new polymath is that the act of remixing does not constitute a drive towards the creation of knowledge in itself, but the new polymath *uses* knowledge to create new knowledge through transdisciplinary manipulation. This is more akin to intelligence, and therefore the polymath's traction lies in the performance of her transdisciplinary intellect and not in the accumulation of knowledge in and of itself.

With this shift in emphasis, the new polymath's identity moves closer to that of the curator. The contemporary curator combines anarchic free play with a responsibility to deliver a clear and artist-led message to the public. As the term curator is increasingly used outside the museum and gallery (picnic curators,[24] curate your closet[25] etc.), the traditional ideal of the curator as custodian of artifacts fades. Curators have become increasingly visible as "choreographers" or "authors" of exhibitions and have effectively co-opted the act of remix so as to render the narrative of the exhibition as sometimes equal to the individual works of art on display. Much like the nature of networked knowledge, this development privileges the exhibition itself (as a type of network), as the primary vehicle of cultural value. Florence Derieux has argued that the rise of the exhibition-as-event has reinforced this position, making current curatorial practice "no longer . . . a history of artworks, but . . . a history of exhibitions."[26]

This blurring in the lines of identity is not new,[27] but serves to demonstrate the wider crisis of the new polymath. The curator question is, in effect, the polymath dilemma—where does a single identity of authority lie when the exhibition itself is the key operator in conveying cultural value? This distancing from the singularity of the polymath is due, partly, to the fragmentation of our worldview. The mass dissemination of information and the sheer volume of (often contradictory) knowledge available online, has warped and splintered our worldview into uncollectable and irreconcilable perspectives. By adopting the everyday tactic[28] of remix, the new polymath hacks the fractured informational terrain, and it is through this optic that the figure of the "DJ of Thought" can be introduced. This parallel is indicated in the quotation at the beginning of this chapter and remains the thesis throughout: the new polymath must operate within the constantly changing and contingent systems of networked knowledge in order for her voice to be heard. She dons a myriad of hats, employs a transdisciplinary strategy and is nomadic in her trajectory. The new polymath raids the boundaries between disciplines, absorbing and appropriating the cognitive and cultural material at her fingertips, performing for the digital commons.

In the next section, the figure of the remixer and the act of remix are more closely examined in relation to the new polymath. While the specialist delves deeper into a niche, often-isolated subject rabbit hole, the new polymath forms active, free associations within a transdisciplinary knowledge ecology. Much like a DJ referencing and assimilating a myriad of musical styles and beats, the polymath in the digital age is defined by her, "operative"[29] act of remix.

Remix Defined

Nadine Wanono writes extensively about détournement in Chapter 28 and Stefan Sonvilla-Weiss's Chapter 3 in Part I, History, also reviews many of these references to visual culture.

From its early roots in classic jazz and disco 12-inches to the anarchic Negativland and the slightly more palatable Hype Williams, remix culture has spread like a virus during the online years. The term *remix* originated from the late twentieth century practice of taking samples from audio tracks and recombining them in new and original ways. Traceable through a varied and sporadic history of cultural tactics, remix can be detected in the cut-up novels of William Burroughs, the practice of *détournement* enacted by Michèle Bernstein, Dadaist Hannah Hoch's photomontages and, most recently, in the artist and poet Kenneth Goldsmith's practice of "uncreative writing."[30]

From a theoretical perspective, remix as a discourse operates within the logic of Deleuze and Guattari's concept of *smooth* and *striated* space.[31] In *A Thousand Plateaus*, Deleuze and Guattari describe smooth spaces as rhizomatic, nomadic and anarchic, while striated spaces are arbolic, sedentary, and hierarchical. These spaces, both smooth and striated, coexist and together form a smooth/striated dyad. Sometimes smooth space is reterritorialized and converted into striated space, while striated space is deterritorialized and converted into smooth space. Remix in this case is identified as a pendulum between deterritorialization and reterritorialization.

The Internet began as a smooth space. Over time, government control and capitalism began to reterritorialize the Net, converting the once utopic vision of it into striated space. Empires classically default to reterritorialization even after they have been deterritorialized—one only has to think of the (re)emergence of racism in decolonized countries. The primary mechanisms of striation in the context of networked knowledge production are the application of offline copyright laws to online material, and increased surveillance of information flow via tracking software. These two processes of reterritorialization and deterritorialization are constantly in a state of flux and are played off each other in the act of remix in the digital arena. Here, the remixer is an agent who deterritorializes the now "corrupted" Internet by challenging the mechanisms of copyright, and subverting surveillance strategies.

Reterritorialization is also evident in the new digital commons where the online public are implicated in the act of consumer remix—prosumption. The prosumer, a term first coined by Alvin Toffler[32] in 1980, is a new class of public who operate as both producer and consumer. Whereas in the broadcast era there was a time lag between experiencing and critiquing, the digital prosumer simultaneously experiences, likes and shares, rates and reviews, remixes and uploads the vast array of content accessible to her.

Prosumers include citizen journalists, and the use of citizen research to complete scientific research papers. Lawrence Lessig defines this as the reviving of Read/Write culture.[33] Michel de Certeau supports the belief in this shift from producer to consumer and, in his seminal text *The Practice of Everyday Life* emphasizes the potential for human agency in everyday acts. This strategy is evident in the act of remix employed by the new polymath and the prosumer.[34] In direct opposition to Foucault's panoptic control,[35] Certeau disagrees that we are passive makers of our own destiny. Following this logic, we can position the polymath and the consumer as active agents of change. With the grid of discipline becoming increasingly extensive, Certeau asserts that it is important to employ everyday practices to evade the mechanisms of control and reappropriate the space occupied by the existing dominant order. Although Certeau is not specifically talking about the Internet, one can convincingly make the analogy, particularly when he describes the potential sites of resistance as "networks of anti-discipline."[36] These disruptive strategies recall the previously cited mechanisms of Deleuze and Guattari's de/reterritorialization, inviting an association with Certeau's description of the "trajectories" of consumers.[37] Nowhere is the digital consumer more directly implicated in this bind than in the realm of social capital.

Blog as Canon

The blogosphere,[38] and more recent micro-blogging platforms such as Facebook and Twitter, act as potential sites of remix for the new polymath. Recently, the mobile micro-blog—emblematic of convergence culture—has seen a fundamental shift in mobilizing the political reach of the Internet.[39] The growing popularity of citizen journalism and news aggregator sites are testament to the demand for remixed counterpoints to mediated mass media news feeds.

However, these platforms are contested genuine sites of cultural remix due to their relatively ephemeral nature and speed, as well as the associated lightweight connotations attached to the often banal, bite-sized pieces of personal detritus circulating throughout the datasphere. The media theorist Geert Lovink asserts that blogging is an essentially nihilist exercise, a digital self-fashioning that actually negates critical engagement, privileging self-promotion over analytic interventions.[40] This view is supported by journalist Andrew Keen who is skeptical of the perceived freedom of expression afforded via the blog format: "If you democratize media, then you end up democratizing talent. The unintended consequence of all this democratization, to misquote Web 2.0 apologist Thomas Friedman, is cultural 'flattening'."[41] The author Nicholas Carr shares this position and states: "In the end we're left with nothing more than 'the flat noise of opinion'—Socrates's nightmare."[42]

However, David Kline declares the blog fertile ground for the aspiring polymath:

> Rather than seeing the proliferation of specialty blogs as an indicator of the fragmentation of our society, we should see this trend as providing a way for citizen-experts to emerge and to bring together global constituencies in many disparate fields."[43]

Indeed, the blog format is becoming more widely accepted as a way for public intellectualism to be acknowledged.[44]

Cultural blogs are often reinterpretations of dense intertextuality[45]—a condition elemental to the polymath. For theorist Julia Kristeva, the concept of intertextuality replaces that of intersubjectivity."[46] She says that we need to acknowledge that meaning is not directly transmitted from writer to reader, but instead is mediated through the "codes" imparted to the writer and reader by other texts. As we are delivered a continuous stream of online content—including blogs via RSS[47] feeds—the fluid and customizable nature of this data inevitably changes the way we read, write, access, and understand text.

The artist Kate Armstrong[48] locates RSS feeds as sites of potential generative, cultural remix. She perceives the automatic relaying of digital textual ephemera as generating new patterns of reading which morph the ontology of the RSS feed into a writer/publisher/consumer hybrid. In the spirit of the avant-garde, Armstrong identifies the cyclical nature of this type of cognitive remix: "It is not only about remixing the world or the work, but remixing the world into the work, and the work into the world."[49] This self-reflexive impulse is personified in the next section by the figure of the fan.

Fan Fiction and the New Polymath

Historically, the polymath was implicated in canon-building by preserving the value of the sources he was referencing.[50] This also holds true for the DJ who is dependent on her ability to remix material from a recognized source in order to cultivate a fandom around her personal practice. However, as we have seen, the value systems and authority structures surrounding the new polymath are highly contingent, and the codependent relationship with the audience is considerably complicated by the decentralized nature of networked knowledge production.

The culture industry now operates on the assumption of the engagement of an active and potentially collaborative prosumer. In this context, the fan is as much an avatar of culture as a consumer. Fan fiction is a specific enterprise within fan culture that has a direct correlation with the new polymath,[51] as it remixes references and narratives from disparate cultural content to produce unique, yet transparent homages to the original content. This reversioning of cultural artifacts reflects the activities of the new polymath and, although fan fiction is not a product of the Internet, the Web has proliferated this literature to proportions greater than those it could have achieved in print.[52]

For the new polymath, the phenomenon of what Henry Jenkins has termed the "interpretive community"[53] is crucial. Jenkins cites Thomas McLauglin's[54] challenge to the positioning of theory as an exclusively academic activity as he invites an expansive vision and cross-disciplinary approach to theory-making which includes the agency of fandom. The interpretive and generative characteristics of fan behavior mirror that of remix as fans appropriate and remix material from the object of their fandom in order to actively rework the material to suit their own needs and interests.

Jenkins suggests[55] works of fan fiction are not just extensions or continuations of the original media material, arguing that these works may "include the active appropriation and transformation of the characters in a different historical context . . . fan fiction is speculative but that does not mean that it is not at its core interpretative."[56] He suggests that the digital technologies available to fans have allowed for more serious public discourse and activism,[57] echoing Certeau's assertion that the power to resist dominant ideologies lies in the use of the very commodities imposed on them by capitalism. Here, Jenkins locates the resistance that Certeau describes when analyzing the media practices of ordinary people and provides a strategy for deterritorialization.

In "Voices from the Combat Zone: Game Grrlz Talk Back,"[58] Jenkins identifies patterns in Third Wave feminism which provide models for subsequent fan activism. For example, Clan PMS and the Game Grrlz movement actively challenged obtuse gender stereotypes in computer games.[59] The participants' claims to fan status gave them credibility and critical leverage within the culture industries they challenged. This repurposing of material is a key function of the new polymath, and one which directly interrogates the historical status of originality and genius.

The Unoriginal Genius

The literary critic Marjorie Perloff uses the term "unoriginal genius"[60] to describe the paradigmatic shift in the figure of the author[61] in the age of networked knowledge production. She identifies writers who exclusively use appropriated material in their work, citing the Conceptual poets Vanessa Place, Caroline Bergvall, and Kenneth Goldsmith as practitioners who "foreground the choice of source text itself, the very selection of that text and its context generating the methods that determine its copy."[62] The radical change in the understanding of what constitutes "genius" has been affected by new technologies, and she argues that a more accurate idea of the genius needs to focus on the individual's mastery of navigating and disseminating information.[63] In her terms, "moving information"[64] is the manifestation of spreading language, online knowledge, and being emotionally affected by this process. She positions the writer as programmer, the maestro of conceptualizing, constructing, executing, and maintaining a writing machine. The poet and artist Kenneth Goldsmith is the poster boy of unoriginal genius as he blurs the lines between authorship and appropriation through his "Uncreative Writing"—writing that has been produced under constrictions which eliminate the author's own creative control over the result. His methods include the use of readymade artifacts as art objects, translating algorithms and the championing of transcription. He asserts that even in a simple act of remix, a creative dimension emerges.

> Even when we do something as seemingly "uncreative" as retyping a few pages, we express ourselves in a variety of ways. The act of choosing and reframing tells us as much about ourselves as our story about our mother's cancer operation. It's just that we've never been taught to value such choices."[65]

Goldsmith's ethos is echoed in Jonathan Lethem's famous 2007 *Harper's* piece "The Ecstasy of Influence: A Plagiarism"[66]—a defense of the history and creative agency of piracy and appropriation in literature. However, many have criticized both Goldsmith and other advocates of the unoriginal genius, particularly within the more traditional academic environment. The main criticism leveled at the open system of knowledge production is how to tell the good from the bad and, consequently, directly challenges the cult of the polymath.

Conclusion

This chapter has suggested possible ways in which remix can provide new contexts for the polymath to be acknowledged in networked knowledge culture. Kenneth Goldsmith suggests that in order for the new author to achieve recognition in the leveled creative playing field of the digital, the role of choice needs to be championed:

Success lies in knowing what to include and—more important—leave out. If all language can be transformed into poetry by merely reframing—an exciting possibility—then she who reframes words in the most charged and convincing way will be judged best.[67]

In truth, we are all edging towards a polymath existence as we navigate and circumnavigate broadening bodies of nonhierarchical knowledge in our everyday lives. In order to construct our own identity we are in a constant state of remix, cast in the almost ubiquitous role of the new polymath. Following this logic, where the polymath has traction as the rules of the game are changed and authorship becomes a fluid, conceptual term, is questionable. This chapter has set out the conditions of the changing status of both the polymath and the value systems defining her. The dynamics of the digital age have placed both the institutions of knowledge and the idea of the polymath in crisis. The tectonic shift in emphasis from knowledge acquisition to knowledge transference means that knowledge is now the property of the network; maybe the idea of the new polymath/DJ of Thought as an individual is outdated and inherently contingent on the context of the specific network in which she operates? As David Weinberger suggests:

> As knowledge becomes networked, the smartest person in the room isn't the person standing at the front lecturing us, and isn't the collective wisdom of those in the room. The smartest person in the room is the room itself: the network that joins the people and ideas in the room, and connects to those outside of it.[68]

In order for a true act of generative remix to take place in knowledge production, the network itself must be acknowledged as the maestro or the new polymath.

Notes

1 Adam Good, "Becoming a DJ of Thought," *The Real Good Adam* (2010), http://www.therealadamgood.com/becoming-a-dj-of-thought/ (accessed August 4, 2013).
2 A term first recorded in written English in the early seventeenth century from the Greek *polymathes*, meaning understanding, knowing, or having learnt in quantity.
3 Michel de Certeau, *The Practice of Everyday Life*, 3rd revised edition (Berkeley, CA: University of California Press, 2011).
4 Good, "Becoming a DJ of Thought."
5 Nico Carpentier and Peter Dahlgren, "Interrogating Audiences, Theoretical Horizons of Participation," *CM Communication Management Quarterly* 21, 2011, http://www.academia.edu/1151340/Interrogating_audiences_Theoretical_horizons_of_participation.
6 Jack Schofield, "Aaron Swartz Obituary," *The Guardian*, January 13, 2013, http://www.theguardian.com/technology/2013/jan/13/aaron-swartz.
7 Historically the polymath was considered to be a male construct, but Parker and Polock argue that the females of the time have been overlooked. Rozsika Parker and Griselda Polock, *Old Mistresses: Women Art and Ideology* (London: I. B. Taurus & Co Ltd, 2013), 82.
8 Ibid.
9 The term originates from Jenkins's *Convergence Culture*. He uses this term to refer to both the tendency of modern media to attract a much greater degree of audience participation than before, and the phenomenon of a single cultural franchise being distributed through and impacting on a range of mobile and distributed media. Henry Jenkins, *Convergence Culture* (New York: New York University Press, 2006).
10 Kevin Kelly, *Out of Control, The New Biology of Machines, Social Systems, and the Economic World* (New York: Basic Books, 1995).

11 Ibid., 147.

12 Common examples are: Wikipedia and Google, news aggregator sites such as Digg and Popurls, and cultural filtering sites such as Boing Boing.

13 Jaron Lanier, "Digital Maoism: The Hazards of the New Online Collectivism," *Edge*, May 29, 2006, http://www.edge.org/conversation/digital-maoism-the-hazards-of-the-new-online-collectivism.

14 Donna J. Haraway, "A Cyborg Manifesto: Science, Technology, and Socialist-Feminism in the Late Twentieth Century," *Simians, Cyborgs, and Women: The Reinvention of Nature* (New York, NY: Routledge, 1991).

15 N. Katherine Hayles, "Unfinished Work: From Cyborg to Cognisphere," *Theory, Culture & Society* 23, no. 7/8 (2006): 159.

16 The Jesuit Pierre Teilhard de Chardin appropriated the term noösphere as an attempt to marry Christian theology with evolutionary theory. The emergence of the noösphere, he thought, was just the latest stage in our teleological progression towards the world's culmination—the Omega Point, at which physical existence would cease. However, it is in its popular appropriation by the Internet community to define the idea of collective intelligence on the Web that noösphere is used in the context of this paper to paint the picture of the terrain of the new polymath. Pierre Teilhard de Chardin, *The Phenomenon of Man* (New York: Harper Torchbooks, 1961).

17 Ibid., 159.

18 The Internet meme is an idea, style or action which spreads, often as mimicry, from person to person via the Internet. It has a persuasive cultural value and is mimetic in intent. An examination of the full relationship between the new polymath and meme culture cannot be fully covered in this chapter, but a strong analogy can be, and is, drawn. See Richard Dawkins, *The Selfish Gene* (Oxford: Oxford University Press, 1989).

19 Olivia Solon, "Richard Dawkins Appears in Psychedelic Show Celebrating Internet Memes," *WIRED*, June 20, 2013, http://www.wired.co.uk/news/archive/2013–06/20/new-directors-showcase.

20 David Weinberger, *Too Big To Know* (New York: Basic Books, 2011), xiii.

21 Ibid.

22 Ibid.

23 The ideal in Renaissance Humanism that it was possible to acquire a universal learning.

24 Picnic curator company: http://gothamist.com/2013/08/07/curated_picnic_basket.php.

25 Closet curator: http://www.ecouterre.com/keep-or-toss-10-slightly-unconventional-rules-for-editing-your-wardrobe/curate-your-closet-1/.

26 Florence Derieux, ed., *Harald Szeemann: Individual Methodology* (New York: JRP Ringler, 2008), 8–10.

27 Historical examples of this are: Judy Chicago and Miriam Schapiro's exhibition Womanhouse, 1972 and Lucy Lippard's Number Shows, 1969–74.

28 Following Certeau.

29 Following Certeau's assertion that subversion and generative acts can be achieved through "ways of operating" in everyday activities within already existing systems.

30 Kenneth Goldsmith, *Uncreative Writing* (New York: Colombia University Press, 2011).

31 Gilles Deleuze and Felix Guattari, *A Thousand Plateaus: Capitalism and Schizophrenia* (London: Continuum International Publishing Group Ltd, 2004), 523–551.

32 Alvin Toffler, *The Third Wave* (New York: William Morrow & Company, 1980), 87.

33 Lawrence Lessig, *Remix: Making Art and Commerce Thrive Beyond the Economy* (London: Bloomsbury Academic, 2008), 28.

34 Certeau, *The Practice of Everyday Life*.

35 Foucault, Michel, *Discipline and Punish: The Birth of the Prison*, 2nd edition (New York, NY: Vintage Books; 1995), 33.

36 Certeau, *The Practice of Everyday Life*, xi.

37 Ibid., 34.

38 A slang term for all the blogs on the Internet, the blogosphere is considered a defined community within the larger environment of the Internet due to the unique ways in which bloggers interlink with one another and with the wider Internet. First used as a term by Brad L. Graham in 1999: http://www.brad-lands.com/weblog/comments/september_10_1999/ (accessed August 15, 2014).

39 Twitter and Facebook arguably played a key role in the Arab Spring of 2011.

40 Geert Lovink, "Blogging, The Nihilist Impulse," *Eurozine*, January 2, 2007. Based on a lecture given at Berlin Institute of Advanced Study, the Wissenschaftskolleg, Berlin, March 27, 2006, http://www.eurozine.com/articles/2007-01-02-lovink-en.html.

41 Andrew Keen, "Web 2.0, The Second Generation of the Internet Has Arrived, Its Worse Than You Think," *The Weekly Standard*, February 14, 2006, http://www.weeklystandard.com/Content/Public/Articles/000/000/006/714fjczq.asp.

42 Nicholas Carr, "The New Narcissism," *Rough Type*, February 17, 2006, www.roughtype.com/archives/2006/02/the_new_narciss.php.

43 David Kline, *Blog! How the Newest Media Revolution is Changing Politics, Business, and Culture* (New York: CDS Books, 2005), 130.

44 The role of academic blogging in scholarship is a much-debated subject and is an example of the systems of value this chapter addresses as part of the analysis of the status of the new polymath. Blogging is now recognized as a valuable part of the wider ecology of scholarship. For a more in depth debate please refer to "Accept No Substitutes: Blogging is a Valuable Supplement to Scholarship and Rightfully Challenges the Status Quo" by Rohan Maitzen: http://blogs.lse.ac.uk/impactofsocialsciences/2013/06/25/blogging-accept-no-substitutes/ (accessed August 14, 2014).

45 The shaping of a text's meaning by another text.

46 Julia Kristeva introduced the "intertextuality" as an interpretation of translation of Mikhail Bakhtin's concept of the "dialogic"—that is, the simultaneous presence, within a literary work, or two or more intersecting texts which mutually contextualize one another. Julia Kristeva, *Desire in Language: A Semiotic Approach to Literature and Art* (New York: Columbia University Press, 1980).

47 RSS stands for Rich Site Summary, RDF Site Summary, or Real Simple Syndication and is an emergent standardized format that makes it possible for information of any kind to be sent as an ongoing feed, creating a world where cultural information is customized and spontaneous.

48 Kate Armstrong is a digital writer and artist who experiments with networked, experimental narrative. http://katearmstrong.com/.

49 Ibid.

50 Whether in science, the humanities, or the arts.

51 Fan fiction is literature written by fans of a particular cultural product, featuring the canonical characters and settings of the work in a new context.

52 Nancy Baym, "The New Shape of Online Community: The Example of Swedish Independent Music Fandom," *First Monday* 12, no. 8 (2007), http://firstmonday.org/ojs/index.php/fm/article/view/1978/1853.

53 Henry Jenkins, *Textual Poachers: Television Fans and Participatory Culture* (New York: Routledge, 1992).

54 Thomas McLaughlin, *Street Smarts and Critical Theory: Listening to the Vernacular* (Madison, WI: University of Wisconsin Press) 1996.

55 Jenkins, *Textual Poachers*, 73.

56 Ibid., 86.

57 Henry Jenkins, *Convergence Culture*.

58 Henry Jenkins, "Voices from the Combat Zone: Game Grrlz Talk Back." In *From Barbie to Mortal Kombat: Gender and Computer Games*, new edition, ed. Justine Cassell and Henry Jenkins (Cambridge, MA: MIT Press, 2000), 328–341.

59 Ibid.

60 Marjorie Perloff, *Unoriginal Genius: Poetry by Other Means in the New Century* (Chicago, IL: University of Chicago Press, 2012).

61 A figure inexorably linked to that of the polymath.

62 Marjorie Perloff, "Poetry on the Brink," *Boston Review*, 2012, http://www.bostonreview.net/forum/poetry-brink.

63 Perloff, *Unoriginal Genius*, 45.

64 Ibid.

65 Kenneth Goldsmith, *Uncreative Writing*, 9.

66 Jonathan Lethem, "The Ecstasy of Influence: A Plagiarism," *Harper's* (February, 2007), http://harpers.org/archive/2007/02/the-ecstasy-of-influence/.

67 Goldsmith, *Uncreative Writing*, 124.

68 David Weinberger, *Too Big To Know* (New York: Basic Books, 2011), xiii.

Bibliography

Baym, Nancy. "The New Shape of Online Community: The Example of Swedish Independent Music Fandom." *First Monday* 12, no. 8 (2007), http://firstmonday.org/ojs/index.php/fm/article/view/1978/1853 (accessed September 12, 2013).

Carpentier, Nico, and Peter Dahlgren. "Interrogating Audiences, Theoretical Horizons of Participation." *CM Communication Management Quarterly* 21 (2011). http://www.academia.edu/1151340/Interrogating_audiences_Theoretical_horizons_of_participation (accessed August 15, 2014).

Carr, Nicholas. "The New Narcissism." *Rough Type*, February 17, 2006. www.roughtype.com/archives/2006/02/the_new_narciss.php (accessed August 28, 2013).

——. *The Shallows*. New York: W. W. Norton and Company, 2010.

Certeau, Michel de. *The Practice of Everyday Life*, 3rd revised edition. Berkeley, CA: University of California Press, 2011.

Chardin, Pierre Teilhard de. *The Phenomenon of Man*. New York: Harper Torchbooks, 1961.

Dawkins, Richard. *The Selfish Gene*. Oxford: Oxford University Press, 1989.

Deleuze, Gilles, and Felix Guattari. *A Thousand Plateaus: Capitalism and Schizophrenia*. London: Continuum International Publishing Group Ltd, 2004.

Derieux, Florence, ed. *Harald Szeemann: Individual Methodology*. New York: JRP Ringler, 2008.

Foucault, Michel. *Discipline and Punish: The Birth of the Prison*, 2nd edition. New York: Vintage Books, 1995.

Goldsmith, Kenneth. *Uncreative Writing*. New York: Colombia University Press, 2011.

Haraway, Donna J. "A Cyborg Manifesto: Science, Technology, and Socialist Feminism in the Late Twentieth Century." *Simians, Cyborgs. and Women: The Reinvention of Nature*. New York: Routledge, 1991.

Harvey, David. *The Enigma of Capital*, London: Profile Books Ltd, 2010.

Hayles, N. Katherine. "Unfinished Work: From Cyborg to Cognisphere," *Theory, Culture & Society* 23, no. 7/8 (2006): 159–166.

Jenkins, Henry. *Textual Poachers: Television Fans and Participatory Culture*. New York: Routledge, 1992.

——. "Voices from the Combat Zone: Game Grrlz Talk Back." In *From Barbie to Mortal Kombat: Gender and Computer Games*, edited by Justine Cassell and Henry Jenkins. Cambridge: MIT Press, 2000.

——. *Convergence Culture*. New York: New York University Press, 2006.

Keen, Andrew. "Web 2.0, The Second Generation of the Internet Has Arrived, Its Worse Than You Think." *The Weekly Standard*, February 14, 2006. http://www.weeklystandard.com/Content/Public/Articles/000/000/006/714fjczq.asp (accessed September 2, 2013).

Kelly, Kevin. *Out of Control, The New Biology of Machines, Social Systems, and the Economic World*. New York: Basic Books, 1995.

Kline, David. *Blog! How the Newest Media Revolution is Changing Politics, Business, and Culture*. New York: CDS Books, 2005.

Kristeva, Julia. *Desire in Language: A Semiotic Approach to Literature and Art*. New York, NY: Columbia University Press, 1980.

Lanier, Jaron. "Digital Maoism: The Hazards of the New Online Collectivism," *Edge*, May 29, 2006, http://www.edge.org/conversation/digital-maoism-the-hazards-of-the-new-online-collectivism (accessed September 13, 2013).

Lessig, Lawrence. *Remix: Making Art and Commerce Thrive Beyond the Economy*. London: Bloomsbury Academic, 2008.

Lethem, Jonathan. "The Ecstasy of Influence: A Plagiarism." *Harper's* (February, 2007). http://harpers.org/archive/2007/02/the-ecstasy-of-influence/ (accessed September 11, 2013).

Lovink, Geert. "Blogging, The Nihilist Impulse." *Eurozine*, January 2, 2007. Based on a lecture given at Berlin Institute of Advanced Study, the Wissenschaftskolleg, Berlin, March 27, 2006, http://www.eurozine.com/articles/2007-01-02-lovink-en.html (accessed May 4, 2014).

Mason, Matt. *The Pirate's Dilemma*. New York: FP Press, 2009.

McLaughlin, Thomas. *Street Smarts and Critical Theory: Listening to the Vernacular*. Madison, WI: University of Wisconsin Press, 1996.

Navas, Eduardo. *Remix Theory*. New York: Springer, 2012.

Parker Rozsika, and Griselda Polock. *Old Mistresses: Women Art and Ideology*. London: I. B. Taurus & Co Ltd, 2013.

Perloff, Marjorie. *Unoriginal Genius: Poetry by Other Means in the New Century*. Chicago, IL: University of Chicago Press, 2012.

Schofield, Jack. "Aaron Swartz Obituary." *The Guardian*, January 13, 2013. http://www.theguardian.com/technology/2013/jan/13/aaron-swartz (accessed March 1, 2014).

Solon, Olivia. "Richard Dawkins Appears in Psychedelic Show Celebrating Internet Memes," *WIRED*, June 20, 2013, http://www.wired.co.uk/news/archive/2013-06/20/new-directors-showcase (accessed September 22, 2013).

Toffler, Alvin. *The Third Wave*. New York: William Morrow & Company, 1980.

Weinberger, David. *Too Big To Know*. New York: Basic Books, 2011.

Part V

PRACTICE

30

CRISES OF MEANING IN COMMUNITIES OF CREATIVE APPROPRIATION

A Case Study of the 2010 RE/Mixed Media Festival

Tom Tenney

On February 27 2010, *The New York Times* published a piece called "The Free-Appropriation Writer," in which Randy Kennedy reported on the controversy over German novelist Helene Hegemann's alleged plagiarism, and questioned whether her use of another writer's work in her novel was theft or an allowable form of "sampling" or "remix." Kennedy defined the modernist concept of the creative writer as one of "the individual trying to wrestle language, maybe even the meaning of life, from his [*sic*] soul," and asked readers to use this ideal while judging the young novelist's actions. Only after she was caught did Hegemann defend her appropriation as "remix"; however, she seemed to be portrayed in the article as a spokesperson for remix culture. Kennedy drew parallels between Hegemann and David Shields (whose masterwork of creative appropriation, *Reality Hunger*, had been released only three days earlier), placing them together on the same side of the "battle lines" between "a culture of borrowing and appropriation on one side and, on the other, copyright advocates and those who fear a steady erosion of creative protections."[1]

What struck me as unfair about this particular article was not only the blanket portrayal in the media of appropriation as an agent of cultural erosion—note the heroic language portraying defenders of copyright as "advocates" while those who appropriate add to the "erosion of creative protections"—but also the tacit equation of two wildly different styles of appropriation. Kennedy's article was just one circumstance inspiring the creation of the RE/Mixed Media Festival[2] in the spring of 2010, an event that has become an annual celebration of appropriation in the arts, approached from the artist's perspective. As opposed to a conference, where appropriated art is only discussed, the festival seeks to provide a voice for artists in the public discourse surrounding copyright and creative appropriation by providing a venue for artists to demonstrate the legitimacy of appropriative techniques using their native language, i.e., the works themselves. The goal of the festival is to provide a response to the growing body of negative press and public opinion that equates creative appropriation with plagiarism and piracy. A primary tactic is to connect the contemporary cultural practice of remix to the rich heritage of appropriation in the arts.

What follows is a case study—a narrative inquiry into the building of the festival during its first year, 2010. As a practicing artist, a student of media history and theory, and a digital media professional, I have dedicated myself to promoting and inviting artists into a contemporary discourse that includes sharing, appropriation and the cultural commons.

Background

Over the past two decades, the proliferation of new production, reproductive, and sharing technologies has enabled authors, such as Hegemann and Shields, as well as visual artists and cultural producers at large to move easily from a modernist-metaphoric to a metonymic, multitextual order of representation through sampling and other appropriative methodologies. Indeed, Lev Manovich has called remix the "dominant aesthetics of the era of globalization, affecting and reshaping everything from music and cinema to food and fashion."[3] Kennedy's article seems to indicate a crisis of legitimation for artists who employ such methodologies. Concurrently, the culture industry seems to be experiencing a crisis of assimilation, an inability to absorb these works, creating tension between artist and industry. In this way, it may be said that these technologies have been both good and bad for artists. On the one hand, they have provided uncompli-

> The Ethics part of this book more thoroughly details the tensions Tenney alludes to here.

cated and affordable means to sample cultural objects for the purposes of aesthetic and social commentary; on the other hand, this proliferation has also led to an increased scrutiny by those with a vested interest in maintaining the economic status quo of the content creators.

As a teenager in the late 1970s and early 1980s, I learned about art through the lens of punk rock, a culture in which it seemed as though everything—music, lyrics, clothing, and attitudes—was appropriated. Jamie Reid's iconic collage imagery for The Sex Pistols was rooted in Situationist *détournement* and The New York Dolls were simply the blues dressed up in red patent leather and painted with postmodern lipstick. In 1986, I portrayed a black-leather-jacketed Hamlet in Robert Wilson's staging of Heiner Muller's *Hamletmachine*, in which Ophelia delivered lines appropriated from Karl Marx, a photograph of the author was torn in half in a nod to Barthes and Foucault, and the great Peggy Lee hit, *Is That All There Is?* was plunked out by a single finger on a piano. More than a decade later, I produced a series of midnight shows in a performance loft in downtown NYC—musical send-ups of pop culture and Giuliani-era NYC politics. The shows were a collection of cherry-picked headlines and personalities, mixing and mashing disparate fruit from the tree of the cultural zeitgeist. The performances were guided by a ten-point manifesto,[4] three of which were :

Figure 30.1 Tom Tenney portrayed a black-leather-jacketed Hamlet in Robert Wilson's 1986 staging of Heiner Muller's *Hamletmachine* (courtesy of Tom Tenney)

- Nothing is original, everything has been done before
- The world is your playground, history your library—borrow from it freely
- Creativity is placing two previously disparate elements side by side.[5]

These principles became the motivational force that led me to, and guided me through, the process of organizing the RE/Mixed Media Festival. What I discovered was not only a crisis of legitimation between industry and artist, but also one of meaning within the remix community itself.

Establishing Parameters

After recruiting three fellow artists—Emilie McDonald, Bruce Smolanoff, and Marie Mundaca—as coproducers, and creating calls for submission, one of our first tasks was to define a set of criteria for the work: Which kinds of art constitute "remix?" Without being too broad or too narrow in our definition, our primary objectives were to challenge the meanings advocated by mainstream media and interrogate the concept of "piracy," and also to explore and celebrate the position creative appropriation occupies as an aesthetic practice in the continuum of art history.

In his influential book, *Remix*, Lawrence Lessig characterizes remix culture as "Read/ Write" (RW) as opposed to "Read Only" (RO), using the vernacular of today's digital technology. He defines RW culture as one in which "ordinary citizens" have the ability to transcend the role of passive media consumers, and become active producers as well. Far from being a new phenomenon, Lessig portrays RW culture as a *return* to the folk culture model dominant prior to the twentieth century when, due to the rise of technologies of reproducibility and repetition, culture became "professionalized" and RO

413

See Chapter 15 for Byron Russell's discussion of a RW culture that supports remix as activism and an activity of self-expression.

became the status quo.[6] It is significant that Lessig characterizes remix culture as the restoration of something that has been *lost*, as opposed to the popular idea, reinforced in Mr. Kennedy's article, that the sharing of cultural artifacts is something new, enabled by digital tools. In my view, artists who are being playful with technology today don't seem substantially different from the amateur tinkerers who created the very media technologies that eventually led to RO culture. Further, creative appropriation in the arts has a long history, and in the twentieth century alone, appropriative practices were employed by the Cubists, Dadaists, Surrealists, Situationists, Pop Artists, and such contemporary artists as Richard Prince and Sherrie Levine, among many others.[7] What differentiates "remix culture" is, among other things, the scale of production—the degree to which anyone can participate in reusing cultural objects for individual self-expression.[8]

Lessig's portrayal of remix as "Read/Write" most closely aligned with the type of barometer we were reaching for, as it provided a characterization rather than a definition. Instead of holding each submission to a precise definition of remix, we instead decided to include work that we felt landed within the long historical continuum of creative appropriation, work that would help create a dialog between artists, scholars, policy makers, and audiences. Therefore, the parameters for acceptance became less about whether a work identified itself specifically as remix, and more about how well it asked the question: "What is remix?" The only questions we asked artists were ones that determined if their work fulfilled the most elementary definition of "creative appropriation." For example, we asked, does the work appropriate an already-existing work?[9] and, does the relationship between combined elements create a new significance not present in each element individually? We began with the idea of remix as a question in the hopes that what we would end up with was not a polemic but a creative expression of our process. While planning the festival, we encountered and considered unexpected challenges dealing with ethics, responsibility, and meaning.

Ethical Considerations

An influential work in planning the festival was Bruce Conner's 1967 film, *Report*, a found-footage collage of media coverage of the Kennedy assassination that uses appropriation to interrogate the mass media's commodification of the cultural mythology surrounding the fallen president. I had heard about the film in 2009 after seeing *A Movie*, another of Conner's film collages. *Report*, however, was unavailable for purchase, so in order to see the film at all, I had to make an appointment to view the 16mm version archived in the Performing Arts Library at Lincoln Center. *Report* is an excellent example of creative appropriation as practiced in late twentieth century experimental cinema, so when I later discovered a bootleg DVD of all of Conner's films on the Internet, I purchased it without hesitation. After receiving the disc, we included *Report* in a YouTube collection called *The Roots of Remix* that we curated in advance of the festival—a playlist designed to showcase a diverse array of appropriated art and cinema.

As far as we knew, our exhibition of *Report* mitigated neither the artistic nor the market value of the film; our intention was to cultivate an awareness of the artist and his work, and provide a historical context for what we refer to today as remix. A month before the festival, I received an email from YouTube informing me that the video had been "disabled . . . as a result of a third-party notification from Jean Conner [Conner's widow], Trustee of the Conner Family Trust claiming that this material is infringing."[10] While this action was certainly Ms. Conner's right under the law, one wonders why she would object to a fan's attempt to bring her late husband's work to a public that may have never seen it, and one that, further, had little *possibility* of seeing it due to its unavailability in the marketplace. My conclusion was that Conner's demand was not about money, but about maintaining *control* over the use of—and therefore the cultural *meaning* of—the work; for once an object is liberated from the purview of the creator and becomes part of the cultural archive, its meaning and relevance are then measured by the public discourse surrounding it.[11] Certainly, contextualizing the film as an antecedent of remix culture couldn't have been intended by the artist. However, there seemed to be an inherent inconsistency in restricting access to a film that was largely created by reassembling newsreel footage.[12] Nevertheless, this incident raised the issue of ownership from a personal, ethical perspective. Our feeling was that this kind of "piracy" respected the work, and could only lead to expanded interest in Conner's body of work. Such an act can be compared to the work of collectors in the 1940s and 1950s who repressed jazz recordings to preserve them from fading into obscurity.[13] Similarly, my intent as a proponent of creative appropriation was to uphold such historical examples in the hope that they would serve as both inspiration to artists, and precedent in the argument for creative reuse of cultural artifacts.

Another ethical question we faced in the planning stages was whether to charge audiences to attend. There is an unavoidable conundrum in setting an admission fee for an event that centers on work appropriated from copyrighted material. Of course, we wanted to recoup our production costs, but were unclear on whether doing so would create ethical, or even legal, complications. Perhaps more importantly, we had to consider and preserve the relationship between remix culture and the gift economy. Ultimately, each and every work that we were presenting relied and drew upon the idea of a "cultural commons," a principle that culture belongs to everyone and no one, and that commercial interests—those that would build a pecuniary fence around art—were destroying the ability of others to create. This is not to say that a work cannot simultaneously exist in both a market and a gift economy at once. Lewis Hyde articulates this dialectical aspect of the gift economy: "Even if we've paid a fee at the door of the museum or concert hall, when we are touched by a work of art something comes to us that has nothing to do with the price."[14] Eventually, we decided to keep the event free for the first year, prioritizing sharing with a wide audience over recouping our costs. This decision seemed to make the most sense in terms of both demonstrating our commitment to the cultural commons, and maximizing the size of our audience, critical in launching an event of this scale.[15]

Artists and Collaborators

Because digital technologies that characterize the work of "remix culture" are, by and large, video and audio technologies, it followed that these constituted the bulk of the submissions we received. Finding works that represented the other arts required more effort and outreach on our part. Our objective was to present remix in ways that audiences might find surprising or unexpected, throughout the 11 hours of festival programming. What follows are descriptions of selected events[16] that represent the overall experience, listed in chronological order of presentation.

Video Program: Remixing Politics and Culture

The first presentation following the keynote was a collection of six videos offering political and social commentary on contemporary culture and politics. Elisa Kreisinger, a remixer from Boston, presented a radical reedit of *Sex and the City* clips entitled *Sex and the Remix* (or, *The Queering of Carrie*), Jonathan McIntosh's video, *So You Think You Can Be President* mashed up the Obama/McCain debates as an *American Idol*-esque reality show, and Kenneth Tin-Kin Hung's *In G.O.D. We Trust* was a stop-motion animation made entirely with images found through Google image search. Other artists screened during this program were Desiree D'Alessandro, Seth Indigo Carnes, and Kat Green.

"Artists Only" Panel on Appropriation, Remix, and Copyright, Moderated by Deanna Zandt

Moby, a popular electronic musician, has been a vocal advocate for copyright reform for several years. At the time of the festival, he had recently launched a website[17] providing independent filmmakers with free access to his music for use in their soundtracks.

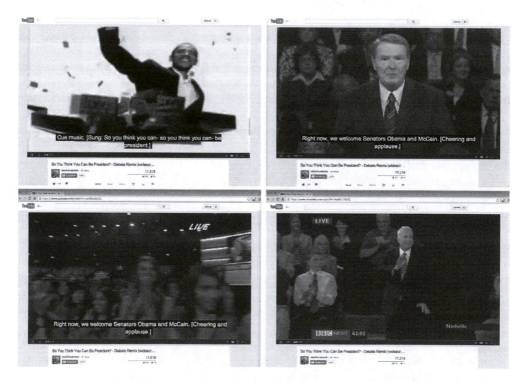

Figure 30.2 Jonathan McIntosh mashes up the Obama/McCain debate as an *American Idol-esque* reality show in *So You Think You Can Be President*. Screen shots from YouTube (courtesy of Jonathan McIntosh)

Including Moby in the festival drew a diverse audience, and his new site was a salient topic of conversation for a panel discussion among artists. Other artists who similarly advocated sharing and copyright reform included Elisa Kreisinger, Seth Indigo Carnes, Kenneth Tin-Kin Hung, and music journalist Christopher Weingarten. However, with so many artists on the same side of the philosophical divide, there was a danger of the discussion becoming doctrinaire, exactly the situation we were trying to avoid. For this reason, we recruited two artists willing to represent a viewpoint that favored stronger copyright protections. Kait Kerrigan and Brian Lowdermilk, two New York City performers who run a website[18] for composers who provide self-published sheet music to musicians for a licensing fee. Their stories provided an intelligent and measured counterpoint to the others. During the 40-minute debate, both sides presented compelling arguments, with Moby referring to copyright as a "strange and antiquated idea," and Kerrigan/Lowdermilk arguing for stronger protections for artists. Elisa Kreisinger offered the centrist viewpoint that copyright is "great when it protects—and it protects [the remixer] with fair use."[19]

Man with a Movie Camera: The Global Remake

Perry Bard is a New York City artist who works on interdisciplinary collaborations for public space. Her Web-based project, begun in 2007 and titled *Man with a Movie Camera: The Global Remake*, invites Web users to remake scenes from Vertov's 1929 silent film, *Man with a Movie Camera*, and upload them to a database. She describes the project as:

> A participatory video shot by people around the world who are invited to record images interpreting the original script of Vertov's *Man With A Movie Camera* and upload them to this site. Software developed specifically for this project archives, sequences, and streams the submissions as a film. Anyone can upload footage. When the work streams, your contribution becomes part of a world-wide montage, in Vertov's terms the "decoding of life as it is."[20]

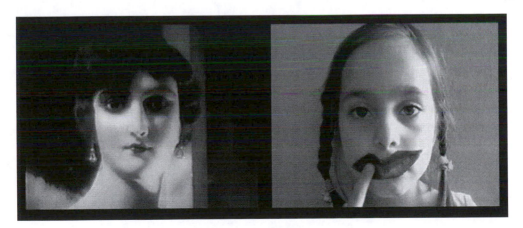

Figure 30.3 Perry Bard's *Man with a Movie Camera: The Global Remake*, invites Web users to remake scenes from Vertov's 1929 silent film. Screen shot from YouTube (courtesy of Perry Bard)

Because the project allows for multiple users to upload the same scene, the software randomly selects one interpretation of each scene and then stitches together a new result for each screening, which is shown side by side with Vertov's original film. The result points to a kind of remix that falls outside even the most radical definitions. Bard's project represents a work where the concept of the author is not only thrown into question, but must be applied to hundreds of artists simultaneously. While Eduardo Navas's classification of "regenerative remix"[21] seems to come closest to describing this type of work, it differs in that no single artistic vision is at play, but rather oscillates between a collaboratively created *work* and an algorithmic *process*. This "algorithm-as-selector"[22] methodology could perhaps more accurately be called "generative" or "procedural" remix, with the artist assuming the role of programmer, and computer processes stepping into the role of author.

Extending Game Culture Panel

Moderated by media professor Josephine Dorado, this panel explored emergent forms of expression sparked by innovations within the game industry and gamer communities. From the release of tools to make user-created content such as custom avatars and maps, to the addition of filmmaking tools, the discussion focused on the large opening that has formed in digital media through which gamers are showing that they are not just passive consumers, but engaged media makers. Panel members included Michael Nitsche, Jesper Juul, Bit Shifter, and ILL Clan.

Video Remix Competition Screenings

As an incentive for participation, the films and videos received through our website submission process were entered into a competition judged by a panel of artists chosen by us—although neither I nor any of the producers were on the panel—with the winner to receive a cash prize of $500. We were delighted with the variety of films we received. Ten advanced to the final round of judging at the festival, a few of which are described below.[23]

Jake Gyllenhaal Challenges the Winner of the Nobel Peace Prize by Diran Lyons mashed up Gyllenhaal's characters from *Donnie Darko* and *Jarhead*, who are seen interrogating Barack Obama on the legitimacy of his Nobel Peace Prize. Of the video finalists, this was an excellent representation of a remix that employs techniques of radical reediting and recontexualization as a method of overt social critique.

Western by Lili White was the longest and most complex of the videos presented in the competition. White's film is a collage of found footage from spaghetti Westerns and original footage of the American Southwest. The soundtrack layers traditional cowboy music over soundtracks of Western films. Throughout, a voiceover tells the story of a filmmaker who dons a military uniform in order to gain passage to the occupied region in Palestine. The layering of multiple meanings serves to reveal a parallel between the American genocide of Native Americans, and the current political struggle in Israel and Palestine.

In *Helping Johnny Remember* by Ashleigh Nankivell, the artist used only one video as a source—an educational film from the 1950s about cooperation and sharing. The originality of the film comes from Nankivell's use of Adobe After Effects to transform

JAKE GYLLENHAAL CHALLENGES THE WINNER OF THE NOBEL PEACE PRIZE
A POLITICAL REMIX VIDEO BY DIRAN LYONS

Figure 30.4 Jake Gyllenhaal Challenges the Winner of the Nobel Peace Prize by Diran Lyons
is a mashup of Gyllenhaal's characters from *Donnie Darko* and *Jarhead*
(courtesy of Diran Lyons)

the children in the film, who complain about the title character's unwillingness to share, into little monsters and demons. In this light, Johnny is seen as an antihero, a rebel loner—an apt, if clichéd, metaphor for the "misunderstood artist." At the end of the film, Johnny exacts his revenge by firing laser beams from his eyes and decimating his classmates, who disappear in spectacular explosions, or shatter like glass into the ether. The film ends with Johnny smiling knowingly to the audience, as he continues to play with his toys alone.

Sweatshoppe

Sweatshoppe was a multimedia performance collaboration between Bruno Levy and Blake Shaw at the intersection of art, music, and technology. The two developed software to construct a 3D visual remix[24] composed of found images, film clips, and vector shapes. The projected visuals were reactive to the electronic music being mixed in real time by the two artists on laptops, both wearing insect masks. The performance represented a remix of different media types and a blending of the languages of representation. These included cinematographic techniques applied to layers of video, photography, and vector graphics, that responded to sound stimulus, all in real time, and all mixed within the metamedium of the laptop computer—a phenomenon Lev Manovich refers to as "deep remixability."[25]

Steinski

Another notable remixer that we recruited was Steven Stein, aka Steinski, a music producer widely known for his analog tape collages in the 1980s such as *The Payoff Mix*, *Lesson 2 (The James Brown Mix)* with his partner Double Dee. We booked him as the last act of the evening, and he remixed music and visuals simultaneously, providing an energetic culmination of a long day.

Crises of Meaning

Since our festival was, at least in part, a theatrical event, we planned to remix a historical event surrounding the first screening of Joseph Cornell's film, *Rose Hobart*—an early example of appropriation in film (and a prototype of the fan-video). In the mid-1930s, Cornell reedited found footage from the 1931 film *East of Borneo* into a 20-minute tribute to the film's star, Rose Hobart, with whom he was allegedly obsessed. Cornell originally screened the film through a filter of blue glass, and replaced the soundtrack with two tracks by Brazilian composer Nestor Amaral. *Rose Hobart* premiered in 1936 in New York City at the Julien Levy gallery on Madison Avenue. Salvador Dali was in the audience and, according to Cornell's biographer, he felt a moment of zeitgeist during the viewing:

> Halfway through the movie, there was a loud crash as the projector was overturned. "Salaud!" came from Dali, which was tantamount to calling Cornell a skunk. Levy yelled for lights . . . After [Dali's] anger had subsided, he lamented to Julien Levy: "My idea for a film is exactly that, and I was going to propose it to someone who would pay to have it made . . . I never wrote it or told anyone, but it is as if he had stolen it."[26]

For the role of Dali, we enlisted performance artist Will "Master" Lee, who is well known in downtown Manhattan performance circles for his off-the-wall portrayals of the bombastic Spanish surrealist. The audience received no indication that this would be a reenactment other than a short sentence in the program and a prop movie projector fashioned from a cardboard box that was placed unobtrusively on the stage, in front of and below the screen. Cornell's film played to a seemingly appreciative audience who, about three-quarters of the way into the film, began to take notice of the agitated rumblings from a man with a flamboyant mustache who sat among them. Suddenly, Master Lee exploded from his seat, rushed onto the stage, dutifully knocked over our prop projector, and launched into a postmodern remix of Dali's tirade. Lee was sure to include all the original elements of Dali's rant but added his own performative embellishments as well. Valmont Sprout, another performance artist, accompanied Lee on stage with an improvised interpretive dance.

After the initial shock, most of the audience realized that this was, in fact, all part of the performance. However, a few moments after Lee stormed the stage, a woman left her seat and approached me in the back—she was a representative from one of our partner organizations who had been peripherally involved in the planning of some of the festival's events. Sounding slightly panicked, she asked what was going on and whether I could do something about this interruption. I reassured her that it was all part of the performance, but she was resistant, and insisted that I remove him from the stage, before angrily making her way back to her seat.

This incident, which ended up being an unintended *enhancement* to the performance, was also a reminder that the value of remix does not rely only on a consensus of definition, but on a negotiation of *cultural meaning* as well. In *The Wealth of Networks*, Yochai Benkler wrote,

> Culture [is not] a fixed artifact. It is the product of a dynamic process of engagement among those who make up a culture. It is a frame of meaning from within

which we must inevitably function and speak to each other, and whose terms, constraints, and affordances we always negotiate.[27]

The woman's reaction to our carefully staged stunt was marginally upsetting to me as a theatrical producer. However, it served as a reminder of the reasons for producing the festival in the first place. In order for free culture advocates—artists, producers, scholars, and activists—to challenge the culture industry's monopoly on meaning, we must first be able to negotiate these meanings among ourselves. This doesn't mean that we always need to agree on definitions, only that a plurality of meanings should be accepted and understood.

Another incident that reinforced this point occurred on the morning of the first day of the festival. While preparing to leave for the venue, I received an email from one of the judges of the video competition, a video remixer known for his satirical political video remixes, who sent a note responding to my request from the judges for their final votes on the video competition. The email read:

> Are these all by a bunch of guys? Not a very good representation of the vast array of styles of remix videos that are out there at all. Honestly I kinda hate most of these, no hard feelings but these represent basically all the stuff I'm trying so hard to work against with my remix videos and advocacy work for fair use. Where are the vidders[28] for instance? I would say my choices are . . .
> (1) *Jake Gyllenhaal Challenges the Winner of the Nobel Peace Prize*
> (2–5) I can't stand to watch all the way through.
> Hope that does not mess up your scoring.[29]

In reality, five out of the ten remixes in the competition were by women, or had a woman as a primary artist. Of greater concern was his accusation that the videos didn't represent a variety of styles of remix. Aesthetic heterogeneity had become of such critical importance to me and the other producers, it had become one of our guiding principles. Finally, I can understand someone simply not liking a particular remix, or even a certain style, but was this artist really trying to "*work against*" them? And what, exactly, could that mean?

This reaction seems to be indicative of a crisis of meaning on a level deeper than simple opinion. The ten videos he was asked to watch were chosen precisely *for* their uniqueness and diversity of style, and although they may not have aligned with this artist's practice—i.e., subverting media objects with the overt intention of achieving a critique of culture or politics—I would argue that simply transforming a cultural artifact is a creative act that also contains within it, inherently, an element of subversion. I believe this for two reasons: (1) a remix, regardless of its political intentions, is the manipulation of a sign in a way that was not intended, subverting the original meaning and bringing about a unique expression of the work; and (2) it also constitutes subversion because, under the current copyright regime in the US, remix is an intentional act of cultural disobedience which asserts the agency of the artist within a cultural milieu that is increasingly prohibitive to this type of act. Looked at from this perspective, even the least political remix can become a profoundly political act.

Both of these incidents served to illustrate one category of complexity that the RE/Mixed Media Festival continues to address—the internal disconnect among the ranks of remix culture. As previously stated, it's not necessary that every artist fall in line behind a singular aesthetic or political perspective. However, an acknowledgement of the variety of ways appropriation has been, and continues to be, used as an aesthetic practice may go a long way towards an understanding of its diversity of meaning in contemporary culture.

Conclusions

Since the inaugural event in 2010, the RE/Mixed Media Festival has undergone two subsequent iterations, each attracting more artists and audience than the last. The progression we have seen—not only in numbers, but in the variety and level of innovation of the artists—has been remarkable. With somewhat less of an emphasis on film and video, the 2011 and 2012 editions of the festival have broadened to include hacker/maker workshops, interactive installations, sculpture, sound art, and theater. Panels have included discussions on remix in literature, hip hop as cultural intervention, and talking back to pop culture through video remix, among many others.

In 2011, Congress's introduction of the SOPA and PIPA bills[30] and the resulting controversy had the positive effect of elevating public awareness of the implications of more stringent copyright regulations, allowing us to continue to challenge hegemonic definitions of terms like piracy and file sharing, which resulted in stronger interest and support from audiences and artists alike. These developments have certainly helped to heal what I have observed to be a lack of consensus on the saliency of remix as a cultural praxis. Additionally, as global market concerns have caused other nations to examine their own copyright laws, interest in sensible reform has become a worldwide concern. For the first time, in 2012, the RE/Mixed Media Festival hosted a total of 18 international artists, representing over one-third of our total roster for that year. We continue to program on a "cross-pollination" model so that each year audiences who come for a specific performance or panel are exposed to several other ideas in the process. In our view, this is how social evolution occurs and culture advances—and how we hope remix and creative appropriation will ultimately be redeemed as a legitimate artistic practice in the twenty-first century.

Notes

1 Randy Kennedy, "The Free-Appropriation Writer," *The New York Times*, February 27, 2010, http://www.nytimes.com/2010/02/28/weekinreview/28kennedy.html.

2 The presentation of the name—RE/Mixed Media Festival—pays homage to V. Vale and Andrea Juno, founders of RE/Search Publications. Since the early 1980s, RE/Search has been publishing books on a variety of underground artists and countercultural trend—books that have helped shape my own aesthetic and to which my interest in remix owes a tremendous debt.

3 Lev Manovich, *Software Takes Command* (New York: Bloomsbury, 2013), 267.

4 Tom Tenney, "Jarmusch's Golden Rules v. Grindhouse Manifesto," Inc.ongruo.us, May 1, 2010, http://inc.ongruo.us/2010/05/01/jarmuschs-golden-rules-v-grindhouse-manifesto.

5 This point was an unintentional paraphrase of Comte de Lautréaumont who, in 1869, wrote, in *The Songs of Maldoror*, "As beautiful as the chance encounter of a sewing machine and an umbrella on an operating table." The phrase was popularized by the surrealist Andre Breton, and is misattributed to him in Jonathan Lethem's February 2007 article in *Harper's*, "The Ecstasy of Influence: A Plagiarism."

6 Lawrence Lessig, *Remix: Making Art and Commerce Thrive in the Hybrid Economy* (New York: Penguin Press, 2008), 28–31.

7 Kembrew McLeod, *Owning Culture: Authorship, Ownership, and Intellectual Property Law* (New York: Peter Lang, 2001), 126–145.

8 Yochai Benkler, *The Wealth of Networks: How Social Production Transforms Markets and Freedom* (New Haven, CT: Yale University Press, 2006), 293.

9 As opposed to a genre or style, in which case we'd consider it more a hybrid form than a remix.

10 Personal correspondence, April 30, 2010.

11 Benkler, *The Wealth of Networks*, 285–294.

12 Conner did not use footage from the Zapruder film, as is sometimes assumed.

13 Alex Sayf Cummings, *Democracy of Sound: Music Piracy and the Remaking of American Copyright in the Twentieth Century* (New York: Oxford University Press, 2013), 35–62.

14 Lewis Hyde, *The Gift: How the Creative Spirit Transforms the World* (Edinburgh: Canongate, 2007), xiv.

15 As this is not a sustainable model without major funding, it has changed in the interceding years. We do now charge a nominal admission fee for the festival, which provides access to everything at the event. No separate admission is charged for any single performance, exhibit, or presentation.

16 A PDF of the full program can be downloaded from http://www.remixnyc.com/2010-Program (accessed August 15, 2014).

17 Moby, *Mobygratis: Music for Independent Film Makers*, http://www.mobygratis.com.

18 New Musical Theatre, http://www.newmusicaltheatre.com.

19 RE/Mixed Media Festival, "Tweets from the 2010 RE/Mixed Media Festival," http://remixnyc.com/tweets-from-the-2010-remixed-media-festival.

20 Perry Bard, "Man with a Movie Camera," http://dziga.perrybard.net.

21 Eduardo Navas, *Remix Theory: The Aesthetics of Sampling* (New York: Springer, 2012), 73.

22 Selector is the Jamaican term for DJ. I actually prefer selector to the American term as it's both more descriptive of its function and more appropriate in its application to other, nonmusic, media.

23 All of the video finalists can be viewed at http://www.remixnyc.com.

24 3D glasses were distributed to the audience.

25 Lev Manovich, *Software Takes Command*, 267–277. Manovich defines "deep remixability" as the combining not only of media content, but also of the languages, techniques, and methodologies used to create their means of expression.

26 Deborah Solomon, *Utopia Parkway: The Life and Work of Joseph Cornell* (London: Pimlico, 1997), 87–89.

27 Yochai Benkler, *The Wealth of Networks*, 282.

28 Vidding refers to the fan practice of constructing new music videos from clips of a movie or television show. See Francesca Coppa, "An Editing Room of One's Own: Vidding as Women's Work," *Camera Obscura* 26, no. 77 (2011).

29 Anonymous, personal correspondence, May 10, 2010.

30 The Stop Online Piracy Act (SOPA) and the Protect IP Act (PIPA) were legislative bills whose ostensible purpose was to restrict foreign websites from providing illegal content. However, provisions included in both bills allowed for the removal of non-infringing Web content as well, including political and other forms of protected speech.

Bibliography

Bard, Perry. "Man with a Movie Camera." http://dziga.perrybard.net (accessed December 30, 2013).

Benkler, Yochai. *The Wealth of Networks: How Social Production Transforms Markets and Freedom*. New Haven, CT: Yale University Press, 2006.

Coppa, Francesca. "An Editing Room of One's Own: Vidding as Women's Work." *Camera Obscura* 26, no. 77 (2011): 123–124.

Cummings, Alex Sayf. *Democracy of Sound: Music Piracy and the Remaking of American Copyright in the Twentieth Century*. New York: Oxford University Press, 2013.

Hatch, Kevin. *Looking for Bruce Conner*. Cambridge, MA: MIT Press, 2012.

Hyde, Lewis. *The Gift: How the Creative Spirit Transforms the World*. Edinburgh: Canongate, 2007.

Kennedy, Randy. "The Free-Appropriation Writer." *The New York Times*, February 27, 2010. http://www.nytimes.com/2010/02/28/weekinreview/28kennedy.html (accessed July 31, 2013).

Lessig, Lawrence. *Remix: Making Art and Commerce Thrive in the Hybrid Economy*. New York: Penguin Press, 2008.

Lethem, Jonathan. *The Ecstasy of Influence: Nonfictions, Etc.* New York: Vintage, 2011.

Manovich, Lev. *Software Takes Command*. New York, NY: Bloomsbury, 2013.

McLeod, Kembrew. *Owning Culture: Authorship, Ownership, and Intellectual Property Law*. New York: Peter Lang, 2001.

Moby. *Mobygratis: Music for Independent Film Makers*. http://www.mobygratis.com (accessed December 30, 2013).

Navas, Eduardo. *Remix Theory: The Aesthetics of Sampling*. New York: Springer, 2012.

New Musical Theatre. http://www.newmusicaltheatre.com (accessed December 30, 2013).

RE/Mixed Media Festival. "Tweets from the 2010 RE/Mixed Media Festival." http://remixnyc.com/tweets-from-the-2010-remixed-media-festival (accessed December 30, 2013).

Solomon, Deborah. *Utopia Parkway: The Life and Work of Joseph Cornell*. London: Pimlico, 1997.

Tenney, Tom. "Jarmusch's Golden Rules v. Grindhouse Manifesto." Inc.ongruo.us, May 1, 2010. http://inc.ongruo.us/2010/05/01/jarmuschs-golden-rules-v-grindhouse-manifesto (accessed July 18, 2013).

31
OF RE/APPROPRIATIONS
Gustavo Romano

Digital media makes possible not just the reproduction of material, but its manipulation as well. Instead of invariability, it offers perpetual mutation; rather than copying: remixing. This has introduced a series of reflections not only regarding the notion of originals and copies—meaningless concepts in the digital realm—but also regarding ideas such as authorship, possession, and art collections.

This text evaluates selected works from the NETescopio archive that share a practice of reappropriation and reuse, but employ it via different strategies. Some of the works, part of the collection, remix and recombine material to yield new creations; others reference the original source while creating a "free version" as its re-creation. There are others that manipulate material on the Web or websites to develop parody, or sabotage the sources' messages. I will also explore artists who operate like collectors, turning their computer's cache into a kind of involuntary *wunderkammer*, or cabinet of curiosities, along with other works based on the recirculation of information and interaction as necessary mechanisms for the creation of meaning. The artist's role on the Web is transformed from creator to "redirector" of information. What follows is a brief reflection on some net art pieces from the exhibition *Re/appropriations*.

Remix

The recombination of materials is a practice that, in the plastic arts, has traditionally been associated with collage above all in relation to fixed images, painting, or photography. In the digital realm, however, when including the temporal element, this practice is closely linked to the notion of cinematographic montage as pioneered by Sergei Eisenstein. Montage, for him, was an idea that arises from the dialectic collision between two entities independent of each other.[1] Couldn't we envision as a kind of montage the remix of what browsers produce as they provide us with a constant mix of text, images, and sounds on our screens?

The digital realm, in addition, not only incorporates linear time—which in cinema is the stage on which that collision of meanings takes place—but also the juxtaposition of potentially infinite time and space as the viewer has an endless range of choices.

If the general public's channel surfing has led to a kind of experimental montage creation thanks to the power of the remote control, today the television screen has exploded, as a result offering multiple viewing possibilities. Today screens connect us via the Internet to infinite elements of content that are remote and distant from each other, not only spatially but in meaning, generating with each click that "dialectic collision"[2] of which Eisenstein spoke, now in potentially infinite directions.

Keeping in mind the early context of cinema, works of NETescopio clearly are part of the cinematic tradition. Starting at the time when Web cameras began to proliferate worldwide—in almost infinite directions—the *Multi-Cultural Recycler*[3] invites the public to take part in a voyeurism which is no longer merely passive or limited to the simple exercise of watching; it is geared towards intervention, and the mixing and remixing of the material that these remote surveillance cameras send to our computers. Selecting two or three cameras at random or choosing mixes made previously by another user, the *Recycler* embarks on a digital process in order to offer the viewer a final image. In this project we find a double recycling effect: one is caused by the use of the cameras (which lose their surveillance function), and the other effect relates to the meaning of the image (which loses its documentary function in favor of one that is metacritical). It is in this strange limbo produced by the random remix of geographical locations that people unknown to each other still share a destiny in cyberspace in which they collide, super-impose, and remain frozen in time.

Increasingly, keywords are used to govern and organize our daily lives. They have become a kind of language without grammar, without modalization, dissonance, or doubt. They are isolated names used to describe our environment, and even ourselves. *youTAG*[4] offers us a device which, using the tags that describe the videos uploaded to YouTube as a starting point, allows users to suggest two words and generate a remix that superimposes the resulting videos.

The mixing of words becomes a war of meanings, and the video space is transformed into a battleground where no one meaning can triumph.

Reinterpretations

Unlike remixes in which materials are taken independently from the narratives, there are a few works which are based on the creations of other artists and which respect their organization in the same way that a musician reads and plays sheet music. Though in music or in cinema this practice is not only standard, but an actual tradition, it is not as established in the area of the plastic arts. Remakes, covers, free versions or even karaoke are somewhat distant concepts, which are associated with and introduced from other disciplines. Various concepts enter into play here, such as authorship, original ideas, and closed works. There are also various strategies used by certain artists in order to generate a "crisis" with these concepts in the digital realm.

There are artists who act as interpreters of other authors, illustrating at times that it is not just ideas but the way they are presented and their contexts that give them mean-ing. Others who play a two-fold role, functioning as actors in territory foreign to them, recreating works in a personal way, are impostors who occupy, without prejudice, the author's place, challenging his role and authorship.

These practices also evoke two processes in the digital realm: identity theft and the system of successive software versions, two issues which come together in the practice of open code software, where we see that its strength lies precisely in free access, simul-taneous authors, and a range of different versions.

The term "remake" describes audiovisual productions that faithfully reproduce the plot, characters, atmosphere, and practically all the other features of a previous work. In theory, one of the many *My Boyfriend Came Back From the War* (MBCBFTW)[5] remixes by Epstein and the new version of the well-known work by Olia Lialina could be considered a remake. In the case of certain works for the Internet, simply replacing image files under the same name leads us to a new version of the work.

In the digital world, on the other hand, the subsequent versions of software always offer us an improvement, better-quality graphics, and improved user-friendliness. Arguably, this is what we see in this mix of parody and homage to a classic work of hypernarration.

Second Life is, by definition, a second part, a second world, a second opportunity. While everything that happens there takes place in real time—the same time that is shared by SL (Second Life) and RL (Real Life)—the "now" offered by SL takes us back to something past, something we knew or experienced previously.

In this respect, the *Synthetic Performances*[6] developed in SL make more sense as reenactments of performances previously carried out in RL.

Another characteristic of SL is the proliferation of multiple personalities, imposture, and identity theft. Consequently, it seems natural to us to see them change skin, changing from one moment to the next into avatars of Marina Abramović, Joseph Beuys, Gilbert and George, Vito Acconci, and Chris Burden.

Reengineering

Though all remixing involves a change in meaning with respect to the original work there are certain works that wage decided attacks on the ideas conveyed by the originals. We will, thus, find works undertaking these attacks with tactics like sabotage, distortion, or aikido-like methods through which one uses his opponent's own effort against him, revealing his weak points.

There are also other tactics comparable to certain living beings' survival mechanisms. The ability to camouflage themselves in their environment, for example, has been developed by species such as the chameleon and some classes of butterflies to keep from being seen by both their prey and predators. We can also compare them to the ploy used by a legendary wooden animal: the Trojan Horse. The computer version being well-known on the Web, Trojan Horses have surpassed viruses as a threat, mainly thanks to their ability to get into our systems by hiding inside other programs like viruses or memes, which are reproduced through a human carrier, who they use as a vehicle. Certain arguments are patiently kept out of sight, only subsequently exploited to achieve maximum "infection."

As advertised, *Reamweaver*[7] features all you need to instantly replicate any website at home, maintaining its design while allowing you to change any image or word you desire.

Various examples illustrate its potential applications: news pages from sites such as CNN, the World Economic Forum, the World Trade Organization, and the Republican National Committee, to mention just a few examples of pages that were distorted by the software which is also free and open due to its GNU software license. This distortion tool allows us to redress the balance between us and powerful companies or institutions. By taking advantage of the Internet, it allows David and Goliath to be on an equal footing and of the same stature. A webpage is just the same as any other webpage, and here all the huge differences which we would face were we to take on these organizations in the real world disappear.

The collaboration of Ubermorgen, Paolo Cirio, and Alessandro Ludovico cannot be described as a group or formal art collective as such, although it does resemble a "band" in many ways. Their previous strike was an attempt to displace Google by reinvesting the money paid to them by Google for advertising in Google shares. In 2006 they planned a new action which targeted the largest online bookseller: *Amazon Noir*.[8] The band dedicated their time to purloining books with copyrights protected by Amazon. com, using a sophisticated technology encoded by supervillain and media hacker Paolo Cirio. They managed to gain access to all the pages of books for sale online, which allowed them to download whole publications and offer them for free on their website as material in the public domain on the grounds of an economy of shared property. The result was a legal contest with Amazon.com which was followed by huge online debates on the limits of intellectual property.

"Re-Collections"

Towards the end of the past century a new "continent" was added to those already known, a continent made of nothing but information, and which is in constant flux. The metaphor for the Internet is that of an endless sea on which the user is like a sailor who uses bookmarks as anchors in an attempt to grant some kind of ephemeral structure to a universe with no land in sight and no stars to guide him. Although we may know where we want to go, a voyage without any coordinates is a voyage without a destination.

This sense of randomness will be essential to our experience as travelers, an eternal act of serendipity which will take us from port to port, making us gradually forget the destination towards which we had embarked. To our surprise, these accidental encounters will have unexpected results, as vestiges of our days are stored in our computer's cache.

Like a collector looking at his list of contacts on social networks, or like a tested seer looking for hidden meanings in the order of a deck of cards, the stars, or the image results on Google, the authors of this section's works will salvage these vestiges, these unintended information collisions, crafting unforeseen associations, circumstantial "bays" and unanticipated "lighthouses" to aid us before we continue our wandering voyage.

In *I Wanted to See All of the News From Today*[9] Martin John Callanan presents us with miniatures of the front cover of more than 600 global publications on one webpage. The navigator is induced to plunge into this impossible collection, in this visual mass, which tells us a great deal about the surface of the news, and very little—if anything—beyond that.

In one way it suggests that this is perhaps the same pointless effort made by the publication itself, by each newspaper and each of its readers. The trapping, the realization today, of what happened yesterday.

People collect the most diverse items: fans, shark teeth, Barbie dolls. There are also those who collect friends on Facebook or Twitter. The project *My_Contacts*[10] invites us to intrude on the world of people's contacts, and enter their respective pages on Flickr. Thus, we can take a look at photos taken by people like Bill Gates, Paris Hilton, the Dalai Lama, Marcel Duchamp, Osama Bin Laden, or George W. Bush. On the Internet, we can all be Hollywood stars, sportspersons, statesmen, or terrorists. And they can be our friends.

Recirculations

Information recirculation and joint authorship are not new concepts, but on the Internet they have found the ideal platform on which to function. The Web's immediacy and its power to go around the world in seconds have allowed humanity to become connected at lightning speed.

In the field of art we have gone from taking turns, with exquisite cadavers for example, to the kind of instant negotiation, discussion, and collaboration permitted by a wiki. The exchange creates a networking behavior, which is now simultaneous and recursive, rather than just sequential.

We can define *networking* as the promotion of social nexuses and the creation of two-way communication tools made possible by the latest technologies. From this perspective we see that not all net art falls into this category, but rather only those works in which art ceases to be an "object" (albeit virtual) made by "artists" and instead becomes a kind of platform, a space, a meaning machine with parts being added constantly, depending upon the participation which it attracts.

In some cases the artist even tries to disappear, to become invisible, hidden behind a "collective." In other cases this isn't even relevant, as the artist adopts a role as a promoter, someone who shines a light on a story in which nobody knows the end, or even the next scene. In others, the artist's work seems to be inspired by Joseph Beuys's idea that "every man is an artist," as one is invited to participate actively and to transform himself from a user into a "networker."

New meanings—in this case generated in an undesirable way—are the result of translation processes. For the translator, the huge differences between the structures of different languages pose a problem magnified by the constant apparition of new languages: the computer languages of each new device, the languages of new urban or cyberurban tribes, the languages of fiction, transhuman languages used to communicate with other species, or those designed for the communication between machines of different "species." Moreover, these languages are growing at a rate much faster than the rate at which old languages become extinct.

Antoni Muntadas deals with this issue in his work *On Translation: The Internet Project*,[11] which forms part of the *On Translation* series that began in 1994. This project, which was a coproduction with äda 'web, Documenta X, and the Goethe Institute, was based on a deconstructed "Chinese whispers" game, in which a phrase is transmitted by means of a chain of people with the resulting changes in meaning. The phrase *"Communication systems provide the possibility of developing a better understanding between people: but in which language?"* was translated by a chain of translators into 23 different languages. The results can be seen in the form of a metaphor in the image of a descending spiral in which the original phrase slides into the abyss. This process not only involved the translation of human languages (English, German, Russian, Korean, Swahili, Japanese, or Spanish); the work carried out by the translators was also affected by the technological transcodification implied by the differences between them: different operating systems, character mapping, keyboards, and so on. Nevertheless, in the end we can see that parallel to this loss of meaning there is a replacement of meaning carried out by each reader/translator. The linear original meaning is converted into a rhizomatic, fertile, unpredictable resignification.

Web 2.0 presents itself to us both as a medium and a system, as a paradigm of coexistence and social contract. Each network requires its communication protocol. All societies need their constitution. Doesn't society in the Internet age deserve an editable protocol, agreed upon in real time? This seems to have been the question posed by a group of Spanish artists that created the *Wiki Constitution*,[12] which transformed the Spanish Constitution into a wiki, a webpage that could be edited by anyone from their browser, turning the clauses and articles of the 1978 Constitution on their head. During the time in which the project was working (the wiki has since been disabled), you could access the index, choose the article that you wished to modify, and edit or change whatever you liked. Each article also had a discussion page to encourage debate.

We could question ourselves and analyze the reasons why the Wiki Constitution project was terminated. While this format has been a tool that generated deferents, which has generated important—to this day indispensable—sources of agreed information, such as that offered by Wikipedia, we should remember that it has also produced fierce virtual battles such as the one centered on the George W. Bush entry during the invasion of Iraq, which led to the open access to its editing being closed permanently. The Internet is presented to us as a space for free navigation and virtual exchange, but it is also a space for dispute, an ephemeral stage for debate, construction, battle, and sanction. Whenever these hundreds of virtual battles and attacks take place, from that first famous Great Hacker War in 1991 before the World Wide Web existed which was fought with weapons already obsolete, we can trace the mark of a warlike cyberchronicler.

Altering the Flows of Information

We could say that the artist's role on the Web is transformed from creator to "redirector" of information. She will play as a kind of pilot helping the navigator through the net, that smooth space, that virtual world made of nothing but information.

On the other hand, the "real" world became a hypercontrolled space, a world where there are no uncatalogued or unlabeled areas, with an endless technological reterritorialization of the public space. And that implies the beginning of a new hybrid space with new cartographers—like Google and the social networks—whose resources come from what might be called a "surplus of intimacy," harnessing people's need to make the private public (e.g., posting their privacy, making it known) and the public private (e.g., obtaining private profit delivering public information).

In a hyperlabeled context that we might call cybergeographic, art has an opportunity to alter the flows of recirculating information, and to generate new relational architectures; an expanded topology from which to exploit differences and to foster both horizontal and point-to-point exchange and cooperation.

Notes

1 Sergei Eisenstein, "A Dialectic Approach to Film Form," *Film Form* (New York: Harcourt, Brace, 1949), 50. "Montage is not an idea composed of successive shots stuck together but an idea that DERIVES from the collision between two shots that are independent of one another . . . As in Japanese hieroglyphics in which two independent ideographic characters ('shots') are juxtaposed and explode into a concept."

2 Ibid., 45. "Thus: the projection of the dialectical system of objects into the brain—into abstract creation, into thought—produces dialectical modes of thought—dialectical materialism—PHILOSOPHY. Similarity: the projection of the same system of objects—in concrete creation—in form—produces ART. The basis of the philosophy is the dynamic conception of objects: being as a constant evolution from the interaction between two contradictory opposites."

3 *Multi-Cultural Recycler*, Amy Alexander, 1996, http://recycler.plagiarist.org/ (accessed August 18, 2014).

4 *youTAG*, Lucas Bambozzi, 2009, http://www.youtag.org/ (accessed August 18, 2014).

5 *My Boyfriend Came Back From the War Remix*, Vadim Epstein, 1998, http://myboyfriendcamebackfromth.ewar.ru/warwara/ (accessed August 18, 2014).

6 *Synthetic Performances*, Eva and Franco Mattes, 2007, http://0100101110101101.org/synthetic-performances/ (accessed August 18, 2014).

7 *Reamweaver*, Amy Alexander, The Yes Men, and Steev Hise, 2001, http://netescopio.meiac.es/en/obra. php?id=141 (accessed August 18, 2014).

8 *Amazon Noir*, Ubermorgen, Paolo Cirio and Alessandro Ludovico, 2006, http://www.amazon-noir.com (accessed August 18, 2014).

9 *I Wanted to See All of the News From Today*, Martin John Callanan, 2007, http://allnews.greyisgood.eu/ (accessed August 18, 2014).

10 *My_Contacts*, Thomson & Craighead, 2008, http://www.thomson-craighead.net/my_contacts/ (accessed August 18, 2014).

11 *On Translation: The Internet Project*, Antoni Muntadas, 1997, http://www.adaweb.com/influx/muntadas/ (accessed August 18, 2014).

12 *Wiki Constitution*, Taller d'Intangibles (Jaume Ferrer and David Gómez, 2004), formerly at: http://www. enlloc.org/constitucion/descongelat/sobre.htm (accessed August 18, 2014).

Bibliography

Barthes, Roland. *S/Z*. New York: Hill and Wang, 1975.

Baudrillard, Jean. *The Transparency of Evil: Essays on Extreme Phenomena*. Translated by James Benedict. New York: Verso, 2009.

Burroughs, William. *The Soft Machine*. Boston, MA: Atlantic Monthly Press, 1992.

Cage, John. *Silence: Lectures and Writings by John Cage*. Middletown, CT: Wesleyan University Press, 1973.

Calvino, Italo. "Cibernética y fantasmas." *Punto y aparte*. Barcelona: Bruguera, 1983.

——. *El castillo de los destinos cruzados*. Madrid: Siruela, 1999.

Cortázar, Julio. *La vuelta al día en ochenta mundos*. México: Siglo XXI, 1968.

Debord, Guy. *La sociedad del espectáculo y otros textos situacionistas*. Madrid: Ediciones de la Flor, 1974.

Deleuze, Gilles y Guattari, Félix. *Mille Plateaux*. Paris: Editions de Minuit, 1980.

Eisenstein, Sergei. "A Dialectic Approach to Film Form," *Film Form*. New York: Harcourt, Brace, 1949.

Nelson, Theodor Holm. *Literary Machines*. Sausalito, CA: Mindful Press, 1993.

Paz, Octavio. *La apariencia desnuda, la obra de Marcel Duchamp*. México: Nueva Era, 1979.

Queneau, Raymond. *Cent mille milliards de poèmes*. Paris: Gallimard, 1961.

32

AESTHETICS OF REMIX

Networked Interactive Objects and Interface Design

Jonah Brucker-Cohen

The construction and design of a successful interactive object and interface requires the seamless integration of several different physical and experiential factors. In particular, the aesthetics of interaction, such as the location, physical proximity, connected data streams, and mindset of the user all contribute to the overall quality of their experience. In interactive media design, there is great attention and detail towards emphasizing the surrounding elements and contexts of the interaction. A remix occurs in digital media when the physicality of the real world is coupled with the intangible nature of online or digital worlds. When a physical input or output is connected to these virtual systems, a clear connection is made between a user and the controls in which they are engaged at the interface level. A seemingly obvious example of this relationship in real life is the way in which our typical interactions with computers is limited due to the tools we are given to interact with them, such as the mouse and keyboard. In *Affective Computing*, Picard writes about the advantage of being "not yet flesh and bone," that computers "perceive their world through cameras, microphones, keyboards, mice, and other sensors. These are their eyes, ears, hands, and skin . . . However, machines need not be limited to human-like sensors."[1] She goes on to say that the computer itself has the ability to augment its sensory attention beyond what humans can perceive so much that eventually the computer could surpass our sensory abilities and "might recognize emotions and other states that humans would not ordinarily recognize."[2] This form of sensory recognition outside of the interface paradigm relates back to the concept of an aesthetically determined interaction with computers and other electronic devices. Interaction is based on the collective input of elements such as the psychological state of the user, the location of the interaction, the interface developed for interaction, or the surrounding factors of the environment where the interaction takes place, such as through a touch screen on a mobile device or another form of tactile physical interface.

In order to interact with traditional computers such as laptops or desktops and other forms of technology, such as mobile and handheld devices, we have to be in a certain mindset. This includes being focused, determined, attentive, and dedicated to the work or game displayed on the screen.[3] This mindset quickly dissipates the minute we leave the screen, stand up to walk around, and observe the world around us. Innately, we stop thinking about what it means for our bodies to be traveling through a space, and our biological ability to disseminate information takes over from our concentrated efforts to understand specificity. When we move through the world we forget about what our bodies are doing and instead concentrate on the environment. Whether navigating a street corner to avoid charging automobiles or moving around an office cubicle, the mind plots the route and the body follows. Despite the seamless adaptability we engender, this close relationship between physical and personal space immediately disappears when physical handicaps are introduced. Whether it is something as minor as a headache or as chronic as blindness, biological obstacles make us notice our physical presence when navigating the world. Physical disabilities suddenly become disruptions in this natural relationship between our surroundings and our bodies.[4]

By integrating these forms of disruptions into technological objects or interfaces, the digital object suddenly becomes more human and transforms into something to which we can directly relate. On the most surface level, when a computer or application suddenly crashes mid-use, the nature of our interaction with the device changes dramatically. On one hand we are upset about losing our work, but on the other we recognize that machines, like us, carry frailties and can almost never reach the form of perfection that they are advertised to maintain. Interactive projects that integrate sensors such as sonar, video, or light detection have the ability to impart human-like characteristics because they are built to react to sudden movements or change their state based on touch inputs through haptic feedback.

I combined (remixed) physical clumsiness with virtual interfaces and networked devices in a project called *LiveWindow*.[5] *LiveWindow* was a browser window controlled by inputs from a physical space such as light, physical movement, vibration, and sound. This project answered the question of why computer software and hardware could not exhibit physical characteristics and other real-world aesthetics such as time-based deterioration and context sensitivity. *LiveWindow* allowed anyone to open a browser window on the Web and see a virtual representation of a particular physical space. The computer hosting the window collected physical (instead of virtual) "hits" as people were encouraged to bump into the computer or hit it with their hand to advance the hit counter. In its initial installation, the project was connected to a geophone sensor that detected vibration and relayed input to a microcontroller connected to the computer. This project allowed for a physical interaction to change and influence a virtual networked entity that could then be relayed over the Internet. This is similar to the way that automated burglar alarm systems function, or more recently a plethora of connected devices that maintain their own online presence.

One such project was the *TweetingSeat* by Chris McNicholl. It sent photos of its users from two camera vantage points via Twitter whenever someone sat on a custom-built park bench. McNicholl explained that the *TweetingSeat* was:

> created to explore the environments in which it is placed and the people whom it encounters. The aim of *TweetingSeat* is for people and communities to form their own relationship with the object through the way in which they choose to use it.[6]

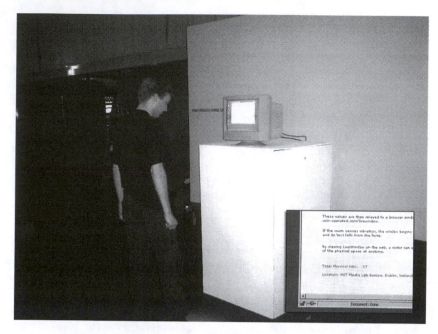

Figure 32.1 LiveWindow, Jonah Brucker-Cohen, 2001. *LiveWindow* is a browser controlled by inputs from a physical space such as light, physical movement, vibration, and sound (courtesy Jonah Brucker-Cohen)

Figure 32.2 TweetingSeat, Chris McNicholl, 2012. *TweetingSeat* is a custom-built park bench that sends photos of its users from two camera vantage points via Twitter (courtesy Chris McNicholl)

This form of connected object gains aesthetic sensibilities from its original incarnation, but the added connectivity and immediacy in its design allows for a closer relationship with users than a typical bench would exhibit. This is because the *TweetingSeat* imparts a social layer that allowed participants to engage with the object outside of the immediate time frame of their engagement with the bench itself. Through the advent of digital media and connectivity, there is an increased ability to add these levels of interaction and engagement to once closed systems such as park benches, thus increasing their aesthetic value and opening their use to a wider audience than those within the bench's local vicinity.

Enabling these experiences from a Do-It-Yourself (DIY) or Make:[7] perspective, the utilization of low-cost electronic hardware and microcontroller boards such as the Arduino[8] gives designers the ability to easily engage with a computer or network by building an endless array of custom interfaces for interaction. By using low-cost or hobbyist electronics, it is now possible to redesign common objects with integrated electronic layers for our existing frameworks of operation and use. Describing the aesthetics of use as a metaphor for contextual relationships, Theodor W. Adorno stated that "the context in which culture is produced determines its meaning and ideological effect."[9] Although Adorno wrote of the difference between the cultural influences surrounding the creation of pop and classical music, this relationship could be construed to fit any form of creative product. Since pop music is usually mass produced and highly standardized it might therefore be considered substandard to classical music. Today, this might engender a similar case for the separation of digital art as a less valid form of art from traditional genres such as painting and drawing. This distinction also distinguishes how the context of use, creation, and exhibition of an object changes people's perception of not only the object itself, but also the aesthetic and cultural specifications it provokes. Thus the aesthetic value of an object relies on both its context of use and its ability to draw attention to itself as something worth using in the first place.

Of particular interest to the realm of aesthetics and computer-based interventions is the coupling—the mashup—of humans and machines and the melding of our habits and instincts into machine code, interactive interventions, or the choices made in the industrial design of an object. In several of my projects related to network decay and interaction, I demonstrate how the future of technological interaction may rely on the moment where our navigation of machines becomes as innate as that of our bodies through the world. With added dysfunction, technology may have the potential to become more like us—thus creating a rift in the idea that humans and machines are unique entities that can never be equated.

A project of mine that explored the idea of creating aesthetic shifts in how software is designed and implemented was *BumpList*, a community email list project commissioned by the Whitney Museum of Art for their "Artport" website.[10] The project was created to reevaluate the structure and culture of email lists and the activities of their participants. The main difference between *BumpList* and traditional email lists was that *BumpList* intentionally limited subscribers, prevented user access to message archives, and publicly presented user activity on the list. By altering the framework of the email list, we explored how these modifications and aesthetic changes to an email list could augment and affect accepted forms of online social discourse. The project also exposed the inherent power structures prevalent in online mailing list systems imposed by their structural design and implementation. The main constraint used with *BumpList* was that when a new person subscribed, the first person to subscribe was "bumped," or

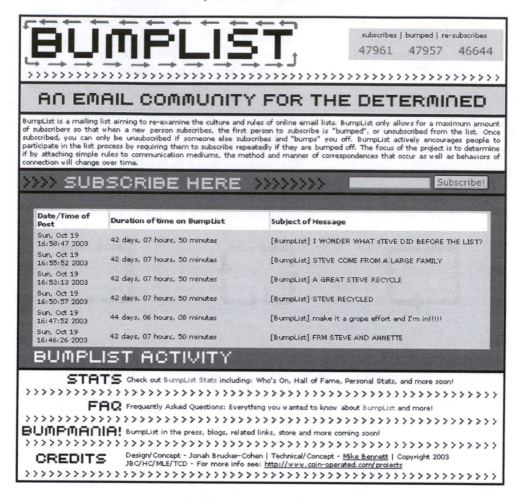

Figure 32.3 BumpList, Jonah Brucker-Cohen and Mike Bennett, 2003. *BumpList* is a
mailing list created to investigate the need to belong to a community
(courtesy Jonah Brucker-Cohen)

unsubscribed from the list. As part of the process, participants' behaviors were tracked,
collated, and examined over three phases of constraints. The results showed how public
statistics that were displayed on the project website such as a Hall of Fame for Most
Subscriptions, Most Bumps, Most Messages Sent, Most Time Spent on the List, and so
on, provided a measure of determination for the participants and how the selective
presentation of these statistics influenced their behavior. This approach to changing
rule-sets for a mailing list offered methods for building upon and enhancing accepted
forms of online discussion lists and changing the aesthetic nature of our interaction with
the social media software of lists. These changes could affect future communication
methods.

Before initiating the project, we found that one element that stood out in mailing list
rules and conventions was that the act of being a member and subscribing to an email
list was the least active aspect for a user. In response to this, *BumpList* was created to

investigate the need to belong to a community. The aim was to emphasize the "belonging" relationship and to establish if this would have an effect on the behavior of the participants subscribed to the list. In effect, this change provoked the aesthetic nature of the experience of being on the list because it foregrounded the challenge to stay subscribed, rather than what a typical passive email list exhibits as a background trait. The list structure was inherently human-like, akin to the game of "musical chairs" which, while music is played, provokes participants to constantly move around a set number of seats and when the music stops, they must occupy one of the seats or they are bumped from the game and one chair is removed.[11] The action of "bumping" in this game and in *BumpList*, in addition to the act of rejoining the activity or in *BumpList*'s case, resubscribing to the list, was enough impetus for the participants to stay engaged and remain loyal to the list. Over the course of its existence from May 2003 to February 2005, *BumpList* accrued 26,084 total subscriptions, 26,080 bumps, and 24,933 resubscriptions. The number of total subscriptions and resubscriptions did not equal the number of bumps because many people either resubscribed to the list or never resubscribed after their first bump. Users of *BumpList* ranged from highly motivated and determined to passive and unresponsive. To an unexpected degree, some of the most determined members managed to stay on the list, get to know each other, and participate in the discussions. For example, some of the most dedicated users sent more than 1,000 emails to the list, accrued more than 30 days total time on the list, and resubscribed more than 1,000 times. More passive members often signed up out of interest, and after getting bumped, never resubscribed. Between these two extremes were a few people who continually subscribed and never posted or who posted and subscribed infrequently. At the height of the list's busiest time there appeared to be 15–20 users fighting for the six spots on the list. The male/female ratio was about 60 percent male, 40 percent female with age groups from 19 to 40 years. A dramatic result of this remix of rules that *BumpList* exhibited was that in addition to large subscription totals, *BumpList* subscribers also produced more than 16,000 email messages in four months. The amount of email traffic in relation to subscriptions changed over the phases of the list and seemed to fluctuate according to the amount of media exposure and the release of a "posting hall of fame" that was placed on the main *BumpList* website in order to present live data to users about how their persistence in subscribing and reliance on the list had measured against other subscribers. As the time between bump rates approached mere minutes due to a constant influx of users fighting for six spots on the list, users had less time in which to respond to messages. This may have caused them to send more messages in shorter periods of time. Similarly, when certain subscribers began competing for top posting records, they tended to post more. A subset of user responses included participants' feelings of rejection after being bumped to optimism after resubscribing. Other survey responses indicated feelings of accomplishment from inclusion in the statistics to surprise after being bumped quickly after signup. The range of responses to getting bumped varied. In the early phases, since user activity was limited, subscribers' responses ranged from surprise to curiosity after being bumped. As the list gained more publicity, and more members joined, the feeling of being bumped sometimes turned into frustration and surprise at the rapid number of bumps over short periods. One user, who stayed on the list more than 14 days with 916 bumps described his first feeling of being bumped: "I felt challenged and determined to return." Another *BumpList* subscriber succinctly described her feeling as "transient frustration." Some of the respondents felt that because they had to actively stay subscribed to the list, their attachment grew stronger. "With so much on the Internet that can be consumed without too much effort, the perceived value is much higher with something that takes some work,"[12] explained one member, who had 722 posts, and 1,034 sub-scribes. A number of members also gained a sense of accomplishment from being included in the hall of fame during the last two phases. One subscriber who resubscribed 146 times, declared his inclusion in the hall of fame as "triumphant." Certain others felt that the hall of fame kept them interested in the list and their subsequent activity while subscribed. A dedicated subscriber stated, "The stats give a sense of accomplishment/ competition for me. I don't know that I would have been so active on the list if there were no stats available." Over time, milestones of subscription and posting activity emerged, causing certain core members to acknowledge each other based on rank. For example, one member sent a message to the list that referred to the number of posts tallied from a fellow *BumpList* subscriber.

> On August 20th, 2003, around 10:13 PM CDT, she was the first person to reach the 1000 post mark. Look at the time she was on the list, versus the number of posts. Kinda brings a tear to your eye.[13]

This idea of making the behaviors associated with using software and hardware more human-like was inspired by the Turing test that aimed to equate machines with harboring human thought.[14] Although the justification as to whether this is beneficial or detrimental has yet to be determined, the chance and opportunity for increased and more developed forms of interaction with computers has the potential to change our lives for the better. For instance, we are context-sensitive creatures. We are aware of our surroundings and change moods, intentions, appearance, and both mental and physical states depending on our location. Our "sensors" are biometric, have narrow bandwidth, and never crash, unless we inhibit them. Technology that typically contains no electronic sensors on it reacts to its context, except when it overheats; contains built-in geographical mapping capabilities to know its location; or is disconnected from power and network connectivity. One possible control mechanism we could impart to change this paradigm is for us to design technology that could relinquish its control over us and in effect "stoop" to our level by becoming more human.

The question remains as to whether computers and their inherent design and functionality control us, or do we control them? When someone clicks a link on the Web, they have to wait for the resulting page to download. At this moment they are "power-less" as the machine and speed of their network connection controls the situation. Why does the network ignore the human's angst of waiting and how can this control be taken back? If technology was more like us, the burdens it might have would be in response to its physical, not virtual, environments.[15] This human-centric approach to interface and interaction design is an area that often becomes apparent when we are using the Internet as stated above. Beginning from the first networked transmission across the Atlantic, the phenomena of fixed-wire infrastructure networks dates back to the invention of the telegraph as an early form of communication. As Neil Postman explained, the telegraph was instrumental in separating information from physical locations and political functions.

> The telegraph removed space as an inevitable constraint on the movement of information, and, for the first time transportation and communication were disengaged from each other. In the United States, the telegraph erased state

lines, collapsed regions, and, by wrapping the continent in an information grid, created the possibility of a unified nation-state. But more than this, telegraphy created the idea of context-free information, that is, the idea that the value of information need not be tied to any function it might serve in social and political decision-making and action. The telegraph made information into a commodity, a "thing" that could be bought and sold irrespective of its uses or meaning.[16]

This shift from location-based information to decentralized systems is one of the reasons why the Internet is so successful as a communication and commerce medium. Despite the seemingly utopian vision of instantaneous communication transmission across borders, accessing the Internet still remains a challenge in some countries. In particular, in developing countries that have less communication infrastructure in place, the chance of connecting to the global Internet is minimal if existent at all. Even in industrialized countries, getting "connected" at home and in private establishments often comes with a price tag. Usually, the more one pays for their Internet connection, the faster that connection tends to be. *Crank the Web* was a project I developed in response to this

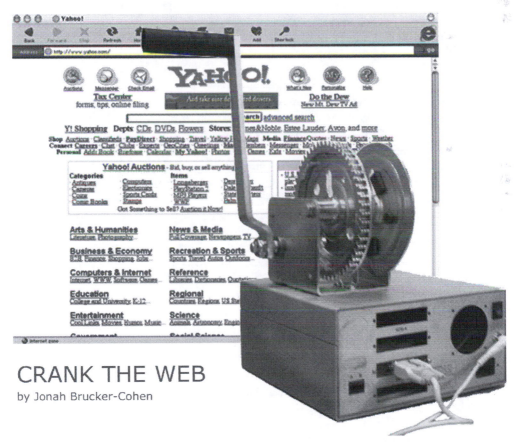

CRANK THE WEB
by Jonah Brucker-Cohen

Figure 32.4 Crank the Web, Jonah Brucker-Cohen, 2001. Users manually download Web content by turning a crank handle (courtesy Jonah Brucker-Cohen)

monetary challenge, as well as the aesthetic and often seamless experience of downloading. The project utilized a mechanical hand crank that was connected to an Internet-connected PC via a serial port. Users typed a URL into a browser on the PC (the same way they would with any computer), and pressed the return key. This opened a blank browser window. The user then turned the crank handle to manually download the website. This process added human movement to the act of retrieving information from the Internet. Although it did not act as a tangible form of navigation from site to site, it did add a physicality and manual action to the process of downloading information on the Web—which is uncommon in today's high-tech world. The idea behind *Crank the Web* was to combine (to mash) ancient forms of automation with contemporary digital telecommunications technology. The crank, a technology that dates more than 1,000 years ago, is a familiar manual process.

The project adopts the belief that it is ultimately up to individuals to use the crank to physically obtain their bandwidth, thus resulting in an Internet connection speed based on personal strength, rather than personal wealth. The project examined how transforming technological processes from intangible to tangible forms could result in a form of democratization where the technology itself becomes both attainable and understandable. The crank also added a sense of motion and transfer to the common process of clicking a link on the Internet. Chun describes the media space as a traversal across vast distances through "teleportation" rather than the "backwards" and "forwards" metaphors that most traditional interfaces (such as Web browsers) often adhere to when navigating these information spaces:

> Even new media reduced to its interface, as navigable space, rewrites the relation between space and tours. Consider, for instance, the experience of "surfing" or "browsing" the Web in 2005. Both Netscape Navigator and Microsoft's Internet Explorer rely on navigational icons . . . In either case, by typing in an address, or by clicking from location to location, you teleport rather than travel from one virtual location to another, and the backward and forward icons do not move backwards and forwards between contiguous locations.[17]

This separation of place with the action of getting there is evident in many Internet-related applications as Chun describes and is a key element of *Crank the Web*. The project added the act of reaching a location into the experience of surfing the Web since a user has to physically exert him or herself to accomplish the final goal of downloading a website. This experience is the opposite of a typical interaction with the Web, something that is instantaneous and requires no effort (besides a click) on the part of the user.

When you wait for a computer to deliver information over the network, you become immediately dependent on the machine, the infrastructure it is connected to and become powerless beyond this connection point. The project circumvented this relationship and literally put the power back into the person's hand that was interacting with the system in question. My intent was to also add the aesthetic element of humor and introspection to the act of visiting a website and downloading content from the Internet. The crank in turn, adds an element of inconvenience to this seemingly automated system and offers a novel perspective on the action and activity of downloading a website. Ideally through using the project, users would be able to understand how physical activities are closely related to the virtual and machine-led processes of downloading and accessing information on the Internet.

Similarly situated in the world of physical motion and manipulation, it should be possible that when someone stands on top of a computer it could be made to notice this interaction and react accordingly. Likewise, when someone tips a monitor onto its side, the windows on the screen would also tip over to acknowledge the change, similar to the way an Apple iPhone screen changes from landscape to portrait mode. When someone pounds hard on the keyboard, the font size, for instance, should increase in response. These types of subtle cues are innate to us as they aid us in manipulating the analog world. They make us human while at the same time distinguish us from other objects. In the design of computer interfaces, it is not enough to simply inject "desktop" metaphors and skeuomorph real-world characteristics into the design of computers and their software. Instead, there has to be a breaking point where the interface between the physical and virtual begins to exhibit and engender similar traits, including those of decomposition, decay, and dysfunction. For instance when billions of people click on the Google search button it should show an element of decay, as a door handle used by thousands of people at a sports arena would fall off or break.

In order for computers and software to change, the stigma of interface as having purely digital characteristics must ideally be separated from technology. Designers should be questioning the very nature of digital systems, metaphors for interaction, and methods of thinking and using computers. Interface should literally mean "in your face," as the interface of our bodies typically overpowers the standard computer interface as we know it. Everywhere we inhabit, physical objects infiltrate our homes, offices, towns, cities, and personal lives. The more we accumulate, the more we forget about the last thing we accumulated. We may have even moved beyond the "Information Age" where, as Castells explains, information and its manipulation become more important than the medium in which it is delivered.[18] Ultimately, the methods we use to gain connectivity to the Internet and its vast wealth of information are becoming standardized to the point where the Internet is transforming into another form of public utility. The network the Internet inhabits has become as vital as the electric grid, phone lines, water, and gas mains. Without it we would be both lost and liberated. Orlik explains that the idea of "technological escapism" includes treating the Internet as something that would ultimately cut people off from society and maybe even reality.[19] For those people who use it every day, most cannot even remember a time when it did not exist. How did we buy airplane tickets? Find out about movie show times? Many people never even participated in auctions until eBay came along. Things that come to us via computer are not only for us but are part of a shared community. How many times have two different people who have never met emailed you the same link? These types of occurrences are now commonplace online, especially within online communities, where information exchanges are as contagious and viral as the common cold. In effect, the shrinking of our world through advances in communications technologies such as the Internet has led to a changing aesthetic and more worthwhile experience for us as users, consumers, and producers of technology and technological artifacts. Whether this is beneficial to us is still under great scrutiny, but the challenge remains as to whether our experience with technology will ever gain the seamless interaction and complacency that we exhibit when we interact with each other and the physical world. This point extrapolates on the concept of remix in machine topologies because of our current and future reliance on all things digital and how the bits of information we manipulate daily must align themselves with our physical selves and the objects and space that we inhabit. Thus our bodies and actions are constantly in a state of remix with intangible data and online culture where we must redefine our lives in response to how well we integrate with the data sphere on a daily basis. Our lives have become a constant state of remix and rediscovery with everything that we do within an increasingly technological landscape.

Notes

1 Rosalind Picard, *Affective Computing* (Cambridge, MA: MIT Press, 2000) 52–53.
2 Ibid., 53.
3 Sonia Aujer and Anke Richter. "The User Intention Oriented Approach to User Interface Patterns," Proceedings of Workshop on HCI Patterns, INTERACT 2005 Rome, Italy, 31.
4 George Taleporos and Marita P. McCabe, "Body Image and Physical Disability—Personal Perspectives," *Social Science & Medicine* 54, no. 6 (2002): 971–980.
5 *LiveWindow*, available at: http://www.coin-operated.com/coinop29/2010/05/02/live-window-2001/.
6 *TweetingSeat*, available at: http://www.chrismcnicholl.com/projects/tweetingseat.
7 Make:, www.makezine.com.
8 Arduino Controller, www.arduino.cc.
9 Theodor W. Adorno, *Aesthetic Theory* (London: Athlone Press, 1997), 67.
10 Jonah Brucker-Cohen and Michael Bennett, *BumpList*, 2003, available at: http://www.bumplist.net.
11 Holly Arrow and Scott Crosson, "Musical Chairs: Membership-Dynamics in Self-Organized Group Formation," *Small Group Research* 34, no. 5 (2003): 523–556.
12 Email message from user 43212, Bumplist.net, 2004.
13 Email message from user 3212, Bumplist.net, 2003.
14 Stuart M. Shieber, "The Turing Test as Interactive Proof," *Nôus* 41, no. 4 (2008): 686–713, http://www.eecs.harvard.edu/shieber/Biblio/Papers/turing-interactive-proof.pdf.
15 Picard, *Affective Computing*, 63.
16 Neil Postman, *Technopoly: The Surrender of Culture to Technology* (New York: Knopf, 1992), 67–68.
17 Wendy Hui Kyong Chun, *Control and Freedom: Power and Paranoia in the Age of Fiber Optics* (Cambridge, MA: MIT Press, 2005), 47, 52.
18 Manuel Castells, *The Internet Galaxy: Reflections on the Internet, Business, and Society* (Oxford: Oxford University Press, 2003), 140.
19 Peter B. Orlik, *Electronic Media Criticism: Applied Perspectives* (Mahwah, NJ: Lawrence Erlbaum, 2000), 128.

Bibliography

Adorno, Theodor W. *Aesthetic Theory*. London: Athlone Press, 1997.
Arduino Controller. www.arduino.cc (accessed May 24, 2013).
Arrow, Holly, and Scott Crosson. "Musical Chairs: Membership-Dynamics in Self-Organized Group Formation," *Small Group Research* 34, no. 5 (2003): 523–556.
Aujer, Sonia, and Anke Richter. "The User Intention Oriented Approach to User Interface Patterns," *Proceedings of Workshop on HCI Patterns*, INTERACT 2005, Rome, Italy.
Brucker-Cohen, Jonah, and Michael Bennett, *BumpList*, 2003, available at: http://www.bumplist.net (accessed August 18, 2014).
Castells, Manuel. *The Internet Galaxy: Reflections on the Internet, Business, and Society*. Oxford: Oxford University Press, 2003.
Chun, Wendy Hui Kyong. *Control and Freedom: Power and Paranoia in the Age of Fiber Optics*. Cambridge, MA: The MIT Press, 2005.
Kurzweil, Ray. *The Age of Spiritual Machines: When Computers Exceed Human Intelligence*, New York: Penguin (Non-Classics), 2000, 63.
LiveWindow, available at: http://www.coin-operated.com/coinop29/2010/05/02/live-window-2001/ (accessed September 2, 2013).
Make:. http://www.makezine.com (accessed May 24, 2013).
Miller, Rose. "Is the Internet the Public Utility of the Future?" *Utne Reader*, September 8, 2005. http://www.utnereader.com/community/istheinternetthepublicutilityofthefuture.aspx#axzz3AkS0Hkgc (accessed August 18, 2014).

Norretranders, Tor. *The User Illusion: Cutting Consciousness Down to Size*. New York: Penguin, 1999, 124.

Orlik, Peter B. *Electronic Media Criticism: Applied Perspectives*. Mahwah, NJ: Lawrence Erlbaum, 2000.

Picard, Rosalind. *Affective Computing*. Cambridge, MA: MIT Press, 2000.

Postman, Neil. *Technopoly: The Surrender of Culture to Technology*. New York: Knopf, 1992.

Shieber, Stuart M. "The Turing Test as Interactive Proof." *Nôus* 41, no. 4 (2008): 686–713. http://www.eecs.harvard.edu/shieber/Biblio/Papers/turing-interactive-proof.pdf (accessed September 1, 2013).

Standage, Tom. *The Victorian Internet: The Remarkable Story of the Telegraph and the Nineteenth Century's On-Line Pioneers*. New York: Walker and Co., 1999, 13.

Taleporos, George, and Marita P. McCabe. "Body Image and Physical Disability—Personal Perspectives," *Social Science & Medicine* 54, no. 6 (2002): 971–980.

TweetingSeat, available at: http://www.chrismcnicholl.com/projects/tweetingseat (accessed September 3, 2013).

33

REFLECTIONS ON THE AMEN BREAK

A Continued History, an Unsettled Ethics

Nate Harrison

It is not uncommon, when engaged in a conversation about copying, appropriation, and remixing, that I hear the terms "copyright infringement" and "plagiarism" used interchangeably. This happens especially in educational settings, though any context is perhaps understandable given that, despite artists' increased awareness of intellectual property issues over the last decade, "plagiarism" as an idea still seems hazy—simultaneously bygone yet ever-present.[1] Its "old school" connotation has somehow been replaced by copyright's digital "tech now." And although related, copyright infringement and plagiarism are significantly different concepts. Simply put, while copyright infringement is a legal violation, plagiarism is better understood in terms of ethical misconduct. One can plagiarize without necessarily infringing a copyright. For instance, assume a scheming dramatist copies a Shakespeare play, hoping to pass it off as an original work. As all of Shakespeare's plays reside in the public domain, no copyrights will be infringed, yet most would regard this appropriation disparagingly as unoriginal and unethical thievery—the secondary user taking something creative and attempting to take credit for it without the due effort or responsibility to its historical significance. Conversely, cartoonists the Air Pirates were found liable for infringing Disney's copyrights in 1978, though clearly the adult comic books in question parodied rather than plagiarized Mickey and Minnie Mouse's perceived wholesomeness.[2]

At their most elemental, what both plagiarism and copyright infringement share is the common act of copying. Over the next pages, my intention is to identify slippages that occur between plagiarism and copyright—between ethical and legal categorization in the cultural life of intellectual property. As a case study, I will detail my own experiences with what is popularly known as the *Amen Break*, a six-second drum beat sample lifted from a late 1960s soul recording. Music remix culture today continues to rely heavily on copies of the *Amen Break*, but it is the particular path the sample travels within the context of a history project and art work I produced in 2004 that can provide further nuance on the sometimes blurry lines that separate copyright infringement and

Figure 33.1 *Can I Get An Amen?* Nate Harrison, Sandroni Rey, Los Angeles, 2007 (courtesy Nate Harrison)

plagiarism. Indeed, as copying, especially using digital tools, has become such a naturalized aspect of communication, it is not always apparent when boundaries are probed, let alone transgressed. I hope that my story-within-a-story inspires the reader to examine his or her own participation in the (re)production of culture through the everyday act of copying.

Can I Get An Amen?

In December 2004 I completed a sound art installation entitled *Can I Get An Amen?* The work consists of a 17-minute spoken word recording (I supplied the voiceover) cut to an acetate record—in DJ jargon a "dub plate"—which plays on a standard Technics SL-1200MK2 turntable (Figure 33.1). The record can be played on a stereo pair of loudspeakers or through headphones. In addition to the audio component, the installation also includes: a color, life-size photo reproduction of The Winstons' 1969 7" single "Color Him Father"; registration documents showing that Richard Spencer, front man for The Winstons, holds the copyrights in both "Color Him Father," and its B-side, "Amen, Brother"; and finally, a printout of the contents of stock audio company Zero G's *Jungle Warfare* breakbeat sample collection, which contains several *Amen Break* loops (unlicensed from The Winstons). All of these materials are mounted on a wall next to the turntable. Their significance is explained throughout the course of my narration in the spoken word recording.[3] I have described *Can I Get An Amen?* as:

An audio project that unfolds a critical perspective of perhaps the most sampled drum beat in the history of recorded music, the "Amen Break." It begins with '60s soul band The Winstons and their pop instrumental track Amen, Brother, and traces the transformation of the song's drum solo from its original context as part of a B-side vinyl single into its use as a key aural ingredient in contemporary, sample and collage-based remix culture. The work attempts to bring into scrutiny the techno-utopian notion that "information wants to be free"—it questions this freedom's effectiveness as a democratizing agent. This as well as other issues are foregrounded through a history of the Amen Break and its peculiar relationship to current copyright law.[4]

My project thus serves as an audio essay that unpacks the history-making journey of one particular drum beat recording through the early postmodern formation of both art and cultural property law.

I won't dwell too much on the content of Can I Get An Amen?; the project is readily available online and I encourage the reader to spend time with it there.[5] Here I'd like to focus on the work's passage through the cultural landscape—to the ways in which it spread and transformed in the ensuing years. After exhibiting the work at CalArts in the spring of 2005, I posted a description and documentation of Can I Get An Amen? on my personal website. Like many artists with online portfolios, my intention was to give potential curators a sense of the conceptual and practical aspects of the project. The project page still includes a QuickTime video of the record playing in its entirety, which makes for a pretty boring visual experience. However, since the emphasis of the project was its audio component, the minimalist video reinforced the importance of the sound. My primary desire was to present an audio work within the visual logic of an art exhibition.

I've always considered the online version of Can I Get An Amen? as a poor substitute for the analog, gallery specific version. Yet its existence on the Web is precisely what catapulted it from a project I made while pursuing my graduate studies into one of the first instances of the "mini documentary" genre now so prevalent on the Internet.[6] As a direct result of YouTube user mobieus32 "appropriating" the QuickTime file from my site and uploading it to the popular social video site, Can I Get An Amen? amassed more than 88,000 views within a year.[7] A short time later, The Winstons' publisher, Holly Bee Music, Inc., contacted me after viewing the YouTube upload, having had no idea of the cultural significance of the Amen drum loop. I initially feared Holly Bee Music would begin legal proceedings against me (for copyright infringement). But the opposite was the case; Holly Bee thanked me for bringing Amen sampling to its attention and wanted to know how they might be able to recover potential lost licensing revenues. I replied that I was not a lawyer, but that I wished them luck in their pursuits.[8] Family relatives of the original band members also reached out to me. Over time Can I Get An Amen? was featured on several music, culture, and intellectual property law websites and radio shows, including the BBC's Radio 1, which dedicated an entire program and DJ mix in honor of the Amen Break.[9] Several electronic music producers, including Wax Tailor and Skrillex, sampled the project for use in their hip hop and dance music remixes.[10] As of August 2013, the YouTube version of Can I Get An Amen? had amassed over 4.3 million views; this in addition to the many occasions the "original" work has been exhibited in gallery and museum settings (i.e., within the institution of Art). One of the aspects of the project that continues to interest me is its travel from "high" to "low" culture and back again.

It is important to note that mobieus32 never asked for my permission to post *Can I Get An Amen?* to YouTube, nor did I ever grant it. I learned of its existence only after a friend told me he had seen the work there. I was surprised by the upload, but excited to see it being shared. I also realized there wasn't much I could do to stop its circulation, short of sending a takedown message to YouTube and removing the QuickTime version from my own website. And I didn't want that; it was important to me that my project, an analysis of the *Amen Break*, traverse the same cultural path that the original sample had: one that required unregulated copying and distribution. "Information wants to be free," as the cliché goes. The online existence of *Can I Get An Amen?*—its form— matched its content.

Amen and Seven Seconds of Fire

While perusing the user comments on the YouTube page in late December 2011, I noticed several viewers were referred to the project through an article published by *The Economist* (Figure 33.2). Intrigued by what a reputable, highbrow, politics and economics journal might have to say about contemporary music sampling, I discovered that it published a story, both in print and online, about the history of the *Amen Break*. The story was remarkably similar to my own—too similar, in my opinion.[11] For the first time since conceiving *Can I Get An Amen?*, it seemed I had been copied *inappropriately*. But I didn't feel as though I had been infringed as much as plagiarized. Compelled to write *The Economist*'s editors, I reproduce here the letter I sent, which explains my ethical dilemma.

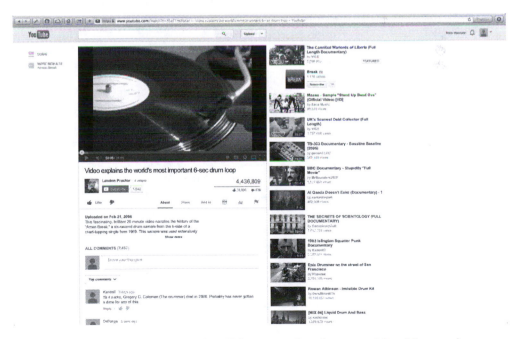

Figure 33.2 Can I Get An Amen? YouTube screenshot (courtesy Nate Harrison)

December 26, 2011

Dear Sir or Madame,

This letter is in response to The Economist article "Seven seconds of fire," dated December 17th, as well as its corresponding Prospero blog entry, "Just a sample" (http://www.economist.com/node/21540676) from December 15th. I would first like to commend the editors at The Economist for putting into print such an important topic. The history of the "Amen break" is recounted in a lively and elaborate tone evoking the excitement all those drum loop permutations have delivered to our ears over the years. More significantly, a whole new group of people (i.e., subscribers) who might not have otherwise known are now aware of an important subculture and its development. Yet the story wasn't entirely new to me; you see, I authored a project, *Can I Get An Amen?* (http://www.youtube.com/watch?v=5SaFTm2bcac) that told an almost identical story, also in December of 2004.

Now, my project and The Economist articles do share some differences. "Seven seconds of fire" contains more specifics (e.g., technical details, quotations) than *Can I Get An Amen?* Likewise, my essay ultimately seeks to raise important copyright issues surrounding not only the Amen break but also cultural production in general, while The Economist text just briefly mentions the ownership aspects of the now infamous drum solo. And The Economist names G. C. Coleman as the original drummer, while I did not (regrettably, researching in 2003 I was not able to confirm with absolute certainty that Coleman played the drums for The Winstons).

With all this said, however, there are simply too many similarities between the works leading me to conclude that it is practically impossible the editors at The Economist—and indeed, their anonymity only adds another layer of complexity—could not have heard *Can I Get An Amen?* I am certain they used it, without citation, as a primary source.[12] Not only is the narrative arc of their story largely the same as my own, they also mirror certain structural elements. For example, the editors write of the nostalgia for the Amen break, as I did. They also ask the question "Why was the Amen so popular?" and offered an analysis based on its formal qualities, as I did. Four of the illustrating songs they posted to the Prospero blog for readers to hear are examples I also used (when there are literally thousands of Amen tracks from which the editors could have chosen to showcase). Finally, at the level of sentence comparison, in 2004 I wrote "It's been used so much, I might argue it's now entered into the collective audio unconscious," while The Economist wrote in 2011 "Coleman's seven-second break had entered the collective aural unconscious of a generation of young Britons." I will leave it for readers to decide.

And indeed some of them already have. In the days following the publication of "Seven seconds of fire," these are just some of the reader comments posted on The Economist website:

"The excellent story caused me to further research the Amen Break. I was amazed to find immediately a twenty-minute very informative lecture on YouTube from 2004 about the subject that nearly follows point by point the author's article. It appears the author may have borrowed—or 'sampled'—quite a bit from the video."

And:

"I liked this article so I wanted to learn more about the 'Amen Break' and I came across the twenty min [sic] YouTube video that others mention. It appears the author is doing the same thing with the material that s/he articulates is happening with this drum riff. Art imitating life? I expect more from The Economist."[13]

Further, from the comments on the project's YouTube page:

"If you are here due to The Economist, ask yourself if The Economist author basically copied this video for his article . . . unless it is one and the same person . . . because the content of the article is exactly the same."

And:

"Brilliant video, and yes, The Economist article is completely biting this."[14]

Now, this puts me in a peculiar situation. I want to be clear that this letter is not some sort of "cease and desist" threat. Writing such a letter would be hypocritical of me, especially given the nature and content of *Can I Get An Amen?* It would also go against my own strong belief and respect for the copyleft movement. Over the last several years, dozens of writers, musicians (including some pretty famous DJs), and students have all contacted me, kindly asking permission to quote/appropriate/remix my work, and I have always (and will always) allowed for it. I am also aware that there are people who will sample my work without my knowing, and there is little I can do about that.

But I do want to distinguish legal from ethical issues here, just as there is a difference between copyright infringement and plagiarism (although I am less interested in whether The Economist is committing either the former or the latter). There is a (now doubled) irony involving anonymous writers at The Economist, who are telling a tale about the largely forgotten band The Winstons and their unrecognized impact on legions of mostly anonymous music producers, by taking portions of another writer's work and not crediting that writer. In other words, The Economist is ultimately reproducing the very dynamic it seeks to critically illuminate. Is this intentional on the editors' part? Some sort of postmodernist sleight of hand, a cunning wink to their more savvy readers? Or plain sloppy journalism? It's especially strange that the editors would use audio examples culled from YouTube videos, which further link to my video, making it easy for curious readers to stumble onto my work and consequently exposing the problem I am detailing here. Given the stalwart reputation The Economist has maintained for so long now, I call upon its editors to do the right thing and give credit where credit is due.

Sincerely yours,
Nate Harrison[15]

Within a few days, Tom Nuttall, deputy/online Europe editor and author of *The Economist* piece, responded to my letter. While admitting that he had encountered *Can I Get An Amen?* online before writing his article, he also stated that he had grown up in London—ground-zero of the *Amen*/jungle scene—and was long aware of the break's sampling and significance. Primarily, Mr. Nuttall answered that he and I both had touched upon the general narrative of the *Amen*, as any proper history should have. And while my work centered on intellectual property issues, *The Economist* piece focused around cultural aspects. I'm not sure I agree with Nuttall's assessment, but, to his credit, he updated the piece online to include a reference to my project, writing, "As a general principle, I think that it is courteous for writers to acknowledge an outstanding and original contribution and so I have linked to it."[16] I was satisfied with this reply.

Amen (So Be It)

My letter to *The Economist* should not be interpreted here as an egotistical gesture, as if my history of the *Amen Break* is *the* history. It certainly is not. I encourage readers to look up Mr. Nuttall's piece, compare it to my work, and decide for themselves what sorts of ethical lines, if any, were crossed. As I wrote above, I not only tolerate but also appreciate the ways in which awareness and use of both the original drum loop as well as my meditation on it have circulated. But the interaction with *The Economist* did give me pause, causing me to reevaluate my attitude towards sampling, appropriation, infringement and plagiarism. And while I remain a committed "copyleftist," I also believe that along with copying comes a responsibility to source material. Such responsibility goes beyond proper citations, or credits in journals; it goes beyond music remix culture in its myriad manifestations—across medicine, architecture, even law itself. As the simple act of copying increasingly becomes first nature across global demographics, it's all the more crucial that what I have previously called a "semiotic integrity" to source material is maintained.[17] That is, every act of borrowing should strive, in its new re-presentation, to acknowledge in some way the circumstances out of which its source material is taken. This could be something as simple as citations in essay writing or as complex as the careful manipulation of (and simultaneous reference to) established visual codes in postmodernist art (as in Sherrie Levine's early work).[18] Context is important. If it ceases to matter, then we are left with what Jean Baudrillard and Frederic Jameson referred to, so many years ago during the emergence of media appropriation, as simulation and pastiche—conditions that attenuate critical thinking in the service of constructing pseudo-history.[19]

Notes

1 A recent example of the crossover between rhetorics of copyright infringement and plagiarism involves the school essay evaluation service Turnitin (http://www.turnitin.com), which scans student work to catch and deter copying. The company hosts an "educational" website (http://www.plagiarism.org) that, in this author's estimation, problematically conflates issues of plagiarism with those surrounding intellectual property. Ironically, a group of students sued Turnitin, claiming copyright infringement due to the company's for-profit use of students' original work. Turnitin prevailed. See A.V. v. iParadigms, LLC (2009), http://www.ca4.uscourts.gov/Opinions/Published/081424.P.pdf.

2 "Walt Disney Productions v. Air Pirates, 581 F 2nd 751 Court of Appeals, Ninth Circuit 1978—Google Scholar," Google, accessed December 4, 2013, http://scholar.google.com.mx/scholar_case?case=1298582 4547460808287&hl=en&as_sdt=2&as_vis=1&oi=scholarr&sa=X&ei=l0MIUsv7I4jZ2AWTn4HwCw &ved=0CCgQgAMoADAA.

See also Bob Levin, *The Pirates and the Mouse: Disney's War Against the Counterculture* (Seattle, WA: Fantagraphics Books, 2003).

3 Can I Get An Amen? can be found on my website. See Nate Harrison, "Nate Harrison," last modified August 15, 2006, http://www.nkhstudio.com/pages/popup_amen.html.

4 Ibid.

5 The recording is also available on YouTube. See Landon Proctor, "Video explains the world's most important 6-sec drum loop—YouTube," YouTube, accessed December 4, 2013, http://www.youtube.com/watch?v=5SaFTm2bcac.

6 By "mini documentary" I am referring to five- to ten-minute, semi-professional video and audio productions made possible by cheaper and more accessible media technologies. With video capabilities present in most phones now, barely a day goes by without a new mini documentary going viral. For an early example, see *The Story of Stuff*, http://www.storyofstuff.org/movies-all/story-of-stuff/.

7 Mobieus32 was the online alias of Landon Proctor, who has since retired the name. Landon Proctor, e-mail message to the author, November 24, 2012.

8 Johnny Moses of Holly Bee Music, in telephone conversation with the author, August 9, 2007.

9 "BBC Radio 1—BBC Radio 1's Stories, The Amen Break," British Broadcasting Corporation, last modified May 2, 2012, http://www.bbc.co.uk/programmes/p00rzp6w. I was interviewed for the segment along with several other musicians and cultural critics.

10 BOL3KiLOL3K, "Wax Tailor—Once Upon a Past—YouTube," YouTube, http://www.youtube.com/watch?v=BiBxh7Mg3OM; CannibalWhirm, "SKRILLEX—I know who you are," YouTube, http://www.youtube.com/watch?v=HuwNw_fVFUY&list=FLKNmY2QCp1ucL6TJOzqeaUg&index=19.

11 See "Seven Seconds of Fire," *The Economist*, last modified December 17, 2011, http://www.economist.com/node/21541707.

12 *The Economist* maintains a policy of editorial anonymity. See http://www.economist.com/help/about-us#About_Economistcom.

13 Comments taken from users "Otto von Kronq" and "y7JUMZwGiq," respectively, who posted responses to The Economist article online.

14 Comments taken from users "davidhelvadjian" and "myoest," respectively, who posted to the YouTube page.

15 With the exception of corrected typographical errors, my letter is unchanged from the version sent to *The Economist*.

16 Tom Nuttall, e-mail message to the author, January 3, 2012.

17 Nate Harrison, "In Fair Use, Freedom Does Not Equal Progress," *Antenna* (blog), June 14, 2013, http://blog.commarts.wisc.edu/2013/06/14/in-fair-use-freedom-does-not-equal-progress/.

18 On Sherrie Levine's early appropriation work, see Howard Singerman and Sherrie Levine, *Art History, After Sherrie Levine* (Berkeley, CA: University of California Press, 2012).

19 On simulation see Jean Baudrillard, *Simulations* (New York, NY: Semiotext(e), Inc., 1983). On pastiche see Fredric Jameson, *Postmodernism, Or, the Cultural Logic of Late Capitalism* (Durham, NC: Duke University Press, 1991).

Bibliography

Baudrillard, Jean. *Simulations*. New York: Semiotext(e), Inc., 1983.

"BBC Radio 1—BBC Radio 1's Stories, The Amen Break." *British Broadcasting Corporation*. last modified May 2, 2012, http://www.bbc.co.uk/programmes/p00rzp6w (accessed August 18, 2014).

BOL3KiLOL3K. "Wax Tailor—Once Upon a Past—YouTube." YouTube video. http://www.youtube.com/watch?v=BiBxh7Mg3OM (accessed August 18, 2014).

CannibalWhirm. "SKRILLEX—I know who you are." YouTube video. http://www.youtube.com/watch?v=HuwNw_fVFUY&list=FLKNmY2QCp1ucL6TJOzqeaUg&index=19 (accessed December 4, 2013).

Harrison, Nate. "Nate Harrison." Last modified August 15, 2006. http://www.nkhstudio.com/pages/popup_amen.html (accessed August 18, 2014).

——. "In Fair Use, Freedom Does Not Equal Progress," *Antenna* (blog), June 14, 2013, http://blog.commarts.wisc.edu/2013/06/14/in-fair-use-freedom-does-not-equal-progress/ (accessed August 18, 2014).

Jameson, Fredric. *Postmodernism, Or, the Cultural Logic of Late Capitalism*. Durham, NC: Duke University Press, 1991.

Levin, Bob. *The Pirates and the Mouse: Disney's War Against the Counterculture*. Seattle, WA: Fantagraphics Books, 2003.

Proctor, Landon. "Video Explains the World's Most Important 6-sec Drum Loop—YouTube." YouTube video. http://www.youtube.com/watch?v=5SaFTm2bcac (accessed December 4, 2013).

"Seven Seconds of Fire." *The Economist*. Last modified December 17, 2011. http://www.economist.com/node/21541707(accessed August 18, 2014).

Singerman, Howard and Sherrie Levine. *Art History, After Sherrie Levine*. Berkeley, CA: University of California Press, 2012.

"Walt Disney Productions v. Air Pirates, 581 F 2nd 751 Court of Appeals, Ninth Circuit 1978—Google Scholar." Google.com. http://scholar.google.com.mx/scholar_case?case=12985824547460808287&hl=en&as_sdt=2&as_vis=1&oi=scholarr&sa=X&ei=l0MIUsv7I4jZ2AWTn4HwCw&ved=0CCgQgAMoADAA (accessed December 4, 2013).

34
GOING CRAZY WITH REMIX

A Classroom Study by Practice via *Lenz v. Universal*

xtine burrough and Emily Erickson

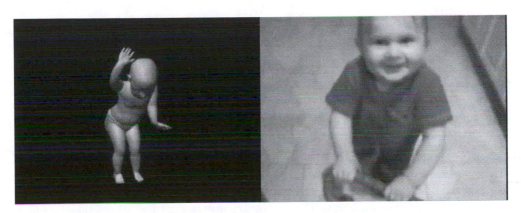

Figure 34.1 Dancing babies: (left) Michael Girard's 3D dancing baby and (right) Holden Lenz dances on YouTube

In the mid-1990s, Michael Girard's 3D dancing baby graphic[1] became an early example of an Internet meme.[2] From email inboxes to the television program *Ally McBeal*, where the clip was inserted during the protagonist's hallucinations. The dancing baby exemplifies Douglas Rushkoff's notion of a "living organism" that travels Richard Dawkins's etymological parallel between genes and memes: "the circulatory system for today's information, ideas, and images."[3] This case study includes yet another baby dancing online, though the author's intent was anything but viral media. In 2007, Stephanie Lenz posted a 29-second video of her toddler dancing to Prince's 1980s hit *Let's Go Crazy* on YouTube (Figure 34.1).[4] The song, playing in a room off-camera, was barely recognizable. However, when Lenz uploaded the video of 18-month-old Holden to YouTube, she titled it *Let's Go Crazy #1*—making it easy for Prince's record label,

Figure 34.2 A likeness to the ubiquitous YouTube "sad face"

Universal Music Group, to find it with a Web crawler and send Google a takedown notice, via the copyright holder's prerogative outlined in the Digital Millennium Copyright Act (DMCA).[5] For the next six months, anyone looking for the video—namely, Holden's relatives—would get the ubiquitous YouTube apology: "We're sorry, this video is no longer available" (Figure 34.2).

After YouTube removed the video, Lenz was warned that additional copyright infringements would force the company to cancel her account. Lenz submitted a counternotification arguing fair use. By the time Google reposted the video months later, Lenz was ready for action. Aided by the Electronic Frontier Foundation (EFF), she sued Universal, arguing that it had violated her First Amendment rights by demanding the removal of her video without considering the likelihood of fair use. Universal filed a motion to dismiss, pointing out that the DMCA makes no mention of fair use. But in August 2008 a US District judge refused to dismiss the case, ruling that copyright owners must indeed consider whether their content has been used within the parameters of fair use before issuing a takedown notice.[6] Recognizing that this precedent could profoundly change the ease with which it currently uses the DMCA, Universal went through several more legal contortions to make the *Lenz* case go away. However, in March 2010, the judge ruled against the company's motion for dismissal again, bringing Lenz closer to the courtroom.[7] In January 2013 Corynne McSherry reported on the EFF's website that the court "clarified that [the] 'consideration'" of fair use, "means making an actual legal determination."[8]

Although Stephanie Lenz's video *was* ultimately reposted on YouTube, her case illustrates how easy it is, under the DMCA guidelines, for content owners to see user-generated content (UGC) removed from the Web when it contains copyrighted material, even if that material is clearly fair use—with no profit motive or likely economic harm to the content owner. Her case also holds the possibility of ending, or at least changing, this current paradigm, in which UGC creators are held guilty of copyright infringement (i.e., losing the right to post their remixes, parodies, mashups, and home videos) until proven innocent.

This case provides a nuanced example of the challenges content creators face. As an educator, this case was low-hanging fruit on the pedagogical tree. My students—who have been bombarded with what Lessig calls the "War on Piracy"[9]—increasingly understand that file sharing is illegal, but are much less clear about other uses of copyrighted content online. This vagueness isn't helped by the massive number of takedown notices issued by content holders—which, as *Lenz v. Universal* demonstrates—is undertaken *without* considering fair use.

I felt good about using the case as a real-world teaching tool, but I also have to admit to my frustration with the politics of the case. It is hard to reconcile a large publishing company antagonizing a mother and her young son. I wanted to contribute to Lenz's battle—I wanted to put up hundreds of videos with that old *Crazy* song in it. Therefore, as we waited for a definitive ruling on *Lenz*, the project in this case study demonstrates one method of online solidarity: bombard them with remixes.

Specs

In the classroom, *Lenz v. Universal* is a didactic tool, used to demonstrate how to create UGC with a rich understanding of fair use doctrine. But for all practical purposes, assigning the remix project was a way to create many more videos, most using the same snippet of Prince's song, that are obviously critiquing or commenting upon the case.

Henry Jenkins writes, "More and more literacy experts are recognizing that enacting, reciting, and appropriating elements from preexisting stories is a valuable and organic part of the process by which children develop cultural literacy."[10] Creating "preexisting stories" with social media could be as simple as updating a Facebook or MySpace page— as 18-year-old Skyler told danah boyd, "If you're not on MySpace, you don't exist."[11] Status updates, and other media published online, are not just technical exercises. These activities aid developmental learning in the growth of digital media literacy for students of the networked era. If students can post status updates to Facebook, they can "rip, mix, and burn"[12] (or upload) for Web participation. The remix project assigned to my students was a call to action and a platform for participation. I hope that students entering college classrooms in the next few years will say, "If you're not creating new commentary, you don't exist."

First, we watched Lenz's original video. I asked a class of 20 students if they recognized the song in the background of the video. While one student could name the song and its author, many failed to notice the background music. We discussed the case, which provided an opportunity to review fair use doctrine. Then we dissected Lenz's video into parts: the aesthetic treatment, the script, camera movements, and so on. My students were to create a remix of Lenz's original video or develop a parody in which it made sense to use Prince's song (Figure 34.3). Their videos had to be exactly 29 seconds (the same as the original) and posted to YouTube as a video response (a feature YouTube no longer supports)[13] to *Let's Go Crazy #1*. I had a feeling Universal would be unlikely to continue issuing takedown notices on or near Lenz's account while they were still avoiding the courts. To this day, only one of my students (and there were more than 100) has received a takedown notice.

Coincidentally, in the process of bombarding Universal with remixes, we were also bombarding Stephanie Lenz. At the time, video responses required authorization for publication on YouTube from the original author. So Stephanie learned of our class

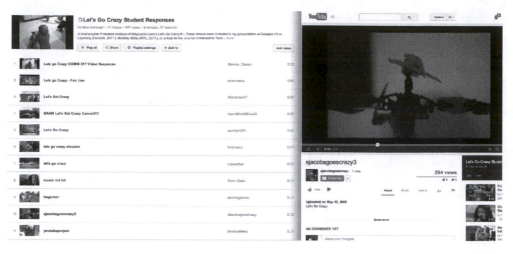

Figure 34.3 Since video responses are no longer available (or searchable), student video responses to Lenz's work can be viewed on the YouTube playlist: http://www. youtube.com/playlist?list=PLC8F47F3AD251E99C (courtesy of xtine burrough)

project the first time students submitted their assignments. As a result, my students interviewed Ms. Lenz and we developed a website for the project to publish their interview (Figure 34.4).[14]

Figuring a Better Way

Lawrence Lessig defines our networked culture as "RW" (read/write), in contrast to the "RO" (read-only) culture that once dominated our media landscape. Since today's communication methods commonly include downloading, editing, recreating, and uploading, Lessig and others call for a reform of copyright law, end-user license agreements, or the definition of "authorship." Lessig writes, "It is time we call a truce, and figure a better way. And a better way means redefining the system of law we call copyright so that ordinary, normal behavior is not called criminal."[15]

The Organisation for Economic Co-operation and Development (OECD) issued the report, "Participative Web: User-Created Content" to understand the newest feature of society and the economy, "wide creative participation in developing digital content, driven by rapidly diffusing broadband access and new software tools."[16] Without a concrete definition for UGC, the committee developed the following guidelines for understanding it: (1) it must be published online; (2) creative effort is necessary;[17] and (3) it must be made outside of professional practices. This portion of the guidelines virtually requires that UGC remain an amateur effort; and Lenz's video fulfills the OECD's definition. It was published online, expressed creativity—in the form of dance, and emerged from an unambiguously personal sphere. As Ian Chuang notes, "the crux of Lenz's argument was that copyright holders cannot, in good faith, order materials taken down without first considering the issue of fair use."[18] This is the argument that would be used in future cases if amateur UGC creators had to defend themselves against (most likely, corporate) copyright holders.

Figure 34.4 The complete interview with Stephanie Lenz is available on letsgocrazy. info/interview.html

A directory of rulings in regards to artworks that rely on mimicking original works, such as those intending to create parody, satire, or appropriation in a fine arts context, demonstrate that this type of expression is risky. Mark Sableman writes, "as with copyright and trademark, several key rulings have placed legitimate artistic use of the content of today's culture at risk."[19] Challenges particular to UGC have to do with authorship and the current licensing process. Laura Heymann suggests the term "author" is used too broadly, as she writes,

> one's notion of how the word should be described might align not only with the kind of creative work one does (or engages with) but also with one's sense of what the scope of the legal rights attached to authorship should be.[20]

Heymann suggests *traditional authors* were motivated by economic forces, unlike *new authors* who create "new and imaginative works, often by incorporating or commenting on the works of others."[21] These new authors are not limited to producing UGC, but for our purposes this is a clear example of Heymann's suggestion. When UGC takes the form of remix, mashup, or parody, the expression necessarily relies on directly referencing contemporary culture.[22] Heymann calls for copyright law to account for authors' motivations and intentions instead of emphasizing the artistic product. Biederman and Andrews's contractual differentiation provides another binary relationship to Heymann's "old authors/new authors" conundrum. The old authors saw content creators and distributors enter into "binding, bilaterally negotiated contracts, including representations and warranties, indemnification clauses, and other familiar language allocating their respective liabilities and designating ownership rights,"[23] while new authors (as in UGC creators) are presented with nonnegotiable end-user license agreements (EULAs). As Biederman and Andrews point out, "UGC copyright ownership issues are usually dealt with at two distinct periods in the content creation process, either: (1) the front end (contractually); or (2) the back end (through litigation)."[24]

Fair use doctrine requires a four-part investigation for balance between: (1) the purpose of the derivative work; (2) the nature of the content (for example, facts versus creative content); (3) the amount of original work used in the derivative; and (4) the effect that the new work has on the actual or potential market value of the original. UGC creators must be aware of how to balance these factors. Since today's students are likely to participate in generating content for the Web, teaching fair use is a pedagogical imperative. However, fair use cases are evaluated individually, so it is often seen as a defense rather than a "category of activity that is not infringement in the first place."[25] Heymann concludes, "too much deference is given to copyright owners' interests and too little to defendants' needs to use copyrighted works";[26] and Rebecca Ganz reiterates, "The main problem with fair use is that it is currently applied on a case-by-case basis."[27]

Cultural production, viewed through the lens of art history, includes practices of collage and juxtaposition. Henry Jenkins alludes to cultural production as "the displacement of folk culture by mass media."[28] Photographer and collage artist John Baldessari argues that since images are so similar to words, neither should be owned.[29] While I appreciate these new possibilities for governance (all related to the second challenge in determining fair use), media creators and educators should focus on the first challenge while developing an understanding of fair use. In university curricula, this means teaching the fair use doctrine alongside the practice-based activities of downloading, editing, recreating, and uploading. In his introduction to *Remix*, Lessig credits Jack Valenti for his insightful question about a college student who admitted to downloading music in violation of the copyright law: "What kind of moral platform will sustain this young man in later life?"[30]

We wish we had the answer. In the meantime, pedagogy combining fair use doctrine with UGC activity develops a moral platform to sustain students until policy makers accommodate Web practices, such as the *Lenz* remix project, that are already protected by the fair use doctrine.

Notes

1 Greg Lefevre, "Dancing Baby Cha-Chas from the Internet to the Networks," CNN, last modified January 19, 1998, http://www.cnn.com/TECH/9801/19/dancing.baby.index.html.

2 The term *meme*—"a unit of cultural transmission"—was coined by Richard Dawkins, in his 1976 classic, *The Selfish Gene* (Oxford: Oxford University Press, 2006 edition), 192.

3 Ibid., 7.

4 Stephanie Lenz, "Let's Go Crazy #1," YouTube, http://www.youtube.com/watch?v=N1KfJHFWlhQ.

5 DMCA 2006: 17 USC § 512.

6 Lenz v. Universal Music Corp., 572 F. Supp. 2d 1150 (ND Cal. 2008).

7 Lenz v. Universal Music Corp., LEXIS 16899 (ND Cal. 2010).

8 Corynne McSherry, "Lenz v. Universal: This Baby May Be Dancing to Trial," *Electronic Frontier Foundation*, January 28, 2013, https://www.eff.org/deeplinks/2013/01/lenz-v-universal-baby-may-be-dancing-trial-0.

9 Lawrence Lessig, *Remix: Making Art and Commerce Thrive in the Hybrid Economy* (New York: Penguin, 2008), xv–xvii.

10 Henry Jenkins, *Convergence Culture: Where Old and New Media Collide* (New York: New York University Press, 2006), 177.

11 danah boyd, "Why Youth (Heart) Social Network Sites: The Role of Networked Publics in Teenage Social Life," in *MacArthur Foundation Series on Digital Learning—Youth, Identity, and Digital Media Volume*, ed. David Buckingham (Cambridge, MA: MIT Press, 2007), last modified March 30, 2010. http://www.danah.org/papers/WhyYouthHeart.pdf, 1.

12 This was the slogan Apple Computers used to sell the first version of iTunes. See Apple Computers, "Archived—Rip, Mix, Burn Defined," *Apple*, February 18, 2012, http://support.apple.com/kb/TA44040?viewlocale=en_US.

13 Josh Ong, "Google is Removing Video Responses on YouTube from September 12 Due to Low Engagement," *The Next Web*, August 28, 2013, http://thenextweb.com/google/2013/08/28/google-is-removing-video-responses-on-youtube-from-september-12-due-to-low-engagement/#!u4u6e.

14 Stephanie Lenz, "Interview, Winter 2009," *Let's Go Crazy! Teaching Media Literacy with Remix Practices*, http://www.letsgocrazy.info/interview.html.

15 Lessig, *Remix*, xix.

16 Directorate for Science, Technology and Industry, Committee for Information, Computer and Communications Policy, "Participative Web: User-Created Content," Organisation for Economic Co-operation and Development, April 12, 2007, http://www.oecd.org/dataoecd/57/14/38393115.pdf.

17 The commission wrote, "a certain amount of creative effort was put into creating the work or adapting existing works to construct a new one."

18 Ian Chuang, "Be Wary of Adding Your Own Soundtrack: Lenz v. Universal and How the Fair Use Policy Should Be Applied to User Generated Content," *Loyola of Los Angeles Entertainment Law Review* 29, no. 2 (2009), 166.

19 Mark Sableman, "Artistic Expression Today: Can Artists Use the Language of Our Culture?" *Saint Louis University Law Journal* 52, no. 1 (2007): 206.

20 Laura A. Heymann, "A Tale of (At Least) Two Authors: Focusing Copyright Law on Process Over Product," *The Journal of Corporation Law* 34 (2009): 1010.

21 Ibid.

22 Sableman, "Artistic Expression Today."

23 Charles J. Biederman and Danny Andrews, "Applying Copyright Law to User-Generated Content," Practice Tips, *Los Angeles Lawyer* 31, no. 3 (2008): 12.

24 Ibid., 14.

25 Heymann, "A Tale of (At Least) Two Authors," 1032.

26 Ibid.

27 Rebecca F. Ganz, "A Portrait of the Artist's Estate As a Copyright Problem," *Loyola of Los Angeles Law Review* 41, no. 2 (2008): 755.

28 Henry Jenkins, *Convergence Culture*, 135.

29 Baldessari says, "I just don't think imagery should be owned, including my own. If it's part of our world, it's like owning words, I mean, how could you own words? I mean, it's stuff to use." *Art21, Inc.*, Producers Wesley Miler, Nick Ravish, 2009, accessed online at Wooster Collective. John Baldessari, "On The Origins of Copy and Paste Culture," http://www.woostercollective.com/2010/02/john_baldessari_on_the_origins_of_copy_a.html.

30 Lessig, *Remix*, 10.

Bibliography

Apple Computers. "Rip, Mix, Burn Defined." *Apple*. Last modified February 18, 2012. http://support.apple.com/kb/TA44040?viewlocale=en_US (accessed August 19, 2014).

Baldessari, John. "On The Origins of Copy and Paste Culture." *Art21, Inc.* Prods. Wesley Miler, Nick Ravish, Wooster Collective, 2009. http://www.woostercollective.com/2010/02/john_baldessari_on_the_origins_of_copy_a.html (accessed February 2010).

Biederman, Charles J., and Danny Andrews. "Applying Copyright Law to User-Generated Content." Practice Tips, *Los Angeles Lawyer* 31, no. 3 (2008): 12–18.

boyd, danah. "Why Youth (Heart) Social Network Sites: The Role of Networked Publics in Teenage Social Life." In *MacArthur Foundation Series on Digital Learning—Youth, Identity, and Digital Media Volume*, edited by David Buckingham. Cambridge, MA: MIT Press. Last modified March 30, 2010. http://www.danah.org/papers/WhyYouthHeart.pdf (accessed August 19, 2014).

Chuang, Ian. "Be Wary of Adding Your Own Soundtrack: Lenz v. Universal and How the Fair Use Policy Should Be Applied to User Generated Content." *Loyola of Los Angeles Entertainment Law Review* 29, no. 2 (2009): 163–191.

Dawkins, Richard. *The Selfish Gene*. Oxford: Oxford University Press, 2006.

Directorate for Science, Technology and Industry, Committee for Information, Computer and Communications Policy. "Participative Web: User-Created Content." *Organisation for Economic Co-operation and Development*, April 12, 2007. http://www.oecd.org/dataoecd/57/14/38393115.pdf (accessed August 19, 2014).

Ganz, Rebecca F. "A Portrait of the Artist's Estate As a Copyright Problem." *Loyola of Los Angeles Law Review* 41, no. 2 (2008): 739–762.

Heymann, Laura A. "A Tale of (At Least) Two Authors: Focusing Copyright Law on Process Over Product." *The Journal of Corporation Law* 34 (2009): 1009–1032.

Jenkins, Henry. *Convergence Culture: Where Old and New Media Collide*. New York: New York University Press, 2006.

Lefevre, Greg. "Dancing Baby Cha-Chas from the Internet to the Networks." *CNN.com*, Last modified January 19, 1998. http://www.cnn.com/TECH/9801/19/dancing.baby/index.html (accessed August 19, 2014).

Lessig, Lawrence. *Remix: Making Art and Commerce Thrive in the Hybrid Economy*. New York: The Penguin Press, 2008.

Lenz, Stephanie. "Interview, Winter 2009." *Let's Go Crazy! Teaching Media Literacy with Remix Practices*. http://www.letsgocrazy.info/interview.html (accessed February 9, 2014).

——. *Let's Go Crazy #1*. YouTube. http://www.youtube.com/watch?v=N1KfJHFWlhQ (accessed October 14, 2013).

Lenz v. Universal Music Corp. 572 F. Supp. 2d 1150. N.D. Cal. 2008.

——. *LEXIS* 16899. N.D. Cal. 2010.

McSherry, Corynne. "Lenz v. Universal: This Baby May Be Dancing to Trial." *Electronic Frontier Foundation*, January 28, 2013. https://www.eff.org/deeplinks/2013/01/lenz-v-universal-baby-may-be-dancing-trial-0 (accessed August 19, 2014).

Ong, Josh. "Google is removing video responses on YouTube from September 12 due to low engagement." *The Next Web*. August 28, 2013. http://thenextweb.com/google/2013/08/28/google-is-removing-video-responses-on-youtube-from-september-12-due-to-low-engagement/#!u4u6e (accessed August 19, 2014).

Rushkoff, Douglas. *Media Virus!* New York: Ballantine Books, 1994.

Sableman, Mark. "Artistic Expression Today: Can Artists Use the Language of Our Culture?" *Saint Louis University Law Journal* 52, no. 1 (2007): 187–218.

35

A REMIX ARTIST AND ADVOCATE

Desiree D'Alessandro

Remix is everywhere. Examples are published on YouTube, televised programming, and songs topping our radio charts. When Robin Thicke's "Blurred Lines" aired, I immediately recognized the reminiscent undertones of Marvin Gaye's 1970s hit "Got to Give It Up."[1] My inner-geek rejoiced when Kickstarter fan pledges helped launch OverClocked (OC) Remix's *Balance and Ruin*, an album inspired by the music of *Final Fantasy* VI.[2] I laughed while watching the 2013 San Diego Comic-Con International panel for AMC's *The Walking Dead,* where producers and cast members joked about character romance fan-fiction in front of a cheering audience.[3] I have attended Metrocon and witnessed cosplayers create costumes that hybridize characters from different series and celebrate user-created Anime Music Videos (AMV) and self-circulated *doujinshi*.[4] All of these exemplify the inherent inclusivity of remix; a quality that I have always embraced and advocated.

In his popular four-part series *Everything is a Remix*, Kirby Ferguson defines remix as the process of combining or editing existing materials to produce something new.[5] Remix is far from being an emergent phenomenon, as appropriation and repurposing strategies are inherent to creativity itself and the very process of cultural production.[6] Remix has evolved to be prominent in a variety of forums—video excerpts, online video, music, literature, fashion, and more. It is exercised by big companies and industries with the finances to handle their own licensing and lawyer fees, as well as by individuals without extensive assets. Unfortunately, these individuals potentially face penalties under the continuous predominant control of the copyright holder. Since the conception of intellectual property, this concept has overpowered that of the common good, resulting in the authority of the copyright holder frequently trumping the creative remix endeavors and potential of the general public.

Remix and Art: My Evolving Practice

Remix has been integral to my evolving practice as an artist. As an undergraduate at the University of South Florida, I created multimedia installations and works that incorporated media from popular culture and audience engagement. In the Fine Art Graduate program at the University of California, Santa Barbara (UCSB), I learned to contextualize my practice through critical theory and was encouraged to explore my interest in the dynamic relationship between source material, the individual, and the social. My work continues to question and investigate a variety of issues through a concept-driven process while exploring a wide range of production methods. The following brief overview of my remix videos hosted on YouTube demonstrates the tone of my practice and outlines some of my history of exercising fair use.

My first "World Fair Use Day" remixes existed as promotional trailers for Public Knowledge's First Annual World's Fair Use Day (WFUD), held in Washington, DC in 2010 (Figure 35.1).[7] Both utilized film footage from *The Ten Commandments* (1956), with the intention of reinterpreting the role of Moses as the messiah of fair use, leading the people out of their copyright-restricted bondage (Figure 35.2).

My next remix, "World Water Shortage vs. Golf Course Consumption," explored water conservation and hydropolitics after I discovered that California is one of the leading golf course-congested states in the US (Figure 35.3).[8] This video aimed to spread awareness and expose how corporations maneuver to convert a critical world resource into a profitable commodity.

Soon after the release of my "World Water Shortage vs. Golf Course Consumption" remix, I faced DMCA violation complications with the UCSB Office of Judicial Affairs (further reflection on this to follow). I created a reactionary video titled "WHAT?! DMCA Violation (*Step Brothers* Remix)" that showcased Will Ferrell and John C. Reilly hysterically reacting to the Internet ban placed on my UC-networked computer (Figure 35.4).[9]

WORLD FAIR USE DAY 01.12.10

Figure 35.1 "World Fair Use Day," Desiree D'Alessandro, via YouTube (courtesy of Desiree D'Alessandro)

WORLD FAIR USE DAY 01.12.10 B

Figure 35.2 Moses as the messiah of fair use, leading the people out of their copyright-restricted bondage, Desiree D'Alessandro, via YouTube (courtesy of Desiree D'Alessandro)

World Water Shortage vs. Golf Course Consumption HD

Figure 35.3 "World Water Shortage vs. Golf Course Consumption," Desiree D'Alessandro, via YouTube (courtesy of Desiree D'Alessandro)

WHAT?! DMCA Violation (Step Brothers Remix)

Figure 35.4 "WHAT?! DMCA Violation (Step Brothers Remix)," Desiree D'Alessandro, via YouTube (courtesy of Desiree D'Alessandro)

Next, "Woman Warrior Exposed (Sigourney Weaver Remix)" featured a cinematic montage that highlighted Weaver's career of conflicting sexualized character personas, though she is presented as an icon of female power in popular culture (Figure 35.5).[10] The iconic horror narrator John Newland from *One Step Beyond* (1959) is utilized to draw public attention to the discord between Weaver's reputation and cinematic record.

Will Ferrell and John C. Reilly were revisited in "Open Video Conference (*Step Brothers* Remix)" to promote the Open Video Conference held in New York City, 2010 (Figure 35.6).[11] The film narrative was transformed to showcase a RIAA and MPAA agent crashing a meeting and getting an appropriate welcome by open video and fair use representatives.

Lastly, "Ronda Rousey—She's a Lady (*UFC* Remix)" is my most recent remix to date (Figure 35.7).[12] This work featured Tom Jones's 1971 hit "She's a Lady" and footage featuring UFC Women's Bantamweight Champion, Ronda Rousey. The intention was to highlight a humorous and simultaneously critical juxtaposition between the emergence of this strong/lethal female celebrity against past tropes regarding female delicacy, domesticity, and decency.

In addition to embracing a variety of addressed topics, my work also incorporates remix beyond the digital playback head. My recent projects mashup the disciplines of performance art and athleticism through boxing, hybridizing the two with the aim to address questions in terms of contemporary sports and gender studies. These pieces were directly inspired by the debut of women's amateur boxing in the 2012 London Olympic games and the profound impact of boxing on my relationship with my father. I remember watching televised fights throughout my childhood and growing up inspired by Sylvester Stallone's performance in the *Rocky* series. With the aim to dissolve traditional fields

Figure 35.5 "Woman Warrior Exposed (Sigourney Weaver Remix)," Desiree D'Alessandro, via YouTube (courtesy of Desiree D'Alessandro)

Figure 35.6 "Open Video Conference (Step Brothers Remix)," Desiree D'Alessandro, via YouTube (courtesy of Desiree D'Alessandro)

Ronda Rousey - She's a Lady (UFC Remix)

Figure 35.7 "Ronda Rousey—She's a Lady (UFC Remix)," Desiree D'Alessandro, via YouTube (courtesy of Desiree D'Alessandro)

and boundaries, I implemented a rigorous artist-turned-athlete training regimen as the focus of my Master's thesis efforts, and shortly after graduation and returning home, I earned the 2012 Florida Novice Middleweight Champion titles for USA Boxing and Golden Gloves. This was a way for me to explore new conceptual ground while operating within the seemingly disparate rings of organized sports and performance art.

Remix and Resistance: Recounting My DMCA Violation

As a preface to the experience I am about to share, I want to emphasize that it is not my intention to speak against the university, given the circumstances that transpired. I am truly grateful for the incredible graduate experience, knowledgeable faculty mentors, and opportunities that the school provided. The lack of institutional support or aid in defense when I faced a first-time DMCA violation is a systemic problem that is in no way exclusive only to the UCSB.

When I first delved into generating online remix videos, I began the process of acquiring source materials to reconstruct and recontextualize new narratives. In order to gather these sources, I did what any digitally savvy remixer would do: I turned to the Internet. Clips were found primarily through YouTube and scarcer sources were acquired through peer-to-peer (P2P) applications. Feeling successful in the remixes I generated, with multiple screenings on campus and the support of my department faculty and peers, I awoke one morning to discover that UCSB had banned my UC-networked Internet connection. Note that Residential Networking (ResNet) registration is mandatory for students who live on campus. The locked new homepage displayed the following alerting red typeface: "THIS DEVICE HAS BEEN BLOCKED DUE TO A DMCA VIOLATION" (Figure 35.8).

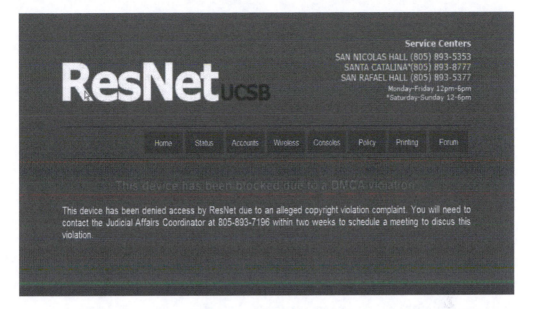

Figure 35.8 Screenshot of the locked UCSB Internet home page (courtesy of Desiree D'Alessandro)

I immediately contacted my campus DMCA Agent and Judicial Affairs Assistant Coordinator to appeal the allegation and lift the ban placed on my computer. To my surprise, the bureaucratic responses from authoritative sources led nowhere. I explained that generating online remix videos requires appropriating sources. They informed me this was not important. When I defended my efforts with numerous department faculty members ready to write letters to attest to the legitimacy of my work, they informed me that this did not matter. There was no opportunity for me to justify the use of the material in my practice or attempt to contextualize the downloaded files.

UCSB does not examine DMCA complaints on a case-by-case basis. Any acquiring and/or sharing copyrighted source materials violates their ResNet Terms of Services.[13] I noted that the UCSB Judicial Affairs Homepage claimed, "All activities, programs, and everyday interactions are enriched by our acceptance of one another, and the knowledge we gain when we learn from each other in an atmosphere of positive engagement and mutual respect."[14] I emphasized that my efforts were not being respected. Though downloading content can lead to illegal copyright infringement, there is a chance that the utilization of such sources could lead to educational purposes and commentary on culture, which is protected by the First Amendment. Through this collective university ban, the opportunity to appropriate for critical and creative expression is withheld from students who have a right to engage in fair use. The assertion of fair use plays a vital role in the broader range of activities that evidence the poor fit between today's copyright policy and the limitations on creative practices.[15]

After all my efforts to explain and defend myself were dismissed, the UCSB DMCA Agent reaffirmed that in order to protect itself and its students the university has a responsibility to uphold its policy against violators, with no exceptions.[16] The Agent said any further resistance would potentially lead to serious repercussions, hefty lawyer fees, and even charges. It was also revealed that in the prior four years (2006–10), no one at UCSB had filed a counternotice, the procedure with which one can appeal with a fair use claim. I was disappointed and frustrated by the steadfast university policy put in place for fear of liability pursuits.

I often wonder what would have happened if I had stood my ground and effectively filed a counternotice. I was forced to choose between potentially facing serious repercussions, or accepting the first-time offense penalty, which entailed residential Internet ban for 30 days. I felt defeated when I was forced to a sign a Notice of Copyright Infringement, in keeping with the policy for a first-time violation. Second and third offenses included an Internet ban for one year or indefinitely, and jeopardized housing and academic enroll-ment status at the university. It would have been useful to maintain official documents to review the specific details of this entire experience. When I requested a physical copy of my case file and the associated accusation list of infringed instances, as well as the name of the company or copyright holder who filed the DMCA notice, my request was denied.

Remix and Advocacy: Towards a Generative Future

Remix is a viable practice and should be encouraged and unrestricted in order to generate new forms of creative expression. Today, lawsuits abound and the widespread fear of "pirates" stealing intellectual property persists. We must remember that remix has been integral to the development of our culture throughout the ages. Inventor and author Stephen Key declares "Anyone who claims to have developed a totally original idea is ignorant . . . Ideas have and do influence all of us, all the time. New ideas are usually formed by mixing and matching older ideas."[17] Science and art rarely spring forth in a vacuum, and the Copyright Act in many ways limits opportunities that build upon, reinterpret, and reconceive existing works.[18] But the battle between the rights of copy-right holders and users has become further complicated through technology as Internet-fueled fears have changed the legal and cultural landscape in dramatic ways.[19]

Consider the Internet and its evolution from the 1960s Advanced Research Projects Agency Network (ARPANET) progenitor. ARPANET was designed to survive network losses and facilitate information sharing and access for researchers. Ironically, its develop-ment is closely tied with the University of California, as UCLA and UCSB played integral roles on the eve of electronic communication. Yet today, every campus in the system has a DMCA Agent on staff and bans information sharing via P2P applications in accordance with the Responsible Use Policy. What was once a progressive academic force has been unfortunately reduced to one of restriction and restraint. DMCA is ineffective because it fails to prevent unauthorized duplication of copyrighted goods and only succeeds in cur-tailing freedoms and criminalizing legitimate research.[20] Harvard political activist, Lawrence Lessig, reminds us of the poignant outcome: an architecture of control.[21]

The complexities of the Internet and our everyday integration with digital technologies have created a world enveloped in copyright consideration. Access to the Internet is criti-cal, social networking sites are widespread, and digitally formatted images, videos, and music are necessary elements of the digital communication system. Lessig explains that digital networks inevitably function by making copies, thus every single use of creative work in the digital environment triggers copyright.[22] With this consideration in mind, Lessig affirms that "If copyright regulates copies, and copying is as common as breathing, then a law that triggers federal regulation on copying is a law that regulates too far."[23]

Lessig is not alone in this sentiment. Remixers, pop culture pirates, and culture jammers are speaking out, fighting back against takedown notices, defending themselves against network surveillance, and taking advantage of the generative technology we now house in our pockets. Enthusiastic individuals including newsmakers, world changers, visionaries, and innovators understand that more respect to the creators must be acknowledged to neutralize the imbalance of power in the current system where the hierarchy of power recognizes the rights of publishers first, authors second, and the public a distant third.[24] This imbalance between individuals and corporations contradicts copyright's constitutional mandate where the monopoly power of copyright was designed first and foremost to benefit society by stimulating new creative works as opposed to providing special private benefits to individuals or corporations.[25] In response, several forward-thinking organizations and universities have already shown how powerful open access to collections, materials, and research can be.[26] Access to digital sources is vital for opportunities of expression and the proliferation of today's user-generated culture, and users should be able to access this content in order to critique the society in which we live.

In closing, I realize that the works that I have generated and events that I have experienced will all help shape and inform my practice in the future. I am grateful for these experiences that have established my emergent career and enabled me to speak about remix at numerous conferences and festivals, in academic journals, and publications in dialog with esteemed remixers. We are in a critical moment in history with copyright reformation inevitably on the horizon. Fueled by our awareness and ignited by the recognition of remixers as viable contributors to our cultural dialog, we must unite in the name of progress to defend our right to articulate our voices in the twenty-first century. I look forward to continuing to explore remix in my practice and participating in part of a much larger collective.

Notes

1 Thicke and song co-writers are involved in an unresolved lawsuit with the Gaye estate. The Gaye estate and publishing company have reached a confidential settlement.

2 The OverClocked Remix, "Final Fantasy VI: Balance and Ruin," http://ff6.ocremix.org. Initial disputes between Square-Enix and album producers were resolved.

3 AMC Network, "Comic-Con Panel 2013: *The Walking Dead*," http://www.amctv.com/the-walking-dead/videos/comic-con-panel-2013-the-walking-dead.

4 Metrocon is Florida's largest anime convention. For more information, see http://metroconventions.com.

5 Kirby Ferguson, "Everything is a Remix Part 1: The Song Remains the Same," Vimeo video, 7:18, 2011, http://everythingisaremix.info/watch-the-series.

6 The Remix Cinema, "What is Remix?" http://archive.today/1NYYF.

7 Desiree D'Alessandro, "World Fair Use Day I," YouTube video, 0:38, http://youtu.be/qWg5U3nKY2Q; and "World Fair Use Day II," YouTube video, 0:45, http://youtu.be/l0W0pA_ZIn8. Both December 26, 2009 and accessed March 15, 2014.

8 Desiree D'Alessandro, "World Water Shortage vs. Golf Course Consumption," YouTube video, 3:12, November 24, 2009, http://youtu.be/UXWSWatszBQ (accessed March 15, 2014).

9 Desiree D'Alessandro, "WHAT?! DMCA Violation (*Step Brothers* Remix)," YouTube video, 0:30, January 3, 2010, http://youtu.be/aFx4yTUFtWY (accessed March 15, 2014).

10 Desiree D'Alessandro, "Woman Warrior Exposed (Sigourney Weaver Remix)," YouTube video, 1:23, August, 30, 2010, http://youtu.be/C_VPriU6te0 (accessed March 15, 2014).

11 Desiree D'Alessandro, "Open Video Conference (*Step Brothers* Remix)," YouTube video, 1:16, October 4, 2010, http://youtu.be/uFRNOEHm2Y8 (accessed March 15, 2014).

12 Desiree D'Alessandro, "Ronda Rousey—She's a Lady (UFC Remix)," YouTube video, 3:21, January 19, 2014, http://youtu.be/svtLnjXwDUc (accessed March 15, 2014).

13 University of California, Santa Barbara, "ResNet: DMCA Policy," Housing and Residential Services, http://www.housing.ucsb.edu/resnet/dmca-policy.

14 University of California, Santa Barbara, "Judicial Affairs: Home," Housing and Residential Services, http://www.housing.ucsb.edu/judicial-affairs.

15 Patricia Aufderheide and Peter Jaszi, *Reclaiming Fair Use: How to Put Balance Back in Copyright* (Chicago, IL: University of Chicago Press, 2011), 15.

16 University of California, Santa Barbara, "ResNet: DMCA Policy."

17 Stephen Key, "What Robin Thicke's 'Blurred Lines' Can Teach You About Stealing Ideas," *Entrepreneur*, August 20, 2013, http://www.entrepreneur.com/article/227986.

18 Ashley Packard, *Digital Law* (Malden, MA: Wiley-Blackwell, 2013), 184.

19 Kembrew McLeod, *Freedom of Expression: Resistance and Repression in the Age of Intellectual Property* (Minneapolis, MN: University of Minnesota Press, 2007), 4.

20 Ibid.

21 Lawrence Lessig, *The Future of Ideas: The Fate of the Commons in a Connected World* (New York, NY: Vintage, 2002), 268.

22 Lawrence Lessig, *Code 2.0: Version 2.0* (New York, NY: SoHo Books, 2010), 268.

23 Lawrence Lessig, *Remix: Making Art and Commerce Thrive in the Hybrid Economy* (New York, NY: Penguin, 2008), 269.

24 Siva Vaidhyanathan, *Copyrights and Copywrongs: The Rise of Intellectual Property and How it Threatens Creativity* (New York, NY: New York University Press, 2003), 11.

25 McLeod, *Freedom of Expression*, 9.

26 James Cuno, "Open Content, An Idea Whose Time Has Come," The Getty: Iris, http://blogs.getty.edu/iris/open-content-an-idea-whose-time-has-come. The Getty, Walters Art Museum, the National Gallery of Art, Yale University, the Los Angeles County Museum of Art, and Harvard University now support digital access.

Bibliography

AMC Network. "Comic-Con Panel 2013: *The Walking Dead*." http://www.amctv.com/the-walking-dead/videos/comic-con-panel-2013-the-walking-dead (accessed March 15, 2014).

Aufderheide, Patricia and Peter Jaszi. *Reclaiming Fair Use: How to Put Balance Back in Copyright*. Chicago, IL: University of Chicago Press, 2011.

Cuno, James. "Open Content, An Idea Whose Time Has Come." *The Getty: Iris*. http://blogs.getty.edu/iris/open-content-an-idea-whose-time-has-come (accessed September 30, 2013).

Ferguson, Kirby. "Everything is a Remix Part 1: The Song Remains the Same." Vimeo video, 7:18. 2011. http://everythingisaremix.info/watch-the-series (accessed March 15, 2014).

Ferguson, Russell. *Out There: Marginalization and Contemporary Cultures*. Cambridge, MA: MIT Press, 1990.

Key, Stephen. "What Robin Thicke's 'Blurred Lines' Can Teach You About Stealing Ideas." *Entrepreneur*. August 20, 2013. http://www.entrepreneur.com/article/227986 (accessed March 15, 2014).

Lessig, Lawrence. *The Future of Ideas: The Fate of the Commons in a Connected World*. New York, NY: Vintage, 2002.

——. *Remix: Making Art and Commerce Thrive in the Hybrid Economy*. New York, NY: Penguin, 2008.

——. *Code 2.0: Version 2.0*. New York, NY: SoHo Books, 2010.

McLeod, Kembrew. *Freedom of Expression: Resistance and Repression in the Age of Intellectual Property*. Minneapolis, MN: University of Minnesota Press, 2007.

OverClocked Remix. "Final Fantasy VI: *Balance and Ruin*," http://ff6.ocremix.org (accessed March 15, 2014).

Packard, Ashley. *Digital Law*. Malden, MA: Wiley-Blackwell, 2013.

The Remix Cinema, "What is Remix?" http://archive.today/1NYYF (accessed August 19, 2014).

University of California, Santa Barbara. "Judicial Affairs: Home." Housing and Residential Services. http://www.housing.ucsb.edu/judicial-affairs (accessed March 15, 2014).

——. "ResNet: DMCA Policy." Housing and Residential Services. http://www.housing.ucsb.edu/resnet/dmca-policy (accessed March 15, 2014).

Vaidhyanathan, Siva. *Copyrights and Copywrongs: The Rise of Intellectual Property and How it Threatens Creativity*. New York, NY: New York University Press, 2003.

36
OCCUPY/BAND AID MASHUP

"Do They Know It's Christmas?"

Owen Gallagher

In this chapter, I will discuss *Occupy/Band Aid Mashup*, a work I produced as part of a series of three critical remix videos in 2011. I will describe the context that led to the concept and creation of this piece, as well as my political and aesthetic intentions and the reasons informing my choice of subject matter. Finally, I will contextualize this work within the field of remix and video art and relate it to my own remix practice over the past decade, as well as my ongoing research in visual culture, focusing on critical remix.

Background and Context

Occupy/Band Aid Mashup was produced and published just before Christmas 2011, three months after the Occupy Wall Street protests began in New York and a year after the Arab Spring uprisings began in Tunisia. I was living in Bahrain (a tiny Middle Eastern island kingdom nestled between Saudi Arabia and Iran), spending Christmas away from family and friends in Ireland for the first time. I had witnessed firsthand the response of Middle Eastern authorities to protesters, including the destruction of a symbolic protest monument, Bahrain's "Pearl Roundabout" in March 2011.[1] By December, a number of related events had occurred within a short time of each other. Arab Spring protests were in full bloom in Syria, Egypt, and Yemen; the Libyan people were celebrating their freedom for the first time in 42 years, following the death of Muammar al-Qadaffi two months earlier;[2] and Occupy Wall Street protesters had just attempted a reoccupation to mark their three-month anniversary, but failed, due to New York city police intervention.[3]

Being away from home, I felt compelled to enter the global conversation with a remix video using news and documentary footage of the Arab Spring and Occupy movements. One of the aims of this remix was to try to bring together a set of visually incongruous material to highlight the similarities and connections between various crises occurring in societies around the world. In the UK, a campaign was in full swing to push the Military Wives Choir music single "Wherever You Are" to the Christmas Number 1 spot, to highlight the public profile of British soldiers on active duty in the Afghanistan War, and to raise the morale of the wives and families they left behind.[4] This campaign, combined with my nostalgia for Band Aid's past Number 1 single, "Do They Know It's Christmas?" inspired me to create a remix in the form of a music video. Coincidentally, the latest version of Band Aid's song had just been recorded and released by the cast of the popular musical TV series, *Glee*.[5]

Band Aid and Live Aid

The original Band Aid single was released in the UK in 1984, followed by new versions featuring different recording artists in 1989, 2004, and 2011.[6] The idea of Band Aid was to raise money for Africa—specifically, Ethiopia—where millions of people were dying of starvation at the time.[7] It preceded the infamous UK and USA Live Aid concerts in 1985 and was the brainchild of Bob Geldof, front man of the Dublin band, The Boomtown Rats, and Midge Ure, Scottish front man of Ultravox. In the US, inspired by the success of the Band Aid charity single, Michael Jackson, Lionel Richie, and Quincy Jones formed a similar supergroup of American musical stars called USA for Africa and released their own charity single, "We Are the World" in 1985, which sold over 20 million copies.[8]

In 1986, Chumbawamba, a UK band, released their album, *Pictures of Starving Children Sell Records*, offering an anticapitalist critique of both Band Aid and Live Aid, suggesting that they were cosmetic spectacles that served to draw attention away from the real political and economic causes of world hunger.[9] The idea that world hunger could be eradicated by purchasing a predictable, self-congratulatory pop song seemed to arouse the suspicions of some who were familiar with the inner workings of the music business. Today, hunger and malnutrition are still significant problems in Africa, although not on the same scale as in the 1980s. In comparison to the rest of the world, Ethiopia still has some of the worst food insecurity, starvation, hunger, malnutrition, and infant mortality problems on the planet.[10] There have been a number of scathing reports in relation to the spending of the Band Aid and Live Aid finances, such as claims that some of the money was used to purchase weapons for militia forces.[11] Despite this, the charities have clearly done some good for the people of Ethiopia, but arguably Band Aid and USA for Africa have done a lot more for the careers, wealth, and fame of those artists whose names were associated with the records and concerts. In addition, the music videos for the various versions of "Do They Know It's Christmas?" which depict the joy and cama-raderie of familiar pop and rock icons singing in harmony, offer a striking visual coun-terpoint to the scenes of violent protest in the Middle East and peaceful occupation in the USA with which they are juxtaposed in the remix video.

Political and Aesthetic Intentions

In producing this remix,[12] I was responding to issues of power and resistance in developing and developed countries. Many developing countries had experienced protests against dictatorial regimes in the name of democracy, while in the USA and Europe protests against the corruption and transformation of liberal democracy into corporatism were on the increase. The original question that was asked by Geldof and Ure when they penned the lyrics, "Do they know it's Christmas time?" referred to starving children in Ethiopia. Thirty years later, in my remix, these lyrics are redirected towards revolution-aries, rebels, and freedom fighters struggling under dictatorial Middle Eastern regimes. This semiotic transferal of meaning occurs as a result of replacing imagery of starving

Figure 36.1 Occupy/Band Aid Mashup, Owen Gallagher, 2011, via YouTube (courtesy of Owen Gallagher)

African children from the original videos, with footage of clashes between protesters and military forces, begging the question, what does Christmas mean for these people? What does it mean for Occupy protesters who spent Christmas huddled on city streets across America? Although the intention of the remix is to highlight Arab Spring protests across many Middle Eastern countries, the majority of footage used focuses on Libya, echoing the connection with Africa evident in the original song.

The remix opens with a four-way split screen depicting images of Occupy sites, introducing the anticapitalist sentiments of US protesters involved in the movement (Figure 36.1). Within a few seconds, as the vocals begin, the viewer sees four different versions of "Do They Know It's Christmas?"—the original 1984 version, the subsequent 1989 and 2004 versions and finally the version recorded for the TV series *Glee* in 2011. From a musical perspective, the songs were recorded in different keys at different tempos, so they do not synchronize. However, the *Glee* version was recorded at a harmonic interval of the original key used in 1984 (C major), meaning that the *Glee* vocal line became a relative harmony (F major) of the original, producing a haunting, atmospheric, evocative effect, prior to the moment when Phil Collins's heavy drum beat kicks in after the first verse. As the song progresses, at various points, different versions of the audio tracks fade in and out, to match the visuals, and to produce the most aurally pleasing harmonies possible within the limitations of the available material. For example, U2 front man, Bono sings the same line "Tonight, thank God it's them instead of you" differently in the 1984 and 2004 versions, both of which are depicted on screen simultaneously, creating a bizarre audiovisual mashup of time and space over two decades. In one version, the singer is seen as a young man early in his musical career and in the other, a middle-aged rock veteran.

Each of the source material music videos depicts crowds of musicians and singers standing side-by-side in recording studios performing the song. This relatively superficial visual solidarity is contrasted with images of protesters standing side-by-side as they occupy public spaces or defend themselves against military attacks. For the first two minutes, three out of the four screens depict pop stars, while the fourth shows Occupy or Arab Spring protesters. The screens go through a gradual transformation, whereby pop stars and protesters compete for space, until two of the four screens show protesters and the remainder, pop stars; then three and eventually all four screens are taken over by protesters, as the song comes to an aural climax during the bridge. During the last section of the remix, images depict increasingly jubilant crowds and successful protests, ending with a placard reading "Nice day for a revolution."

Influences

Musically, this work is influenced by the mashup genre, as exemplified by the work of one of my favorite artists, DJ Le Clown,[13] who juxtaposes popular songs from different musical genres, recombining them in creative ways with often unusual and memorable results. In the case of *Occupy/Band Aid Mashup*, the techniques of production are similar, but the difference is that the same song is being mashed together with itself, albeit using different versions recorded by various artists over a period of almost 30 years. Visually, this work is inspired by the work of Nam June Paik, particularly his pieces that explore the potential of multiple screens within a larger frame, such as *Electronic Superhighway*,[14] one of his many "video wall" projects (Figure 36.2). It is also influenced by the video art work of Emergency Broadcast Network (EBN), which often employs the technique of "picture-in-picture," as exemplified in their piece *Electronic Behavior Control System*.[15] More recently, these techniques have been advanced somewhat by the use of software such as Adobe After Effects, and the work of Joe Sabia makes particularly good use of technology to bring this technique to the next level, as demonstrated in *Prime Time Terror: How TV Dramas Depict the War On Terror*.[16] Kutiman's remixing of YouTube videos in his Thru-You project was also a strong influence on this work.[17] Lev Manovich has written extensively about this phenomenon, the technique of viewing multiple images in one frame, which he has termed "spatial montage," whereby elements are no longer necessarily replaced on the screen over time—instead, they coexist in the same space for longer periods.[18]

As part of my research, which involves the analysis of critical remix videos (CRVs) from semiotic, rhetorical, and ideological perspectives, I frequently use Manovich's notion of spatial collage to enable the presentation of multiple sections of a particular remix on screen simultaneously. For example, when analyzing Vote Different,[19] a 60-second remix video based on Apple's famous 1984 commercial, by dividing the video into individual shots, then looping and repositioning these shots into a single frame using Adobe After Effects, it becomes possible to view the entire remix video at once. This enables the potential for multiple research opportunities, such as the ability to make instant visual connections between shots that may otherwise go unnoticed. This technique was expanded in the creation of the Critical Remix Video Wall,[20] an ongoing media art project, which presents multiple categories of CRVs on screen at once, enabling each one to be selected and viewed, down to the level of the individual shot (Figure 36.3). These shots can then be recombined in new sequences, or combined with shots from other CRVs to produce entirely new compositions using remixed samples as raw material.

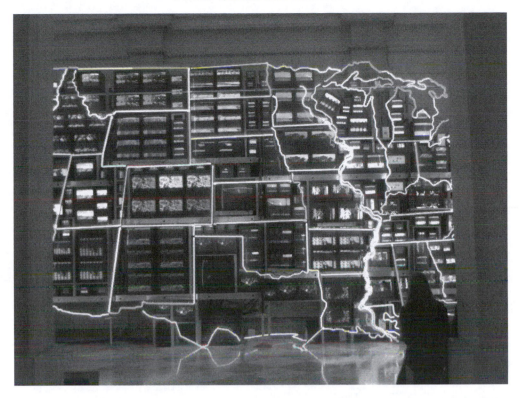

Figure 36.2 Electronic Superhighway, Nam June Paik, 1995 (photo courtesy of user Libjbr on Wikimedia Commons)

Remix Practice

Occupy/Band Aid Mashup was produced as part of a series of three remixes, all produced and published in December 2011 as part of my ongoing research, each of which explored a different political issue. The other two remixes were *State of the Nation: Enda Kenny Recut*,[21] and *Man of the Year 2012: How Jon Stewart Became President*.[22] The first of these took the form of a speech delivered by the Taoiseach (Prime Minister) of Ireland, Enda Kenny, in which the dialog was reedited to reflect a more truthful, if somewhat bizarre version of contemporary Ireland than had originally been broadcast. The second remix portrays a fictional narrative in which Obama's 2012 reelection campaign is taken over by comedians, Jon Stewart and Stephen Colbert, who compete against him for the office of president, including a national televised debate, which ultimately leads to Stewart's illegitimate election. All three remix videos are connected by their focus on serious global political issues mixed with a playful sense of irreverence, and their reuse and transformation of previously published material to produce new works with different meanings. Each of these works is a type of remix video, however they adopt very different forms—a music mashup, a video recut, and a transformative narrative remix—the distinguishing feature being their reuse of sampled material.

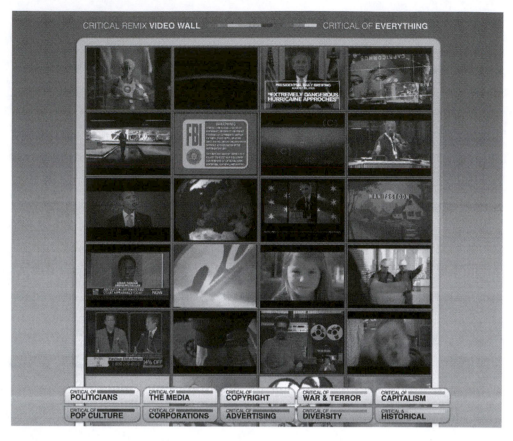

Figure 36.3 Critical Remix Video Wall, Owen Gallagher, 2014–, via criticalremix.com
(courtesy of Owen Gallagher)

Since being uploaded to YouTube and Vimeo, *Occupy/Band Aid Mashup* has been reposted to a number of blogs and webpages, including the largest Live Aid group on Facebook, and I have received a number of comments and emails in support of the work. Although this piece has not gone viral, with just over 8,000 views on YouTube,[23] it has become part of a meme cluster featuring remixes, covers and variations of the song "Do They Know It's Christmas?" and frequently appears in related content lists and targeted search results. In July 2013, it was displayed in the White Cube exhibition as part of the Repeat, Remix, Remediate summer school, which took place in Hamburg, Germany.[24] Surprisingly, this remix video has not received any takedown notices from copyright holders, even though the song and video content are still clearly recognizable, albeit significantly modified and remixed. One of my most recent remix videos, *Miley/O'Connor Mashup: Nothing Compares to a Wrecking Ball*,[25] has been blocked in some countries as a result of a copyright claim made by Sony Music Entertainment. This has been a problem for me and many other remixers in the past, however it is possible to successfully dispute such a claim by filing a counternotification, if the work in question has a strong case for fair use. I have personally overturned a number of takedown notices in this way during the past seven years and had my remix videos reinstated in each case.[26]

Conclusion

My hope for *Occupy/Band Aid Mashup* is that it might become even a fraction as enduring as the song that inspired it. Thus far, the potential seems to exist. Every Christmas since it was uploaded, I have received fresh comments and emails from people who have just discovered the remix for the first time. The specific protests depicted in the video will surely age with time, however the broader issues to which they draw attention are unlikely to be resolved in the near future. As such, my hope is that this remix video will help to raise awareness of these issues, encouraging people to ask questions and perhaps contribute in some small way to ongoing global struggles against injustice.

Notes

1 Ethan Bronner, "Bahrain Tears Down Monument as Protesters Seethe," *The New York Times*, March 18, 2011, http://www.nytimes.com/2011/03/19/world/middleeast/19bahrain.html?_r=0.

2 *The New York Times*, "Arab World Uprisings: A Country-by-Country Look," *The New York Times*, last updated December 12, 2011, http://www.nytimes.com/interactive/world/middleeast/middle-east-hub.html.

3 Dominique Debucquoy Dodley and Jesse Solomon, "50 Arrested in Occupy Wall Street Demonstration," *CNN*, December 18, 2011, http://edition.cnn.com/2011/12/17/us/new-york-occupy-arrests/.

4 *BBC News*, "Military Wives Choir Captures Christmas Number One," *BBC*, December 25, 2011, http://www.bbc.com/news/entertainment-arts-16285101.

5 *The Telegraph*, "Glee to cover Band Aid's Do They Know It's Christmas," *The Telegraph*, December 12, 2011, http://www.telegraph.co.uk/culture/music/music-news/8950294/Glee-to-cover-Band-Aids-Do-They-Know-Its-Christmas.html.

6 Kyle Anderson, "Looking Back at Live Aid: 25 Years Later," *MTV.com*, July 12, 2010, http://www.mtv.com/news/articles/1643506/looking-back-at-live-aid-25-years-later.jhtml.

7 Kate Milner, "Flashback 1984: Portrait of a Famine," *BBC News*, April 6, 2000, http://news.bbc.co.uk/2/hi/africa/703958.stm.

8 David Breskin, *We are the World: The Story Behind the Song* (Hollywood, CA: Image Entertainment, 2004).

9 Fraser McAlpine, "A Few Thoughts About Chumbawamba," *BBC America*, July 10, 2012, http://www.bbcamerica.com/anglophenia/2012/07/a-few-thoughts-about-chumbawamba/.

10 Roger Thurow, "Ethiopia's Lasting Legacy of Famine," *The Telegraph*, May 27, 2013, http://www.telegraph.co.uk/news/worldnews/africaandindianocean/ethiopia/10083186/Ethiopias-lasting-legacy-of-famine.html.

11 Emma Alberici, "Live Aid Funded Ethiopian Rebels," *ABC News*, November 17, 2010, http://www.abc.net.au/news/2010-03-04/live-aid-funded-ethiopian-rebels/349434.

12 Owen Gallagher, *Occupy/Band Aid Mashup*, YouTube.com, December 23, 2011, YouTube video, http://www.youtube.com/watch?v=-ImjjCSpgh0.

13 Philippe Maujard, "DJ Le Clown Profile Page," *SoundCloud.com*, https://soundcloud.com/dj-le-clown.

14 Nam June Paik, "Electronic Superhighway," American Art Museum, 1995–96, http://commons.wikimedia.org/wiki/File:Electronic_Superhighway_by_Nam_June_Paik.jpg (accessed May 16, 2014).

15 Emergency Broadcast Network, "Electronic Behavior Control System," YouTube.com, August 20, 2012 (1995), YouTube video, http://www.youtube.com/watch?v=oQZsKWV4mDo.

16 USC Annenberg, *Primetime Terror: How TV Dramas Depict the War on Terror*, YouTube.com, September 6, 2011, YouTube video, http://www.youtube.com/watch?v=8XIUcJ9ymrs.

17 Kutiman, "Thru-You—01—Mother of All Funk Chords," YouTube.com, March 7, 2009, YouTube video, http://www.youtube.com/watch?v=tprMEs-zfQA.

18 Lev Manovich, "The Archaeology of Windows and Spatial Montage," *Manovich.net*, September 1, 2002, formerly available at: http://www.manovich.net/DOCS/windows_montage.doc.

19 Philip DeVelis, *Vote Different*, YouTube.com, March 5, 2007, YouTube video, http://www.youtube.com/watch?v=6h3G-lMZxjo.

20 Owen Gallagher, "Critical Remix Video Wall," *criticalremix.com*, 2014 and ongoing, http://criticalremix.com/videowall.

21 Owen Gallagher, *State of the Nation—Enda Kenny Recut*, YouTube.com, December 24, 2011, YouTube video, http://www.youtube.com/watch?v=W_SJGSDvNVY.

22 Owen Gallagher, *Man of the Year 2012: How Jon Stewart Became President*, YouTube.com, December 19, 2011, YouTube video, http://www.youtube.com/watch?v=kOuu1b81ogU.

23 Gallagher, *Occupy/Band Aid Mashup*.

24 University of Hamburg, "Repeat, Remix Remediate Summer School," Research Center of Media and Communication, July 29–August 2, 2013, http://repeat-remix-remediate.com/ (accessed May 16, 2014).

25 Owen Gallagher, *Miley/O'Connor Mashup—Nothing Compares to a Wrecking Ball*, YouTube.com, October 3, 2013, YouTube video, http://www.youtube.com/watch?v=44VjE5WcgjA.

26 I have received and successfully responded to takedown notices from BBC Worldwide, Paramount Pictures and 20th Century Fox for my remix videos, "Bertie Ahern on Dragons' Den," "Napoleon Dynamite PSA," and "Shrek Recut," among others.

Bibliography

Alberici, Emma. "Live Aid Funded Ethiopian Rebels." *ABC News*, November 17, 2010. http://www.abc.net.au/news/2010-03-04/live-aid-funded-ethiopian-rebels/349434 (accessed May 16, 2014).

Anderson, Kyle. "Looking Back at Live Aid: 25 Years Later." *MTV.com*, July 12, 2010. http://www.mtv.com/news/articles/1643506/looking-back-at-live-aid-25-years-later.jhtml (accessed May 16, 2014).

BBC News. "Military Wives Choir Captures Christmas Number One." *BBC*, December 25, 2011. http://www.bbc.com/news/entertainment-arts-16285101 (accessed May 16, 2014).

Breskin, David. *We are the World: The Story Behind the Song*. Hollywood, CA: Image Entertainment, 2004.

Bronner, Ethan. "Bahrain Tears Down Monument as Protesters Seethe." *The New York Times*, March 18, 2011. http://www.nytimes.com/2011/03/19/world/middleeast/19bahrain.html?_r=0 (accessed May 16, 2014).

DeVelis, Philip. *Vote Different*. YouTube.com, March 5, 2007. YouTube video. http://www.youtube.com/watch?v=6h3G-lMZxjo (accessed May 16, 2014).

Dodley, Dominique Debucquoy, and Jesse Solomon. "50 Arrested in Occupy Wall Street Demonstration." *CNN*, December 18, 2011. http://edition.cnn.com/2011/12/17/us/new-york-occupy-arrests/ (accessed May 16, 2014).

Emergency Broadcast Network. *Electronic Behavior Control System*. YouTube.com, August 20. 2012 (1995). YouTube video. http://www.youtube.com/watch?v=oQZsKWV4mDo (accessed May 16, 2014).

Gallagher, Owen. *Man of the Year 2012: How Jon Stewart Became President*. YouTube.com, December 19, 2011. YouTube video. http://www.youtube.com/watch?v=kOuu1b81ogU (accessed May 16, 2014).

——. *Occupy/Band Aid Mashup*, YouTube.com, December 23, 2011. YouTube video. http://www.youtube.com/watch?v=-ImjjCSpgh0 (accessed May 16, 2014).

——. *State of the Nation—Enda Kenny Recut*. YouTube.com, December 24, 2011. YouTube video. http://www.youtube.com/watch?v=W_SJGSDvNVY (accessed May 16, 2014).

——. *Miley/O'Connor Mashup—Nothing Compares to a Wrecking Ball*. YouTube.com, October 3, 2013. YouTube video. http://www.youtube.com/watch?v=44VjE5WcgjA (accessed May 16, 2014).

——. "Critical Remix Video Wall." *criticalremix.com*, 2014 and ongoing. http://criticalremix.com/videowall (accessed May 16, 2014).

Kutiman. *Thru-You—01—Mother of All Funk Chords*. YouTube.com, March 7, 2009. http://www.youtube.com/watch?v=tprMEs-zfQA (accessed May 16, 2014).

Manovich, Lev. "The Archaeology of Windows and Spatial Montage." *Manovich.net*, 2002. formerly available at: http://www.manovich.net/DOCS/windows_montage.doc (accessed March 2014).

Maujard, Philippe "DJ Le Clown Profile Page," *SoundCloud.com*, https://soundcloud.com/dj-le-clown (accessed May 16, 2014).

McAlpine, Fraser. "A Few Thoughts About Chumbawamba." *BBC America*, July 10, 2012. http://www.bbcamerica.com/anglophenia/2012/07/a-few-thoughts-about-chumbawamba/ (accessed May 16, 2014).

Milner, Kate. "Flashback 1984: Portrait of a Famine," *BBC News*, April 6, 2000. http://news.bbc.co.uk/2/hi/africa/703958.stm (accessed May 16, 2014).

Paik, Nam June. "Internet Dream." *ZKM*, Centre for Art and Media, 1994. http://www02.zkm.de/digitalartconservation/index.php/en/exhibitions/zkm-exhibition/nnnnnnam-june-paik.html (accessed May 16, 2014).

The New York Times. "Arab World Uprisings: A Country-by-Country Look." *The New York Times*, last updated December 12, 2011. http://www.nytimes.com/interactive/world/middleeast/middle-east-hub.html (accessed May 16, 2014).

The Telegraph. "Glee to cover Band Aid's Do They Know It's Christmas." *The Telegraph*, December 12, 2011. http://www.telegraph.co.uk/culture/music/music-news/8950294/Glee-to-cover-Band-Aids-Do-They-Know-Its-Christmas.html (accessed May 16, 2014).

Thurow, Roger. "Ethiopia's Lasting Legacy of Famine." *The Telegraph*, May 27, 2013. http://www.telegraph.co.uk/news/worldnews/africaandindianocean/ethiopia/10083186/Ethiopias-lasting-legacy-of-famine.html (accessed May 16 2014).

USC Annenberg. *Primetime Terror: How TV Dramas Depict the War on Terror*. YouTube.com, September 6, 2011. YouTube video. http://www.youtube.com/watch?v=8XIUcJ9ymrs (accessed May 16, 2014).

37

REMIXING THE REMIX

Elisa Kreisinger

I came to video remixing at the height of the "Web 2.0" era, and this surge of online participation was most noticeable to me in feminist and queer online communities where users were quick to publish smart and snarky responses to popular culture. It was 2008, before the movie *Bridesmaids* and the award-winning HBO series *GIRLS*, and as indicated by the popularity of these shows, young women were tired of compromising their gender politics to be entertained. While there is a long academic tradition supporting the criticism of popular culture, women with only an Intro to Gender Studies seminar under their belts were suddenly negotiating the fine line between fan and critic publicly, in real time through GIFs, blogs and vlogs. These viewers were no longer passive victims of the media, they were creators of it, able to talk back and generate content that commented on the misrepresentation or marginalization of their communities. Platforms like Tumblr and Jezebel were one year old and they were hungry for content. It was the perfect climate for feminist video remixing: there was an already-engaged audience that pop culture seemed to repeatedly misrepresent, and multiple platforms to disseminate work. But, of course, it was not so simple.

Hosting platforms such as YouTube were struggling to curb piracy and keep copyright holders happy. Unfortunately, remixers got caught in the middle. In June 2007, YouTube began trial-testing their automated detection system, known as Content ID[1], to help the entertainment industry identify uploaded videos that infringed their copyright. By 2011, Content ID was wrongfully flagging remix content for potential copyright violations as it still cannot identify a fair use of copyright content over an infringing one. Users found the dispute process to be an intimidating and arduous process, often taking weeks to resolve, highlighting how private agreements between copyright holders and hosting platforms undermine the safeguards for fair use built into the law and leave remixers confused about their rights, with no choice but to abide by the interests of the copyright holder.

But before I address the conflicts embedded in remix practice, I want to define it and highlight its position as an artistic practice heavily influenced by a postmodern framework.

Video Remix and a Postmodern Framework

Video remix is a DIY form of grassroots media production whereby creators appropriate mass media texts, reediting them to comment, critique, satirize, or pay homage to the source material and produce a newly transformed piece of media intended for public viewing on video-sharing sites such as YouTube. Because remix requires the physical deconstruction of mainstream images of identity similar to the deconstruction of identities associated with a postmodern framework, it easily serves as an effective tool for questioning socially constructed images of gender and, I would like to argue, is itself a queer act.

In "Bodily Inscriptions, Performative Subversions,"[2] Judith Butler argues that stationary racial, gendered, and sexual identities are harmful, used to justify power over another and foster a binary. Deconstructing these identities, Butler argues, reveals the arbitrary characteristics and rigid categorization on which oppression is based, thus destabilizing systems of oppression. Building off of this theory, the physical deconstruction and recontextualization of popular culture's depictions of gender, race, and sexuality that remix requires, allows creators to produce multiple and fluid concepts of identity, disrupting the binaries on which oppression and hierarchy are based.

Additionally, the remix process itself can be considered a queer act. If queer is defined as any act that challenges, questions, or provokes the normal, the acceptable, and the dominant, then remix's required rejection of the dominant and acceptable notions of copyright challenges the author/reader and owner/user binaries on which it is based.

Putting Theory into Practice

My goal in 2008 was to create a digital product heavily influenced by Butler's writings that would capture the existing level of critical discourse around women in the media already happening on blogs and Tumblr in video form. I hoped that by physically deconstructing female characters in mainstream TV shows and reediting them into subversive, feminist ones, I could rearticulate and recontextualize normative identities in a recognizable narrative structure so that both the remix form and the pop-culture content mirrored each other's purpose: to redefine the way we are represented.

To start, I sought out the most highly gendered source material targeted at women. The source material had to have characters immediately identifiable by women, even if they had no knowledge of the storyline. The right show had to carry enough weight in our collective cultural consciousness to be recognizable by nonfans so that viewers could identify that it was taken out of context and was now a new, transformed narrative. That show was *Sex and the City* (*SATC*); it was a groundbreaking and innovative female-driven pop-culture text that was as subversive as it was problematic. *SATC* championed staying single under societal pressure, it was sexually frank and the story was told from a woman's point of view, seemingly in her own voice. But it appropriated the language of radical feminism only to retell old patriarchal fairy tales.

> Carrie:
> No, it's not about the money. I don't care about the money.
> I'm talking about a woman's right to shoes.
> Why did she have to shame me?
> Miranda:
> Because she's trapped in a hell of her own making.
> No wait, that's me. Oh.[3]

Why were these women, in all their sexual candor and frankness, abandoning their postfeminist thinking? Or, why was it so easy to use the language of radical feminism to tell the story but so hard to give up on those patriarchal fantasies within the narrative?

481

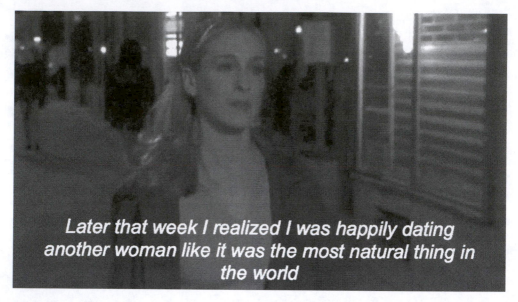

Figure 37.1 The Queer Carrie Project, Elisa Kreisinger, 2008 (courtesy of Elisa Kreisinger)

These contradictions made for infinite reworkings of storylines. From a production standpoint, there were enough cutaways, B-roll and uninterrupted dialog-driven scenes per season of footage to reedit into a three-part narrative narrated by the main character, which I titled *The Queer Carrie Project* (Figure 37.1). I built a script database from fan-made transcripts found online and took apart each season of the show, assembling a new narrative that follows Carrie Bradshaw out of the closet, confronting those patriarchal fantasies head on, ultimately rejecting the candy-coated ending of the original and opting for a more tragic turn of events.

Because popular culture is such a reflection of our own societal norms, when we fail to see ourselves and our communities represented our sense of identity disintegrates within that community. It is not my intention to queer every cast of women who have strong friendships on TV. However, when a community is culturally "poor" in terms of representation, both queer and feminist, one must reuse what they have access to, whether it be for subtext, entertainment, or critique.

One of the problems with *The Queer Carrie Project* was that the show was ten years old. While still discussed across blogs thanks to the movie *Sex and the City* released in 2008 (followed by *Sex and the City 2* in 2010 and the TV series *The Carrie Diaries* in 2013), the source footage was standard definition, the aspect ratio was 4×3 and the fashion was passé. The dated source material significantly limited viewership. If my goal was to rearticulate and recontextualize normative identities in a recognizable narrative form, I had to find identities that were more current, with source material airing weekly and discussed, reviewed, and recapped in public discursive spaces to attract maximum viewership and conversation.

In 2010, there had been four seasons of the hour-long AMC series *Mad Men* when lengthy license fee talks between AMC and Lionsgate pushed the fifth season's air date to 2012. The situation provided enough footage and time for a new remix series to be made in anticipation of the long-awaited premiere.

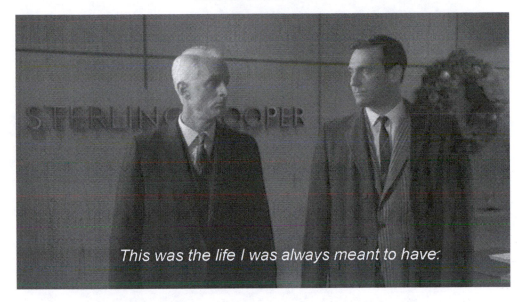

This was the life I was always meant to have.

Figure 37.2 *Don Loves Roger*, Elisa Kreisinger, 2012 (courtesy of Elisa Kreisinger)

Don Loves Roger mashes up every season of *Mad Men*, creating a remixed narrative about two men who once preserved established notions of manhood and masculinity but then found relief and happiness in each other, becoming a threat to the very same patriarchal system on which their power and privilege was based (Figure 37.2). *Don Loves Roger* gives Don an opportunity to subvert rather than sell traditional masculinity.

In *Mad Men: Set Me Free*, Betty, Joan, and Peggy form an entirely female-framed version of *Mad Men* that rearticulates their feminist frustrations amidst rigid gender roles, with the help of the 1966 Motown hit "Keep Me Hanging On."

Both *Mad Men* remixes garnered more views than the official AMC *Mad Men* trailers; however, the videos were disabled by YouTube via the copyright holders, Lionsgate, for wrongful copyright infringement (but they remained on Vimeo) (Figure 37.3). It is important to stress that the claim of infringement was wrongful, as it points to the disturbing ability for YouTube to pick and choose who is allowed to exercise their fair use rights. The Web's transformative remix works are highly eligible to be protected under fair use, a section of US copyright law that allows for copyrighted content to be sampled and quoted without the permission of the copyright holder for the transformative purposes of comment, critique, satire, or homage.[4] Fair use provides a safeguard against private censorship by copyright, allowing creators to build upon old culture to create new. However, YouTube's Content ID system, which automatically scans 100 hours of user-uploaded-video every minute for copyright violations,[5] is unable to distinguish between a fair use of copyrighted content and an unlawful one.[6] As a result, the automated system regularly removes, blocks, and monetizes user-generated content on the basis of copyright infringement, even though it may not be in violation. The fear of unlawful removal of content due to an inaccurate claim of copyright infringement has chilling effects that illustrate the disconnect between copy culture and copyright.

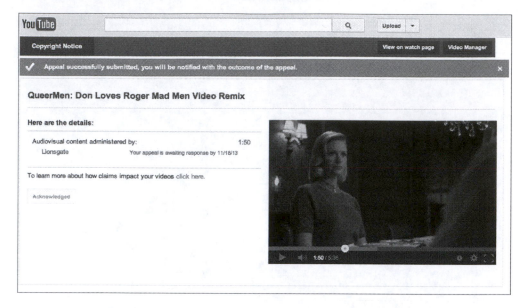

Figure 37.3 Mad Men: Set Me Free, Elisa Kreisinger, 2012 (courtesy of Elisa Kreisinger)

Conflicts Embedded in the Genre

This was the first conflict I encountered upon entering the world of content creation as an appropriation artist in the YouTube era. It became illustrative of the dichotomies embedded in the genre. While we live in a brave new world of participatory media where the barriers to entry are so low that nearly anyone can make a viral video, in reality, uploaded content is likely to be matched for copyright violation, regardless of whether or not it is a remix or "original" content. The most telling example of the flaws embedded in YouTube's automated system occurred in a 2012 video *Simple Living: Picking a Wild Salad* where the user Simple Living documented himself picking eatable wild greens in a field. Content ID matched the bird chirping sounds in the background upon upload. As he stated in the information section below his video,

> Basically, their system identified this video as containing copyright infringing music owned by Rumblefish. They put ads on it, with the proceeds of the ads going partly to Rumblefish, partly to Google.
>
> Since there's no music in my video, I disputed the claimed copyright violation, and Rumblefish was sent a link to my video to check it and see if Youtube's [sic] automated system had made a mistake.
>
> They checked the video, and told Youtube [sic] that there was no mistake, and that they do own the music in the video. So the dispute was closed, and there was seemingly nothing else I could do.[7]

So while we live in a participatory culture where everything is a remix, the reality of content creation is that YouTube users are so often presumed guilty of copyright violation upon upload that they have given up defending their work. In a 2013 nationwide survey of content creators I conducted as an artist-in-residence at Eyebeam Art and

Technology Center in collaboration with DC-based consumer rights organization Public Knowledge, I found that the majority of respondents did not attempt to dispute a copyright violation because the process was too confusing or time consuming[8]. In fact, Content ID places the fate of the video in question in the hands of the copyright holder. As *Reclaiming Fair Use* author and attorney Peter Jaszi notes in the Center for Media & Social Impact's video *Fair Use is Your Friend—Remix Culture*, "fair use is a right, as the Supreme Court has recognized, and it's rooted in the First Amendment. But like any right, its reality depends on its exercise. We must use it or risk losing it."[9]

The flaws of Content ID threaten fair use's effectiveness as an important legal exemption to copyright, leaving fair users confused about their rights with little choice but to abide by the interests of the copyright holder. Private agreements between copyright holders and hosting platforms such as Content ID undermine the safeguards for fair use built into the law. But the question remains: What kind of obligation does a private company built on fair use (Google image search, Google books, etc.) have to its users to allow them the same ability to easily access and defend their rights?

Conclusion

Remix practice itself can be considered a queer act as it demands that producers physically deconstruct copyright images, identities, and narratives to create a new, transformative work, displacing and, thus, queering, the binaries on which copyright, ownership, and authorship are based. This physical deconstruction of mainstream images of identity that remix requires is similar to the deconstruction of identities associated with a postmodern framework, making remix serve as an effective tool for questioning socially constructed images of gender. *The Queer Carrie Project, Don Loves Roger*, and *Mad Men Set Me Free* were inspired by Butler's writings and the robust critical discourse surrounding gender depictions in the media throughout the Web. Through these videos, I hoped I could rearticulate and recontextualize normative identities in a recognizable narrative to redefine the way we are represented. However the challenges of doing so highlight the conflicts embedded in the genre. Private agreements between copyright holders and hosting platforms such as YouTube's automated Content ID system make it difficult for all users, especially remixers who depend on the fair use of copyright content, to upload and share their work. Such challenges simultaneously undermine the safeguards for fair use built into the law. One of the wonderful by-products of video remix is that its recontextualization of images forces viewers to reflect upon popular culture's role in society. With nearly one out of every two people on the Internet visiting YouTube and a monthly audience equivalent to ten Super Bowl audiences,[10] it is troublesome that such important work cannot be sustained in this space.

Notes

1 Kevin J. Delaney, "YouTube to Test Software to Ease Licensing Fights," *The Wall Street Journal*. Last modified June 12, 2007. http://online.wsj.com/news/articles/SB118161295626932114.

2 Judith Butler, "Bodily Inscriptions, Performative Subversion," *Gender Trouble: Feminism and the Subversion of Identity* (New York, NY: Routledge, 2011), 175–193.

3 "Season 6, Episode 9." *Sex and the City*. 2003. New York: HBO.

4 Patricia Aufderheide and Peter Jaszi, "Code of best practices in fair use for online video," Center for Media and Social Impact, June 2008, http://www.cmsimpact.org/sites/default/files/online_best_practices_in_fair_use.pdf.

5 YouTube, "Statistics," YouTube video, http://www.youtube.com/yt/press/statistics.html.
6 Shenaz Zack, "Official Blog: Content ID and Fair Use," YouTube Official Blog, last modified April 22, 2010, YouTube video, http://youtube-global.blogspot.com/2010/04/content-id-and-fair-use.html.
7 Simple Living. "Simple Living: Picking a Wild Salad." YouTube, February 24, 2012, YouTube video, http://www.youtube.com/watch?v=nPBlfeuZuWg.
8 Elisa Kreisinger, "Fair Use(r) Survey Results," Pop Culture Pirate, last modified December 2, 2013, formerly available at: http://www.popculturepirate.com/fair-user-survey-results/.
9 Center for Media & Social Impact, "Fair Use: Fair Use Is Your Friend—Remix Culture," YouTube, May 2, 2013, YouTube video, http://www.youtube.com/watch?v=alKh7IMEAoE#t=88.
10 The YouTube Team. "Official Blog: YouTube Hits a Billion Monthly Users." YouTube Official Blog, last modified March 20, 2013, http://youtube-global.blogspot.co.uk/2013/03/onebillionstrong.html.

Bibliography

Aufderheide, Patricia, and Peter Jaszi. "Code of Best Practices in Fair Use for Online Video." Center for Media and Social Impact, June 2008. http://www.cmsimpact.org/sites/default/files/online_best_practices_in_fair_use.pdf (accessed August 20, 2014).

Butler, Judith. "Bodily Inscriptions, Performative Subversion." *Gender Trouble: Feminism and the Subversion of Identity*, 175–193. New York: Routledge, 2011.

Center for Media & Social Impact. "Fair Use: Fair Use is Your Friend—Remix Culture." YouTube, May 2, 2013. YouTube video. http://www.youtube.com/watch?v=alKh7IMEAoE#t=88 (accessed January 3, 2014).

Delaney, Kevin J. "YouTube to Test Software to Ease Licensing Fights." *The Wall Street Journal*. Last modified June 12, 2007. http://online.wsj.com/news/articles/SB118161295626932114 (accessed August 20, 2014).

"Season 6, Episode 9." *Sex and the City*. 2003. New York: HBO.

Jenkins, Henry. "Locating Fair Use in the Space Between Fandom and the Art World (Part One)." Confessions of an AcaFan. http://henryjenkins.org/2009/03/locating_fair_use_in_the_space.html (accessed July 25, 2013).

Kreisinger, Elisa. "Fair Use(r) Survey Results." Pop Culture Pirate. Last modified December 2, 2013. Formerly available at: http://www.popculturepirate.com/fair-user-survey-results/ (last accessed December 2, 2013).

Simple Living. "Simple Living: Picking a Wild Salad." YouTube. February 24, 2012. YouTube video. http://www.youtube.com/watch?v=nPBlfeuZuWg (accessed January 3, 2014).

Smith, Roberta. "Rays of Light and Menacing Shadows." *The New York Times*. http://www.nytimes.com/2013/12/15/arts/design/roberta-smiths-2013-art-highlights-and-some-concerns.html?pagewanted=all&_r=0 (accessed December 14, 2013).

Steinhauer, Jillian. "Are Art Professionals Afraid of Fair Use?" Hyperallergic. http://hyperallergic.com/106741/are-art-professionals-afraid-of-fair-use/ (accessed February 3, 2014).

The YouTube Team. "Official Blog: YouTube Hits a Billion Monthly Users." YouTube Official Blog. Last modified March 20, 2013. http://youtube-global.blogspot.co.uk/2013/03/onebillionstrong.html (accessed August 20, 2014).

YouTube. "Statistics." http://www.youtube.com/yt/press/statistics.html (accessed January 5, 2014).

Zack, Shenaz. "Official Blog: Content ID and Fair Use." YouTube Official Blog. Last modified April 22, 2010. http://youtube-global.blogspot.com/2010/04/content-id-and-fair-use.html (accessed August 20, 2014).

38

A FAIR(Y) USE TALE

Eric S. Faden

In early 2006, I began a collaborative film called *A Fair(y) Use Tale* with several of my Bucknell University undergraduate students (Figure 38.1). This short film remixed over 400 unlicensed animated clips from the notoriously litigious Walt Disney Company. Their aggressive lobbying in favor of the Sonny Bono Copyright Extension Act of 1998 put Disney in the middle of an intellectual property storm and we hoped our film might act as a lightning rod. During *A Fair(y) Use Tale*'s production, we wanted to get a fresh opinion on the cut and showed an early version to a class of first-year students. About two minutes into the movie, a young woman in the front row was visibly uncomfortable while watching the film. Soon after, she urgently raised her hand and I paused the film. She asked, "Are we going to get into trouble for watching this?" At first, her question confused me but I quickly realized she was concerned that simply *watching* the film might qualify as criminal activity. This was the moment when I knew that today's institution of copyright protection had become *insane*.

The next year, Stanford Law School posted *A Fair(y) Use Tale* online, The Media Education Foundation released the film on DVD, and shortly thereafter the film appeared on YouTube.[1] To date, the film has received over 14 million views online and is regularly used as a pedagogical resource in high schools, colleges, law schools, and even featured on Google's YouTube copyright education page. More impressively, my students and I continue to enjoy a life of freedom unencumbered by fines or jail time over copyright infringement. This essay details how and why we got away with it.

The Remix Mediascape in the Early Twenty-First Century

A Fair(y) Use Tale is a product of my frustration with the vagaries of copyright law and academic publishing in the age of electronic journals. In the late 1990s, I was a graduate student in Film Studies at The University of Florida. While writing my dissertation, I hit a roadblock trying to articulate various concepts, theories, and observations of patterns I saw while analyzing films. For me, describing visual or sonic material through text proved dissatisfying—no matter how vivid the prose, the words never approximated the screen's complexity, poetics, and nuances.

As a result, I began making short videos that illustrated my textual analysis using basic remixing of filmic texts (Figure 38.2). Initially, these were purely analog affairs: Using a stack of VHS decks and a video mixer with text generator, I manipulated and annotated film clips by slowing or freezing the action and adding arrows and a small amount of text to indicate points of interest. In other cases, I put two (or more) clips side-by-side or used superimposition to illustrate common visual patterns (Figure 38.3). Sometimes

Figure 38.1 Stills from the video *A Fair(y) Use Tale*, Eric S. Faden, 2006 (images courtesy of the artist)

straight cuts produced the jarring juxtaposition or radical similarity between different films I wanted to illuminate. Even at this early stage, I saw how editing and annotation could make the films "speak" in a new way. Remix allowed the films to talk to each other—to comment, illuminate, critique—rather than standing stoically in historical and cultural isolation. The art of remix became a scholarly spotlight to expose material otherwise difficult to observe.

These fledgling video illustrations so successfully communicated my ideas that my dissertation director Robert Ray suggested I combine the films together as a companion piece to my dissertation—a kind of multimedia, alternate version of my textual, scholarly work. Adding original footage, voiceover, and music to the remixed clips created 20–30 minute video essays. Problems, however, quickly arose.

These problems weren't so much with the content in my videos but with their mode: The academy, in the large sense of the word, wasn't prepared to receive video as a scholarly medium. In the late 1990s, doctoral dissertations were purely textual affairs. Thus, my videos could not be included as part of my finished dissertation. Further, this type of work did not fit into the standard hierarchy of academic publishing, which counts conference papers, peer-reviewed journal articles, and books from established scholarly presses toward tenure and promotion. For example, proposing a video at a film studies conference in lieu of a traditional paper read aloud resulted in immediate rejection. Thus, I had to follow a "bait and switch" strategy where I proposed a paper and then

Figure 38.2 Stills from the video *Mass Ornament Revisited*, Eric S. Faden, 1998 (images courtesy of the artist)

substituted my video work during the actual presentation. Indeed, in a cruel irony, one of my first published journal articles was a transcription of an earlier video essay called *Crowd Control*.[2]

As print journals gave way to electronic journals in the early twenty-first century, another problem arose: copyright. Traditional print-based journals never dealt extensively with appropriated material. Publishers had long established quotations from other texts as fair use. Images or film stills accompanying scholarly books or journal articles were often licensed at reasonable rates or treated as fair use and litigation was practically nonexistent. Yet, the move from print to electronic journals potentially opened a Pandora's box of intellectual property concerns. After all, with the simultaneous rise of affordable computers that easily copied, combined, and transformed text, images, film, and music plus expanding access to the Internet's potential for instantaneous worldwide distribution, many scholarly publishers and university legal departments were rightly concerned about copyright infringement. In short, the ability to create, appropriate, and remix media far outpaced the legal framework and "best practices" for distributing media. From a publisher's legal viewpoint, the path of least resistance was simply to reject any work—no matter the quality—that might contain problematic content.

Indeed, my 2006 film *The Documentary's New Politics* was initially caught in a copyright/fair use catch-22. The film used extensive amounts of remixed, unlicensed, appropriated footage to provide a scholarly analysis and critique of recent trends in feature

Figure 38.3 Stills from the video *Crowd Control*, Eric S. Faden, 1999 (Images courtesy of the artist)

documentaries. In each case, I used the footage under the auspices of fair use, carefully including unlicensed material only for the purposes of supporting a particular scholarly argument or illustrating an analytical point. The online journal where I submitted my film rejected it despite peer reviews that recommended publication. The journal editor told me they could publish the video after I licensed or cleared every appropriated clip. Because a court determination of fair use is not predictable, many scholarly journals and publishers rejected any responsibility of holding an intellectual property "hot potato," should a content-owner decide to litigate.

A Fair(y) Use Tale

These difficulties with publishing and distribution led me to make a film specifically about copyright and fair use. While I did not have a clear concept in mind, I felt the film should educate and remind potential publishers (and the public at large) about the fair use clause of copyright law in the digital age. Moreover, I wanted "a worst case scenario" for fair use; something so dependent on fair use, that any future films that appropriated material would seem uncomplicated to publishers and distributors. As a general rubric, I make films that are *about* something while simultaneously *demonstrating* the thing, itself.

A small group of Bucknell undergraduate students—Craig Staufenberg, Saskia Madlener, Janine Merolla, Reanna Truck, and David Lopera—agreed to help. We spent considerable time developing ideas but nothing stuck. Then, Craig Staufenberg proposed a film composed *exclusively* of copyrighted material, using short clips of individual words mashed together to enunciate the dialog. We collaboratively wrote a script about copyright, boiling down the thick legal concepts into something short and straightforward.

As the script developed, we devised a screen test, a kind of proof of concept, that cobbled together two lines of dialog from an assortment of movies. It is safe to say that the initial screen test was an abysmal disaster. While we found individual words to fit our script, the cutting from black and white to color or from wide screen to full screen proved too distracting. Moreover, each film carried various amounts of vague historical or cultural "baggage"—narrative backstory and star personas that distracted from the content. Viewers invested more time mentally identifying each film fragment rather than listening to the newly remixed dialog. Finally, the soundtracks also proved challenging. Because narrative feature films evenly mix dialog with sound effects and music, individual words proved difficult to cleanly isolate. Even worse, contemporary films frequently employed overlapping dialog that made individual words incoherent out of context. There was, however, one genre that was less preventative: animated films.

In fact, animated movies had several advantages. First, the aesthetics provide a consistent visual quality and also more consistent aspect ratios. Thus remixing different animated films wasn't as visually jarring as live action films. Second, the films were largely iconic and familiar. As a result, viewers focused less on identifying individual films and more on the dialog's message. Third, we discovered that dialog was much easier to isolate in animated films. Perhaps because the films were intended for a younger audience, dialog was clearly enunciated and mixed higher in the soundtrack.

Within minutes of these realizations, we knew The Walt Disney Company should supply our film's dialog since they had a distinct reputation for zealously defending their intellectual property. If we could make an educational film that exclusively appropriated material from Walt Disney under the rubric of fair use, then we could appropriate anything. Our film—by deliberately poking the biggest copyright bear with a sharp fair use stick—hoped to establish a small precedent for how technology, remix, and scholarship might push the law forward.

The Process and Aesthetics of Remix in A Fair(y) Use Tale

With a script finished, we started the laborious search for individual words of dialog from the Disney canon. We used three main strategies for finding dialog: crawling the Internet for film transcripts, watching the films with closed captioning, and relying on two students—Janine Merolla and Reanna Truck—who simply had an encyclopedic knowledge of (and love for) all things Disney.[3] We particularly looked for matching words that began or ended a sentence since those proved easier to sonically isolate and provided the most intelligibility. Once found, we captured the clips (via an analog capture process) into a nonlinear editing workstation. Beyond dialog, we appropriated clips illustrating various legal concepts as well as various types of reaction shots.

At first glance, A Fair(y) Use Tale appears to be a mashup of different snippets of dialog strung together like a digital video ransom note. Yet, the film actually contains many different presentational modes (plus some original footage as well as licensed material).[4] For the remix, we wanted to clearly have three distinct modes: material representing the audience's viewpoint; expository material explaining legal concepts; and material commenting on, critiquing, or illustrating the expository material. For the audience's viewpoint, the remixed material mainly focused on the posing of questions ("what the heck is the public domain?") plus various (often silent) reaction shots of confusion, contemplation, or understanding. These reflective moments indicated how the audience might likely react to the expository material but also provided much needed visual and sonic relief from the rapid cutting. The expository material focused on describing the state, scope, and history of copyright law as accurately and objectively as possible. This goal proved to be a give and take between the script we wrote and the words we found. The script endured many revisions to help fit the available catalog of words supplied by the source films. Surprisingly, however, several Disney films (*Aladdin* and *Robin Hood*, in particular) largely focus on legal concepts and were chock full of key terms.[5] Finally, we remixed dialog that provided a reaction or commentary on the expository material. This material was more subjective and argumentative in nature—a literal critique of the law that advocated for change.

Another important aesthetic consideration of remix concerns the relationship between the nature of the source material and the nature of the remix—the larger the degree of repurposing, the bigger the remix's critical impact. Disney markets their films exclusively as commercial entertainment. Given that the material is largely promoted to young children, audiences and popular media critics perceive their films as simple, harmless, and escapist in nature. Our remix's sharp critical edge emerges from the repurposing of escapist entertainment into the noncommercial arena of *education* about a serious and complex topic.

Even A Fair(y) Use Tale's brusque form undermines, opposes, and transforms the original material's style. After all, the original Disney canon remains *immensely* pleasurable, escapist, and entertaining. Their editing, animation, and sound design skillfully draw audiences into a seamless narrative universe that obscures any production labor. Our remixing, however, purposely ruins that pleasure by highlighting the editing and denying the audience a familiar narrative. In fact, as *A Fair(y) Use Tale*'s expository material explains, the film's grating style results from the law itself—the fair use exemption dictates that only short excerpts may be used. We embraced that exemption by borrowing only small fractions (usually less than 1 percent) of the original source material.

Fair Use and Transformation

Remix's transformative nature represents another important concept of fair use. Courts increasingly consider whether material is appropriated whole and untouched or whether the material was transformed to serve a new purpose. Obviously, the more transformative the remix, the more likely the usage will be deemed "fair." For *A Fair(y) Use Tale*, we considered two particular acts of transformation. First, on a macro level, was the shift in the nature of the material as discussed above. The very act of editing and remixing the material changes its nature from entertainment to education. Moreover, we wanted the editing to be an obvious tour-de-force to show the labor, time, and energy invested in the film's construction.

On a micro level, however, there were also significant changes to the source material. For example, the film's first third significantly slows down the animation and dialog as a way of "acclimating" audiences to the remix. As viewers adjust to the staccato editing, we gradually sped up the cutting pace and source material. We digitally "massaged" nearly every clip in some way—scaled frames to highlight an individual character or gesture, sleight-of-hand speed changes, audio pitch shifting, mapping different dialog onto existing animation, and looping reaction shots. Thus, while the film's overall "look" appears Disney-esque, the individual shots remain altered.

Fair Use as an Offensive Weapon

Above I outlined various ways that *A Fair(y) Use Tale* employed the fair use exemption to avoid copyright infringement. Yet, the reality is, Disney very well could have litigated against us and that litigation would prove so expensive as to make it impossible to defend in court. Many potential fair use cases never make it to trial as the cost of defending copyright infringement is prohibitively expensive. As a result, a kind of economic censorship exists where content owners quash potential fair use cases by monetarily draining those appropriating material prior to a court determining infringement.

During production, *A Fair(y) Use Tale* received significant support and legal guidance from Stanford Law School's Lawrence Lessig and Anthony Falzone as part of Stanford's Center for Internet and Society. Attorney Falzone, in particular, advised us to embrace fair use as an offensive weapon rather than a defensive strategy. The film not only demonstrates a thorough understanding of the legal concepts at play, it also highlights in the film's credits that intellectual property attorneys stand ready for Disney to react. To paraphrase Heath Ledger's Joker character from *The Dark Knight*, *A Fair(y) Use Tale* wasn't about making money, it was about sending a message. The film's continued existence establishes an unofficial precedent for fair use in the digital age. My hope is that the film dissuades content owners from censoring critical commentary while also showing emerging filmmakers, artists, and scholars how to properly and creatively appropriate material for critical and artistic purposes.

Notes

1 Stanford Law School, The Center for Internet and Society: http://cyberlaw.stanford.edu/blog/2007/03/fairy-use-tale. *A Fair(y) Use Tale* is included on the DVD of Kembrew McLeod's Freedom of Expression (Media Education Foundation, 2007, US): http://www.mediaed.org/cgi-bin/commerce.cgi?preadd=action&key=127. The video can be found on YouTube at http://www.youtube.com/watch?v=CJn_jC4FNDo (all accessed August 20, 2014).
2 Eric S. Faden, "Crowd Control," *Journal of Film and Video* 53, no. 2/3 (2001): 93–106.
3 Several commentators assumed we ripped the DVD closed captioning and then searched those text files for appropriate words. That would have been a really good idea but unfortunately it never occurred to us to do that!
4 The chapter backgrounds include original artwork by painter Hope LeVan who, ironically, did character concept paintings for Disney in the 1980s. Similarly, the music by Rick Benjamin's Paragon Orchestra was cleared and used with permission. In another touch of irony, that orchestra also supplied the music for Disney Theme Park's Main Street Parade.
5 One of the more difficult words to find was "fourteen," which we needed to express the original duration of copyright terms—14 years. Fortunately in *101 Dalmatians*, there is initially a litter of 15 puppies but one is initially thought to have died. We were put in the awkward position of gleefully celebrating that puppy's near death.

Bibliography

Faden, Eric "A Fair(y) Use Tale." In *Freedom of Expression (DVD)*. Kembrew McLeod, Media Education Foundation, 2007. http://www.mediaed.org/cgi-bin/commerce.cgi?preadd=action&key=127 (accessed August 20, 2014).
——. "Crowd Control." *Journal of Film and Video* 53, no. 2/3 (2001): 93–106.

39

AN AESTHETICS OF DECEPTION IN POLITICAL REMIX VIDEO

Diran Lyons

Political remix video (PRV) appropriates media familiar to the general public: film, TV, news broadcasts, sometimes even still photography. The video editor exploits this familiarity to critical effect. When one sees, for example, George W. Bush or Barack Obama in a political remix, they no longer espouse the platitudes and clichés of US foreign policy, the state of the US economy, or other official governmental positions. The new video work recalibrates its sources in order to repudiate the ideologies embedded within them, positing what the artist holds to be a corrective lens to the postures initially propagated by mainstream media, Hollywood, and other powerful institutions.

When I first encountered the PRV community online in the fall of 2007, I saw the art form as an exciting new tributary for my creative pursuits. It conjoins an aesthetics of deception, video art, and the topical politics that my work often engages with in other media. My artistic oeuvre is difficult to classify: I make objects and sculptural installations, large-scale paintings, performance art, and video, incorporating these elements into a use of art that develops the idea of the aesthetic object as something that intrinsically peddles in deception.[1]

In all my work, the main objective is to blur the distinctions between fiction and nonfiction, subjectivity and objectivity, and a concrete truth versus what one could describe as a "creative lie." Through different types of illusion, the creative lie intentionally imbues the work of art with an inability to tell the truth immediately or straightforwardly. Rather, it pulls the wool over a viewer's eyes to encourage the contemplation of a greater truth that lies behind it. In what follows, I examine three political remixes I created between 2010 and 2012 with respect to their capacity to offer alternative viewpoints through illusion.

Jake Gyllenhaal Challenges the Winner of the Nobel Peace Prize (2010)

Less than a full year into President Obama's first term in office, I uploaded to YouTube *Jake Gyllenhaal Challenges the Winner of the Nobel Peace Prize*, a seven-minute remixed narrative that distinguished itself as the first within the PRV genre to reach #1 on the

Figure 39.1 Jake Gyllenhaal Challenges the Winner of the Nobel Peace Prize on IMDB.com

IMDb most popular shorts ratings (Figure 39.1). The video addresses US foreign policy under Obama's direction and provides a clear example of fabricating a convincing inter-action between characters from unrelated sources. Formally, it is also associated with what contemporary film theorist Gilles Deleuze calls a time-image.

The time-image disrupts the continuous movement of cause and effect through dis-continuity, alluring a viewer to ponder the time between shots.[2] While planning the remix, I decided that propelling the transformative story via a linear procession of events would be less effective for what I wanted to accomplish. In order to accentuate the "coming of age" trope, I opted to present haphazard timelines, jumping back and forth between future and past. As such, the narrative repeatedly foregrounds their difference and at times even creates a fictitious simultaneity between the two: The montage effec-tively pictorializes a type of temporal circuit where future and past timelines appear to conflate. This artifice takes place most forcefully toward the middle of the remix, where the younger Gyllenhaal character (from *Donnie Darko*) stares at the elder version (in *Jarhead*) on a TV screen. The latter's facial expression suggests disappointment toward his counterpart, creating one of the more poignant moments in the video.

That juncture is the dividing point in the story where Gyllenhaal begins to radically revise his perspectives. Over the course of the remix, he changes his thinking so thoroughly that in the video's closing moments he fervently contradicts the initial prop-ositions he first espoused. At the beginning of the video, Gyllenhaal approaches a microphone to address the president and pronounce that Obama's citation of the Golden

Rule (in the 2009 Nobel Peace Prize acceptance speech) was the worst advice he had ever heard. However, after experiencing some of the brutality of war—I use footage from *Jarhead* that depicts him fighting overseas, flirting with death under enemy fire, and seeing Iraqi civilians burnt to a crisp by US bombing raids—the video concludes with Gyllenhaal taking odds with Obama's admonition that those who desperately want peace must understand that sometimes war is necessary. Certainly Gyllenhaal and Obama never actually sat down together to discuss foreign policy, but the video manufactures the illusion of a Hollywood actor rebuking Obama for his prowar rhetoric, something that unfortunately still remains a rarity four years after the remix's debut.

Obama Likes Spending (Project 12, 3/12) (2010)

A little over a year later, I established a rigorous code to shepherd the production of a remix that pokes fun at the US government's spendthrift proclivities. The result was *Obama Likes Spending (Project 12, 3/12)*, a tedious, six-and-a-half minute supercut (Figure 39.2). A supercut is a rapid and obsessive succession of clips focused on a specific phenomenon, usually a behavior, word, or phrase from mainstream media.

The stricture of rules for the video was as extensive as it was obsessive. The only sources permitted in the video were those from the White House video archive. The time I chose to post the work online had to playfully triangulate the month of the year, the number of years Obama had served in office, and the video's position within my *Project 12* series, which was a year-long undertaking that featured a new upload on the twelfth day of each month.[3] The video satisfied this stipulation by being posted during the third month of 2011, in the third year of Obama's presidency, and as the third video of *Project 12*. The US budget, the Troubled Asset Relief Program, and the Recovery Act (otherwise referred to as Obama's stimulus package) were the objects of great controversy during the many months leading up to the video, so immediately after completing the second installment of *Project 12*, I committed to locate each instance of Obama's use

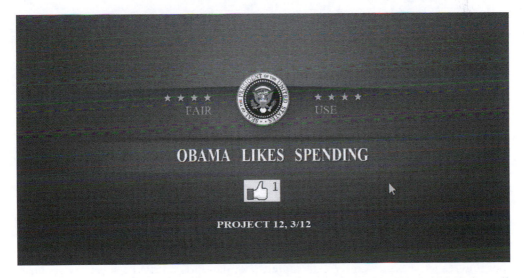

Figure 39.2 Obama Likes Spending (Project 12), 3/12, Diran Lyons, 2010 (6:24), http://youtu.be/K-JuE9esfUc (courtesy of the artist)

of the words "spend," "spent," and "spending" throughout his term in office.[4] The instances had to be in reverse chronological order, i.e., from March 12, 2011 backward and noted at the bottom of the screen. Every 60-second interval had to feature at least one humorous phrase, such as "Spend money to spend it," "I spent your tax dollars," "Spend money on out of control government spending and spending," etc. The phrases could be contrived through editing or unaltered as they exist in the original video documents, but their function was to break up an otherwise relentless relay, featuring over 600 examples.

The supercut form usually exposes an actual phenomenon viewers may tend to overlook. However, as the key function of a creative lie is the use of illusion to inculcate the consideration of alternative viewpoints, *Obama Likes Spending* underscores our national leader's repetitive script and reduces him to a consumerism-pushing, bobblehead doll. The rigor required to generate the video was overwhelming, but it is also overwhelming to watch. "Spending" begins to lose its meaning and transforms into a type of audiovisual water torture, where each utterance of the word leaves the viewer increasingly desensitized and disarranged. It is in this state that new modes of thinking hopefully lead the viewer toward considerations of fiscal responsibility at a time when the national deficit is $17.5 trillion.

Through its straightforward gesture, remix also suggests a dark underbelly of the federal government's exorbitant spending spree amidst the worst financial crisis since the Great Depression. While many of the video's excerpts derive from contexts in which Obama argued for investment in US education and infrastructure, the remix forges the illusion that Obama enjoys entrenching US taxpayers into deeper debt and debasing the purchasing power of the dollar in concert with the Federal Reserve's "quantitative easing," i.e., printing trillions in fiat money to buttress the fragile economy.[5] Even if financing the federal budget by printing money temporarily averts financial collapse, there is a great deal of legitimate concern about the amount, the execution, and the excessively high expectations created by the president himself for how well this will work in the long-term.

99 Problems (Explicit Political Remix) (2012)

My *99 Problems (Explicit Political Remix)* employs fragments of public speeches by President Obama to the instrumental of hip hop artist Jay-Z's song by the same title (Figure 39.3). The lyrics present many of the original's key statements, the majority of the profanity, and a comparable dialog to Jay-Z's argument with a racist policeman. In the remix, Mitt Romney performs the cop's role, antagonizing Obama in a type of rap battle. A side-by-side comparison of the two songs makes plain the degree of fidelity the new work has to its referent. Of the 481 total words Jay-Z wrote in the first two verses, the remix preserves over 50%. Where the words diverge, the video offers nonpartisan criticism of both candidates, though as is appropriate it speaks truthiness to the man who had the most power at that time.

Before further examining the content of the song, a word about the lyric construction is in order. It is here that the creative lie is most evident. Viewers in the video's comment section wondered how the lyrics featured words Obama had not used in his public speeches. *Entertainment Weekly* inaccurately speculated that I used a source of profane recordings by the president.[6] Fundamental to the completion of the work was engaging the atomic structure of political remix: New meanings can emerge through extracting

Figure 39.3 99 *Problems (Explicit Political Remix)*, Diran Lyons, 2012 (2:35), http://youtu.be/2C22wBf2h5k (courtesy of the artist)

indivisible phonemes, the strategic juxtaposition of these units forms morphemes (a linguistic term for words), and this diachronic linguistic process makes it possible to augment a cultural meme, or catchphrase, like the one found in the chorus of Jay-Z's track, a hook he himself appropriated from an early 1990s song by Ice T.

By using the precision of digital video editing software to separate the sounds of a given word into irreducible parts, it becomes possible for an editor to extract the smallest audible bits and recombine them with sounds from other words. This process opens the possibility of making a remixed speaker appear to say any word the editor wants. For example, separating the *f* from a word like *f*undamental and pairing it with the final three letters in t*ruck* enabled me to create the convincing appearance of Obama cursing. Moreover, Obama never used the word "conspiracy" in his first term in office, but a subtle blend of the words *con*sider, *spir*it, and democra*cy* provided the requisite phonological relationships. I filled the video with literally dozens of words, explicit or otherwise, that underwent such revision. Similar to how a painter might celebrate the texture of brushstrokes rather than intentionally conceal their presence in a representational painting, on some occasions I allowed the original imagery to remain coupled with its audible component in order to visually expose the adjoining cut in my process of forging new words. The imagery toggles in the middle of a word from one portrait of Obama to another, thereby revealing the sound manipulation. In most instances, however, I located imagery of lip movements which are visually similar to those of the explicit words I coerced Obama to say. A clip of Obama saying "funding," for example, suffices as a realistic surrogate for the gerund form of the curse word I alluded to above.

Although an undertone of the remix questions Obama's association with a pop culture icon whose songs over the years have included filthy language, misogynist lyrics, and homophobic slurs, the mashup centers on the 2012 presidential election and the performance of our first African American president. The commentary begins with a statement about the 2011 left-leaning Occupy Wall Street protests, maintaining that Obama works for the banks. Contrary to the Tea Party protests of 2009, the Occupy movement ventured to critique corporate capitalism. Like his predecessor Bush and despite his many tough words, Obama supported the bank bailouts, received record Wall Street campaign contributions, and surrounded himself with economic advisors and appointees from financial institutions. The opening lines of the first verse declare that Obama will side on behalf of his "Wall Street brothers," i.e., corporate controllers. Because his allegiance is to the financial megaliths, the remix's prognosis is a reelection victory with no reason for trepidation in facing Mitt Romney.

Obama starts the second verse by describing the condition of the US economy following his rise to the White House:

> The year is 2009 and the White House is mine
> But the economy's in full mother (expletive) decline
> My choices at the time were to (expletive) on the poor
> Or fellate the banks to get elected once more

Instead of punishing the biggest financial institutions for their carelessness in the lead-up to the economic meltdown of 2008, they remained unscathed under Obama, receiving a second set of bailouts after Bush issued the first. Conversely, the financial situation of many Americans continued to erode on Obama's watch. For example, he did not honor campaign promises to protect homeowners from foreclosure through the Home Affordable Modification Program, spelling catastrophe for nearly a million people.[7]

In Jay-Z's version of the second verse, he gets pulled over by a racist police officer while transporting cocaine inside the trunk. In the Obama–Romney battle, instead of asking to search his trunk, Romney challenges Obama to verify his citizenship:

> I ain't steppin' down from (expletive) 'cause this president's legit
> (Romney) Well, do you mind if we see that birth certificate?
> All my records are blocked, you conspiracy hack
> And I know my rights. So, you gon' need a warrant for that

This passage takes a shot at both candidates, making Romney pander to the Tea Party in its unremitting incredulity of Obama's citizenship, while blaming the president for allowing the issue to fester and ultimately hijack political discourse. Had Obama presented the document when the concerns first emerged, the entire distraction likely could have been avoided.

Finally, the outro problematizes the comparison of Obama to Martin Luther King, Jr. Echoing outspoken critics such as Chris Hedges, the closing lines accuse Obama of war profiteering:[8]

> Criminal, fraud, repression, deceit
> I murder and I plunder for the world elite
> We invade countries till we have all they own
> (King) I have a dream
> Well, I have a drone

Some commentators esteemed Obama's 2009 election as the realization of Dr. King's "dream," as articulated in MLK's "I Have a Dream" speech. The mic drop quickly manifests the contrast between the two figures. King's dream and predator drones are irreconcilable: He contested militarism and called the United States "the greatest purveyor of violence on the planet."[9] Regrettably, Obama's foreign policy perpetuated and intensified the violent political scene he inherited, lacking the commitment to restraint in the pursuit of peace that King preached.

Concluding Remarks

Part of my motivation in making these works was to address progressives still invested in the left-versus-right political dichotomy. In conversations with liberals during Obama's first term, I repeatedly heard the argument that Bush made this whole mess, and we should give Obama more time to fix it. I disagreed with the latter and reflected that, in terms of illusion, nothing is worse than self-deception. It should be axiomatic that a candidate backed by record bank contributions will not resist business as usual. A tree is known by its fruits. Obama pushed for more bank bailouts as soon as he got into office. The peace laureate expanded the wars and started new preemptive military actions in Libya and Pakistan, threatening others along the way. He failed to deliver on promises to close Guantanamo Bay. He escalated the use of drone attacks, crafted secret kill lists, and refused to investigate the Bush Administration on rendition and domestic spying. He reauthorized the Patriot Act, signed the National Defense Authorization Act (which authorizes the disappearance of US citizens without trial), presided over the installation of intrusive full-body scanners at airports, and defended the National Security Agency's totalitarian surveillance of the public.

In each case, had McCain or Romney done the same, the progressive left likely would have pushed hard against them. However, since Obama is a Democrat, many I talked with concocted a litany of justifications. As a card-carrying Democratic Party supporter since reaching the legal age to vote in 1996, I knew the risk involved in making the videos. For me, though, it was a matter of political consistency and conviction: I could not oppose Bush as vociferously as I did and then give a Democratic president an uncritical pass. In short, we should resist "hope and change" sponsored by Goldman Sachs, the corporate elite, and the military industrial complex, striving to advance discourse that catalyzes the creation of a more peaceful and prosperous world.

Notes

1 This estimation reflects Friedrich Nietzsche's writings on aesthetics.

2 Gilles Deleuze, *Cinema 2: The Time-Image*, trans. Hugh Tomlinson and Roberta Galeta (Minneapolis, MN: University of Minnesota Press, 1989), 41.

3 *Project 12* utilized a film production model where I directed the videos and collaborated with different script co-writers, including Stephen Mears, Vrüden Jakov, and Desiree D'Alessandro.

4 The remix fell short of this specific ambition at the deadline, locating Obama's words only through the summer of 2009.

5 Paul Craig Roberts, "How Economists and Policymakers Murdered Our Economy," January 25, 2014, http://www.paulcraigroberts.org/2014/01/25/economists-policymakers-murdered-economy-paul-craig-roberts.

6 Hillary Busis, "Obama's Got 99 Problems, but a Mitt Ain't One—NSFW VIDEO," September 28, 2012. http://popwatch.ew.com/2012/09/28/obama-99-problems-remix.

7 Neil M. Barofsky, "Where the Bank Bailout Went Wrong," *The New York Times*, March 29, 2011, http://www.nytimes.com/2011/03/30/opinion/30barofsky.html?_r=0.
8 Chris Hedges, "Time to Get Crazy," Truthdig, July 2, 2012, http://www.truthdig.com/report/item/time_to_get_crazy_20120702.
9 Martin Luther King, Jr. "Why I Am Opposed to the War in Vietnam," April 30, 1967, Riverside Church, New York. Media Resources Center, Moffitt Library, UC Berkeley, http://www.lib.berkeley.edu/MRC/pacificaviet/riversidetranscript.html.

Bibliography

Barofsky, Neil M. "Where the Bank Bailout Went Wrong." *The New York Times*, March 29, 2011 http://www.nytimes.com/2011/03/30/opinion/30barofsky.html?_r=0 (accessed on April 14, 2014).

Busis, Hillary. "Obama's Got 99 Problems, but a Mitt Ain't One—NSFW VIDEO." September 28, 2012. http://popwatch.ew.com/2012/09/28/obama-99-problems-remix (accessed April 14, 2014).

Deleuze, Gilles. *Cinema 2: The Time-Image*. Translated by Hugh Tomlinson and Roberta Galeta. Minneapolis, MN: University of Minnesota Press, 1989.

Hedges, Chris. *Time to Get Crazy*. Truthdig, July 2, 2012. http://www.truthdig.com/report/item/time_to_get_crazy_20120702 (accessed on April 14, 2014).

King, Martin Luther, Jr. *Why I Am Opposed to the War in Vietnam*. April 30, 1967, Riverside Church, New York. Media Resources Center, Moffitt Library, UC Berkeley. http://www.lib.berkeley.edu/MRC/pacificaviet/riversidetranscript.html (accessed on April 14, 2014).

Roberts, Paul Craig. "How Economists and Policymakers Murdered Our Economy." January 25, 2014. http://www.paulcraigroberts.org/2014/01/25/economists-policymakers-murdered-economy-paul-craig-roberts (accessed April 14, 2014).

40
RADICAL REMIX
Manifestoon
Jesse Drew

Viral clips of appropriated, reused, and recut commercial and governmental video and sound have by now become standard weapons of political discourse in our media-saturated societies. The content of these no-budget, amateur, and often legally dubious video clips range from mild sarcasm and mockery to cinematic salvos against multinational corporations or governments. With the growth of the Internet and relatively easy access to new digital tools, the speed and viral nature of remix video has propelled the form from a somewhat fringe-practice within the fine arts to a mass cultural phenomenon.

Manifestoon

My contribution to the arena of political remix is the bricolage *Manifestoon*,[1] an homage to Marx and Engels's *Communist Manifesto*. The impetus for *Manifestoon* was the dissolution of the Soviet Union, and the widespread implication that any alternative to the neoliberal economic ordering of society was no longer possible. I had spent some time in East Germany as the Berlin Wall was coming down and produced a film (*Deutschemarks Uber Alles!*)[2] based on East German activists who advocated a "third way" to govern, negotiating the polarity between Soviet-style state control and West German capital. In the aftermath I was inspired to go to the source of what is perhaps the most influential piece of writing in modern history, *The Communist Manifesto*.[3] I was surprised to find how contemporary the 1848 *Manifesto* sounded in the 1990s, and noted how little had changed since its publication. I was reminded of how Marx referred to revolutionary ideas as an "old mole" that kept being driven underground, only to reappear again throughout history. This "old mole" conjured up a comical cartoon figure, and I soon began seeing the *Manifesto* through the eyes of anthropomorphic cartoon characters. Reflecting on my own cultural upbringing, I realized how important cartoons had been to my stance in life, particularly the "good guy" character Bugs Bunny, who always defeated the bad guys thanks to his wits, street smarts, determination, and sense of humor. In using cartoons as a vehicle to relay Marx and Engels's message, I stripped the words from the historical baggage that surrounds them. My intention was that by mixing the *Manifesto* with popular, beloved cartoons, people could consider Marx and Engels's ideas without prejudice, with a sense of humor rather than a grim countenance. I chose early American cartoons, not only because of my familiarity, but because they embodied the type of labor Marx and Engels discuss in their writing. Early cartoons were handmade, cell by cell, rather than by automation and computers. Aesthetically, cell animations are beautiful works of art in their own right.

Using the common remix strategy of harvesting images, I set my VCR to record a two-hour time slot every morning, capturing traditional Looney Tunes and Merry Melodies cartoons. Every morning I would run downstairs to my basement before I had to get my daughter off to school and make sure the "trap" had sprung. Later in the evening, I would scan through the tape to see what I caught. I downloaded the text of the *Manifesto* online from Project Gutenberg and redacted it to make it shorter and less cumbersome, cutting the more polemical aspects of it written to respond to debates of the day. I recorded a friend reading the version, and laid down that track on the tape. From that point on, I pulled appropriate images from the capture tape and insert-edited them into the master. The entire project was done on a cuts-only Super VHS tape machine that had the added advantage of a time-base corrector to allow minimal color correction. The title was done with an Amiga Video Toaster that was connected to the system.

When the master was complete I created a dub for viewing, showing mostly to friends at video gatherings where remixers and culture jammers often met. It was then shown at Other Cinema in San Francisco, where it was met with appreciation. I dubbed more copies and sent them to film festivals, resulting in dozens of public screenings. I took the tape to an industrial copy service and made 100 more copies, made labels, and sent them to venues and festivals around the country, with much success. The tape was picked up for distribution by the Video Data Bank, arguably one of the largest distributors of video art in the United States. They included it in a special packaged anthology of new work, called "The New McLennium,"[4] which was played at many venues internationally and nationally.[5] A highlight was its selection by the German Zentrum für Kunst und Medientechnologie (ZKM) to be played on German national television as one of the best videos of their festival. For the ZKM, *Manifestoon* was described as:

> an homage to the latent subversiveness of cartoons. Though American cartoons are usually thought of as conveying consumerist and individualistic ideologies, as an avid fan of cartoons as a child, these ideas were secondary to a more important lesson—that of the "trickster" nature of many cartoon characters as they mocked, outwitted, and ultimately defeated their stronger, more powerful adversaries. In the classic cartoon, brute strength and heavy artillery are no match for wit and humor, and justice always prevails. These cartoon clips are all from different cartoons, with the exception of one or two, and reflect a broad range of the classic traditional Hollywood animations. In *Manifestoon*, the image of Mickey running over the globe has new meaning in the current media-scape in which Disney now controls one of the largest concentrations of media ownership in the world. But it could be asked, is he gaining ground, or could he be running away from the revolt of the dispossessed 'toons?[6]

Eventually, the festival outlets became saturated and the tape received less and less festival play. I prepared to put *Manifestoon* out to pasture, pleased that an experimental video remix with political intent had been widely seen. After that, I had not paid attention to its activity until one day in 2006 when I heard from a friend that he saw it on YouTube—a surprise, as I never uploaded the file. I ran a Google search. The sites I came upon not only hosted *Manifestoon*, but had more than one million total hits on YouTube. It was also on many other sites as well. A positive review of it on Boing Boing[7] accelerated its distribution tremendously and I lost track of the sites posting it. I then began to notice it in different languages, both subtitled and overdubbed. I began receiving emails with requests for versions of it without the narration, so they could dub it into their own language. I also received emails asking for the text of the piece, to ease writing subtitles for it, and I happily complied. I have seen *Manifestoon* in at least ten different languages, including Greek, Arabic, French, German, Italian, Turkish, and others. The power of Internet distribution is shocking, as the global audience reached was simply not possible with the tape and festival route that had been the norm only a few years before. The impact of *Manifestoon* was truly on a mass and international scale, and more democratic in many ways, as it was reaching people who would not normally attend festivals or otherwise participate in an underground culture. One of the most inspiring notices was from an indigenous political community in Brazil, who wrote telling me how much they enjoyed the tape and that they used it at their community gatherings.

Splicers, Glue, and Flatbeds, Oh My

Along with *Manifestoon*, in the 1990s there were many other political remixes on the VCR-analog/computer-digital cusp that flashed on video screens across networks of alternative film venues, night clubs, galleries, museums, and living rooms. One of the most influential remix artists to emerge in the 1980s and 1990s is San Francisco-based montage/collage filmmaker Craig Baldwin, an artist who stubbornly clung to working in actual celluloid against the intrusion of video tape. *Tribulation 99*[8] is Baldwin's epic sci-fi homage, a dense, visually rich hallucination that cuts, mixes, and clashes popular "conspiracy theory" stories with actual political conspiracies, slashing together CIA plots and political assassinations with moon creatures and alien pyramid builders. Subsequent films such as *Sonic Outlaws*,[9] *Spectres of the Spectrum*,[10] and *Mockup on Mu*[11] have cemented Baldwin's place in the pantheon of radical remixers and found-footage artists. Baldwin's proselytizing has helped develop a global appreciation for the radical remix, along with the slogan "Copyright Violation Is Your Greatest Entertainment Value." Much of Baldwin's work tears into the heart of corporate censorship and the main enemies of remix work—the copyright police and the limitless aggressive legal tactics of trade groups like the MPAA (Motion Picture Association of America) and the RIAA (Recording Industry Association of America). Baldwin's work has often championed the media pirates who resist what he considers legal censorship. *Sonic Outlaws* for example, highlights Negativland, the music group that has been in the forefront of resisting cultural censorship, tangling with the Irish rock band U2 as well as pop music personality Casey Kasem.

While artists such as Baldwin continued to work with the medium of film, others became enthralled with the dual VCR technique, as it allowed access to readily available images from commercial television, and did not require much technical knowledge or the specialized equipment used by filmmakers: splicers, glue, winders, flatbeds, and other equipment. In the late 1980s and early 1990s, the proliferation of consumer-level television production equipment fueled an upsurge in radical remix, allied with the practice of culture-jamming that included billboard alteration, graffiti, doctored advertising posters, and audio remixes. According to author David Cox, "culture jamming is sabotage at the symbolic level."[12] The culture-jamming phenomenon was spurred along by glossy Canadian magazine *Adbusters*, which regularly solicited and printed the reworking of ads by readers. *Processed World*, a magazine published in

San Francisco, was also a rich source of culture-jamming graphics and illustrations. The advent of Photoshop and the introduction of low-cost flatbed scanners also energized the culture-jamming communities. Graphic artists, fine artists, musicians, and video remixers cross-pollinated, influencing each other and stimulating a prolific period of memorable video remixes. One such memorable video remix starred Ronald and Nancy Reagan as they launched their newly founded "war on drugs."[13] In the video, made by Cliff Roth, the Reagans' national address was mocked, as Ron and Nancy were remixed to explain the benefits of hard drugs and the fact that "they are hooked on heroin." Artists of the Emergency Broadcast Network (EBN) spread the word through their performative video remixes geared for the club scene.[14] EBN remixes included rapid paced, danceable remixes on such themes as psychoactive drugs, the Gulf War, and violence in popular culture. *Special Report*[15] by Bryan Boyce was an equally hilarious critique of television news, hijacked so that "respectable" television broadcast personalities were mixed with the voices of low-budget horror movies and confessed to conspiratorial plots to take over planet earth.

Phil Patiris, a renowned found-footage remixer, operated out of a rundown storefront in San Francisco, surrounded by banks of salvaged VCRs that he kept on record/play, capturing thousands of hours of broadcast footage. On a bare-bones computer, he would log each tape, which he recorded on six-hour speed, entering keywords that would allow him to find the clip or program or ad at a later time. One of the most popular programs that remixers would set their VCRs for was the US Super Bowl, the premiere venue for high budget commercials and superpatriot hype in the US. Patiris became the go-to source for important media moments or broadcast bloopers that remixers craved. When the First Gulf War erupted, the so-called Desert Storm, Phil's operation was a hub of activity, as the "media war" became great fodder for political remixers who wanted to point out the prowar, government collaborationist slant of the major broadcasters. Patiris's own work, *The Iraq Campaign*,[16] became one of the most widely viewed remixes of the war, ingeniously mixing the science fiction film *Dune* with the coverage of Desert Storm. *The Iraq Campaign* specifically focused on the over-the-top slick graphics and animation openings of the networks, as they sought to glamorize and heroicize the massacres happening on the ground in the Middle East.

The widespread availability of remixing and mashup software tools and skills has made the political remix standard fare and part of millions of people's inboxes, to the point where such work becomes a daily comment, rather than a crafted work of art to be viewed and discussed more carefully. This is the promise and the peril of radical remix in the digital age. Not long ago, the Bryan Boyce mashup video that inserted George Bush Jr. into the children's utopia of *Teletubbies*[17] was a humorously shocking construction to behold. Today remix is less novel, but still delights and surprises viewers. No one asks anymore, "How did they do that?" On the other hand, the instant commentary it provides allows it to become an instantaneous audio/visual expression that can enrich and extend public discourse. The acquisition of media tropes and the quick remix of them into memes is a lively demonstration of such language. On the University of California, Davis campus, the casual pepper-spraying of protesting students captured on cell phone cameras sparked its own meme, allowing respondents the opportunity to place the image of brutality across history, from Renaissance paintings to rock 'n' roll album covers. The public deployment of the political remix has moved the practice out of the realm of the skilled craftsperson and the fine artist and moved it within easier reach of the general public. While some may argue that in doing so it has lost its power,

Figure 40.1 Still from *Manifestoon* by Jesse Drew, 1995 (image courtesy of the artist)

it could also be argued that in doing so it has spread its roots ever more deeply into the popular political consciousness, challenging the public to respond to media spectacles rather than passively ingest them.

Notes

1 Jesse Drew, *Manifestoon* (1995, Mission Creek Video), video, 9:00, https://archive.org/details/Manifestoon.
2 Jesse Drew, *Deutschemarks Uber Alles!* (1990; San Francisco, Mission Creek Video) (not online), video, 58:00, referenced at http://www.worldcat.org/title/deutschemarks-uber-alles-the-failure-of-east-germanys-silent-revolution-a-documentary/oclc/27065180.
3 Karl Marx and Friedrich Engels, *The Communist Manifesto* (1848), full text at http://www.gutenberg.org/ebooks/61.
4 "The New McLennium," video series by Video Data Bank (1998, Chicago, Video Data Bank) referenced at http://www.vdb.org/titles/new-mclennium.
5 For a partial list of screenings, http://www.jessedrew.com/*Manifestoon*.html.
6 ZKM Award Notes (1998, Karlsruhe, Germany) http://on1.zkm.de/zkm/e/IMKP50/3.
7 Cory Doctorow, "Communist Manifesto Remixed from Vintage Toons," *Boing Boing*, November 14, 2006, http://boingboing.net/2006/11/14/communist-manifesto.html.
8 Craig Baldwin, *Tribulation 99* (San Francisco, CA: Other Cinema, 1991), video, 1:37:00, http://www.othercinema.com/cbfilmography.html.
9 Craig Baldwin, *Sonic Outlaws* (San Francisco, CA: Other Cinema, 1995), video, 1:27:00, http://www.othercinema.com/cbfilmography.html.
10 Craig Baldwin, *Spectres of the Spectrum* (San Francisco, CA: Other Cinema, 1999), video, 1:31:00, http://www.othercinema.com/cbfilmography.html.
11 Craig Baldwin, *Mockup on Mu* (San Francisco, CA: Other Cinema, 2008), video, 1:50:00, http://www.othercinema.com/cbfilmography.html.
12 David Cox, *Sign Wars: The Culture Jammers Strike Back* (Australia: LedaTape, 2005), 140.

13 Cliff Roth, *The Reagans Speak Out on Drugs* (1988), YouTube video, http://www.youtube.com/watch?v=La5jrfobfTM.

14 Emergency Broadcast Network, EBN, online videos at https://www.youtube.com/playlist?list=PLTebmulFR8XzkxrJviGycCa7ZMormNuvn.

15 Bryan Boyce, *Special Report* (1999), YouTube video, http://www.youtube.com/watch?v=n1h2rPvrUr8.

16 "*Iraq Campaign 1991* by Phil Patiris Now Online," *Boing Boing* (July 28, 2009), http://boingboing.net/2009/07/28/iraq-campaign-1991-b.html

17 "Bryan Boyce," in Kate Horsfield and Lucas Hilderbrand, eds., *Feedback: The Video Data Bank Catalog of Video Art and Artist Interviews* (Philadelphia, PA: Temple University Press, 2006), 67.

Bibliography

Baldwin, Craig. *Tribulation 99*. San Francisco, CA: Other Cinema, 1991. Video, 1:37:00. http://www.othercinema.com/cbfilmography.html (accessed August 21, 2014).

——. *Sonic Outlaws*. San Francisco, CA: Other Cinema, 1995. Video, 1:27:00. http://www.othercinema.com/cbfilmography.html (accessed August 21, 2014).

——. *Spectres of the Spectrum*. San Francisco, CA: Other Cinema, 1999. Video, 1:31:00. http://www.othercinema.com/cbfilmography.html (accessed August 21, 2014).

——. *Mockup on Mu*. San Francisco, CA: Other Cinema, 2008. Video, 1:50:00. http://www.othercinema.com/cbfilmography.html (accessed August 21, 2014).

Boyce, Bryan, *Special Report*. 1999. YouTube video. http://www.youtube.com/watch?v=n1h2rPvrUr8 (accessed August 21, 2014).

"Bryan Boyce." In Kate Horsfield and Lucas Hilderbrand, eds. *Feedback: The Video Data Bank Catalog of Video Art and Artist Interviews*. Philadelphia, PA: Temple University Press, 2006.

Cox, David. *Sign Wars: The Culture Jammers Strike Back*. Australia: LedaTape, 2005.

Doctorow, Cory, "Communist Manifesto Remixed from Vintage Toons." *Boing Boing*, November 14, 2006. http://boingboing.net/2006/11/14/communist-manifesto.html (accessed August 21, 2014).

Drew, Jesse, *Deutschemarks Uber Alles!* San Francisco, CA: Mission Creek Video, 1990. Video, 58:00. Not online, referenced at: http://www.worldcat.org/title/deutschemarks-uber-alles-the-failure-of-east-germanys-silent-revolution-a-documentary/oclc/27065180 (accessed August 21, 2014).

——. *Manifestoon*. San Francisco, CA: Mission Creek Video, 1995. Video, 9:00. https://archive.org/details/Manifestoon (accessed August 21, 2014).

Emergency Broadcast Network, EBN. Online videos at https://www.youtube.com/playlist?list=PLTebmulFR8XzkxrJviGycCa7ZMormNuvn (accessed August 21, 2014).

"*Iraq Campaign 1991* by Phil Patiris Now Online." *Boing Boing*, July 28, 2009. http://boingboing.net/2009/07/28/iraq-campaign-1991-b.html (accessed August 21, 2014).

Marx, Karl, and Friedrich Engels. *The Communist Manifesto* (1848). Full text at http://www.gutenberg.org/ebooks/61 (accessed August 21, 2014).

"The New McLennium." Video series by Video Data Bank. Chicago, IL: Video Data Bank, 1998. Referenced at http://www.vdb.org/titles/new-mclennium (accessed August 21, 2014).

Roth, Cliff. *The Reagans Speak Out on Drugs*. Filmed 1988. YouTube video. Posted March 2, 2012. http://www.youtube.com/watch?v=La5jrfobfTM (accessed August 21, 2014).

ZKM Award Notes. Karlsruhe, Germany, 1998. http://on1.zkm.de/zkm/e/IMKP50/3 (accessed August 21, 2014).

41

IN TWO MINDS

Kevin Atherton

This chapter is about a performance art work that I remixed using video footage from the 1970s to generate a dialog with my former self. *In Two Minds* began straightforwardly enough in the winter of 1978 when I first performed it at the Project Arts Centre in Dublin. At that time I had no intention of presenting it again over 30 years later. In its current form in 2014 its claim to a place within remix culture rests on the extent to which the live performance reframes the work's original meanings and intentions into a new and convincing whole. Unlike many of my previous performance pieces from the Seventies, this one was documented (Figure 41.1). Previously I had rigidly adhered to the tenets of performance art, which driven by its bid to distinguish itself from theater, had two key rules. The first was that there should be no repeat performance; the second

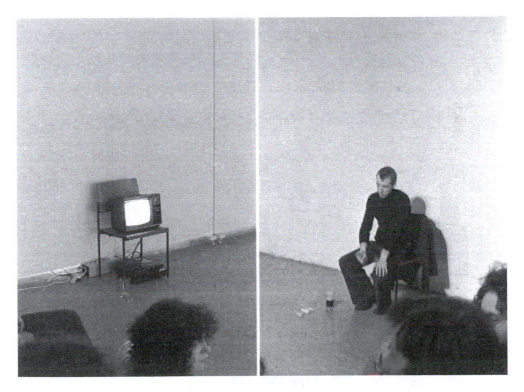

Figure 41.1 In Two Minds, video performance, Project Arts Centre, Dublin, March 1978 (photo: Nigel Rolfe)

was that there must be no documentation, or, as I realize now looking at the grainy black and white negatives from that night in 1978, at least no *decent* documentation.

The particular evening in March at the Project Arts Centre, the gallery space was arranged with a video monitor sitting on a chair placed opposite an identical, empty chair. The audience were also positioned facing one another sitting in two rows— "Wimbledon-style"—either side of the corridor of space between the two facing chairs (Figure 41.1). The performance began when I walked forward to the empty chair and sat down. On the facing monitor a videotape I had recorded earlier that day began to ask questions: "Is this a video work or a performance?" In response to the question I replied: "It's a video work." When my recorded self quickly replied with: "But surely you're performing right now," the performance got its first laugh as the audience responded to the uncanny nature of the interchange between the live and recorded versions of myself. The performance continued in this vein for 30 minutes, with the questions ranging across a number of topics concerning video, performance, and television.

During a month in 1978 I performed the "first" version of In Two Minds three times, each time recording a new question tape,[1] in Dublin and Farnham in Ireland, and Belfast in Northern Ireland, and although each performance received a strong response from the audience, I felt at the time that I had pushed it as far as I could go. That might have been it if I hadn't been selected by the artist Stuart Brisley to be in a group exhibition at the Serpentine Gallery in London. Chosen as one of five artists to share the Serpentine Gallery and given the opportunity of having a space to myself for the three weeks of the "Spring Show" the logical thing to do was to record the answers on videotape as well and to make In Two Minds as a video installation that, with a little bit of technical help from the gallery assistants, could play throughout the run of the show on its own.

At the Serpentine, in keeping with the Dublin performance, the audience was divided into two groups facing one another sitting on two gallery benches (Figure 41.2). Like spectators at a tennis match, the audience had no option but to swing their heads from side to side, as they followed the dialog between the two monitors while questions and answers were verbally batted backward and forward across the space. Now an installation in a gallery and unable by its very nature to respond to a live audience, the work nevertheless continued to be humorous in nature but extended its largely self-referential frame of reference to include questions that challenged the primacy of the gallery. With no intention of repeating the work, I was happy that when the Serpentine exhibition came to the end of its three-week run, In Two Minds—Installation Version and In Two Minds in general, as a series of performances, would come to an end as well.

Twenty-eight years later in 2006, more as a reaction to the trauma of the death of my wife than as a career maneuver (at the time my art career was the last thing on my mind), I rerecorded a new answer tape to In Two Minds—Installation Version and thus "reentered"[2] the work as a part of the process of producing a new installation, which this time around would for the first time involve video projection (Figure 41.3). To make the work, I wore similar clothes to those that I'd worn in the Serpentine video installation in 1978, and sitting on a table, recorded myself answering the questions put to me by my 27-year-old self on the original Serpentine tape. Although this time I was talking across a 28-year gap I felt very much that I had reentered the original 1978 "space" of the work, which from a therapeutic perspective was also proximate to the time that my wife Vicky and I were married.

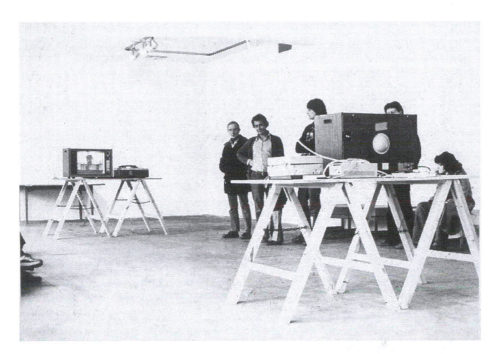

Figure 41.2 *In Two Minds*, video installation, Serpentine Gallery, London, April 1978 (photo: Steve James)

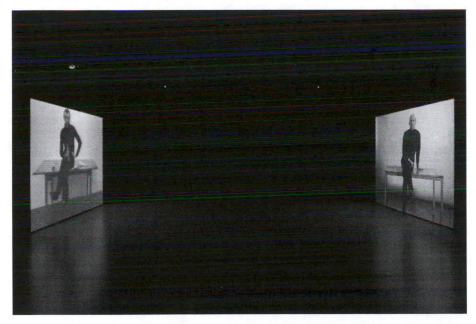

Figure 41.3 Kevin Atherton, *In Two Minds—Past Version, 1978–2006*, The Studio Sessions, 2009 San Francisco Museum of Modern Art installation view (photo: Ian Reeves, courtesy SFMOMA). Two-channel video installation with sound, 25.00; dimensions variable; courtesy the artist (© Kevin Atherton)

It was within this potent period of deeply felt emotions regarding loss and mortality that in 2006, with an acute awareness of the obligation to sustain the original conceptual rigor in relation to video art as a radical practice, I also began to perform live again with the original Serpentine installation question tape.[3]

On first performing the new version of *In Two Minds*, I became instantly aware of the destabilizing effect that I was having through the mixing of past and present in a live situation.[4] As I, as the performer, enter the frame of the video projection, the synchronized nature of the relationship between my recorded self and my live self, as we begin to move in the same space, creates a visually engaging mirror effect, which functions well within the performance in gaining the audience's initial attention. The contrast in appearance between my present and my previous self, once the audience realizes that it is the same person in both, is then amplified when the conversation between the younger and older man deepens. At this point, the disorientation of the piece is experienced. However, as the work progresses there are as likely to be almost as many misconnects as there are connections in our joint conversation, but this only endorses the verisimilitude of the performance as being like a real conversation where the participants frequently talk over or misunderstand one another. The audience members become sufficiently distant witnesses from these social faux pas to be able to enjoy them for their comic effect.

When compared over time, the recorded questions on the original tape of course remain fixed, the same as they were in 1978. If, however, we compare the difference between my answers during the first time around with my present-day answers, we get a sense of the work becoming much more layered over time as it shifts away from its self-referential formalist precepts of the Seventies. My live self, fashioned by life events and informed by the intervening debates that have shaped contemporary fine art, is now able to steer the recorded questions in new directions. By doing so, my younger self is cast in a different light.

The first question on the videotape recorded in 1978 is: "Okay, I've got some questions I'd like to ask, the first one is, why isn't there anything on the walls or on the floor? Can you answer that?" Originally recorded an hour or so afterwards, the young and rather defensive me in the 1978 Serpentine Gallery tape answers: "Quite simply, I'm not a painter and I'm not a sculptor, I'm about this, this is what there is. Why should there be things on the wall?"

In 2011, as a 60-year-old, and a far more relaxed performer, live at Circa Projects in Newcastle upon Tyne (Figure 41.4), I reply: "Well, there are things on the wall and on the floor, we're in an exhibition called 'Seeing in the Dark' in Newcastle so you needn't really worry about that."[5]

Because of an awareness of the situation shared with the audience as the performance unfurls, as the performer, I'm able to collude with them against my recorded self. In this manner, as the dialog develops, I cultivate the conspiratorial nature of the relationship with the audience throughout the performance, as together we join sides in highlighting the shortcomings of the younger interviewer. The following transcription of the live performance in Newcastle exemplifies this:

Question: "You've made this, this time around, you've made it an installation and you've lost the biggest thing of all, you've lost a live audience. Is that a problem?"

Answer: "No, I have a live audience back here now in Newcastle upon Tyne. Thirty-three years later. So play it to this audience then—if you can?"

Figure 41.4 *In Two Minds—Past Version,* video performance, Circa Projects, Newcastle upon Tyne, 2011 (photo: Adam Philips)

Q:	"Because you've got to get that lift somewhere."
A:	"Well, we will."
Q:	"You've got to pull it off."
A:	"Well, let's do it then."
Q:	"Do you think you can do it?"
A:	"Let's do it."

Proceeding in this reflexive manner, because of the nature of the live answers, the work begins to reflect upon itself over time in a way that is impossible for the original tape on its own. The following section of the same performance at Circa Projects in Newcastle shows how a question about time asked in 1978 is seemingly fixed in the time of its recording in the 1970s. When conscripted into the performance in 2011 the same question becomes a meditation on the passing of time, which significantly is now happening *over* time:

Answer:	" . . . but the piece has changed. It was about the parameters of video art, now."
Question:	"But that's not directly."
A:	"It was and now something else has happened called life and there's a thirty-three year gap between you and me. So it begins to talk about other stuff, more interesting stuff like premature hair loss."
Q:	"But you don't know, you don't know."
A:	"I do know, you don't know."
Q:	"Because you're not in the same time and space as they are."
A:	"No, no, you're not here in the same time and space as we are—that's the problem and we know it. You don't even know that I'm asking this!"

Here the unifying conspiracy between the audience and myself as the live performer deepens and our union is consummated through my use of the word "we" rather than "I." My self as a survivor into the present moment reneges on my former self in a peculiar voice-throwing exercise that projects my voice backward and forward through time reminiscent of the act of ventriloquism. The live me manipulates the situation as it occurs while the recorded me has no option but to stick to the script.

The audience laughs nervously suspecting that it's only a matter of time before the tables are turned and my recorded self jokes at the expense of my live self. Stephen Feeke, in an illuminating catalogue article, reveals this process when he writes:

> The act of ventriloquism can be a process of liberation, since the dummy can take the blame for whatever the performer says. Moreover, a performance is more than simply a matter of suspending disbelief. Recent analysis suggests a deeper significance: that ventriloquism as a social phenomenon is confessional and that the act that we witness is a conversation between the ventriloquist and their alter ego.[6]

Jacqui McIntosh also picks up the theme of the alter ego specifically in relation to *In Two Minds* in her 2007 review in *Magill Magazine* when she says:

> He is [in the original footage] like the provocative young student questioning everything in the world whilst here, he is the relaxed very mature teacher. The result is a fantastically humorous work, which on the surface deals with very abstract questions about the nature of the work and performance, but which ultimately becomes a revealing portrait of Atherton himself.[7]

The idea of repetition comes under scrutiny in revealing ways when thinking about *In Two Minds*. Undoubtedly there is a repetition in the playing of the original 1978 question tape, which; even when issues of equipment legacy[8] are taken into account, always remains basically the same. However, it is the "open," or "incomplete," nature of the video recording itself that is crucial in permitting a "reentering" of the work rather than a straightforward repetition of it. In making the original installation version for the Serpentine it is once again worth being reminded that at that time I had no intention of repeating the work beyond that occasion. Likewise, the gaps that were left in the original Serpentine recording were intended to be filled by recorded answers, which; although argumentative in tone and radical in content, can now be regarded as the "correct" or matching answers. The openness of the work resides in the persistence, not as one might first think, of the original questions, but in the original silences that continue to give the illusion of listening whenever the work is played or performed. Clearly related to Samuel Beckett's *Krapp's Last Tape*[9] my Seventies silences differ from Beckett's pauses primarily because they puncture not just the performance, but real life. The recorded silences are crucial in *In Two Minds* because they permit a reentering; and with the audience's tacit involvement, a remaking, of the original work rather than simply a restaging of it.

In the conclusion to her doctoral thesis in Irish art history, Margaret O'Brien articulates this continually changing scenario when she writes:

> Undoubtedly, the most influential factor in the radical transformation of meaning of *In Two Minds* is the lifetime it spans and from the voyeuristic position of

the audience, glimpses of Oscar Wilde's *The Picture of Dorian Grey* emerge fleetingly. The repeat aspect of the live performance is a mechanism that facilitates the entry of immense personal and contextual changes into the work. Not only do the circumstances of receivership change with the condition of the repeat performance, but with each performance the work continues to be made, and far beyond the context of its origination. In this capacity, *In Two Minds* cannot be compared to an object based artwork that is reviewed or reconsidered outside the context of its making. Although the conditions of receivership and the context for viewing may alter for a painting or sculpture, the making of the work ceases at a particular moment and subsequently the materials remain constant. This is not the case with *In Two Minds*, in which the material is Atherton, the conditions of making and the contexts of receivership remain variable, endorsing mutability in a subjective interpretation of the work.[10]

While happy to have reconnected with my former self in *In Two Minds*, I'm even happier, that in true Wildean fashion, and for three decades, I literally kept the original videotapes in the attic. Conscious now of the growing gap between the time of the 1970s recording and the present time, the trick I'm realizing is to keep them both spinning in the air together.

Notes

1 All erased shortly afterwards by being recorded over. At the time this was one of the great things about video; as opposed to film, you could use the same tape again and again.

2 As opposed to "restaging," which in its attempt to remain faithful to the original has a different aim.

3 I had occasionally performed with the Serpentine question tape in the early Eighties in order to demonstrate the original work within a lecture context.

4 Described by Sonny Hayes, a professional illusionist friend, as: "Juggling with time."

5 Kevin Atherton, *In Two Minds* (excerpt), performed at Circa Projects, Newcastle upon Tyne, 2011, Vimeo video, 8:21, http://vimeo.com/31444775.

6 Stephen Feeke and Jon Wood, "Introduction," *With Hidden Noise—Sculpture, Video and Ventriloquism*, exhibition and catalogue (Leeds, UK: Henry Moore Foundation, 2004), 9.

7 Jacqui McIntosh, "Images in Motion," *Magill Magazine* (February 2007): 48.

8 Made in 1978, a decade before the advent of easily accessible video projectors, the recorded "question tape" was originally always played on a video monitor, which in those days was as likely to be as deep as it was wide, now I'm able to perform with a life-size (or even larger) projected version of myself which greatly alters the piece.

9 I saw Beckett's *That Time* at the Royal Court in 1976 but didn't see *Krapp's Last Tape* (1958) until 2009.

10 Margaret O'Brien, "Repetition: A Semiotic Mechanism of Destabilization in Art—A Study of *In Two Minds* by Kevin Atherton and Box (abhareturnabout) by James Coleman, Dublin," (MPhil thesis, Trinity College Dublin, 2011), 81.

Bibliography

Atherton, Kevin. *In Two Minds* (excerpt). Performed at Circa Projects, Newcastle upon Tyne, 2011. Vimeo video, 8:21. http://vimeo.com/31444775 (accessed August 21, 2014).

Feeke, Stephen, and Jon Wood. "Introduction." *With Hidden Noise—Sculpture, Video and Ventriloquism*. Exhibition and catalogue. Leeds, UK: Henry Moore Foundation, 2004.

McIntosh, Jacqui. "Images in Motion." *Magill Magazine* (February 2007) Dublin.

O'Brien, Margaret. "Repetition: A Semiotic Mechanism of Destabilization in Art—A Study of *In Two Minds* by Kevin Atherton and *Box* (abhareturnabout) by James Coleman, Dublin." MPhil thesis, Trinity College Dublin, 2011.

INDEX